MIGRATING TO OBJECT TECHNOLOGY

LIMITED WARRANTY AND DISCLAIMER OF LIABILITY

MIGRATING TO OBJECT TECHNOLOGY

Ian Graham Swiss Bank Corporation

▲▲ **Addison-Wesley Publishing Company**

Wokingham, England • Reading, Massachusetts • Menlo Park, California • New York
Don Mills, Ontario • Amsterdam • Bonn • Sydney • Singapore
Tokyo • Madrid • San Juan • Milan • Paris • Mexico City • Seoul • Taipei

Cover designed by Hybert Design and Type, Maidenhead
and printed by The Riverside Printing Co. (Reading) Ltd.
Typeset and illustrated by PanTek Arts, Maidstone, Kent.
Printed and bound in the United States by R. R. Donnelley & Sons

First printed 1994.

ISBN 0-201-59389-0

British Library Cataloguing-in-Publication Data
A catalogue record for this book is available from the British Library.

Library of Congress Cataloging-in-Publication Data applied for

Acknowledgement
The publisher wishes to thank the following for permission to reproduce material in this book. Figure 1.1 reproduced from Mackenzie K. D. (1991), The Organisational Hologram: The Effective Management of Organisational Change, Boston: Kluwer Academic; Figure 8.1 adapted from Sowa J.F. (1984), Conceptual Structures: Information Processing in Mind and Machine, Reading MA: Addison-Wesley; Quote p.342 from Booch G. (1994) Object-oriented Design with Applications, 2nd edition, Redwood City CA: Benjamin/Cummings; Figure 12.3 adapted from Birrel N.D. and Ould M.A. (1985), A Practical Handbook for Software Development, Cambridge: Cambridge University Press; Quote pp.326–7 from Shelton R.E. (1993), Proceedings of OOP'93, Munich pp.61–70, New York: SIGs Publications; Quote p.303 from Sakkinen M, (1988), SIGPLAN Notices 23(12) p.38; Quote p.422 Jordan V (1993), NeXTWorld, December.

FOREWORD

Although fewer companies these days view object technology as a suspicious innovation, most of those which adopt it, whether for pilot projects or on a large scale, still require guidance through the jungle of concepts, methods, tools, languages and slogans. Thanks to Ian Graham's encyclopaedic knowledge of the field, they will find much in this book to help them.

The roster of topics includes many of the expected aspects of object technology but also a few less predictable incursions. For example, you will find a detailed discussion of user interface design and a chapter on building expert systems.

The 'two books in one' mentioned by the author in his preface – the first part on migration and the second one on SOMA, his second-generation analysis and development method – are unified by the distinctive features of the author's tone: his eagerness to represent fairly the views of many different authors and organizations, often coming from distant locations on the spectrum of Information Technology; his extensive industrial practice, nourishing the presentation of the concepts with the solid experience of many object-oriented projects; his familiarity with countless software tools; his willingness to say 'I' when the context calls for a personal comment; and more than all this his constant effort to explain and apply the concepts of object technology in terms of what they mean for a corporation that is trying to improve itself to confront the turbulent last years of the nineteen-nineties.

Bertrand Meyer
Goleta, California
September 1994

For The Balham Nobblers: Robert and Sam.

PREFACE

Given that many commercial organizations have decided to adopt object technology, practitioners are faced with the problem of how to get from where they are now to where they want to be. They cannot often dispose of their entire investment in conventional computer technology but must work out a migration strategy. This strategy must protect existing investments but not preclude a totally object-oriented future scenario; nor must it preclude other innovations. The strategy must cover technical, managerial and educational issues. It must also, as I shall argue, include a comprehensive method for object-oriented analysis, design and development. The prime objective of this book is to present such a strategy and such a method. It is based on my researches into the literature on object technology, my own research and, most of all, on my involvement with organizations facing exactly this migration problem in the context of particular projects. It emphasizes object technology as a migration strategy for organizations moving to distributed, open systems with modern graphical user interfaces and, perhaps, expert systems components and for those where rapid development practices are being adopted.

My secondary objectives in writing this book were mainly twofold; to add to the material in *Object-Oriented Methods* and to bring a detailed and more leisurely exposition of the Semantic Object Modelling Approach (SOMA) before the public. In addition I wanted to present my solutions to a number of problems facing those people who have moved beyond merely exploring object technology and are building real systems. In particular these problems include:

- How can we migrate existing systems to object technology?
- How can we reuse their best parts in concert with object-oriented extensions?
- How can we describe systems in a language independent, object-oriented manner without losing information in the process and without *unnecessary* rigour and formality?
- Is there an appropriate method for describing both conventional and object-oriented systems in a unified framework?
- How can we build successful graphical user interfaces and work-flow automation systems?

- How can object-oriented methods help build expert systems and advanced database systems?
- Is there a suitable object-oriented method for enterprise modelling?
- Can the methods be used effectively for business process re-engineering?

As a guide to good practice, the book places a strong emphasis on standards and I have attempted to follow the existing and projected standards of the Object Management Group where applicable and recommend others in areas such as interoperation, expert systems and human–computer interaction (HCI).

Object technology (OT) is such a rapidly changing field that almost anything substantial written about it needs to be revised regularly. Thus, when the first edition of *Object-Oriented Methods* was completed and published it almost immediately became necessary to do two quite contradictory things: prepare an updated second edition and write a completely new book going into more detail in several areas and adding material on new developments and issues. The area that interested me most was that of object-oriented analysis and my first thought was to embark on a comprehensive survey of this subject and write it up together with the first complete exposition of SOMA, the method that I was developing during and after the writing of *Object-Oriented Methods*. In the event, my work took me into so many other areas, all of which seemed strongly linked to issues of object-oriented analysis and SOMA in particular, that I realized that SOMA, object-oriented analysis and the serious issues facing organizations migrating to object technology could not be presented in isolation. This book is the result. The survey material was consigned to an updated and expanded second edition of *Object-Oriented Methods*. Like the first edition, that was to some extent a survey of the collective wisdom of the object-oriented community.

This book is in two parts. Part I also has the character of a survey but this time of the application areas to which object technology can be applied. It concentrates on applications and the practical issues facing developers who have already accepted that object technology is an advance on older approaches and who therefore need less basic education and sermonizing. It addresses itself specifically to the issue of how software development organizations can move from where they are now to where they want to be and to applications that are especially important for adopters of object technology. The focus is on issues of concern to organizations migrating from conventional to object technology, and SOMA is located squarely in this context as a tool for understanding systems of all types and as a springboard for migration. This part also deals with the intermediate stages; issues such as the interoperability of conventional and object-oriented components, packages and systems. It also covers the main application areas where these issues are likely to arise in particularly sharp forms. In a sense, Part I acts as a kind of Volume II for *Object-Oriented Methods* in covering the issues that were omitted from that book. However, this book is entirely self-contained.

Object-Oriented Methods introduced the basic concepts of object orientation and surveyed several of the emerging object-oriented analysis and design methods. Out of a critique of these, and experience of several projects, a new method, SOMA, evolved and early work on SOMA was described in my earlier book. The present volume provides a much more complete description of SOMA and the results of some practical experience of using it.

Part II is intended as a complete and detailed exposition of SOMA covering all stages of the systems development life cycle (SDLC) and organized approximately according to the Object Management Group (OMG) reference model, although SOMA covers more issues than those within the scope of the OMG model, notably coordination and reuse. The method is described in detail, emphasizing its support for business and other rules, its representational and semantic richness and its use for building reversible descriptions. It has been argued that this kind of knowledge-rich method is particularly apt from the points of view of organizations wishing to migrate an existing system, build an enterprise model or build applications where the requirements are complex or vaguely expressed. The other notable or novel characteristics of SOMA are its approaches to requirements capture, business process re-engineering and its fully object-oriented life-cycle model.

SOMA has now been used on a number of practical projects. Much of the material in this book is the distillation of this experience although, in many cases, I am unable to reveal the names of organizations or the details of the applications. However, a number of these applications are included as case studies, wearing a false nose and a beard where necessary.

WHO SHOULD READ IT? The intended readership is divided into two groups. The first consists of the same people who would have read *Object-Oriented Methods*; that is, the IT profession, software engineers and, generally, people who work with computers whether in user organizations, consultancies, universities or manufacturers. Managers and project planners will read it to gain an understanding of how to utilize technology in the immediate future to be able to plan more effectively for change and tackle the more tricky issues that object technology gives rise to. Consultants, project managers, systems analysts and designers will read it to deepen their understanding of the technology and, I hope, use the techniques explained in their day-to-day work. Programmers will read it to broaden their horizons in this area. These people will now be broadly familiar with object-oriented concepts and want to move to a deeper and more practical grasp of the subject. The second group is those who have used object-oriented methods and find a need for advice on issues such as how to impose discipline on the development process, how to build certain kinds of applications or how to deal with knotty issues such as interoperability between object-oriented and conventional systems, the measurement of object-oriented projects and continuous process improvement.

This volume, like *Object-Oriented Methods*, is intended to be accessible to readers who do not have deep specialist knowledge of theoretical computer science, but at the same time it attempts to treat the important issues accurately and in depth.

Part II of this book describes the SOMA method in detail and is intended as a reference source on it. It will be used by people seeking an object-oriented method for specifying and analysing applications in semantically rich domains such as enterprise modelling, business process re-engineering, expert systems, advanced database systems and the like.

The book could be also be used as a text in an academic context. In conjunction with *Object-Oriented Methods*, to which it adds, it provides the basis for a (probably one-term postgraduate) course in object technology within a software engineering methods curriculum, perhaps complementing an earlier course on object-oriented programming and methods. This would be of interest to teachers of computer science, business systems analysis, information systems and possibly artificial intelligence. Much of the material has been used as the basis for commercial training courses for project teams building their first, second or third major object-oriented system and for the development of management awareness programmes. Secondly, researchers may be interested in the book for the description of SOMA and the accompanying software *SOMATiK* (the SOMA Tool Kit), which can be used to set practical analysis exercises. Some of the material on migration is original and may also interest researchers. They may also find some of the commentary scattered through the book thought-provoking or controversial.

SOMATiK Like most other object-oriented analysis and design methods, SOMA is tedious to use without some sort of automated support. Since I was using SOMA on project work and since no CASE tool both known to me and within my budget could support my notation in a way that I liked, I had been forced to consider writing my own CASE tool or graphical tool kit and editor. A daunting prospect! Furthermore, this was an entirely unofficial, spare-time project at that stage, so both time and budget were tightly constrained. I had first thought of using Smalltalk V for Windows or Actor, but the price of these products was too great for my personal purse to tolerate. Then, Microsoft announced Visual Basic for an astonishingly affordable price. I decided to write an experimental prototype in this language. After running the tutorial I had a working, usable prototype up and running within little more than seven or eight working hours; a better advertisement for the language, I think, than for my rather rusty programming skills. This was given away to a few friends and colleagues and used by myself and others on an even smaller number of projects for clients. Bugs were found and removed and a few extra features requested and added. This additional investment meant that I could no longer claim that it had been written 'over the weekend'. Thus was born a first prototype of *SOMATiK*. It remained incomplete and I still regarded it as a prototype of something far more complete. However, I used it and it worked. It was given away to a number of organizations and individuals who asked for a copy. Because giving away software involves copying and posting floppy discs, it is boring and time consuming. I decided to make the distribution less painful by including it with this book, the rationale being that if the reader is interested in using SOMA then s/he will immediately need some sort of tool to record specifications.

At this point it became clear that a more robust and complete tool was required and a company was formed to develop *SOMATiK* on a commercial basis. I advised on the design but had no other formal connexion with that firm. The product was developed in its present form by Bezant Object Technologies of Wallingford, UK. Bezant sell a commercial version that is a very long way ahead of my original prototype. They kindly produced a cut down, but still very powerful, version for this book. It is, as far as I know, the only free software tool of its kind. However, this free version of *SOMATiK* is actually a complete tool for the support of Rapid Applications Development (RAD) workshops, production of documentation and object-oriented systems analysis and logical design using SOMA; and it collects all the SOMA metrics automatically. The commercial version also permits the creation of a reuse repository with sophisticated browsing facilities and the remarkable ability to animate and execute SOMA specifications. Clearly no software house is keen to supply such features in the 'freeware' version. The version supplied here is, nevertheless, a fully working product that will enable readers to carry out simulations based on the case studies in Chapter 13 and run small projects of their own. Certain limits have, however, been introduced and some of the advanced features, such as animation of models, support for event traces, object/objectives matrices, source code cross-referencing and syntax checking have been withheld. The main omission is the repository management features that larger organizations will require. *SOMATiK* is also useful as a learning aid, because it contains some knowledge of the SOMA rules and, while it does little to enforce them, reminds the user that they are there. It is my belief that *SOMATiK* is both a radical departure from and a huge improvement over all existing object-oriented CASE tools which, in many instances, are little more than drawing tools with consistency checks. *SOMATiK* is, in this sense, an anti-CASE tool; it does most of the drawing for you. Its power lies in its ability to capture a specification purely in terms of business object descriptions within a single, unified model. Its repository management and browsing features make it potentially the core of an organization's migration strategy.

Appendix B contains an introduction to *SOMATiK* and installation instructions.

KEY FEATURES The chief features that differentiate this work, more or less, from other substantial books on object technology are as follows.

- The book is really two books in one: a book on migration strategy and a complete exposition of the SOMA method.
- There is extensive coverage of the important issue of interoperability between conventional and object-oriented systems.

- Practical advice on migration to object technology and the reuse and integration of existing components is given.
- There is coverage of the key application areas for object technology.
- The SOMA method of object-oriented analysis is described in detail, covering all areas of the SDLC, object modelling, enterprise modelling, business process re-engineering, analysis and design, HCI design principles, Graphical User Interface (GUI) construction, coordination and reuse, object management and distribution.
- It draws on case study experience.
- Several controversial topics are addressed and problems solved.
- The book acts as a second volume to *Object-Oriented Methods* but remains as self-contained as possible by repeating a small amount of key material from that work.
- The *SOMATiK* graphical CASE software tool kit is supplied free with the book.

READING MAP The book is intended to be read sequentially, but the two parts may be read independently and the SOMA material does not depend heavily on the application chapters. The reader who finds the material in Part I tedious may confidently skip straight to Chapter 6. Any missed, relevant material may be tracked down using the subject index, should the need become apparent.

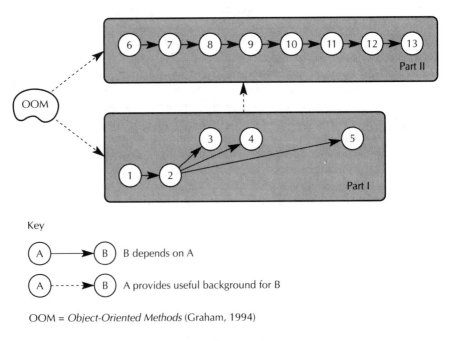

Key

A ──────▶ B   B depends on A

A ------▶ B   A provides useful background for B

OOM = *Object-Oriented Methods* (Graham, 1994)

Reading map

Equally, those readers who do not need to know the details of SOMA may omit Part II, though this would throw their migration strategy back on some other method. The above reading map is a guide. The first two chapters are suitable for managers with no need for a deep technical background. A little more technical background is required for Chapters 3 to 5 and these may be skimmed or omitted at a first reading. Equally, the reader should be able to read Chapter 5 independently of the preceding chapters if so desired. Part II is intended to be a self-contained methods manual and should require no special background. Notwithstanding these remarks, I have assumed that the reader has consumed a basic knowledge of computing and of object-oriented methods from other books. I hope, of course, that they have used my earlier book on the subject but any other introduction should suffice.

ACKNOW-LEDGEMENTS

I would like to acknowledge the help and influence of several other people and organizations. My thanks to Nick Evans of ISA for offering some profound insights into GUI design, providing some case studies for Chapter 4 and suggesting Visual Basic to me, and to Alan Cooper for the language's original conception in the form of Ruby. Tim Lamb of Equitable Life helped with the very first inklings of the SOMA method as applied to enterprise modelling. Thank you Sally Davies, Rob Radmore and David Welton of BIS Banking Systems for providing a first really hard problem to test SOMA on and to Al Vilcius of CIBC, Toronto for adding some interesting insights. Robin Crewe, Al-Noor Ramji and Kerry Williams of Swiss Bank Corporation provided an opportunity to apply my ideas to several large, mission-critical projects and, in doing so, make SOMA more complete and robust. Subsequently, many of my other colleagues at SBC have been massively supportive and have contributed many of the ideas to be found herein. The complete list would contain about 50 names but the following deserve special thanks: Nigel Backhurst for his contributions to Chapter 11 and several useful tips; Steve Birkbeck, Malcomb Dick and Chris Lees for their contributions to Chapter 11; Richard Walker for his contribution to Chapter 9 and many discussions. Other contributions were made by the following colleagues and friends at SBC: Dave Clark, Armando Ferreira, Tim Gee, Thomas Grotehen, Margaret Lyall, René Schwarb, John Taylor, Ulrika Thyssen, Colin Prosser; Brian Thal; John Walsh, Rose Watson and Marcus Zemp. My apologies to those others that I forgot to list in my haste to finish the manuscript.

Peter Jones and Mark Lewis of Bezant Ltd and Blaise Rhodes of ObjectWise Ltd contributed many original ideas during the production of the *SOMATiK* tool. Bezant also supplied much of the material for the appendix on *SOMATiK* . The various readers of *Object-Oriented Methods* who have commented on the stylistic points they liked and the foibles that irritated them have enabled me, I hope, to make stylistic improvements herein.

Participants in the various presentations I have given over the past few years have also helped me greatly by their questions and comments. The British Computer Society OOPS group organized several meetings that contributed ideas, as did SIGS Publications through organizing meetings and through their various publications on this topic. The organizers of the TOOLS series of international conferences deserve similar praise.

Various anonymous referees have made useful suggestions but particular thanks are due to Nigel Backhurst, David King, Martin Fowler, Brian Henderson-Sellers, Mark Lewis and Andy Novobilski for their most thoughtful and thorough reviews of the manuscript and various other comments and good ideas. Despite all this help, there may still be imperfections for which I accept the sole responsibility.

Finally, I should thank my wife, Sue Miller, for her help, patience and sacrifice and apologise to her and to Masters Samuel Thomas and Robert Graham Miller for their dad's neglect of them during the book's gestation.

Despite some reviewers' comments and political correctness, I would remind all readers that my occasional use of so-called 'gender specific' expressions refers to *grammatical* and not to sexual gender throughout. Political correctness is achieved by overthrowing evils, not by tinkering with language.

Ian Graham
September 1994

CONTENTS

Foreword by Bertrand Meyer   v
Preface   vii

PART I Migration, interoperation and applications   **1**

1   The need for object technology   **3**
   1.1   The adaptable business   4
   1.2   The productive developer   12
       1.2.1   Getting started with object technology   17
   1.3   The satisfied user   19
   1.4   OT as the 'Oly Trinity   22
       1.4.1   The key concepts of object technology   23
       1.4.2   Which concepts are the characteristic ones?   27
       1.4.3   Benefits   30
       1.4.4   Market opportunities   32
       1.4.5   Problems with adoption   34
   1.5   Summary   36
   1.6   Bibliographical notes   38

2   Interoperation, reuse and migration   **41**
   2.1   Interoperation of object-oriented systems with conventional IT   42
   2.2   Data management strategies   46
   2.3   Practical problems with migration to object technology   48
   2.4   Reusing existing software components and packages   51
   2.5   Combining relational and object-oriented databases   53
   2.6   Wrappers for expert systems and blackboard systems   59
   2.7   Using object-oriented analysis as a springboard   61
       2.7.1   Three sources of object technology   62
       2.7.2   Object-oriented analysis and knowledge based
          prototyping   64
   2.8   Object technology as a migration strategy in itself   66
   2.9   Summary   69
   2.10 Bibliographical notes   71

xv

3	**Building graphical user interfaces**	**73**
3.1	The need for GUIs	74
3.2	Designing the HCI	76
	3.2.1 Selecting the hardware	78
	3.2.2 Styles of interaction	80
	3.2.3 Fundamentals of cognitive psychology	82
	3.2.4 Principles of HCI design	86
	3.2.5 Guidelines for user interface design	93
	3.2.6 Task analysis	99
	3.2.7 The MVC metaphor	102
	3.2.8 Research issues	103
3.3	GUI standards	104
3.4	Multimedia systems, virtual reality and optical storage	107
3.5	GUI tools and languages	108
	3.5.1 Choosing the right tools	108
	3.5.2 Using tools to reduce risk and cost	115
3.6	Case studies	117
3.7	Summary	119
3.8	Bibliographical notes	122
4	**Distributed systems, databases and object management**	**125**
4.1	Modelling distributed systems	126
4.2	The client/server model	133
4.3	Distributed databases and full-content retrieval	137
4.4	Collaborative work, work-flow automation and groupware	139
4.5	Network and architectural issues	144
4.6	Object request brokers and distributed objects	146
4.7	Case studies	153
4.8	Difficulties in implementing distributed and client/ server systems	155
	4.8.1 Research issues	159
4.9	Summary	160
4.10	Bibliographical notes	163
5	**Building expert systems**	**165**
5.1	Fundamentals of expert systems	166
	5.1.1 The components of a knowledge based system	166
5.2	Knowledge representation	169
	5.2.1 Rules and production systems	171
	5.2.2 Knowledge and inference: cognition and activity	173
5.3	Inference in knowledge based systems	175
	5.3.1 Inference methods and logic	176
	5.3.2 Forward, backward and mixed chaining strategies	178
	5.3.3 Inference in expert system shells	188
5.4	Fuzzy rules and fuzzy objects	193

	5.4.1 Fuzzy inference strategies	195
5.5	Frames and objects	199
5.6	Script theory	200
5.7	Blackboard architectures	204
5.8	Fuzzy, neural and hybrid systems	205
5.9	Implementation in an expert systems environment	206
	5.9.1 Knowledge based systems tools	206
	5.9.2 Database management and rapid development tools	209
5.10	Summary	209
5.11	Bibliographical notes	210

PART II Migration using SOMA: The Semantic Object Modelling Approach **213**

6	**Object modelling**	**215**
6.1	Basic philosophy	217
6.2	What is an object-oriented analysis method?	219
6.3	The OMG and abstract object models	219
6.4	The models of software engineering	222
6.5	Objects	227
6.6	Layers	230
6.7	Finding objects	233
6.8	Structures	234
	6.8.1 Classification structures	234
	6.8.2 Composition structures	240
	6.8.4 Associations	244
	6.8.3 Usage structures	245
6.9	Responsibilities	247
	6.9.1 Attributes	247
	6.9.2 Operations	249
6.10	Rules and rulesets	250
6.11	State model notation	258
6.12	Fuzzy extensions	260
	6.12.1 Fuzzy rules	262
	6.12.2 Defuzzification	262
	6.12.3 Fuzzy quantifiers	264
	6.12.4 Fuzzy attributes	264
	6.12.5 Fuzzy inheritance	264
	6.12.6 Fuzzy objects, fuzzy quantifiers and non-monotonic logic	268
	6.12.7 Control rules for fuzzy multiple inheritance systems	270
	6.12.8 Design theory for fuzzy objects	271
	6.12.9 Objects versus attributes	271
	6.12.10 Tautological objects and maximal decomposition	272
6.13	Deliverables	274
6.14	Summary	274
6.15	Bibliographical notes	276

7	**Requirements capture and analysis**	**277**
	7.1 Object-oriented analysis methods	278
	7.1.1 Object modelling	278
	7.1.2 The process of object modelling	279
	7.2 The requirements capture process	281
	7.3 Context modelling and the environment model	283
	7.4 Task analysis: task scripts, subscripts, component scripts and side-scripts	286
	7.5 Identifying objects	290
	7.5.1 Techniques for leading group discussions and interviewing	292
	7.5.2 Task analysis	293
	7.5.3 Other techniques	298
	7.5.4 Textual analysis	301
	7.5.5 Further guidelines	304
	7.6 Building the object model	305
	7.7 Refining the task scripts to identify responsibilities	307
	7.8 Creating class cards and walking through the system	308
	7.9 Objects with complex states	313
	7.10 Setting priorities and running object-oriented RAD workshops	313
	7.10.1 Business objectives	313
	7.10.2 Running the workshop	314
	7.10.3 Deliverables from RAD workshops and preliminary analysis	315
	7.11 Summary	315
	7.12 Bibliographical notes	317
8	**Strategic modelling and business process re-engineering**	**319**
	8.1 Object-oriented enterprise modelling	320
	8.2 The Zachman framework	322
	8.3 Modelling and re-engineering the business	329
	8.4 Business policy and fuzzy models	334
	8.5 Deliverables	337
	8.6 Summary	338
	8.7 Bibliographical notes	341
9	**Life cycle**	**343**
	9.1 What must an object-oriented method do?	343
	9.2 Life-cycle models	346
	9.2.1 Waterfall models and V models	346
	9.2.2 The X model	347
	9.2.3 Spiral models	347

	9.2.4	The fountain model and MOSES	348
	9.2.5	Fractals, conches and ammonites	353
9.3	RADs, time-boxes and evolutionary development		354
9.4	The SOMA process model		356
	9.4.1	Project initiation stage and activity	363
	9.4.2	RAD workshop activity: Subactivity I – Scoping	364
	9.4.3	RAD workshop activity: Subactivity II – Detail	366
	9.4.4	Rapid object-oriented systems analysis	368
	9.4.5	Time-box planning	371
	9.4.6	The main build time-box	372
	9.4.7	Rapid object-oriented design and programming within the time-box	377
	9.4.8	User review activity	380
	9.4.9	Consolidation, reuse evaluation and documentation	380
	9.4.10	Evaluation	382
	9.4.11	Implementation planning	385
	9.4.12	Project planning activity	386
	9.4.13	Domain modelling and repository administration activity	388
9.5	General project management tasks		391
	9.5.1	Fagan's inspections	391
9.6	Rôles, skills and responsibilities		392
	9.6.1	Project rôles	392
	9.6.2	Developers	393
	9.6.3	Users	394
	9.6.4	RAD workshop rôles	394
	9.6.5	Mentors	396
	9.6.6	Other rôles	396
9.7	Hacking as a structured activity		397
9.8	Summary		397
9.9	Bibliographical notes		398
10	**Metrics, estimation and testing**		**399**
10.1	Metrics, measures and models		399
10.2	Estimation techniques		405
	10.2.1 Function points		405
10.3	Metrics for object-oriented systems analysis		408
10.4	The SOMA metrics		412
10.5	Testing techniques		414
	10.5.1 What does testing mean?		415
	10.5.2 Types of test		416
	10.5.3 Testing object-oriented systems		418
10.6	Summary		421
10.7	Bibliographical notes		422

11	**Coordination and reuse**	**423**
	11.1 Component management and reuse	424
	11.1.1 Code-level versus specification-level reuse	426
	11.1.2 Logistics and management of the software infrastructure team	429
	11.1.3 Rewarding for reuse	431
	11.2 Class libraries and library control	432
	11.3 The process environment and tools	435
	11.4 Designing for reuse	436
	11.5 Repositories, frameworks and CASE tools	437
	11.6 Cross-project coordination	438
	11.6.1 Models of reuse	440
	11.7 Summary	442
	11.8 Bibliographical notes	444
12	**Moving to physical design and implementation**	**445**
	12.1 Converting rules to assertions	445
	12.2 Physical design and implementation in an object-oriented language using Booch'93	448
	12.3 Implementation in a conventional language	452
	12.4 Code generation and class libraries	453
	12.4.1 Using code generators	453
	12.4.2 Integration of class libraries	454
	12.5 Modelling system dynamics	455
	12.5.1 Petri nets and augmented Petri nets	455
	12.6 Formal methods and logic	458
	12.6.1 VDM, Z and object-oriented extensions	460
	12.6.2 Type theory	462
	12.6.3 Intuitionistic type theory	462
	12.7 Converting classes to types	464
	12.8 Specification as implementation in a rule based system and the benefits of prototyping	465
	12.8.1 Prototyping and reversible systems	465
	12.9 Deliverables	467
	12.10 Summary	468
	12.11 Bibliographical notes	468
13	**Case studies**	**469**
	13.1 SOMA in SOMA	470
	13.2 An object-oriented process model for migration	471
	13.3 Building a simple trading system	473
	13.4 Building an order processing application	476
	13.5 Other applications	479

Appendix A   **Notation summary**   **481**

Appendix B   **Using the *SOMATiK* software tool**   **485**

References   **529**

Name index   **539**

Subject index   **542**

Trademark notice

Actor™ is a trademark of Symantec
ADABAS™ is a trademark of Software AG
ADS™ is a trademark of Tanzic, Incorporated
ADW™ is a trademark of KnowledgeWare
Application Manager™ and Crystal™ are trademarks of Intelligent Environments, Incorporated
Beyond Mail™ is a trademark of Beyond, Incorporated
CBR Express™, ART-Enterprise™, ART-IM™ and ART™ are trademarks of Inference
    Corporation
CEO™ is a trademark of Data General
COBOL Workbench™ and MTS™ are trademarks of Micro Focus
Commander™ and System W™ are trademarks of Comshare, Incorporated
CommonView™ is a trademark of Glockenspiel
CORBA™ is a trademark of Object Management Group
CorVision™ is a trademark of Cortex, Incorporated
CP/M 86™ is a trademark of Digital Research
Dataflex™ is a trademark of Dataflex Corporation
DCE™ and Motif™ are trademarks of Open Software Foundation
DOE™ is a trademark of Sunsoft
DOME™ is a trademark of Object-Oriented Technologies Ltd
DOMS™ is a trademark of Hyperdesk, Incorporated
Eiffel™ is a trademark of Interactive Software Engineering Corporation
Ellipse™ is a trademark of Cooperative Solutions, Incorporated
Encina™ is a trademark of Transarc Corporation
Enfin/3™, Easel™ and ENFIN™ are trademarks of Easel Corporation
Epic/Workflow™ is a trademark of Computron
ES/KERNEL™ and ObjectIQ™ are trademarks of Hitachi Corporation
Express™ is a trademark of Information Resources, Incorporated
FCS™ is a trademark of Thorn EMI Software
Filenet (+ Workflo)™ is a trademark of Filenet
Foundationis a trademark of Andersen Consulting
Generis™ is a trademark of Instrumatic Ltd
GeOde™ and Gemstone™ are trademarks of Servio Logic Corporation
Gupta/SQL Windows™ is a trademark of Gupta Technologies, Incorporated
IDMS™ is a trademark of Computer Associates
IEF™ is a trademark of James Martin Associates
Imageflow™ is a trademark of Plexus
ImageFlow™ is a trademark of Recognition Equipment
Ingres Windows™ and INGRES™ are trademarks of Ingres Corporation
Intuitive Solution™ is a trademark of Intuitive Software Ltd
Ipsys™ is a trademark of Ipsys Ltd
ITASCA™ is a trademark of ITASCA, Incorporated
KBMS™ and Intellect™ are trademarks of Al Corporation
Knowledgeman™, MDBS™ and Guru™ are trademarks of MDBS
KnowledPro™ is a trademark of Knowledge Garden, Incorporated
Leonardo™ and SOMATiK™ are trademarks of Bezant Ltd
Liant C++/Views™ is a trademark of Liant
Lisa™, MacApp™, User Interface Toolbox™, HyperCard™ and Macintosh™ are trademarks
    of Apple Computer, Incorporated
Lotus 1-2-3ᴿ is a registered trademark and Lotus cciMail™, Lotus Notes™, Lotus SmartSuite™
    and AmiPro™ are trademarks of
Lotus Development Corporation
MagicCap™ is a trademark of General Magic
McCabe Tools™ is a trademark of McCabe, Incorporated
Netware™ is a trademark of Novell
NeWI™ is a trademark of Softwright Systems
NFS™ and OpenLook™ are trademarks of Sun Microsystems, Incorporated
Object Maker™ is a trademark of Mark V Software
Object Management Workbench™, Kee Connection™, KEE™, ProKappa™ and Kappa™ are
    trademarks of Intellicorp, Incorporated

ObjectCenter^{TM} is a trademark of Centerline, Incorporated
Objective C^{TM} is a trademark of Stepstone Corporation
Objectivity/DB^{TM} is a trademark of Objectivity, Incorporated
Objectory^{TM} is a trademark of Objective Systems SFAB
ObjectStore^{TM} is a trademark of Object Design
Open Client^{TM}, OpenServer^{TM}, NetGateway^{TM}, Replication Server^{TM} and Sybase^{TM} are
    trademarks of Sybase, Incorporated
OpenStep^{TM}, InterfaceBuilder^{TM} and NeXTStep^{TM} are trademarks of NeXT Corporation
Oracle^{R} is a registered trademark of Oracle Corporation
ORBIX^{TM} is a trademark of lona Technologies
ORION^{TM} and Carnot^{TM} are trademarks of MCC
Paradigm Plus^{TM} is a trademark of Protosoft
Paradox^{TM}, OWL^{TM}, ObjectVision^{TM} and Object Windows Library^{TM} are trademarks of Borland
    International, Incorporated
Pharos^{TM} is a trademark of NatWest
Pilot^{TM} is a trademark of Thorn EMI
PowerBuilder^{TM} is a trademark of Powersoft
Presentation Manager^{TM}, AS/400^{TM}, OS/2^{TM}, Visual Age^{TM}, DB2^{TM}, CICS^{TM}, AIX^{TM}, SOM^{TM},
    Folder Application Facility^{TM}
and SNA^{TM} are trademarks of International Business Machines Corporation
ProcesslT^{TM}, CO-OPERATION^{TM} and TOP END^{TM} are trademarks of NCR
Ptechis a trademark of Associative Design Technology, Incorporated
Raima^{TM} is a trademark of Raima
Reveal^{TM} and ProcessWise^{TM} are trademarks of ICL
Rooms^{TM} and Sigma^{TM} are trademarks of Xerox Corporation
ROSE^{TM} and Booch Components^{TM} are trademarks of Rational, Incorporated
Rumba^{TM} is a trademark of Wall Data
Sapiens^{TM} is a trademark of Sapiens Corporation
SAS^{TM} is a trademark of SAS Institute
SELECT^{TM} is a trademark of Select Software Ltd
Simula^{TM} is a trademark of Simula AS
SIR^{TM} is a trademark of SIA Ltd
Smalltalk 80^{TM}, VisualWorks^{TM} and ObjectWorks^{TM} are trademarks of ParcPlace Systems
    Incorporated
Smalltalk V^{TM} is a trademark of Digitalk, Incorporated
Software through Pictures^{TM} is a trademark of Interactive Development Environments
Staffware^{TM} is a trademark of Staffware
Standard Components^{TM} and Tuxedo^{TM} are trademarks of USL, Incorporated
Statice^{TM} and Joshua^{TM} are trademarks of Symbolics, Incorporated
Studio^{TM}, Shorthand^{TM} and ONTOS^{TM} is a trademark of Ontologic, Incorporated
System Engineer^{TM} is a trademark of LBMS plc
System Architect^{TM} is a trademark of Popkin Software, Incorporated
System/4^{TM} is a trademark of Snowbirch
TeamRoute^{TM}, VAX^{TM}, RdB^{TM} and Forte^{TM} are trademarks of Digital Equipment Corporation
The Coordinator^{TM} is a trademark of Action Technologies, Incorporated
Toolbook^{TM} is a trademark of Assymetrix, Incorporated
Tools.h++^{TM} is a trademark of Rogue Wave
UNIX^{TM} is a trademark of AT&T
VERSANT^{TM} is a trademark of Versant Object Technologies
VisualBasic^{TM}, SQLServer^{TM}, Word^{TM}, Word for Windows^{TM}, Microsoft Access^{TM},
    MS Windows^{TM}, ODBC^{TM}, Microsoft
Foundation Classes^{TM}, MS Office^{TM}, OLE^{TM} and Excel^{TM} are trademarks of Microsoft
    Corporation
VSF^{TM} is a trademark of National & Provincial Building Society
WaveFlow^{TM}, OpenODB^{TM} and NewWave are trademarks of Hewlett-Packard, Incorporated
WordPerfect^{TM} is a trademark of WordPerfect Corporation
X Windows^{TM} and Mach^{TM} are trademarks of Massachusetts Institute of Technology
Xi Plus^{TM} is a trademark of Expertech Ltd
XShell^{TM} is a trademark of Expersoft, Incorporated
Xt Intrinsics^{TM} is a trademark of X-Open
Zinc^{TM} is a trademark of Zinc Software, Incorporated

Part I

Migration, interoperation and applications

1

The need for object technology

Needs must when the devil drives.

English proverb

Object technology (OT) has succeeded rapidly in establishing itself within most large software houses as their chief way of building quality software in a cost-effective manner. It is rapidly making inroads into the information systems (IS) departments of large user organizations. The technical reasons for this are clear. Object technology is the most promising way of delivering systems based on reusable modules which can be adapted and changed without having to re-examine the existing source code minutely. As explained in *Object-Oriented Methods* (Graham, 1994a), this is achieved by utilizing the two chief characteristic features of object-oriented systems: encapsulation and inheritance. It is difficult to believe that these merely technical benefits are sufficient to explain the sudden success of OT. After all, it was around for about 25 years before anyone in mainstream information technology (IT) took any notice. Partly we can look to improvements in the power of hardware for an explanation, but I remain convinced that it is the political economy of the situation that has dictated the swing. In this chapter I will argue that there are two primary and opposed forces leading to the necessity of adopting a technology that gives the benefits of object orientation. These are the related needs for businesses to be more adaptable and more flexible in the face of a changing world, together with an even more profound need to drive up the productivity of labour for both developers and users of systems. Automation is the traditional solution to increasing the productivity of labour but traditional automation – especially production line automation – inhibits flexibility. This is why the two forces are opposites. Resolving the contradiction, I will argue, leads to greater satisfaction on the part of users as well as developers.

The move to object technology is the target for many modern enterprises. Once we know where we are going, we must find out how to get there. In the next chapter and much of this book we will explore the question of how existing investments in technology can be protected during the transition to object

3

technology without compromising the aims of the new approach. In this chapter I will discuss the things that make the move unavoidable and, in doing so, reprise some of the key concepts of OT.

1.1 The adaptable business

There are several reasons why the effect of external change on companies is becoming a more important problem than it once was. Taylor (1992a) identifies four 'wedges' or forces for change in modern business: globalization, decentralization, customization and the acceleration of the rate of business change itself caused by technological, social and organizational factors. Global operations imply multiple currencies, regulations and languages, which increase complexity. Decentralization implies multiple standards, dealing with different cultures and the distribution of data and functions. Customization is the trend towards applying large-scale production techniques to achieve economies of scale while producing products tailored to the needs of the customer; even those of an individual customer. These forces underpin the need for a software technology that can deliver extensible, tailorable, modular products and do so without hitting insuperable complexity barriers, as current techniques have been shown to do.

Tom Peters (1987) deduces that the organizations that thrive on chaos and rapid change are the ones that succeed. In his later work (1992) he adds to this the view that businesses must continually invent new products and new ways of doing things. The keys to this are continual innovation and business process re-engineering. The term 'business process re-engineering' (BPR) is due to Hammer (1990). He, Peters and many other management thinkers and practitioners now argue for flatter organizational hierarchies, an emphasis on modelling business processes rather than functional specialization and using information technology to 'empower' the workers at the 'coalface'. Given access to the information resources of the organization, workers can take decisions and provide services without constantly having to refer to their superiors up through the organizational hierarchy. This information can now be provided using computer systems. People must still be responsible for taking sensible decisions but it is the information that makes this de-Stalinization of business possible. Furthermore, the information systems must be easier to use than ever before. Not only can work be democratized in this way using BPR, whole swathes of unnecessary work can be eliminated. Hammer's motivating example was Ford's accounts payable (purchase ledger) system. Ford employed around 500 souls in their Accounts Payable department. They spent much of their time processing invoices and chasing queries concerning them. Ford conceived that a 20% reduction in staff could be achieved by automating some aspects of this process using computers and consultants were engaged to explore this. It was discovered at this time that Mazda operated with a relatively tiny department of five people, although their scale of operation was not proportionately smaller. How could this be so? The solution was found by focusing on the business process that reflected the true business requirement (paying suppliers) rather than the existing functional solution (processing invoices). Ford solved the problem by providing a computer system in the Goods Inward department that enabled delivery checkers to see whether the goods had been ordered when they arrived. If so, Ford then paid the supplier. The whole question of invoices became irrelevant and Ford made a saving of 75% in headcount. This clearly shows the potential benefit of focusing on process instead of function. It is remarkable that the emphasis in object-oriented modelling is exactly similar.

Object models too emphasize models of real-world processes as networks of communicating agents and eschew functional decomposition and procedural emulation. Despite the success of this approach to business modelling there is still a problem. Business process re-engineers need somehow to have 'the great idea'; ignoring invoices in the case of Ford. Where does this idea come from? In Ford's case they had Mazda as an existence theorem but this will not always be the case. Of course, human ingenuity is a source of good ideas too but this sometimes needs stimulation. I will argue later that object models can be regarded as enterprise simulations that enable organizational what-if analysis and help the imagination of human modellers to seek and discover 'the great idea'. This is only one area where object technology can contribute to the management of changing businesses and Chapter 8 is devoted to this topic.

Organizations are increasingly subject to change and, because of the rapid nature of commercial change, they have to be much more adaptable than they have been hitherto. In addition, the world they face is increasingly complex, so the systems that they have to build are also increasingly complex. Therefore, looking into the future is useful because it enables people involved in the development of information technology to see what can be used, what should be avoided, what should be waited for, what should be taken up now and above all what strategy can be adopted for the effective utilization of new developments. Let us therefore gaze into the crystal ball for a while.

It may help our clairvoyance if we try to remember forecasts made in the past. More than ten years ago, had I been asked where IT was going over the next period, I would probably have first thought about the then current wave of new technologies. The personal computer (PC) was just emerging into people's consciousness as something that could be used to do serious business things, not just play games. We were at that point still reeling under the impact of interactive computing and the minicomputer. PCs seemed to be a natural extension to the process. In the context of interactive computing we also knew that the wide area, international network would have considerable impact on business reporting and financial control. PCs, wide area networks and interactive computing were all going to be important during the next period.

The other thing that was emerging from the research laboratories into the commercial world at that point was the now familiar relational database, replacing the *ad hoc* database techniques that existed up until then: IMS and the CODASYL databases. Relational technology is now mature and in wide use. Another application, significant in the area of interactive computing at that time, was financial modelling and around about 1979–80 we saw the first of the 'Visi-clones'. VisiCalc had done something remarkable in making computing far easier for the end user. The effect of that revolution in financial modelling, I would have then predicted, would be to empower the user, thus making it possible for users to describe their business problems to computers directly, rather than have programmers misunderstand their requirements and convert them into specifications which were then converted into designs which were then converted into programs that the end users didn't have any control over whatsoever and which had probably lost most of the original requirements in the translation. Maybe this view was over-optimistic, but it is certainly the view that I would have taken at that time, and I think could have defended reasonably well. Interactive computing, personal computers, networks, relational databases and spreadsheets, as we now call them, all promised to make the world a better place. In nearly every case the technological reason that computers were easier to use was the enrichment of the data structures within their application systems. If, with Wirth (1976), we agree that PROGRAM = ALOGORITHM + DATA STRUCTURE then it can be seen that the richer, but more application-specific, data structures of spreadsheets or DBMSs made the development of algorithms far simpler. Knowledge based systems took this trend further under the slogan: PROGRAM = KNOWLEDGE BASE + INFERENCE ENGINE (Graham and Jones, 1988).

Now, of course, we have the benefit of hindsight. All these developments have matured and have been incorporated into conventional IT; but if you go to the average IS department these days, very little has changed. I was recently in the office of an organization that was using an interactive, mid-range computer system that, if I had seen it ten years ago, I would have regarded as really rather primitive, even though this was a brand new system. The reason for this lack of change is that the problems that the IS department faces haven't changed much. What is data processing after all? It is moving data about from one place to another, and from one form to another. A datum is entered into the computer, it is moved to some location in the computer, combined with other data and ultimately put out to a device in amended form. Usually very little calculation beyond simple arithmetic takes place. That is what IT has been all about; and because the requirement hasn't changed, the tools to do the job haven't changed either, or had a significant impact on the way we do our work.

The world has inherited well over 70 milliard lines of COBOL code: 7×10^{10}. It is indisputable that the vast majority of those lines of COBOL are very bad code indeed, leading to huge maintenance problems. We are also building new systems because of new demands. Even though they are of the same type as the demands of ten years ago, they are often new demands from new business areas. Further, the businesses are bigger. It is not just size that causes complexity in systems. As the business requirement becomes more intricate, rather than just bigger, the complexity of the systems that we build has to reflect that increased complexity.

Another thing that has happened over this period is that we have suddenly become aware – as we always should have been – that users have rights. They should be involved in both the development and the use of systems. The current generation of graphical applications is emphasizing in a very sharp manner the fact that user involvement should be event driven, rather than driven by the design of a preordained dialogue sequence. Users will demand more and more systems of that nature and those systems, because they are event driven, are going to be an order of magnitude more complex to program and maintain. Is this at all avoidable? Surely, complexity is a bad thing. It is attractive to avoid complexity in the provision of good interfaces, but one can only exclude the user from consideration if one wants to risk losing out in the face of the competition's use of IT. At the root of this are the issues of productivity and usability, to which we will return.

Another facet of the complexity of our systems is contained in the trend to make systems 'open'. *Open systems*, a term embraced by many hardware manufacturers, signifies this: if you built a system ten years ago, on a particular manufacturer's mainframe, using a particular language, then you could not move that system to another machine easily. If the manufacturer went out of business, or the line of machine was discontinued, that meant that your IS department had big problems, usually involving a substantial conversion exercise, or in some cases, a complete rewrite of the system. Now, it would be pleasant if we could think that the systems that we are writing today would not suffer from that element of risk. Open systems are all about addressing that problem. The idea of an open system is that you can build your system on one manufacturer's machine and move it to another's without change to the application code, or with only minor changes. The secondary meaning is that if you have several different manufacturers' machines in use on your site, or in your organization, which might be distributed throughout the world, connected by a network, then those applications should be able to interwork or communicate with each other, to transfer information and carry on working when new manufacturers' machines are added to the network and new applications are written. Thus, open systems have this double aspect of future-proofing applications against the exigencies of commercial hardware manufacturing, and also enabling the systems to work together and cooperate in a way that can be understood and utilized by the business. Open systems are an important factor for the IT manager contemplating new developments. The other thing that makes systems more complex is the rapidly changing nature of current requirements, which leads me back to the subject of adaptability.

The first concept that springs to mind, when the adaptability of computer systems is mentioned, is summed up by that tired old phrase: *competitive edge*. Marketing wisdom teaches that the most important thing about, say, motor-car manufacturing is not the amount of profit being made, but the market share, though both are important. If you can convince your customers that you have some feature on your motor car that no other motor car has, then you can gain an edge in the perception of your product and an edge therefore over your competitors, increasing your market share. Anyone who wants to sell you a computer system will tell you that it increases your competitive edge, and when you ask how it will do so, or how to quantify the benefits, they will often reply: 'Well, of course you can't quantify competitive edge.' Therefore, the term *competitive edge* has to be treated with great care. I like to look at it this way. Every large organization has a sort of corporate radar with which they scan the horizon, looking at competitors. A good example is the UK clearing banks. These banks used to look at other banks to see what they were doing. Midland Bank watched NatWest, NatWest watched Lloyds and so on. Companies looked at companies in their own business. Banks who were watching other banks were taken unawares by the deregulation of the mid-1980s, because suddenly everyone and his cousin could become a bank. Mortgage lenders and all sorts of financial services organizations were suddenly in the business of banking; even the high street multiples such as Marks and Spencer began offering financial services in their stores. Where is the competition going to come from? The answer is that you cannot tell. In this age of deregulation, competition can arise from totally unexpected quarters, which means that businesses have to be totally adaptable. It also means that any plans are subject to an increased element of risk.

In future, businesses will have to be designable to order, rather than fixed in bureaucratic modes of operation. If one thinks back to Victorian times, business administration did not change for generation after generation. This was a totally different situation to the one that I have grown up with all my working life and I'm sure will be familiar to most readers, where businesses change regularly, at least every five years, probably every year to a smaller extent. Victorian businesses did not change from great-grandfather to great-grandson. We have inherited this philosophy of the Victorian business in our IT operations. I remember being told when I was first in IT, certainly in consultancy, that the one thing you can't do is change the system: 'Don't try to change the system, you'll lose. The system is a given.' All you can do is build a computer system that mimics or supports the existing business process or makes merely technical innovations. Victorian businesses did not change because, in the days of quill pens and high desks, the labour cost would have been astronomical. The only reason businesses can change rapidly now is precisely because of the power of information technology. IT makes businesses **able** to change, but the 'age of the designable business' concept goes far beyond that, because not only can businesses change, they can use the ability to change in order to survive. That is the real meaning of competitive edge in relation to information technology. IT can be used to meet any challenge much more rapidly than it could be met by changes in procedures using purely manual techniques. Peters (1992) demonstrates that business process re-engineering can enable organizations to strip away bureaucracy and become more responsive and innovative. Mackenzie (1991) takes this even further by arguing that a new organizational form, which he calls the organizational hologram, is emerging. By this he means that the organization's entire structures are replicated in each of its smaller operational units, thus allowing for

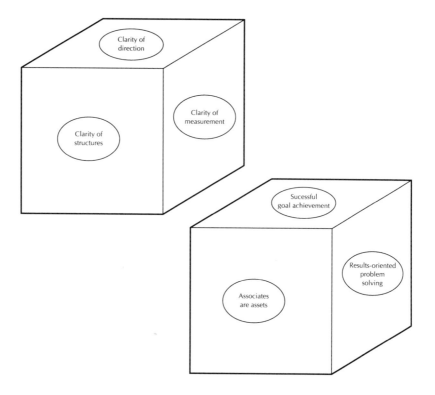

Figure 1.1 A glimpse of Mackenzie's holonomic cube.

greater responsiveness and resilience. He identifies six critical factors that the units and the organization should possess. The interaction between the factors is interpreted by 12 processes. These factors and processes are represented by the faces and edges of a cube – the holonomic cube (Figure 1.1) – which is used as a critical tool in analysing the health and trend of a business. Davenport and Short (1990) emphasize the automatic support for business processes rather more than Hammer, who emphasizes the obliteration of work. In the second part of this book we will be looking at computer-supported business process re-engineering using object-oriented models of organizations.

The need for adapting to competitive pressure itself leads to increasing complexity in systems. Any system that changes rapidly is *a fortiori*[1] more complex. Also, the specifications of our systems are now subject to rapid change. Therefore, if we write a system in the traditional, structured manner where one writes the specification, converts the specification into a design, converts the design into a piece of code, and then delivers the system after two years, then

---

[1] With stronger reason

of course that code is totally out of date, because the specification, by no manner of means, meets the real need as it is now, as opposed to what it was two years ago. Specifications are going to have to evolve during systems development and many existing structured methods do not allow for that. The other thing that we need, in order to capture the fact that the specification might be a moving target, is the idea of **explicitness** in our system specifications. If you take a typical COBOL, FORTRAN or BASIC program, and try to read it seeking the original intention of its designers, you cannot. The semantics, the meaning, of the specification is lost irretrievably in the process of converting the specification to design and then to code. Therefore automatic reverse engineering is impossible. This will dismay the vendors of reverse engineering tools but it is true. In fact, with current methods you cannot even reverse engineer from analysis to a business process description because information is lost in passing from the process description to a data flow model. For example, when I send a message to someone I could say that data flow from me to that person. If I record this in a data flow diagram (DFD) then how can I record the implicit assumption that I expect an answer or acknowledgement? It is certainly not current practice to show a return-value data flow for every data flow on a diagram. It is almost certain that I am trying to accomplish some goal by the interaction. The DFD cannot capture this information either. The DFD also loses sight of the events that caused the data to flow in the first place: the triggers. All such information is lost or corrupted. We need reverse engineering badly because of the huge legacy of badly written systems on which modern enterprises rely. I will argue in this book that properly constructed object-oriented systems will be able to support reverse engineering in future, provided that a semantically rich approach (whereby no information is lost) is adopted from the outset. My approach will be object-oriented, but it must be realized that many other object-oriented approaches are semantically mediocre if not downright impoverished, offering little support for the explicit capture of business policy in their models.

Since systems have to be more adaptable, we must realize that some fast-path and evolutionary techniques for systems development are going to be *de rigeur* in the IT department in future. Prototyping, which has had a lot of bad press over the past few years, is a technique that can be used – with strict management controls and proper IT management practices – to facilitate fast-path developments, and not only fast-path developments, but fast-path changes to existing systems, providing those systems are written with this view in mind from the beginning.

In general, the strategist cannot know what a business is going to need over the coming period. All I can say is that planners are going to have to be watchers of technology and companies are going to have to have people in the organization who understand, at least in broad strategic terms, what the technologies are, what they are likely to be useful for and what they are likely to cost in terms of both effort and money. I would like to close this section with some trite slogans:

Tom Peters is famous for the phrase 'stick to the knitting'. Never mind what changes come about in the competition, respond to them in such a way that you stick to what your company does well. This is a good slogan.

'Be a lateral thinker' is a slogan that can be attributed to Edward de Bono. In other words, one should be prepared to throw out all one's prejudices about systems design when necessary. When the competition forces you to do things that you can't do easily with existing methods, be prepared to rethink them. That doesn't mean chuck them out for the sake of innovation. It means throw them out when they are worn out and outdated and holding you back. Incidentally, this slogan applies to object technology too.

Standards are important. My third slogan is of my own devising: 'don't standardize on a product, productize on a standard'. For example, there are too many companies that use a standard manufacturer, which locks them in to changes in the manufacturer's strategy that they can't predict, whether it is on price or product line; the very opposite of an open systems view. There are even more companies that have a standard word processing package, say. When a product becomes out of date, organizations that have adopted it as a standard suffer. What they should be doing is standardizing on standards. Taking the word processing example, there are several perfectly acceptable standards for document interchange among word processors such as RTF (Rich Text Format) and IBM's DCA (or Revisable Format Text). It seems reasonable that the standard of word processing that companies ought to adopt is not WordPerfect, AmiPro, Word or any other particular package, but any word processor that has certain features and functions that the company requires, supports a document interchange standard, and will work with the suitable graphics, spreadsheet and electronic publishing packages that are in use within the company as well. DCA is a fairly low-level standard and does not admit the transfer of graphics; nor do most of the filters provided to convert directly between word processor formats. RTF is a standard that supports graphics but the definition of RTF is still somewhat unstable due to continuous improvement in word processing technology. Perhaps PostScript would be a better standard. Another possibility is imposing an interoperability standard such as Microsoft's OLE, IBM's SOM object model or the OMG's CORBA. There is a move in government circles to move to using SGML (Standard Generalized Mark-up Language) as the universal interchange standard. Whatever the standard, the important thing is that it is supplier independent and widely agreed on. Therefore don't standardize on products, productize according to standards that are laid down. This applies to system development methods as well as software products.

The last slogan is originally George Cox's[2]: 'be a designable business'. This relates back to all the others. In a world that inexorably keeps changing, if you are not in a designable business you won't be in a surviving business.

---

[2] Cox was a founder of the Butler Cox Institute, now CSC Index.

So in summary, be a lateral thinker, don't standardize on a product – productize on a standard, stick to the knitting, but above all be a designable business within that context.

Adaptable businesses require development techniques that will handle complexity without increasing testing and maintenance costs exponentially. They need software technology that promotes reuse and extensibility so that extensions can be made without compromising existing code. This would be a complete prescription for object technology were it not for the fact that object identity has escaped mention and I have failed to emphasize that objects help with modelling the world using things that correspond to real-world entities. Adaptable businesses require that the conceptual model of the business correspond to the system model. They also need productive developers who will become so by the use of productivity-enhancing tools.

1.2 The productive developer

Developers like to be productive. It is a fundamental characteristic of humankind to enjoy production, albeit of use value rather than exchange value. Producers like a small amount of effort to be rewarded with a useful and powerful end product. That is why high-level languages were developed. However, high-level languages offer puissance at the expense of both performance and flexibility. Peters (1992) provides concrete evidence of this human characteristic in the form of case studies, but indicates that strong management direction and close customer contact are required to ensure that it is exchange value that is produced. The most productive developer works in small, highly focused teams with no bureaucracy and full autonomy within agreed project objectives.

In Peters' examples the underlying assumption is that the teams of highly productive workers have total and immediate access to their organization's information resources. This implies friendly, distributed computer systems – on demand. The purpose of these systems is to enhance and amplify communication between users, not to do work in their own right. Such systems should be built with an awareness of the social nature of knowledge. Collins (1990) provides both persuasive argument and empirical evidence that knowledge is seldom located in the heads of individuals but more often in the historically determined social nexus that they inhabit. This implies that artificial intelligence is, in a sense, impossible and that a system is not completely described without reference to the messages that flow to and from users. Collins argues, for example, that a calculator cannot do arithmetic; it can only assist its user to do arithmetic. Compare the response of the two-metre European human arithmetician who is asked to give his height in imperial units. He would probably respond with 6′7″ and not 78.74015748031 inches as the calculator in MS

Windows tells me he should. I first had to remind it that there were 2.54 centimetres to the inch. One immediate practical consequence of this for system developers is that we must model the tasks of the user before analysing systems. This also makes it possible to produce test scripts before completing the analysis and maps onto another current management science fashion: defining quality first. In Chapter 7 a formal approach to this is presented in detail.

Software tools are always intended to enhance productivity, but the modern requirement is for tools that can produce highly distributed, easy-to-use, natural systems. These systems must support – and even permit the automation of – work-flow and amplify the abilities of their users who will be undertaking many unrelated and unpredictable tasks. For this reason the development tools must permit rapid development, great flexibility and the ability to deal with increased complexity without hitting barriers.

Object technology is productive because of the potential to reuse existing components via their specifications or 'contracts'. Class libraries, whether for code or specifications, are the repository of productivity. Furthermore, these components can be tailored to individual requirements using inheritance. Object technology assists productivity because object-oriented models are easier to debug due to their richer semantic content. It is also more productive because of the semantic richness of its models and because they are models rather than procedural, imperative descriptions.

'Object-oriented' is already a much over-used phrase. On the one hand, this is a good way of keeping student programmers interested in their courses, and journalists in business. On the other, there are aspects of object technology that are of critical significance for IT. OT first took off as a programming style but now has spilled over into the whole software development life cycle. It starts with the idea that you can model the world on the basis of the objects in the world, rather than the objects in the computer, which is what computer languages have done hitherto. The abstractions in FORTRAN are abstractions about computers, not abstractions about real things. Object-oriented programming deals with abstractions that are related to the business directly; and those abstractions, called objects of course, contain data, just like tables in relational databases, but they also contain behaviour. They have programs embedded in the entities, so that when you ask an entity to do something it knows how to do it. This is a very important way of modularizing systems. One benefit of this object-oriented approach to programming, and to design and analysis where the benefits are at an even higher level, is that writing systems in this way enables them to be readily extended. You can add a module to a system without having to take the whole thing offline, recompile and retest it. Extensibility is a benefit that comes from a feature of object-oriented systems called inheritance. Another benefit is potentially even greater: the benefit of reuse. Since we can isolate the program code with the data in these abstractions called objects, we have the potential to reuse objects in different systems. This is delivered through libraries of objects that can be bought. These library objects can then, if you understand them well enough, be reused, offering us the chance to do something we have always wanted to do: build systems from reusable components. After all, if you build a car you don't go and forge an engine block, you buy an engine block and you buy piston rings and you buy spark plugs and you put the thing together. You assemble a car. You assemble a personal computer from circuit boards and disc drives. You do not build the thing by blowing silicon chips or extruding copper wire. Instead a catalogue lists all the bits you need, and you assemble the system. Object orientation offers us the prospect of assembling software systems rather than coding them.

Object technology holds out the promise of high productivity in relatively low-level languages. A good example is the NeXTstep environment which integrates Objective-C into an awesomely productive environment for some UNIX machines and PCs. NeXTstep was originally built on top of the object-oriented and message based Mach kernel but the move to OpenStep will make the environment platform independent. Taligent, the company set up jointly by Apple and IBM, are producing a similar object-oriented machine and environment and Microsoft's Cairo project has announced similar aims.

Technology is important, but it has to be treated with care. Technology is not the answer to all our problems. We cannot predict with certainty the technologies that will be used in any organization over the next few years. There is nevertheless a profound need for IT management to be aware of technology, so that when an opportunity arises, it can be grasped vigorously. Let us pause to review some potentially high-productivity tools.

As I have already argued, at the beginning of the 1980s personal computers, networks, and relational databases were the important new technologies. One of the things that we keep being promised now as an important new technology is parallel hardware. In the world of databases this offers tremendous opportunities and the software database suppliers are now experimenting very vigorously with parallel implementations. IBM has announced its next generation of mainframes based on a parallel architecture and some scaleable UNIX machines are based on the same principle.

We are also told that formal methods will be important. When you write a computer program, as Turing pointed out as early as 1948, it is theoretically conceivable that the specification can be formally, that is mathematically, tested for consistency and completeness, and there has been a lot of research and development in that area over the past few years. I am quite sceptical about whether formal approaches will be of any use in a commercial environment apart from safety-critical systems and defence-related applications, though IBM has had some success in specifying CICS in this way.

Knowledge based systems technology is an enabling technology for diagnosis, for scheduling, and for capturing rare skills that managers have, something that can't be overlooked as a technology for the future. However, it has to be pointed out that many knowledge based systems projects have foundered on the reef of isolation. That it to say, people have tried to build expert systems in isolation from their conventional information systems. Luckily, that tendency seems to have come to an end and there are now several expert systems embedded in conventional information systems in many businesses; and this, I believe, will be the trend.

Communications technology will be very important indeed well into the next millennium. We have seen the increasing importance of Electronic Data Interchange (EDI) and Electronic Funds Transfer at the Point Of Sale (EFTPOS). Multimedia graphical interfaces, where not only text but also pictures are transmitted, require an enormous amount of bandwidth from the communication channels and there will be some significant developments in this area over the next five to ten years. Telephone companies are among those busy installing cable television networks. There is so little of value on the ordinary television that I can't imagine why anyone would ever want to watch cable television, but there must be a few; after all there are one or two subscribers to the dreadful satellite services. Why are people spending a lot of time and effort developing this cable technology? I believe it has nothing to do with television at all. I believe that the reason that many companies in this field are investing so heavily in the technology is because only via cable, which is optical fibre based, will we have enough bandwidth to get IT into the home. Being able to talk as businesses to customers in their homes will give some competitive edge. If our competitors do it then we will have to do it as well. It is only cable networks that will open up enough bandwidth to even begin to deliver the kind of services that modern businesses will be delivering. You will have to be aware of the technology in order to make rational decisions. High-bandwidth communication and multimedia software to support it are technologies that we ought to watch very carefully, because the market effects are unpredictable and could be vast. Certainly the existing telephone network doesn't have enough bandwidth to take the traffic that the forecasters envisage developing, even within five years.

We will need to adopt different system development methods in order to make our IT operations more effective because current methods are so costly. The commission-hungry salesman selling software tells us that CASE tools are going to be very important. I am sceptical, because the current generation of CASE tools are just not very good. In fact, surveys by the Butler Cox Foundation have shown that, of all the structured techniques in use, only two gave any significant benefits – and those two were structured walkthroughs and prototyping. The other structured techniques increased the cost of developing systems by approximately 10%, and led to no significant benefit or time saving whatsoever. All the hype and brouhaha about CASE have to be treated with a good deal of scepticism. I don't think that this necessarily means that we can dismiss the technology. CASE tools are evolving, new ones are coming about. New structured methods are coming about in response to developments in programming languages and systems in general. We will have to watch the methods area very carefully, but I am very sceptical about the existing state of the art. The opposite point of view says that CASE merely raises the level of abstraction at which developers work, in the same way that high-level languages do. This view sees CASE tools primarily as code generators and, as such, I cannot disagree that something like CASE, or visual programming, will displace much coding activity in the long run. The weakness of current CASE is based on the weakness of current methods. If the next generation is to be based on the object-oriented approach then I may find myself a convert.

Our colleagues sometimes tell us that we are living in the age of the demise of the mainframe and the age of downsizing. As with all myths, there is a rational basis for this argument. If we were to compare MIPS (millions of instructions per second) against the cost per MIPS of a computer we would find that a typical mid-range computer is about an order of magnitude less expensive on this measure than a mainframe. We would also find that a PC solution is two orders of magnitude cheaper. Now, this has got to be a very powerful argument indeed for the person in control of the IT budget. It seems that two zeros can be knocked off the hardware bill; but of course there is a flaw in the argument. If you want to be up in the 500 MIPS region, which you will want to be for a whole range of applications, then you cannot do that on a PC. It just doesn't have enough power. It might be cheaper per unit of power but there is not a 500 MIPS PC around. Perhaps there will be in a few years time since their power is going up continually. However, with ten 50 MIPS PCs you have 500 MIPS, but you also have the overhead in buying a network. Even so, you can still say that a network of PCs might be a whole order of magnitude cheaper than a mainframe. So isn't there still an argument for downsizing? Again there are other flaws in the argument. What mainframes are good at is handling channel capacity; they can run bank Automated Teller Machines (ATMs) and airline reservation systems. Their MIPSage is not terribly important, it's the other things that mainframes do that are important. Also, it has been found that the cost of ownership of downsized systems is rather higher than one might think, due *inter alia* to increased support and training costs, and the figures are further complicated because most mainframe users negotiate a price far lower than the manufacturer's published price. Therefore I do not foresee the demise of the mainframe, but something of the argument can be salvaged. I foresee that mainframes will be increasingly utilized to do what they are good at, that is, handling channel capacity, and not calculation. PCs and UNIX workstations will be increasingly used as MIPS servers on networks that include mainframes to do channel handling and transaction processing tasks, where the computationally intensive tasks are passed over the network to MIPS servers using techniques such as remote procedure calls or message broker services. This approach has become known as 'rightsizing'. The mainframe is going to be with us for a long time, but we will see increasing use of distributed computing, networks and workstations to take away from the mainframe those tasks that mainframes are bad at, in other words, computation. The model and metaphor for this is client/server computing which is discussed in Chapter 4.

There is a range of new software tools and a range of new developments in computing and software engineering. The effects of these technological opportunities on businesses are very difficult to predict. What we don't want is

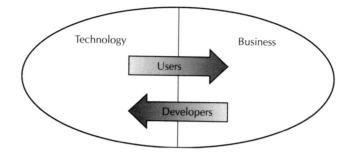

Figure 1.2 Users and developers mediate the contradiction between the evolution of business and the freezing of solutions in technology.

solutions looking for problems. We want our businesses to drive our use of technology. It could be argued that there is a contradiction between adaptability and complexity or, indeed, between a flexible organization and an organization that uses a lot of technology. The more complex the technology the more it inhibits change; the faster the requirements change the harder it is to build tools to support them. The resolution of this contradiction is to be found in the mediation of users and developers illustrated in Figure 1.2.

Users apply technology to transform their businesses. Developers bring the business reality to the models built. Users reflect the business with technical models that developers turn into technically supported business processes. There is a further contradiction between developers and users in that they have different views of both the business and the model. The reflexion[3] of the business in the technology is the system model and the reflexion of the technology in the business is the working, supported business process.

1.2.1 Getting started with object technology

Development managers often ask how to get started with a particular new technology, be it object orientation or electronic document image management. I usually like to answer the question with a parable, because giving abstract answers isn't very helpful in this sort of situation. The parable I prefer is the one about the early use of expert systems. This is how it goes.

At the beginning of the 1980s when a company I worked for was involved in early expert systems developments, one of the senior management

---

[3] The word *reflexion*, with the same root as *reflexive*, is to be distinguished from *reflection*. I use the former in the same way as Lekorsky (1984) to emphasize the rôle of the active subject in cognition, as opposed the passive *reflection* of real-world entities in consciousness. Here it is used to signify the internalization of an aspect of a contradiction within the opposite aspect.

team in the IT department of a very large corporation went to a seminar on expert systems and became extremely excited about the potential of expert systems technology. He thought an important window of opportunity was opening and had been convinced that this was a 'strategic technology'. He wanted to get started in expert systems, so he decided to set up a little project to look at the technology. Next, he surveyed the corporate horizon looking for someone with the spare time to do this job. He went first to the IT manager who said: 'Yes, of course we'd love to get into that, but we have a terrible backlog at the moment and we can't spare anyone'. A further survey of the corporate horizon revealed the operational research department, which of course in those days was out of favour, hadn't done anything useful for a few years and wasn't doing much now. The head of OR therefore was only too pleased to look at expert systems. He looked around his department and saw a couple of folk sitting in the corner with very little to do. They probably had little to do because they lacked either skill or motivation. Our manager said: 'Why don't you look at expert systems?'. They jumped at the chance because they would be able to add it to their résumés. The manager assigned them an absolutely minuscule budget with which they were able to buy a PC and a couple of expert systems shells. They went off and played, and the last thing they had was a clear set of objectives from the business. In the end little progress was made. They probably built a help desk adviser. Remember the help desk? Every week in the trade press we used to read that someone had written an expert system to help with the help desk. Why the help desk? The thought process goes something like this: If we build something that the business is going to see and it goes wrong we are going to be in trouble, so we better build something that isn't too visible. Many help desk projects may have succeeded but even if they did, no one noticed; so expert systems technology has ended up with a pretty bad name as a result. A minuscule budget, no objectives, invisible application: a recipe for disaster. That is not the way to get into new technology. If you want to get into new technology you certainly don't risk the business on it, you don't risk an arm and leg but you have to at least risk a finger. You need to give a serious budget to good people – and that means the people you can probably least afford to spare, not the ones who are sitting around doing nothing – for a significant amount of time with clear business objectives. You pick an application that is visible in the business that is going to be, if it succeeds, understood as a success in the business and, if it fails, the business is going to learn the lessons of the failure. That is the right way to do it, not the wrong way as the man in the parable did. Fortunately, much of the experience on which this book is based has been gathered from projects that have been business-critical, adequately funded, clearly scoped and staffed with talented, and sometimes expensive, developers.

Changes in business are going to be an important reason for introducing new technology because the existing technology doesn't do the job. If you want to live in a designable business then you have to think about some of these technologies. No one can predict which ones. Techniques of systems analysis and the management of software are undergoing rapid evolution and this is going to be an important area where costs will have to be kept down. If we can write reusable specifications, never mind reusable code, we stand a chance of reducing our analysis and design costs. Extensibility will reduce the cost of upgrades. Prototyping will make those upgrades more successful. The problem with these new technologies – and it applies to nearly all of them – is that the investment profile for the introduction of this kind of technology is a bit different from what you are used to, and this is the bad news. If you are going to build a reusable piece of software, I assert that the costs of building such a reusable piece of software are going to be higher. The old way of doing it – interview users, specify it, design it, code it, test it, deliver it – involves a fairly even investment. Although the gurus in the methods area are always telling us we should spend more on analysis, typically we don't and that is probably the reason there are some failures. However, the profile is still reasonably flat. Building reusable objects, reusable code and extensible systems is going to cost even more up front. Of course, in a period of high interest rates that is bad news indeed, because all the costs of development have to be borrowed and discounted back at current interest rates, so when you build something that is reusable you have got to be damn sure that you are going to use the software over and over again, and the chances are, in one business, that you won't be able to do so. I would venture to predict that more and more applications are going to be built from reusable components developed by software houses and consultancies outside the business, because only such organizations can justify the investment in terms of future reuse. That's the bad news: more investment up front, but that can be offset against the chance to go for out-sourced or packaged solutions in the form of object libraries.

We have examined the contradiction between technology and the adaptability of businesses that use it. We have also considered the developer: the first mediator of the conflict. Now we turn to the second mediator: the user.

▱ 1.3 The satisfied user

Systems are written to satisfy users, though they rarely do. A minority satisfice[4]. It is remarkable that, to this day, there is almost nothing decent one can read about user interface design in textbook form, despite the fact that its importance is almost universally acknowledged. Barfield (1993) argues that this will always be the case because of the creative nature of the task and the impossibility of laying down a fixed set of rules in this area. While agreeing in general with this point I think that an overall approach can be discovered and taught. I believe that object technology is exactly right for user interface development

---

[4] A contraction of *satisfy* and *suffice* meaning to satisfy sufficiently; a term introduced originally by Simon (1981).

precisely because the message passing metaphor maps well onto the process of human–machine interaction. It still permits bad designs, but at least the model enables us to predict the effects of design.

Research has shown that users who learn to compute fare badly in promotion and perform their main jobs less well than those who do not. It seems that this is because they become fascinated with computing itself and forget the original reason for their interest in it; accounting, say. Perhaps this is partly because the user interface makes it necessary to have considerable understanding of how the system works internally. To overcome this problem there have been several suggestions: that the user interface should be based on a familiar metaphor such the desktop, that user controls should form a separate layer on top of the application view and that icons and images should be used in preference to textual commands. From its inception these approaches to human–computer interaction (HCI) have been associated with object technology.

One way that object orientation is going to affect many businesses in the immediate future is in the area of the construction of event driven, graphical user interfaces (GUIs). That is, Windows systems: Presentation Manager, MS Windows and the UNIX based X Windows systems. Graphical user interfaces of this kind, because they are event driven, that is, driven by the events in the business world rather than events in the computer, are very costly to design using conventional techniques. For example, if you want to write a simple program that prints 'hallo' on the screen in Microsoft Windows, it takes approximately 90 lines of C program code and of course this productivity loss is unacceptable. In object-oriented languages designed for the purpose of building graphic user interfaces, such as Actor, Smalltalk and various libraries attached to C++, things are different. These systems enable 'hallo world' to be put on the screen with really only a few lines of code, as we would have expected with nongraphical interfaces. This will be a very significant use of the technology in any customer service business over the next few years. Already, banks and insurance companies are investing heavily in this area. I suspect that anyone involved in delivering added value services via computers to their customers – and to their staff indeed – are going to be interested in the technology. They will be forced to consider the use of object-oriented techniques for programming, design and analysis, where the benefits – because they occur earlier in the life cycle – can be even greater than if applied at the programming stage.

One of the areas of computing most influenced in practice by object technology is HCI and this is so especially in the context of GUIs. In support of object technology, Thimbleby (1990) points out that if a language helps the programmer 'to model artefacts available to the user, the user interface will inevitably be cleaner'. This is because objects encapsulate information about their visual form so that programmers are less likely to embed knowledge as fixed, inflexible procedures. Such 'procedural embedding' is analogous to compiled knowledge in humans (skills like bicycle riding are the most frequently quoted examples) and tends to make systems narrow, contrived and inflexible when applied to a machine. Further, as Thimbleby points out, if every window, menu or button is also an object then when the program is improved from a programming point of view the interface tends to be improved from the user's viewpoint too. Many others have pointed to the power and naturalness of the so-called desktop metaphor that was ushered in with Smalltalk. Chapter 3 will take a detailed look at HCI issues in general and especially their relationship to object technology. We shall see there that many of the apparent inventions of object technology were quite well known in HCI under different names. Jacobson's use-case techniques appear to have as much in common with HCI task analysis as they do with Schank's scripts (see Chapter 5). Tasks involve users and users have knowledge that lets them perform tasks well and adaptively. Chapter 3 also discusses the knowledge analysis of tasks, which is an area where knowledge engineering and HCI interact. In Part II we will see how to apply these observations to build an approach to object-oriented requirements capture that goes beyond user interface design and applies the principles of user- and task-oriented design to specifying all sorts of systems.

Like all capital equipment, computers cannot perform labour and create value on their own. Value is created by users who use computers as tools. Users will be satisfied best when the tools they use are 'ready-to-hand' and do not intrude upon and interfere with the task in hand. The tool must contribute to the satisfaction of a goal. A goal is achieved by performing certain tasks. Therefore a computer system must assist with the specified tasks. Tasks may be characterized by sentences in which operations are performed by and on objects and which return results. Tasks can be classified, aggregated, associated and related by messages. This is no more and no less than an object model. The user will be satisfied when s/he understands that the processes going on in the machine correspond to understandable processes that could go on in the business.

It is now a commonplace that one of the great advantages of object-oriented computing is its ability to be regarded as a modelling and simulation tool as opposed to a tool for procedural description of algorithms. A homely example of the difference may by discovered by considering the problem of giving directions to a friend. If you were now with me and wished to go home by train I could direct you by saying: 'Leave this room by the door I am pointing at. Take a pace forward (to avoid the wall) and turn left. Go forward to the front door and open it. Proceed to the street and turn left. Continue until the road bends and follow the bend. Take the next turning left.' ... and so on. These directions would eventually lead you to Balham station. However, if a tree had fallen across the road or there was some other unexpected obstacle or hazard then you would have to retrace your steps and ask for new instructions. The plan would have broken and could not be repaired – to use the jargon of AI. If I had sketched a map of the area you could have repaired the plan yourself and avoided the obstacle by finding a new route. This is the difference between a procedure and a model and I hope you can see that the modelling strategy is better in most cases, especially where the system has to take account of unexpected events, as in a real business. Object-oriented systems are models of the objects in a business and the processes in which they can participate, modelled by message passing.

Object-oriented modelling benefits the user by giving a greater correspondence between the pre-existing mental model of the business and that of the system. The system is therefore easier to understand, use and change. OT also helps by closing the gap between the technical language of systems and the language of the business domain. Finally, it can help by making it easier for the system to contain a model of the user as well as of the business objects. This user-modelling aspect requires features from object technology, expert systems and HCI theory to be effective.

As we shall see in Chapter 4, object technology supports the construction of effective client/server systems and this helps the user by placing more power on the desktop so that the interface to systems can respond better to the user's needs. The use of powerful object-oriented interfaces enhances usability by permitting object-then-action dialogues where appropriate; that is, point at the object (a document, say) and then decide what to do to it (print, say) or even ask what can be done to it. This reduces the knowledge needed to operate the system. This style of interaction also supports event driven styles of interaction, which is important when customers are involved in a dialogue. The client/server approach not only supports better interfaces to many, often widely distributed, information resources, it also places the computer power where it is most needed due to its greater flexibility. This 'rightsizing' approach helps the users' craving for cost-effective solutions as well as friendly ones.

Lastly, the presence of powerful, easy-to-use engines on many users' desks promotes one of the major goals of business process re-engineering: empowerment. We will return to this topic too in subsequent chapters. Chapter 3 covers the whole issue of human–computer interaction in some detail and prepares the reader for the use that is made of this theory in Part II, notably in the chapter on requirements capture, Chapter 7. Chapter 4 looks in more detail at client/server computing.

1.4 OT as the 'Oly Trinity

We have been discussing some of the benefits of and motivations for using object technology. We divided enterprises between business and technology (labour and capital) and then briefly examined the principal mediators of the contradiction: the developer and the user (production and consumption). We now turn to the technology itself – and in so doing take the opportunity to introduce, discuss and redefine the basic ideas of the subject. Object technology is now to be regarded as the syntheses of the business, the developer and the user, internally reflected in either the business or the technology; a dual trinity. Since this is a technical book we will focus for the present on the technical aspects. Users and developers may be viewed as opposites, united by the organization but divided by the technology. The unity arises from their common organizational purpose but technology intervenes, often preventing the user from carrying out certain tasks or at least separating the skills of users from those of developers. This latter separation corresponds to a useful division of labour, leading to increased productivity, so the schism represented by technology is not always a bad thing. If we have adaptable systems, satisfied users and productive developers, we can achieve most of the goals of IT within a business context. In this section we will examine how this can be accomplished and, in doing so, introduce the fundamental ideas and benefits of object technology.

1.4.1 The key concepts of object technology

According to a recent International Data Corporation white paper, object technology (OT) 'will be one of the most fundamental software technologies of the 1990s' and is already 'mature enough to put into production'. Improvements in quality and reliability together with productivity gains of over 14:1 have been realized by some early users. So what is all the fuss about, and how can IT departments exploit the potential?

A conventional computer system can be regarded as a set of functions together with a collection of data. This static architectural model is illustrated in Figure 1.3 which also indicates that, when the system runs, the dynamics may be regarded as some function, f(1), reading some data, A, transforming

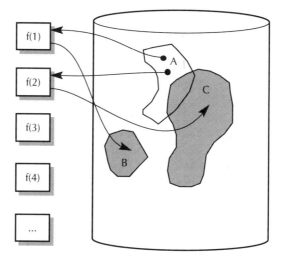

Figure 1.3 The architecture of a conventional computer system.

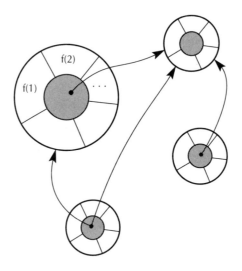

Figure 1.4 The architecture of an object-oriented system.

them and writing to B. Then some other function, f(2), reads some data, perhaps the same data, does whatever it does and writes data to C. Such
overlapping data access gives rise to complex concurrency and integrity problems but these can be well solved by using a database management system. The
question that I will ask you to consider before reading on is: what must be
done when part of the data structure has to change?

Considering this from the point of view of a maintenance programmer,
the only conclusion that one can come to is that every single function must be
checked to see if it may be destabilized by the change. Good documentation
can help with this but it is rarely available in practice. Part of the reason for
this is that good documentation for this task would itself consist in an object-
oriented description of the system and is unlikely to be divorced from an
object-oriented implementation, or at least design. Furthermore, every function that is changed to reflect the new structure may have side-effects in other
parts of the system. Perhaps this accounts for the extraordinarily high costs of
maintenance; up to 95% of all IT costs has been claimed. Figure 1.4 illustrates
a completely different architectural approach to systems. Here, all the data that
a function needs to access are encapsulated with it in packages called *objects*
and in such a way that the functions of no other object may access these data.
Following a suggestion of John Daniels and Steve Cook (1993), these objects
may be regarded as boiled eggs. The yolk is their data structure, the white consists of the functions that access these data and the shell represents the
signature of the publicly visible operations. However, as it stands, there is a
problem with this model. Suppose that every object contains a function that
needs the same datum. In that case the potential for data duplication is stag-

gering and the approach would be quite impracticable. The solution is to permit the objects to send messages to each other. In this way object X may need data A but not encapsulate them. Provided that X stores in its yolk the identity of another object, Y, that does contain the required data, it may send a message requesting the data or even some transformed version of them. This, in a nutshell, is 50% of the idea behind object technology. The other 50% involves allowing the objects to be classified and related to each other in other ways. Notice that with this approach the maintenance problem is localized and thus greatly simplified. When a data structure changes, the maintainer need only check the functions in the albumen that encapsulates it. There can be no effect elsewhere in the system unless the shell is cracked or deformed; that is, if the interface changes. Thus, while we may claim to have reduced the mainte- nance problem by orders of magnitude, we now have to work very hard to ensure that we produce correct, complete and stable interfaces for our objects. This implies that sound analysis and design are even more worthwhile and nec- essary than they were for conventional systems. This extra effort is worthwhile because object technology leads to some very significant benefits.

With this basic metaphor in mind let us proceed to discover and appreci- ate the basic concepts of the subject. Object-oriented software engineering is usually said to be characterized by the following key concepts.

- **Objects** The basic units of construction, be it for conceptualization, design or programming, are instances organized into classes with common features. These features comprise attributes, and procedures called *opera- tions* or *methods*. Strictly speaking, methods are the functions that implement operations and operations are the abstract specifications of methods. Objects should, as far as possible, be based on the real-world entities and concepts of the application or domain. Objects can be either classes or instances, although some authorities use the term *object* synony- mously with *instance*. I object to this usage since there is scope for confusion when two words are used for the same thing and, as Berard (1993) has also observed, in some languages a class can itself be an instance of some higher-level class or metaclass. Throughout this book I shall use the term *object*, as if it were slang, to mean either a class or an instance. The precise term will be used where the difference matters.
- **Identity** Objects, whether classes or instances, have unique identities throughout their lives. This distinguishes object-oriented models from, say, relational ones.
- **Encapsulation** The data structures and implementation details of an object are hidden from other objects in the system. The only way to access an object's state is to send a message that causes one of the meth- ods to execute. Strictly speaking, the attributes are shorthand for methods that get and put values. This makes classes equivalent to abstract data types in programming. Some of the methods of an object may also be hidden behind the interface. The interface is best regarded as a public

declaration of the *responsibilities* of the object. Attributes may be regarded as *responsibilities for knowing* and operations as *responsibilities for doing*.

- **Messages** Objects, classes and their instances, communicate by message passing. This eliminates much data duplication and ensures that changes to data structures encapsulated within objects do not propagate their effects to other parts of the system. Messages are often implemented as function calls. An object can only send a message to another if it stores that object's identity. This may be regarded as a weakness of the object-oriented metaphor when it is necessary to broadcast messages to many objects, though we will see in Chapters 2 and 5 that there are ways round the problem.
- **Inheritance** Instances (usually) inherit all and only the features of the classes they belong to, but it is also possible in an object-oriented system to allow classes to inherit features from more general superclasses. In this case inherited features can be overridden and extra features added to deal with exceptions. Inheritance implements the idea of classification and represents a special case of a structural interrelationship between a group of objects.
- **Polymorphism** The ability to use the same expression to denote different operations is referred to as polymorphism. This occurs where + is used to signify real or integer addition and when the message 'add 1' is sent to a bank account and to a list of reminder notes; the same message should produce quite different results. Polymorphism represents the ability of an abstraction to share features. Polymorphism is often implemented by dynamic binding which, a droll commentator once observed, is the computing equivalent of picking up the cutlery after having selected the meal. Inheritance is a special kind of polymorphism that characterizes object-oriented systems. Some authorities claim that polymorphism is the central idea in object-oriented systems, but there are non-object-oriented metaphors that take this point further, as exemplified in languages such as ML or Miranda.

I think that the terminology in wide use still suffers from some degree of confusion as to which concepts are central and which incidental. Abstracting from this turmoil, I believe that there are two key characteristics of object-oriented systems which are central and these are encapsulation and inheritance (or classification). Strictly speaking, inheritance implements the structure of classification – sometimes called *generalization/specialization* – but I will relax the distinction when no confusion can arise. There is a tension and opposition between these abstractions. Inheritance violates encapsulation because sub-objects may have privileged access to the implementation of their super-objects' methods.

Object technology is **class-oriented** in the sense that instances derive their features from classes which in turn may derive their features from more abstract ones up through a hierarchy or network of classes. Another way to achieve the benefits of the object-oriented approach is to use a classless approach where each object is regarded as a prototype in the following sense. Every object is an instance that is regarded as typical. Other instances may be created by making slight variations to the features of an existing one. Thus, the typical dog has four legs and is called Fido or Rover. There are several instances of dogs with different names all derived from the pattern or prototype provided by Fido. My friend's dog lost a leg in an accident and was called Spock. Spock thus was thoroughly Fido-like except in having three legs. Languages that support this model of inheritance such as SELF (Ungar and Smith, 1987) are known as **prototype languages** and are said to support **classless inheritance**. AI frames and scripts can be regarded in this way as prototypes although they may also use class based inheritance. As a language independent method, SOMA supports both points of view. This may lead purists to the view that SOMA is not strictly object-oriented since it supports a more general model than Smalltalk.

1.4.2 Which concepts are the characteristic ones?

There is a continuing debate on what the key concepts of object technology are. Because there is so much controversy over these a short philosophical digression is in order. This digression can be omitted by readers unhappy with philosophical disputation of this type without endangering their understanding of later sections.

Henderson-Sellers and Edwards (1994) suggest a triad or triangle of concepts consisting of:

(1) Polymorphism/inheritance
(2) Abstraction
(3) Encapsulation/information hiding

Berard (1993) points outs that the last three are closely related, abstraction being the process of identifying what information is important and visible, encapsulation the technique used to package these decisions and information hiding the general principle that design decisions should be hidden. Further, I shrink from triads of this sort, which I do not believe occur in nature or thought and can obfuscate understanding. My approach is to look for the principal contradictions in terminology as in things. Thus, we could approach this question of finding the key concepts by starting with polymorphism (having many forms) and opposing it to monomorphism (having a single form or identity). These opposites interpenetrate each other. Every system is both polymorphic and monomorphic. However, it is a capital mistake to consider form in isolation from content. At this level, abstraction can be seen as the process that gives (ideal) form to (material or concrete) content. The opposite of abstraction is realization, which can be thought of as the instantiation of form: classes, concepts or structures. These processes mediate the contradiction between form and content but yet are at too high a level to be useful. Let us examine one side of the dichotomy in more detail, the category of form. Form can be singular (monomorphic) or manifold (polymorphic) as illustrated in Figure 1.5. When we classify objects, we posit the oneness of their multiplicity. When we encapsulate, we collect variation and give it a single, but polymorphic, identity. Encapsulation collects individual operations and groups them into a multifaceted unity. Thus encapsulation and classification (inheritance) become the key concepts mediating the contradiction between the oneness and multiplicity of system components. Now, this analysis has glossed over the fact that classification is merely a special case of relationship; that is, that relationship corresponding to the verb *to be* or the copula *is*. Strictly, the arrow in the figure should be labelled 'relationship' or 'structuring', but classification is a very special, distinguished kind of relationship. Other distinguished relationships are composition (or aggregation) and usage. The arrows representing encapsulation and structuring can also be viewed as the internalization of abstraction and instantiation within the category of form. All structures imply some sort of inter-object visibility. Where such structures interact we also have replicable 'patterns' (Coad, 1992; Madsen *et al.*, 1993). The general term we will use for the formation of patterns from objects is therefore 'structuring' but for simplicity we will sometimes talk of classification as a representative of this process. This is justified because this particular form of structuring characterizes object-oriented programming languages, which often do not have direct support for composition structures or patterns.

Figure 1.5 can be read as follows. Consider a thing. Abstract from it to discover its form. That form has identity and may be looked at from many points of view. Now realize this form as a concrete instance. You have returned to the original thing but now it is an abstract model rather than the original. Conversely, if we start from an idea, a form such as a class, we can instantiate it and then ask what abstract properties the instance has. This is illustrated in Figure 1.6 which expands the content aspect of the contradiction.

Figure 1.6 also shows how the concepts of object identity and message passing (visibility) arise as a result of the conflict between encapsulation and classification. Visibility is the internal reflection in the category of content of the polymorphic within the monomorphic, which means that when you encapsulate a concept you do so within a context that needs to refer to it. Identity internalizes the singleness of the object within its manifoldness by classifying it as such.

In these rather abstract terms, we can see that the most fundamental concepts of all are content and form; in particular polymorphism. In practical terms, however, the fundamental concepts are those that let us deal with the content and form of systems and their mediating processes of abstraction and

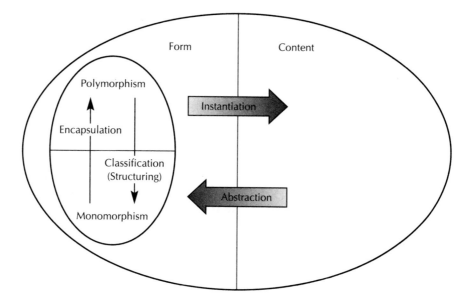

Figure 1.5 Analysis of fundamental terms (form).

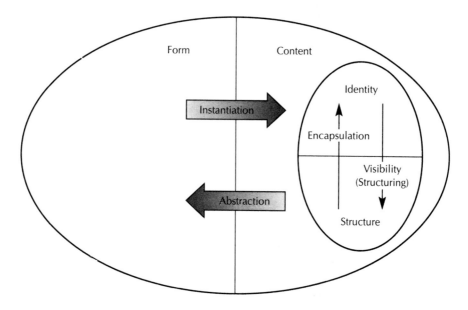

Figure 1.6 Analysis of fundamental terms (content).

realization. These are encapsulation and classification (or more generally structuring). We should avoid taking polymorphism as the fundamental concept since, like structuring in general, it is not definitional for object-oriented languages. There are polymorphic languages, such as ML, that are not object-oriented. This leaves us with encapsulation and classification as the fundamental, definitional concepts of OT. This argument has also shown that polymorphism, abstraction, structuring, usage (message passing) and identity are also key concepts and how they are related. The ladder of concepts need not end or begin here and a deeper exploration is required to discover the nature of the relation between structuring and classification. However, we have made this diversion merely to emphasize the central concepts of object technology as encapsulation and structure, with classification being singled out as a particularly important kind of structure just as inheritance is a particular kind of polymorphism. I fear that completing this exploration would take us too far from the purposes of this text, which is chiefly practical in nature.

1.4.3 Benefits

Equipped with a clear and adaptable understanding of the key concepts, we may now proceed to a discussion of the benefits of object technology. A number of such benefits have been recognized by commentators including:

- higher quality, arising from the reuse of previously used and tested components;
- faster development, arising as much from prototyping as from reuse though not at all from faster development of new code;
- greater flexibility, arising chiefly from inheritance;
- increased scalability, because subsystems can be tested independently and extended easily utilizing inheritance;
- less maintenance in the face of changing requirements;
- better correspondences between the business and its software systems.

The key benefits usually promised by purveyors of object technology are reusability and extensibility. That is, object-oriented systems are to be assembled from pre-written components with minimal effort and the assembled system will be easy to extend without any need to tinker with the reused components. Encapsulation makes objects the unit of reuse. Inheritance provides the ability to extend the system easily. The main advertised benefit of OT is the claim that objects constitute units of reusable code. This requires additional investment but, once produced, the objects can be used with full confidence in their quality. Unfortunately, no two applications are exactly the same, so that reuse will not work unless exceptions can be readily dealt with. This is where the second major feature of an object-oriented system, inheritance, comes in. Objects are organized into classes in a hierarchy and subclasses can be defined.

For example, if we have defined classes for current and deposit accounts it is easy to add the definition of a class for 'interest-bearing current account' that inherits all the features of current account and adds the interest calculations.

A third key benefit is the semantic richness of object-oriented models. Object-oriented systems are models of the business processes rather than imperative descriptions of business functions. Since they mimic the application's real-world objects, concepts and structures directly, they can constitute a rich representation isomorphic to the system being modelled. This is why, for example, object-oriented methods are so suitable for modelling client/server systems and GUIs. It also implies an implicit reversibility from object-oriented code back to requirements not found in conventional systems. The objects in the program correspond directly to real-world active entities and this makes it easy to see how object models can be used to solve problems in business process re-engineering, as we shall see in subsequent chapters.

While there are very many object-oriented programming languages, OT goes far beyond mere programming. There are now object-oriented databases offering hundredfold performance gains over their relational equivalents for some applications while retaining the flexibility of relational systems. There are about a dozen commercial object-oriented databases available. They are all remarkable not only for their efficiency but in their facilities for automatic version control and distribution.

It has also been found that conventional structured methods hinder progress in adopting OT, so that new methods of object-oriented analysis and design have emerged. There have been over 60 suggestions for object-oriented analysis and design methods.

OT can be applied to almost any problem but the chief areas of application at present are connected with building client/server systems, graphical user interfaces, complex engineering and CAD/CAM applications and software products themselves where traditional approaches have fared very badly. Other important ones include building front-ends to legacy systems, distributed computing, multimedia systems, CASE tools and repositories, engineering databases, simulation, process control and geographic information systems. Currently, the most popular language is C++ but Smalltalk is gaining ground rapidly. This is partly because C++ is a frighteningly complex language to write well and partly because IBM has shown great interest in Smalltalk recently. Eiffel is rapidly gaining ground in the educational world. Micro Focus, Realia and other suppliers have announced object-oriented COBOL compilers too. I feel that C++ programmers should start with comprehensive training in methods of object-oriented analysis and design before embarking on their projects and, preferably, should learn a language like Smalltalk or Eiffel first, because the latter enforce the correct use of object-oriented concepts while C++ does not. The first step should be to train developers in proper object-oriented analysis concepts and methods. Since industry-wide standards such as the Object Management Group's CORBA have begun to emerge and become accepted, there is also a need for training programmes to take account of them.

This book is partly based on the observation and belief that reuse is easier to achieve and more beneficial at the specification level than at the code level. Part II emphasizes the construction of a repository of object and task specifications which can be linked to reusable code but which have an independent value in their own right.

1.4.4 Market opportunities

When new technology is first developed it has low capability and is largely unknown to the market. Gradually, through its lifetime, this capability will increase until some saturation level is reached or its potentialities are exhausted. However, the reputation that the technology acquires represents its perceived value and may be driven up by hype out of all proportion to its real capability. This is illustrated by the curves in Figure 1.7. Eventually, as the hype fades and early users try out the technology, gloom sets in. It is discovered that there are problems and the exaggerated claims of both suppliers and journalists are debunked. At this point expectations fall to the level of the initial real capability. However, in the meantime the capability of the technology has improved and the two curves cross over at point Q in the diagram. Now, price is based on exchange value, which is based on demand, which is in turn based on expectations and not on use value or capability. Thus, buyers in the period between points P and Q have been paying a premium for the technology. After the crossover they may purchase at a discount until normality is restored at point R.

The only difficulty in using this model is estimating where one is on the expectation curve. The technical press is a good indicator of expectation and experts in the technology will usually be able to estimate its real capability. At

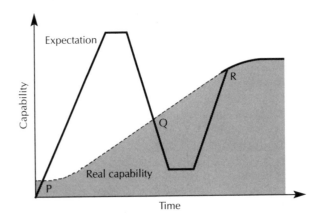

Figure 1.7 Capability and perceived value curves for new technologies.

the time of writing (1994) I believe that we are somewhere near the peak of the expectation curve, which is flatter than the diagrammatic representation. This applies to object-oriented programming, object-oriented methods and object-oriented databases about equally, though object-oriented programming is slightly more advanced than the other two areas. Crossover should occur within two years. This is my judgement but other experts may take different views. The latest market surveys (from Ovum for example) forecast very rapid growth in this market but predict a flattening out in the growth rate within two years, which tends to confirm my view. Since it takes about two years for an organization to understand and adopt a new approach, this is exactly the right time for users to begin education and training programmes in order to be ready for the crossover.

The implications of this analysis for object technology are that:

- Vendors can charge high fees for services and products in the immediate future;
- Buyers will pay premium rates to gain competitive advantage from the technology and build their understanding and skills in preparation for the crossover point when they will be able to apply the technology on a more massive scale and buy at a discount in a mature market;
- The initial projects will be demonstrators and pilots except for organizations where the benefits are especially important.

Market trends that are evident from my experience are upward and changing in character. In 1990 user organizations were attending awareness briefings and gathering information. By 1991 a vendor's OT capability had become important in winning bids for more general work in computing but a few mission-critical projects using it had begun. The market for training courses in object-oriented programming and methods began to mature in 1992 and advanced users were completing their first pilot projects. In 1993 OT was beginning to be used on the first large-scale, mission-critical projects in the mainstream of data processing; and a very small number of advanced users had completely switched to object-oriented development for new systems while continuing to maintain conventional legacy systems pending migration. One head of IT for such an organization, Swiss Bank Corporation, claimed (*Computing*, 19th November 1993) that the chief motivation was rapid development because systems that came in over budget might detract from performance by 8% while those that came in late would affect the bottom line by over 30%. OT contributes to rapid development in several ways but principally through reuse and extensibility. A comprehensive approach to object-oriented rapid application development is presented in Part II.

The current buyers of object technology may be classified as large software houses, smaller software houses and end users. Large software houses such as Borland, Microsoft and even IBM are already committed to OT and the others will inevitably be dragged along, kicking and screaming, with these leaders. The Object Management Group has united these organizations in their determination and practically every significant player is now a member of this organization. These firms will mainly use OT to gain productivity from reuse. The smaller software houses are using OT to develop complex products such as CASE tools and CAD systems. These firms have shown a strong interest in object-oriented development methods as well as languages. They will gain productivity from reuse and use the technology to enter new markets. End users are building pilots, buying mentoring services and showing an interest in methods. Their key applications are client/server systems and graphical user interfaces. They will gain from extensibility and the better modelling ability of OT. Very few have switched over totally. Those that have done so successfully will be rôle models for the future.

1.4.5 Problems with adoption

Management must fully appreciate the benefits, pitfalls and consequences of adopting OT. Many organizations adopting OT have special needs and a customized training programme is often best. Mentoring has been highly successful as a means of knowledge transfer. This means that an experienced object technologist works with a development team offering guidance and practical help.

The danger is to see OT as merely the next 'silver bullet'. We should view it with circumspection but I still believe that most modern companies will be unable to ignore it in the coming years in so far as it remains distinguishable at all from that activity which I like to call 'building computer systems'.

Perhaps the key question facing managers concerns getting from where we are now with a legacy of conventional, difficult to maintain but essential systems to where we want to be with object technology. This is the question of migration strategy and it is the subject of the next chapter and, implicitly, of the remainder of this book.

Before an organization can contemplate migrating to object technology it must first review where it is currently in terms of the classes of tools, products, methods and languages in use. It is often helpful to convince COBOL programmers that many of the concepts of object technology are already familiar and that many of the principles of object-oriented design are already known to them under the heading of 'good software engineering practice'; principles such as modularity, information hiding, low coupling, and so on. This helps them to accept any required changes far more readily. It is worth pointing out that a traditional module can be viewed as a set of interface functions with a shared data structure.

Organizations migrating to object technology must understand that there is some good news and some bad news due. The good news concerns better usability, rapid development, easier re-engineering, the ability to deal with more complex systems, higher reuse levels and greater flexibility. The semantic richness of object models makes specifications more reversible and supports rapid application development directly. Extensibility gives immediate benefits. Sound object-oriented analysis helps to deliver the benefits of OT much earlier in the life cycle. Reuse can slash development costs and some organizations have doubled productivity annually over the past two years or so because of this. The bad news is that reuse is not free and its successful adoption may involve major cultural changes and high levels of investment. Organizations migrating to object technology will have to implement major changes in the reward structures, with reuse specialists being rewarded quite differently from developers and developers being rewarded for speed and quality more explicitly. Key personnel will have to be taken away from the maintenance of important legacy systems in order to bring sufficient business knowledge to new, object-oriented developments. Every manager in the organization will have to be completely re-educated in the new approach, otherwise we shall merely re-create the nightmares of the waterfall model and the structured perspective with object-oriented tools. This requires clear, positive leadership and immense clarity and single-mindedness about the benefits and the risks inherent in object technology.

The range of applications of OT is almost endless. Object-oriented systems analysis produces semantically rich models and helps to support business re-engineering projects. There are now many advanced users of OT in manufacturing, finance, computing itself and other sectors. The National and Provincial Building Society in the UK has focused on business process re-engineering in its adoption and utilization of object technology. By mid-1993 it had at least three major object-oriented projects running and had modified CASE tools to support its methods for BPR and object-oriented analysis. It plans to build a code reuse library and is contemplating the same for specifications. My own company, Swiss Bank Corporation, has adopted OT as the solution to its migration problems in moving from centralized mainframes to distributed, open systems. All new international banking and investment systems development is now done in this way. Other organizations that are using or beginning to make the commitment to OT include (in alphabetical order) Banque Paribas, Boeing, Borland, the Canadian Imperial Bank of Commerce, the Civil Aviation Authority, Credit Suisse, General Electric, Hewlett Packard, IBM, ICL, Microsoft, NYNEX, Union Bank of Switzerland, United Artists and Westinghouse. There are, of course, many other banks, building societies, insurers, retailers, hospitals, police departments, computer manufacturers, telephone companies, software houses and mining consortia that cannot be mentioned in the space available.

The main points of this book may now be summarized as follows:

- The computing industry requires object technology to solve the problems of satisfying users in increasingly adaptable businesses in a productive manner.
- There are four ways to migrate legacy systems: object wrappers, object request brokers, object-oriented databases and DIY methods. A key issue is the interoperability of old and new systems during the migration stages.

- Object-oriented methods facilitate systems with complex, graphical and event driven interfaces. They help enhance usability.
- Object-oriented methods facilitate distributed, rightsized solutions.
- There is a close relationship between the ideas of object-oriented programming and those of expert systems. Expert systems can be built better using object-oriented methods and object-oriented methods can benefit from the introduction of ideas from artificial intelligence and conceptual modelling.
- The key to successful migration is the adoption of a comprehensive approach to object technology throughout the systems development life cycle, from early requirements capture to implementation.
- Such a comprehensive approach is presented in Part II. The approach encompasses object modelling, requirements capture, enterprise modelling and business process re-engineering, a truly object-oriented process model that fits in with an evolutionary (rapid development) approach, transition to design using both object-oriented and conventional languages, databases and tools, measurement and estimation, and coordination and reuse management.

1.5 Summary

There are two forces leading to the necessity of adopting OT: the need for businesses to be more adaptable and more flexible in the face of a changing world, together with an even more profound need to drive up productivity. Resolving the contradiction leads to greater satisfaction on the part of users and developers.

Object technology is potentially able to help modern organizations deal with increasing complexity while remaining responsive to external change. However, the investment in existing systems is vast and cannot be abandoned overnight. A migration strategy is therefore needed.

Business change is endemic to the modern enterprise. Business process re-engineering can help organizations respond to change. Object technology provides a means of building business models based on networks of cooperating agents rather than on functional specializations. These models support and enable BPR.

Increased complexity and the need for technical solutions imply that we need to watch the ever-expanding range of new computer technologies closely. New applications, new open and distributed platforms and the move to event driven styles of interaction drive inexorably towards the adoption of OT. Increased competition heightens uncertainty. Rapid change can only be enabled by IT. This implies the adoption of radical process innovation in the business. The basic ideas of BPR were introduced to this end. IT needs to reduce its time-to-market. Since systems have to be more adaptable, evolutionary techniques for systems development are *de rigeur*.

Adaptable businesses need software technology that promotes reuse and extensibility. They also need productive developers. Objects help with modelling the world, using things that correspond to real-world entities. The method described in this book emphasizes semantic richness and explicit, understandable specifications. Developers like to be productive. The most productive developers work in small, highly focused teams with no bureaucracy and full autonomy within agreed objectives. Tools that can produce highly distributed, easy-to-use, natural systems must support work-flow and amplify the abilities of users. OT is productive because of the potential for reuse. Class libraries are the repository of productivity. These components can be tailored to individual requirements using inheritance. Object-oriented models are easier to debug due to their richer semantic content. OT promises that we might be able to assemble software systems rather than code them.

We looked at some technology futures including emerging object-oriented operating systems, parallelism, formal methods, expert systems, communications technology and methods. We will need to adopt different system development methods in order to make our IT operations more effective because current methods are so costly. The weakness of current CASE is based on the weakness of current methods.

The mainframe is going to be with us for a long time but we will see increasing use of distributed computing, networks and workstations to take away from the mainframe those tasks that mainframes are bad at.

Systems are written to satisfy users, though they rarely do. Object technology is exactly right for user interface development precisely because the message passing metaphor maps well onto the process of human–machine interaction.

One of the great advantages of object-oriented computing is its modelling and simulation ability. Such systems are easier to understand, use and change. OT closes the gap between the language of technicians and that of users.

OT will be one of the most fundamental software technologies of the 1990s and is already mature enough to put into production.

Section 1.4 introduced and discussed the fundamental concepts of OT. Its chief benefit is the localization and consequent reduction of maintenance costs. However, interfaces must be correct, complete and stable. This implies that sound analysis and design are even more worthwhile and necessary than they were for conventional systems. Object-oriented software engineering is usually said to be characterized by the following key concepts: objects, encapsulation, messages, inheritance and polymorphism – but there are two key characteristics of object-oriented systems: encapsulation and inheritance. Prototype languages that support classless inheritance were introduced. AI frames and scripts can be regarded as prototypes although they may also use class based inheritance. As a language independent method, SOMA supports both points of view.

OT can be applied to almost any problem but the chief areas of application at present are connected with building client/server systems, graphical user interfaces, complex engineering and CAD applications and software products themselves.

We discussed some of the marketing issues surrounding OT and a model of technology adoption. The danger is to see OT as a silver bullet. We should view it with circumspection but most modern companies will be unable to ignore it.

There are four ways to migrate legacy systems: object wrappers, object request brokers, object-oriented databases and DIY methods. A key issue is the interoperability of old and new systems during the migration stages.

There is a close relationship between the ideas of object-oriented programming and those of expert systems. Expert systems can be built better using object-oriented methods and object-oriented methods can benefit from the introduction of ideas from artificial intelligence and conceptual modelling.

The key to successful migration is the adoption of a comprehensive approach to OT throughout the systems development life cycle, from early requirements capture to implementation. The semantic richness of object models makes specifications more reversible and supports rapid application development directly. Sound object-oriented analysis helps to deliver the benefits of OT much earlier in the life cycle. Organizations migrating to OT must understand that better usability, rapid development, easier re-engineering, the ability to deal with more complex systems, higher reuse levels and greater flexibility are offset because reuse is not free. They will have to implement major changes. Every manager in the organization will have to be re-educated in the new approach. This requires leadership and immense clarity and single-mindedness about the benefits and the risks inherent in object technology.

☰ 1.6 Bibliographical notes

The seminal papers on business process re-engineering are probably those by Hammer (1990) and Davenport and Short (1990). Other influential papers include Short and Venkatramen (1992) and Woolfe (1991). Recent popular books on the subject include Hammer and Champy (1993) and Davenport (1993). Tom Peters' various books (1987, 1992) offer insights with a slightly different emphasis while making very similar points. Jacobs (1992) discusses the relationship between BPR and knowledge based systems and Fichman and Kemerer (1993) its relationship with OT.

Taylor (1992b) provides a management level introduction to OT as does Taylor (1992a) which goes into more depth. Graham (1994a) is a more technical survey of the whole field of object technology and provides all the background required to understand this book, though the latter is designed to be read independently.

Collins (1990) is a fascinating discussion of the limitations that the social nature of knowledge places on the possibilities for artificial intelligence. Graham (1994c) also discusses this point.

Harmon and Taylor (1993) give details of 19 successful applications of object technology.

Computer Finance, a publication of APT Data Services, regularly presents empirical surveys of the costs of client/server versus mainframe computing.

2

Interoperation, reuse and migration

Between two evils, I always pick the one I never tried before
Mae West (Klondike Annie)

To travel hopefully is a better thing than to arrive.
Robert Louis Stevenson
(Virginibus Puerisque)

Many people and organizations are convinced of the wisdom of shifting their systems development activities towards an object-oriented style. This may be because they have absorbed the lessons of the previous chapter, seen other companies succeeding in this way or even for that worst of reasons: because OT is new and fashionable. Even in the latter, misguided, case these companies may gain from the experience because, even should the project in hand fail, they may gain a better understanding of existing systems and development practices through the construction of an object model. They have several reasons for replacing or extending older systems. For example, a package vendor may see the move to object technology as closely tied to the move to an open platform and, in turn, see this as a way of achieving greater market share since there are usually potential customers who do not (and perhaps will not) own the proprietary platform on which the old product currently runs. They may wish to compete more effectively by adding value to the existing product with graphical user interfaces, management information system (MIS) features or delivery on distributed platforms. User organizations may wish to take advantage of new standards, downsizing, and friendlier interfaces along with the benefits of the move to OT itself that were discussed in Chapter 1. Both types of organization will be looking to slash maintenance costs, which can account for a huge proportion of the IS budget, and reduce time-to-market. However, while overnight migration is highly desirable it is seldom possible. Furthermore, gradual migration may take too long for its benefits to be worthwhile. Often the solution is to reuse existing conventional components or entire systems and packages. So, there are several available options: interoperation, reuse, extension, and gradual or sudden migration. These options are closely related but we will deal with interoperation first.

In this chapter, we will examine various proposed and actual strategies which meet the requirements of organizations facing migration and interoperation problems, emphasizing the concerns of a developer who wants to develop an object-oriented application that needs to use the services provided by applications that incorporate other programming styles such as expert systems, 4GLs, procedural libraries (for example, the NAG FORTRAN library), concurrent systems, parallel processing systems, relational databases, hypermedia, structured designs or even fuzzy controllers. We must ask whether the non-object-oriented features of these old systems can be reused. If so, what are the fundamental issues in designing and building interoperation tools? Is it better to replace non-object-oriented features? If so, are there any rules or recommendations on migration techniques? How do you deal with those critical COBOL or Assembler applications? What is the rôle of new object-oriented analysis and design techniques within this kind of migration? Is there a strategy that enables you to metamorphose an existing procedural application into an object-oriented application without disrupting services to the existing users?

This chapter and much of the remainder of Part I of this book will attempt to answer these questions on the basis of such techniques as object wrappers, object request brokers and blackboard systems and cover such problems as how to wrap an old application that exists in a large number of different versions. We will also explore the ways in which object-oriented analysis in particular and object technology as a whole can be used as a migration technique. In fact, this chapter sets the tone for the remainder of the book wherein we will first look at a few specific application areas where the strategies can be applied and then, in Part II, expose a complete development approach that takes account of migration, reuse and interoperability issues.

2.1 Interoperation of object-oriented systems with conventional IT

There are a number of scenarios in which an object-oriented application should interoperate with existing non-object-oriented systems. These include:

- the evolutionary migration of an existing system to a future object-oriented implementation where parts of the old system will remain temporarily in use;
- the evolution of systems that already exist and are important and too large or complex to rewrite at a stroke and where part or all of the old system may continue to exist indefinitely;

- the reuse of highly specialized or optimized routines, embedded expert systems and hardware-specific software;
- exploiting the best of existing relational databases for one part of an application in concert with the use of an object-oriented programming language and/or object-oriented database for another;
- the construction of graphical front-ends to existing systems;
- the need to build on existing 'package' solutions;
- cooperative processing and blackboard architectures may involve agents that already exist working with newly defined objects;
- the need to cooperate with existing systems across telecommunications and local area networks.

The main issue this chapter addresses is how to tackle the migration of a vast system that is almost invariably very costly and tricky to maintain. The first strategy recommended here is to build what is known as an object *wrapper*. Object wrappers can be used to migrate to object-oriented programming and still protect investments in conventional code. The wrapper concept has become part of the folklore of object orientation but, as far as I know, the term was first coined by Wally Dietrich of IBM (Dietrich *at al.*,1989) though it is also often attributed to Brad Cox and Tom Love, the developers of Objective-C, but in a slightly different context. There are also claims that the usage was in vogue within IBM as early as 1987.

The existence of large investments in programs written in conventional languages such as Assembler, COBOL, PL/1, FORTRAN and even APL has to be recognized. It must also be allowed that the biggest cost associated with these 'legacy' systems, as Dietrich calls them, is maintenance. Maintenance is costly because, in a conventional system, any change to the data structure requires checking every single function to see if it is affected. As we saw in the last chapter, this does not occur with object-oriented systems due to the encapsulation of the data structures by the functions that use them. However much we would like to replace these old systems completely, the economics of the matter forbids it on any large scale; there just are not enough development resources. What we must do is build on the existing investment and move gradually to the brave new world of object orientation.

It is possible to create object wrappers around this bulk of existing code, which can then be replaced or allowed to wither away. Building object wrappers can help protect the investment in older systems during the move to object-oriented programming. An object wrapper enables a new, object-oriented part of a system to interact with a conventional chunk by message passing. The wrapper itself is likely to be written in the same language as the original system, COBOL for example. This may represent a very substantial investment, but once it is in place virtually all maintenance activity may cease; at least this is the theory.

Imagine that the existing COBOL system interacts with users through a traditional menu system, each screen offering about ten options and with the

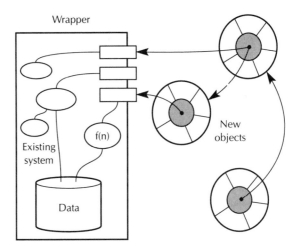

Figure 2.1 Object wrappers.

leaf nodes of the menu tree being normal 'enter, tab and commit' data entry screens. This characterizes a very large number of present-day systems. The wrapper must offer all the functions of the old system as if through the interface of an object, as illustrated by the 'Gradygram' in Figure 2.1 where the small rectangles on the boundary of the wrapper represent its visible operations, which in turn call the old system's functions and thereby access its data too[1]. Effectively, the wrapper is a large object whose methods are the menu options of the old system. The only difference between this new object and the old system is that it will respond to messages from other objects. So far, this gives little in the way of benefits. However, when we discover a bug, receive a change request or wish to add a new business function the benefits begin; for we do not meddle with the old system at all but create a new set of objects to deliver the new features. As far as the existing users are concerned, they may see no difference when using the old functions, although their calls are being diverted via the wrapper. Wrappers may be small or large, but in the context of interoperation they tend to be of quite coarse granularity. For command driven systems, the wrapper may be a set of operating system batch files or scripts. If the old system used a form or screen-based interface, the wrapper may consist of code that reads and writes data to the screen. This can be done using a virtual terminal. This is fairly easy to accomplish on machines such as the VAX though it is not always possible with systems such as OS/400 where some spe-

---

[1] The term *Gradygram* was coined to stand for the icons with operations indicated by small boxes on the boundary of a rectangle representing the object, which have been used by Grady Booch since his work on design for Ada in the mid-1980s. The Booch'93 method uses them for its module diagrams to this day and variants have appeared in several other methods.

cialist software or an object request broker may be required. All new functions or replacements should be dealt with by creating new objects with their own encapsulated data structures and methods. If the services of the old system are needed, these are requested by message passing and the output is decoded by the wrapper and passed to the requester.

So much for the propaganda! Implementing wrappers is not as easy as it sounds in several respects. Much of the literature on wrappers is aimed at deriving the necessity of either object-oriented databases or object request brokers, which we will cover in more detail in Chapter 4. When these are not available, for whatever reason, developers have to face up to the implementation details directly. One such issue concerns granularity. Most of the theoretical arguments and a good deal of the practical experience of object-oriented programmers indicate that small objects are usually more reusable than large ones. Recall the usual set of guidelines for object design from your favourite text on the subject: interfaces should be small and simple; no more than about 17 operations per object; and so on. However, with the legacy system we are faced with a *fait accompli*; the system is as it is. There are irreducibly large-grain 'objects' often present in the design of legacy systems. Object request brokers are specifically aimed at dealing with this kind of coarse-grain reuse. The question is whether, without such a broker, we can still gain from the use of a handmade wrapper. Some developers find that coarse-grain objects arise naturally even with new requirements and deduce that object-oriented models are not always appropriate. Brice (1993) for example found this in the context of geometrical image transformation software. The data structures were straightforward but the processing required pages of equations to describe it and data flow models were found to be the most natural thing to use[2]. Here is a case where wrappers may be beneficial even with greenfield developments.

The wrapper approach to migration is not the only one available. Other options include the use of object request brokers (ORBs), employing object-oriented databases and proceeding in a completely *ad hoc* manner. The *ad hoc* approach is often the correct one, but there are so many ways of approaching a particular problem that few sensible generalizations can be made. ORBs are discussed in Chapter 4 and discussion of their use as a migration tool is deferred until then. The *ad hoc* approach was the only one available until the quite recent appearance of ORB and object-oriented database (OODB) products. One leading financial institution, for example, built a straight-through trading system to connect its front and back office systems using objects that effectively comprised self-describing data packets. The result was observed *post facto* to be an application-specific object request broker but the work was completed before any stable commercial CORBA compliant distributed object

---

[2] Rumbaugh too (1993) has suggested using the data flow models in OMT to model numerical computation – a better use I think than that originally intended by Rumbaugh *et al.* (1991).

management system had come to market. Further, this application went beyond the CORBA specification by using self-describing data. Object-oriented databases are an ingredient of most object request broker products but can be used alone to act as a repository for a handcrafted infrastructure. Object-oriented databases are discussed and compared by Graham (1994a).

One of the biggest problems with the concept of object wrappers concerns data management. Using the wrapper is easy until you need to split the storage of data across the old database and some of the new objects.

2.2 Data management strategies

The object wrapper approach seems ideal at first sight but closer examination reveals some severe data management problems. Where building a wrapper makes it necessary to duplicate or share data across the new and old system components, there are four possible strategies:

(1) Carry a duplicate live copy of the common data in both parts of the system and keep both copies up to date. The problem with this is that storage requirements could double. Worse still, there are real integrity issues to worry about. It is almost certainly not a viable strategy for either migration or reuse of any commercial-scale system. We will call this the **tandem** or **handshake** strategy because it requires constant synchronization of updates and retrievals. It only works when there is little or no overlap between the data of the old and new systems.

(2) Keep all data in the old system and copy them to the new objects as required. Messages to the old system cause it to handle updates. This is known as the **borrowing** strategy because data are borrowed temporarily from the wrapper. It is similar to what is done in many existing, conventional MIS applications where data are downloaded nightly from a mainframe to workstations and updates transmitted in batch too.

(3) Copy the data to the new objects and allow the old system's data to go out of date. Again there may be integrity problems, and the wrapper may have to send messages as well as receive and respond to them, which greatly increases its complexity. Call this the **take-over** strategy by analogy with a company making a take-over bid for another.

(4) Carve out coherent chunks of the database together with related functions. This is difficult and requires a sound method of object-oriented analysis capable of describing the old system as well as the new and/or a translation technique from original systems design documents such as DFDs. On balance, it seems the most promising approach to migration. This is called the **translation** strategy because one must translate the design to an object model. It is easiest to do when the old system was originally written around critical data structures using a technique such

as stepwise refinement. These structures and the programs that use them will migrate naturally to the objects of the new system. A refinement of this strategy is to reverse engineer a data model from the existing system and to identify all file access operations in relation to this model using, for example, a CRUD (create, read, update, delete) matrix approach. CRUD techniques are often used to organize conventional systems around their data structures. These calls can then be replaced as new objects are constructed around the entities. This improved version of translation can be called **data-centred translation**. Whether it is feasible will depend on the difficulty of obtaining a data model and the complexity of the code in which the database calls are embedded. Reverse engineering tools may prove useful within this strategy and, as Reiss (1991) points out, the most useful tools would contain an understanding of the system semantics. When doing this, one should beware of normalized entities in any data model.

The habit of normalization is rooted deep in the data analysis community and one must be aware that normalized tables do not necessarily correspond to real-world entities. Take a look at any reasonably large data model and you will almost certainly find entities with strange, hyphenated names that correspond to absolutely nothing in the vocabulary of users. Thus, one must first de-normalize to get rid of first normal forms which obfuscate the description of aggregate objects and then reconstruct objects that correspond to run-time join operations. So far as reverse engineering is concerned, I will argue in Section 2.6 and Part II that a semantically rich version of object-oriented analysis is an indispensable tool and that its representations need not be as large or complex as Reiss maintains if they are well structured and automated (for example, hypermedia or CASE) support is available.

These strategies may be variously appropriate according to whether we are migrating the system to an object-oriented implementation, reusing its components, extending it or building a better or a distributed front-end. Assuming that our chief aim is to migrate the old system to a new object-oriented one rather than merely to reuse its components, which strategies are feasible? The handshake strategy is flawed for all but the smallest systems, and then there must be little overlap between new and old components. The borrowing strategy may well involve tampering with the old system and is not usually viable for the purposes of system migration unless there is a clean separation between existing functions and new requirements. Borrowing does not permit data to move permanently outward across the wrapper boundary. This means that there will come a time when a huge step must be taken all at once to migrate the data out, unless a DBMS has been used for all data accesses. These strategies, as migration strategies, do grievous violence to the whole idea of building wrappers. Only the last two strategies promise to be feasible if our intention is to migrate the functions of the old system to a new one, and there are some systems where neither seems to be practical. It is also the case that the type of system, its structure and the quality and type of its documentation will affect the choice of strategy. Dietrich's original application of the wrapper concept was to a solid modelling system of considerable complexity but whose intricacy resided in its code rather than in its data management. Furthermore, his primary concern was with the reuse of the functions of a stable system rather than its reconstruction. Hence, there has been little publicly documented experience of solving the problem under consideration here.

Strategy 4, translation, will work most often, provided that the old system can be decomposed around coherent data sets and if there are, say, some existing DFDs to transform objects from by encapsulating their data stores. If not, one is faced with building a wrapper of much greater complexity using takeover: strategy 3. The latter is a far costlier option.

2.3 Practical problems with migration to object technology

Another problem arises when the old system exists and is maintained in multiple versions. For example, a commercial package for a particular industry may, over the years, have been adapted for the needs of particular clients. The cost of building a wrapper for each version is usually prohibitive. The wrapper approach will only work if there is a core system common to all the versions, and the modifications will have to be maintained separately in any case until they can be reimplemented. This was the situation on a project that I was involved with where there were around 70 versions of the product customized for particular sites scattered across the globe, with local, dedicated maintenance teams in many cases. Also, the decomposition of the existing system into coherent chunks was exceedingly hard because of the long modification history. The strategy adopted was to model the system using object-oriented analysis and first wrap the core system in such a way that *new* functionality (an MIS component) could be added using object-oriented methods, leaving the core system largely untouched at this stage. Unfortunately, I am not permitted to reveal all the details of this development, but one feature of the problem is accessible to and worthy of comment. It turned out that the hardware on which the system had to run, pending a move to UNIX at some future date, did not support an object-oriented language of any form. Thus, in the short term, the new object-oriented components had to be implemented in a conventional language. To ensure that the new system could be fully object-oriented in the future we had to find a way to minimize the cost of so doing. This led to the use of an object-oriented analysis approach and the conversion of its products to conventional code. It also led to the use of an object request broker, NeWI, that was able to let the developers treat the system as object-oriented while still writing code in C. The analysis approach will be described fully in Part II and object request brokers more fully in Chapter 4. We also attempted to produce an object-oriented description of the existing system to clarify understanding and help carve out separate reimplementable chunks following a translation strategy. It emerged that treating some functions as objects instead of methods was useful. The bulk of the early effort went into designing additional features and their interface, via a wrapper, to the core of the existing system, translation tasks being deferred to the near future. Thus, it proved wise to proceed in steps:

(1) build a wrapper to communicate with new object-oriented components using (most probably) the borrowing strategy;
(2) perform an object-oriented analysis on the old system;
(3) use translation or data-centred translation to migrate;
(4) utilize an ORB to implement.

Grass (1991) argues that wrappers work well for mature systems that are essentially frozen, in the context of a requirement to reduce the maintenance burden which she characterizes as 'extremely aggravating' with the panache of understatement. Her main point is that ill-structured legacy systems are costly to understand and wrap. However, even this is worthwhile if the potential maintenance savings are large enough. Like Dietrich's, Grass' principal application (a parser for regular grammars) was complex functionally but not primarily a data-intensive application.

One may conclude that, until much more experience has been accumulated, the best approach to migration of legacy systems with significant data management complexity is to build wrappers that support object-oriented front-ends and to build the required new functions within the front-ends. The tandem strategy can be used only when there is little overlap and separate databases will have to be maintained. The exceptions to this are when the existing system already has a coherent data-centred structure that facilitates translation or when the benefits of the migration are large enough to justify the cost of building a very complex wrapper along the lines of the take-over strategy. If there is an existing DBMS this can be wrapped as a whole and maintained for a long time as the wrapped functions are gradually migrated. Then, at some point, one can move all the data at once to an object-oriented database if desired and eliminate the database wrapper. This is a special variant of the translation strategy where the database is one huge 'coherent chunk'. It is probably the ideal option for many organizations already obtaining satisfactory performance from their relational databases. A good wrapper for INGRES, Oracle or Sybase, probably written in C++, is a very sound investment in terms of migration strategy.

Having decided to build a wrapper and a new front-end one needs tools for building them. There are no specific products offering wrapper technology for migration at present but there are several ORB and GUI tools that may help with reuse.

A key problem faced by many IT organizations is one I have often heard called the *goulash* problem. It exists where there is a mixture of essentially incompatible hardware and software that somehow has been made to work together over the years. Conceptually it is easy to see that this goulash can be modelled as a system of large objects communicating by passing messages with parameters. The wrapper approach is appropriate when just one of these systems is to migrate to an object-oriented, open platform. Rather than build a wrapper for each old system, which would be expensive to say the least, it is better to wrap the communication system in some way. One approach to this problem is the object request broker idea covered in Chapter 4.

Many windowing environments now include good, usable GUI class libraries. Good examples are VisualWorks, NeXTstep, and NewWave. Hewlett Packard's NewWave, which started life as an extension to Microsoft Windows, is an object management facility with a special application programmer interface (API) for several graphical user interfaces. It enables objects from several different applications to be used together and applications (running in different windows) to be permanently linked. One thing that makes NewWave particularly interesting is its facilities for developing object wrappers, so that existing, conventional user interface (UI) code can be utilized. NewWave supports the idea of object wrappers by permitting non-object-oriented applications to be embedded, and is particularly suitable for developing multimedia user interfaces. Microsoft's OLE is beginning to exhibit similar features and lets one treat existing applications as if they were wrapped. There are now several distributed object management systems (DOMS) that support wrappers, ranging from coarse-grain DOMS like the ones from Iona Technologies and DEC to class libraries that help with finer-grain wrapping and distributed object management such as XShell, FORTÉ and DOME. Microsoft is working with DEC to make OLE interface with DEC's CORBA product, Objectbroker. Other examples of useful object libraries for GUI development include Borland's OWL, Microsoft's C++ foundation classes, Booch Components, ObjectCenter, ENFIN/3 and Zinc.

In the product migration project referred to above, it turned out, for the reasons given, that there were no suitable software tools at the outset. Therefore our main tool was our object-oriented analysis approach itself. It was originally intended that the products we produced would conform to OMG standards, including CORBA. We will return to these two subjects later. In the outcome, the NeWI product was used to support both distributed object management and the use of C for object-oriented programming. NeWI is not fully CORBA compliant because, like XShell, its messages carry routing information. This is actually an improvement over CORBA but I expect the suppliers either to force compliance at some limited level or to convince the OMG that their standard should permit such enhancements at some point in the future.

Another requirement was for some sort of CASE tool or repository that would support the recording of object and structure definitions. No such tool could be found. Most existing tools allow the user to draw diagrams but are weak on the recording of textual information. The project ended up by creating its own repository tool based on existing AS/400 software. The approach was similar in some respects to that of the *SOMATiK* software included with this book, though lacking in the latter's graphical features.

We need to deal not only with the evolution of existing systems that are important and too large or complex to rewrite but also with the evolutionary migration of an existing system to a future object-oriented implementation. This implies the need for techniques that will let us reuse components of existing functionally decomposed systems or even entire packages within our new or evolving object-oriented systems. To this issue we now turn.

2.4 Reusing existing software components and packages

So far we have considered the wrapper technique from the point of view of migration. Now we must consider also the problem of reusing existing components when there is no explicit need or intention to reimplement them in an object-oriented style. Dietrich's (1989) work has shown in principle how the reuse of highly optimized algorithms or specialized functions can be accomplished using the object wrapper strategy. This can be done by defining application-level classes whose methods call subroutines in the old system. The legacy systems can be wrapped in groups or as individual packages, with the latter option offering greater potential for reuse.

There is also a need to build on existing 'package' solutions. Once again a wrapper that calls package subroutines or simulates dialogue at a terminal can be built. The alternative is to modify the packages to export data for manipulation by the new system, but this fails to reuse existing functional components of the old one. Also, package vendors may not be prepared to support or even countenance such changes.

Some problems which must be solved in building such a wrapper are identified by Dietrich as follows.

- The designer is not free to choose the best representations for the problem in terms of objects since this is already largely decided within the old system. Here again there is a possibility that the wrappers will represent very coarse-grain objects with limited opportunities for reuse.
- The designer must either expose the old system's functions and interface to the user or protect him from possible changes to the old system. It is very difficult to do both successfully. Generally, one should only allow read accesses to the old system, which tends to preclude the take-over data management strategy.
- Where the old system continues to maintain data, the wrapper must preserve the state of these data when it calls internal routines. This militates against the translation strategy.

- Garbage collection and memory management and compaction (where applicable) must be synchronized between the wrapper and the old system.
- Cross-system invariants, which relate the old and new data sets, must be maintained.
- Building a wrapper often requires very detailed understanding of the old system. This is even more true when migrating but still a significant problem when reusing.

Because access to the internals of package software is seldom available at the required level of detail, the wrapper approach described above will not usually work. A better approach is to regard the package as a fixed object offering definite services, possibly in a distributed environment. This is discussed further in Chapter 4.

Whereas data-centred translation is the best approach to migration and replacement of existing systems – while borrowing strategies fail to work – where reuse is the main concern, borrowing is a perfectly viable approach. If the existing system or package largely works, for the functions it provides, and can be maintained at an acceptable level of cost (however large that may be) then when new functions are required it may be possible to build them quite separately using an object-oriented approach and communicate with the old system through a wrapper. This wrapper is used to call the services of the old system and give access to its database. New functions are defined as the methods of objects that encapsulate the data they need, in so far as they are new data. When data stored by the old system are required, a message must be sent to the wrapper and the appropriate retrieval routines called, borrowing the needed data. Updates to the existing database are treated similarly, by lending as it were.

It may well turn out that, in the fullness of time, the new object-oriented system will gradually acquire features that replace and duplicate parts of the old system. Data-centred translation then becomes necessary instead of borrowing for the affected parts of the system. Therefore the step-by-step strategy recommended in the last section is indicated for many commercial systems projects.

We may summarize the conclusions of this chapter so far in Table 2.1. In this table a 'Y' indicates that a wrapper data strategy may be worth considering

Table 2.1 Suitability of data communication strategies for different purposes.

Strategy	Purpose			
	Migration	Reuse	Extension	Front-end
Handshake	N	N	N	N
Borrowing	N	Y	Y	Y
Take-over	?	N	N	N
Translation	?	N	Y	Y
Data-centred translation	Y	N	Y	Y

for a particular class of problem but not that it is guaranteed to work. An 'N' indicates that it probably will not be suitable. A '?' means: 'It all depends.' The four strategies defined in Section 2.2 are compared with four possible reasons for building wrappers: migrating a complex legacy system to a new object-oriented implementation; reusing its components without changing the core system; extending its functionality without changing the core; and building a possibly distributed front-end to provide additional functions. Note that the last three purposes are very similar and the last two have identical Y/N patterns.

The subject of constructing front-ends to existing systems, especially graphical ones, using object-oriented techniques will be covered extensively in the next chapter.

2.5 Combining relational and object-oriented databases

As we have seen, there are four approaches to migration and interoperability: wrappers, request brokers, object-oriented databases and a do-it-yourself approach. For developers and maintainers of commercial systems, many of which have a substantial data management component, exploiting the best of existing relational databases for one part of an application in concert with the use of an object-oriented programming language or even an object-oriented database for another is a key issue. Generally, the interoperation of legacy relational databases and object-oriented programming languages is best viewed as a special case of the client/server model and will be dealt with in Chapter 4. The reason for considering an object-oriented database is that there are several commercial applications that relational databases are very bad at dealing with. Examples include bills of materials, document handling and, in fact, any application where there are complex, structured objects. Older-generation databases were just too inflexible to use for highly evolutionary applications such as text management. For these reasons it is still the case that most of the data owned by businesses are not in a computer system at all; up to 90% according to some estimates. Further, these data do not include the business and technical knowledge on which these organizations depend. As businesses strive for competitive edge there is an ever-increasing demand to computerize all these data along with the need to build a knowledge base, and object-oriented databases offer a partial solution. For an application involving many complex objects, an object-oriented database can be 100 times faster than its relational equivalent and retains the flexibility of the relational approach in terms of schema evolution too. Furthermore, object-oriented databases offer enhanced facilities such as support for long transactions and version control. However, since most organizations have a monstrous investment in existing database systems and, besides, the relational approach works well for most record-oriented IS applications, it

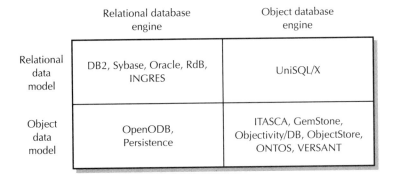

Figure 2.2 Types of database product with examples.

is imperative that moving to object-oriented databases should not involve the abandonment of all this existing work.

There are two options available: a pure object-oriented database or a relational system extended with object-oriented constructs. There are several pure object-oriented products in existence but they have not yet matured fully. These are surveyed in Graham (1994a). Further, there is a class of applications where a relational system may be not only a more mature solution but a faster one; typically those involving few large joins such as ledger applications. Version 6 of INGRES is fundamentally a relational database but has various object-oriented extensions. Oracle too has announced its intention to move to an object-oriented database by Version 8 and the other suppliers will, no doubt, do much the same. Thus, one alternative is to continue with the relational model extended in various ways. The other is to try to make our new object-oriented database applications interoperate with existing database systems. The first may give performance problems for certain applications, judging from early experiences, so the second is at least worth considering.

The option of extending the relational base with an object-oriented front-end as in INGRES can be taken further and HP's OpenODB does so, being a fully formed ODBMS based on an object model built on an implementation based on a relational data model. Friedman (1993) has pointed out that there are four options all supported by existing products as illustrated in Figure 2.2.

The promise of an object-oriented extension of SQL offers some hope of smooth interoperability, if it can be delivered – though this has yet to be seen. Loomis (1991) argues cogently for this approach but, personally, I am sceptical, because it seems to me that the whole idea of a non-procedural enquiry language is fundamentally incompatible with a pointer-based database such as an object-oriented one. As Loomis admits: 'Years ago, it was established that it was impossible to automatically translate [sic] record-at-a-time logic (à la hierarchical and network DBMSs) to SQL table-at-a-time logic.' Nevertheless, attempts are under way to define an object-oriented extension of SQL called

SQL3. If SQL is non-procedural and pointer-based enquiry is procedural, how can this be done without a danger of paradox? It turns out that SQL3 is not only object-oriented, supporting classes and inheritance, but that it is also a procedural extension of SQL. This reflects the various procedural extensions of SQL that have already been delivered by the various database vendors and SQL3 will at least standardize the confusion of multiple extensions. It will not, however, be SQL anymore, in the sense that SQL is a non-procedural language based on the relational calculus. Further, what is a relational system expected to do with messages based on these inevitable extensions to the language in Object SQL or SQL3? Whether I am right or not, Object SQL can never be much more than the carrier of messages. We still need to define an approach to interoperation.

The obvious approach suggested in the foregoing is to build a generalized wrapper for the DBMS itself. For example, a C++ wrapper could be written for Sybase that converts between messages and SQL queries. Thus the object wrapper approach described above will go through in many cases and the interoperability considerations for database systems are not really any different from those discussed for general computer systems. One feature of database systems however does deserve separate attention, and that is the issue of data modelling, because modern database systems are nearly always based on a data model and such a model is based on real-world entities – bearing in mind my remarks about normalization above.

One of the great advantages of a conventional database management system is the separation of processes and data, which gives a notion of data independence and benefits of flexibility and insulation from change, because the interface to shared data is stable. The data model is to be regarded as a model of the statics of the application. With object orientation, processes and data are integrated. Does this mean that you have to abandon the benefits of data independence? Already in client/server relational databases we have seen a step in the same direction, with database triggers and integrity rules stored in the server with the data. With an object-oriented approach to data management it therefore seems reasonable to adopt the view that there are two kinds of business object: **domain objects** and **application objects**. This terminology is derived from that of David Redmond-Pyle (Redmond-Pyle and Graham, 1992) though his co-worker Cameron (1992) uses the terms *shared objects* and *user objects*. As Daniels and Cook (1993) point out, objects that must be shared are nearly always persistent. Domain objects represent those aspects of the system that are relatively stable or generic and application objects are those that can be expected to vary from installation to installation or quite rapidly from time to time and that share the services of the domain objects. This approach resurrects the notion of data independence in an enhanced, object-oriented form. The domain objects are based on the data model and include persistent aspects of the model, constraints, rules and dynamics (state transitions, and so on). The goal is to make the interface to this part of the model as stable as possible. The application objects (including the user interface objects) use the services of the domain objects and may interact through them. This approach is reminiscent of the approach taken in the KADS expert systems development method with its knowledge-level, task-level and application-level models of a domain (see Hickman *et al.*, 1989). It is also compatible with Smalltalk's 'MVC paradigm' if we introduce non-business objects called **interface objects** to represent the controllers. The interface controls share access to the services of the application objects while the application objects share access to those of the domain objects. So-called 'database aware' controls appear to give direct access to domain objects but may be implemented via intermediate application objects. Typically domain objects will be found in the domain or business model and will be maintained by a team separate from application development teams; they are the central repository of reuse for business-level objects.

The distinction between domain, application and interface objects is often hard to make. A window object might need to be shared in a multi-user conferencing system and a domain object might need the protection of complex access privileges. Also, sharing objects leads to higher overheads as we shall see in Chapter 4. Nevertheless, the distinction remains a useful one for the analyst and designer.

The obvious candidates for domain objects are the de-normalized relations or views of a legacy database wrapped with the behaviour of the corresponding business objects. Where a database that offers the capability of storing procedures in the server – such as Sybase – is in use this is even more straightforward though discipline is required to prevent direct access to data structures via SQL. All calls to the database must be via stored procedures representing the wrapper interface. In the extreme case this could be implemented by the database administrator closing off all access privileges to all users, except to the stored procedures. Developers should thus be able to refer to a clean, object-oriented conceptual model while designing their access operations from application objects.

How then should the object-oriented component of our database or data model interoperate with the relational part? Incidentally, I am assuming that you will eventually want to migrate all your old CODASYL and IMS applications to an object-oriented database.

The possibilities are as follows.

(1) Object wrappers can be built for the relational system as a whole, treating it as an entire domain model. This approach offers minimal opportunities for the reuse of domain objects but may nevertheless be viable and the database wrapper can be replaced easily later.

(2) Coherent chunks of the database can be wrapped individually, perhaps allowing a phased approach. The use of stored procedures and a published object model are highly beneficial here. Opportunities for reuse are maximized by this strategy where it is feasible.

(3) SQL can be used to communicate with the relational system, which means that the new system must be able to generate SQL calls and inter-

pret the resulting tables based on knowledge of the data dictionary and its semantics. This will usually involve the use of fairly complex AI techniques such as those used in natural language query systems such as Intellect.

(4) The relational system could be addressed through an object request broker (see Chapter 4) provided it either conforms to the CORBA standard or a conformant wrapper is built. Once again, use of an ORB tends to deal with the legacy system as coarse-grained and the reuse potential is not as high as option 2.

A good example of interworking between relational and non-relational databases is provided by geographic information systems (GIS). Most GIS store two kinds of data: mapping data and data concerning the attributes of the objects mapped. The performance of relational systems is poor on mapping data because of their inability to store complex, structured objects and their need to do joins to reconstruct them. For this reason the mapping data are usually stored in a proprietary file system. The attribute data are often stored in a relational database and also often shared with other applications. In many applications a change to mapping data must be reflected in changes to the attributes and vice versa. This close coupling has been a significant task for product developers. Relational systems that support BLOBs (binary large objects) can be used but they cannot interpret the data. CAD systems developers have faced similar problems. The most recent geographic information systems, such as Smallworld, have opted for an object-oriented approach to storing mapping data.

Loomis (1991) identifies three problems and three approaches to object–relational interoperation. The three problems are to:

(1) build object-oriented applications that access relational databases;
(2) run existing relationally written applications against an object-oriented database;
(3) use an SQL-like query language in an object-oriented environment.

The three approaches are to:

(1) convert the applications and databases completely to object-oriented ones;
(2) use standard import-export facilities;
(3) access the relational databases from the object-oriented programming languages.

The first of these approaches is complicated and expensive, and works badly if some old system functions are to be reused or migration is gradual. The same problem referred to in Sections 2.1 and 2.2 arises, in that coordinating updates across heterogeneous databases is problematical. However, if you can do periodic downloads of data to the new system, the approach can be tolerated. This is exactly what we did when migrating from IMS to DB2 and building MIS extensions. The second approach relies on standards having been defined, which will depend on the application; for example, standards exist in the CAD and VLSI design worlds but not in general. The best variant of this approach is to use an object-oriented database that supports SQL gateways to your relational databases, as does GemStone for example. Here though, the application must provide a mapping between table and object views of data and, except for the simplest cases, this can be complicated. The third approach implies developing an Object SQL. If possible, this would perhaps be the best approach but there is yet no standard or even consensus and I have already expressed my doubts on theoretical grounds.

Conventional databases let one store relations, such as 'all the children who like toys', in a table, but not the rule that 'all children like toys'; nor do they permit one to store the fact that when one field is updated another may have to be also. Both of these kinds of relationship are easy to express in, say, PROLOG or in any knowledge based systems shell. For some time now Sybase and INGRES have extended the relational model to allow database triggers to capture the latter kind of rule. In frame based systems the support for rules is more general and less procedural in style, but there is undoubtedly a trend to enriching the semantic abilities of databases in this way. INGRES, in addition, now offers facilities for defining abstract data types so that it can deal with complex data types exactly in the manner of an object-oriented database. The latest announcement from Oracle indicates that Version 8 of this product too will have a full range of object-oriented features. At present no object-oriented database product known to the author offers explicit support for declarative rules, but this could also change in the immediate future as they are applied to real, commercial problems.

One way to enhance interoperability, we are told, is to place system syntax and semantics in enterprise repositories. These days, nearly all new repository products such as those being produced at Amdahl and DEC are based on object-oriented database technology. In some cases a mixture of I-CASE and expert systems technology is used. See, for example, Martin and Odell (1992) for the arguments for this approach. Such repositories will store an interface library and this will help systems to locate and utilize existing objects.

All these developments suggest the need for a systems analysis technique that captures not just data, process and dynamics but rules and facts of the type found in knowledge based systems. Object-oriented databases and extended relational databases will also make it imperative that business rules are captured explicitly during the analysis process. Part II of this book will show how this can be done.

⊟ 2.6 Wrappers for expert systems and blackboard systems

A free-standing or embedded expert system can be wrapped as described in Sections 2.1 to 2.4. In both cases, the input to the system consists of goals to seek or assertions of facts and the output is the possible conclusions. These define the parameters of the wrapper messages quite clearly. Further, modern expert systems have often been constructed in an object-oriented fashion using platforms such as ADS, ART, Kappa, KBMS, KEE, Leonardo or Nexpert Object and so the translation problems are minimized. However, most object-oriented analysis methods fail to provide means for handling goals in the interface or for describing rule based systems. We will be examining the issue of migrating expert systems along with that of building expert systems in an object-oriented fashion in Chapter 5. There is one important point that need be made here.

Recall that object-oriented systems are bound together by the objects storing the identities of objects to which they can send messages. They cannot broadcast messages to the general population of objects. This is often seen as a major weakness in the object-oriented perspective. One way round it is to use a control technique from artificial intelligence, known as the blackboard system approach.

Blackboard systems have been applied in trading rooms, speech-understanding systems and several military applications. For example, a fighter pilot has to process vast amounts of incoming data in order to select from a limited range of actions. The model is one of several independent knowledge based systems monitoring the input and advising the pilot when something interesting occurs; for example, when a real target or threat is identified among many dummy targets or threats. The financial trader is in a similar position, being the recipient of vast quantities of data from several information feeds, all of them in need of analysis to determine (1) if anything interesting has occurred requiring further analysis and (2) what the appropriate action should be.

A blackboard system is so called because it imitates a group of highly specialized experts sitting around a blackboard in order to solve a problem. As new information arrives it is written up on the blackboard where all the experts can look. When an expert sees that s/he can contribute a new fact based on specialist knowledge, s/he raises a hand. This might be to confirm or refute an hypothesis already on the board or to add a new one. The new evidence will now be available to the other experts who may in turn be prompted to contribute to the discussion. The chairman of the group monitors the experts and selects their contributions in order, according to an agenda visible on the board. Common storage is the blackboard, and the agenda is under the control of a specialized inference program. In the trading context, our experts might be represented by a technical analysis expert system, a fundamental analysis system, an option strategy adviser and so on. If, for example, new price information arrives from the wire, the chartist might detect a possible reversal of trend but need to await confirmation before a sell signal is issued. However, the fundamental analyst only needed this small piece of confirmatory evidence to suggest a flagging in the security's fortunes. The combined evidence may be enough to generate a valid signal and thus, incidentally, beat all the pure chartists to the winning post. Perhaps, also, this action of selling the security will attract the attention of the option strategist who now sees a need to modify positions in order to maintain a risk-free hedge or to avoid an otherwise unexpected exercise in now unfavourable market conditions.

If the components of a system need to communicate there are essentially two methods of achieving this. Object-oriented systems allow objects to send and receive messages that have definite destination objects when sent. In blackboard systems the messages are posted to a common object called the blackboard which is accessible to other objects. However, each object must periodically poll the blackboard to see if there is anything interesting on it. Alternatively the blackboard can regularly send its state to every other object, though this is generally rather inefficient. Sometimes the blackboard is partitioned into pigeonholes and some objects may declare an interest only in certain pigeonholes to speed things up and give more structure to the conceptual model. Usually, messages must be dealt with according to the order in which they arrive and the state of the receiving object at that time; thus all such systems tend to look like real-time systems and would benefit greatly from parallel hardware architectures. Having said this, one of the earliest blackboard systems was the sequential Hearsay-II, which was addressed to the problem of speech understanding, which is only implicitly a real-time problem. Most applications since then have been in military, real-time communication, command and control systems, so that little has been published openly. More recently, however, work has begun on blackboard systems in plant process control and complex currency dealing decision support systems.

A typical way to implement a blackboard system is to set up a family of objects representing a community of cooperating experts. Each object has (in CLOS terminology) a *slot* containing a 'trigger' and one indicating the priority of execution of the methods attached to the object. Some objects will fire their methods on the trigger value denoting the start of processing and these are, *ceteris paribus*[3], executed in order of priority. The priorities may be subject to dynamic alteration as earlier methods write facts on the blackboard. Demons may be used to detect critical changes to the blackboard's data and amend the

---

[3] Other things being equal.

appropriate objects. Other objects are triggered directly by certain values in the database. To implement a broadcast model, as is necessary in ORBs for example, it is usual to have objects 'register' their interest in receiving updates from the blackboard. This reduces message traffic but is not always suitable for the most complex AI applications where it is difficult to predict the incidence of the need for information. In such a case all objects must periodically send a message to a blackboard to see if it has altered since the last look.

Open systems, networks and shared resources make it possible to deal with problems that admit a coarse-grained partitioning into tasks that can run on separate processors with minimal cooperation, although cooperation among such systems is theoretically possible by means of a separate scheduling machine operating as a sort of blackboard system (see for example Graham (1987)).

Cooperative processing and blackboard architectures may involve agents that already exist working with newly defined objects and the object wrapper techniques described above may be used to facilitate their interface. Here there is usually no question of rebuilding the existing modules and the borrowing strategy is often the best one. Where networks are involved, the wrappers need to conform to standards as discussed in Chapter 4. Since object-oriented approaches are very suitable for constructing blackboard systems it may be prudent to build or rebuild the overall system as an object-oriented system and reuse individual expert systems components by wrapping them and treating them as entire objects. We shall return to this topic briefly in Chapter 5. Some distributed object management systems such as XShell now include facilities for incorporating broadcast protocols into conventional object-oriented systems without using an explicit blackboard object.

2.7 Using object-oriented analysis as a springboard

The burgeoning interest in object technology has led to the widespread use of object-oriented programming languages for software development. With this growth has come a realization that current structured methods for software engineering not only fail to support such developments but actually impede them in many cases. Typical applications where this applies are GUI development, client/server computing, use of object-oriented databases and use of extended relational databases. The need for a disciplined approach to such developments has now led to a massive proliferation of methods for object-oriented analysis. These methods vary in complexity, scope and in their degree of conformance to the object-oriented perspective.

Another area where there is a need for methods is expert system development, and here object-oriented approaches are strongly indicated by the presence of inheritance structures in frame based expert systems.

In the case of interoperation between object-oriented and conventional system components we have already seen that it is often necessary to reverse engineer an older system in order to find a description of it in terms of coherent entities. Some technique of object-oriented analysis is clearly required for this, especially if migration to OT is contemplated. Thus, I am suggesting that object-oriented analysis can be used as a fast path to the object-oriented future in the face of interoperability problems and immature language technology.

2.7.1 Three sources of object technology

There are three distinct ways in which the concept of objects has entered computer science. The programming language community developed the object-oriented perspective from its own concerns with simulation, user interface development and so on. Database theorists in need of abstract models to help model data introduced various semantic data modelling techniques, the best known being that of Chen – the Entity Relationship (ER) model (Chen, 1976). These models dealt with abstract objects and inheritance but focused on the data aspects of entities, ignoring the procedures that entities might be able to perform. The artificial intelligence community went a step further with their concept of frames and allowed entities to have procedures attached to attributes that can be used to search for missing values and cause side-effects, but frames are static data structures and offer no specific facilities for specifying the behaviour of entities declaratively. These procedures are often external, though linked to the frames, and not encapsulated as such. Further, frames are closer in spirit to prototypes than objects. This means that there are no definitional classes with instances that inherit all their features, merely instances that are more or less prototypical of some concept. The solution is to allow classes to be treated as prototype definitions; that is, the instances may not have all of the features of the class as in object-oriented programming. In this way a three-legged, alcoholic dog can be an instance of dogs, which have four legs and drink water by choice. There are languages such as SELF (Ungar and Smith, 1987) that are based on prototypes rather than classes. Incidentally, this means that if object-oriented analysis techniques are to be truly language independent they must allow the modelling of prototypes, as indeed does SOMA, by allowing overriding at the instance level. If we permit such relaxations, the object technology movement offers the richest set of means to overcome the obstacles of the semantic data modeller, the knowledge based systems builder and the programmer alike.

Let us take a brief look at each of these perspectives.

THE SEMANTIC DATA MODELLING PERSPECTIVE This perspective has derived from practical database applications as well as from research efforts. It is at the root of the client/server metaphor and of database triggers and server-embedded business rules. Semantic data modellers use rules and inheritance structures extensively but have not been greatly concerned with the issue of encapsulation. Nowadays there is considerable cross-fertilization between this field and object technology. See for example Hughes (1991) or Gray *et al.* (1992).

In this section we will consider only two of the three perspectives in detail. The semantic data modelling perspective is concerned only with data and is largely encompassed by the other two. The reader wishing to know more at an introductory level is directed to Hughes (1991) or Graham (1994a).

Let us begin with the program-level issues.

THE OBJECT-ORIENTED PROGRAMMING PERSPECTIVE
The techniques of object orientation are mainly derived from work on the programming language Smalltalk and its environment, developed at Xerox PARC during the 1970s. There are now many object-oriented languages, including C++, Eiffel, Object PASCAL, Object COBOL, Classic Ada, Simula and Objective-C, among many others. Their developers had various programming-theoretical concerns such as speed, correctness, type safety and denotational expressiveness.

As explained in Chapter 1, in the object-oriented style an 'object' is an entity with three features: *unique identity*, *encapsulation* of a set of attributes, which store data and a set of 'methods' or procedures which can fire when activated and can access the internal data structures of the attribute base of the object, and *inheritance*. Encapsulation means that objects (either classes or their instances) consist of an interface of attributes and methods together with a hidden implementation of their data structures and processes.

As we have seen, the key benefits of this approach are that objects are inherently units of reusable code and that systems built from them are extensible, using inheritance to add new or exceptional features to a system.

THE AI PERSPECTIVE
A frame, on the other hand, is usually described as having a set of attributes which themselves can be attached to procedures although these procedures are not usually stored with the object as in object-oriented programming. Interestingly, this is also the approach taken in most object-oriented databases with the notable exception of GemStone and ITASCA. The difference between frames and objects is the lack of emphasis in the former on the encapsulation of the data and procedures together, hidden behind an interface. Secondly, in AI, the procedures may be regarded as rulesets instead of procedural code. Another difference between object-oriented and AI approaches is that AI work has provided very rich methods for dealing with inheritance compared to object technology (OT). Nevertheless, the similarities outweigh the differences, and someone wishing to take advantage of the benefits of object-orientation (that is, reuse and extensibility) might as well proceed using a Leonardo or a Kappa as a Smalltalk. The advantages are the richer inheritance features and the ability to express relationships as rulesets. The disadvantages are that the level of encapsulation (and thus reuse) is lower and, for some applications such as GUI development or CASE tool construction, existing class libraries or database managers may make the pure object-oriented approach more productive.

2.7.2 Object-oriented analysis and knowledge based prototyping

It is often claimed that the two main obstacles to the proliferation of the object-oriented programming style are performance problems and the habit of trying to apply traditional life-cycle and design techniques. An obstacle to the migration of existing systems or even the construction of object wrappers for them is that object-oriented languages are not yet fully mature or not even available at all on some older platforms. For many users a migration path to open systems is required and an object-oriented future is clearly signposted. However, there is a profound need for an intermediate, conventional implementation strategy. This is due to the lack of stable, mature object-oriented programming languages on the machine currently in use and could be characterized as the 'waiting for ObjectCOBOL' syndrome. Also, for software product suppliers, their customers may not wish to migrate or, worse still, run on two types of machine at the same time. For these and other reasons the pure object-oriented migration path, with or without wrappers, is often inappropriate and we need a strategy for such circumstances.

Why not perform object-oriented analysis and implement in, say, COBOL now – with a view to later migration? The advantages of this approach are that it avoids risks arising from the still evolving language technology and the danger of choosing a strategic object-oriented language which is not the one that will eventually be accepted as the industry standard.

Any decent object-oriented analysis approach should be language independent. The disadvantages are that the specification cannot be tested and that the system cannot be delivered and used. The answer to both problems is prototyping. A prototype can be used to agree the specification with users and can even be implemented incrementally, pending a final rewrite in the object-oriented language of choice should performance or some other factor make this desirable. However, what we build as a model in the prototyping language needs to be *reversible* in the sense that it is possible to discover the intentions of the analysts and designers by examining the code. This should also be true of the paper analysis itself, leading to a requirement for a semantically rich analysis language and a readable declarative prototyping one.

The two areas of IT where such tools have become available are expert systems and advanced databases, themselves under the influence, it has to be said, of artificial intelligence. Expert systems offer declarative, semantically rich programming languages. Advanced databases allow business rules to be coded as stored procedures (the Sybase term) and database triggers but not always declaratively. It is really rather hard to extract the original rules as expressed by the users from such a system. Thus, there is a need for declarative rule based modes of expression and, so far, only INGRES and the semantic databases offer anything like this. Even object-oriented databases fall short in this respect. It seems that this situation will change and the database community are certainly aware of the problem. Furthermore, several database workers now accept that business rules should be attached to the entities or objects of the data model. As Andleigh and Gretzinger (1992) put it: 'Clear documentation of the business rules *and which objects each rule is associated with* ensures that the application of the rules is perceived clearly and is well understood by the user before the coding of the rules.' (My emphasis.)

We may conclude that knowledge based systems and advanced database products, or perhaps both in concert, can help build reversible prototypes. However, this is best done in conjunction with a machine independent analysis exercise using a semantically rich and therefore reversible notation.

This was confirmed within my personal experience by the ARIES expert systems project (Butler and Chamberlain, 1988) where we built systems on a workstation with the conscious intention of transporting them to PCs at a later date. At every stage, including prototyping, implementation independent representations or, more succinctly, paper models were built. Porting then became very easy indeed because we ported not the code but the paper model; the paper model was reversible because it was written in the expressive language of knowledge engineers and not the irreversible products of software engineering.

As expert systems software has advanced and moved closer to object orientation I have come to regard knowledge based systems as first-rate prototyping tools in their own right. This is mainly because of their excellent and expressive inheritance features. I am quite happy to see this removed at implementation time to enhance reusability, but for analysis inheritance is indispensable. Knowledge based systems are also inherently reversible because they express knowledge as rules and objects and not in procedural code or obscure diagrammatic conventions. The use of such an approach to specification and prototyping requires a matching analysis notation and approach so that the expert system prototype can be reversed into a reversible, object-oriented paper model or CASE tool. I will describe a complete, hybrid object-oriented analysis and systems development approach designed to be reversible and to suit using expert systems tools for prototyping in Part II.

One important issue for practitioners is to find analysis and design methods that support the rich features available in existing systems. Another question is: how are we to make immediate use of available technology? One answer is to utilize knowledge based systems as prototyping tools, basing these developments on a semantically rich analysis and design technique. For the time being we may have to compromise at the implementation stage for performance reasons or even implement in COBOL, but since most of the investment in system building is not implementation, this approach is not only viable but an investment in the future. We shall return to this topic briefly in Chapter 12.

▤ 2.8 Object technology as a migration strategy in itself

Up to now I have been arguing, perhaps rather circuitously, that the key to migration to object technology (OT) lies in the approach taken to analysis and design. We shall be returning to this issue. However, I now want to turn the issue on its head and argue that OT is not an end in itself any more than systems analysis is. The real issues for modern business are how to be both more flexible and more productive and simultaneously to cut costs. One approach to this is rightsizing or, put more bluntly, getting rid of the mainframe or reducing it to mere 'channel server' status. This involves many technical and cultural changes and is generally agreed to be a very hard thing to do right. However, my recent observations lead me to the conclusion that OT itself, together with clear vision and positive leadership, is the answer to this particular, corporate maiden's prayer.

We analyse systems to help build them. We computerize businesses to help run them better. Good analysis should lead to better systems. Good systems ought to lead to better businesses. What then is a good system? This of course is highly arguable, but I think few these days can resist the view that good systems are those that are *inter alia* cost-effective, open, flexible, robust, usable and maintainable. How can object technology contribute to these aims? Cost-effectiveness, of course, will be enhanced by reuse and flexibility and maintainability by the use of inheritance but the other issues are not so directly related to programming with objects. Usable systems are generally regarded these days as having a graphical interface and Microsoft, for example, have pinned their whole marketing strategy on 'making it easier' with GUIs. Of course, it is still possible to build a totally unusable graphical user interface. Perhaps the most important features of all for modern businesses are the costs of operating the computing infrastructure and the costs associated with change in this area. Here the great hopes for some time have been distributed and 'open' systems.

The cost per MIPS of UNIX and PC platforms is thought to be at least an order of magnitude less than that of mainframe systems, though some vested interests still wave the banner of hidden costs and avidly publicize the failures. These hidden costs are largely those associated with not having a successful migration strategy, in my opinion. Further, these smaller platforms are associated with graphical user interfaces and interoperability. Thus, most modern companies would like to move as many applications as possible to such platforms. Unfortunately there are some pretty big difficulties facing them. Their staffs have the wrong training. Distributed computing is far more complex. Few people know the principles of user interface design well enough to produce consistently usable GUIs. And then there is reuse.... Even experts in object technology argue about how it can be achieved and managed successfully.

The object-oriented perspective is capable of describing the distributed nature of systems in a very natural way since message passing is central to both. Further, the fact that object technology offers a way of managing complexity through encapsulation and inheritance means that it at least becomes possible to think about very complex distributed architectures.

Object-oriented tools for GUI development both make it easier and impose a style and consistency that itself contributes to usability. They enhance productivity enormously and can be used to impose standards for user interface design and promote reuse in this area. Similarly, object-oriented tools for expert system construction are beginning to be common, capitalizing on inheritance schemes to reduce the complexity of rule bases and thus deliver friendlier, more natural dialogues between people and their applications.

It has also become apparent that experienced COBOL programmers can learn the object-oriented approach and several companies have proved this in practice.

The problems that remain are largely methodological and organizational. Good object-oriented systems analysis is still the key to the methodological aspects in my view and I have argued this point already. The real nightmare is the organizational issue.

All change management exercises are fraught with peril and the move to object technology is no exception. People often resist change merely because they doubt the benefits will actually accrue to them or their organizations. As Machiavelli (1961) put it: 'there is nothing more difficult to arrange, more doubtful of success, and more dangerous to carry through than initiating changes'. Those who prospered under the old order and stand to lose will oppose you vigorously, while those who might gain will only provide lukewarm support. The potential gainers are 'generally incredulous, never really trusting new things unless they have tested them by experience'. To win them over, one must demonstrate success early on. Further, one must be sure of not backing the wrong horse. This is the danger of the silver bullet. I wonder how many hours of people's lives have been wasted backing a good technical solution that never survived commercially: the Xerox Sigma, APL, CP/M 86 and perhaps now even the Mac. I work in an IT organization that has traversed successfully a good length of the road to open, downsized, distributed systems. We achieved this by a positive turn to object technology, by strong leadership and clear vision and by hedging our bets on technology. I do not intend to write a history of this organization's experience. That would take too long and be too specific to be of general use. What I can offer is a distillation of advice.

There is no point in dithering. The aim of the migration strategy should be clearly stated in the form of a mission statement. It has to come from the top. People will accept it or vote with their feet in that case. One might announce that the mainframes are to be replaced within two years or that productivity will be doubled in three; ambitious targets which may not be fully met but which provide direction. These aims should be related to technology so that one might argue that reuse, using objects, is the basis for productivity growth. Next, one must select some technology. It is doubtful that one can be sure, in a new field, of what will survive or what will work. Therefore, rather than choosing just one language or one OOA/D method one should choose two or three, giving project managers some leeway to optimize their own performance. Typically the language choice should encompass different programming styles, so that a selection of C++ and Ada would be quite wrong. Suitable pairs might be Objective-C/NeXTstep with Eiffel or CLOS with C++. Different types of project can now be run with what appears to be the most suitable language and lessons learnt by the organization. Similarly, one may give project managers the authority to select from a short list of object-oriented design methods such as Booch'93, OMT and Shlaer/Mellor. The analysis method, however, should not be treated in this way for, if it is, the reuse programme may be endangered. What is required is a sound method that imposes a definite life cycle and guides requirements capture, systems analysis and logical design. In this way, objects can be captured and placed in a repository from the earliest stages of a project. If the method is language independent these objects can be reused regardless of the language used. Think of the dismay that might be caused if a switch of language meant that the reuse library had to be ditched or even substantially redesigned. The sort of method I have in mind is (perhaps unsurprisingly) SOMA (described in Part II) or MOSES (Henderson-Sellers and Edwards, 1994).

The development staff are critical too. The main choice that most organizations will face is that between traditional developers with many years in the business and great experience and newcomers with skills in OT and modern methods. In fact, neither type will do. The newcomers must be used to educate the oldsters and provide mentoring. Obversely, the young Turks must diligently learn about the nature of the business from their predecessors. It is a process that requires a deep and lasting trust between the two groups and establishing such trust is a key management task. Reward schemes that encourage both cooperation among workers and the reuse of other people's objects need to be devised.

Finally, the sponsors of computer developments must be rewarded too. The obvious rewards that can be aimed for are lower costs through reuse and shorter time-to-market. The quality of the product is thereby enhanced as well. Inheritance means that maintenance costs can be reduced and systems changed more easily in response to business change. Reuse successes lead to funding but are hard to achieve. Most developers expect to get reuse at the code level but this is very difficult to manage and often takes place informally. I believe that a reuse programme should start at the specification level and I will be discussing how to do this in Part II.

☰ 2.9 Summary

This chapter examined various strategies for organizations facing migration and interoperation problems, emphasizing the concerns of a developer who wants to develop an object-oriented application that needs to use the services provided by applications that incorporate other programming styles. It covered techniques such as object wrappers, object request brokers and blackboard systems and discussed how to wrap an application that exists in a large number of different versions.

The biggest cost associated with 'legacy' systems is maintenance. However much we would like to replace these old systems completely, the economics of the matter forbids it on any large scale. We must build on the existing investment and move gradually to object technology.

The first strategy recommended was to build object *wrappers*. Building object wrappers helps protect investments in older systems during the move to object-oriented programming. An object wrapper enables a new, object-oriented part of a system to interact with a conventional chunk by message passing. This may represent a substantial investment, but once it is in place virtually all maintenance activity may cease.

Implementing wrappers is not as easy as it sounds in several respects. One issue is granularity. Small objects are usually more reusable than large ones. With legacy systems we are often faced with irreducibly large-grain 'objects' present in the design. Object request brokers are specifically aimed at dealing with this kind of coarse-grain reuse.

The wrapper approach to migration is not the only one available. Other options include the use of object request brokers, object-oriented databases and proceeding in a completely *ad hoc* manner.

One of the biggest problems with the concept of object wrappers concerns data management. Using the wrapper is easy until you need to split the storage of data across the old database and some of the new objects. Four possible strategies for dealing with these problems were defined as follows. The **handshake strategy** involves carrying a duplicate, live copy of the common data in both parts of the system and keeping both copies up to date. It only works well when there is little or no overlap between the data of the old and new systems. The **borrowing strategy** keeps all data in the old system and copies them to the new objects as required. The **take-over strategy** involves copying the data to the new objects and allowing the old system's data to go out of date. There may be integrity problems, and the wrapper may have to send messages as well as receive and respond to them, which greatly increases its complexity. The **translation strategy** carves out coherent chunks of the database together with related functions. This requires a sound method of object-oriented analysis capable of describing the old system as well as the new. It seems the most promising approach to migration on balance. A refinement of this strategy is to reverse engineer a data model from the existing system and to identify all file access operations in relation to this model. These calls can then be replaced as new objects are constructed around the entities. This version of translation is the **data-centred translation** strategy. These strategies may be variously appropriate according to whether we are migrating the system to an object-oriented implementation, reusing its components, extending it or building a better or a distributed front-end.

When the old system exists and is maintained in multiple versions, the wrapper approach will only work if there is a core system common to all the versions. Use a phased approach that builds a wrapper to communicate with new object-oriented components using (most probably) the borrowing strategy. Perform an object-oriented analysis on the old system. Use translation or data-centred translation to migrate.

Having decided to build a wrapper and a new front-end one needs tools for building them. There are no specific products offering wrapper technology for migration at present but there are a number of ORB and GUI tools that may help with reuse. Rather than build a wrapper for each old system it is sometimes better to wrap the communication system in some way. One approach to this problem is to use an object request broker. Many windowing environments now include good, usable GUI class libraries and facilities for developing object wrappers, so that existing, conventional UI code can be utilized. Sometimes the main tool can be the object-oriented analysis approach itself but good CASE tools are then required.

The wrapper technique can be used for migration or for reusing existing components when there is no explicit intention to reimplement them in an object-oriented style. Some problems that must be solved in building such a wrapper were listed. Table 2.1 summarized the applicability of the four strategies to four migration problems.

We discussed object-oriented databases and the issues surrounding interoperation with them. Object-oriented databases and extended relational databases make it imperative that business rules are captured explicitly during the analysis process.

We saw how expert systems can be wrapped and discussed the use of blackboard systems to help object-oriented systems simulate broadcasting.

We saw that object-oriented analysis could be the main springboard for a company's migration strategy and that object technology was itself a migration strategy. The problems that remain are largely methodological and organizational.

All change management exercises are fraught with peril and the move to object technology is no exception. Management style and the quality of the development staff are critical. Most developers expect to get reuse at the code level but this is very difficult to manage and often takes place informally. A reuse programme should start at the specification level.

⊟ 2.10 Bibliographical notes

Dietrich's (1989) paper is the original source on object wrappers and is well complemented by the analyses of Reiss (1991) and Grass (1991). Some of the panels in the OOPSLA proceedings (Meyrowitz, 1987, 1990) contain useful insights.

Graham (1994a) contains an introduction to the whole area of object technology, a very extensive survey of object-oriented analysis and design methods and a partial exposition of SOMA and the philosophy behind it. It also contains summary descriptions of and comparisons between object-oriented database products and comprehensive bibliographical references.

There are numerous good introductions to expert systems available. Material on blackboard systems is scarcer but the book by Englemore and Morgan (1989) contains most of the seminal papers on the subject.

My articles in *Object Magazine* during 1993 and 1994 were based on early drafts of the material in this chapter, which originated as a tutorial presentation at Object Expo Europe.

3

Building graphical user interfaces

I have multiplied visions, and used similitudes

Hosea viii. 10

User interfaces originated with the very first computers in the form of cathode ray tube displays showing base-32 arithmetic for output and plug boards for input. Programming was thus like rewiring the hardware and interpreting the magic symbols that came out. The early machines also made a noise so that experienced operators could guess what sort of thing they were doing and detect abnormalities such as endless loops (a constant whirring sound). Later Hollerith punched cards were used for input and batch line-printers for output. This represented a significant advance in user friendliness – until you dropped a large box of punched cards. The main problem with this approach occurred when the programmer missed a comma from a line of code and discovered that the program would not compile – only after a day or so – because of this simple slip. Paper tape was not so subject to being dropped but tore easily. Paper tape, incidentally, was the nearest thing there was to a hardware independent data interchange medium for many years. Long turn-round times began to be addressed when conversational remote job entry (CRJE) was introduced, whereby the programmer could submit jobs via a golf-ball teletype machine attached to a remote computer via a modem. As television technology became cheaper to manufacture, these terminals were gradually replaced with screen terminals which emulated CRJE devices, but quietly. For this reason, these character display terminals were known as 'glass teletypes'. In the 1970s these displays began to be used by users who were not programmers and command line interfaces gave way to simple menu systems and tab-and-fill data entry screens. Meanwhile, Doug Englebart had invented the mouse but no one had yet exploited its potential.

The first well-known commercial application of the mouse came out of the work at Xerox PARC on the Star interface and later emerged in the form of the Apple Lisa and Macintosh. Rodents[1] made it possible to conceive of an

---

[1] We have to call them that because foot-operated mice which run along the floor have been developed and these and the large mice used for specialist graphics work are sometimes knows as **rats**.

entirely different style of user interaction with the display based on the metaphor of pointing and choosing rather than instructing and describing actions. Now there is a great variety of advanced input and output devices and we will discuss them later. The Xerox/Apple style was emulated by many others and eventually standardized into the systems we are now familiar with: MS Windows, Presentation Manager (PM) and the two flavours of X-Windows (Motif and OpenLook). There have been recent attempts to go beyond a 'windows' style interface, some based on virtual reality techniques, but little consensus on the next standard is yet evident. Most improvements, such as NeXTstep, General Magic's MagicCap and Xerox's Rooms are merely extensions of the original idea. Most interface innovations include the features of earlier interface styles to some extent, though command lines are considered most unusual by Macintosh users.

This chapter seeks to explain why object technology is suitable for GUI development, review some of the productivity tools available and their benefits, explain the principles behind GUI design and expose some important techniques used in human–computer interaction (HCI) specification. It supports much of what I will have to say about object-oriented requirements capture in Part II in introducing the technique known as hierarchical task analysis. Those readers already familiar with the literature on human–computer interaction may wish to skim this material quickly but should read at least Sections 3.3.6 and 3.3.7, which provide background for Part II.

The guidelines for interface design given in this chapter should be thought of as part of SOMA. Work to formalize this is in hand at the time of writing.

3.1 The need for GUIs

Graphical user interfaces (GUIs) are popular because it is widely believed that they are easy to use, enhance user and developer productivity and lead to a greater degree of comfort and less stress. Evidence for this is to be found in a report that was commissioned by Microsoft and carried out by Temple, Barker and Sloan (1990) which reported that users were 35% more productive and completed 23% more tasks with a graphical user interface. Experienced users made a third of the number of mistakes and could use more applications. Further, they reported 50% less frustration. The funding by Microsoft throws some doubt on the independence of the survey, but there is little validated evidence to the contrary. Independent studies by Butler Cox (now CSC Index) in 1991 and Apple-sponsored research between 1987 and 1988 support these findings and found that users took 1.8 hours to learn the basics of how to use a Mac compared with 20.4 hours for a DOS PC and that new applications could be mastered in a third of the time required for DOS software. An earlier report from Butler Cox had shown that ease of use was the main user concern, followed closely by interface standards and interoperability. A report produced by

Arthur D. Little in 1994 compares MS Windows with the Mac and concludes that the Mac is substantially easier to learn and use. This warns us that a GUI in and of itself is not the secret of productivity; it is a well-crafted GUI that is required. Anecdotal evidence suggests that ease of use and increased productivity are only achieved after quite a lot of time is invested in learning to use such an interface. It certainly took me much more than 1.8 hours just to master the physical coordination needed to control my first mouse, never mind learning the interface, and I have no physical handicaps that I am aware of. Interface usage also depends on the type of task being undertaken, as we shall see later. For me, greater benefits derive from the consistency of the interface. For example, no matter what application is running, the File menu is always in the top left-hand corner of the screen and Help is always the rightmost pull-down menu. Even if you have no mouse, in MS Windows, Alt-F-X **always** closes the application. The exploratory style means that users can explore the structure of the application without commitment to actions. This is often achieved by 'greying out' inapplicable menu entries in the current mode; for example, you cannot *cut* unless you have selected something but you can see that cut and paste is supported in the system. An *undo* facility also promotes exploration since it is possible to try an action and then recover from it if the effects are undesirable. A further benefit is the use of a metaphor, the so-called desktop metaphor, to help users transfer knowledge from manual tasks to using the computer. I will discuss such transfer effects in more detail in Section 3.3.

The uses to which GUIs can be put are manifold. They can be used to hide multi-language implementations: systems connected by loosely coupling systems written in different products. For example, Inference Corporation's CBR Express is a case-based reasoning tool aimed at building automatic help-desk, diagnostic and field service systems. CBR Express is built using Toolbook for the display, graphics and animation management, a database manager and an expert system shell. The interface acts as a platform for communication among diverse tools. The MS Office suite of products combines its multiple applications using OLE to support sophisticated drag and drop facilities and NeXTstep and Microsoft's projected Cairo take this even further. Similarly, a very common use of GUIs is to protect users from the interaction style of old mainframe systems or the complexities of networks. All these usages can be viewed as examples of object wrappers, when the GUI is built using an object-oriented language. In such cases the GUI often contains functionality beyond that of the systems it conceals and is a key part of an implicit or explicit migration strategy.

In some cases the GUI is used to enhance the quality of a product. A good example is word processing where AmiPro and Word for Windows are an order of magnitude easier to use and, in practice, more powerful than their DOS equivalents. The use of toolbars, embedded graphics, drag and drop text, and the like all contribute enormously to my productivity – and indeed joy – as a writer. Those writers who persist in using non-graphical software and argue for its benefits are often concealing their reluctance to change their views of the work-flow inherent in document production where writing, typesetting and graphics preparation used to be separate tasks.

The construction of graphical front-ends to existing systems is currently a very widespread use of object technology. Object-oriented languages, special tools and class libraries now exist to simplify the task. Usually, these tools also offer support for building client/server systems because the front-end will often have to access a mainframe database or an existing system. In the latter case the problem becomes very much like the reuse problem discussed in the previous chapter and the wrapper approach may be considered. Because the front-end is merely using an entire existing system, the borrowing strategy is appropriate. Otherwise, there are no special considerations worthy of comment above and beyond what has already been said about wrappers for reuse.

The special skills and techniques required for the successful design and construction of GUIs is an important subject that is discussed in Section 3.3. Another peculiar issue that does deserve attention is that of cooperative processing or client/server computing, which does seem to characterize many GUI applications. This is discussed in Chapter 4.

The apparent, main benefits of graphical user interfaces are consistency, ease of use, learnability and the ease with which multiple applications can be combined. However, there are drawbacks, including extra software, hardware, operational and support costs and more complex software development. The fact that the size of the memory required for an entry-level PC has more than quadrupled in two years and the hard disk size gone up by almost an order of magnitude is a tribute to the hardware hunger of GUIs. On the other hand the cash price of such a machine has not changed appreciably in the same period. Whatever one thinks about this there is no doubt that most organizations will install and standardize around GUIs. These companies will inevitably be using object-oriented tools and will need corresponding software engineering methods. All these extra costs will be paid for by better, more usable, more flexible applications and the consequent business benefits.

The next section introduces the theory behind user interface design and some practical guidance.

3.2 Designing the HCI

Design for human–computer interaction (HCI) is like other design problems and the same principles apply. Designed artefacts should be fit for their purpose. They should be natural in behaviour and conform to users' expectations. There should be no unpleasant surprises except where these are introduced deliberately as alarms. Use of the artefact should give feedback on progress of the task being undertaken. They should fit the mental and manual abilities of users. A very common example of bad interface design outside the context of computers concerns door handles. Recently I was walking through an office building with a colleague and, meeting a closed door, I grasped its handle and pushed. Nothing happened because the door only opened towards me. My colleague laughed and remarked that his old headmaster would have shouted: 'Stupid boy! Can't you see that the handle is there to be pulled?'. I had to explain that I had worked for over two years in a building that had handles on both sides of all the doors and that I had often strained myself by pulling doors that should be pushed. In the end I had become totally disoriented in my relationships with all doors. I still find the stupidity of builders or architects that design in this way quite exasperating. Further, someone paid them for the work; more stupid yet! I know of at least two systems that include the helpful advice: Press Enter to Exit. As long as users continue to buy them, designers will continue to deliver such daft interfaces.

Similar examples of inane design abound in computer interface design. Lotus cc:Mail is a fairly rudimentary electronic mail package. The Windows version has a toolbar with some sensibly labelled buttons such as 'Prepare' and 'Send'. There is also a button labelled 'Reply'. Quite often you will receive a message that consists of a message that you have sent earlier with a reply added to the top. What do you think is the right interpretation of the Reply button? I guessed that, on reading a message, I should type the reply above the received text and then press Reply. I did this for weeks before realizing that none of the replies were being received. What I should have done was press Reply, type my response and then press Send. Equally logical I suppose – but the offensive fact is that I received no feedback nor any indication that my text was being lost. That is a typical example of thoughtless user interface design. My feeling is that a good design is one that supports a conversational style of interaction. In English, the sentence 'I have replied' has the same status as 'I have sent'. Therefore the buttons should have the same status too. Barfield (1993) compares a computer with a human servant and pillories bad interface designers by asking how we would respond if such a servant replied to simple requests with sentences like 'Error code 42 Sir!'. Worse, he argues, if it behaves like the servant who, when asked to put a fiction writer's new manuscript in the filing cabinet, returns with the comment: 'Sorry Sir, the filing cabinet was full so I burnt the manuscript'. Something like this has happened to me recently while using Lotus AmiPro and MS Windows on a machine with a full hard disk. I do not know which product was to blame, but it didn't endear either to me. I think it would be an interesting exercise to take the guidelines on user interface design given in this chapter and compare the two leading Windows word processors, AmiPro 3.0 and Word 2.0 (which I am using now), point by point. I have not done this formally but I know which one I would bet on – the one developed first on the Macintosh! Here, though, we enter the world of prejudice and software bigotry and I desist.

Criticizing other people's design is far easier than designing something well yourself. This long section attempts to set out a series of guidelines for good UI design, including good practice in the analysis required to design well. A key feature of the section is an exploration of task analysis, which is widely used by successful designers. We will see in Chapter 7 that task analysis has uses far beyond the design of user interfaces and can be put to service in capturing requirements for all kinds of systems. The key observation here is that user-centred design and, especially, the task-centred design favoured by most UI theorists are important for creating usable, useful, correct systems – even where the interface element is not the primary consideration. First, we look at the hardware issues.

3.2.1 Selecting the hardware

Hardware for the user interface may be conveniently divided into hardware for input, output or both. There are many kinds of input device available, including plug boards, punched cards, paper tape, keyboards (QWERTY and otherwise), mice, tracker balls, light pens, pressure pens, joysticks, data gloves, graphics tablets, touch screens and microphones. In this section we will pause to review the advantages and disadvantages of some of these before returning to the issue of how to design a system to support them.

Keyboards are flexible, cheap and good at supporting unstructured tasks. However, they take ages to learn how to use well and are bad for tasks such as cursor positioning and especially disliked by casual users or those on the move.

Mice and *tracker balls* have very high resolution and a typically low error rate. They require the user to learn no commands and their rate of movement is nearly maximal with respect to eye–hand coordination. On the other hand there are some rules to learn (use the left button) and continuous use can cause fatigue and even repetitive strain injuries. Like keyboards, they need desk space and they are very poor devices for character input. Despite the naturalness of pointing with a mouse, there is an extra cognitive load compared to direct pointing devices such as touch screens or pen computers. Mice can have between one and three buttons. I have never been able to train my hand to work the centre button on a three-button mouse and a one-button mouse loads the interface designer with a task that is very difficult. I suspect the two-button mouse will outlast other designs.

Touch screens offer natural hand–eye coordination and a low cognitive load. There are no commands to learn and no extra desk space is required. They are useful in clean environments such as hospital operating theatres since they can be sealed and cleaned easily. Furthermore, touch screens are as programmable as any normal graphical interface. Their disadvantages include a limited bandwidth due to the minimum size of screen targets discriminable by the human finger, the fact that continuous use causes fatigue and the fact that the optimal viewing position is not the optimal touching position. Furthermore, there is a danger of breakage. An example of this occurred in a commodity dealing room into which touch screens were introduced. The traders had been used to operating the dealer boards (by which they were connected to other dealing rooms by telephone) with their telephone handsets. Strangely perhaps, they seemed to find the habit hard to break when the dealer boards were replaced with glass touch screens, with predictable results. Fortunately, no one was actually injured by an imploding screen.

There are several types of touch screen including scanning infra-red, surface acoustic wave, capacitative overlay, conductive or resistive membrane types. This is not the place to discuss these in detail but continuous capacitative touch screens are probably agreed to be best for most kinds of application.

Pen computers overcome some of the disadvantages of touch screens and build on the user's familiarity with writing. Finger size is no longer a problem. However, they have so far only been popular for applications where portability is important, typically replacing clipboard data capture.

The advantages of *graphics tablets* are that no part of the screen is hidden, they are programmable and they are more accurate than touch screens. As disadvantages, they require a lot of desk space, are harder to program than touch screens and there is a danger that magnetic bomb-sights (devices that are used to read or digitize data using some graphics tablets) might damage discs.

In the common imagination, *voice input* must be the ideal form of input for the majority of tasks. There is no learning time because we mostly know a natural language already. It leaves our hands and eyes free and imposes a very low cognitive load due to the commonplace character of speech. On the other hand there are many disadvantages. Speech can be noisy and distracting to others in the work environment and voice input itself needs silence since ambient noise can interfere with the interpretation. Complex software is needed and in practice there is a trade-off between the training time required and a limited vocabulary. Correct interpretation can be affected by illness, alcohol, the weather and so on.

Though voice input is attractive for many applications, especially those where the user's hands are not free, there are problems with the recognition of continuous speech. To see why this is so consider the sentence: IT'S VERY HARD TO WRECK A NICE BEACH. Now try saying it out loud a few times, rapidly[2]. There are now continuous speech recognition systems but their vocabulary is very limited. The topic remains essentially in the research domain. Most speech input systems make fairly precise impositions on what can be said and how. A recently installed commodity trading floor trade capture system required that its users underwent a training course before using the hand-held devices it used: a course on how to speak!

As well as devices for input, there are several options for the output devices including screens, printers and loudspeakers. Networks are both

---

[2] If there was someone within earshot while you were doing this, they are probably agreeing with you by now that it is indeed very hard to recognize speech.

input and output devices. Only input devices, such as screens, raise serious HCI issues, not mostly concerned with physical ergonomics. Therefore, and to keep the discussion concise, in this chapter we shall ignore the details of non-graphical devices from here on.

Studies have shown that there is no 'best' input or output device. What is most appropriate and usable depends not only on the application but on the precise task or set of tasks being carried out. One unpublished study, carried out by Logica, concluded that foreign exchange traders would benefit from a keyboard but that a bond trader might do better using a graphics tablet for input. Given changes in both the task and the technology, whether these results apply today is unclear.

3.2.2 Styles of interaction

There are many different ways of interacting with a computer system. These include menus, forms, command languages, natural language and graphical user interfaces. As with input and output devices, the best style of interaction depends mainly on the task being undertaken. There is no generic best style.

Menus have the advantage that they can be learned quickly. They generally require fewer keystrokes than other styles and can use dialogue management tools. Menus help to give structure to the dialogue and make it far easier for the designer to manage errors. However, there are several disadvantages too. The menu tree may be deep and difficult to remember and navigate. This may slow frequent users down significantly. Menus consume screen space, are inflexible and impose a need for a rapid display rate. The most significant factor with menu interfaces is the need for the task analysis to be complete.

Forms-based interfaces are mainly suitable for data entry and tend to make it easier. Users of such interfaces require modest training but they are not very good for casual users. They too consume screen space and tend to be inflexible. On the plus side, form generators can readily be used to cut down development times compared to coding everything at the 3GL level.

Modal dialogue boxes, where the dialogue is constrained strictly to the questions and values in the current box, represent a sort of combination of the forms- and menus-based approaches.

Command languages have the advantage of infinite flexibility and are usually tailorable with macros or a programming language. However, they are notoriously hard to learn, hard to remember and easy to make errors with.

The oldest command languages are natural languages and it has often been remarked that the computer should speak the user's language and interact via English or some other natural language. This would mean that the users had no new commands to learn but there are several very serious disadvantages. Natural languages are expressive but verbose and ambiguous. In work situations, even without computers, a more formal or structured subset of language is often used.

Consider, for example, the use of 'roger' in military communications or technical jargon in most trades. Natural language conversations are invariably based on implicit, shared understanding and the fact that when this breaks down clarification is often needed – and this will slow dialogues unbearably. This and the context sensitivity of language means that artificial intelligence techniques are required. Unfortunately these techniques are not very advanced as yet and some of us believe that a speaking computer would be a thinking computer and that that is either impossible or so far beyond the scope of rational human engineering as to be absurd (Graham, 1994c). Natural language front-ends to databases have been written and exist as commercial products, such as Intellect, but these do not attempt to solve the general language understanding problem, preferring rather to permit natural enquiries in a restricted context, based on a shared model of the data dictionary and its structure.

Graphical user interfaces combine the advantages of several of the above styles. They are easier to remember than command languages because they provide visual aids to memory and can be quite flexible. They encourage exploration while at the same time making it possible to encourage consistency and enforce a standard interface across different software products. Novice errors can be constrained by warnings or modal dialogue boxes. However, graphical user interfaces are very costly indeed to write and may need extra and more expensive hardware, though this must be judged against falling hardware prices.

Despite the extra cost, people and organizations are gradually moving to graphical interfaces for a number of reasons. They believe that GUIs will help enhance productivity. Further, GUIs are making a number of new applications possible that would not have been attempted with older approaches. A good example occurs in industries which I would characterize as customer service industries: banks, insurers, retailers and so on. One used to be faced, on entering a bank say, with a glass screen behind which was a teller. Pieces of paper were exchanged under the screen and one left satisfied. Nowadays, the glass screens have gone and there are desks in an open plan area, behind each of which are 'financial consultants'. These financial consultants (ex-tellers with a short training course behind them in some cases) mediate their conversations with the customer through the use of a terminal which gives them access to the information resources of the bank and sometimes (as with NatWest's Pharos) to an expert system (Figure 3.1). Without this support they would be little better than the old tellers. The trouble with the customers, however, is that they will refuse to ask their questions and present their answers in an order compatible with the order built into the menu system of an application. Thus, banks and other similar customer service organizations are turning to GUIs to provide an event driven dialogue. Traditional interfaces could not handle such event driven dialogues and modern GUIs are largely able to do so only because the controls on the screen are seen as passing messages to system objects. Thus, most of these developments are being built using some sort of object-based technology, usually with built in client/server links to mainframe databases.

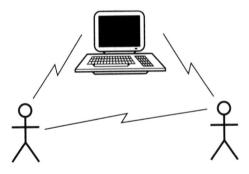

Figure 3.1 Dialogues between customers and 'consultants' are often mediated by a machine.

3.2.3 Fundamentals of cognitive psychology

In order to design a good user interface it is necessary to know a little about the way the human mind and body works. In particular it is useful to know how memory storage and retrieval works, how the eye responds to colours, what positions lead to fatigue and so on. The bodily aspects of human–computer interaction are often referred to as ergonomics, though strictly this subject encompasses the mental aspects as well.

According to current theories of cognitive psychology, **long-term memory** (LTM) stores knowledge and data. To be used these memories must be activated and this takes time. They are normally stored in an inactivated state though not necessarily in a separate location from those immediately accessible in what used to be called short-term memory. **Working** or **activated memory** is limited and transitory. Items in working memory can be accessed directly and quickly. The activation of the linkages to these memories decays over time. Miller (1956) discovered that activated memory could hold a maximum of between five and nine items or chunks before filling up in some sense. These limits depend on the meaning of the material and an expert's chunk can represent far more knowledge than that of a novice. It is a crude mistake to interpret this as meaning, for example, that there should never be more than 7±2 items presented on a screen. For example, when a novice sees a display of a chess board s/he sees 32 pieces. A grand master however may see only five high-level game patterns which s/he has chunked through long practice. Further, the units are stored in classification, composition and other structures which assist recall. **Rehearsal** of cues helps storage in LTM and retrieval, through reinforcing commonly used activation paths in the brain's neural network. Another way of activating these paths more quickly is **prim-**

ing where recalling one item helps to activate another semantically related one. Priming helps activate concepts in working memory (WM). When a user moves from one system's interface to that of another there are **transfer effects** due to both rehearsal and priming. These transfer effects can be both positive (beneficial) and negative (harmful) from the point of view of usability. The more user interface designers are aware of memory characteristics, the better they can do their job.

Other memory effects that may be significant include **interference**, which occurs when priming may activate the wrong things or at least activate memories that interfere with what should be recalled. This is an example of a negative transfer effect. Positive transfer effects can exploit the ability of users to classify their knowledge and this helps with the consistency and coherence of an interface. Generally speaking, positive effects will occur when the designer copies the structure of existing and well-known tasks. The success of the desktop metaphor that Xerox and Apple promoted can be regarded as evidence for this proposition as can the popularity of tricks such as 3-D button controls that appear to depress as they are clicked. Xerox have recently generalized this metaphor to one of Rooms wherein each 'room' has a set of windows associated with it. Rooms can be thought of as a multi-desktop metaphor and it is yet to be established whether the average user will be comfortable with this view of things. An example of negative effects is the use of the F3 key for the help function in WordPerfect when most packages use F1. When a WordPerfect user presses F1 the wrong things are primed and when trying to recall what key gives help there is no such support. An example of the exploitation of positive transfer effects is the support for Lotus syntax in Excel.

Structure and organization help priming. This can be seen readily by examining Figure 3.2. In Figure 3.2(a) related items are adjacent and the lines emphasize this. In Figure 3.2(b) there is no such organization and the menu is confusing to read and difficult to remember.

Priming effects occur between semantically related words. For example, saying CAT primes DOG; showing *ITALIC* may prime **bold**. Another example of the beneficial exploitation of priming effects in a user interface occurs when the actual appearance of an item is used to reinforce the memory of what selecting that item may imply, often using a visual cue or an icon. Figure 3.3 illustrates this with an example of two different menu designs for the typeface selection within a word processor. The rightmost menu clearly helps the user remember what typefaces like Courier and Times Roman look like. However, this can go too far. A user unfamiliar with the Greek alphabet might well be very confused by the Hellenic appearance of the Symbol face. Priming is a context-sensitive effect and this should be understood by designers. For example, CAT could prime X-RAY rather than DOG in the context of medical diagnosis.

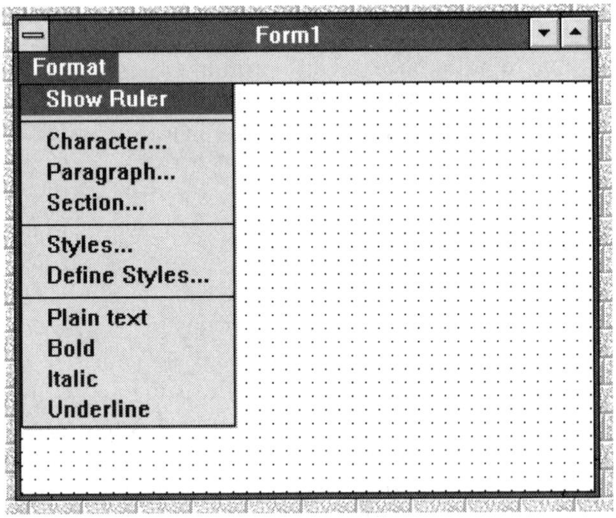

(a)

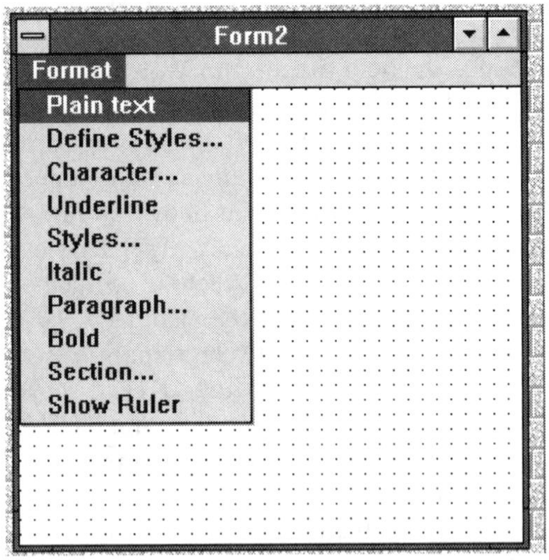

(b)

Figure 3.2 (a) Structured menu; (b) unstructured menu.

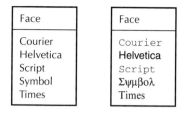

Figure 3.3 Priming the memory of typefaces.

Exercise: Devise a similar menu that overcomes both problems.

This example raises a general point about the use of symbols, icons and mnemonics. Icons are culturally dependent and their use depends on background knowledge that may not be shared by all users. For example, consider the symbol shown in Figure 3.4 for a moment. You either know what it means immediately or, I suggest, will never guess. Here is a clue. Most European or American readers over 30 will have used a device with this icon in its interface. The answer will be given later in the chapter. It is usually a good idea to reinforce icons with words.

There are several guidelines that can be deduced from a knowledge of how users act when reading displays. Research has shown that the first items read from a list tend to be stored more readily in LTM. This is known as the **primacy effect**. The last items in a list tend to be stored in WM; the **recency effect**. One corollary of this is the need for interfaces to be standardized across applications and stable in time. Standard interfaces also exploit the classification structures of memory.

Standard user interfaces are important because of the memory limitations of users. The chief advantage for me of a GUI such as X or MS Windows is that most applications work in the same way and I can utilize positive transfer when closing a window or calling for help because the positions of the features are standard. In my opinion, this is more important than ease of use itself.

Figure 3.4 An icon.

Another important principle of user interface design that derives from an understanding of psychology is exploiting **closure**. We are all familiar with the 'I came in here for something but can't remember what' syndrome. It occurs because of the human tendency to be satisfied with closed tasks and once we have achieved closure in one respect we tend to omit to complete ancillary tasks. For example, when using a bank ATM the sequence:

1. Insert card
2. Enter PIN
3. Enter option
4. Enter cash amount
5. Take cash (closure reached)
6. Take card
7. Take receipt

is likely to cause errors because once you have the cash (closure of main task) you are likely to depart, forgetting the card and receipt. Thus, most ATM programs force you to take the card before taking the cash. Unfortunately for the street sweepers the same principle is rarely applied to the receipt as well.

Cognitive dissonance occurs when a false consciousness is created to explain a bad design. Users create explanations for doing stupid things. If you do something often enough and have worked hard to learn how to do it, you will often invent reasons for continuing to do so. In this way bad designs become right by usage and bugs become features. Having invested the learning time you can make yourself an indispensable resource as the source of knowledge about the product. Now you can be the expert to whom others refer, even though a better designed product would eliminate the need for any expertise. I have observed this often with impenetrable mainframe operating systems, otiose programming languages such as RPG and write-only macro languages such as that of Lotus 1-2-3 and its ilk. Perhaps the QWERTY keyboard could be regarded as a particularly well-known example of this phenomenon.

Given this very high-level knowledge of psychological principles, we can now establish some practical principles and guidelines for HCI design.

3.2.4 Principles of HCI design

Human–computer interaction (HCI) involves computers, users, tasks and requirements. For a time, user-centred design was emphasized. However, it is now widely realized that the user is not a stable given, because users adopt varying rôles in interacting with a computer system. The stable feature is often the task being performed for the rôle. Therefore, this section and this whole book focus on task-centred design. HCI uses principles from computer science, psychology, sociology, anthropology, engineering, aesthetics and many other areas. This book emphasizes the insights from psychology, software engineering and knowledge engineering but attempts to take account of all other influences. The main insight from knowledge engineering is that the user interface includes the user's knowledge of the system and the system's model of the user. A personal insight that has greatly influenced this presentation is that most user interfaces are dreadful.

It is crucial that the interface designer, like the software engineer, does not stop at analysing and automating existing manual practices. Computers can change the tasks they were designed to assist with and this is often their largest contribution. Word processing has largely changed the nature of work in many offices already and groupware and hypermedia systems are continuing the trend.

HCI design involves the following issues:

- Functionality: How does the interface help users carry out tasks and how does it impede them? Does the interface itself make something possible or impossible?
- Usability, covering:
  - Learnability
  - Memorability
  - Productivity
  - Propensity to errors
  - Support for tasks (task analysis)
  - Safety
  - Range of users
  - Suitability for different locations and conditions
- Aesthetics
- Acceptability
- Structure
- Reliability
- Efficiency
- Maintainability
- Extensibility
- Cost

Object-oriented programming contributes to maintainability, extensibility and some aspects of usability. Prototyping is widely seen as essential for the production of usable interfaces. Some authorities recommend the use of specialist graphic or industrial designers as part of the development team and some go further, suggesting the complete separation of the UI development within the life cycle. I think that this is a mistake and that sound practices of software engineering and object-oriented methods should integrate the specialist skills of interface designers into those of software developers in general.

It is remarkable that the most liked features of a given GUI are often the aesthetic ones. One of the most popular innovations in windows systems for example was the 3-D push button that appears to depress when clicked or held clicked. It apparently contributes nothing but is loved by users to the extent of being a prerequisite for all such systems nowadays.

General HCI principles are rare, though some have been suggested. IBM's Common User Access (CUA) (1991a) gives a set of remarkably clear and complete guidelines that are compatible with an object-oriented approach. It incorporates task analysis, user surveys, site visits and usability testing within the approach and constructs three models representing user, designer and programmer views on the interface and underlying system. CUA emphasizes reducing user memory load, consistency and placing the user in command of the interface. In particular, in support of the last principle, it recommends not blaming users for errors, parsimonious use of modes with pre-emption to control them, immediate feedback, undo, accommodating users with different skill levels, providing helpful messages, customizability and transparency of the interface. Memory loads are reduced by using meaningful class interfaces to control interaction and using concrete instances and examples wherever possible. The CUA approach to consistency is well known and exploits the principles of aesthetics, continuity and priming via clear standards and visual metaphors.

STUDIO (Browne, 1994) is an attempt to provide a traditional structured approach to user interface design and construction. While it contains much that is of value and is one of the first attempts to provide a comprehensive framework, it suffers from several weaknesses from our present point of view. First, it assumes that UI work is a quite separate activity from system building and requires separate skills. This leads to the need to tie it in to an ordinary software engineering process model and the model chosen is a conventional, rather than object-oriented, one. The fact that such a process model cannot support object-oriented development further reinforces the view that HCI design must be handled separately. My view is that a good method must support both and help integrate the skills of designers so that all aspects of systems are designed with and for the user.

Thimbleby (1990) introduces the concept of Generative User-Engineering Principles (GUEPs) – for both designers and users. Typical GUEPs he identifies include the following.

- Recognize and exploit closure.
- WYSIWYG = What You See Is What You Get!
- Fix the documentation and then make the program conform to it.
- The designer should be able to explain the interface concisely and completely.
- The designer must ensure that the user can construct an appropriate internal model of the system.

He also introduces a number of formal or algebraic GUEPs as follows.

- *Idempotence* $[T = T^2]$. Some operations should have no effect when reiterated. For example, when the escape key returns to the main menu, hitting it twice should have no further effect. When deleting files, one should not be able to re-press the delete key to delete the next file without some other interaction intervening. The cut, copy and paste actions should also be idempotent. Idempotence is particularly important when the type-ahead buffer is active since unintentional actions might otherwise be performed when the machine cannot keep pace with typing.

- *Distributivity* [A*(B+C) = A*B+A*C]. This GUEP says that distributing operations over their arguments can enhance usability and convenience by reducing input. For example: 'delete file1; delete file2' should be equivalent to 'delete file1, file2'. In the MS Windows 3.1 File Manager, *delete file* distributes over *select file*, so that you can select a whole bunch of files and delete them at one stroke.
- *Commutativity* [A*B = B*A]. This says that the order of operations should not be important unless order is significant. For example, cursor movement (except at the screen boundaries) with the right and left arrow keys successively should leave the cursor position unchanged. This principle tends against the common modern innovation of permitting mouse wrap-around where the mouse appears on the opposite side of the screen when moved past the boundary.
- *Substitutivity* means putting an expression in place of a constant, as can be done in most programming languages or spreadsheets.
- *Associativity* [A*(B*C) = (A*B)*C]. This principle is equivalent to that of modelessness.

Modes in a user interface are defined as 'variable information in the computer system affecting the meaning of what the user sees and does'. In a modal (or modey) system the user is required to know what mode the system is in because the same action may have quite different effects in different modes.

It is commonly agreed that modes should be avoided but that they are sometimes necessary. For example, having *user* and *novice* modes is widely agreed to be almost a principle in its own right. Certainly the system should inform the user of the current mode and it is good practice to attract attention to the change by a change of colour in the mode indicator, a status bar or some such device. Examples of modes in an interface include: pressing the ON button on a typical calculator, where the mode is either *on* or *off* and the effect is different in each case; a 'Cannot save file – disk not formatted' message reveals a mode; as does 'Overwrite existing file?'. Dialogue boxes are usually modal in that the behaviour of other visible options is suspended while they appear; the behaviour of part of the screen has thus changed. The notion of modes is closely related to that of polymorphism; polymorphic interfaces are precisely modal. However, what is useful in a language is not necessarily good in an interface.

It is very helpful to provide users with information about the context within which their actions will be interpreted. This includes information on state dependencies and modes and should explain the current task with its preconditions, postconditions and side-effects. Modes should only be used where it is absolutely necessary to restrict the user's freedom of interaction. Temporal modes can be used to enforce a certain sequence of operations but this implies burdening the user with a heavy load on memory. This should never be done useless out-of-sequence actions are catastrophic. The commonest example of this is the excessive use of cascaded modal dialogue boxes where a simple data entry form would do better. Spatial modes are common when several things are possible but only one can be done at a time. Highlighting icons and changing the mouse pointer are good ways to draw attention to spatial modes. Other contextual information can be given in a status bar, such as the state of the irritatingly-close-to-the-main-keyboard 'insert' key on most PCs.

It is generally wise to include *undo* and *redo* facilities to encourage exploratory learning and protect users from catastrophic errors. However, *undo* and modelessness are incompatible as Thimbleby (1990) adequately demonstrates, though the argument is too intricate to summarize here. This is largely because undoing multiple actions may change the state of the system in other ways.

Thimbleby gives the following GUEPs for modes, breaking them down into GUEPs for pre-emptive, inertial, input and output modes along with a general principle of *equal opportunity*.

- *Pre-emptive modes*. You should be able to do anything anywhere (for example, there should be no Y/N questions or immovable dialogue boxes).
- *Inertial modes*. The layout of successive screens should change as little as possible. When you go back everything should be as you left it. The most [recently|likely|frequently] used menu selection should be highlighted.
- *Input modes*. The system should be sufficiently consistent to use with the display switched off (for example, q or Alt-F-X for quit).
- *Output modes*. WYSIWYG.
- *Equal opportunity*. Output can become input and vice versa (for example, aperture or shutter priority cameras).

A well-known example of equal opportunity is Query By Example (QBE), a widely used query method for relational and pseudo-relational databases. QBE offers the user a blank form such as the one in Figure 3.5. The user may then type fixed values for Dept and Salary and QBE will return all records that match the pattern. This is not dissimilar in principle from what occurs

Name	Dept	Salary
?	Sales	>10,000

Figure 3.5 Query By Example in database enquiry systems.

with PROLOG queries which are resolved by pattern matching too. The equal opportunity arises because the user may choose **any** value to fix and is not constrained to a fixed, pre-designed dialogue, such as:

Enter Dept: Sales
Enter Salary: >10,000
<list of matching records>

Cut and paste facilities usually give equal opportunity, or at least should do. For example, if you are in a search routine you should be able to search for the last item cut.

Thimbleby gives the example of a calculator of the sort illustrated in Figure 3.6. Simple calculators are not equal opportunity because the result and the operands are not interchangeable. For example, I can put in 13 * 4 = and I will (with luck and a good battery) get 52; but I cannot put in ? * 4 = 52 and expect the unknown to be computed. Incidentally, these devices have poor feedback in the interface. If you want to check that 0 * 0 = 0 you may equally well believe that the device is not working as that the algebra is vindicated.

Figure 3.7 illustrates an improved design based on this GUEP; set the symbols for the two button displays and put in any two numbers, and the third will display a consistent result. We could further improve the design by not using 0 as the default display.

Some other design principles that have been proposed include the following.

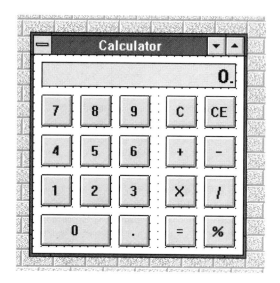

Figure 3.6 A simple calculator.

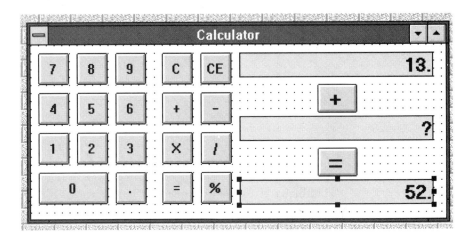

Figure 3.7 An equal opportunity calculator.

- WYSIWYG. I have mentioned this term already without explaining it. It stands for What You See Is What You Get and implies the principle that all forms of output should be the same; for example, the layout, fount and size of characters that appear on a screen will be exactly what the printer produces.
- WYSIWYCU stand for What You See Is What You Can Use. If there is an object on the screen you should be able do something to it or with it and what that something is should be as natural and obvious as possible. Future computer systems may, I hope, generalize this to: WYKAIWYCU (What You Know About Is What You Can Use). I know about cut and paste. Why can't I use it in a typical modal dialogue box?
- The principle of *commensurate effort* states that it should be as hard to delete something as to create it; as hard to undo as to do. Steve Jobs' slogan 'Simple things should be simple, difficult things should be possible' is a rephrasing of this principle.
- The interface should provide *a sense of progress*. Feedback is needed for this because effects can thus be related to causes and it allows the user to see if the results of each step are contributing to the overall task. Slow tasks or network delays should be made visible in this way, so that the user can tell if the system has really crashed or is just plain slow. Changing the mouse pointer to an hourglass is a helpful and often used technique but one can still wonder whether the system has hung. Providing an estimate of the anticipated time in the form of a gauge is useful in such contexts.
- *Non-pre-emption.* This is a good principle because it restricts the flexibility of the interface and the range of tasks to which it can be applied. On the other hand there is sometimes a real need for pre-emption to prevent

catastrophic, inadvertent errors. The user might erase several pages by accident, delete or overwrite files unintentionally, forget to save some important work, lock the keyboard or system inadvertently or fill memory and abort the session by accident. Such dangerous moves are candidates for pre-emptive prompts.

- *Self-demonstrability*. Consider context-sensitive help, tutorials and – best of all – a completely intuitive interface based on transfer effects from a suitable metaphor.
- *Options should be settable by the user*. For example, the latest Microsoft mouse driver offers options for wrapping the pointer round to the opposite screen edge and snapping its position to the latest OK button to appear in a dialogue box. Both these options are useful, but to the experienced user they just lead to 'mouse creep' as the physical position is constantly at variance with his expectations. Fortunately they can be switched off.
- *Avoid frequent channel switching*. Frequent switching of input between keyboard and mouse is evidently undesirable. Distracting messages from screen areas other than the one where attention is directed should be avoided, as should moving the focus of attention around too much.

So much for abstract principles, now for some more concrete, practical advice on user interface design.

3.2.5 Guidelines for user interface design

In the context of a user interface, both the user and the system must fulfil their responsibilities towards each other. The responsibilities of the user include knowing what tasks can be attempted, being able to perform the procedures needed to accomplish these tasks, understanding and interpreting messages (including their interpretation under different modes) and being able to use the appropriate I/O devices.

The responsibilities of the system include those of helping the user to carry out the tasks specified during design, responding correctly to commands, pre-empting destructive input, meeting performance constraints and sometimes explaining itself to the user.

These responsibilities are task oriented rather than user oriented because the same user may have quite different responsibilities when adopting a different rôle, when a different set of tasks is implied. For example, the same user might approach the system as a manager enquiring on performance or as a data entry clerk adding new financial assumptions.

Designers should remember that there are considerable variations among users. Icons – images – are culturally dependent, as demonstrated by the icon in Figure 3.4. For those who have still not guessed the meaning of this icon, it represents the choke of an automobile. Recognizing it depends either entirely on memory or on the knowledge that a carburettor contains within it a 'butterfly', a device consisting of a flat metal plate that pivots about an axial pin to allow more or less air into the combustion process. Once you know this, the meaning is obvious. If you don't have this fundamental engineering knowledge, you have to remember the meaning. Furthermore, users vary widely in their visual ability and will react accordingly. In addition to this natural variation in ability there may also be very great variation due to handicaps such as colour blindness, fingers missing, fatigue, illiteracy, memory disorders, deafness and so on.

The **power law of practice** says that practice has a log-linear effect on skill or that practice makes perfect. The more opportunity the users have to explore the interface the better they will become at using it. This implies that both regular use and an exploratory style will help. It also tells us that systems that will be used by infrequent users need more attention to the user interface.

Users come to the system with different backgrounds and knowledge levels. Psychology tells us that during skill acquisition knowledge is first stored as **declarative knowledge**, often in the form of rules and objects to which those rules apply, and can be directly recalled as such. Practice helps people store associations between items and form chunks based on these associations; this is **associative knowledge**. More practice compiles the rules into **procedural knowledge** by which stage it is often inaccessible to consciousness, as with the knowledge of how to ride a bicycle or read a sentence. On this basis designers should design for the knowledge level of the users they anticipate using the systems and preferably provide both novice and expert modes.

Here are some commonly used heuristics for user interface modelling which add to the above principles.

- ■ Use strong, natural metaphors and analogies.
- ■ Keep it simple.
- ■ Model the domain objects directly.
- ■ Use semantic structures (classification, composition, usage, association).
- ■ Minimize semantic primitives.
- ■ Capture rules.

Note the similarity with guidelines for constructing object-oriented models to be found in Part II.

Remember that documentation, training and the user's knowledge are all part of the user interface.

DIALOGUE DESIGN

Dialogue design is a problem for all user interfaces, graphical or otherwise. Much work outside computer science may be drawn upon. Relevant fields include discourse analysis and semiotics. Speech act theory (Austen, 1962; Searle, 1969) is particularly relevant to groupware systems (Winograd and Flores, 1986) and has influenced SOMA's approach to task modelling as discussed in Chapter 7. Suchman (1987) applies anthropological and ethnomethodological principles to the design of photocopiers. Johnson (1992) describes a number of research attempts to formalize interaction using command language grammars and task action languages. Neither approach is yet proven to yield significant improvements in practice. Perhaps the most important observation that can be made in this context is that dialogues depend on shared understanding and knowledge of a common domain. This has long been known to designers of computerized natural language systems where it would be a wonderful achievement to get a computer to understand the sentence 'time flies like an arrow' because of the use of simile, but how much harder it is to expect the same machine to respond intelligently, and soon after the last remark, to the observation that 'fruit flies like a banana'.

Dialogues are used for several reasons: to give commands, to refine a common goal and plan tasks to achieve it, to convey information, data or knowledge, to pass the time. Most system dialogues are concerned with commands and conveying information and data. Commands imply a commitment on the part of the recipient to carry out the task mentioned. All interactions initiated by the user should therefore give an observable result, either confirming that the task is complete and giving any resultant information or reporting an exception. In other words, well-designed systems are *helpful*. They should also be *forgiving* of user errors.

Expert systems often include explanation facilities though the latter are more costly to write than is often supposed. Sometimes therefore a dialogue consists of an explanation that modifies the user's model of the system. If the user has a good model of a system, s/he will find it easier to use. Good feedback as well as explanation help the user to develop and refine a model. If the system has a model of the user it will be able to respond more appropriately. Examples of the latter occur frequently in intelligent computer-aided learning where the system asks easier questions of novices based on their test scores, or in systems that have a *novice* and *expert* mode switch of some sort.

Here are some commonly used heuristics for dialogue design:

- Minimize input movements.
- Maximize input bandwidth/channels.
- Use words and language carefully.
- The interface should look good.
- Be consistent (keys, positioning, and so on).
- Keep the system modeless or provide a high level of context-sensitive feedback.
- A natural response time is desirable.
- Process continuity should be sought.
- Ease of use should be paramount.
- Make your system customizable.
- Make it non-pre-emptive.
- Follow standards.

Table 3.1 Use of language in error messages.

Error message	Evaluation
ABORT: error 451	Bad
I'm tremendously sorry but I have discovered that a file you want to use is already open (error number 451).	Better but verbose
Error number 451. File already open. This error normally occurs when you forgot to close the file at the end of a previous subroutine.	Better but tedious
Error number 451: File already open. Explain?<Y/N>:	Good-ish
Left as an exercise for the reader!	PERFECT

Good dialogue design requires consistency, informative feedback and simple error handling. Frequent users should be able to take shortcuts. The system should exploit and indicate the phenomenon of closure. Undo/redo facilities are often useful but can be problematic in cases where some actions cannot be consistently undone or redone. Dialogues should be user driven and not modal, when possible. The designer should attempt to reduce the load placed on the working memory of the user – exploiting priming, transfer effects, closure and other devices. Some designers stress that the use of words and language itself can be important. It is reported, for example, that some female users are disturbed by words like *abort*. Table 3.1 illustrates this point.

Error messages should be consistent, friendly and constructive, informative, precise and use the users' terminology. Multiple levels of message are often helpful. Hypertext help systems are a simple way to meet most of these requirements, though hypertext design has problems of its own.

Command languages should exhibit uniform abbreviation rules, be consistent and follow standards. Counter-examples from DOS include multiple ways of abbreviating directory commands (CHDIR, CD, DIR, ...). Also, in different operating systems from the same manufacturer it used to be common to find several words being used for the same purpose; for example, CATALOG/DIRECTORY, HELP/ASSIST/AID, and so on.

GAINING ATTENTION AND USING COLOUR

There are many tricks that designers employ for getting the users' attention to focus on a particular screen location, datum or message. Galitz (1981) reports that the guidelines provided in Table 3.2 have proved effective. Colour is useful for gaining attention but one should be aware that the eye is not colour-sensitive at the periphery. It can help in emphasizing the logical organization of a screen, facilitating subtle discrimination and improving aesthetics. Use it parsimoniously. Beware of monochrome ports; that is, people running an application on a black and white screen that was developed on a colour one and finding that certain contrasts obscure a function. Beware of poor contrast combinations. Allow users to change the colour scheme and above all be consistent. Another reason for avoiding indiscriminate use of colour is the very large number of people, especially men, who have some degree of colour blindness.

Table 3.2 Gaining attention.

Intensity	Up to 2 levels
Point size	Up to 4
Founts	Up to 3
Blinking	2–4 Hz
Colour	Up to 5
Sound	Soft tones except for emergencies
Symbols	Bullets, arrows, boxes, lines

Other guideline are identified by MacDonald (1993) and, adding some deriving from my own experience, may be summarized as follows.

■ Use colour parsimoniously. Use no more than 12 colours and only five for critical tasks.
■ Use colour to increase information flow. Colours should relate semantically connected items. Colour changes should nearly always be used to indicate mode changes to attract attention to them.
■ Take advantage of colour associations such as red/danger but beware of cultural variations (white is the colour of mourning in China). Use industry-standard associations where possible; for example, the colour coding of electrical wiring or red and yellow for healthy tissue in medical applications.
■ Allow for human limitations. The eye is usually more sensitive to yellow and green than red or blue. The latter are therefore poor for displaying detail or small text. The luminance ratio between foreground and background should be 10:1. Embolden dark characters on light backgrounds. Use desaturated colours for backgrounds to avoid fatigue. Avoid bright colours at the display extremities to avoid flicker effects. Grey is usually best for this. Use complementary colours to avoid problems for colour-blind users.
■ Consider the task being performed. Typeface design matters for textual presentation. Realism matters for pictures.
■ Treat colour as part of the whole interface. Let the user change the colour scheme. Be consistent. Use colour as you use menu design – as a simplifier of tasks.
■ Think about how the user will cope with motion, especially when using a mouse. When I upgraded my processor recently I found that drag-and-drop, a feature I made much use of, had become unusable – simply because the screen scrolled too quickly for me to control the drop point. Mouse movement and screen refreshment or scrolling should accelerate in proportion to the time the button is depressed to overcome such problems.

It is often effective to prototype in monochrome and introduce colours later. Further, one should not clutter the display. The same technique, sound or colour should indicate related items. Response times should normally be under 1 second. Messages should indicate significant variations. Pace-induced stress should be avoided. Novices should be allowed more time.

USABILITY TESTS AND METRICS

Evaluation of the user interface is very important. HCI reviews and expert walkthroughs are usually enormously useful. Other valuable evaluation techniques include questionnaires, observational studies and test script reports. Useful GUI metrics include the time it takes to learn an operation or to use a whole system, the time it takes to carry out a particular task, the average user's error rate, satisfaction indices and skill retention over time. These metrics imply that a budget for experimentation and data collection be created. Also, it should be noted that the existing system should be measured with respect to these metrics during requirements capture if the metrics are to be of use in assessing benefits.

For mass market products it is often worth investing in full-scale usability workshops wherein trial users are recorded, observed and measured carrying out common operations. This is usually too expensive for custom developments but would be worthwhile for systems going into very wide use or where paybacks are very high and sensitive to usability. Observational studies of any kind imply the need for usability metrics to be agreed. One can measure learnability by comparing task execution times before and after extended use. Other metrics have already been discussed. Usability testing is easier if it is supported by specific software support tools although this is most beneficial for a mature product where comparisons with earlier versions are possible. Usability testing also uses task analysis as a key technique.

Usability tests should examine users' rôles, skill levels, frequency of use and the possible social, cultural and organizational variations. The method exposed in Part II emphasizes the centrality of user rôles; that is, neither the users nor their rôles but the combination of a user adopting a rôle: an actor. This notion combines the skill level and organizational rôle in a single, finer-grained concept. Usability studies may further distinguish computer and application skill levels and most approaches to HCI use a simple knowledge-level model such as:

(1) Beginner (no knowledge)
(2) Learner (knowledge incomplete, encoded as rules)
(3) Competent (knowledge complete, compiled and not accessible to consciousness)
(4) Expert (knowledge subject to critique and refinement).

Usability testing requires careful experimental design and statistical analysis. It is therefore expensive. At the simplest level it must identify the categories of the most frequent users, such as: frequent, competent with computers, domain learners, English-speaking or well educated. The tests should take account of transfer effects between different environments and this may, for example, lead to the need for a user interface that looks the same on different platforms. An additional difficulty with testing GUIs arises from their graphical nature. Whereas a command line interface can be tested by producing a test harness that compares textual output across trials, often GUI tests have to compare bitmaps of output. This is complicated by the need to ignore irrelevant variations, such as the final position of the mouse pointer, which makes careful design of the tests very important. For all this, studies of two projects at IBM have shown that big savings can result from thorough usability engineering; as much as $2 saved by productivity gains for every dollar spent.

3.2.6 Task analysis

One of the most important techniques available to the interface designer is task analysis. Early versions of task analysis were developed independently, and somewhat differently, in the USA and Britain during the 1950s. In both cases, the motivation and background was mainly training needs analysis to help overcome a chronic post-war labour and skills shortage. The British concentrated on the hierarchical decomposition of tasks and on taxonomies of human skills while the Americans focused on issues such as psychometric testing. Substantive tasks were decomposed into their requisite psychological abilities, viewed as perceptual, motor and problem-solving skills. The model of human cognition was fairly primitive at this time and not able to analyse complex tasks such as programming.

A **task** is an activity or set of actions undertaken by an agent assuming a rôle to change a system's state to some goal state. Goals may have subgoals and be achieved by executing procedures (sets of actions). It is a matter of some skill to set goals at the appropriate level; neither too abstract nor too specific. Tasks involve objects, actions and taxonomies (classification structures). Sometimes the goals are clear. In other cases the goal is not known at the start or may change during the task, as new factors emerge. UI designers should consider people, rôles, organizations and technology in their approach. A goal is a desired state and a task is the means of reaching it. For example, my goal might be to stop feelings of hunger. The corresponding task is to eat. This may involve setting subgoals (or implied tasks) such as finding food, chewing, and so on.

There are two kinds of task: **internal tasks** are the tasks that the user must carry out to use the system (having knowledge, depressing certain keys in sequence, and so on); **external tasks** are those tasks that the user must perform using the system to support them (interpreting reports, writing documents, and so on). Internal tasks enable external tasks.

Just as there are two kinds of task, there are two approaches to design. We can attempt to merely support each of the external tasks. This approach does not challenge the underlying business processes or attempt to change them and Barfield (1993) suggests that it amounts to building 'intelligent notebooks'. The alternative is to attempt to build a model underneath the task level including some understanding of what is being done and why. If the existing task can be modelled then the model can be criticized and optimized. This may lead to suggestions as to how to improve the business processes. Building internal task models is tantamount to building a knowledge model in cases where the task is not merely a sequence of simple external tasks. The skills of the knowledge engineer are then useful. When the task normally involves group interaction, as with CASE or group work, then some internal task knowledge may become externalized. Typically these kinds of system are the hardest to model and Barfield points out forcibly, and correctly in my view, how this is evinced by most CASE tools, which usually enforce too many trivial tasks and sometimes miss out the important ones.

To be useful for system builders, task knowledge should be central, typical and representative. **Centrality** means that the task is critical to achieving the goal. If most users mention it, it is likely to be central. **Representativeness** holds when the mental model corresponds closely to the domain model that experts would hold. **Typicality** occurs when the task knowledge is typical of most users.

There are many strong links between task analysis and object-oriented programming, AI planning theory and knowledge based systems and these can be exploited in object-oriented analysis. The use cases of Jacobson's Objectory (Jacobson *et al.*, 1992) are reminiscent of tasks and this observation enriches the Jacobson theory by adding a notion of hierarchical and recursive decomposition to use cases. They are also similar to the scripts of Schank and Abelson (1977) to be described in Chapter 5. Script theory in AI was developed to model knowledge of typical behaviour by actors. The canonical example is the restaurant script, which goes roughly: 'Enter restaurant, attract waiter's attention, sit, order, eat, pay and leave'. The link to planning theory results simply from the idea that an actor searches for subgoals in order to execute a task, just as in constructing a plan in a domain such as job-shop scheduling. A synthesis of all these ideas is part of the SOMA approach to requirements capture and is described in detail in Chapter 7. They apply equally to UI design and general systems design.

There are three fundamental activities (which may be regarded loosely as steps) involved in task analysis. These activities are: to define the objectives of the system, perform task knowledge elicitation and finally carry out a knowledge analysis – looking for the knowledge and skills involved in task performance. Again there is a strong link here to the domain of expert systems and the skills of the knowledge engineer. Typically, knowledge engineers carry a tool bag of more or less formal knowledge elicitation techniques which includes such approaches as task analysis itself, topic analysis, Kelly grids and card sorts, rating scales and frequency counts, skill profiles and taxonomies of human performance. These techniques will be described further in Chapter 7 when we deal with the object identification techniques within SOMA. Other techniques include reading about the domain, introspection, examining sample output, observation (both direct and indirect), structured and focused interviews, protocol analysis (both concurrent and retrospective), brainstorming, questionnaires and having the analyst perform the task after instruction from the user or expert (also called teachback). Direct observation involves the physical presence of the observer whereas indirect observation could utilize video recordings. Both are time consuming and may be intrusive. Concurrent protocols require the expert to give a running commentary on the task being performed while retrospective ones are reports on task performance given afterwards.

Tasks are usually expressed in a simple task-action grammar whereby each task has the form:

Subject – Verb – Direct.Object – [Preposition – Indirect.Object]

When we use this form in Part II we will call them SVDPI sentences. Typically, the verb will be a transitive verb. The subject corresponds either to an actor or to some active component of the system. For example, a deal capture task could be expressed as 'Dealer enters bargain details', where there is no indirect object, or a deal confirmation task as 'System sends confirmation to counterparty', where there is. It is important, in our approach at least, that tasks are only decomposed to **atomic** level; that is, to the lowest level that introduces no terms extraneous to the domain. We would thus exclude tasks such as: 'Dealer enters bargain details with keyboard'. The term 'keyboard' is not within the trading domain. Lee (1993) gives similar advice when he forbids tasks such as 'transfer selected text to current application' since that assumes a 'cut-and-paste style of interaction communication ... which is a user interface design issue'. I shall have more to say on this point in relation to metrics in Chapter 10. Another more complex, but useful, way to represent tasks is as scripts with slots, props (in the theatrical sense) and exception handlers. This is discussed in Chapter 5 and used in Part II.

SOMA requirements capture and task analysis will be dealt with more fully and in greater generality in Chapter 7. Only the briefest outline of the approach is appropriate here. The first step establishes a context model including events and messages. These are used to establish goals and their related task scripts. Task analysis is then used to decompose the tasks and to identify objects and actions. This leads to a complete object model where the objects are tasks. We then construct an object model using textual analysis and other knowledge elicitation techniques to transform the task object model to a business object model and complete the object-oriented analysis. The task scripts and event traces based on them are kept for testing purposes. During this process we capture any relevant business rules and assertions concerning the objects. Prototyping is then used to specify the interface and/or other system components.

Task analysis is central to HCI practice. I now believe it should be central to object-oriented analysis too, as we will see in Part II. The strategic options available to future system developers are manifold, but fundamentally they have the choice between doing nothing, completely rebuilding existing systems to include graphical user interfaces, re-engineering these legacy systems or building object wrappers as described in the preceding chapter.

3.2.7 The MVC metaphor

The Model-View-Controller (MVC) 'paradigm', as it is sometimes called, is a modelling metaphor with its origins in Smalltalk (Figure 3.8). In the context of UI design, a **model** implements the interface to the application. A model is typically an object or objects with methods; for example, draw, move, rotate, and so on. This subsystem represents the application and handles messages sent to it from the controller objects and sometimes from the view as a result of changes to the view state. It then broadcasts changes to its registered views and controllers. A **view** displays aspects of a model and sends messages to a model to get its state and display it. Views include graphical displays, data from the model and interaction views. The latter can present images of controls. Views typically have a hierarchical structure. A **controller** interprets user actions and changes the model. Buttons, list boxes, and so on are examples of controllers; often also called **controls**. These can sometimes be thought of as combinations of a view and a controller; for example, menus.

Almost any system's interface may be interpreted in this way. The way a word processor stores text is not the way it is displayed. A simulation model may give the user access to some variables but block others, if changing them would violate the integrity of the model, say. Most GUI environments use an event handler to capture mouse and keyboard actions. This can be modelled as the controller that sends messages to the methods of the application.

The MVC metaphor has influenced several visual programming languages including non-object-oriented ones such as Visual Basic. Advanced MVC tools are gradually being added to modern Smalltalk environments and other object-oriented languages and development environments.

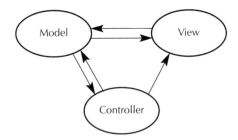

Figure 3.8 The MVC metaphor. The model can access both controls and views. Controls and views change when the model changes. The controller can be used to change the view but not vice versa.

3.2.8 Research issues

Johnson (1992) describes current research into command language grammar (CLG) and other, as yet unproven, formal approaches to task analysis.

CLG (Moran 1981) offers a top-down, input/output model of interaction. CLG describes the interface as composed of three components at two levels of abstraction. The conceptual component has a task and a semantic level, so that task hierarchies are constructed and then objects and procedures to accomplish each task are expressed in a LISP-style language. The communication component has syntactic (the command language) and interaction (physical actions) levels. Finally, the physical component has spatial and device levels. The approach is largely unproven.

Reisner's (1981) Task Action Language uses BNF-style grammar rules to describe user interfaces formally, and therefore provides a basis for measurement and comparison. This approach is promising but also unproven as yet.

Programmable User Models (Young *et al.*, 1989) treat the user as just another processor or object in the system. They draw the designer's attention to usability and cognitive aspects of a design and are intended to help with measuring usability. The approach has much in common with object-oriented user interface design.

Johnson's (1992) Task Action Grammar extends Reisner's approach by incorporating insights from cognitive psychology and ideas about user modelling. It develops a rule based model of the user's competence.

One of the oldest formal approaches to UI design is GOMS (Goals, Operators, Methods and Selection rules) and cognitive complexity theory (Card *et al.*, 1983). The approach is task and rule based and predicts training time. It is based on a rather outmoded theory of human cognition that says there are three cognitive subsystems: perceptual, motor and cognitive. A model is built and decomposed to the level of these primitive skills. We first identify a goal or task sequence (a method) leading to each high-level user goal. Each task is accomplished by a sequence of perceptual, motor or cognitive operators such as: see icon, move finger, recall password. Selection rules tell us when particular methods are appropriate. For example, we could find a book in a library by sequential search or by using an index.

The trouble with these types of approach is that they are complex, time consuming and often need a trained psychologist. GOMS task descriptions can be extremely verbose too. Furthermore, GOMS assumes that a prototype exists to be measured so that the approach cannot be used in the early phases of requirements capture. In fact, most of the approaches discussed in this section are mainly useful for evaluative studies rather than original elicitation of the user interface.

Lee (1993) offers a sensible, slightly simplified version of the GOMS approach which has some common features with the approach of SOMA described in Part II.

GOMS was seminal in the development of much of the theory of task analysis but is weakened by a crude, rule based conception of cognition. Johnson (1992) presents a synthesis of ideas from task analysis and expert systems called Knowledge Analysis of Tasks that emphasizes not only the tasks but the user's knowledge of them. This is a promising area of research that deserves to be explored further. The approach adopted is much simpler and depends on expressing tasks as simple sentences concerning actions on objects with indirect objects.

There are a number of general frameworks and so-called 'architectures' for user interface development. Frameworks give a general model of the structure of interfaces while architectures provide a developers' tool kit based on such a model, though it is not always explicit. Frameworks and architectures are sometimes referred to as User Interface Management Systems or Development Environments (UIMSs or UIDEs). UIDEs provide tool kits, usually in the form of object libraries, and help with dialogue design and UI management. Typical of such systems are Sassafras (Hill, 1986), TUBE (Hill and Hermman, 1989), GARNET (Myers, 1991) and IDL (Foley *et al.*, 1989). PAC (Coutaz, 1987) and MVC (Goldberg, 1984) provide object-oriented frameworks for describing and limiting the connectivity of interfaces by classifying objects as concerned with presentation, abstraction or modelling and control. Many GUI class libraries are based on these frameworks.

MVC may be viewed as a UIMS and is the most widely adopted. Johnson (1992) describes several research tool kits for user interface development. Object-enhanced and object-oriented tools such as Visual Basic, Visual Age, ENFIN, Zinc, CommonView, ObjectWorks/VisualWorks, and so on are now making the research a commercial reality.

3.3 GUI standards

The various style guides from Apple, IBM, Microsoft, NeXT, OSF and Sun all adopt a broadly object-oriented approach to user interface design. Therefore, given a sufficiently correct and expressive object model, these guides may be used to select standard components to represent the objects in the model. This is especially easy when there is an interface object library available. Apple provides MacApp and the User Interface Toolbox. Microsoft Windows can be approached with the Microsoft Foundation Classes or the Borland Object Windows Library (OWL). NeXT provides possibly the best combination of ease-of-use and power in an integrated environment. OSF and Sun provide 'widget' libraries both based on X-open's Xt Intrinsics. All these support the 'look and feel' recommended by the appropriate style guide. However, each one uses a different terminology for common features. A mild example is the term 'mouse-down' (Apple and Microsoft) which appears as 'ButtonPress' in X-Windows variants. Some concepts, such as 'mouse-over', are not supported uniformly across all styles. Also the class libraries have very different classification structures and this can be confusing for developers moving from platform to platform. Further, the structures might well be incompatible with those of an earlier object-oriented analysis, leading to the need for careful implementation remodelling.

IBM's CUA'91 (IBM, 1991a, 1991b) provides a standard look and feel for Presentation Manager applications and, in fact, for DOS, AIX and Windows applications too. The intention was to make all CUA compliant applications look and behave similarly on all platforms. CUA'91 also contains guidelines on how to go about designing a user interface and amounts to the rudiments of a structured method for graphical user interface design. Microsoft (1992) has also published similar, detailed guidelines on user interface design when the context is MS Windows. Apple, Sun and the Open Systems Foundation have all published style guides defining a standard for the Mac (Apple Computer Inc., 1987), Open Look (Sun Microsystems Inc., 1989) and Motif (OSF, 1990) workstations respectively, with the Apple document being generally regarded as the paradigm for all the others mentioned so far. Most of these standards give a lot of detail including: positioning standards for controls (for example, the Cancel button should be 3 mm below the OK button or to its right), standard control types and layouts (such as those shown in Figure 3.9), standards for menus and naming conventions. Visual Basic includes an on-screen, tutorial style guide.

There are certain things that all the style guides have in common, despite terminological variations. All permit the display of one or more windows that can be divided into panes or child windows and used to provide views of different parts of an object, file or document. One may have either modal or modeless dialogue boxes to give additional information or contextual clues. The windows contain objects to be acted upon and there is a menu bar detailing the actions permissible. The style guides agree on issues such as the use of single words for menu items. Most require a status bar at the bottom of the screen and 'grey out' unreachable menu options. They all support push buttons, radio buttons, check boxes, text fields, scroll bars, gauges and some kind of hierarchical menu display. Only some have spin buttons, list boxes, combo boxes, hierarchical scrolling lists, scrolling menus and so on, but there is usually an equivalent way to implement such features. Lee (1993) gives a high-level list of the features of these style guides.

Sometimes it is more profitable to look at a really first-rate implementation than to read the style guide. I think that Word for Windows Version 2.0 was a paragon of user interface design using the Microsoft style. It uses

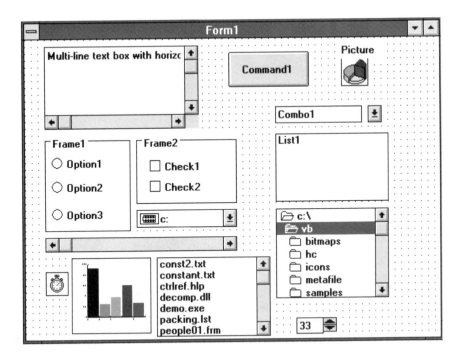

Figure 3.9 Some typical CUA-style objects.

depressed buttons to show active attribute values, such as the bold/italic status of the current text, and uses colour to indicate whether the screen area is subject to user modification. Others would cite the design of the Macintosh interface, where the Word design originated in any case. I actually rather prefer Windows with its useful keyboard short cuts. NeXTstep and OpenStep offer an improvement over both the Mac and Windows interface styles which all designers can learn from.

International standards exist in this area too. ISO 9126 covers UI evaluation processes and ISO 9241 deals with ergonomic and safety requirements for displays. The latter is to be extended to deal with how to specify usability. There is also a European Community directive on health and safety that refers to software usability.

One word of caution about these interface standards is in order. These are early days. These documents do contain some standards – on issues like control positioning, colour and so on – but they mostly contain only guidelines on design. It is a capital mistake not to be willing to vary your design away from the standard when you can justify the deviation as an improvement that is at least roughly compatible with the guidance.

⊟ 3.4 Multimedia systems, virtual reality and optical storage

GUI design becomes more complex when new interface technology arrives but the principles remain much the same. The arrival of new multimedia, virtual reality, full-content retrieval and optical storage technology presents a new challenge for interface designers. At present, little is known about the implications but this short section makes some general observations.

Document images may be scanned and displayed with annotations in Document Image Management systems. This can lead to huge savings in the costs of storing paper records and the time used in getting access to information. Voice storage is also possible and the two approaches can be used together to attach voice memos to documents. Video animation and the presentation of high-quality photographic images are now popular in computer-assisted education and fault diagnosis expert systems. The human–computer interaction principles elucidated in this chapter will have to be refined and extended to deal with this new richness and experience will have to be collected. For example, it is already emerging that there is a need for new ways to deal with voice-mail systems since it can take far longer to deal with a backlog of lengthy voice messages than with their textual equivalent on a conventional e-mail system. Moderation in the use of such techniques is required and new methods of classifying and filtering information are needed. However, the general psychological basis of the principles will not be altered and, if properly applied, they should remain useful. With extensive use of video, it has been suggested that developers will have to acquire the skills of the film producer. Here the real question is whether outside specialists are better than retrained developers, as with GUI design in general. Only time will tell.

When optical storage devices are in use, designers will have to take account of their quite different performance characteristics. Byte-addressable CD-ROMs work well for music replay but are slow as file systems. Erasable drives are about an order of magnitude faster in terms of access time but offer low transfer rates because erasure must precede writing. WORMs (Write Once Read Many devices) offer a compromise and are suitable for archival applications. The point here is that the interface design must take account of the longer access times when such devices are used.

Storage technology has developed far more quickly than retrieval technology. Object-oriented repositories of code and of specifications presuppose the need for far more sophisticated retrieval methods, using the methods developed for databases together with those of library information management systems. This too presents new challenges for the user interface designer. We will return to the topic in Chapter 11. In fact, object technology provides precisely the correct basis for structuring documents and repositories so that powerful, understandable access methods can be used.

Virtual reality, which immerses the user in a simulated world and provides feedback through multiple senses as well as multiple media, offers perhaps the greatest challenge of all to user interface designers. Fortunately, all interactions in such a world can be described as interactions with objects satisfying contracts. The method of object-oriented analysis presented in Part II of this book takes the issue of contracts very seriously and thus should support the description of such systems. However, it is not yet clear what the new psychological factors associated with such immersion are. Many of the basic UI principles may need amendment and much care will be needed since there are many medical and social dangers.

3.5 GUI tools and languages

GUIs are very hard to build compared with character based and command interfaces. Recalling that even the simplest 'hallo world' program requires nearly 90 lines of C using the MS Windows API – which itself conceals much pre-written code – confirms this graphically. The API itself is extremely rich and complicated which makes learning to use it very hard work. Writing a GUI application in C is tantamount to programming at the level of the operating system. What is required for successful GUI application building is high-level languages that contain reusable graphical objects which may be extended. These must be supported by sound analysis and design methods. The events that may occur during a session, such as the user clicking or double-clicking the mouse in different positions, cannot be sequenced in advance, which means that traditional structured methods are useless for this kind of application, as is admitted even by Yourdon (1992). The bulk of this book is devoted to a method that does permit the description of event driven systems, as do most object-oriented methods.

3.5.1 Choosing the right tools

There is a massive number of tools that are suitable for building systems with a GUI component. These include the database management systems with GUI tools attached such as Omnis, Oracle with Oracle Card, INGRES with Simplify, Superbase, MS Access, SQL Windows and Paradox with Object Vision to name only a few. There are database 'drill-down' tools such as Forests & Trees which give read only, graphical access to multiple database products. There are scripting languages such as Hypercard and Toolbook. There are languages with specialized graphical libraries such as Interviews,

Actor, Andrew, C++ with CommonView, Smalltalk with VisualWorks, Object Pascal, Visual Basic and Zinc. There are authoring systems such as Choreographer, GUI Master, Easel and ENFIN. Finally one can use C and the operating system API (the Windows SDK for example) to build the interface. There is even the option of configuring an existing application such as Excel or Word for Windows using a macro language. The choice is great and the decision is therefore difficult.

These approaches can be categorized according to their performance, complexity and ease of use. Generally speaking, the shorter the development effort, the worse the performance and vice versa. Many developers have exploited reuse strategies at the product level, building systems by assembling them largely from existing products. For example, one might use a database with an expert system shell and tie it all together using Toolbook or Actor. Sometimes network tools such as Netware or NFS will be involved in such a development.

It is important to use the right tools for any job. Let us examine the requirements for tools for software development of all kinds. We want our analysts, designers and programmers to be as productive as possible; that is, able to get as much done as possible for the least effort. This requirement will be supported by tools that offer four key features:

(1) Reusability
(2) Extensibility
(3) A high-level procedural programming language
(4) A visual programming environment

These same four features are especially important for graphical user interface development where productivity without them can be greatly impaired. Not only for UI development but for all kinds of system we usually want the system we are building to be flexible in use and able to meet rapidly changing business requirements. The same four features are required for this reason and, in addition, we require the following three:

(5) A common data dictionary (or object repository) of some form
(6) A high-level, non-procedural data access language
(7) A high-level modelling language or decision support system tools

These extra features reflect the fact that flexibility in the application domain depends on flexible access to the stable data of the business. The final universal requirement is for computational richness; that is, the system should be able to express in simple form anything we wish. Here features 3, 5, 6 and 7 must be complemented by one more:

(8) A low impedance between the modelling and programming language and the data management system

Thus all systems should be able to store persistent data, permit the import of existing data and schema definitions, support quick changes in front of users for prototyping purposes – at least where the changes are simple ones – and permit the production of system descriptions in the form of diagrams, schema descriptions, screen layouts, business rules and method or process outlines. Interactive screen painting and visual programming are highly desirable and the language should be computationally rich and expressive. Reversibility is important too; so that the worst possible way to develop a system is to use something like Lotus macros, which lead to effectively write-only code. Limits on the amount and structure of help text are also to be avoided in tools. Nonprocedural, preferably visual, report generators also contribute greatly to productivity for most applications.

Where specification, throwaway or **revolutionary** prototyping, as I have called it, is to be used there is an additional set of requirements, the most important of which is semantic richness. This leads to the need for three more features:

(9) Rule based programming languages
(10) Abstract data types
(11) Object modelling with multiple inheritance and/or prototypes

Prototypes provide a form of classless inheritance as discussed in Chapter 1.

Evolutionary prototyping requires that the tools should perform at the required service levels on volume data and work loads. They should support efficiency, portability and correctness. These requirements lead to the need for the following five additional features:

(12) Links to 3GLs from the high-level languages
(13) A tool that runs unchanged on a wide range of hardware and operating systems; or
(13a) A tool that fully conforms to open systems standards
(14) A formal specification language or its equivalent
(15) Support for some kind of structured method or approach

The above 15 required features represent a pretty formidable list. What kind of products are there that satisfy these requirements? It would be impossible to survey all the many tools available. To make the problem more tractable, products may be classified into generic types. Products for software development may be classified into the categories shown in Table 3.3, each of which is typified by the products named. The classification, howsoever done, will be highly arguable and the reader may wish to alter the classification and especially the selection of exemplars chosen here. The argument will be largely unaffected, I think.

Table 3.4 shows the extent to which each product category meets the criteria 1–15 above. From this table we can see that object-oriented 4GLs come out well for most purposes. The problem here is that there are few such products at present and *no* mature, widely practically tested ones yet. However, there is a small number of 4GL products, claiming to be object-oriented, which have successful applications to their credit. Typical of such products are Dataflex, INGRES Windows4GL, ProKappa and System/4 from Snowbirch.

Table 3.3 Software development product categories and typical products.

Product category	Typical products
3GLs	C, COBOL, PASCAL, FORTRAN, BASIC, Visual BASIC
4GLs based on an RDBMS	Oracle, INGRES, Sybase, Rdb, Informix, DB2
Open relational 4GLs	Uniface, Unify, Gupta
Other conventional 4GLs	FOCUS, dBase III, MANTIS, NOMAD, Paradox, ObjectVision
4GLs based on semantic data models	Generis, DAPLEX, ADABAS ENTIRE, Sapiens
Object-oriented languages	Smalltalk, C++, Eiffel
Object-oriented 4GLs	Shorthand/Studio/Ontos, GeOde, O2, ProKappa, Nexpert Object, ADS, KBMS
Front-end building tools and 4GLs	Easel, Intuitive Solution, GUI Master, Choreographer, Visual BASIC, ENFIN, Application Manager
CASE tools and code generators	IEF, ADW, Paradigm Plus, SELECT, System Architect, VSF, Object Maker, Ipsys, StP, Ptech, System Engineer, CorVision, Rational ROSE
Knowledge based 4GLs	Nexpert, Kappa, ADS, KBMS, Leonardo, Crystal, Xi Plus, Guru, KnowledgePro
Decision support systems and executive information systems	Express, System W, FCS, Pilot, Holos, Commander, Knowledgeman, MDBS, SAS, SIR, SPSS

For specification prototypers, semantic databases and knowledge based systems tools score well precisely because of their ability to manipulate high-level business rules. Evolutionary prototypers or rapid developers will probably still choose a 4GL based on a relational database for many mainstream commercial applications for the time being, even where there is a strong client/server element where the open 4GLs will be preferred. This will change as object-oriented databases and 4GLs mature. For now, I recommend using object-oriented analysis and design techniques with conventional products to provide a future migration path and because it is the most natural way to describe a client/server system. Object request brokers will be important in this setting too. This is discussed in Chapter 4.

Graphical user interface builders will do best with OO4GLs eventually but, for the present, Actor, Smalltalk, Objective-C (under NeXTstep) or one of the special purpose authoring systems such as ENFIN or Intuitive Solution will suffice. Personally, I have found that a combination of Visual Basic and C produces remarkably good results, although this reveals me to be a closet BASIC programmer I fear, or at least an unreconstructed hacker.

Overall, I can conclude that object-oriented 4GLs need to absorb several features from other product categories before they become ideal tools. In particular they must take on decision support system modelling features, KBS rule languages and inferencing techniques and all the features of object-oriented database management systems. Until better tools are available we must use existing tools and integrate them within our overall approach to system development.

Table 3.4 Product types versus product features.

	Reus-ability	Extens-ibility	High-level language	Visual prog-ram-ming	Data dict-ionary	Non-proc. data access	Model-ling	Low impe-dance	Rules	ADTs	Object modelling & mult. inherit-ance	3GL links	Port-able	For-mal lang-uage	Struct-ured meth-ods
Normal 3GLs	No	No	No	Few	No	n/a	No	No	No	No	No	n/a	Yes	No	Yes
4GLs based on an RDBMS	No	No	Yes	No	Yes	Yes	No	No	No	Some	No	Yes	Yes	No	Yes
Open relational 4GLs	No	No	Yes	No	Yes	Yes	No	No	No	No	No	Yes	Yes	No	Yes
Other conventional 4GLS	No	No	Yes	Few	Some	No	No	No	No	No	No	Yes	No	No	Yes
4GLs based on semantic data models	No	Yes	Yes	No	Some	Yes	No	No	Some	Some	Yes	Yes	No	No	Yes
Object-oriented languages	Yes	Yes	n/a	No	No	No	Some	Yes	No	Yes	Some	Some	Some	Some	Yes
Object-oriented 4GLs	Yes	Yes	Yes	Some	Some	No	No	Yes	No	Yes	?	Yes	?	?	Yes
Front-end building tools & 4GLs	Yes	Some	Yes	Yes	No	No	No	No	No	?	No	Some	Some	No	No
CASE tools and code generators	No	No	Yes	Some	Yes	n/a	No	No	No	No	Some	Some	No	No	Yes
Knowledge based 4GLs	No	Yes	Yes	Some	No	No	?	No	Yes	Some	Yes	Yes	Some	?	?
Decision support system and executive information systems	No	No	Yes	No	Some	Some	Yes	No	No	No	No	Some	?	No	?

As we have already seen, there is now a vast array of tools for GUI building available. These include tools with minimal genuflections toward object technology, such as Easel, through special purpose 4GL/GUI development systems, such as Choreographer, GUI Master and Windows4GL (INGRES), and object-enhanced languages, such as Powerbuilder and Visual Basic, to complete OO graphical programming environments, such as Smalltalk/ObjectWorks/ VisualWorks and ENFIN/3. There are also a few products derived from expert systems environments, such as Kappa and ART-Enterprise. This is not the place for a survey of all these tools but a few remarks are in order.

Actor is an object-oriented language with a syntax reminiscent of C. It was originally developed by the Whitewater Group and more recently acquired by Symantec. The professional version comes equipped with an object library to support GUI building, database access and some network protocols. Its user base is quite large but nowhere near the size of the Smalltalk community.

Toolbook is a Windows development system based on object-oriented ideas and with particularly strong animation features. Like many other modern tools its core is a high-level scripting language. Borland's ObjectVision goes a little further by attempting to make its scripting language a visual one. Programs are written by drawing decision trees and selecting built-in functions at nodes. This is appealing at first but soon becomes tedious for a skilled programmer.

ENFIN/3 is a complete object-oriented 4GL built with Smalltalk and giving access to that language. It is mainly used as a GUI development tool in a client/server context but could find more general use. Smalltalk V for Windows is an AD/Cycle SAA language and is integrated with Micro Focus' COBOL Workbench. It contains an extensive GUI library and also runs on Macs and under PM. Objectworks is also available for C++ under UNIX.

Kappa is a programming environment that includes class libraries and both a procedural capability through C and a rule language. OMW is a CASE environment based on the Ptech method (Martin and Odell, 1992; Graham, 1994a) that generates Kappa applications and will compile them into C.

Visual Basic is a conventional programming language which nevertheless contains built-in objects called **controls**. It does not (yet) support inheritance among these controls but they do contain skeletal operations that are used to implement event or message driven behaviour. Visual Basic is an **object-enhanced** language in the sense that one cannot define new classes – without resorting outside the language to C – but there is a predefined set of classes, some of which can be instantiated with the *new* operator, so that for 'small' controls instances can be created at run time. Typical controls are command buttons, text boxes, file boxes and radio buttons. A command button contains empty methods for such events as Click (the user left-clicks the mouse in the button's area) and DragDrop (the user depresses the left button inside the area and holds it down while dragging the mouse to a new position before releasing the button, typically thus dropping the control in a new position). Controls have attributes such as position, visibility, colour and fount, which can all be changed. The language also contains built-in methods applicable to the controls such as PrintForm. The simplest example I can think of to demonstrate how programming is done in Visual Basic is as follows. Open a window called Form1. Create a command button by selecting the appropriate icon from the toolbox, positioning the mouse pointer on the form and dragging it out to the correct size. Edit the attribute called CtrlName and change its value to 'Cancel'. You will now have a cancel button in a window but it will not do anything when pressed. To make it cause the application to terminate, open the code window and edit the Click procedure which currently reads:

```
Sub Cancel_Click ()
|
End Sub
```

Position the pointer between these two lines and type 'end'. The syntax is checked automatically and if correct, the cancel button now has a method to respond to mouse clicks and the application can be run in interpreted mode to test it. If it works it can be compiled. All this takes about 20 seconds; it would take hours using the Windows SDK.

Many object-oriented languages now include GUI libraries. Borland C++ includes the OWL graphical library and MS Visual C++ contains the Microsoft Foundation Classes library. They have similar intentions but a very different style. These are specific to Windows but there is a small number of cross-platform libraries and tools now, including Liant C++/Views, WNDX, XVT and Zinc (Table 3.5). One problem with all the other libraries is that they impose a way of working that is not always appropriate to the application. An example that springs to mind is the Microsoft Foundation Classes for C++ which make it very easy to build an interface using cascaded, modal dialogue boxes but offer little support for other styles of interaction. This problem is

Table 3.5 Platform independence of tools.

System	Development platform	Other platforms	Implementation
Choreographer	OS/2	MS Windows (projected)	Interpreted (threaded-compiled)
ENFIN	MS Windows		Interpreted (threaded-compiled)
Actor	MS Windows		Interpreted (threaded-compiled)
Objectworks	X-Windows	MS Windows	
Liant C++/Views	Macintosh, OS/2, Windows, X/Motif	Macintosh, OS/2, Windows, X/Motif	
WNDX	"	"	
XVT	"	"	
Zinc	"	"	

compounded by the use of Wizards that offer a fast start to the application but impose what might be an inappropriate interface early on. The cross-platform tools do not lock you into a platform even if they lock you into themselves as development products. They provide an API and a set of libraries that remove your application a step from the operating system. Each, except the Liant product, provides tools for constructing graphical elements and linking them to code. Liant C++/Views is more like a Smalltalk-style language.

3.5.2 Using tools to reduce risk and cost

There are various trade-offs to be made in deciding how to go about building a GUI or a system in which a GUI is a significant part. We must assume that the computational and data access components of such a system are previously solved problems. The complexity will then lie in the interface. Using existing tools for data management and highly optimized algorithms, rather than writing the whole system from scratch, can significantly reduce development costs and enhance quality, though performance may be degraded. Generally speaking, this coarse-grain reuse pays dividends in terms of time-to-market and reduces risk due to the fact that third-party products have been tested. One is placing reliance on the suppliers of the tools for future support and there may even be a royalty to pay on distribution of the application. This trade-off has to be managed in the concrete context of the development against its longevity, significance and urgency.

There is a general trade-off of development cost against efficiency. Smalltalk is slower than Actor which is slower than C++ which can be, in turn, slower than C if it is not used with great care. However, the richer development environments and the higher level of the slower languages mean that the development costs are in inverse proportion to efficiency. As a consequence, things can be both done and undone quickly and it is worth musing that long analysis and design phases are much harder to justify in these circumstances. If mistakes at the coding stage are expensive then it is worth spending a lot of money to make sure that they do not happen. If they are cheap to fix then the precautions are harder to justify.

There is a trade-off between the high risk and dependency on the tool being able to do the job when a relatively new (to the developers) tool like Smalltalk is used on the one hand and a high dependency on correct analysis and design when a language such as C++ is used on the other (Table 3.6). The more familiar you are with both the problem and the tool the less this is so. Low-level tools like C++ act as a barrier forcing developers to concentrate on the tool rather than the problem, though high-level class libraries, such as ObjectWorks, Borland's OWL and Microsoft's Foundation Classes, help a lot. The use of the object-oriented metaphor helps with this because the solution is expressed in the same language as the problem if a proper analysis approach is used.

Table 3.6 Trade-offs in tool selection.

Low design costs, higher system risk	High design costs, higher project risk
Course-grain reuse (package software)	Fine-grain reuse (class libraries)
High-level language	Low-level language
Relatively inefficient	Maximum efficiency
Loosely bound	Tightly bound

There is a fourth trade-off of tightly versus loosely bound solutions. Tightly bound environments offer multiple tools integrated via DLLs, call-return protocols and so on. This gives high performance. Loosely bound environments use DDE, OLE or even the clipboard to pass data among separate tools. This gives slower performance but is more flexible. Examples of the former include CBR Express (discussed above) which uses Raima DLLs for data management bound into Toolbook. Examples of the latter are MS Office or Lotus Smartsuite. A tightly bound approach requires object-oriented analysis and design and an iterative approach to development. A loosely bound approach requires a good overall view of the features of available tools and of the likely application difficulties. Tightly bound developments typically use IT staff and are proactive and technology driven. Loosely bound developments can involve end users and are reactive and need driven.

As Novobilski (private communication) has pointed out, tightly bound systems must meet users' needs exactly or they will remain unused whereas loosely bound systems will benefit greatly from a strong design effort, to minimize the performance penalties that derive from badly structured code. The main difference between the two approaches is to do with the relative ease of reusability and extensibility. Correctly designed new classes, when added to a loosely coupled system, should work well if they conform to the framework. On the other hand, all class descriptions in a tightly bound system generally need to be rebuilt to link them into the system properly.

All four trade-offs affect the development costs and the risk of the project and must needs be managed carefully. Rapid development nearly always wins out over phased development and powerful, object-oriented tools are the most powerful, flexible tools to use for the UI. Given that development can be further shortened by combining and integrating existing products, there is substantial potential for the approach when time-to-market and cost are critical factors – as they nearly always are. When the risk associated with third-party products is unacceptable one is forced to think of reusing products or classes developed in-house. The approach in Part II is geared to both situations.

Object technology is highly beneficial for GUI developments because it is almost unique in being able to model event driven interaction in a natural way. It contributes to productivity through the reuse of graphical objects, hiding complexity and helping to enforce standards by the (re)use of library classes. This contributes to lowering maintenance costs. The higher level of object-oriented languages and the strength of the metaphor help to reduce development costs massively, after the initial learning process. Inheritance lets the developer focus on the exceptions; the things that make his application different. This implies that developers can work within generic *application frameworks* for GUI building rather than invent the solution anew on each project.

Of all the frameworks available to the object-oriented developer, the GUI frameworks are the oldest and most successful. Nevertheless, we can still produce a thoroughly bad interface using a thoroughly good framework or class library. Object technology provides no magic in this respect and sound design practices and methods are still required.

3.6 Case studies

ISA Limited of London, England, developed a data capture and analysis expert system for a major management consultancy who wanted a system to support strategic audits of their clients. Typically these clients would be assessed in three dimensions: business strategy, IT strategy and human resources strategy. The purpose of the audit was to discover how compatible and integrated the three strategies were. The manual audit used questionnaires and consultants' analytical skills but this was very labour intensive. The new system automated data capture and storage from the questionnaires and provided graphical and tabular analyses and recommendations based on the conclusions of a simple expert system. The recommended actions could be edited and the colours changed by the consultant, and could be printed on a very wide range of printing devices. ISA reports that its cost for building this system was half that of its nearest competitor even though their fee rates were higher. The reason is that ISA used a combination of existing tools: Windows device drivers, Actor and its libraries, the SQLServer database manager and an existing inference engine, rather than constructing the application from scratch. GUIs, as integration tools, help achieve lower development costs.

ISA have a catalogue of similar experiences. Tillinghurst provides actuarial and risk management consultancy to insurance companies. The UK Financial Services Act 1986 resulted in many changes to the use these companies made of brokers and it became necessary to justify the costs of direct selling very carefully. Tillinghurst, in particular, advises its clients on the viability and cost of maintaining a direct sales force. PRISM (PRedictive Insurance Salesforce Model), a system written in a mixture of Actor and C, enabled Tillinghurst to consider individual agent types and their typical career in terms of productivity, remuneration, promotion or termination. These agents were notionally added to new or existing branches and the branch running expenses computed. Head-office sales projections were then added to complete the forecast for up to ten years into the future. The output

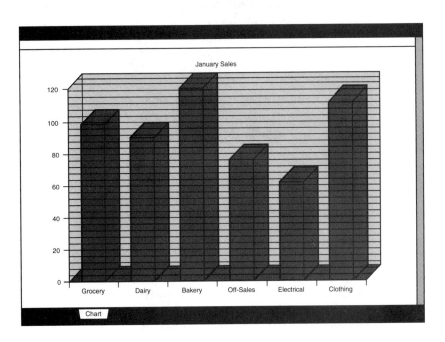

Figure 3.10 Pathfinder permits the use of various tools to display its results.

had to be highly graphical to encourage use and facilitate understanding. Furthermore, it had to be easy to change as the system was to be sold into different countries with differing conditions in their markets. The C routines were introduced to speed up the more complex array computations where Actor performed poorly. Otherwise, Tillinghurst reported that the system had enabled them to do a very critical forecast in hours that took three days using spreadsheets and is more flexible (Dalton, 1992). Global Financial Engineering used ISA and Smalltalk V to build a blackboard system for financial trading with complex graphical presentation and an element of machine learning. This system supported automated bond futures trading and repaid 50% of capital employed in the first year (O'Connor, 1991). ISA liked Smalltalk V so much that, when they could find no suitable CASE tool to support both the OMT notation and reverse engineering, they used it to write their own: EVE. The productivity of the language makes this possible even for a small company like ISA. Imagine writing your own graphical CASE tool under Windows in C! Having been involved in rewriting *SOMATiK* in C++ I can testify that the task is daunting.

Pathfinder-SQL is an advanced database query tool which runs under Windows. It allows users to access corporate data under most databases and formulate complex queries without having to know anything about database navigation or the SQL query language. The result of five years research by one of the largest petroleum companies in the world, Pathfinder-SQL provides a simple graphical view of user's data, enabling them to access information quickly without the need for support form the IT department. Normally, the job of explaining the structure of the database to a query tool would take some hours. However, Pathfinder removes the necessity for that set-up task. Using AI techniques Pathfinder can understand the structure and content of a database from existing descriptions. Pathfinder understands the underlying structure of database, using that understanding to create a syntactically correct query based on the information required. It then retrieves the data into the PC Windows environment and either presents it using Pathfinder's own data presentation and graphing mechanism or passes it to a presentation tool such as Excel. A fundamental goal of the Pathfinder system is close integration with other tools on the Windows desktop. Pathfinder supports integration with most common Windows applications using both the clipboard and DDE (Dynamic Data Exchange) facilities to ensure that data within reports are automatically updated.

Many companies derive benefits directly from the GUI itself together with standard, linked applications such as word processing and spreadsheets. An example is Pepsi Cola, which was an early adopter of MS Windows as part of its downsizing strategy in the UK head office. Pepsi report savings arising mainly from e-mail and fax facilities. New recruits are given a half-day training course, which is adequate due to many tasks being automated with macros.

Bass, the UK brewer and the world's largest hotel operator, aimed to have 50% of all new corporate systems running under Windows by 1993, representing about 6000 machines. Bass claims that this has 'virtually revolutionized personal computing' (Costello, 1992). Other users need to become serious GUI developers. Britvic, a subsidiary of Bass, used Gupta/SQLWindows to develop a sophisticated product formulation application.

Reuters use Windows as a platform for their foreign exchange and commodity information product. For them multitasking capability and features such as DDE are critical. The Norwegian nationalized telephone company, Televerket, emphasizes the benefits deriving from consistency and the ability to wrap legacy applications. It uses Motif on a variety of UNIX platforms for office automation. The clear trend for such users is to turn to object-oriented development tools to enhance their ability to produce the more complex GUI applications.

⊟ 3.7 Summary

This chapter explained why object technology is suitable for GUI development, reviewed some of the productivity tools available, explained the principles behind GUI design and exposed some important techniques used in HCI. Well-designed GUIs are popular because they are easy to use, enhance user and developer productivity and lead to a greater degree of comfort and less stress.

Design for HCI is like other design problems. Artefacts should be fit for their purpose. They should be natural in behaviour and conform to users' expectations. Use of the artefact should give feedback on progress. They should fit the mental and manual abilities of users. Task analysis has uses far beyond the design of user interfaces and can be put to service in capturing requirements for all kinds of systems. The key observation here is that task-centred design is important for creating usable, useful, correct systems even where the interface element is not the primary consideration.

We surveyed the chief types of hardware for I/O. The relative merits and weaknesses of keyboards, mice, tracker balls, touch screens, graphics tablets and voice input were discussed. Studies have shown that there is no 'best' input or output device. What is most appropriate and usable depends not only on the application but on the precise task or set of tasks being carried out.

Methods of interacting with a computer system include menus, forms, command languages, natural language and graphical user interfaces. The best style of interaction depends mainly on the task. Graphical user interfaces combine the advantages of several of these styles. However, graphical user interfaces are very costly to write and may need more expensive hardware. Despite the extra cost, people and organizations are gradually moving to graphical interfaces.

The fundamentals of cognitive psychology were introduced, including such concepts as long-term memory, activated memory, Miller's law, rehearsal, priming, closure, cognitive dissonance, transfer effects, primacy effects, recency effects and interference. Icons are culturally dependent and their use depends on background knowledge that may not be shared by all users. Standard interfaces exploit the classification structures of memory. Standard user interfaces are important because of the memory limitations of users. We also established some principles for HCI design, including not stopping at analysing and automating existing manual practices.

Thimbleby's concept of Generative User-Engineering Principles (GUEPs) was discussed and modes in a user interface defined. Modes should be avoided but are sometimes necessary. A number of heuristics for user interface modelling were identified and we noted the similarity with guidelines for constructing object-oriented models.

In the context of a user interface, both the user and the system must fulfil their responsibilities towards each other. These responsibilities are task oriented rather than user oriented. Designers should remember that there are considerable variations among users. Icons – images – are culturally dependent.

The power law of practice was introduced and we distinguished the different types of knowledge acquired during skill acquisition: declarative, associative and procedural knowledge. Dialogue design was discussed. Well-designed systems are *helpful*. They should also be *forgiving* of user errors.

Commonly used heuristics for dialogue design and for using colour effectively were enumerated.

We discussed HCI reviews, GUI metrics and usability workshops. SOMA emphasizes the centrality of user rôles; that is, neither the users nor their rôles but the combination of a user adopting a rôle: an actor. Usability studies are expensive but big savings can result.

There was an important discussion of task analysis. Tasks involve goals, objects, actions and classification structures. UI designers should consider people, rôles, organizations and technology in their approach. There are two kinds of tasks: internal tasks and external tasks. Just as there are two kinds of tasks, there are two approaches to design. We can attempt merely to support each of the external tasks. This approach does not challenge the underlying business processes or attempt to change them. The alternative is to attempt to build a model underneath the task level including some understanding of what is being done and why. There are many strong links between task analysis and object-oriented programming, AI planning theory and knowledge based systems. These can be exploited in object-oriented analysis.

A rapid preview of SOMA's requirements capture approach was given. Tasks are usually expressed in a simple task-action grammar whereby each task has the form:

Subject – Verb – Direct.Object – [Preposition – Indirect.Object]

Tasks are decomposed to **atomic** level; that is, to the lowest level that introduces no terms extraneous to the domain. Another more complex, but useful, way to represent tasks is as scripts with slots, props and exception handlers. Task analysis is central to HCI practice. It should be central to object-oriented analysis too.

The Model-View-Controller (MVC) metaphor was introduced and several research issues related to HCI were discussed. Next, various style guides and standards were discussed.

The arrival of new multimedia, virtual reality, full-content retrieval and optical storage technology presents a new challenge for interface designers. Virtual reality offers perhaps the greatest challenge of all to user interface designers. Fortunately, all interactions in such a world can be described as interactions with objects satisfying contracts. SOMA takes the issue of contracts very seriously and supports the description of such systems.

GUIs are very hard to build compared with character based and command interfaces. Sound analysis and design methods are needed. The events that may occur during a session cannot be sequenced in advance. Traditional structured methods are useless for this kind of application.

We examined the requirements for tools for software development and classified the types of tool. Until better tools are available we must use existing tools and integrate them within our overall approach to system development. Many object-oriented languages now include GUI libraries. One problem with libraries is that they can impose a way of working that is not always appropriate to the application.

There are trade-offs to be made in deciding how to go about building a GUI. These are between development cost and efficiency, between the risk of new products and the obsolescence of old ones, between coarse- and fine-grain reuse and between tightly and loosely bound solutions. All four trade-offs affect the development costs and the risk of the project and must be managed carefully. Rapid development nearly always wins out over phased development. Object-oriented tools are the most flexible tools to use for the UI.

Object technology is highly beneficial for GUI developments because it can model event driven interaction. It contributes to productivity through the reuse of graphical objects, hiding complexity and helping to enforce standards by the (re)use of library classes. This contributes to lowering maintenance costs. Inheritance lets the developer focus on the exceptions; the things that make his application different. This implies that developers can work within generic *application frameworks* for GUI building rather than invent the solution anew on each project.

A small number of case studies were presented, showing that a combination of tools can reduce both costs and risk. Many companies derive benefits directly from the GUI itself together with standard, linked applications. Sometimes the benefits derive from consistency and the ability to wrap legacy applications. The clear trend for such users is to turn to object-oriented development tools to enhance their ability to produce the more complex GUI applications.

▤ 3.8 Bibliographical notes

Schneiderman (1992) has been a standard text on user interface design for some time, and is particularly good on the use of specific types of hardware for input and output. Laurel (1990) discusses the art of user interface design in general and in relation to several emerging technologies, and collects together several papers on the design aspects of systems using advanced UI technology, including virtual reality. Laurel's most interesting work is concerned with applying the principles of Greek drama to interface design. I am still waiting for my first experience of catharsis when using a computer but still consider this work as very important. Suchman (1987) applies anthropological and ethnomethodological principles to user interface design and gives, as an example, the case study design of a photocopier interface at Xerox Corporation. Suchman approaches design from the point of view that the user is acting within the context of a certain situation and that the machine should be sensitive to this situation as far as possible. Her book is highly recommended.

Johnson (1992) deals with task analysis and especially the knowledge analysis of tasks. There are many other references on task analysis that may be usefully consulted too. Thimbleby (1990) is one of the most thoughtful contributions to the subject available and many of the principles presented in this chapter are derived from his work.

Norman (1988) is essential background reading for user interface designers and some consider that the same is true for Alexander (1964, 1977, 1979) who, in writing of architecture, considers design patterns. Design patterns are closely related to object-oriented application frameworks.

Barfield (1993) is a recent, intelligent and welcome addition to the literature on HCI. Its humorous style only adds to the important messages it carries about good design and the need for humanity and intelligence on the part of designers. Read together with the books by Thimbleby, Johnson and Schneiderman it forms the basis of an excellent introduction to the subject.

Lee (1993) gives a reasonably complete and well-structured approach to GUI design based on object-oriented principles. The emphasis is on task analysis and interface design principles. Lee describes how to perform usability studies and bases his method of task analysis on the traditional 'Goals, Operators, Methods and Selection rules' model. He simplifies this model by expressing tasks as simple subject/predicate sentences and explains the approach well using a running personnel administration example. Especially clear guidelines on the use of user interface metaphors such as the desktop metaphor are provided and the architectural design of GUIs is covered briefly. Most usefully, he compares the approaches adopted in the style guides for several environments: Apple, IBM SAA/CUA, Microsoft Windows, NeXTstep, OSF Motif and Sun OpenLook. Browne (1994) also offers a structured approach but one located squarely in the structured tradition of SSADM and separated from the development of the non-interface components. It does however contain some useful insights.

Baecker and Buxton (1987) provide a comprehensive collection of source papers on early user interface design theory including many that pre-date the arrival of graphical interfaces. The proceedings of the various annual conferences on the subject of HCI and nowadays on object technology too, such as OT'9X, Object Expo, TOOLS and OOPSLA, are all that is available to take the reader further.

Khoshafian *et al.* (1992) provide a readable, non-specialist introduction to a wide range of current office technologies including optical storage, full-text retrieval, video, groupware, e-mail, data and voice networking and repositories. The book's main value is in the descriptions of how the various hardware and software technologies work but it essays to be a manifesto for object-oriented, distributed office systems of the future.

If you are embarking on an HCI project it may be useful to read the appropriate manuals and style guides for the system that you will use. IBM's CUA guides (1991a,1991b) are intended for Presentation Manager developers but are excellent guides to general principles as well. They are now published in book form (IBM, 1992). The Apple (1987) *Human Interface Guidelines* is a classic reference of the same type. For UNIX developers the X style guides from OSF (1990) and Sun (1989) and that from NeXT (1991) may be of use. Microsoft publishes various guides to Windows development (for example, Microsoft, 1992). A very useful comparison of cross-platform GUI development tools appeared in the January 1994 edition of *Byte*.

4

Distributed systems, databases and object management

From each according to his abilities, to each according to his needs!
K. Marx (Critique of the Gotha Programme)

The theme of this chapter is sharing: the sharing of both data and functions by different systems and across different platforms. This leads us to the consideration of the technology of distributed systems, client/server computing, distributed databases and Computer Supported Cooperative Work (CSCW). Distributed systems are composed of nodes that offer services according to their definitions to other nodes as and when required. We will also take a critical look at the buzz-words spawned within this area of computing: terms such as 'downsizing' and 'rightsizing'. Naturally in this book, the emphasis is on the practical issues of migrating from centralized, conventional systems to these distributed systems and we must be aware at the outset that some of the components that are to be distributed will remain conventional while others will be built using object-oriented programming. Above all I will emphasize the rôle of object-oriented models as a way of describing and understanding distributed systems. Many modern companies are determined to base their future computer infrastructure on distributed workstations as far as possible. If there are mainframes, they will be there for specialized applications with high transaction processing requirements or to act as data servers when an existing corporate database cannot be replaced economically. There are obvious cash and infrastructural benefits associated with the move to lower cost workstations but there are also some latent costs and difficulties to be overcome before these benefits can be realized.

Distributed computing is in some sense a return from the chaos (or freedom) of the PC to the golden (or dark) age of the mainframe. Early computers were single user machines with low storage capacities. Time-sharing operating systems offered the possibility of using the same hardware architecture to support multiple cooperating users. When international wide area networks (WANs) arrived, this cooperation could extend across the planet and still only need a few central points of management and integrity control. Workstations, when they arrived, took us right back to single user machines where we did our own backups and so on and were once again isolated from other users with whom we might wish to share and cooperate. LANs end this quarantine but reintroduce all the complexities of operating a mainframe; only now the mainframe is distributed and harder than ever to manage. Nevertheless, on balance, the advantages seem to outweigh the extra complexity. Distributed computing is, in principle, more resilient, fast, flexible, scaleable and open.

The main purpose of this chapter is to introduce the basic ideas of distributed systems as well as to explain the notions of distributed object computing. The reader who is already familiar with this topic may wish to skim the chapter lightly or go directly to Section 4.7 where object request brokers are discussed.

4.1 Modelling distributed systems

Distributed systems, as discussed in this chapter, are to be thought of as networked computers that do not share memory as, for example, multiprocessors do. This means that the nodes must communicate by message passing. This immediately indicates that object-oriented models may be appropriate for modelling such systems. Also, objects provide a natural metaphor for combining data and control and are the natural units of distribution. Performance is enhanced by the implicit parallelism involved. Expensive, under-utilized resources such as printers can be shared to reduce costs. In a well-designed system there may be no single point of failure or it may be possible to duplicate services so that higher availability and greater resilience become possible. Nodes can be added and the system can be reconfigured piecemeal, to reduce costs or facilitate upgrades – rather like component hi-fi systems. These and other advantages must be weighed against the additional overheads of maintaining a complex network and the increased difficulty of understanding and describing such a complex. To continue the simile, music centres are much easier to install and use than component hi-fi, though their power, quality and flexibility are lower.

The operating systems of distributed systems can be *distributed* or *networked* (Tanenbaum and van Renesse, 1985). In the former case the operating system is itself distributed over all the nodes in fragments and the network is largely invisible to the user. Networked operating systems give every node a full copy of its own operating system and the network is visible.

Jazayeri (1992) defines three data management strategies for distributed computing: centralized, replicated and partitioned. Centralized management involves placing the data at one node and routing all requests there. The advantage of this is that changes need be made only once. The disadvantage is that all accesses result in a message across the network. Replicated management makes copies of the data where they are most often needed. This avoids the need for two-phase commits but may lead to a user working with out-of-date data unless complex additional measures are taken. Where read accesses are more common than writes this is a good strategy. Partitioned data management stores data across several nodes, usually based on access demand predictions. This necessitates two-phase commits but can be efficient when the partitioning follows some natural division of data ownership in the business. Object-oriented decomposition is even better because not only ownership but conceptual stability drive the decomposition. Nowadays, database vendors offer a choice between two-phase commits and replication as distribution strategies. Sybase Release 10 is an example of a relational, distributed database that offers replication.

Apart from the kind of operating system and the details of data management, there are several different kinds of distributed computer architecture and it is easy to become confused among them. **Client/server** computing involves a single server with one or many clients and most of the intelligence is located in the clients. Often the server is a file-store or a database, although the terminology may be used to include print servers. This is a simple form of distribution but it is extremely important commercially and Section 4.2 deals with it in more detail for this reason. The next level of complexity is the **multi-client/multi-server** system where there may be several servers but the servers may not communicate directly; in other words: nodes cannot be both clients and servers. Several database products support this architecture. A more technical definition in terms of database architectures is given in the next section but you will find that few publications agree on the exact definitions. The most general case occurs when every process node may be both a client and a server (in general simultaneously) though this is rare at present. This case involves **peer-to-peer** communication between nodes. Nodes may represent processors or task images within a processor. Messages may be split, relayed and combined as they pass from node to node. Implementing this kind of system is not without its difficulties.

Another way of viewing the different types of distributed architecture is presented in Figure 4.1. Here, we distinguish four models: the database server model, the transaction server model, the peer-to-peer model and the distributed front-end model. The database server model offers a limited choice as to where to locate the functions of the system while the transaction server model is a more effective way to balance the processing load between nodes and reduce network traffic; data-intensive tasks can be handled by the server and interface manipulation and secondary computation by the client. Further, SQL queries can be precompiled to improve performance and there is a central point of maintenance.

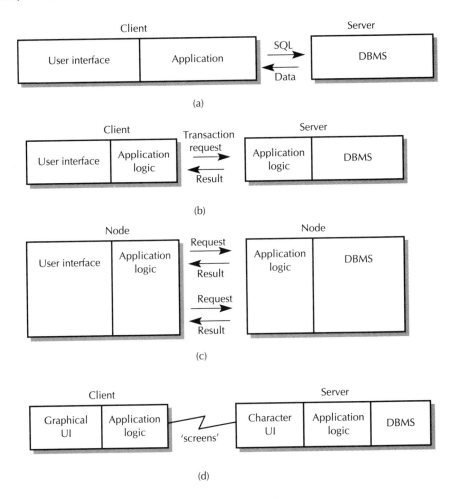

Figure 4.1 Distributed computing architectures: (a) database server model; (b) transaction server model; (c) peer-to-peer model; (d) distributed front-end model.

The peer-to-peer model is the most flexible and general but the most difficult to program and manage. In applications such as real-time process control, CSCW and groupware it is almost mandatory. The distributed front-end model is really only used as a sort of wrapper strategy when there is a legacy mainframe with a character interface based on synchronous protocols such as 3270. Here, the workstation client should be envisaged as remapping between its own and the host screen format and transmitting or receiving the results.

Distributed computing brings with it problems additional to those of a centralized approach. For example, every user in a different department may work with a different definition of the business entities such as *customers*. A customer could be a company or a person within a company. Is a child a customer when a parent pays but the child chooses? At what point does a prospect become converted to a customer? These questions merely hint at the difficulty. With a centralized system the differences do not matter so much because users can take copies of the data they need and add their own view. The distributed totality is never assembled to reveal any discrepancies. A distributed system therefore means that it becomes necessary for all to agree on definitions, which can be very hard to do. There is a contradiction between the need to have all applications interoperate with each other and the need to permit each department to work in its own way. Housekeeping too becomes a more complex task. On the one hand, users may not consider routine backups and disc purges as part of their job but, on the other, nothing is more annoying than when the Information Systems Stasi comes round and erases all those useful little files on your hard disc over the weekend. One possible solution is automated housekeeping but the danger of a totalitarian approach remains.

There are yet other areas where distributed systems increase complexity. In a centralized system the operators and administrators take backups and tune the system. In a distributed one each user must be both operator and administrator. Physical distribution often makes central backups and software release control impractical. Network shared file servers help but they fail to provide a complete answer. A true distributed system implies a distributed operating system that makes the multitude of systems look like one system as far as the user is concerned. Such a system must ensure both fault tolerance and parallelism. That is, no single part failing should bring the system down and there must be interconnected units containing both processor and memory. The first requirement implies that the system nodes must share state or, in the present context, that objects must be replicated.

The sheer cost of a simple solution may also increase complexity. Fully interconnected networks are simple but expensive; and thus the need for complex routers and scheduling techniques. Mullender (1989) illustrates this point well by comparing the operating policy of a railway connecting two towns with a track in each direction, one being a single track, possibly plus sidings for passing. This example also illustrates the concept of **latency** in networks, which is too often ignored by designers of distributed systems. At 60 mph a single track network (with no sidings) connecting two points 120 miles distant has a latency of 2 hours while the double track railway has a latency of almost zero. Latency in a computer network is the time taken to call another thread of control. High-latency networks often have severe clock synchronization problems. Latency is an important concept in the design of any object-oriented system, distributed or not. In that context it refers to delays due to blocking sends.

Early adopters of distributed approaches and especially client/server systems involving graphical front-ends to existing systems have discovered the hard way that existing structured methods not only contribute little but actually impede progress in many areas. This is because the methods of functional decomposition and the separation of data from processing offer no representational techniques for describing communication between autonomous actors (objects). Thus, there is, in these organizations, a profound need for object-oriented analysis methods to help describe the systems being built. Also, new skills are needed, some specifically to do with distributed computing itself, but more significantly in terms of the different kinds of hardware and software platforms that will be used.

Object technology provides a natural way of modelling distributed applications. In conventional systems, library interfaces are usually procedural. In distributed systems they are more involved. Just as an object's state is encapsulated, it is easy to see that its location can be 'hidden' in the same way – the location is part of the state. However, some means of finding these objects must be provided. When an object references another (that is, sends a message) the routing of the message is of no concern to the sender. Providing there is some sort of global address table, the sender should not need to care whether the receiver is even on the same machine. This must be the case for an object-oriented system because objects have unique identity for their lifetimes – regardless of location. In other words the object-oriented model both assumes and implies **locational transparency**.

Realizing that locational transparency is possible in principle for object-oriented systems does not lead to the conclusion that implementing such systems is trivial. In fact, a great deal of programming is required to set up the requisite support services and environment, and this involves several technologies as well as networking. Several system software vendors, such as Apple, HP, IBM, Microsoft, Sun and DEC have been working towards developing object-oriented environments for distributed computing. Most commercial products resulting from this enterprise will conform to the OMG's CORBA distributed messaging standard as well as other, more proprietary, standards in some cases.

Guttman *et al.* (1993) describe the approach to distributed object management used within NCR's CO-OPERATION workgroup application suite. The CO-OPERATION system uses a directory services table structured similarly to that of the X500 E-mail standard. References to distributed objects are obtained from the directory as surrogates that are copied to the task space of the requester. Messages are sent to the surrogate and it relays them to the real object transparently. In fact, the distributed object manager itself is responsible for this. Figure 4.2 illustrates this remote method invocation model.

There remain problems that are not directly to do with message passing. These include concurrency, recovery from node failures, optimal object location for efficient access, how objects should be physically distributed when there are conflicting demands from different users and whether and how large objects can be decomposed into their components and distributed. CO-OPERATION divides objects into active and passive types. Active objects provide services to others, can be copied as surrogates and need concurrency control. A printer might be an active object. Passive objects may be physically distributed when their services are required. A trivial example of a passive object is a number. There are three strategies for determining the location of active objects in this framework:

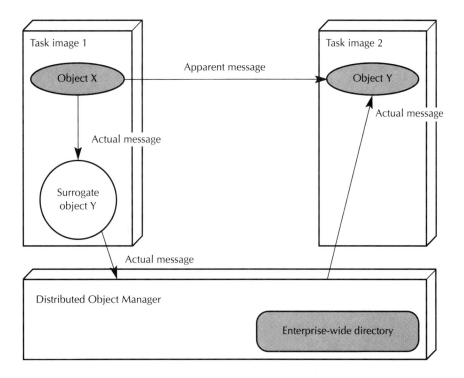

Figure 4.2 Remote method invocation in CO-OPERATION.

(1) Set the location explicitly.
(2) Set the location, statically or dynamically, on the basis of the resources it needs and those available.
(3) Allow the requester to set the location dynamically.

This separation of active from passive objects is useful provided that the split can be made or the objects redefined to support it, the processing requirements of active objects can be defined and mapped onto physical hardware and the passive object mapping can be decided upon.

The options available to those wishing to implement distributed systems are:

■ Build the necessary infrastructure, network support, remote procedure calls, and so on by hand.
■ Build a wrapper.
■ Use some proprietary tool or tools; for example a client/server application development system.
■ Utilize the features of an object-oriented database.
■ Utilize an object request broker (ORB).

Before the advent of ORBs remote invocations were typically accomplished by writing remote procedure calls (RPCs). Problems that need to be addressed by designers who use RPCs include naming and binding conventions, locating the procedure, minimizing latency, dealing with multiple machine types and languages, concurrency, connexion efficiency and locational transparency. It is not easy. This is precisely why special tools are popular. In addition, the developer must face up to all the data management issues discussed in Chapter 2 where object wrappers are constructed or object-oriented databases are used.

Network nodes can be regarded as abstract data types or objects. However, inheritance and composition links shouldn't cross the network. Associations that span the network should be minimized for reasons of efficiency. Typically, a system layer should be implemented at a single node. In fact, nodes are best regarded as layers in the sense of SOMA (see Chapter 6).

Daniels and Cook (1993) discuss the particular problems that arise when objects must be shared by different applications or workstations. They define sharing as 'controlled, simultaneous, multi-user access to objects'. As I have pointed out in Chapter 2, we can solve the migration problem in three ways: using object-oriented databases, wrappers or object request brokers. These authors take a similar position and view ORBs as a short-term compromise pending the development of technology to enable systems where every object is potentially shared and would be located by following pointers from known objects; all this at a fine level of granularity. They also offer four strategies for linking object-oriented systems to persistent storage that correspond roughly to the other two of mine. Their 'jump the gap' strategy comprises mapping objects onto an existing file system or database. This strategy can be improved by automating the mapping by defining a general procedure using a standard protocol such as SQL. This they call 'building a bridge'. The problem with this approach is that there is nothing to stop developers violating the encapsulation of the data stores. The other two possibilities are to use the services provided by an advanced, partly object-oriented, relational database or to use a full-blown object-oriented database. These last two strategies reduce or completely fill the gap between the programming language and storage representations. The former involves using at least two languages however and there are doubts as to whether the efficiency of object-oriented databases can ever be approached in this way.

Distributed computing using objects combines object-oriented (OO) with client/server notions. The modular nature and benefits of OO systems are combined with the scaleability and distribution of client/server systems. Applications in future will be constructed from collections of distributed objects that interact to carry out some task.

▤ 4.2 The client/server model

Client/server computing (CSC) can be defined as the division of processing and data between one or more front-end client machines that run applications and a single back-end server machine that provides a service to each client. This is often taken to mean that the machines are connected by a network and that the clients are workstations running a graphical user interface. More generally, a client/server system can be defined as one in which some element of the computation, user interface or database access is performed by an independent application, as a service to another; possibly on the same machine. In this broader sense all object-oriented systems are client/server systems, though the converse is not true. Evans (1992) offers a simple classification of systems as an *aide-mémoire*. His three types are illustrated in Figure 4.3.

Client/server computing, as we have seen, is a special case of distributed computing but does not usually involve a distributed database, though it may. One should avoid the temptation to confuse it with terminal emulation on workstations or with purely graphical front-ends. Further, CSC is not a new invention. In the 1970s terminals were often attached to front-end processors (usually small minicomputers) which switched the services of a mainframe application (often a database or modelling system). By the 1980s we were using PCs for terminal emulation and a small amount of the application logic, often concerned with display, had migrated to the PC. CSC became a mature possibility with the advent of multitasking PC operating systems so that the user could maintain links with a remote server while running a local application as well.

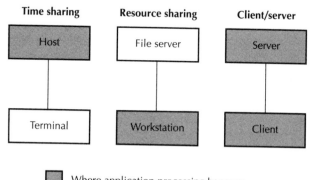

Figure 4.3 Three simple kinds of distributed architecture.

More and more it is users themselves who are demanding CSC systems. This increases their control over their work process but has a tendency to upset IT managers who feel that corporate control may be lost and maintenance costs run out of hand. The move into the unknown also violates the feelings of security that have been laid down over the years by 'total solutions' providers such as IBM.

Factors encouraging the adoption of CSC include cheaper workstations, better LAN software and the rightsizing economics which we visited briefly in Chapter 1. Also, there have been advances in software technology connected with peer-to-peer communications, starting with RPCs and arguably culminating in ORBs (see Section 4.7). Examples of the application of CSC include access to corporate databases via spreadsheets and other modelling systems, use of shared file servers and printers, e-mail with shared directory services as in X500 and many other office automation tasks.

It is worth noting that resource sharing systems such as file servers are not in the same category as database servers. With a file server, the client application requests a file which is then locked and transferred to the client for processing. If the access is for update, the file may be locked until the client releases control. All the processing is done by the client. With a database manager running on the server, the client issues queries and updates. The server processes these and returns only the result. Processing is shared, network traffic is reduced and locking is minimized.

Most currently installed client/server systems are of the database server type. However, as Flint and Macdonald (1992) point out, there is a hierarchy of types going beyond these, as depicted in Figure 4.4. The division between client and server can occur at any horizontal line in the diagram. Application servers correspond exactly to objects and object wrappers. We could slightly generalize the idea of a database server to that of a domain object server and differentiate it from an application object server. This point of view emphasizes a layered architecture rather than a single division between client and server as in the figure. We then begin to see that object-oriented systems are nothing

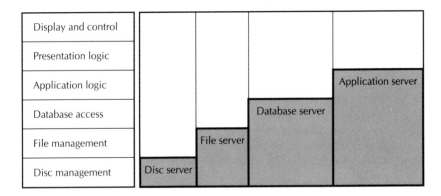

Figure 4.4 Levels of abstraction of client/server systems.

other than, possibly layered, multi-client/multi-server or peer-to-peer systems. The Smalltalk MVC metaphor uses three layers. Figure 4.4 suggests six. The right number depends on the application.

It is considered axiomatic that CSC, as with other distributed computing services, should offer locational transparency. That is, the user should not need to be aware of the physical location of the services being requested at any time. Even where this is true logically, network delays will sometimes make it only too apparent that requests are being processed remotely. Even finer distinctions become possible when the services are accessed by a mixture of local and wide area networks whose response characteristics are very different. Remote procedure calls (RPCs) violate locational transparency because the client application needs to know where the remote procedure is located to address it. This is sometimes hidden from the user by clever network software such as Sun's NFS and the reusable network services of the OSF's DCE but it remains a problem in principle. The extent to which the services offered by these systems are packaged as objects varies but such packaging, especially of the API, definitely represents a trend. We will see how distributed object systems overcome this problem in a general way later.

DCE (Distributed Computing Environment) is a software architecture that supports multi-vendor distributed data and process sharing. It protects the user against variations in communications protocols but relies almost entirely on remote procedure calls (RPCs) and is thus rather threatened by the emergence of object request brokers and Sunsoft's DOE (Distributed Objects Everywhere) and OpenStep initiatives, discussed below.

Conventional database tools are often organized around the client/server metaphor. One of the earliest commercial products to do this was Sybase, with more recent versions of INGRES, Oracle and other products working as multi-client/multi-server systems. The original Sybase approach offered each client a single access point to a multithreaded server. There was one process and each user represented a thread of control within it. This is efficient in terms of memory utilization but cannot be exploited by modern multiprocessor machines or parallel processors. The multi-server approach offers each client a single-threaded process of its own and is thus far better able to exploit parallelism even through slightly more hungry for memory. These kinds of tool assume network support and adherence to certain standards. The client and the server applications communicate via an API (such as the Sybase 'Open Client' API), connectivity software (such as 'SQL Connect') and some network protocol (such as TCP/IP, IBM's LU6.2/APPC or Novell's SPX/IPX). With the relational products, what is transmitted through all these filters is usually SQL, but this need not be so for object-oriented databases or other kinds of application. Again, with relational systems, the ones that make use of stored procedures can reduce network traffic considerably. This is because whole transactions are not fragmented into separate statements and they may be pre-compiled to further improve performance. Object-oriented systems, of course, give these benefits automatically, provided that the methods really are stored with the corresponding objects. (For a discussion of the way object-oriented database products handle method storage see Graham (1994a).)

Stored procedures in relational systems provide not true object orientation but the possibility of regarding the database server as one huge object; that is, of creating a wrapper. The difficulty is that the encapsulation is not enforced by the system and the discipline of a robust approach to object-oriented analysis must be enforced by the standards, procedures and QA policies of the organization. It is quite possible for the undisciplined – or badly educated – developer to access the database structure directly using SQL rather than by going through the access routines supplied as stored procedures. One rather unwieldy solution to this problem is for the database administrator to remove all access privileges from all users so that the only access must be via stored procedures; but this also removes most of the advantages of a relational database in terms of being able to perform *ad hoc* associative queries.

A special case of distributed computing, often confused with CSC, which is of particular interest is **cooperative processing**. This is usually understood as offering peer-to-peer communication between servers. A client may request a service from one server which in turn requests another service from another server in order to complete the servicing of the request. For example, if the request were for a loan, the loan accounting system might request the services of the credit rating server before completing its transaction. Obviously, this can be described very easily in terms of a network of objects communicating by message passing. Indeed, it is difficult to imagine any other kind of description being anything short of baroque.

The benefits of the client/server approach most often claimed are that it permits organizations to:

(1) reduce the incremental cost of meeting the demands of users for increased functionality and access to corporate systems;
(2) reduce hardware and development costs by allowing the use of tools optimized for particular tasks;
(3) reduce development times;
(4) reduce hardware costs by utilizing low cost workstations (downsizing) and optimizing the utilization of other hardware (rightsizing);
(5) increase competitive edge and empower users; and
(6) ease integration by hiding the complexities of communication between machines and adopting open standards.

Large organizations rely heavily on their corporate data resources. Even with mainframes these databases are often spread out and isolated due to having grown organically over long periods. CSC permits the combination of these resources. This can add value from sheer completeness or could, with the addition of rule induction or other machine learning techniques, permit data mining: the exploration for and extraction of unanticipated relationships. For example, think how much advertising budget a fast-moving consumer goods (FMCG) company could save if it discovered that 98% of its customers never watched television.

Centralized computing offers the advantages of security, economies of scale and easier enforcement of management and accounting disciplines. However, operating costs can be high, systems inflexible, development and maintenance costly and the user has little control – and often limited access. Furthermore, most mainframes are poor calculating machines so that the users' need to build models of business processes is hard to cater for in this way. This has led to considerable demand for end-user computing and CSC but there are still difficulties such as network bottlenecks, failures when not all machines are switched on, costs due to under-utilized CPUs, security breaches, data integrity and file locking delays. New skills are required within many IT organizations and change management is nearly always advisable to ameliorate the level of resistance to change. IT staff need not only their old mainframe skills but skills with PCs, networks and new, complex communication standards. In my view, they will benefit most from an understanding of the principles of OT and above all a sound grasp of object-oriented analysis. This too involves extra costs, often significant, in terms of recruitment, consultancy, education and training.

The potential benefits have attracted many users and suppliers have not been slow to climb aboard the bandwagon as well. For example, Andersen Consulting sells a CASE tool, Foundation, specifically aimed at supporting client/server development and IBM created a specialist business unit to deal with client/server products and consulting at the end of 1992.

Though CSC architectures usually involve two or more machines, in principle both client and server can reside on the same machine. The distinction is logical as well as physical. Multi-client/multi-server systems extend the CSC model to give users heterogeneous access to several servers without the need to know where the services are located. There are several relational database management systems that support a client/server or even multi-client/multi-server model. All object-oriented databases do so.

There are now several TP monitors for UNIX machines and PCs including Ellipse from Cooperative Solutions Inc., Encina from Transarc Corp., MTS from Micro Focus, TOP END from NCR, Tuxedo from USL Inc. and even IBM's CICS. The latter, it is reported, had its internal design heavily influenced by object-oriented ideas taken from Smalltalk and became notorious by winning a Queen's Award for the development team's use of formal specification using Z.

4.3 Distributed databases and full-content retrieval

Object-oriented databases are good at distribution but so are some modern relational products able to work on networks. SQL can be used to connect clients to servers but is usually only used in this way for *ad hoc* queries. More complex applications call for application-dependent code on the server, usually in the form of stored procedures that are not written in the standard part of SQL but in a procedural extension of the language. API standards represented by such products as Sybase's Open Server or Microsoft's rather similar ODBC make it possible, and fairly straightforward, to implement client/server systems in the context of relational databases. The model here is that of a single server. Genuine distributed databases are not yet well supported. Locational transparency, node failure resilience, error handling and latency are all severe practical problems. Non-relational databases can often supply data to relational ones via gateways but the interface to these gateways, and to other relational systems, is usually dependent on a proprietary API of some sort. Standards like ODBC, on the other hand, oblige database vendors to modify their client-end products so that all PC applications can talk to any database. However, this only works for single user workstations and the need for support for multi-user clients is driving some users towards the adoption of object request broker technology.

Khoshafian *et al.* (1992) argue that the solution lies not so much in ORBs but in a combination of object-oriented, relational and rule based databases that they dub 'intelligent' databases. They also suggest that such databases should incorporate the full-content retrieval capabilities normally associated with library Information Retrieval (IR) systems. The presence of BLOBs or memo fields containing complex information underlines the need for this extension. Further, as databases go beyond the storage of text and numbers to embrace visual and aural media, the indexing and search problem becomes at once more pressing and more complex. Users need to be able to access the content – the meaning – of a stored object without reading it or viewing its content.

IR systems that have to deal with documents whose content changes infrequently can use inverted indexing, concept classification and thesaurus techniques. For more volatile applications, the system's documents may be scanned and their contents compared with a set of keywords or other tokens. Another approach is to build a signature table for each document by hashing keywords into a small numerical signature. This can then be compared against the signature of an arbitrary query. This is a probabilistic approach that does not guarantee that all matching documents will be retrieved or that all those retrieved will match. The best concept indexing systems require people with good knowledge of the subject matter to prepare keyword tables, synonym lists, thesauri and so on. Khoshafian *et al.* (1992) provide a brief but reasonably detailed introduction to the subject of full-content information retrieval systems in the context of general office automation systems and include a discussion of the retrieval of sounds and images as well as text. They also give a reasonable amount of detail on the different technical approaches to data refinement, data capture, parsing and understanding structure, expert system based query languages, indexing and compression.

Context is also a problem and IR faces similar problems in this respect to those faced by AI natural language systems. Manual indexing is usually too expensive an option to be worth considering so that some workers have explored automatic indexing systems. Van Rijsbergen (1993) supports the use of statistical techniques and suggests that IR can be regarded as theorem proving with non-Boolean logic. He also refers to the recent work of Barwise and Devlin on situation theory, which defines a primitive unit of information: the *infon* (Devlin, 1992).

A particularly important application of this theory in the context of this book is its use in retrieving data from a reuse repository. Storing information is a relatively easy problem. The central problem of IR is that of finding the information you require. This has particular significance for object-oriented developers because of the need to retrieve information about class libraries. There have been two basic suggestions: organize the references in the form of a hierarchy and use classification to gain access or index all class specifications according to keywords and search on them. Neither approach is ideal. Successful reuse of library code objects and specifications can only be achieved through a combination of classification and keyword based retrieval. Further, it is possible to extend both approaches to encompass uncertainty calculi. For example, the thesaurus of an IR system will often permit the user to ask for a match on a keyword or class specification and then ask that the search be recomputed using a narrower or broader meaning of the term. SOMA object models can be used in much the same way as Khoshafian's semantic nets to describe the structure and semantics of information and, in one respect, SOMA object models are more powerful. This is because of the incorporation of fuzzy rulesets into objects and fuzzy inheritance. *SOMATiK* extends the idea of hierarchical search using four orthogonal structures and permits fuzzy matching on keywords. This is discussed further in Chapters 6 and 11.

⊟ 4.4 Collaborative work, work-flow automation and groupware

While labour in manufacturing has seen massive increases in its productivity in the recent past, the productivity of office workers has stagnated despite increased usage of computers (Brynjolfsson, 1993; Roach, 1991). According to the Association for Image and Information Management and other researchers (Wang, 1989) between 94% and 95% of office information still resides on paper and 15% to 30% of office workers' time is spent in locating it.

This section deals with some technology for amplifying the productivity of office workers. It is variously known as computer-supported cooperative work (CSCW), work-flow automation, groupware and collaborative work support. It involves various technologies from document image management, scanners, CD storage, multimedia display, broadband networks, full-content database retrieval, and specialized technologies based on insights from linguistics, AI, biology, anthropology and other social sciences. There are also strong links to the ideas of business process re-engineering (BPR).

Durham (1992) suggests that the definition of **work-flow** software is that it automates existing, repetitive, multi-actor processes while **groupware** supports *ad hoc* forms of cooperation and coordination. Some software products support both approaches. The split reflects a dichotomy within the business process re-engineering community, which emphasizes either the automation and streamlining of existing processes and the enforcement of 'best practice' or the entire obliteration of unnecessary work. Successful introduction of groupware correlates with flat organizational structures where the norm is people working in teams to solve problems rather than individuals reporting upwards in order to have their decisions authorized.

Recall from Chapter 1 that BPR redefines jobs by making corporate information accessible to all and giving those in direct contact with the task the power to make decisions. Unfortunately, it is largely an art rather than a science because the analyst has to leap intuitively to what is sometimes called 'the great idea'. The examples quoted in the literature all have such a great idea; for example, Hammer (1990) and Davenport and Short (1990). We have already seen how Ford was able to reduce the size of its Accounts Payable headcount from 500 to 125 by paying for goods on receipt rather than matching invoices and orders. This was enabled by a computer system, but the great idea was generated from the observation that Mazda had an equivalent department with only five people in it. Mutual Benefit Life similarly reduced its underwriting turn-round from 24 to 4 hours by making a 'case manager', equipped with expert systems technology, responsible for the whole process. Here it seems the great idea arose directly from the technological potential of expert systems combined with the propensity to think outside current organizational constraints. I think the main lesson to be learnt from these and many other case studies is that a more systematic approach is necessary. Re-engineers need representational and simulation tools so that they can perform 'what-if' analyses on a model of the existing or projected business process; tools that do for the re-engineer what spreadsheets have done for management accountants. Object technology offers a solution here because business processes can be modelled as arrangements of communicating objects with state, responsibilities and, importantly, knowledge of business policies and rules. Chapter 8 shows how SOMA supports this activity directly. Another lesson is that IT makes BPR possible. A story is told about the managing director of an insurance company who was at his desk at 7 p.m. when the telephone rang. Since he had access to the company's work-flow model via a terminal he was able to call up the customer's records and deal with her problem there and then.

IT helps eliminate unnecessary flows and makes managers into clerks as much as it makes clerks into decision makers (a better word might be executives). This questions the classical conceptions of the division of labour of Adam Smith and Frederick Taylor in a fundamental way. In fact, the arguments of the modern management science gurus are faintly reminiscent of the argument used by Lenin in his *State and Revolution* (Lenin, 1964)[1], where it is argued that in a genuinely free and productive society the division of labour would wither away. His slogan was 'the administration of things – not the management of people'. This sounds very much like Tom Peters' exhortations to empower the workforce and eliminate chains of permission to act. However, the evident conclusion from matching these disparate political views is to ask whether current politico-economic structures will either tolerate or support such radical restructuring of the way work is done. Peters evidently believes it will, but it is unproven and unlikely that the beneficial effects of empowerment will continue to apply when spread from a handful of advanced companies to all the world's enterprises unless there are concomitant social changes. Another, more immediate, social issue that arises with work-flow systems is the fact that managers can use them to monitor employees' work. This could lead to resentment against snooping. Gary Marx (1992) argues that if managers think such monitoring is useful, they should submit to it themselves.

The BPR literature emphasizes that businesses organized around functional models are rigid and inflexible due to excessive functional specialization. No one in this circle has suggested that object models are better but it is widely agreed that the unit of analysis should be the business process. The rôle of objects is to provide direct support for modelling processes as flows of communication between actors. I would assert that any natural language description of a business process translates naturally to an object model – at least when rules can be represented. This is discussed further in Chapter 8, where we will see that the rule based, object-oriented, description may be animated to provide business process simulations that may be used for scenario modelling to help find the 'great idea'.

To see where a business can benefit most from groupware it is often effective to construct an application grid of the type shown in Figure 4.5. In this figure we compare the level of social interaction required to carry out the task with the management level at which the task usually occurs. The cells of the grid contain some typical applications and it can be seen that groupware may be suitable for a range of applications across all management levels at the high interactivity level. More surprising is that medium interactivity applications tend to be concentrated at the operational level, again emphasizing collaboration and the empowerment of line workers. Further, work-flow applications, emphasizing control, are more appropriate at the low interactivity end of the scale. Where organizational change is expected it would seem prudent to adopt systems flexible enough to cover both control and collaboration applications.

---

[1] Lenin was undoubtedly familiar with Taylor's ideas, as evinced by his famous slogan: 'Electrification + Taylorism = Socialism'.

Management level

Interaction	Operational	Middle	Top
Low	Database access	Reporting	Executive information systems
Medium	E-mail, resource sharing	Scheduling meetings	Decision support systems, expert systems
High	Informal discussions, meetings, panics	Decision support systems, expert systems	Group decision support

Figure 4.5 Application grid for groupware and work-flow systems.

Tools for work-flow automation fall into three main classes. They are either document image management (DIM) systems such as Filenet with its integral Workflo language, office automation systems or specific groupware products. Such systems are highly effective in large bureaucracies such as local government departments where paper flow and rule adherence are considered to be important factors in public accountability. The amount of paper storage and concomitant costs can also be dramatically reduced in these contexts. Products like Lotus Notes enable incoming documents to be scanned, stored and distributed by e-mail. This helps to avoid massive waste where many photocopies are circulated to people with no interest in the information while genuinely interested parties are omitted from the circulation. Many products offer two modes: one for developers and one for users. The developer mode usually utilizes some kind of high-level scripting language. Some products, such as Beyond Mail, attempt to apply rules to the mail routing problem to support work-flow applications. It is possible, for example, to store and send a standard reply to mail from nominated individuals – useful for junking junk mail, I would hazard. The approach need not be restricted to a local LAN. Boldon James' Enterprise Mail already supports the X400 and X500 protocols and most other e-mail products will do so soon.

As discussed in the previous chapter, HCI concentrates on the detailed performance of specific tasks. This is fine for analysing the use of a computer system by an individual at a workstation but less so in work-flow environments where many users have to cooperate. HCI draws heavily on work in cognitive psychology, as we saw in the last chapter, and this means that the results of HCI can be extended to CSCW. Work on this at Xerox' research centre in Cambridge, England has emphasized the use of contributions from the other social sciences such as anthropology, ethnomethodology and social psychology. Ethnomethodology, for example, is concerned with the relationships between people, groups, work patterns and technology. It has considerable application to studying the organizational impact of IT. Group work emphasizes the social aspects of work and thought and CSCW has emphasized this further. In fact, Diaper (1993) has claimed that CSCW is little more than HCI for groups. Ethnomethodologists may film people at work in groups and record physical movement, gestures, eye focus, posture and their relationship to conversation. Conversation analysis provides notations for recording such things and the results can be surprising. For example, it turns out that sound cues are very important, and when a door is heard closing at the end of a conversation via a multimedia system, this augments user satisfaction because it helps them achieve closure. Subtle hand positioning and movement can provide cues for the counterparty to begin speaking. People in video conferences are less sensitive to small but significant movements in peripheral vision than in face-to-face conversations. Some users learn to exaggerate their gestures for this reason. However useful in the video context, this can make people look very silly when viewed from across the office. I have also heard it reported that users of an early video-conferencing system in a large corporation gave up using it when they realized that the unreality of the experience led to tarnished images within the organization. An extreme case was a senior manager who had a tendency to pick his nose throughout video meetings. He did not do this in real meetings. Obviously I cannot name the company.

It is often useful in designing work-flow and groupware systems to analyse what Jacobson *et al.* (1992) call use cases and what I generalize as **task scripts**. Each task script is associated with a set of objects, which will often be documents or database records. A task script analysis leads directly to an object-oriented description as detailed in Chapter 7 and this model may be used to critique the current work-flow in order to obliterate some work. A process view is integral to many object-oriented analysis and design methods, notably methods such as Ptech which was actually named as a contraction of Process technology long before it became fashionable to describe the method as object-oriented.

The quality movement and the more recent interest in BPR have both emphasized process over functional specialization. An orientation towards process, it is said, helps to produce:

- increases in efficiency and effectiveness;
- cost reductions;
- greater process flexibility and therefore adaptability;
- greater job satisfaction; and
- higher quality products.

It has become commonplace to appoint a 'process engineer' to oversee the delivery of these benefits. We will see in Part II that these lessons can be applied to the process of software engineering itself and, with object-oriented developments in mind, the rôle of the process engineer will be largely adopted by the domain modeller – see Chapters 8 and 9.

It would be a mistake to assume that the benefits of collaborative computing arrive without costs being incurred. Beyond the costs of the new software there are training and change management costs. I would assert that this style of working requires that every member of staff has a workstation of their own, for example. Where this is not already the case, it must be paid for. On the other hand there are some latent benefits too. Instant access to information can speed up time-to-market considerably. For example, a first-rate e-mail system can reduce the number of meetings required to reach a critical decision, since no one has to go off to collect missing information and reconvene the meeting later.

There are several groupware tools, ranging from Lotus Notes to Action Technologies' The Coordinator. Other relevant products available at the time of writing include Beyond Inc's BeyondMail, Computron's Epic/Workflow, DEC's TeamRoute, HP's WaveFlow, IBM's Folder Application Facility, ICL's ProcessWise, NCR's ProcessIT (part of CO-OPERATION), Plexus' Imageflow, Recognition Equipment's ImageFlow and the eponymous Filenet and Staffware. Many of these tools rely on object technology. For example, ProcessWise claims that object-oriented techniques are used to let it build business process simulations and to develop the computer systems needed to support business process re-engineering. ICL's approach involves finding measurable improvement objectives and using ProcessWise WorkBench to build the simulations to be measured against these objectives. ProcessWise Integrator then helps to develop the work-flow management system. This approach is remarkably similar in some respects to the approach of SOMA to modelling both enterprises and systems but still has a data flow emphasis. It also illustrates the intimate connexion between groupware products and business process re-engineering. Organizations that claim to have benefited from BPR in this manner include IBM, National & Provincial Building Society, British Telecom, Lucas, Nabisco and Rank Xerox.

Many current IT practices help to lock organizations into their existing methods of working. This is chiefly because changes to computer systems take too long. The move to rapid development is thus very important for IT within the adaptable business that is adopting BPR. OT supports this move by providing programming environments that are very flexible, based on the polymorphic characteristics of the languages and dynamic binding. Prototypes can be built quickly and evolved easily. Reuse libraries make rapid development even faster, where they exist. Finally, object-oriented methods like SOMA pay close attention to the flexibility of the life-cycle model. In Chapter 9 we will see exactly how this is so.

4.5 Network and architectural issues

Distributed systems use more network capacity than centralized ones and it is a common error to underestimate the demand. It is a good idea therefore to involve users – who can often forecast what they want to do, network and operating systems specialists and application builders. These three groups together should be able to produce a reasonable forecast of network loading and avoid the situation where people are taking half an hour to move their gigabyte database across the LAN and, incidentally, preventing anyone else from moving data.

Peer-to-peer communication can be used to build big systems out of relatively small computers. The prototype for this was DECnet. IBM's APPN protocol and TCP/IP follow the same model, though TCP/IP is more widely supported and less proprietary. OSI networks are yet to reach the mature stage of development reached by TCP/IP.

One of the most urgent questions facing an organization migrating to object technology is that of systems, application and network architecture. It is essential that new and legacy systems must be able to interoperate during the migration period. Often the *status quo* is a goulash of different systems, machines and networks. Figure 4.6 shows a simplified version of a typical architecture of the sort required by the migrating organization.

In the figure, the mainframe may be running all sorts of COBOL, FORTRAN, DB2 or VSAM applications and using proprietary network standards, such as SNA, for connectivity. The key component that must be added to the mainframe is some software that allows clients to interact directly with the

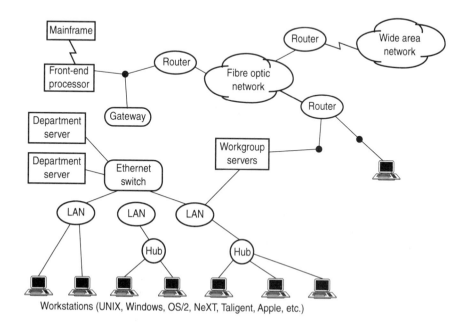

Figure 4.6 A typical network architecture during migration.

mainframe relational database, using SQL, or execute COBOL routines remotely. A second key component is the gateway. This is some special software that would normally run on a dedicated machine and which acts as a bridge between UNIX clients and the mainframe network. Several database vendors can supply suitable software. For example, Sybase offer a CICS connectivity product called OpenServer and a gateway product called NetGateway. Routers connect different LAN and WAN technologies and hubs permit point-to-point wiring between workstations. Ethernet switches help to maximize both flexibility and throughput. Various other equipment is needed but this is not a book on network architecture and the simplified view presented here will suffice. In future, object request brokers will simplify the picture considerably and it is this development that we consider next.

4.6 Object request brokers and distributed objects

The need to cooperate with existing systems and other object-oriented systems across telecommunications and local area networks and packages that support this is our next subject.

The requirement here is to represent applications and services on a network through a common object schema consisting of objects to represent every entity and with all locations and implementations transparent to the user and other objects. Most systems houses have made this aim a part of their strategies for the 1990s. However, not all the theoretical problems have yet been solved and this is a rapidly evolving area. Typical unsolved problems concern abstract models of distributed objects, multi-user servers, security, maintaining locational transparency without overloading the network and lack of standards. However, standards are beginning to emerge.

One important way in which future packages and applications will interoperate is through the Object Management Group's Common Object Request Broker Architecture (CORBA).

The Object Management Group (OMG) is a large group of influential companies committed to establishing broad agreement between vendors on both the terminology of object orientation and on 4GL style and interface standards – possibly based on existing technology from suppliers such as DEC, Hewlett Packard and Hyperdesk. Companies originally involved in the OMG included Borland, Microsoft, Hewlett Packard, Data General, AT&T, Prime, Wang, ICL, Sun, DEC and most of the leading hardware, software and object-oriented suppliers, along with several major users such as Boeing and British Airways. Now almost every seriously interested party is a member. Meetings of the OMG Technical Committee rotate between Europe, the USA and the Far East, helping to ensure an international base. The OMG is committed to the fast production of published standards, faster anyway than the official stan-

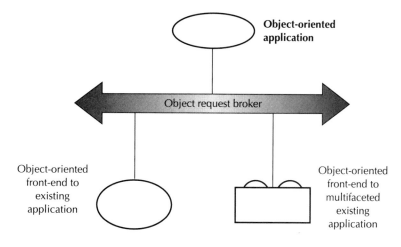

Figure 4.7 The Object Request Broker concept.

dards bodies can operate, and has already published an architecture guide, a standard for object request brokers (ORBs) and a high-level object-oriented abstract data model. Already several suppliers have announced ORB compliant products and many more will soon follow. The fast growth of the OMG suggests that the industry is highly aware of both the potential of object technology and the need for standards.

An ORB is a transparent data highway connecting object-oriented applications and object-oriented front-ends to existing applications (Figure 4.7). It is analogous to the X500 electronic mail communications standard wherein a requester can issue a request to another application or node without needing detailed knowledge of its directory services structure. In this way, the ORB removes much of the need for complex RPCs by providing the mechanisms by which objects make and receive requests and responses transparently. It is intended to provide interoperability between applications on different machines in heterogeneous distributed environments and to connect multiple object systems seamlessly. It provides a means of using an abstract description of applications and the relationships between them and provides services for locating and using these applications across multi-vendor networks. Applications need not be written in an object-oriented manner since the ORB effectively provides a wrapper and they can be entire third-party packages. Packages and in-house applications can be reused and combined to deliver brand new cross-platform, distributed business systems. As Ewald and Roy (1993) succinctly put it, ORBs bring the benefit of OT to the world of systems integration.

The ORB fits in with the OMG architecture model (Figure 4.8) in which objects are classified as Application Objects, Common Facilities and Object Services. Application Objects are specific to particular end-user applications

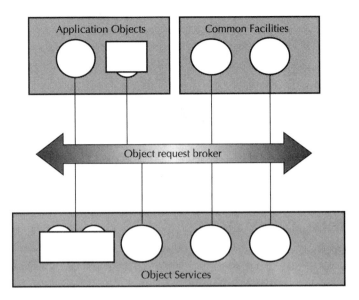

Figure 4.8 The OMG architecture.

such as word processing or spreadsheets. Common Facilities are objects which are useful in many contexts such as help facilities, browsers, e-mail and so on. Object Services provide basic operations for the logical modelling and physical storage of objects and might include object-oriented databases, directory and file services or transaction monitors. In the ORB, a request names an operation and its parameters, which may be object names. The ORB arranges the processing of the request by identifying and running a suitable method and returning the result to the requester.

Object request brokers work by acting on requests from all other types of object. They bind these to objects and route requests to other ORBs for binding. They can be regarded as either communication managers or systems integrators since they either route requests to the correct destination object or understand the syntax and semantics of each request by maintaining an object model, or both. They replace the need for much complex RPC programming and are a small step towards truly intelligent networks. In future, I anticipate expert systems and machine learning techniques being used to take this development even further.

An ORB makes use of the principles of data abstraction using its object model. In this model the **interface classes** specify the services of the applications known to the broker while the implementation classes represent the object wrapper code. To define an interface class one should specify the class in terms of its superclasses, attributes and operations. An Interface Definition Language (IDL) supports both dynamic and static binding to cater for different performance and extensibility requirements. All location services are handled transparently by the broker. This is handled by implementation classes but CORBA does not yet include a language for specifying these. Vendors are still free to innovate in this area.

ORBs extend the polymorphism of normal object-oriented systems based on features such as inheritance to allow the user to choose at run time between different objects that perform the same function. So users can select a favourite word processor to perform editing functions based on their skills and preferences, thus maximizing their productivity within an albeit standardized environment. Other common facilities, such as spreadsheets or graphics servers, may be treated in the same flexible but disciplined manner. In this way, ORBs – for all their weaknesses – address some of the fundamental points made about productivity in Chapter 1.

The CORBA standard claims to address five key problems for distributed object systems: integration, interoperation, distribution, reuse and group work. Integration is addressed by providing a standard Interface Definition Language (IDL). Hitherto, the problem of distribution had been solved using very low-level RPC programming and every developer, notably those in the banks, invented their own frameworks.

One of the first commercial products to emerge was Hyperdesk's DOMS. In fact, the creators of this product were influential in setting up the OMG in the first place. They started building a replacement for Data General's ageing CEO office automation products within that company. HP's NewWave technology was unsuccessfully tried as a basis for this work. In the late 1980s the group was spun off from DG as a separate company and Chris Stone left to form the OMG. Companies such as Sun, HP, DEC and NCR all had ideas on how to solve the distributed office computing problem with objects at this time.

There were two basic approaches, a static approach originating from Sun and HP and a dynamic, but less efficient, one coming from Hyperdesk and DEC. The dynamic model requires a single request-building API and a single message-unpacking mechanism. In the static model there was one code stub per operation and each request was made by a different subroutine. Each object bound in skeletons specific to each operation. Each skeleton delivered parameters as if the requester were a subroutine. CORBA represents a synthesis of the static and dynamic models of object request brokers and every CORBA compliant implementation must support both approaches, though DOMS emphasized the dynamic approach. Objects and their methods could be modified dynamically without full recompilation or a system restart. The DOMS kernel was implemented as a server that was responsible for locational transparency, authentication, method binding and so on. The server kept track of a global name space for all registered objects and their interfaces using an object-oriented database (at one point this was ObjectStore) as illustrated in Figure 4.9. In general, in distributed systems, a name service must be provided to map names to attributes – such as mapping file names to file identifiers or mail aliases to mail addresses. Such services are needed to maintain locational

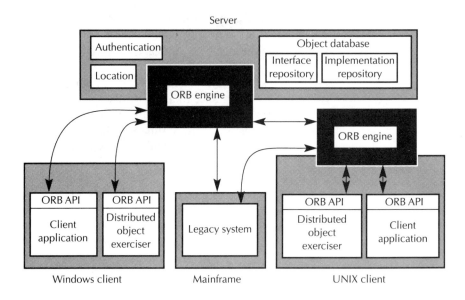

Figure 4.9 The Hyperdesk Distributed Object Management System.

transparency. The IDL can express information about an object's attributes, operations, inheritance and containment. IIDL (Implementation and Interface Definition Language) extended IDL to deal with the implementation of objects. DEC's CORBA product contains similar features.

DOMS includes a set of C++ class libraries for creating distributed applications. In the figure, the object exerciser provides a single point of access to the DOMS libraries for creating applications.

A number of criticisms have been levelled at DOMS. These mainly revolve around the claim that it cannot deal with fine-grain objects well; it lacks full support for languages other than C++ and its packets contain too little information. Furthermore, most commercial ORBs are closely tied to C++ or C environments, leaving Smalltalk users somewhat isolated.

Another important CORBA compliant object request broker is ORBIX from Iona Technologies in Eire. NeWI from Softwright Systems is an ORB that does not comply with all of the CORBA standard and has two major advantages as a result: the information packets can contain additional information on routing and the data packets sent as messages are self-describing within a single string so that there is no reliance on positioning. This allows amodal working and helps to support polymorphism. The router allows NeWI to support object replication. The XShell system has a similar facility. NeWI permits and encourages the use of C or even COBOL to construct applications which NeWI can then wrap up as objects, allowing a high-level object-oriented view of a system that may be written on a machine that does not support a C++ compiler – as was the case with the AS/400 machine for some time. This would be useful for porting a legacy system where the users would not all consider migrating to a new platform but who require new features and some of the benefits of object technology.

CORBA compliant products such as DOME from Object-Oriented Technologies Ltd are based on the view that packaged ORBs may be too restrictive for some users, especially systems integrators. Rather like XShell, DOME is supplied as a C++ tool kit with which one can construct an ORB.

Several DOMS, such as NeWI and XShell, offer interest registration facilities so that broadcast messages can be supported without the need for an explicit blackboard object. The target object is sent a message registering the interest of some other object. When an event occurs in the target object the interested object is sent a message.

The OMG is still developing and filling gaps in CORBA. Suppliers like Softwright are lobbying for a richer definition of packets in IDL and it is likely that CORBA 2 will support a standard naming convention for objects – to increase portability. Attention is also being paid to the question of making ORBs from different suppliers interoperate – which they do not at present – without sacrificing local efficiency. CORBA 2 was expected to be released during 1994 though there have been setbacks due to inter-vendor disagreements.

Most users will have to wait for ORB compliant products to emerge from major suppliers to gain the interoperability benefits potentially on offer. It will be interesting to see how existing products and *de facto* standards such as Microsoft's OLE are positioned in relation to the ORB and Microsoft is collaborating with DEC on this issue at the time of writing. Nor do we yet know whether Cairo will support CORBA. One hopes that there will be no conflict but proprietary considerations may dictate otherwise. In the meantime it would be wise to become at least a subscribing member of the OMG, which is not vastly expensive, if you are engaged in the development of any major system that could benefit from interoperation with other systems in future, and perhaps try to comply with the standard in advance. If this strategy takes off it will mean that organizations building object-oriented front-ends to existing applications will benefit even more than they anticipated.

ORBS, WRAPPERS AND DISTRIBUTED COMPUTING ORBs are closely related to object wrappers since access to an object or package on another system takes place via the broker, which at once defines the protocol via IDL and locates the service. The IDL interface could be to an object-oriented system or it could be to an entire package that is treated as if it were wrapped – provided that the IDL standard is observed by the wrapper.

The client/server model is not without its problems as discussed in Section 4.8, but the ORB offers some hope that these problems are not insuperable. In Hyperdesk's implementation, object services manage class, instance, state, security, version and so on for other objects. Different implementations of object services are supported simultaneously, so that multiple database managers and multiple naming systems can execute as required by the network's application and common facilities objects. These object services need not be stored in an object-oriented database although their interfaces must meet the standard; that is, they must be suitably *wrapped*. In this system, definition objects store the system's class structure and attributes. Life-cycle objects define the intrinsic methods used to manipulate and store objects and manage their values. Naming service objects encapsulate the implementation of object location functions or, in other words, know where all objects are within the network. What is emerging is the spectre of future networks being quite smart as regards what is connected to them. Other ORB products will begin to see daylight very soon and this will alleviate many of the problems of interoperation and of client/server systems in general.

Distributed, object-oriented systems proffer a number of benefits. The standardization of interfaces, brought about by object request brokers and initiatives such as SunSoft's DOE (Distributed Objects Everywhere) project, offers the possibility of reusing a wide range of commercially available, tested objects in bespoke applications. DOE will incorporate NeXTstep technology to provide a better operating system and infrastructure (OpenStep) on top of DOE and the Taligent and SOM (System Object Model) projects of IBM will inevitably combine to offer similar facilities. Environments like these combine languages, GUIs, class libraries, programmer and project support tools and database access tools in an integrated application development environment. These tools will have to use the same object-oriented language for extensions and class description. Conformance to standards such as the OMG's CORBA and COSS (Common Object Services Standard) will allow applications to be portable to multiple platforms. All the object-oriented benefits – reuse, extensibility, localization of maintenance, assembly of applications from software ICs (integrated circuits), and so on – will then apply in distributed environments. Further, this will provide scaleability up to the largest systems imaginable on multi-machine systems implemented under several different distributed architectures. Complex network interfaces and APIs are being replaced by powerful locationally transparent mechanisms that manage messaging, locations and global naming of objects.

DOE is a good example of this kind of development. It consists of an application library, interface builder, database kit and distribution manager. The application library provides GUI objects and classes for opening and closing files, event management, text editing, graphics display, printing and multimedia support. The interface builder, based on that of NeXTstep, provides advanced GUI and program development facilities. The database kit provides wrappers for multiple databases and permits databases to be separated from the application in much the same manner as more conventional products, like Uniface. Perhaps the most significant feature of DOE is its support for distribution. It includes CORBA compliant locational transparency and IDL mappings to allow applications written in different languages to communicate. The OpenStep interface specification is published so that other vendors can work with it, though DOE has evident commercial ambitions of its own. Similar products are emerging and this type of approach to computing is likely to become very widespread soon. All computing will be distributed computing.

4.7 Case studies

The first half of the 1990s saw many organizations undergoing major changes in technology, principally moving away from systems based on centralized mainframes – usually from a single supplier – to distributed systems. PCs and UNIX workstations became desirable platforms for both development and applications due to their increased and more accessible power and the ease of building usable graphical interfaces on them. This was associated with a greater emphasis on rapid response to changing business needs and the use of prototyping. The existence of immovable legacy systems meant that interoperability was a key issue during the migration. Developments in hardware and relational database software also led to increased demand for and reliance on client/server architectures. One of the industries where this kind of migration was prevalent was finance and the remarks in this section are based on the experiences of a number of anonymous financial service organizations in the City of London and Wall Street. Typically these organizations operated with a goulash of mainframe systems, departmental minis and standalone or networked PCs running word processors or spreadsheet applications. The mainframes ran both relational and non-relational databases and record-oriented applications written in COBOL or Assembler.

As new applications began to appear the first need was for them to access information on the mainframes. This could be accomplished by nightly downloads but the more advanced solution was to build a bridge using open gateway software that could convert between systems such as IMS on the mainframe and Oracle or Sybase on UNIX servers. Often this software was supplied by the relational database vendors themselves, a typical product being Sybase's NetGateway which requires a complementary product called OpenServer on the mainframe to support 'straight-through' SQL access to DB2 and via COBOL routines to other databases. In this way, data could be both retrieved and updated rather than merely copied, thus removing the necessity to rebuild terminal data entry screens for new applications. This approach was found to offer considerable locational transparency to users and made database interaction far easier.

Server applications are now being largely written on UNIX machines and these are accessed from X-terminals or PCs running suitable emulators. The predominant experience is that users are happier with the systems that result and that IT departments are offering a far more rapid response.

One of the complex migration issues that was faced by most of the organizations studied was that of network architecture, resilience and management. One organization viewed its networks as offering a hierarchy of service layers. The highest level enabled users to connect their workstations to various local servers. The next level provided workgroup server support. Both these layers relied chiefly on LAN technology and the workgroup level used matrix switching. The third layer linked the previous two to departmental and database servers using Ethernet switches. Finally, there was a massively complex connectivity layer that supported gateways to the mainframe-based legacy systems, access to WANs and message routing. Security is an important issue in the financial services sector and one company took it very seriously indeed. They adopted the Open Software Foundation's DCE security services standard, Kerberos, within their network management system. Routers were employed to connect different LAN systems such as Ethernet and Token Ring and to provide fire walls between network segments.

Within two years their distributed computing architecture enabled one company to construct several complex, business-critical and flexible applications. Typical systems move trading data from a mainframe network database and combine them with prices from a market data feed. The data are placed in server-based relational systems, validated interactively and then returned to the mainframe and passed simultaneously to local workstations. Other systems provide seamless 'straight-through' links between previously incompatible front and back office systems. Simpler client/server applications also can be implemented rapidly in this kind of environment.

The key technical features in this environment are distribution, connectivity and flexibility. These factors have led away from the waterfall-structured mainframe mind-set to a rapid development, evolutionary, downsized culture. To support the move it was soon realized that not only were advanced, object-oriented programming environments essential to exploit prototyping and describe the parallel, distributed, message based world but also the company would have to adopt object-oriented analysis and design approaches. Without sound object-oriented analysis and a project management culture that accepts its implications, the distributed solution will soon become even more cumbersome to manage than the mainframes it replaced. The key task for the companies studied in this section, at the time of writing, is the definition of such a sound approach. Part II of this book offers a modest suggestion as to what they should do in this respect.

Even without object technology, a number of successful applications of the CSC approach have received wide publicity. Taunton Cider claims significant benefits, in the context of information management, from switching from a centralized ICL mainframe to Sequent UNIX machines with INGRES.

The 1992 Winter Olympics used a client/server system based on a central DB2/CICS server and OS/2 clients with touch screens, to gather and distribute the scores from events, schedules and even weather predictions. It also handled over 10 000 e-mail messages using OfficeVision and was used by 40 000 officials at 13 sites. The touch screens were necessary because the system had to be used by people who were not only untrained but who often were wearing bulky cold-weather gloves.

Airline seat prices fluctuate hourly. By the time a customer confirms a booking the prices may have changed, allowing a cheaper seat to be found. However, a mainframe airline reservation system could not have computed the new situation quickly enough. One novel application of the client/server idea moves these calculations to a network of PCs. Here the client is the mainframe and the PCs are servers. This application offered savings to customers of up to $1 million per week. A survey carried out by KPMG in 1992 found that more than 90% of organizations that had downsized claimed they had achieved cost savings, though over 35% met resistance to change.

▤ 4.8 Difficulties in implementing distributed and client/server systems

These success stories should be juxtaposed with the increasing number of reports of unexpectedly high costs, abandoned projects and other indications that all is not well. The UK Performing Rights Society, which collects royalties for musicians and others, cancelled a huge downsizing project, writing off large sums. This was initially attributed to poor estimation of performance and project difficulty but ultimately ascribed to bad management. Similarly, the London Ambulance Service was forced to abandon a costly PC based command and control system and geographic information system (GIS) in 1992. However, close examination reveals that the problem was not so much the hardware and software chosen as the management issues and the overriding imperative to skimp on public expenditure – even at the risk of lives in this case. It turned out, incredibly, that the lead contractor didn't think it was the lead contractor. Another major downsizing project was abandoned in 1994, this time by Prudential Assurance.

It is evident that these failures cannot be blamed purely on the technology, since other organizations have succeeded, and one is forced to the conclusion that issues such as change management, development methods and staff motivation must have been the most significant factors.

The main pitfalls of CSC seem to be that:

(1) capital outlay is higher;
(2) getting the strategy right and managing change is always problematical;
(3) business may be temporarily disrupted by the changeover;
(4) control may be lost;
(5) skills may not be available;
(6) estimation is even harder than before; and

(7) existing 'structured' approaches offer no tools to manage the additional complexity.

There are other, more technical, problems such as the synchronization of clock times across machines. CSC is just more complicated to manage and this problem is compounded by the likely mix of technology from different manufacturers. Further, the purchase cost of equipment is only a tiny fraction of the cost of ownership. In 1992 the annual cost of owning a PC written off over five years was about £1,000 compared with a purchase price of just under that amount. Additional hidden costs, according to KPMG again, bring this annual figure up to nearly £5,500.

These pitfalls have resulted in a veritable onslaught on downsizing, largely orchestrated by companies and individuals with a vested interest in the perpetuation of the centralized, mainframe culture. Mainframe consultancy Xephon, for example, collected statistics to show that the mainframe was far more cost-effective per user for organizations over a certain size – roughly 200 users (Xephon, 1992). The bigger the system, the bigger the savings! They also emphasize the advantages of integrity, security and manageability and claim to be able to show that the relative costs will continue to favour the mainframe for some time and even decrease. Finally, Xephon warns that the savings that result from downsizing will not outweigh the disruption within a five-year period. However, the majority of case studies point the accusing finger at management-related problems rather than technology.

Mainframes also have their hidden costs. For example, the larger the system is, the greater the chance of a disaster. One advantage of client/server systems is that they consist of several smaller systems and each can be sized and customized for its task. The greater resilience of distributed computing can help with the problem of massive failure, though designing such a system is not trivial.

One of the main problems with distributed and client/server computing (CSC) compared to centralized computing is that the software becomes far more complex, and a strategy is required for managing or reducing this complexity. This is where object technology can help by providing tractable modelling techniques based on message passing, class libraries to protect developers from complex APIs, purpose-built routers and full-blown object request brokers to simplify location management and interprocess communication even further.

Distributed systems have to be far more complex to prevent problems that just do not arise with conventional systems. If one processor fails while another proceeds, the application may end up in an inconsistent state – leading to the need to be able to roll back portions of an application selectively and intelligently. Imagine what would happen if you posted a cheque to a country whose postal service failed, after you had deleted the money from your account on the assumption that it would be credited to that of the recipient.

There are also problems when two processors access the same data and when the network itself goes awry. Most of us have experienced network errors that are far more frequent than on standalone machines and consequently increased our save rate during tasks such as word processing. In fact, the trade-off between independent communicating nodes and a single network operating system is strongly reminiscent of the trade-off between planned, integrated, cooperative human societies and rampant individualism; each has its advantages – at least for some members.

CSC is far easier to implement in a workstation or PC environment than when mainframes are involved but, inevitably, the mainframe will remain the repository of corporate data for some time in many organizations. Most database vendors provide middleware to handle client/server connexions for their UNIX versions. They usually use Windows or OS/2 with TCP/IP. The lower-level, interpreted, drill-down type products use SQL strings as a protocol but for production systems this middleware must use precompilers that create compiled enquiries on the server and support RPCs invoked at run time. Sadly, the precompilers usually only work with one supplier's database product. Often the middleware cannot be tuned in terms of the number of rows fetched at a time or the size of network packets. This can lead to huge network bottlenecks.

The problem with mainframes is not that they cannot support a client/server system but that they cannot do so if the client and the server are on separate boxes. It is the network that causes part of the problem. TCP/IP provides far better services in this respect than do most mainframe interconnexion protocols such as LU6.2. Furthermore, UNIX systems do not require a specialized TP monitor (for example, CICS) to be added to the basic operating system. Doing so adds an overhead that is not often small.

Several proprietary products have emerged to address some or all of these difficulties. An example is Wall Data's RUMBA, which simplifies building client/server systems based on an AS/400 or 370 server. Also, standards are beginning to emerge to make database interconnectivity simpler. The SQL Access Group consists of over 30 database vendors concerned about this issue. Microsoft's ODBC is one result and Sybase's, quite similar, NetGateway technology can be used to provided gateways into quite old-fashioned databases such as IDMS or IMS.

As pointed out already, experience with client/server and downsizing in general suggests that migration is not simple. However, analysis of the downsizing disasters at both the London Ambulance Service and the Performing Rights Society indicates that management and design issues were chiefly responsible rather than any of the particular tools and techniques used.

Although many organizations are convinced that the client/server approach is safer and more flexible than earlier centralized or distributed approaches, recent experience studied by Coopers & Lybrand has also indicated that the reality of delivering the approach is not so easy. Working out where data should be handled for efficient processing, storage costs due to partitioned servers, deciding where the business rules should be stored, locking problems when data are kept on the server and locking delays due to two-phase commits all make life harder. The approach really requires much more intelligent networks that will be able to work out who handles what, based on current loadings, and know when to call the server and when to bundle requests. Not all applications are suitable for this approach but – for those that are – object orientation offers the most promising approach to design; for there is still no agreed method for client/server system development. Thus, while savings of around 30% are possible over a five-year period, according to a CSC Index report, without object-oriented methods and a sound migration strategy they are unlikely to be realized. In any case, a 30% improvement is just not enough for modern businesses.

Experience so far suggests that the main problem has been that latent support, training and culture change costs have exceeded the benefits expected from downsizing. However, it must be remembered that other benefits derive from the move to distributed, open, rightsized systems. Surveys have shown that the relative costs of CSC, while still high, are declining and that the initial cost of building the infrastructure has distorted early perceptions. A survey of 70 sites showed that migration costs to UNIX were up to three times higher than to mainstream platforms but these costs began to be recovered eventually – leading to high levels of saving along with gains in terms of user satisfaction. At one company, while the per-seat costs of CSC were slightly higher, productivity and time-to-market were vastly improved. Additional training costs were trimmed by increased use of computer based training. (*Computer Finance*, 1993b, 1993c, 1993a.)

Suppliers such as Hyperdesk and some users believe strongly that object request brokers are the right way to overcome the problems of client/server implementation. The chief, practical alternative is to base the move to CSC or distributed computing on the services offered by an object-oriented database. Here much of the middleware, locational transparency, message routing, version control, and replication services will be provided by the package, leaving the user free to concentrate on applications rather than infrastructure. The main differences between these two approaches are those of granularity and openness.

Most commercial object-oriented databases offer such support, though their architectures vary greatly in terms of how they handle the sharing of storage and computation between the client and server components. The advantage of this approach is that one can maintain a consistent, fully object-oriented model for the whole application. Also, storage, recovery, transaction management, concurrency and, often, version control are handled automatically by the database. The disadvantage is the potentially large cost of converting existing data and/or applications if the new system is to take advantage of the conceptual model, performance benefits and the possibilities of extending the system using object-oriented programming languages. As Ewald and Roy (1993) point out, where migration in the context of extensive legacy systems is contemplated, the disbenefits can predominate. They remark that existing applications often already have their own methods for instance management, whether as proprietary file management systems or relational database systems. They conclude that ORBs are often a better solution even though the latter may sacrifice a pure object-oriented style for flexibility. They are flexible precisely because they permit the use of existing applications, packages and other resources within the object-oriented framework. Reuse of such resources, however, is a coarse-grain reuse, sometimes violating the principle of small interfaces (Meyer, 1988; Graham, 1994a). Also, an ORB will not dictate exactly where and how applications should be coupled with pre-existing systems.

I believe that the key to successful distributed systems is the use of sound object-oriented analysis and design approaches and I have argued for this in Section 4.1. However, even here there are problems, mainly concerned with the need to compromise encapsulation for efficiency. For example, replicating data from an object seems to compromise encapsulation *prima facie*. Fortunately, ORBs and systems like CO-OPERATION attempt to remove the problem to a physical level by presenting the developer with a clean logical model that hides this complexity.

On balance, I think that the arguments for CSC will win out over the disadvantages and additional costs that early adopters have had to face in some cases. This will only be true, in the short term at least, for those organizations that face up to the cultural and change management problems that beset all migration projects.

4.8.1 Research issues

Distributed or shared object systems lead to complex problems in overcoming poor performance. Two-phase commits and replication inevitably slow things down a great deal. Daniels and Cook (1993) define two approaches to sharing: **single representation** and **multiple representation**. In the former there is one copy of the object that is sent messages. In the latter, a local copy receives messages and the system performs the necessary housekeeping. Single representation involves the complexities of remote procedure calls and can be inefficient. Further, in a language where object identity is maintained only locally, as with most object-oriented languages, programming becomes tricky. Therefore surrogate objects are usually used. We have seen an example of this approach in CO-OPERATION. Solving this problem is both a research problem and one that several practitioners have solved pragmatically, by force of necessity.

A similar open issue is the problem of concurrent control. Multiple accesses need to be serialized in some way and the simplest way seems to be to insist that each access with a thread of control takes place within a transaction.

The Carnot project at MCC is developing a suite of tools for building distributed, heterogeneous systems that will also act as a bridge to legacy systems. The project works closely with the SQL Access Group and is particularly concerned with database interoperability, perhaps using the Remote Database Access (RDA) protocol for client/server communication. Carnot ensures that updates are replicated in all locations to maintain consistency rather than relying on a centralized server. This makes it unlikely that there can be a single point of failure. Sybase's Replication Server follows a similar philosophy to avoid the delays inherent in two-phase commits. Carnot allows updates to be flagged as 'pending' where immediate commits are not possible, subject to some time limit – from hours to many months. Carnot is based on a suite of several independently developed systems including the ORION object-oriented database, the CYC knowledge base (see Lenat and Guha (1990) for details of CYC or Graham (1994a) for an overview of both projects), the Rosette parallel computation manager and the GIE interface builder. Just as the ORION project eventually led to the commercial product ITASCA and influenced several others, it is likely that the Carnot research will be highly influential on future interoperability products though it seems unlikely that such a huge and ambitious amalgam of advanced technologies could be marketed widely in its current state.

Distributed systems are obvious candidates for object-oriented modelling. Network nodes can be viewed as coarse-grain, active objects defined by their operations, with message passing as the invocation mechanism. There have thus been several attempts to extend object-oriented programming languages to deal with concurrency. However, such attempts have not always been efficient because existing operating systems are not compatible with the approach in terms of both architecture and granularity and an impedance mismatch often results. Research into concurrent object-oriented languages is very active but has produced few clear results so far.

4.9 Summary

Object technology makes the sharing by different systems possible. This chapter emphasized the rôle of object-oriented models as a way of describing and understanding distributed systems.

Distributed computing is in some sense a return from the days of the PC to those of the mainframe, only now the mainframe is distributed and harder than ever to manage. Nevertheless, the advantages outweigh the extra complexity. Distributed computing is, in principle, more resilient, fast, flexible, scaleable and open.

The operating systems of distributed systems can be *distributed* or *networked*. There are three data management strategies for distributed computing: centralized, replicated and partitioned. We examined several kinds of distributed computer architecture: client/server, multi-client/multi-server and peer-to-peer. We distinguished four distribution models: database server, transaction server, peer-to-peer and distributed front-end. The peer-to-peer model is the most general but the most difficult to program and manage. Latency is an important concept in the design of any object-oriented system, distributed or not.

Existing structured methods contribute little and impede progress with distributed systems. Object technology provides a natural way of modelling distributed applications. Network nodes can be regarded as abstract data types or objects. However, inheritance and composition links shouldn't cross the network. Associations that span the network should be minimized for reasons of efficiency. Typically, a system layer should be implemented at a single node. Nodes are best regarded as SOMA layers. The object-oriented model both assumes and implies locational transparency.

Distributed systems can be implemented by building the necessary infrastructure, network support, remote procedure calls, and so on by hand, building a wrapper, using proprietary tools, utilizing an object-oriented database or using an object request broker.

Client/server computing was defined as the division of processing and data between one or more front-end client machines that run applications and a single back-end server machine that provides a service to each client. Client/server computing is a special case of distributed computing. Object-oriented systems are nothing other than, possibly layered, multi-client/ multi-server or peer-to-peer systems. RPCs violate locational transparency but this is sometimes hidden from the user by clever network software. Cooperative processing is a special case of distributed computing that offers peer-to-peer communication between servers.

Database tools are often organized around the client/server metaphor. With relational systems, the ones that make use of stored procedures are able to reduce network traffic considerably. The difficulty is that encapsulation is not enforced and the discipline of a robust approach to object-oriented analysis is required. Object-oriented systems give these benefits automatically.

We discussed several benefits of and difficulties with the client/server approach.

Genuine distributed databases are not yet well supported. In future, databases should incorporate the full-content retrieval capabilities of information retrieval (IR) systems. A particularly important application of this theory is its use in retrieving data from a reuse repository. SOMA object models can be used to describe the structure and semantics of information. The central problem of IR is that of finding the information you require. This has particular significance for object-oriented developers because of the need to retrieve information about class libraries.

The productivity of office workers has stagnated despite increased usage of computers. Computer-supported cooperative work amplifies the productivity of office workers. There are also strong links to the technology of BPR. Work-flow software automates existing, repetitive, multi-actor processes while groupware supports *ad hoc* forms of cooperation and coordination. Re-engineers need tools that perform 'what-if' analyses. Object technology offers a solution because business processes can be modelled as arrangements of communicating objects. SOMA supports this activity directly. We discussed the contradictions inherent in arguments for increasing empowerment without questioning the economic *status quo*. Any natural language description of a business process translates naturally to an object model; at least when rules can be represented. A rule based, object-oriented description may be animated to provide business process simulations that may be used for scenario modelling to help find the 'great idea'. A task script analysis leads directly to an object-oriented description and this model may be used to critique the current work-flow in order to obliterate some work.

Many current IT practices lock organizations into their existing methods of working. The move to rapid development is thus very important for IT within the adaptable business that is adopting BPR.

ORBs remove much of the need for complex RPCs. Applications need not be written in an object-oriented manner since the ORB effectively provides a wrapper. ORBs bring the benefit of OT to the world of systems integration.

The history of the OMG was outlined and the architecture of a typical DOMS described. Some ORB products are not CORBA compliant but this means, in some cases, that they have extra benefits. Some DOMS have features to support blackboard architectures. The standardization of interfaces, brought about by object request brokers and initiatives such as SunSoft's DOE project, offer the possibility of reusing a wide range of commercially available objects in applications. DOE will incorporate NeXTstep technology. Soon, all computing will be distributed computing.

A number of successful applications of the approach have received wide publicity. These success stories should be juxtaposed to reports of failures; but, mainframe systems are not without problems. On balance, the advantages of CSC outweigh its problems. OT helps with the management of the additional complexity. However, it is the management issues that predominate.

The first half of the 1990s saw many organizations undergoing major changes in technology; principally moving away from systems based on mainframes to distributed systems. Some of these experiences were discussed. Where the target is a distributed computing environment object technology **is** a migration strategy, possibly the only one available.

The key technical features in this environment are distribution, connectivity and flexibility. These factors have led away from the waterfall-structured mainframe mind-set to a rapid development, evolutionary, downsized culture. Advanced, object-oriented programming environments are essential to exploit prototyping and describe the parallel, distributed, message based world. Object-oriented analysis and design approaches are needed. Without sound object-oriented analysis and a project management culture that accepts its implications the distributed solution will soon become even more cumbersome to manage than the mainframes it replaced.

We examined some research issues, including those raised by the Carnot project and its particular contribution to interoperability.

≡ 4.10 Bibliographical notes

Mullender (1989) is an advanced, comprehensive – but slightly dated now – introduction to most of the issues of distributed system development. Daniels and Cook (1993) offer a penetrating discussion of the issues surrounding the sharing of persistent objects together with useful comments on locking strategies and other important related issues. Shafer and Taylor (1993) describe, in outline, NCR's CO-OPERATION workgroup computing application.

Durham (1992), in what must be the best concise and accurate survey of the topic of groupware I have seen, describes the state of the art and covers the practical issues in collaborative computing. Incidentally, Tony Durham's *IT Horizons* is probably the best value and highest quality condensed news analysis service concerning itself exclusively with advanced IT issues. More information can be obtained from Tony on +44-181-960-0536 (Tel.) or tdurham@cix.compulink.co.uk (e-mail).

Ovum (1992) has produced a report on work-flow software that describes some enlightening success stories. The field of CSCW is surveyed in Greenberg (1991) and Wilson (1990). Diaper (1993) is a collection of papers on the state of the art. There are also several journals devoted totally or partially to the subject including *CSCW* (Kluwer), *Collaborative Computing* (Chapman & Hall) and *The Interdisciplinary Journal of Human Computer Interaction* (Butterworth).

Khoshafian *et al.* (1992) is a manifesto about building office automation systems using a combination of techniques from relational databases, object-oriented databases, expert systems, CSCW, graphical user interfaces, multimedia storage systems, network technology and full-content information retrieval. They are effectively proposing a product to meet the needs of office automation and, presumably, are building such a thing for sale. However, the book is a useful survey of the underlying technology covering a broad range of topics not usually brought together.

Andleigh and Gretzinger (1992) provide much useful background information on software engineering, databases and distributed processing. The method is applied in some detail to the design of a distributed financial trading system.

Bapat (1994) offers a comprehensive discussion of how to apply object-oriented design to modelling computer networks.

Agha *et al.* (1993) is a collection of papers discussing many of the difficult issues related to concurrency in object-oriented systems and the tension between the two areas of research. A special issue of *Object Magazine* was devoted to distributed object management in February/March 1993. The September 1993 edition of the *Communications of the ACM* is devoted to concurrent object-oriented programming and contains several important papers.

5

Building expert systems

Machines will be capable, within twenty years, of doing any work that a man can do.

Herbert Simon (The Shape of
Automation for Men and
Management, 1965)

It is easy to deride Simon's error with hindsight; it is harder to see how it could have arisen. His error was not just excessive optimism concerning computers but relates to an erroneous view of the nature of tools and of human intelligence. Tools help us to perform labour; they do not perform labour themselves. Should they do so, they would become intelligent beings and not mere artefacts. What then constitutes an intelligent being and could a computer be one? Simon, and most workers in artificial intelligence since, have regarded intelligence as a property of the organism. Views differ as to whether it is rule based (cf. Chomsky, 1980), based on a society of symbolic mental agents (Minsky, 1985b) or emergent from a complex neural network of simple processors. What these views have in common is that they all hold that the individual brain is the seat of intelligence. Even major critics of the programme of AI such as the Dreyfus brothers (1986) acquiesce in this model of a human society composed of atomic intelligences. They argue that artificial intelligence is impossible because the individual's emotional and mental needs are related to his environment and context but fail to see that the intelligence of humans is actually distributed among social individuals. What is obvious for ants is somehow impossible to accept for humans. I cannot accept any of these views since, it seems to me, intelligence only arises in the historical context of human society, human interaction and cooperative production. Harry Collins (1990) gives striking empirical evidence for this in a study of the sociology of knowledge related to a particular skill: growing experimental semiconductor crystals. Collins and a colleague, Rodney Green, adopted completely different approaches to knowledge acquisition. The latter applied expert system knowledge elicitation techniques and tried to model the knowledge in a computer system, as well as trying to gain his own level of expertise. Collins, by contrast, became an apprentice to the subject-matter expert and essayed to increase his expertise in this way. The book reports the results and shows that symbolic representations cannot capture what scientific communities know. The abilities of machines come about only because they are embedded in our society. Even Collins' expert is said to have relied heavily on the knowledge of others. This view of the social nature of intelligence becomes of significant practical importance in object-oriented analysis when, as discussed in Chapter 7, we are interpreting task scripts to model the requirements for a new system.

The purpose of this chapter is twofold. Its primary purpose is to show how object technology can be applied to building expert systems or, more importantly, systems that have an important knowledge-based component. This leads us to look at expert systems tools and the influence that object-oriented ideas have had on them. The second purpose is to introduce the reader to some concepts from artificial intelligence (AI) that will be useful in Part II, notably rule based representation of knowledge and the theory of scripts.

5.1 Fundamentals of expert systems

Object-oriented programming has been associated with AI research for many years and has affected the technology of expert systems greatly. Many expert systems packages incorporate object-oriented features. This means that expert systems built with such tools can potentially deliver the key benefits of object orientation: reusable and extensible code. However, many current products only apply principles such as encapsulation to a limited extent.

The term **expert systems** as used here is a general one that describes a mode of building computer systems that can give advice or make decisions in a narrowly defined area at or near the level of a human expert. There are two kinds of such systems: systems that take decisions, which are chiefly process controllers, and systems that act as decision support systems, giving advice but not making decisions. This definition is couched in terms of what expert systems do. More importantly, expert systems are defined by how they do it; by their architecture. The most important architectural feature is that knowledge about a problem is stored separately from the code which applies the knowledge to the problem in hand. Expert systems are sometimes called **knowledge based systems** to emphasize this point.

5.1.1 The components of a knowledge based system

The repository of chunks of knowledge in an expert system is referred to as the **knowledge base** and the mechanism that applies the knowledge to the data presented to it as the **inference engine**. This characteristic architecture is illustrated in Figure 5.1.

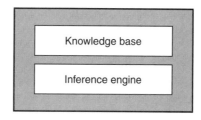

Figure 5.1 The architecture of expert systems.

It is now widely accepted that there are essentially three components of a knowledge based computer system. Firstly, there is the underlying environment of symbol and value manipulation which all computer systems share and which can be thought of as the programming languages and support environment; editors, floating point processors, data structures, compilers, and so on. This is represented by the grey area in Figure 5.1. Secondly, we have the structure of the knowledge base itself including methods of representation and access, and lastly there must be some techniques for applying the knowledge in a rational manner to the problem at hand. This third element is the inference engine.

The knowledge base and the inference engine are separated from one another to facilitate maintenance. After all, in most cases knowledge will change over time and one does not want to rewrite the inference engine whenever a new rule is added. In real systems this separation is achieved to a greater or lesser extent and may be regarded as an ideal to be striven for. However, from another point of view it is clear that this separation is artificial. The manner of reasoning with knowledge is affected profoundly by the way it is presented to us and represented by us. Conversely, the essential nature of our knowledge about objects is characterized to a large extent by our innate logical processes. Cognitive and social processes also play a part in human knowledge if not in computer systems also.

Knowledge about causal relationships is usually stored in the form of **rules** of the form 'IF A THEN X'. Unlike the if/then statements found in conventional languages like COBOL or FORTRAN, rule languages in expert systems are typically **declarative** or equivalently **non-procedural**; that is, the order in which the rules are written is not important. Knowledge about entities or objects is sometimes stored in structures known as objects or **frames**, also called classes or units. Frames are similar to relations in databases, except that attributes can be created at run time and both attributes and values may be inherited. They are also very similar to objects except that the procedures are attached to visible attributes and there is no notion of encapsulation. The latter presupposes that the frames are organized into a classification network whereby, for example, the frame for an employee inherits all the attributes and operations of a person frame, of which it is a special case. Inheritance avoids much of the need for repetition in coding and in storage. In artificial intelligence the attributes of frames are called **slots**. Attributes may contain procedures as well as data. Procedures that fire automatically when a slot is referenced are called **demons**. Though lacking in terms of encapsulation, frames are very similar to the objects found in object-oriented programming systems, although the details of inheritance may differ slightly. If anything, frame systems have more generalized and powerful inheritance régimes. Another important way to represent knowledge is as **procedures**, as found in conventional languages. There are various other ways to represent knowledge, but rules, procedures and frames are the main ones used in commercial expert systems at present.

An inference engine offers one or more means of applying knowledge to data. The most common strategies are known as **backward chaining** and **forward chaining**. Backward chaining or **goal-directed** reasoning is typical of diagnostic or advice-giving systems. It involves deriving a plausible reason for some given fact. For example, given the fact 'the patient has spots' a medical expert system might reason that the patient could have been among young children recently since young children often have measles and measles causes spots. Forward chaining or **data-directed** inference takes all data present and attempts to discover as much as possible by applying as many rules as possible to them, or filling as many frame slots as possible. This is typical of process control and scheduling applications. Most expert systems involve a mixture of backward and forward chaining and other strategies to reduce blind search.

An **expert systems shell** is an expert system that has had the knowledge base removed and some means of putting in new knowledge added – an editor usually. Thus, a shell is a software tool that allows expert systems to be built more rapidly.

Two other features that separate expert systems from other computer systems are that they can:

- provide an explanation of their reasoning;
- incorporate qualitative or judgemental reasoning and manage uncertainty.

If the last two features are both present, expert systems can offer multiple conclusions ranked by a measure of confidence. Both features, if required, tend to increase the cost of system building. Built-in explanation facilities in the shell are useful debugging aids but are rarely suitable for user enquiries. Useful facilities for explanation of the system's reasoning to users usually must be handcrafted.

There are several techniques for managing uncertainty, the most common being:

- Reasoning explicitly using verbal labels for uncertain terms
- Certainty factors
- Bayesian probability

- What-if facilities
- Fuzzy sets
- Truth maintenance systems

Reasoning about uncertainty adds to the complexity of a system, and the knowledge acquisition associated with specifying it, but permits it to tackle more complex problems.

We will examine the knowledge base and the inference engine separately in the following sections. In the next section the reader is asked to bear in mind that object modelling will be regarded in this book as a form of knowledge representation.

☐ 5.2 Knowledge representation

Starting from the point of view of computer science, most of us are familiar with the notion of data; that is, unstructured sets of numbers, facts and symbols. These data can convey information only by virtue of some structure or decoding mechanism. In the limiting case this distinction can be illustrated by two people who may communicate via a channel that may only carry one message consisting of a single symbol. The datum, the symbol itself, carries no information except by virtue of the presence of the channel, whose structure determines that the receiver may learn from the absence of a symbol as well from its transmission. This structure is, in turn, determined by the shared knowledge of the sender and receiver. Two points emerge from this example. Information always has a context while data may be context free; thus if I say 'she shot up', that is a datum for which I would need to explain whether the person in question was an astronaut or a heroin addict in order to convey unambiguous information. Knowledge is usually seen as a concept at a higher level of abstraction, and there is a sense in which this is true. For example, '1000' is a datum, '1000 millibars at noon' could be information about the weather in some situations but 'Most people feel better when the pressure rises above 1000 millibars' is knowledge about barometric information and people. The realization that much knowledge is expressed in the form of heuristic descriptions or rules of thumb is what gives rise to the conception of knowledge as more abstract than information.

Apart from asking what it is, epistemologists have traditionally raised several other problems concerning knowledge, including:

- How it may be classified;
- How it is obtained;
- Whether it has objective reality;
- If it is limited in principle.

As a preliminary attempt at classification we might note that there are several evidently different types of knowledge at hand; knowledge about objects, events, task performance, and even about knowledge itself. If we know something about objects such as tomatoes we will probably know that tomatoes are red. However, we are still prepared to recognize a green tomato as a tomato; so that contradictions often coexist within our knowledge. Object knowledge is often expressed in the form of assertions, although this is by no means the only available formalism and OO-style objects or frames are particularly well suited to this purpose. Here are a few typical assertions:

(1) Tomatoes are red.
(2) Zoe is very lively.
(3) This house is built with bricks and mortar.

Knowledge of causality, however, is expressed typically as a chain of statements relating cause to effect. A typical such statement might be:

If you boil tomatoes with the right accompaniments, chutney results.

Such knowledge is well represented by sets of rules that can be chained together or by logical propositions within a particular logical calculus.

To perform a task as commonplace as walking requires a very complex interacting system of knowledge about balance, muscle tone, and so on, much of which is held subconsciously and is deeply integrated with our biological hardware. Knowledge about cognition, often called meta-knowledge, also needs to be represented when such questions as 'What do I know?' and 'How useful or complete is a particular knowledge system or inference strategy?' are raised. This, I hope, shows that there is no clear boundary between knowledge and inference, as practices. Each interpenetrates the other; we have inference with knowledge and knowledge about inference.

There are various dimensions along which knowledge can be evaluated:

Scope	What does it cover?
Granularity	How detailed is it?
Uncertainty	How likely, certain or plausible is it?
Completeness	Might we have to retract conclusions if new knowledge comes to light?
Consistency	How easily can we live with its contradictions?
Modality	Can we avoid its consequences?

The above dimensions are all connected with some form of uncertainty. This arises from the contradictory nature of knowledge. Knowledge presents itself in two basic forms, as absolute and relative. To understand this, consider the whole of the history of science, which is an attempt to arrive at a knowledge of the environment we inhabit and change our relationship with it. The scientist develops various theories that explain the experimental evidence and are further verified in practice. S/he never suspects that any theory is comprehensively correct, at least not nowadays. Newton's models overthrew the theories of earlier times and were in their turn overthrown by Einstein's. If nature exists beyond, before and apart from us then it represents, in all its complexity, an absolute truth which is (in principle) beyond knowledge because nature is not in itself human and knowledge is. To assume otherwise is to assert either that nature is a totally human construct or that the whole may be totally assimilated by a fragment of itself. This is not to say that the finite may not know the infinite, only that the knowledge may only be relative. Otherwise the finite would contain the infinite and thus become infinite itself. Thus all truth seeking aims at the absolute but achieves the relative and here it is that we see why all knowledge must perforce be uncertain. This is why the correct handling of uncertainty is one of the primary concerns for builders of knowledge based systems of any sort.

The dimensions of knowledge mentioned above all will have some bearing on the techniques used to represent knowledge. If we choose logic as the representation then, if our knowledge is incomplete, non-monotonic logic will be required in preference to first-order predicate logic and in the presence of uncertainty a logic capable of handling it will be required. Similar remarks apply to inconsistent knowledge where contradiction must be handled by either the logic or the control structure or metalogic. Modality will require the use of a logic that can deal with necessity and possibility.

If, on the other hand we choose objects, frames or semantic network representations, the scope and granularity will affect the amount of storage we can expect to use. For this, it is useful to have some metrics. Granularity is often measured in **chunks**. Anderson (1976) defines a chunk to be a learnt configuration of symbols which comes to act as a single symbol. The passage between levels of representation is an important theme in AI research and has great bearing on the practical question of efficiency of storage and execution. Generally speaking, you should choose a granularity close to that adopted by human experts, if this can be discerned, and use chunking whenever gains are not made at the expense of understandability.

5.2.1 Rules and production systems

The concept of reducing systems to a few primitives plus production rules for generating the rest of the system goes back to Post – Post, Church and Turing all worked on the idea of formal models of computers independently. Post's original work was concerned with the theory of semigroups, which is of interest in algebraic models of language. Newell and Simon (1963) introduced them in the form in which we find them in knowledge based systems as part of their work on GPS, the general problem solver, which was an attempt to build an intelligent system which did not rely for its problem-solving abilities on a store of domain specific knowledge but would *inter alia* generate production rules as required. For example, Marvin the robot wants to go to Boston. He is faced with an immediate problem before this goal can be satisfied: how to get there. He can fly, walk/swim, ride a bus or train, and so on. To make the decision he might weigh up the cost and the journey time and decide to fly, but this strategy will not work because he is not at an airport. Thus he must solve a subproblem of how to get to an airfield that runs a service that takes him close to Boston. In production rules his reasoning so far (he hasn't solved the whole problem yet) might look like this:

1. If I want to go to Boston then I must choose a transport mode
2. Flying is a mode of transport which I will choose
3. If you are at an airport then you can fly
4. I am not at an airport
5. If I want to be at an airport then I must choose a transport mode

Incidentally, we should note the distinction between Marvin's goal, being in Boston, and his tasks, the steps to be taken to get there. All reasoning of this nature can be equally well viewed as goal decomposition or task decomposition. This viewpoint will prove important in Chapter 7.

The five statements above consist of assertions and productions and together these represent some of the knowledge Marvin needs to begin reasoning about his problems. There are many reasoning strategies or inference methods he can employ. For the time being we are interested in the representation of knowledge by production rules, as these IF/THEN constructions are known.

The left hand side, A, of a production rule of the form:

If A then X

is called its **antecedent** clause and the right hand side, X, its **consequent**. It may be interpreted in many ways: if a certain condition is satisfied then a certain action is appropriate; if a certain statement is true then another can be inferred; if a certain syntactic structure is present then some other can be generated grammatically. In general, A and X can be complex statements constructed from simpler ones using the connectives AND and OR and the NOT operator. In practice only A is permitted this rich structure so that a typical production would look like this:

IF (animal bears live young AND animal suckles young)
OR location is mammal-house
THEN animal is mammal

The parentheses disambiguate the precedence of the connectives and avoid the need to repeat clauses unnecessarily. Production systems combine rules as if there were an OR between the rules; that is, between the antecedents of rules with the same consequent. A production rule system may be regarded as a machine that takes as input values of the variables mentioned in antecedent clauses and puts out values for the consequent variables. Clearly, it is equivalent to a system with one machine for each consequent variable unless we allow feedback among the variables. When feedback is present we enter the realms of inference.

Production rules are easy for humans to understand and, since each rule represents a small independent granule of knowledge, can be easily added to or subtracted from a knowledge base. For this reason they have formed the basis of several well-known, large-scale applications such as DENDRAL (Barr and Feigenbaum, 1981), MYCIN (Shortliffe, 1976) and PROSPECTOR (Duda *et al.*, 1976). They form the basis of nearly all expert system shells. Because the rules are, in principle, independent from each other, they support a declarative style of programming which considerably reduces maintenance problems. However, care must be taken that contradictory rules are not introduced since this can lead to inefficiency at best and incorrect conclusions at worst. Another advantage that has been exploited in expert systems is the ease with which a production system can stack up a record of a program's use of each rule and thus provide rudimentary explanations of the system's reasoning. Lastly, productions make fairly light demands on a processor, although a large amount of memory or secondary storage will typically be required.

Precisely because they are memory intensive, production systems can be very inefficient. Also, it is difficult to model associations among objects or processes. This makes taking short cuts in reasoning difficult to implement. The declarative style makes algorithms extremely difficult to represent and flow of control is hard to supervise for a system designer. Lastly, the formalism – as described so far – makes no allowances for uncertain knowledge. For these reasons, it is now becoming more common to find that knowledge based systems use several different kinds of knowledge representation, usually a mixture of rules, objects and procedures. The formalism can be directly extended to cope with some kinds of uncertainty.

5.2.2 Knowledge and inference: cognition and activity

The question of how human beings store and manipulate knowledge is a question we only touch upon here. The questions of how knowledge comes about and how it may be substantiated, what philosophers call the problem of cognition, or epistemology, is sufficiently neglected in the existing literature of knowledge engineering to deserve a little attention, though. We also ask how the interconnexion between knowledge and inference is mediated. In my view, it is this relationship that leads to the need for uncertainty management in expert systems.

Consider two important questions about the representation of knowledge. First there was the question of how knowledge is represented in the human or animal brain, and now there is that of what structures may be used for computer representation. The first question is the concern of cognitive psychology and psychoanalysis and will not exercise us greatly here. However, the theories of psychologists and psychoanalysts have much to offer in the way of ideas and we will be using several of them in Chapter 7 as object discovery techniques. The interdisciplinary subject of artificial intelligence has been defined as 'the study of mental faculties through the use of computational models' (Charniak and McDermott, 1985); exactly the reverse of what interests builders of knowledge based systems. Perhaps this is why there is such confusion between the fields today. One important point to make categorically is that no one knows how the human brain works and no one could give a prescription for the best computer knowledge representation formalism even if they did. Until some pretty fundamental advances are made, the best bet for system builders is to use whatever formalism best suits the task at hand, pragmatically.

Apart from its ability to be abstract at various levels, knowledge is concerned with action. It is concerned with practice in the world. Knowing how people feel under different atmospheric conditions helps us to respond better to their moods, work with them or even improve their air-conditioning (if we have some knowledge about ventilation engineering as well). Incidentally, it also assumes the existence of various socially evolved measuring devices, such as the barometer, thermometer and so on. Knowledge is a guide to informed practice and relates to information as a processor of it; that is, we **understand** knowledge but we **process** information. It is no use knowing that people respond well to high pressure if you cannot measure that pressure. Effective use of knowledge leads to the formulation of plans for action and ultimately to deeper understanding. This leads to a subsidiary definition that knowledge is concerned with using information effectively. The next level of abstraction might be called 'theory'.

From this point of view, inference is to knowledge as processing is to information. Inference is the method used to transform perceptions (perhaps via some symbolic representation) into a form suitable for reconversion into actions. It may also be viewed as an abstraction from practical activity. In our experience of the world we observe, both individually and collectively, that certain consequences follow from certain actions. We give this phenomenon the name causality, and say that action A 'causes' perception B. Later (both in ontogenesis and philogenesis[1]) we generalize this to include causal relations between external events independent of ourselves. From there it is a short step (one originally taken at the end of the Bronze Age) to the idea that ideas are related in a similar way; that symbol A can 'imply' symbol B. This process of abstraction corresponds, according to Piaget, to the process of child development. Historically, it corresponds to the development of the division of labour. In other words, just as tool making and social behaviour make knowledge possible, so the interdependencies of the world of nature are developed into the

---

[1] Ontogenesis is the origin or developmental history of the being (the individual in this sense) and philogenesis the origin of the species. I deliberately choose these terms to remind the reader of the ancient and famous Greek aphorism: 'Philogenesis recapitulates ontogenesis'.

abstract relations of human thinking; part of this system of relationships corresponding to inference.

Of course, computers do not partake of social activity, nor yet do they create tools (although they may manufacture and use them if we include robots in our perception of computing machinery). As far as inference is concerned we cannot expect computers to encompass the richness and depth of human reasoning (at least not in the foreseeable future). For many thousands of years it has been convenient, for certain applications in the special sciences, to reason with a formalized subset of human reasoning. This 'formal logic' has been the basis of most western technological developments and, while not capturing the scope of human informal reasoning, is immensely powerful in resolving many practical problems. Thus, we are converging on a definition of inference which will serve the purposes of knowledge engineering. Inference in this sense is the abstract, formal process by which conclusions may be drawn from premises. It is a special kind of meta-knowledge about the abstract relationships between symbols representing knowledge.

Many philosophers have questioned whether true artificial intelligence is possible in principle. In my view the question is merely maladroit. Clearly, if we are able in future to engineer genetically (or otherwise) an artificial human being there is no reason (excluding spurious religious arguments) why the constructed entity should not be 'intelligent' by any normal criteria. If, on the other hand, the question is posed as to whether electronic computers of the type currently existing or foreseeable can pass the Turing test, then matters are a little different. Human cognition is a process mediated by both society and the artefacts of Man's construction. It may well be that no entity (be it a computer or a totally dissimilar organism from outer space) could ever dissemble its true non-social, non-tool-making character sufficiently to deceive the testers. My belief is that artificial intelligence in this sense is impossible (cf. Graham, 1994c) but that useful results are to be obtained by trying to achieve an approximation.

Let us now descend from these abstract considerations and ask how computers can be made to simulate reasoning.

▤ 5.3 Inference in knowledge based systems

Given that knowledge is stored in a computer in some convenient representation or representations, the system will require facilities for navigating through and manipulating the knowledge if anything is to be achieved at all. Inference in the usual logical sense is this process of drawing valid conclusions from premises. In our wider sense it is any computational mechanism whereby stored knowledge can be applied to data and information structures to arrive at conclusions which are to be plausible rather than valid in the strict logical sense. This, of course, poses problems in relation to how to judge whether the conclusions are reasonable, and how to represent knowledge about how to test conclusions and how to evaluate plausibility. Thus, we can see that knowledge representation and inference are inextricably bound together, though as opposites. Before exploring the inference strategies of expert systems we introduce some ideas from formal logic. We first deal with the rules for making individual inferences. The next subsection contains a little more in the way of mathematical notation than other parts of this book and may be safely omitted by readers who find this sort of thing off-putting, who may skip straight to Section 5.3.2.

5.3.1 Inference methods and logic

Before moving on to the more complex inference strategies to be found in expert systems, we must first look at the basics of simple inferences as found in Aristotelian logic. In doing this we follow closely the treatment to be found in McCawley (1981). We start with some definitions. A **formal system** comes equipped with the connectives:

$\wedge$ (and), $\vee$ (or), $\neg$ (not), $\Rightarrow$ (implies), $\Leftrightarrow$ (if and only if) and (sometimes) $=$

There are (at least) two quantification symbols: $\forall$ (for all) and $\exists$ (there exists at least one).

The primitive symbols are usually taken to include only $\forall$, $\wedge$, $\vee$, $\Rightarrow$ and $\neg$. These symbols can be used together with propositions to make up sentences, and these are valid sentences when they follow, by specified rules of inference, from a few selected sentences called axioms. The rules of inference we will use here fall into two classes, called rules of introduction and rules of elimination. The introduction rule for $\wedge$ says that, for example, if the sentences:

1. Jim is American
2. Sophie is English
3. Anders is Norwegian

are all true, then we may infer that the sentence:

4. Jim is American and Sophie is English and Anders is Norwegian

is also true. The corresponding elimination rule says that if the previous sentence is true then we may infer that any one of the earlier three holds. Similarly, we can state rules for the other connectives and the quantifiers. We may state all these rules more succinctly in the following rather general form as **rules of inference** as shown in Figure 5.2, where the horizontal lines denote the inference step. The statements of the missing rules are left as an exercise for the reader.

The rules of $\neg$ introduction and elimination are known as **reductio ad absurdum** and the law of the **excluded middle** respectively. They are not valid in

∧ introduction	∧ elimination	∨ introduction	∨ elimination
p q r —————— p ∧ q ∧ r	p ∧ q ∧ r —————— p	p —————— p ∨ q ∨ r	p ∨ q ∨ r —————— one of p,q,r

⇒ introduction	⇒ elimination (*modus ponens*)
p ⇒ q q ⇒ r —————— p ⇒ r	p ⇒ q p —————— q

∀ introduction (generalization)	∀ elimination
p —————— ∀ x, p(x)	∀ x such that q(x) ⇒ p(x) q(a) —————— p(a)

∃ introduction	...
p(a) —————— (∃ x) p(x)	

Figure 5.2 Some rules of inference.

all logical systems. For the purposes of reasoning, one of the most interesting rules is ⇒ elimination which is also known as *modus ponens*. This rule sanctions inferences of the form:

1. If Gaius is a man, then he is mortal
2. Gaius is a man
3. Therefore: Gaius is mortal

The rule of ⇒ introduction just says that implication is transitive and sanctions the following type of argument:

1. Whoever committed the murder left by the window
2. Anyone leaving by the window would have mud on his boots
3. If the butler committed the murder, then he left by the window
4. Therefore he has mud on his boots
5. So, if the butler did it he has muddy boots

Returning to *modus ponens* as a model of reasoning forwards from premises to conclusion, we can put the case as follows. From a fact p and a rule $p \Rightarrow q$ we may deduce a new fact q with certainty. Two other rules of inference which follow from those given above are *modus tollens* and the *resolution* principle, which latter is the basis of many automatic theorem-proving systems (Robinson, 1965).

Modus tollens	*Resolution*
$p \Rightarrow q$	$p \lor q$
$\neg q$	$\neg q \lor r$
———	———
$\neg p$	$p \lor r$

Modus tollens is apparently very different from *modus ponens*; we are reasoning backwards from the falsity of a conclusion to the falsity of the premise. If the butler does not have muddy boots then he is not guilty but if he does, no conclusion can be drawn. *Modus tollens* is much harder for humans to understand and compute with although it is similar to a lot of problem-solving behaviour, as we will see later when we encounter backward chaining. For example, suppose p = 'It is raining' and q = 'It is cloudy', then the two kinds of inference are exemplified by:

If it is raining then it must be cloudy
If it is not cloudy then it can't be raining

In the latter case we are implicitly invoking the rule of *modus tollens* on the implication 'if raining then cloudy'.

5.3.2 Forward, backward and mixed chaining strategies

Up to now we have only considered the problem of how to infer the truth value of one proposition from another using a rule of inference in just one step. Clearly however, there will be occasions when such inferences (or proofs) will involve long chains of reasoning using the rules of inference and some initial suppositions (or axioms). We now turn to the generalizations of *modus ponens* and *modus tollens* which feature strongly in all expert systems and are supplied as standard code in many expert system shells and in the *SOMATiK* rule engine. Understanding these forward and backward reasoning strategies will be crucial in interpreting and using rules to describe contracts for objects as discussed in Chapter 6.

FORWARD
CHAINING

To fix ideas, consider an expert system whose knowledge is represented in the form of production rules and whose domain is the truth of abstract propositions; A, B, C, ...

The knowledge base consists solely of rules as follows.

Rule 1: A and B and C   implies D
Rule 2: D and F   implies G
Rule 3: E   implies F
Rule 4: F   implies B
Rule 5: B   implies C
Rule 6: G   implies H
Rule 7: I   implies J
Rule 8: A and F   implies H

To start with, assume that normal two-valued logic and *modus ponens* are available, and that the expert system has been asked whether proposition H is true given that propositions A and F are true. We will show that the system may approach the problem in two quite distinct ways. Assume for the present that the computer stores these rules on a sequential device such as magnetic tape, so that it must access the rules in order unless it rewinds to Rule 1.

What I am about to describe is the forward chaining inference strategy. This itself has several variants. We may pass through the rules until a single rule fires, we may continue until all rules have been processed once, or we may continue firing in either manner until either the conclusion we desire has been achieved or the database of proven propositions ceases to be changed by the process. A little thought shows that this gives at least four different varieties of forward chaining. This will become clearer as we proceed.

The assumption is that A and F are known to be true at the outset. If we apply all the rules to this database the only rules that fire are 4 and 8 and the firing of Rule 8 assigns the value true to H, which is what we were after. Suppose now that Rule 8 is excised from the knowledge base. Can we still prove H? This time only Rule 4 fires, so we have to rewind and apply the rules again to have any chance of proving the target proposition. Below we show what happens to the truth values in the database on successive applications of Rules 1 to 7.

Iteration number	0	1	2	3	4	5	6	7
A	T	T	T	T	T	T	T	T
B		T	T	T	T	T	T	T
C			T	T	T	T	T	T
D				T	T	T	T	T
E								
F	T	T	T	T	T	T	T	T
G						T	T	T
H							T	T
I								
J								

So, H is proven after five iterations. Note, in passing, that further iterations do not succeed in proving any further propositions in this particular case. Since we are considering a computer strategy, we need to program some means by which the machine is to know when to stop applying rules. From the above example there are two methods: either 'stop when H becomes true' or 'stop when the database ceases to change on rule application'. Which one of these two we select depends on the system's purpose; for one interesting side-effect of the latter procedure is that we have proved the propositions B, C, D and G and, were we later to need to know their truth values, we need do no more computation. On the other hand, if this is not an important consideration we might have proved H long before we can prove everything else.

It should be noted that we have assumed that the rules are applied 'in parallel', which is to say that in any one iteration every rule fires on the basis that the data are as they were at the beginning of the cycle. This is not necessary, but we would warn of the confusion which would result from the alternative in any practical applications; a knowledge based, and thus essentially declarative, system should not be dependent on the order in which the rules are entered, stored or processed unless there is some very good reason for forcing modularity on the rules. Very efficient algorithms, notably the RETE algorithm, have been developed for this type of reasoning.

These strategies are known as **forward chaining** or data directed reasoning, because they begin with the data known and apply *modus ponens* successively to find out what results are implied. In expert systems, this strategy is particularly appropriate in situations where data are expensive to collect but potentially few in quantity. Typical domains are financial planning, process control, scheduling, the configuration of complex systems and system tuning.

In the example given, the antecedents and consequents of the rules are all of the same type; propositions in some logical system. However, this need not be the case. For example, in industrial control applications the inputs might be measurements and the output control actions. In that case it does not make sense to add these incommensurables together in the database. Variations on forward chaining now include: 'pass through the rules until a single rule fires then act'; 'pass through all the rules once and then act'.

BACKWARD CHAINING

There is a completely different way we could have set about proving H, and that is to start with the desired goal 'H is true' and attempt to find evidence for this to be the case. This is **backward chaining** or goal directed inference. It is usual when the only thing we need to do is prove H and we are not interested in the values of other propositions.

Backward chaining arises typically in situations where the quantity of data is potentially very large and where some specific characteristic of the system under consideration is of interest. Most typical are various problems of diagnosis, such as medical diagnosis or fault finding in electrical or mechanical equipment. Most first-generation expert system shells were based on some form of backward chaining, although some early production rule languages such as OPS5 used forward chaining.

Trying to prove H
Try rule 6
Trying to prove G
Try rule 2
F is true, trying to prove D
Try rule 1
A is true, trying to prove B
Try rule 4
It works. B is true
Backtrack to trying rule 1
Trying to prove C
Try rule 5, it works C is true
Apply rule 1, D is true
Apply rule 2, G is true
Apply rule 6, H is true

Figure 5.3 Proof by backward chaining or recursive descent.

Returning to our original eight rules, the system is asked to find a rule that proves H. The only candidate rules are 6 and 8, but 6 is encountered first. Let us ignore Rule 8 for the present. At this point we establish a new subgoal of proving that G is true, for if we can do this then it would follow that H were true by *modus ponens*. Our next subgoal will be to prove that D and F are true. Recall that we have told the system that A and F are true, so it is only necessary to prove D (by ∧ introduction). The whole proof proceeds as shown in Figure 5.3.

The observant reader will have noticed that we could have proved H in one step from Rule 8. The point is that Rule 8 was not reached and the system could not know in advance that it was going to be quicker to explore that rule than Rule 6. On the other hand if the original line of exploration had failed (suppose Rule 4 was deleted) then the system would have had to backtrack and try Rule 8. Figure 5.4 illustrates the proof strategy more pictorially.

Backward chaining can thus be viewed as a strategy for searching through trees built in some solution space. The strategy we have described is usually called depth-first search in that context. We now look at other strategies.

MIXED STRATEGIES AND TREE SEARCH

I have introduced two fundamental forms of inference, forward and backward chaining. In practice most reasoning is a mixture of at least these two. Given some initial assumption, we infer a conclusion by reasoning forwards and then apply backward chaining to find other data that confirm these conclusions. Alternatively, we start with a goal, backward chain to some plausible reason and then forward chain to exploit the consequences of this new datum. This is often called **opportunistic chaining** or, less succinctly, 'backwards reasoning

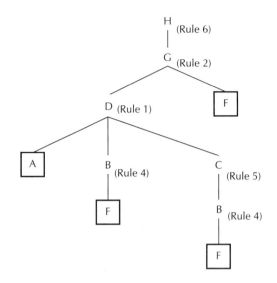

Figure 5.4 A proof tree. Propositions in boxes are those found in the database (that is, those known to be true).

with opportunistic forward chaining', because the data directed search exploits the consequences of data as they become available 'opportunistically'. This method is commonly found in the better expert systems shells and is the default mode for executing rulesets in *SOMATiK*. Another way of looking at it is to observe that every rule becomes a demon.

These inference methods can be represented as searches through a branching network or tree, and trees may be searched in a number of ways. We turn briefly now to some of the available methods. The subject of tree search is so well covered in the existing literature on expert systems that we will not attempt exhaustive descriptions of every technique, but try to give the general idea for each one with a view to giving some intuition as to when a particular technique is likely to be appropriate to a problem.

Methods of searching trees may be conveniently divided into blind search and informed search. The latter is often called heuristic or intelligent search. The two basic methods of blind search are called depth-first and breadth-first search. Depth-first search corresponds to what we did in the example given in the preceding section. It is important however not to confuse backward chaining with depth-first search totally. The terms backward and forward chaining refer to the relationship between goals and data, whereas a depth-first search may be applied to either and refers only to the solution strategy. It is convenient sometimes to blur the distinction and think of depth-first search as the 'usual' way of doing backward chaining.

Depth-first search proceeds broadly as follows. Look for the leftmost (or first) node beneath the goal node (or initial data in the case of forward chaining) and check if it is terminal (that is, proven or a goal); if not establish it on a list of subgoals outstanding. Start again with the node reached as goal. Once there are no lower-level nodes then, providing the current node is not terminal, go back to the last subgoal on the outstanding list and take the next route of descent to the right. If the tree has an AND/OR structure then success indicates going back to the last AND node, while failure indicates a return to the last outstanding OR node. Since we do not know in advance how deep the search may go only to find a failure or dead end before backtracking, it is sometimes convenient to place a restriction on the maximum depth of any one exploration. The search may go on for ever with infinite trees, in which case the only course is to set a limit. This is called a depth bound. The danger, of course, is that the required solution may be one step below the bound level. There are two principal methods of implementation for this kind of search, although they are formally equivalent. In languages like PROLOG, which depend on the idea of pattern matching, the implementation technique is called 'backtracking' and is as we have described except that explored paths are explicitly deleted and blocked and variable bindings undone at that stage, whenever failure is encountered. Backtracking accounts for much of the declarative nature of the PROLOG language since it is relatively transparent to the user. The other method, prevalent in lower-level languages like LISP, is known as recursive descent. In this case the route recording has to be hand-crafted and the garbage collection done later (in most LISPs automatically). Recursive algorithms need to beware of one subtlety. If, in the above example, we had rules of the form $A \Rightarrow B$ and $B \Rightarrow A$, then there is every possibility that the search could continue for ever in a loop. This must be explicitly checked.

Breadth-first search expands all the nodes immediately below the initial node. Then, working from left to right, it expands all these nodes until a solution is reached or the tree is completely expanded. This procedure has one striking advantage over the depth-first method: it guarantees that the shortest solution is found, if it exists. On the other hand, breadth-first search in large solution spaces can lead to huge computational costs: the so-called combinatorial explosion. This is because the cost of expanding the nodes at any level is typically the square of that on the previous level.

In some cases it is appropriate to assign costs (other than computational costs) to each link of the tree. A good example is the 'travelling salesman' problem, which is essentially the problem of how to optimize the delivery route of a vehicle which must visit a number of sites once and only once on its tour. The generalized cost in that case is a linear combination of distance, time, fuel and risk costs. In a tree with costs, both depth- and breadth-first techniques may be used but will be modified to expand the nodes with lowest cost first. This is one example of informed search. Clearly, if an optimal solution is required, breadth-first search will tend to be better.

Combining the ideas of forward and backward chaining with that of breadth-first search leads to the notion of bidirectional search. In this, a goal is expanded backwards and the initial data expanded forwards until the two trees being built can be joined, leading to a complete path. This can sometimes be much more efficient than other blind strategies. The problem we mentioned in the last section, of how to avoid blind alleys or unnecessarily long searches, can be dealt with in a number of ways. In our current example, we might choose, during a depth-first search, to expand those nodes with the smallest number of clauses in the antecedent. As it happens, this is the wrong strategy in this case, although it does seem a plausible one for this type of problem in general. The reason it is plausible is that it makes the tacit assumption that the computational cost of expanding a node is roughly proportional to the number of its descendants.

In a tree with costs, a slightly more intelligent way to proceed is not to expand the nodes with lowest cost but to store the cumulative cost of the exploration so far and expand the node whose expansion keeps the costs at a minimum. This strategy restores to breadth-first search the optimality property. One can go one step further and make an estimate of the cost of completing the search from a particular node and then minimize the sum of the two functions. This is the basic idea behind the A* algorithm. An algorithm designated B* has been suggested by Berliner (1981), which makes much more use of knowledge to terminate the search. These algorithms have been particularly important in game-playing programs.

DEDUCTION,
ABDUCTION
AND
INDUCTION

Deduction is reasoning from certain, known facts and assumptions to new facts. Using *modus ponens* and breadth-first search to arrive at conclusions is an example of deduction. So are all the other methods we have mentioned. Forward chaining lets us deduce the consequences of an assertion, and backward chaining allows us to deduce or abduce a cause for some stated situation or to find a potential cause for a goal. It is possible for a fact to support the truth of a proposition even though it does not prove it in a strict deductive manner. **Abduction** is deductive reasoning where the minor premise is uncertain. In the case of backward chaining under uncertainty we can only abduce that the patient has measles from the presence of spots, because there may be other causes of spots. We are saying that if a consequence of a thing can be proven, then at least there is nothing to contradict its truth, and that this provides evidence of its plausibility. Mixtures of the two main strategies also have a deductive or abductive character. It becomes especially important when multivalent logic is in use. Suppose that, in the example given above, we can only assign probabilities to propositions A, E and G. Then, it is plausible that F is caused by them but not certain. For example, if a friend says she feels tired and hot and is sneezing we may abduce that she is suffering from the common cold from the implication 'colds cause sneezing, high temperature and lassitude'. The fact that she has pneumonia will be discovered by further questioning, we hope. In other words, abduction is non-monotonic. It is nonetheless an invaluable method in expert systems, as in human reasoning.

The third principal mode of inference is **induction**. Broadly, induction enables us to infer new rules from collections of facts and data. The word 'induction' has two senses: the Aristotelian sense of a syllogism in which the major premise in conjunction with instances entails the generalization, and the sense of empirical generalization from observations. A third sense, the principle of mathematical induction, need not concern us here. It is with the second sense we shall be concerned. Most authorities (for example, Braithwaite, 1953; Haack, 1978; Hempel, 1966) talk about induction in terms of probabilities; if we observe that sheep on 200 hillsides all have wool and four legs, then we may induce the generalization 'all sheep have wool and four legs'. Every observation we then make increases the probability of this statement being true, but never confirms it completely. Only one observation of a shorn, three-legged merino is needed to refute the theory. From our point of view, this cannot be correct. There are many kinds of uncertainty, and it can be said equally that our degree of knowledge, belief or the relevance of the rules is what is changed by experience rather than probability. The obsession with probability derives (probably) from the prevailing empiricist climate in the philosophy of science; experience being seen only as experiments performed by external observers trying to refute some hypothesis. Another view is possible. The history of quantum physics shows that we can no longer regard observers as independent from what they observe. Marcuse (1955) develops the alternative point of view especially clearly. Experience takes place in a world of which we humans are an internal part but from which we are able to differentiate ourselves. We do this by internalizing a representation of nature and checking the validity of the representation through continuous practice. However, the very internalization process is a practice, and practice is guided by the representation so far achieved. From this point of view induction is the process of practice which confirms our existing theories of all kinds. The other important general point to note is that the syllogism of induction moves from the particular to the general, whereas deductive and abductive syllogisms tend to work in the opposite direction, from the general to the particular.

The probabilistic definition of induction does have merit in many cases, especially in the case of new knowledge. It is this case that current computer learning systems always face. In nearly every case, computer programs that reason by induction are presented with a number of examples and expected to find a pattern, generalization or program that can reproduce and extend the training set.

Suppose we are given the following training set of examples.

Name	Eye colour	Hair colour	Sex	Job
J. Stalin	blue	blond	male	programmer
A. Capone	grey	brown	male	programmer
M. Thatcher	brown	black	female	analyst
R. Kray	brown	brown	male	operator
E. Braune	blue	black	female	analyst

The simplest possible algorithm enables us to infer that:

> IF female THEN analyst
> IF male AND (blue eyes OR grey eyes) THEN programmer
> IF brown hair AND brown eyes THEN operator

However, the addition of a new example (brown eyes, brown hair, female, programmer) makes the position less clear. The first and last rules must be withdrawn, but the second can remain although it no longer has quite the same force.

The first attempts at machine learning came out of the cybernetics movement of the 1950s. Cybernetics, according to its founder Wiener (1948), is the science of control and communication in animal and machine. Several attempts were made, using primitive technology by today's standards, to build machinery simulating aspects of animal behaviour. In particular, analogue machines called homeostats simulated the ability to remain in unstable equilibrium; see Ashby (1956). Perceptrons are hinted at in Wiener's earliest work on neural networks and, as the name suggests, were attempts to simulate the functionality of the visual cortex. Learning came in because of the need to classify and recognize physical objects. The technique employed was to weight the input in each of a number of dimensions and, if the resultant vector exceeded a certain threshold, to class the input as a positive example. Neural network technology has now overcome an apparent flaw discovered by Minsky and Papert (1969), and impressive learning systems are beginning to be built.

Rule based learning systems also exist. Quinlan's (1979) interactive dichotomizer algorithm, known as ID3, selects an arbitrary subset of the training set and partitions it according to the variable with the greatest discriminatory power using an information theoretic measure of the latter. This is repeated until a rule is found which is added to the rule set as in the above example on jobs. Next the entire training set is searched for exceptions to the new rule and if any are found they are inserted in the sample and the process repeated. The difficulties with this approach are that the end result is a sometimes huge decision tree which is difficult to understand and modify, and that the algorithm does not do very well in the presence of noisy data, though suitable modifications have been proposed based on statistical tests.

One of the problems with totally deterministic algorithms like ID3 is that, although they are guaranteed to find a rule to explain the data in the training set, if one exists, they cannot deal with situations where the rules can only be expressed subject to uncertainty. In complex situations, such as weather forecasting or betting – where only some of the contributory variables can be measured and modelled – often no exact, dichotomizing rules exist. With the simple problem of forecasting whether it will rain tomorrow it is well known that a reasonably successful rule is 'if it is raining today then it will rain tomorrow'. This is not always true but it is a reasonable approximation for some purposes. ID3 would reject this as a rule if it found one single counter-example. Statistical tests, however useful, require complex independence assumptions and interpretative skills on the part of users.

A completely different class of learning algorithm is based on the concept of adaptation or Darwinian selection. The general idea is to generate rules at random and compute some measure of performance for each rule relative to the training set. Inefficient rules are deleted and operations based on the ideas of mutation, crossover and inversion are applied to generate new rules. These techniques are referred to as **genetic algorithms**.

Genetic algorithms are also closely related to neural nets as pattern classification devices. Genetic programming is a form of machine learning that takes a random collection of computer programs and a representation of some problem and then 'evolves' a program that solves the problem. It does this by representing each program as a binary vector, or string, that can be thought of as a chromosome. The chromosomes in each successive sample can 'mate' by crossing over portions of themselves[2], invert substrings of their bodies and mutate at random. Programs that score well against some objective function that represents the problem to be solved are allowed to participate in the next mating round and, after many generations, there is a good chance that a successful – but not necessarily optimal – program will evolve.

Another approach to machine learning is represented by the work of Lenat and his colleagues. As a graduate student Lenat produced a program called AM (which stood for Artificial Mathematician) whose remit was to discover number theory from a base of pre-numerical concepts from set theory (Davis and Lenat, 1982). AM succeeded, admittedly with a fair amount of guidance from its author, in pointing out the interestingness of prime numbers and conjecturing (it had no theorem-proving capability) a number of results of number theory, including Goldbach's conjecture: every even number is the sum of two primes. No one has proved or disproved this yet, incidentally. AM, like most mathematicians, thought it was fairly obvious. The next project was EURISKO which, like AM, was based on the idea of frames for which new slots can be created as part of the learning process and meta-rules or heuristics that affect the way rules are generated and generalized. An amusing example of this heuristic approach occurred early on in the development of EURISKO which noticed that rules inserted by humans were generally better than its own attempts at that stage. Thus it generated the meta-rule 'If a rule is machine generated then delete it'. Fortunately, this was the first rule deleted under the new régime. EURISKO had a number of successes. It participated in the design of a new tessellated VLSI and embarrassed the Pentagon by winning the annual war game several times. On one occasion it did so by blasting its own crippled ships out of the water and steaming on to victory. The real success was that the rules were subsequently changed to disallow this rather bloodthirsty option. It should also serve to warn of the very real danger of

---

[2] Given two binary strings (representing chromosomes) 110101 and 111000, their crossover (at the fourth place) could either be 110000 or 111101. Crossing over at the first place corresponds to choosing one of the original strings.

entrusting dangerous activities like war or nuclear engineering to computer systems. But we digress. Lenat's current project, CYC, is concerned more with knowledge representation than with learning, since it was the power of the representation language that made EURISKO so successful, as well as the meta-rule approach to learning. CYC aims to encode and make available as an expert system all the knowledge contained in the Encyclopaedia Britannica (Lenat and Guha, 1990).

5.3.3 Inference in expert system shells

In this section we move from the theoretical consideration of the various available inference strategies to the consideration of commercially available products, in particular the second generation of expert system shells. These products have made the commercial exploitation of the technology of expert systems both relatively easy and cost-effective. We will compare the inferencing capabilities of three products: Crystal (IEL, 1986), Guru (Holsapple and Whinston,1986) and Leonardo (CLL, 1987). We are concerned here with the practical issues, but first let us take a brief look at the history of knowledge representation languages and expert system shells.

There have been several attempts to construct computer languages specifically for knowledge representation. The best known, early languages are probably KRL (Bobrow and Winograd, 1977) and OPS5 (Forgy, 1981). The basic form of representation in OPS5 is production rules and in KRL it is frames. OPS5 achieved notoriety because it was used in the highly successful XCON system, which is used by Digital Equipment Corporation (DEC) to configure orders for VAX^{TM} computers. The fact that a large chunk of XCON, concerned with database access, was written in the procedural language Bliss32 is rarely mentioned, but that does not change the fact that the knowledge incorporated in the system is the key to its success. DEC's success rate in the configuration task increased by a factor of more than two, resulting in huge savings. Even more important is that XCON enabled DEC to maintain its distinctive policy of delivering just what the customer asks for, however non-standard. The maintenance of the OPS5 rule base is in fact a vastly costly operation, because of the continual updates in the product range.

Two major types of productivity aid have emerged as commercial products: expert system shells at the lower end of the market and sophisticated special-purpose software to enhance knowledge based system development at the top end. These latter environments are usually based on hardware optimized for a symbol manipulation language such as LISP or PROLOG or sometimes several. On top of these languages are added context-sensitive editors, graphics, object-oriented features, knowledge representation languages and usually some form of built-in inference method. Typical such systems are KEE and ART. The idea is to speed system development by providing many of the more commonly used programs and tools. The idea is similar to the one behind fourth-generation languages, where program generation is facilitated by exploiting common data processing patterns. If all else fails, these systems give access to the basic languages so that flexibility is not sacrificed; code can be hacked out in LISP, POP11 or C++ as a last resort. Also programmers can add their own tools to the environment. One problem with the early systems, apart from high cost, is that it is not always easy to run systems written in LISP or suchlike on conventional machines at the required speeds. A more serious problem is the lack of more conventional tools, such as database management, modelling and reporting software. The advantage of such systems is the relative freedom given to the developer to explore ideas – a distinct advantage when building prototypes.

The other kind of product is the shell. The early expert systems such as MYCIN, DENDRAL and PROSPECTOR contained very narrow specific knowledge about the subject matter of medicine, mass spectography and geology. It was realized very quickly that it could be useful to excise this knowledge, leaving the 'shell' of the inference mechanism, and add some means for easily plugging in new knowledge. Thus the shell based on MYCIN (EMYCIN for 'empty MYCIN') could be used to build an expert system in another domain without the overhead of building a knowledge application system. Unfortunately, it was soon found that the inference methods required varied significantly from one domain to another, and that a shell that was good at diagnosing faults in machinery couldn't be used for a system to tune that machinery or to control it. Ignoring the fact that the systems on which the shells were based were not without problems – MYCIN could not be turned into a training aid for doctors because it contained no knowledge about its reasoning – attempts to build really flexible shells have generally failed. Modern products have tended to remove the distinction between shells and AI environments and are often now presented as object-oriented development tools.

There are several products that run on PCs. Many of these provide basic forward and backward reasoning mechanisms but have no means of expressing uncertainty other than by the granularity of the terms used. All these systems come equipped with a fixed inference strategy and allow knowledge to be entered in rule form. They have found a number of applications, principally in domains similar to the PROSPECTOR and MYCIN archetypes, such as fault diagnosis and classification of data.

The more elaborate environments such as ART and KEE typically provide support for LISP and fairly flexible built-in control strategies together with more complex knowledge representation methods as well as production rules; frames for example. Inference is still not under rule control but the degree of flexibility is much greater and a wide range of applications has been tackled. The price to be paid for the additional flexibility is that systems do take longer to build and the systems are, of course, much more expensive. The

```
1.                                    /*Rule 1
2.   if investment is 'lump sum'
3.   and growth is desirable
4.   and pension is desirable
5.   and life.cover is unnecessary
6.   then advice is annuity
7.                                    /*Rule 2
8.   if investment is regular
9.   and growth is not desirable
10.  and income is desirable
11.  and pension is not desirable
12.  and life.cover is desirable
13.  then advice is 'unit trust'
14.                                   /*Rule 3
15.  if investment is regular
16.  and growth is desirable
17.  and risk.aversion is low
18.  and life.cover is desirable
19.  and funds are ample
20.  then advice is equity
21.                                   /*Rule 4
22.  if investment is regular
23.  and growth is desirable
24.  and risk.aversion is high
25.  and life.cover is desirable
26.  then advice is 'with profits endowment'
27.                                   /*Rule 5
28.  if investment is regular
29.  and growth is desirable
30.  and life.cover is desirable
31.  and funds are limited
32.  then advice is 'whole life assurance'
33.                                   /*Rule 6
34.  if no.of.children > 0
35.  then children is yes
36.                                   /*Rule 7
37.  if no.of.children <= 0
38.  then children is no
39.                                   /*Rule 8
40.  if married is yes
41.  then life.cover is desirable
42.                                   /*Rule 9
43.  if children is yes
44.  then life.cover is desirable
45.                                   /*Rule 10
46.  if married is no and children is no
47.  then life.cover is unnecessary
48.
49.  seek advice
```

Figure 5.5 A small ruleset in Leonardo.

modern descendants of these AI environments are ART-IM and ART-Enterprise and Kappa and ProKappa. These systems require a reasonably powerful workstation or PC. At the low end of the market there are a few products with more modest requirements. Now we turn to a comparison of inference in three products of this type.

The incomplete Leonardo ruleset reproduced in Figure 5.5 is intended to represent the knowledge of an insurance salesman about the suitability of life assurance products. Some explanation of the abbreviations may help. The variable investment refers to the type of saving under consideration; permissible answers to the question generated are restricted to the Allowed Values specified in the Leonardo variable frame structures. For example, the variable investment has allowed values of unnecessary and desirable. Growth refers to the desirability of capital growth as opposed to regular income, and risk.aversion refers to the nervousness of the investor. The meaning of the remainder of the variable names should be clear from the context, excepting the values taken by the advice variable.

When we execute these rules in Leonardo, we are asked questions in an order partly determined by the answers we give. A typical consultation might go as follows. The style of the user interface, of course, is nothing like that represented below.

Leonardo	User	Commentary
investment?	regular	Rule 1 is now excluded
growth?	desirable	
income?	unimportant	Now Rule 2 is knocked out
risk.aversion?	low	
married?	no	
no.of.kids?	2	Rule 9 now fires
funds	ample	Rule 3 can now fire

The advice generated is 'equity' in this case, and at this point a bit of purely procedural code takes over to present this advice to the user in a prettier and more understandable form. One point to note is that the user is never asked to supply a value for 'life.cover'. This is a result of the backward chaining inference being performed, which causes the machine to search for a rule with 'life.cover'in the consequent clause, thus asking the 'married' question in this case. The explanation facilities built into the shell enable the exploration of the chain of reasoning, following it backwards until a point is reached where either the value has been read from some database or put in by the user.

Almost identical rules can be entered into Crystal with identical results in this simple case. In Guru the coding of the rules is usually a little more tortuous. For example, Rules 1 and 6 in Figure 5.5 would appear in Guru as follows.

RULE: R1
  IF: INVESTMENT = 'lump sum' AND GROWTH = 'desirable'
   AND PENSION = 'desirable' AND LIFECOVER = 'unnecessary'
  NEEDS: INVESTMENT,LIFECOVER,GROWTH,PENSION
  THEN: ADVICE = 'annuity'
  REASON: For someone who wants capital growth and a pension
      but has no need of life cover, the best use of a lump sum
      is the purchase of a deferred annuity
RULE: R6
  IF: NOOFKIDS > 0
  THEN: CHILDREN = 'yes'
  REASON: I need to know if you have any children

The NEEDS clause changes the order in which the inference engine deals with the variables. This is an example of the great flexibility built into the Guru inference engine which has literally hundreds of fine-tuning devices available. The price paid for this flexibility is the complexity of coding and the need to understand inference and uncertainty at a fairly profound level. Taking the three selected shells along the dimension of flexibility, let us look at an even simpler example. Here are three rules expressed in an arbitrary style:

IF A AND B THEN C
IF A AND B THEN D
IF C THEN E

The point to note is the apparent redundancy of the second rule. In a pure backward chaining inference strategy this rule is never visited, and so the variable D never has a value assigned. Crystal prides itself on the speed with which it can process large volumes of rules (all three of the shells dealt with here are actually very fast rule processors) and so it operates in the most efficient way on this example and D is not assigned a value – Rule 2 is not processed. The difficulty with this approach is that in a more complex application with many more rules, D may be required as part of the antecedent of some rule. In such a case efficiency may dictate that it would have been better if all rules had fired as soon as their antecedents were satisfied, propagating the consequences throughout the database at the earliest opportunity. This opportunistic chaining strategy is, in fact, the default method in Leonardo. Thus Leonardo would assign a value to D if the above rule base were consulted, storing the value of the object D for future use. Leonardo supports, in addition to this default strategy, both pure backward and forward chaining, although these are regarded principally as debugging aids. The situation in Guru is a little more complex. Guru's 'environment control variables' allow the designer to control the inference strategy closely. The default strategy is the same as Crystal's, but changing the values of the control variables makes it possible to simulate the mixed strategy of Leonardo along with a large number of others. Understanding which is the correct choice for a particular problem, however, is a distinctly non-trivial exercise and many users would be happier to be told what to do by the shell.

5.4 Fuzzy rules and fuzzy objects

Traditional production rule systems admit as their antecedent and consequent clauses assignments to or testing of values of variables that take numbers, strings or lists as values. If the antecedent clause is satisfied then so is the consequent, with no shade of uncertainty apart from that expressed in the terms themselves. This section deals with fuzzy expert systems and provides some background to the fuzzy extensions to SOMA. It should be emphasized that these fuzzy extensions to the method are optional. Therefore, and because this section contains some advanced material and assumes some mathematical background knowledge, this section may be safely omitted or skimmed at a first reading.

The only difference with fuzzy rules is that the variables involved in the antecedent and consequent clauses may be function valued rather than point valued. In other words a new primitive data type, the fuzzy subset, is permitted. A fuzzy set is a set whose boundaries are imprecise. Instead of membership being a matter of *yes* or *no*, with a fuzzy set, membership can be partial. A membership function representing a typical fuzzy set, the set of tall buildings in London, is illustrated in Figure 5.6(a). The Canary Wharf tower is definitely tall; in fact it's the tallest. The Post Office tower[3] is tall too; it used to be the tallest. It has a membership value of 1. My house (two stories) has a value of 0; it is definitely not tall by London standards. However, my office building might be regarded as tall to degree 0.2 say, having five stories.

Just as ordinary logic is modelled by set theory, one can construct a fuzzy logic modelled by fuzzy set theory. All the propositional operators are available: AND, OR and NOT. The definitions will be given in the next chapter. There are also additional operators called hedges. Figure 5.6(b) shows how a new fuzzy set representing 'very tall' buildings is constructed – by raising the tall membership function to the power 2. We could similarly create 'fairly tall' by taking the square root. These operations are known as power **hedges**. There are also shift hedges available but this is not the place to go into such details.

Fuzzy logic models possibility not probability. Both the mathematics and the interpretation are different. In general, we could also allow probability distributions as primitive data types. Normally however, it would be dangerous to allow both simultaneously without some complex supervisory structure to avoid the mixing of different kinds of uncertainty.

---

[3] For those readers who think I have misnamed it, I don't think landmarks should be renamed just because their owner changes.

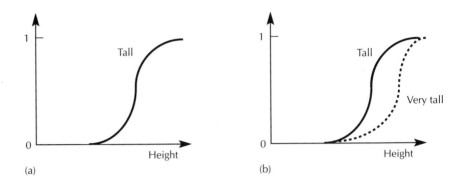

Figure 5.6 Fuzzy sets and hedges: (a) a fuzzy membership function; (b) a hedge.

1. OUR PRICE SHOULD BE LOW
2. OUR PRICE SHOULD BE ABOUT 2∗DIRECT.COSTS
3. IF THE OPPOSITION.PRICE IS NOT VERY HIGH THEN OUR PRICE
   SHOULD BE NEAR THE OPPOSITION.PRICE

Figure 5.7 A fuzzy ruleset concerning product marketing strategy.

The most striking advantages of fuzzy rules over the conventional formalisms are that hedges may be used and that truth values are automatically
propagated through the rules, obviating some of the need for a complex control strategy. This is to say that the logic plays a fundamental rôle. The upshot,
from the point of view of knowledge representation, is that rules may be
expressed in a formal language which comes much closer to modelling the
process of natural reasoning. Figure 5.7 shows some knowledge represented by
fuzzy production rules. The examples are based on the way a product manager
for fast-moving consumer goods might express knowledge based on experience
and knowledge about marketing strategy. Note that there are actually two
kinds of knowledge represented. First, knowledge about causality or transformation is represented, as with all production systems, but in a strikingly clear
fashion. The second kind is actually hidden in words such as 'high' and 'very',
which are predefined by the knowledge engineer in the form of functions which
assign truth values to various input values for variables and transformations
(hedges) which modify such functions in the presence of words such as *very*.
We shall discuss the representation and manipulation of fuzzy sets and hedges
further in Chapter 6 and their application in Chapter 8.

The same kind of extension of functionality can be applied to frames or
objects by permitting slots or attributes to be filled with fuzzy valued variables.
Detailed consideration of this idea is deferred to the next chapter. The general
idea is obtained by considering a frame for the notion of a man, which might

include slots for height, weight, generosity and beauty; these slots might contain the 'values': 5′10″, 140 lbs, 'mean' and 'ugly'. The last two values are arrays representing fuzzy subsets chosen from term sets of values describing possible levels of generosity and beauty, to which it would be inappropriate to give exact numerical values here. The linguistic variables are, of course, represented on some arbitrary numerical interval scale.

The next subsection describes how fuzzy rule-based systems implement inference. It is a little more mathematical than other passages but may be omitted safely at a first reading if so desired.

5.4.1 Fuzzy inference strategies

Usually, in dealing with inference, we assume that the value of propositions can only be either true or false. In the case of most practical reasoning, uncertainty is involved. There are cases where it is difficult to decide whether the adjective 'cloudy' is exactly true. For example, if the cloud cover is exactly 55% then are we to say it is insufficiently cloudy to imply rain or not? The extension principle (see Graham and Jones, 1988) allows us to fuzzify both *modus ponens* and *modus tollens*. Suppose that p='it is raining' is true to the extent 0.7, then the minimum degree of truth we would wish to assign to q='it is cloudy' is 0.7. However, if we only know the implication $p \Rightarrow q$ to the extent 0.5 then our confidence in the conclusion is further diminished to a number which depends on the way in which the uncertainty is to be interpreted, or the fuzzy logic in use. If we are dealing with probability, the value would be 0.5*0.7=0.35; if possibility, then min(0.5,0.7)=0.5. It is easier to see what fuzzy *modus ponens* does if we consider not just individual truth values, but the entire fuzzy sets underlying them. To see this, suppose 'raining' is a fuzzy set defined on the variable 'inches of rain per unit time' and given by the vector:

$$[0 .4 .7 .9 1]$$

and that cloudy is similarly defined over 'percentage of cloud cover' by:

$$[0 .3 .7 1].$$

Then the fuzzy relation describing $p \Rightarrow q$ is:

$$\begin{bmatrix} 1 & 1 & 1 & 1 \\ .6 & .6 & .7 & 1 \\ .3 & .3 & .7 & 1 \\ .1 & .3 & .7 & 1 \\ 0 & .3 & .7 & 1 \end{bmatrix}$$

From this, given a value for p we can infer a fuzzy set for q. The procedure is known as *fuzzy modus ponens*.

It is usual, in practical applications, to require that the answer be a single truth value rather than a fuzzy set and the fuzzy implication rule can be chosen from either the mean of the maxima or the centre of moments of the resultant fuzzy set. We must, however, point out that the implication function given above is not the only one possible.

Applying these ideas to the ruleset of Figure 5.7 enables us to see how most fuzzy expert systems are implemented. All assertions are processed first and in parallel, as if an AND stood between and connected them. Then all IF statements are processed in parallel as if an OR stood between and connected them. The inference strategy can be thought of as one-shot forward chaining. The details of this particular example are discussed in Chapter 8. In this strategy there is no notion of chaining since all rules fire together and just once. The results combine to give the output.

We now turn to the question of how to propagate uncertainty through a search tree. This is problematical whether certainty factors, Bayesian probabilities or fuzzy sets are used due to the way that any measure of certainty is reduced under conjunction.

To illustrate the problem consider the situation in a courtroom where a jury is trying to reach a decision based on the evidence presented. It is known that the witnesses have made the following two statements:

1. There was mud outside the open window
2. The butler had mud on his boots

However, statement 1 is corroborated by the independent evidence of several witnesses and statement 2 is based purely on the evidence of the housekeeper who, incidentally, stands to inherit a large fortune as a result of the untimely decease of the Major.

We might model this by assigning degrees of belief to each statement and, indeed, to our rules of inference. Suppose that we assign the values as follows.

Statement 1: 0.95
Statement 2: 0.30

Using the operations of standard fuzzy logic the possibility that 'the butler did it' cannot be greater than 0.30. Here we are invoking the judicial principle that a man is innocent until proven guilty (which holds perfectly in who-dun-its if not in real life) and assuming that the jury will give the accused the benefit of any reasonable doubt. The outstanding difficulty is to set a 'cut off' point below which to acquit. Is 30% belief sufficient proof?

These difficulties apply in all backward or forward chaining inference schemes, and it is still a matter of experimentation to set cut-off levels in such a way as to reproduce expert decisions in knowledge engineering applications. The other problem is that one has to decide whether to backtrack if a truth value falls below a given level or only if it reaches zero. In practice there will be many more than two truth values and a whole stream of deductive inferences to process. How this problem is solved depends strictly on the particular application.

Graham and Jones (1988) proposed a solution to the problem of fuzzy backward chaining as follows. The objective is to provide a convenient method of generating structure amongst a set of fuzzy rules. Instead of being executed exactly once each in parallel, the rules are compiled into a tree structure and evaluated using a generalized backward chaining algorithm. Adding some form of opportunistic forward chaining could easily be considered, but I will not do so here for reasons of clarity of exposition.

Consider a rule base containing several fuzzy productions. This system of productions is to be regarded as a complete description of our knowledge of how to compute the value of y, given the definition of the appropriate term sets. The rules are:

1. If x is low then y is solution1
2. If a is medium then y is solution2
3. If b is medium then y is solution3

The approach to computation can be summarized as follows.

(1) Obtain the (scalar) values of x, a and b.
(2) Compute the truth level of the antecedents of each production, based on these scalars and the definitions of the term sets. For example, if low $=\{1.0, 0.9, 0.7, 0.4, 0.2, 0.1, 0.0, 0.0, 0.0, 0.0, 0.0\}$ over the interval $[0,10]$ and x is found to have the value 3, then the truth of the antecedent of rule 1 is 0.4.
(3) Generate the consequent fuzzy sets for each production, according to the selected method of inference. Combine these sets using the selected disjunction operator, and thus generate the resultant fuzzy set representing the value of y.
(4) Using the selected method of defuzzification, reduce the resultant fuzzy set representing y to a scalar and an associated certainty factor for actual use.

If we now expand the system of productions by incorporating the three additional rules shown below, then we no longer expect to acquire the value of x as an immediate datum.

4. If p is true then x is low
5. If q is true then x is medium
6. If v is true then x is high

Instead of this, we have to suspend the task of evaluating y, and compute x from its own set of productions. This is fine up to step (3) of the algorithm, but at stage (4) we must take note of a difficulty. Suppose, at this stage, that $x=\{0.80, 0.90, 0.95, 1.00, 0.50, 0.20, 0.00, 0.00, 0.00, 0.00, 0.00\}$. Were we to use the 'maximum' method of defuzzifying x at this stage, x would be returned as 3 from this nested task. Then the computation of y would proceed as described above, and indeed yield an identical value.

However, a loss of information has occurred. Representing the fuzzy set x as a scalar is an unwarranted approximation, and the earlier part of the task must return the full fuzzy set instead. Otherwise, later stages cannot begin with comparably rich data, since we have no really compelling evidence on the basis

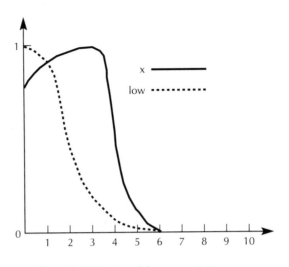

Figure 5.8 Results of the computation.

of which to assign a value in its domain to the variable in question. Evaluation of the antecedent clause 'x is low' is much better treated as a matter of comparing the output fuzzy set for x with 'low'.

There are obviously many ways in which this could be done. One way is to define the dissimilarity of two fuzzy sets, A and B, by the least-squares distance metric:

$$d(A,B) = \sum_{i=1}^{N} \frac{(\mu_A - \mu_B)^2}{N}$$

where N is the number of sample points in the domain of A and B, and the μ's denote their membership functions. This metric, although a somewhat arbitrary choice, has the virtues that if $A=B$ then $d(A,B)=0$ (in common with all metrics) and if A and B are such that $\mu(A)=1$ and $\mu(B)=0$ then $d(A,B)=1$. In the current example $d(x,\text{low}) = 0.05$, and the similarity of the two fuzzy sets, defined as the complement of the dissimilarity, is thus 0.95. The impact on the computation of y is clear, since the truth of the antecedent in production 1 is now 0.95 rather than 0.4.

Thus, given an unstructured set of fuzzy productions, along with the nomination of a goal object, our fuzzy backward chaining algorithm differs from the classical formulation in the following significant ways.

(1) No goal object value (that is, no specific hypothesis) is fixed at the inception of the task. Rather, an evidence gathering mechanism is employed to seek the most plausible value of the goal object.

(2) Recursively, all productions contributing evidence as to the value of the current (sub)goal object are processed together, in the manner of the forward chaining evaluation process.

(c) The full value (that is, the generated consequent fuzzy set) of all objects is retained as the search unwinds, maximizing the value gained from the information obtained.

As with all backward chaining algorithms which permit multiple values in the antecedent, it becomes difficult to implement a 'what if' facility in a universally satisfactory way, but this is not a consequence of the use of fuzzy sets; it applies equally to those algorithms based on probability or certainty factors. Explanation facilities remain implementable.

5.5 Frames and objects

We have concentrated up to here in this chapter on the representation of knowledge using rules, hinting only at the use of objects. Clearly, in a work of this nature, emphasis is on using objects. Artificial intelligence and expert systems software use a construct called the **frame** rather than the object of object-oriented programming. Frame systems are similar to object-oriented ones and support inheritance, if anything, even better than object-oriented systems. However, they do not encapsulate their implementation. SOMA offers a synthesis of ideas from AI and object technology and its approach to representing knowledge using objects is covered in great detail in the next and subsequent chapters. Therefore it is inappropriate to reproduce that material here. Only a few remarks about frames are in order.

Frames are used in AI to capture knowledge about objects and types in the domain under consideration. Allowing rules to be quantified over such data structures enormously reduces the number of rules required in a rule based system. Permitting inheritance reduces their number even further. For example, in a knowledge base concerning the choice of house plants we might find rules such as the following.

1. If position is sunny and temperature is warm then best.plant is cactus
2. If position is shady and temperature is average then best.plant is aspidistra
3. If position is shady and temperature is cool then best.plant is fern

and so on.

Each rule has the same pattern and there must be at least one for every possible conclusion (plant name). Some product formulation and configuration expert systems have literally millions of potential conclusions and this approach is completely untenable, since even rule bases of over 500 rules are practically impossible to maintain. The solution is to introduce a single rule that refers to plant types rather than individual plants. Then the richer the classification structure is, the smaller the number of rules we need. Frames could be constructed, perhaps corresponding to botanical classification, to represent plants that like warm, sunny conditions and so on.

The other primary use of frames has been to represent understanding. The attributes of frames and their attached operations are stored in **slots**. When all the slots are filled with values the system can be said to have an **understanding** of the object in question. If values are missing the operations can search – using backward, forward or mixed strategies – for a value. This corresponds to performing inference on the objects and can be used to represent a semantic network of associations between concepts and objects in the domain. The structures of an object model are thus a form of semantic network. This permits efficient reasoning about highly structured domains. A special case of this approach is the theory of scripts dealt with in the next section.

In most expert system shells the frame system is subordinate to the rule system. Rules are created and compiled and, usually, the frames are created as a side-effect of this compilation. The rules then **refer to** the frames rather than the reverse. In SOMA, as we shall see, the situation is reversed and rulesets are attributes of objects. This has several advantages, not least that we can encapsulate and inherit rulesets (more on this in Chapter 6). Making the rules separate from the objects creates several practical difficulties. First, there are maintenance problems associated with the lack of encapsulation. Second, it is difficult to build systems that are models of objects exhibiting rule based behaviour. Third, it is hard to navigate from rules to frames to procedures and back to rules and so on during reasoning, which restricts the kinds of applications that can be easily dealt with. Making rules dominate comes from assuming that they are the primary or best way of representing knowledge. There is no best way and we should be able to approach a problem using any or several representational formalisms: rules, objects, logic and procedures.

5.6 Script theory

Whereas frames are primarily useful for capturing knowledge about objects, there is a related structure in the AI research literature called a 'script' which is designed to be more appropriate to the description of event knowledge and its structure. Both frames and scripts have been advanced as theories of human cognition; of how we think and understand. I will regard them in this book merely as useful computational structures, however. Scripts, according to Schank and Abelson (1977), are structures that describe sequences of events pertinent to a context. They were originally designed to be particularly useful in forming an internal representation of meaning in a universal form suitable for understanding stories written in natural language and summarizing them. Consider, for example, the following story.

Wendy went to her golf club. She stayed there for over three hours. The next day she needed an aspirin.

It is difficult to understand the meaning of this story unless we refer to our knowledge of golf clubs as places where hangovers can be acquired by drinking too much alcohol. Scripts (assuming that they are part of our cognitive repertoire) enable us to leave out the boring details when relating a story in the safe knowledge that our auditors can fill in the gaps from their own knowledge of what is usual or expected. Like a frame, a script is made up of slots and requirements as to what can fill those slots. The structure is an interdependent whole, in which the contents of one slot can influence what can be in another. As with frames, 'understanding' occurs when all the slots are filled.

Scripts are predetermined, stylized, stereotyped sequences of actions that define well-known situations and are not subject to much change once stored. This fixed nature means that intelligent behaviour requires some methods for handling exceptions and, indeed, for learning new scripts as the need arises. Thus planning and goal seeking are important adjuncts to any script based system.

Every script has associated with it a number of **rôles** that the actors can assume. The script is written from the point of view of a particular rôle and this rôle is the stereotype for the default actor, if unnamed. Schank and Abelson break down all actions to a set of primitive actions and evaluate them according to predefined 'scales' such as HEALTH (dead, ill, average, well, superfit). Their theory of conceptual dependency is not our chief concern here, but we will introduce a fragment of it to speed our discussion of scripts as a form of knowledge representation. The primitive actions of conceptual dependency theory are:

```
ATRANS  –  Transfer abstract relation between actors
PTRANS  –  Transfer object
MTRANS  –  Transfer mental state
PROPEL  –
MOVE    –
GRASP   –
INGEST  –
EXPEL   –
MBUILD  –  Construct new mental state
SPEAK   –  Display information
ATTEND  –
DO      –  Perform unknown act
```

The meanings of the unlabelled primitives should be obvious. The assumption is that this is a complete list, which is probably not the case but seems to have worked well in the limited domain in which Schank and Abelson worked. The theory enables sentences to be understood as sequences of causal primitives consisting of:

r – an ACT results in a STATE
E – a STATE enables an ACT
dE – a STATE disables an ACT
I – a STATE initiates a M(ental)STATE
R – a MSTATE is a reason for an ACT

It allows two abbreviated combinations of these primitives:

IR – an ACT or STATE initiates a thought which is a reason for an ACT
rE – an ACT results in a STATE which enables an ACT

For example, the sentence 'John gave Wendy an aspirin for her hangover' is represented by the causal chain:

John ATRANS aspirin to Wendy
                rE
Wendy INGEST aspirin
           r
Wendy HEALTH(positive change)

Fairly complex stories can be handled this way. To aid understanding let us have a look at a fragment of the script system for golf clubs.

Script: Golf club
Track: The Boondoggle Golf Club
Props: Irons,Fairway,Chairs,Drinks,Glasses,Plates,Food,Money,...
Rules: M – member
         G – guest
         O – official
         S – staff
         C – caddie
Entry conditions: M has money,...
Results: M has less money, O happier, M happier, ...
Scenes:
       Scene1: Entering(member)
                 M MBUILD M thirsty(high)
                 M DO (SIGN-IN-GUEST script)
                 M ATTEND eyes to bar
                 M MBUILD S(barmaid) present
                 M PTRANS M to bar
                 M MTRANS signal to S
                        ...
       Scene2: Drinking
                        ...

The key early use of and motivation for scripts was understanding stories – notably news stories concerning the Vietnam war – and skimming news stories for new content so that humans don't have to read press releases that say much the same thing as those that came over the wire yesterday. The SAM program (Schank and Abelson, 1977) understands stories about restaurants and is provided with appropriate scripts to make this possible. It can paraphrase and answer questions about these stories. PAM is a similar system for understanding stories based on plans rather than scripts. TALESPIN uses similar methods and assigns the actors goals with the result that it can invent children's stories in a limited domain. Later, several banks applied the technique to decoding and processing natural language elements of SWIFT funds-transfer telexes, saving a good deal of money thereby.

In explaining the idea of scripts it is common to use a description of the 'restaurant' script. The idea is that one **always** does the same thing when visiting a restaurant. One **always**:

1. Enters the restaurant
2. Attracts the attention of a waiter
3. Takes one's seat
4. Reads the menu
5. Chooses a meal
6. Eats it
7. Pays
8. Leaves

This is certainly a good stereotype of the situations normally encountered. However, no visit to a restaurant follows this script exactly. One may, for example:

1. Enter the restaurant
2. Attract the attention of a waiter
3. Go to take one's seat
4. Slip on a banana skin ...

The script is broken and must be repaired before our culinary cravings can be assuaged. This is accomplished by permitting what I will call **side-scripts**[4] that deal with stereotypical exceptions. In this particular case the side-script we need might proceed:

1. Get up
2. Brush oneself down
3. Look around to see who is laughing
4. Abuse them verbally or punch them
5. Return to interrupted task

---

[4] Schank and Abelson call them 'sub scripts' but I will use this term in Part II to capture the notion of more specialized scripts.

In practice scripts are very complicated indeed and have to allow for many exceptions; for example, what happens when the bill arrives and you find you have lost your wallet? However, the point is that the script describes a well-known and stereotypical situation, one that has been encountered many times before. They do not assist in dealing with the unexpected or unusual as such. For that, the ability to form plans is required and this is a major theme in AI research. Of course the same remark applies to frames; they cannot take account of objects whose properties are not known and cannot be inherited from those of more general objects or computed from default procedures. To do this, objects and scripts must be able to send messages to each other, as we shall see in Chapter 7.

In Part II we will be using this idea of scripts to motivate an approach to task-centred requirements capture for object-oriented systems.

5.7 Blackboard architectures

Blackboard systems have already been discussed in Chapter 2 and there is little that needs to be added here. Recall only that a blackboard system simulates several cooperating knowledge sources, each of which could be a separate expert system. Object-oriented languages are ideal for implementing such systems but the developer should be aware that the metaphor is slightly different.

Blackboard systems permit object-oriented systems to support the broadcasting of messages via the blackboard. Smalltalk's call-back mechanism fulfils a similar purpose by allowing objects to register with an object in such a way that they receive notification whenever that object changes. Call-back is often used to support distributed systems and blackboard systems often assign a scheduling responsibility to the blackboard. This was certainly the case with Logica's Taurus project (unpublished) whose design included a rudimentary call-back like mechanism consisting of a small interface to the blackboard showing what had changed since the last access. The blackboard metaphor seems to me to be a highly general model that can be used to synchronize many classes of distributed systems, whether or not they include expert systems as components. However, in my experience, the model works best when the separate, distributed components are working, in some sense, towards the same end or are solving the same or related problems by different means. The paradigms for such problems are expert systems with multiple knowledge sources and computer supported cooperative work.

I once attended a workshop on object-oriented design that used building a simple blackboard system as the exercise. In most study groups an argument developed over whether the blackboard itself was an object. This did not happen in my group because it was utterly obvious to us that conceptual structures were objects just as much as buttons and bows are. This, I think, indicates an important distinction between the approach of methods like SOMA and some of the early object-oriented design methods that were concerned more with representing programs than with representing knowledge. You may not implement the blackboard as an object but there is no other way to **conceive** of it. SOMA is concerned with modelling the world and the world includes the object, the subject and the relationships between them. This includes concepts as well as physical things.

5.8 Fuzzy, neural and hybrid systems

Fuzzy controllers and expert systems based on approximate reasoning, or fuzzy sets, are making something of a comeback for two reasons. The first is that the Japanese consumer goods industry has had significant financial success with products that incorporate fuzzy controllers. Examples include cameras, washing machines, vacuum cleaners, lifts and even a passenger train. The recent Japanese exploitation of fuzzy theory in consumer goods has led to increased interest in the USA where a number of fuzzy software products aimed at process control applications now exist. The second reason is the extreme computational efficiency of fuzzy algorithms for inference. It has been shown by Bart Kosko (1991) that every neural network is equivalent to a system of fuzzy rules. The set of fuzzy subsets of a set can be regarded as points in the unit hypercube. The corners of the hypercube correspond to the lattice of crisp subsets. Now, regarding an evolving neural net as a 'brain state in a box' in this way, where the activations of the neurons trace a path through the cube to one of its corners corresponding to a matched pattern, allows us to conclude that every neural net is equivalent to an expert system with rules that associate fuzzy subsets, such as 'if temperature is *high* then control action is *reduce slightly*'. This means that cost trade-off decisions can be taken by engineers building systems as to which is the most effective technology. This also makes it possible to construct adaptive fuzzy systems which can effectively learn like neural nets but which have the structural comprehensibility of rule based expert systems; the best of both worlds. Whether you accept these arguments or not, it is undeniable that system components may in future be generated by neural nets or genetic algorithms or both. This will promote adaptive computer systems that learn as they are used. Such components must be designed as objects in future.

Treating these neural or fuzzy systems as entire objects, either by designing them as such or by wrapping them, will enable large complex systems to call on their services as required with significant benefits in terms of efficiency and functionality. Hitachi's ES/KERNEL expert systems development system combines an object-oriented approach to expert systems with fuzzy rules. Until recently, it was only available in a Kanji version but the Romanized version is now available and is called ObjectIQ. It is significant that all the fuzzy features are disabled in Object IQ, probably due to the narrow-mindedness of many Western AI experts. One cannot but wonder whether this lack of market differentiation is responsible for the relative lack of success in Western markets. ES/KERNEL has over 4500 users in Japan but ObjectIQ has had less success in Europe. For a survey of the use of fuzzy sets in expert systems see Graham (1991b, 1991c). In future ObjectIQ will include a hypertext-based, code-level reuse management tool called ORL (Object Reuse Librarian).

The range of applications for an object-oriented, rule based technology with appropriate tools and analysis and design methods is very wide. CASE tool vendors have already used AI techniques in their products, and are now reimplementing their repositories using object-oriented databases. Intelligent user interfaces have been a field of endeavour for expert systems builders, and graphical user interfaces are now understood to require object-oriented techniques. A combined approach is clearly indicated. Conventional systems require that systems capture business rules and constraints in a declarative fashion to support reverse engineering and would benefit greatly from the reusability and extensibility of object-oriented approaches. In AI itself, frames and objects promise easier ways to model temporal logic, evidential reasoning and uncertainty. The SOMA method described in Part II demonstrates one aspect of this by supporting fuzzy objects; objects that support partial properties and partial inheritance (see Chapter 6 for details).

5.9 Implementation in an expert systems environment

The products that combine rules and objects are of two basic types: either AI products based on frames or database products of various kinds that comprehend the need to express business rules. This section closes the chapter and the first part of the book with a brief discussion concerning such current products. Since the market for expert systems products has not expanded as rapidly as the vendors of these products would have liked, there is a tendency to re-badge them as 'object-oriented development' systems. We will examine the merits of such claims.

5.9.1 Knowledge based systems tools

A number of AI environments and second-generation expert system shells were heavily influenced by object-oriented ideas as well as by frames. Originally, they were mostly based on applicative languages such as LISP although modern systems are often based on imperative languages such as C. FLA-VORS was an extension of LISP in which frames were called *flavors* and whose terminology of message passing closely resembles that of Smalltalk. Many of the ideas developed in FLAVORS are present in the industry-standard object-oriented extension of LISP, CLOS (Common Lisp Object System) with its rich and libertarian notion of multiple inheritance.

Constructing knowledge based systems using object-oriented or frame-based expert systems development systems, such as Leonardo, Kappa, AionDS, KBMS, Prolog++, Nexpert Object or the like, usually proceeds by eliciting two things from users and domain experts: the key entities and concepts of the problem area and the rules for coming to conclusions. The traditional approach, to a diagnostic problem for example, starts with a goal to be searched for and chains of rules that might lead to this goal. These rules mention objects that are either program variables or more complex 'frames'. A frame is a data structure rather like a conventional entity type except that its attributes or slots may contain procedures which can be used to search for missing values. In a few systems, such as KEE, rules themselves are stored as frame structures. As we have seen, frames and objects are similar in that they both contain data and processes but the way this is described varies between the AI literature and that of object orientation. Further, encapsulation is not enforced in frame systems. On the other hand the support for inheritance is usually better and less restrictive, with multiple inheritance as a standard rather than the exception.

Intellicorp's KEE also makes use of the message passing metaphor and is based on LISP. Frames, or 'units' in KEE terminology, consist of slots which may contain numbers, text, lists, complex data structures, rules or methods (written in LISP). Slots may be inherited and each slot has sub-slots or facets to store defaults, data type information, constraints and demons. Facets provide facilities for specifying how multiple inheritance conflicts are to be handled. What KEE lacks is an object-oriented database to help manage persistent data. KEE Connection, which offers links to a conventional SQL database, is perceived as inadequate because of the need to convert between data structures represented as units on the one hand and tables on the other – the so-called 'impedance mismatch' problem. Symbolics Inc. faced up to this problem by developing a knowledge representation system called Joshua together with an object-oriented database called Statice based on the functional data model. ProKappa is very similar to KEE in its approach though it is implemented in and integrated with C. The internal language of ProKappa is either C++ or a PROLOG-influenced OO language with procedural elements too. A compiled C version of applications can be generated. Kappa is a cut-down version that runs on PCs. ProKappa is probably one of the AI products that is closest to a true object-oriented system. However, rule based knowledge predominates still and there is some way to go before all object-oriented purists will be satisfied with the claim. Intellicorp supply a CASE tool based on Ptech called OMW (the Object Management Workbench) that generates C code via Kappa.

ART has a similar pedigree and function to KEE albeit with a slightly stronger emphasis on temporal logic and truth maintenance systems. Just as Intellicorp have moved from KEE to the C-based Kappa, Inference Corp. has redeveloped ART as ART-IM for the PC and now ART-Enterprise is sold as a general-purpose, object-oriented development tool. The remarks made about ProKappa in the preceding paragraph could be made equally well about ART-Enterprise. One of the key uses for the product is said to be enterprise-level business modelling.

ProKappa has now attracted the attention of James Martin, who also conceives it as a vehicle for companies building enterprise models that will generate Kappa code and draw models from CASE tools such as KnowledgeWare's ADW. A joint project between James Martin & Co. and Intellicorp will use ProKappa to build expert systems tools for modelling company structures and operations, incorporating Martin's latest methods of Object-Oriented Planning and Analysis and Intelligent Enterprise Engineering. These tools will lay the basis of an object-oriented CASE tool which will let business rules, goals and policy be expressed in the model and used for code generation. Business simulations and scenario modelling also become possible with such an approach. The danger I see here is that this whole approach is still completely 'structured'. The method advanced in Part II of this book is intended as an antidote to such structured complaints.

Gradually the frame-based knowledge based systems tools such as Kappa, ART-Enterprise, Nexpert Object, Leonardo and ObjectIQ are all becoming gradually more compliant, though not completely so, with the object-oriented model. It is important that they do not lose the power of their rule based approach in the process. Equally, we can expect conventional tools to adopt a more rule based approach. We have seen this process at work with CASE tools. The key issue is to define the nature of the relationship between rules and objects clearly. Either the rules control the objects or the objects encapsulate the rules; there seems to be no alternative that works. SOMA takes the latter view as discussed in the next chapter but can model both approaches if desired. The full version of *SOMATiK* will enable specifications to be animated (executed) using *inter alia* rule based techniques. So far as I know, *SOMATiK* is the first and only tool built on this model.

Knowledge based systems (KBS) tools support features lacked by object-oriented tools and vice versa. Conventional tools can benefit from both in terms of reusability, extensibility and a level of reversibility arising from the rule based approach. However, conventional systems analysis techniques are inadequate in this respect. The approach of this book is intended to address all types of development tool. For KBS tools we can create objects consisting of nothing but rules and relate them to other objects representing data. With conventional and object-oriented tools, rules are used to capture business rules and object constraints.

5.9.2 Database management and rapid development tools

Generally speaking, the vendors of database products have not jumped on the object technology bandwagon to the same extent as the knowledge based system vendors and have not needed to. Very few such products provide explicit rule support, the only really notable exception being INGRES, though most relational products support triggers, which can be thought of as rules. This functionality is not critical in the market usually and is not emphasized. Some vendors however will claim that their database or 4GL is rule based but, when pressed, will reveal that the rules are no more than integrity constraints or validation ranges for attributes. Beware of such vendors.

To my knowledge, no commercial object-oriented database offers support for rules yet, though some research prototypes do. I hope the topic of object-oriented databases is adequately discussed in *Object-Oriented Methods* (Graham, 1994a) and in Chapter 2 of this book to support the formulation of a migration strategy in their respect.

Several development methods for knowledge based systems such as Gemini and KADS (Schreiber *et al.*, 1993) have been developed over the past five years or so. The trouble is that these methods are largely based on existing structured methods. The strength of such methods is that they are systematic and communicable to other developers. Their weaknesses include a massive overhead, the difficulty of learning them, the barrier they present to communication with users and the fact that they retain much of the batch orientation of all structured approaches. They are bureaucratic and have little to say about maintainability, reuse, reversibility or extensibility compared to object-oriented methods. They deal with three separate notations, leading to problems that we will discuss in the next chapter. Systems developed with them thus soon hit a complexity barrier. We know that structured methods impede the development of object-oriented systems. Why should expert systems be any different? Expert systems developers need a development method that is fully object-oriented and the existing crop of object-oriented methods has little to say about this kind of application. They need a method with a single, unified notation that captures the semantics of knowledge-rich applications and structures models around domain objects and experts' concept structures. This method must take the best aspects from object technology, prototyping, knowledge based systems, graphical user interface and distributed computing approaches. The remainder of the book is devoted to presenting and explaining SOMA, an approach that is intended to meet all these objectives.

▤ 5.10 Summary

This chapter introduced the reader to some fundamental aspects of the technology of expert systems that will be useful in understanding the techniques of SOMA introduced in Part II. We saw that an expert system consists of a knowledge base separated as cleanly as possible from an inference engine. We also considered the way in which uncertainty mediates this separation. This architectural characterization was contrasted with a functional characterization in terms of systems that perform expert tasks in narrow domains. It was also noted that some expert systems can explain their reasoning process to a user. Throughout, I emphasized that expert systems are not, and cannot be, intelligent. They are, like all computer systems, tools to support intelligent users.

The basic forms of knowledge representation were introduced: rules, semantic networks, frames (objects), logic and procedures. Rule languages are usually non-procedural or declarative languages.

The basic inference methods of forward and backward chaining were explained in detail to help the reader see how non-procedural descriptions could be executed. Variations and combinations of the two basic methods were also presented and various techniques for inductive reasoning or machine learning introduced.

An expert system shell is an expert system with its knowledge base emptied. Several such commercial systems were described briefly and discussed along with other more general AI environments. This discussion provides the basis for understanding the rule syntax of SOMA introduced in the next chapter.

It was shown how a practical system using fuzzy rules could be built and how this led to a much more readable syntax for business rules. For completeness, fuzzy inference was also discussed.

The relationship between the notions of frames in expert systems and objects was discussed. Frames reduce the complexity of rule based systems and are very similar to classes in OT. A particular variant of the idea of a frame was discussed in detail because it will be a key idea in the SOMA requirements capture approach described in Chapter 7. This is the notion of a script. Scripts describe stereotypical sequences of actions or tasks and will be used to generalize and simplify use-case analyses.

Blackboard architectures and their relationship to the ideas of OT were discussed. The relationship between fuzzy logic and neural computing was explained. Finally, we discussed the use of expert systems development tools – and advanced databases with knowledge based extensions – to implement systems and their key rôle in prototyping.

The chief purpose of this chapter was to prepare the reader for the use of the concepts of rules, inference, fuzzy rules and scripts in SOMA.

5.11 Bibliographical notes

For an introduction to the field of expert systems in general, the reader may consult Edwards (1991), Forsythe (1989), Hayes-Roth *et al.* (1983), Jackson (1986) or one of the several works available. For one particularly compatible with the views expressed here, and one emphasizing fuzzy logic, Graham and Jones (1988) may be recommended.

The book by Brachman and Levesque (1985) is a collection of seminal papers on the theory of knowledge representation and provides an excellent introduction to the issues of that subject that are of importance in object technology too.

Collins' (1990) book is highly recommended as an expansion of the basic view of artificial intelligence set forth in this chapter. The interested reader may wish to read a fuller exposition of my views on the topic of the social character of intelligence, which differ slightly from those of Collins (Graham, 1994c).

Goldberg (1989) explains the basic mechanisms of genetic algorithms. It covers nearly every key issue in the field, including the robustness of algorithms, suitability of operators, and knowledge based guidance of search and applications. He illustrates all major techniques with copious Pascal source code and worked examples. Koza (1992) presents the same theory in a simple and appealing way, emphasizing that genetic programming is a very general perspective that subsumes many others, including neural networks and statistical analysis. He gives examples of applications from a large range of topics such as process control, function approximation, artificial intelligence, planning, forecasting, game playing, decision problems and programming cellular automata. Code samples are in LISP. For a more practically motivated introduction there is Forsythe's (1989b) *Machine Learning*. The most important distinguishing feature of this collection is its scope. Most contemporary books on this subject have reduced machine learning to simple classification-based rule induction. This book takes a wider view and deals with neural networks, genetic algorithms and the philosophical perspective. An excellent paper by Anna Hart puts the conventional (that is, ID3) wisdom in perspective and the jewel in the crown is the contribution from Rechenberg, who carried the torch for genetic algorithms through the dark days of the sixties when AI ran roughshod over such biologically inspired approaches.

Schank and Abelson (1977) give, so far as I know, just about the only decent introduction to the widely influential notion of scripts.

The expert systems and AI equivalent of Durham's *IT Horizons* mentioned in the last chapter's Bibliographical notes is Goodall's *AI Watch. AI Watch* offers concise, accurate, up-to-date summaries of commercial and research developments in the field at reasonable subscription rates, though not quite so reasonable as *IT Horizons*. More information can be obtained from Alex on +44-1865-59872 (tel./fax). Other useful sources of current information include the excellent *Machine Intelligence News, AI Magazine, IEEE Expert, Expert Systems Applications*, and the weekly and monthly trade press.

Part II

Migrating using SOMA
The Semantic Object
Modelling Approach

6

Object modelling

Read not my blemishes in the world's report
I have not kept the square, but that to come
Shall all be done by the rule.

W. Shakespeare (Antony and
Cleopatra)

Πάντα ῥεῖ, οὐδὲν μένᾳι[1]

Herakleitus of Ephesos

This chapter describes one of the central and most basic parts of SOMA, its approach to systems analysis and modelling at the logical level. As the opening chapter of Part II, it describes the object modelling component of the SOMA method for object-oriented development in some detail, emphasizing its support for reuse and packaging through subject area layering, its support for business and other rules, its representational and semantic richness and its use for building reversible descriptions. The primary subject matter of the chapter is object modelling and specification. That is, it covers methods, techniques and notations which help in the elicitation of business models, user requirements, descriptions of existing systems and domain knowledge and with the analysis of these to produce a specification written purely in terms of objects. Requirements capture uses the modelling techniques developed here and is therefore presented after this material in the next chapter.

SOMA is particularly aimed at applications with the following characteristics: GUI development, distributed and client/server systems, use of object-oriented databases, work-flow and groupware applications, expert systems, object wrapper construction and use of extended relational systems that support active data (for example, Sybase or INGRES). It may also be used for business process re-engineering projects as we shall see in Chapter 8. Its principal novel features compared with other methods are:

- the use of a Task Object Model to capture requirements and the transformation of the products of this model into a Business Object Model – a transformation to be dealt with in the next chapter;

[1] All is flux, nothing stands still

- the encapsulation of rules in objects, which permits global properties to be locally encapsulated and inherited, allows an object's contract to be formulated without recourse to excessively formal notations and supports inferencing over class invariants;
- the use of a HOOD-like levelling technique to provide precise semantics for subsystems, thus supporting a reuse and delivery strategy based on subject area layers and object wrappers;
- its genuine language independence whereby conventional, prototype, functional and object-oriented languages can be accommodated equally well;
- its insistence that precise semantics at the analysis stage restrict the expressive power of the notation and the simplicity of the notation itself.

These features are as they are because the true purpose of SOMA is to build a bridge between the language used by system developers and that used by their customers. This will become even more evident in subsequent chapters.

This book uses a particular notation for exposition. However, SOMA is largely 'notation free' in the sense that other graphical icons may be substituted for those recommended here. Some guidance on this is given. Fuzzy rules and inheritance can be supported if appropriate. The chief application of the fuzzy extensions described in Section 6.12 is in strategic modelling and business re-engineering as described in Chapter 8, though there are applications to building fuzzy knowledge based systems as well.

A development using SOMA begins with requirements capture which is followed by object modelling and then development. This progress assumes that the developers are also aware of the overall life-cycle model of SOMA dealt with in Chapter 9. It may be asked why we begin in the middle of the process, rather than explain the life-cycle model and requirements capture techniques first. The reason is simple. The philosophy of the life cycle cannot be justified without an understanding of object modelling and the requirements-oriented Task Object Model in SOMA (described in Chapter 7) is itself an object model. We also assume that object-oriented development is a modelling process first and foremost. Therefore, there is no other place to begin.

At the end of object modelling, the development organization should have a set of potentially reusable object descriptions, with a set of metrics, which can be placed in a specification library. Such a collection of soundly engineered, semantically rich, reversible object descriptions can be used as the basis for kick-starting a company's reuse programme. In my experience, this is an easier place to start than with a library of source code objects that may not be documented properly, may be inconsistently documented or may not be documented at all. SOMA encourages the organization to build the reuse library incrementally, starting with new developments, storing analysis-level descriptions first, adding code components as they are built and tying them to the specifications in the library, and only later reverse engineering the existing code resource. The specifications can then be used to navigate the library. The SOMA metrics are described in Chapter 10. More on the subject of reuse will be found in Chapter 11.

The reader is assumed to be broadly familiar with the basics of conventional software engineering, database management systems, object-oriented methods and – to a lesser extent – expert systems. In the first four sections of this chapter we will review a few general issues that are crucial to understanding what follows.

6.1 Basic philosophy

The burgeoning interest in object technology (OT) has led to the widespread use of object-oriented programming languages. With this growth has come a realization that current structured methods for software engineering not only fail to support such developments but actually impede them in many cases. Within my own experience, developers using an object-oriented programming language who are presented with a set of entity-relationship diagrams and function decompositions often find them totally unhelpful and are forced to fall back on their skills as hackers in the absence of pertinently expressed requirements. Furthermore, the sheer bureaucracy and amount of documentation required by structured methods is a severe impediment to productivity in itself.

The need for a disciplined approach has now led to a proliferation of methods for object-oriented analysis and there are well over 60 published suggestions in existence (Graham, 1994a). In principle, the users of an object-oriented analysis method could implement now in C or COBOL, say, with a view to later migration to an object-oriented programming language. The advantages of this approach are that it avoids risks arising from the still evolving language technology and the danger of choosing a strategic object-oriented language which is not the one which will eventually be accepted as the industry standard. Equally, if an object-oriented language has been chosen then object-oriented analysis imposes some discipline on the development process without forcing developers to adapt their designs from 'structured' functional descriptions of the problem and the outline solution. Thus, any decent object-oriented analysis approach should be language independent. The disadvantages of this are that the specification cannot be tested and that the system cannot be delivered and used. The answer to both problems is prototyping.

A prototype can be used to agree the specification with users and can even be implemented incrementally pending a final rewrite in the object-oriented language of choice, should performance or some other factor make this desirable. However, what we build as a model in the prototyping language needs to be **reversible** in the sense that it is possible to discover the intentions of the analysts and designers by examining the code. This should also be true of the paper analysis itself, leading to a requirement for a semantically rich analysis language and a readable, declarative prototyping one. The two areas of IT where such tools have become available are expert systems and advanced databases – themselves under the influence, it has to be said, of artificial intelligence. Expert systems offer declarative, semantically rich programming languages. Advanced databases allow business rules to be coded as stored procedures (the Sybase term) and database triggers – but not always declaratively. It is really rather hard to extract the original rules as expressed by users from such a system. Thus, there is a need for declarative, rule based modes of expression and, so far, only INGRES and the semantic databases offer anything like this. Even object-oriented databases fall short in this respect. It seems that this situation will change and the database community are certainly aware of the problem. Furthermore, several database workers now accept that business rules should be attached to the entities or objects of the data model. As Andleigh and Gretzinger (1992) put it: 'Clear documentation of the business rules *and which objects each rule is associated with* ensures that the application of the rules is perceived clearly and is well understood by the user before the coding of the rules.' (My emphasis.) We may conclude that knowledge based systems and advanced database products, or perhaps both in concert, can help build reversible prototypes. However, this is best done in conjunction with a machine independent analysis exercise using a semantically rich and therefore reversible notation. Environments such as NeXT's Interface Builder also support rapid prototyping well, though it requires greater programming skills (in Objective-C) than the former options.

SOMA is a method which overcomes the weaknesses of traditional methods in relation to knowledge based systems, graphical user interfaces, and systems to be built using extended relational database managers such as Sybase, INGRES or Oracle. We will see why this approach enriches the semantics of the description and makes such a description more traceable and reversible. While this chapter only describes the object modelling aspects of the method, we shall see in subsequent chapters that SOMA covers the entire software development life cycle.

SOMA also synthesizes best practice and permits use of notations from other well-known object-oriented analysis methods. Notable influences include Booch (1994), de Champeaux *et al.* (1993), Coad and Yourdon (1991), Desfray (1992), Jacobson *et al.* (1992), MOSES (Henderson-Sellers and Edwards, 1994) and OMT (Rumbaugh *et al.*, 1991).

Anticipating the next chapter somewhat, SOMA proceeds by constructing a model of the tasks that the system supports. This task model is used to create an object model of the business or system under consideration and then this Business Object Model is either implemented directly or converted into a design (or implementation) object model with the precise semantics of a particular language for especially complex systems. This Implementation Object Model may be expressed in SOMA notation if a high-level language (Smalltalk, O2 or ENFIN for example) is to be used. More usually we convert to a suitable object-oriented design notation and method such as Booch'93 (for C++) or BON (for Eiffel). The mapping is method independent but we will assume in this book that Booch'93 is used for clarity of exposition[2].

---

[2] Despite the fact that Booch's book carried the copyright imprint of 1994, he insists that the method contained in it should be referred to as Booch'93.

☐ 6.2 What is an object-oriented analysis method?

A method consists of *at least*: a modelling technique, a process and a notation. The notation could just be natural language so that it may be regarded as optional if we restrict the usage of 'notation' to graphical notation. A method, in my opinion, should minimize the amount of notation that must be learnt, minimize the number of mandatory deliverables from the process and minimize the number of foundation concepts in the modelling approach. It should maximize the information content or semantic richness of the models and deliverables produced. As such, it should be complete (rules help with this) and consistent (*pace* Gödel[3]). Ideally, it should be proven in practice on significant projects.

At the time of writing SOMA has, to my knowledge, been used by relatively few organizations, but has been used successfully on quite large and important commercial projects in banking, insurance and IT itself.

A method should be scaleable and generally applicable across small and large-scale projects, across real-time and commercial applications, by average and virtuoso developers and in all different hardware and programming language cultures. SOMA now covers all of the issues of the OMG OOA/D reference model, as all good methods should. In fact it goes further in offering guidance on coordination and reuse – a topic that is outside the scope of the reference model at present.

Tools that support the method should exist. This book includes a version of such a tool: *SOMATiK*. We are often told that methods should be based on a recognizable theory. SOMA is based on the theory expounded in this book.

Finally, SOMA differs from most software engineering methods in de-emphasizing the drawing of pictures as the only way to describe, or begin describing, a system. SOMA does include graphical techniques, especially at the requirements stage, but makes it possible for most of the graphics to be generated automatically from a textual characterization of the model. The textual description is the basis for a repository. The *SOMATiK* software demonstrates the benefits of this approach quite clearly. This almost equips SOMA with a slogan: away with drawing as the only place to begin; in with text-based description and a rich repository. At the root of this approach is an insistence that the principle of encapsulation is strongly enforced throughout SOMA.

☐ 6.3 The OMG and abstract object models

The Object Management Group have defined a high-level reference model for object-oriented analysis and design. Its purpose is to cover all imaginable issues in object-oriented software engineering but it is not a method in itself,

---

[3] Gödel's theorem states that a system complex enough to contain arithmetic cannot be both complete and consistent; but this refers to infinite systems of course.

rather a framework within which methods may be evaluated. Schematically the reference model is described in Figure 6.1 with the equivalent SOMA terms in brackets; though, in SOMA, business object modelling and logical design are largely merged into a continuous activity.

Object modelling provides a set of terms and concepts for representing everything within the scope of analysis and design in terms of objects. It defines standard terms. SOMA, as described in this book, provides a complete object modelling approach and covers all the other issues, as subsequent chapters will reveal. **Strategic modelling** (or enterprise modelling) covers enterprise and business process modelling, requirements capture and development planning. **Analysis modelling** covers the process of obtaining and recording a description of the problem domain. **Design modelling** (called logical design in this book) consists in adding non-public information to class specifications and producing a solution to some particular problem including system and interface objects. **Implementation modelling** is physical design and involves designing modules, the distribution strategy and taking account of the specific software and hardware to be used.

The shaded areas in Figure 6.1 indicate those areas that are the concern of the reference model. Unshaded areas are outside its scope. SOMA covers all the shaded areas and, additionally, that of coordination and reuse (Chapter 11).

The OMG Abstract Object Model for object-oriented analysis and design (AOM) sets out to define, at a reasonably high level, the semantics of the main

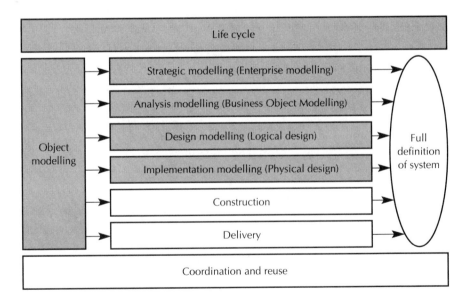

Figure 6.1 The OMG Reference Model. Only the shaded areas are within the scope of the model.

object-oriented analysis and design constructs. Keeping the level high is especially important since, while there is a good consensus about the basic concepts at the programming level, there is still little agreement at the analysis level. Fixing too much too early would stifle innovation. The chief innovation of the abstract object model itself, at least from the standpoint of the object-oriented programmer, is the introduction of constructs from semantic data modelling. Thus, visible attributes are recognized as equivalent to two standard methods: Get and Set. Encapsulation is interpreted as the hiding of the implementation of state, not the abstract state itself. Furthermore, relationships between objects are introduced, allowing the analyst to express concepts of adding and removing instances and navigating around the model. There are two kinds of entity in the AOM, objects and characteristics, with various subclassifications as shown in Table 6.1.

There is minimal normative structure in the OMG Reference Model. You can use a waterfall or prototyping approach. You can start at any point from business strategy modelling to code. The OMG special interest group (SIG) who developed the Reference Model considered over 30 methods and none of them were excluded by the result. Interestingly, the SIG viewed functional models as being to do with grouping and views rather than as a part of the analysis model. The Reference Model embraces the Abstract Object Model and is now quite widely agreed upon. The need for the Object Model arose because of the large variance in meaning given to terms like 'object' and 'method' in the literature. For example, people had generally failed to agree whether 'object' meant instance or class. The Object Model now declares that **object type** shall be the correct term for class, although strictly speaking a **class** is the implementation of an object type. Some of us will continue to say 'object' for short, just as data modellers say 'entity' for entity type. **Methods** are defined as the implementation of **operations**. This book will use this standard terminology as far as possible and point out any deviations. Table 6.1 sets out the terminology of the Object Model and the various specialization relationships between terms.

It should be noted that some prominent methodologists have questioned the applicability of the OMG OOA/D models.

One of the side-effects of the activities of the OMG's object-oriented analysis SIG has been to prompt methodologists to extend their methods into more areas of the reference model, and the work reported here is influenced by the model, though SOMA includes the topic of coordination and reuse as within its scope and some aspects of delivery too in the sense that maintenance is regarded as evolutionary development.

In SOMA, **analysis** provides a description of the problem domain. **Logical design** extends analysis by including descriptions of alternative solutions and logical interface definitions. This involves no techniques different from those of analysis but more detail and the extension of the scope into the architectural domain. This is what is meant when it is claimed that object-oriented analysis offers a continuum of representation. **Physical design** provides a description of the structure of the implementation, taking account of languages, devices and so on. Moving from logical to physical design, it is less clear that the continuum can be maintained since a definite choice of hardware and language must be made and an abstract SOMA model is just not the same thing as a C++ program.

⊟ 6.4 The models of software engineering

Analysis is the decomposition of problems into their component parts. In computing it is also to be understood as the process of specification of user requirements and system structure and function independently of the means of implementation or physical decomposition into modules or components. Analysis is traditionally done top-down using structured analysis or an equivalent method based on functional decomposition combined with separate data analysis. Often, the high-level, strategic, business goal driven analysis is separated from the systems analysis. Here we are concerned with both and will eschew any distinction between business and systems analysis. This is necessary for sound systems analysis and possible because object-oriented analysis permits the system to be described in the same terms as the real world; the system abstractions correspond more or less exactly to the business abstractions.

Object-oriented analysis is analysis, but also contains an element of synthesis. Abstracting user requirements and identifying key domain objects are followed by the assembly of those objects into structures of a form that will support physical design at some later stage. The synthetic aspect intrudes precisely because we are analysing a **system**, in other words imposing a structure on the domain.

According to the conventional wisdom in software engineering, there are three primary aspects of a system. These are respectively concerned with: (1) data, objects, concepts and their static structure; (2) functional architecture or atemporal process and (3) dynamics or system behaviour. We shall refer to these three dimensions as data, process and control. Object orientation combines two of these aspects – data and process – by encapsulating and localizing behaviour with data. We shall see later that it is also possible to encapsulate some aspects of control.

In this book, I present a synthesis and extension of the suggestions contained in other approaches. The resultant method was originally published in incomplete form in various places (Graham, 1991a, 1992a, 1993, 1994a, 1994b). It is a filter for ideas present in other conventional and object-oriented methods. In this chapter a default notation is offered for those who do not wish to use one they already know or one which they have decided is particularly

Table 6.1 The OMG Abstract Object Model concept hierarchy (reprinted from Graham, *Object-Oriented Methods,* 1994a, by kind permission of the publishers).

Term	Specializations
Value	Object Non-object Concept
Non-object	Relationship
Concept	Modelling concept Object model concept
Modelling concept	Strategic modelling concept Analysis modelling concept Implementation modelling concept Deliverable Activity type Technique
Object model concept	Rule concept Object behavioural concept Group and view concept Object structure concept
Rule concept	Constraint Assertion
Object behavioural concept	Operation Event State Transition Message
Message	Request
Group and view concept	Diagram Schema Quality concept Strategic model G&V concepts Analysis model G&V concepts Design model G&V concepts Implementation model G&V concepts
Object structure concept	Attribute type Object type Relationship type
Object type	Strategic model object type Analysis model object type Design model object type Implementation model object type
Relationship type	Association Aggregation Specialization Instantiation Usage

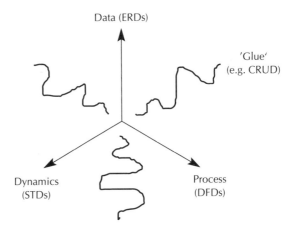

Figure 6.2 The three dimensions of software engineering.

appropriate for their application domain. Unlike most other methods, SOMA includes prescriptive techniques for requirements capture and the discovery of objects and has a strong focus on business re-engineering applications. At the same time it attempts to remain close to the concerns of the coder by expressing specifications in textual rather than graphical form.

As remarked above, it is usual to express system models in three dimensions: those of process, data and control – or dynamics (Figure 6.2). The data dimension corresponds to entity-relationship diagrams (ERDs) or logical data models. The process models are represented by data flow or activity diagrams of one sort or another. Finally, the dynamics is described by either a state transition or entity life history notation. To ensure that these diagrams are consistent, structured methods usually insist that some cross-checking documents are created to 'glue' the model together. For example, to check the consistency of a model between the entity-relationship and data-flow views, a CRUD matrix might be constructed. CRUD stands for Create, Read, Update, Delete and checks which processes use which entities and how they are used. There must be similar cross-checks for the relationships between the dynamic model and both process and data; for example, the Effect Correspondence Diagrams of SSADM. This approach creates a potentially enormous overhead in terms of documentation alone. However, it does ensure that all aspects of a system are covered, assuming the requirements capture or knowledge elicitation is not deficient. It also has the advantage that where two techniques are used to reach the same conclusion then, if the results agree, the level of confidence in them both is raised. This conceptual division spreads control across the dynamics and process dimensions. In SOMA, we resolve this problem by restricting the dynamic model to individual objects and generalizing the process model to model message passing, as discussed in Chapter 7.

Data-centred approaches to software engineering begin with the data model while process-oriented approaches start with data flow diagrams (DFDs). Some real-time approaches begin with finite state machines or state transition diagrams (STDs); but this is unusual for commercial systems developers. Data structures are more stable than functional decompositions and so data-centred approaches are preferred in most cases.

There is a rich theory of semantic data modelling going far beyond the normal use of ER diagrams. This theory encompasses many of the concerns of object orientation such as inheritance and abstract types. It also illuminates our understanding of relationships or **associations**, as we will call them, between entities by highlighting the fact that they may be ternary as well as binary and that they may themselves have attributes and states. Until recently much of this work has been ignored by workers in object technology and in AI as thoroughly as these two areas have ignored each other.

Object-oriented analysis and design methods fall into two basic types, those that mimic existing structured methods by having three separate notations for data, dynamics and process, and those that assert that, since objects inherently combine processes (methods) and data, only one notation is required. I will call these two approaches **ternary** and **unary** respectively.

Ternary approaches have the advantage that existing practitioners of structured methods will be broadly familiar with the philosophy; proceeding in this way helps to ensure a smooth transition to object-oriented approaches for those already skilled in traditional methods. Against this, unary approaches are (1) more consistent with the metaphor of object orientation and (2) easier to learn from scratch.

Of the ternary approaches the clearest examples are OMT (Rumbaugh *et al.*, 1991), the modified Ptech of Martin and Odell (1992) and Shlaer/Mellor OOA (Shlaer and Mellor, 1988, 1992). Of the unary ones, the best known are CRC/RDD (Wirfs-Brock *et al.*, 1990; Lorenz, 1993) and Coad/Yourdon (Coad and Yourdon, 1990,1991a,1991b). There is also a growing number of hybrid methods of both types, such as FUSION (Coleman *et al.*, 1994), Syntropy (Cook and Daniels, 1994) and MOSES (Henderson-Sellers and Edwards, 1994). Some methods, such as Coad/Yourdon, are simple but lack support for describing system dynamics. Some, such as Rumbaugh's OMT and Shlaer/ Mellor, are richer but very complex to learn. Methods like OMT also offer little to help express business rules, contracts and constraints. You will search long for advice on how to combine the products of the three separate models into a coherent single model. None of these methods supports rules.

SOMA provides a unary notation for object-oriented analysis that uses knowledge based systems style rules for describing contracts, constraints, business rules, global system control, database triggers and quantification over associations (for example, 'all children who like toys like each other'). It also addresses in this way the issue of reversibility and thus is ideal as the analytic precursor to prototyping.

Although SOMA seems to be unique as an analysis method in combining objects and rules, several software products already do this, notably expert systems shells such as Leonardo, Nexpert Object, ProKappa, and ObjectIQ/ES/KERNEL and a few database products such as INGRES. There seems to be no suitable analysis approach for such products. One of the weaknesses of all existing object-oriented analysis methods is in the way rules and constraints are added almost as an afterthought. It turns out that extending the object model to encapsulate not only attributes and operations but rules too is a profound step. It enables an object-oriented description of rule based systems, advanced databases and enterprise models, with the attendant benefits of reuse and extensibility, and also increases the semantic richness of descriptions of conventional systems. SOMA is also unique in supporting fuzzy classification, which is important for requirement specification in some domains such as enterprise modelling, business process re-engineering and process control, though unfashionable in many software engineering circles.

There seem to be only two ways to introduce rules into an object model. Either they are encapsulated in objects or they are placed separately in the model. In the latter case, encapsulation can be violated. In actual implementations, such as in the tools mentioned in the preceding paragraph, the tendency is to make the rules control the objects in the system, which are created as a side-effect of rule compilation. This too violates most of the principles of the object-oriented metaphor.

There is a general problem in distinguishing object-oriented analysis methods from object-oriented design methods which does not arise for conventional methods. Because of the continuum of representation and philosophy in object-oriented software engineering, from analysis at least up until logical design, it is often hard to tell where one begins and the other ends or, indeed, if there is any difference at all. This is good news for the developer and maintainer but bad news for the project manager and estimator because it is harder to construct a work breakdown structure. In this book, we will take the view that there is little real difference between analysis and logical design, though physical design can be profoundly different because of language and hardware dependencies. The concerns of the project manager are addressed by the object-oriented life-cycle model of Chapter 9.

At the time of writing there are over 60 more or less (but mostly less) complete object-oriented methods in existence, ranging from incomplete suggestions to arguably complete methods. This is clearly an unsustainable situation, especially as none of them is really complete and many merely represent opinions on what is important at various points in the life cycle. Until recently, most users would have had to synthesize a complete method from fragments of the published ones. The danger is that this could lead to random combinations of method fragments with little coherence. The method described here is the result of a more careful synthesis arrived at from using some of the existing published methods on projects.

The remainder of this chapter describes SOMA's object modelling component. It is intended to be simple yet refines the semantics of subject areas or subsystems (called layers in SOMA). Usage, classification and composition structures are supported along with general associations and various ways of classifying objects and annotating their attributes and operations. Assertions (pre-, post- and invariance conditions) are also supported. Lastly, it adds expert system style rules to objects to enhance the semantic richness of the analysis models in all cases and to help model the analysis of advanced database and knowledge based systems. Rules generalize class invariants by allowing them to be chained together and inferences performed. At design time these rules can be converted to logical assertions. This enables the transformation of a SOMA model to a model in some particular object-oriented design notation such as that of Booch (1994). SOMA is unique in providing support for fuzzy objects and fuzzy inheritance.

The activities within SOMA object modelling, in no particular order, are as follows:

- Identify objects
- Identify layers
- Identify association, usage, classification and composition structures
- Add attributes to objects
- Add operations to objects
- Add rulesets to the objects where appropriate
- Add state models for objects with significant, complex states

We will now look at each of these activities in turn.

6.5 Objects

First, let us establish some notational points. An **object** can be a **class** or an **instance** of a class. By default, objects in SOMA are displayed in the form shown in Figure 6.3(a). If the icon has sharp corners it represents an instance, if round – as in the figure – a class. To help remember this, realize that you can cut your finger with an instance of a knife but that the class of all knives can never hurt anyone. Thus, an object has an identifier and three lists: attribute and association names, operation names and ruleset names. Each of these has additional information, or facets, attached as we shall see.

Surrounding a class icon with a box as in Figure 6.3(b) says that the class is not an **abstract class**. In other words, the class may have instances; it is a **concrete class**. This also tells us that any subclasses that there are do not form an exhaustive list of possible subclasses; for example, Cars is probably a concrete class because I am unlikely to know the names of all the cars in production and I want to be able to store an instance of a car of unknown type when it arises.

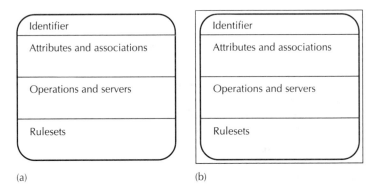

Figure 6.3 (a) A SOMA class; (b) a SOMA class with instances.

When it is convenient, the icons may be reduced to show only the identifier. Instances seldom arise during analysis modelling, although sometimes one will want to distinguish a particular instance; for example, the Reuters data service. One might also wish to represent the instance myCompany separately from the class Companies. It is usually best to use a small filled circle for such instances with a name written nearby. Analysts do not often work with particular instances or need to represent them. Occasionally, however, this is required. Class identifiers should be named in the plural and instances in the singular. This is deliberately the opposite convention from that used in data modelling.

SOMA permits the use of other notations with suitable extensions where rules are used. For instance, adopting an icon with sharp corners for a class corresponds to adoption of the OMT Object Model notation with an extension to cope with rulesets. This is permitted but must be applied consistently. The class icon can be shrunk to either a button (SOMA), a box (OMT) or a cloud with dotted outline (Booch) according to taste. This is illustrated in Figure 6.4. In all cases a shadow indicates a utility class (only illustrated for Booch). An instance would be a rectangle (SOMA), button (OMT) or cloud (Booch). Note the danger of confusion where rectangles are used. The view of the object in Figure 6.3 is called 'zoomed in' and those views in Figure 6.4 'zoomed out'. The zoomed-out view shows only the identity of the object and any external associations or structural links. The zoomed-in view gives access to some or all of the details of its superclasses, parts, servers, associations, attributes, operations and rules. We will use the SOMA notation in this book from now on.

It is often claimed that the explicit treatment of attributes violates the principle of information hiding. However, as we have seen, the complexity of the data structures present in most commercial systems – compared to simple programming abstractions like windows or stacks – leads to the need to make attributes explicit and visible. Thus, in this method we retain the attributes window. To retain some object-oriented purity, we regard each attribute in this

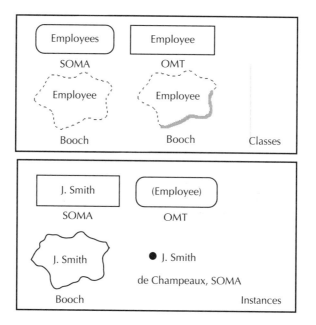

Figure 6.4 Available notations for classes and instances when 'zoomed out' to reduce detail.

window as a shorthand for two standard methods. For example, the attribute Name: is short for the operations GetName and PutName. Special versions of these operations may be included in the operations window, in which case they override the standard operations. Each of these operations is regarded as containing standard security checks, which may be overridden. Validation and other conditions must be specified for each attribute as facets. All attributes may have **facets**, which add details such as type, ownership, defaults, valid ranges, and so on. See Section 6.9.1 for more details on attribute annotations.

A **feature** of an object is either an attribute, association, operation or ruleset. All features may have facets.

The operation name may contain (along with facets for the details of the method's function, parameters and type information) invariance, pre- and postcondition facets: conditions that must hold when the method is running, fires and terminates respectively. These are called **assertions**. In this way, a part of the control structure is encapsulated in the object's methods.

Another important facet of each operation is its list of servers and the messages sent to them. Some operations may be sequentially nested, where several operations are executed together in a fixed sequence. These should be represented as 'subroutines' of an operation representing the combined effect. Such subroutines can also be invoked directly by messages unless otherwise indicated by a 'private' facet.

The facets of a ruleset are its rules and its inference régime.

We distinguish between application and domain objects. **Domain objects** are those considered to be generally useful throughout an enterprise and which are likely to be servers for other objects. **Application objects** are more contingent; they arise in specific applications and may never be used again. Classes such as Orders or Customers are likely to be domain objects. Classes such as Students may be specific to an educational application. This distinction is imprecise but is intended to assist with assessing the need for generalization for reuse and with providing a form of data independence. A third category available is that of **interface objects**. These are the new objects introduced during logical design that are not strictly business objects at all.

The complete details of a class are recorded on a **class card**. The layout of class cards will be shown later in Figure 7.11.

6.6 Layers

Large systems must be decomposed for work packaging and to understand them better. Therefore, some notion of subsystems or layers is required. Layers in SOMA are not just a convenient way to decompose the problem domain, as in most other methods; they are first-class objects in their own right with the semantics of objects. Layers are the units of delivery and may be units of reuse. Layers differ from other objects in two ways: (1) they exist at the top of a composition structure; (2) each of their operations may be implemented by an operation of some object within that structure. This means that layers can be arrived at top-down or bottom-up during the Identify Structures activity. Further, the requirement that every operation must have either an implementation or a properly terminated implemented_by link (an idea borrowed directly from HOOD) assists in completeness checking during top-down design. Equally the analyst can ask, during a bottom-up analysis: 'What does this operation implement for the Layer?'.

In most methods only heuristics such as 'maximize cohesion and minimise coupling' are given as guidance on how to identify layers. Coad suggests that a subject layer should contain 7±2 objects. This is based on (a misunderstanding of) Miller's Law in cognitive psychology which states that humans can retain 7±2 'chunks' in activated memory. What constitutes a chunk varies with the expertise of the human subject. For example, a novice at chess sees up to 32 men on the board or 18 (2×9) types of man, while a Grand Master sees perhaps only seven strategic arrangements of those same pieces.

A layer is an object with at least two 'parts' and may (optionally) have implemented-by links delegating a top-level operation to an operation of a part. In principle, an operation can be implemented by the operations of more than one part but this would need to be described in detail at the composite level. It is better to split the operation at that level in the first place. It follows from the definition that layers can be components of other layers.

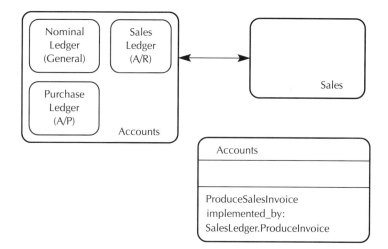

Figure 6.5 Layers for the Accounts subsystem.

Notationally, layers may be shown in the notation of Figure 6.3 but a 'Gradygram' notation as in Figure 6.6 is sometimes preferable since it is easier to show implemented_by links in this way.

Example: a commercial system might have the layers: Marketing, Sales, Accounts and Production. The Accounts layer is an object representing the Accounts department as a whole and may have a operation called ProduceSalesInvoice. Accounts is composed of three objects or layers: PurchaseLedger, SalesLedger and NominalLedger. The ProduceSalesInvoice operation is implemented_by the ProduceInvoice operation of the SalesLedger object, denoted: SalesLedger.ProduceInvoice. This is illustrated by Figure 6.5.

The sales people should not need to know that there is an AP department. This is part of the internal implementation of Accounts. If they ask Accounts to send an invoice, that should be the end of the matter from the message sender's point of view. Accounts encapsulates the decomposition into GL (general ledger), AR(accounts receivable) and AP(accounts payable) which implement most of its functionality. It **delegates** the responsibility along the implemented_by link.

In the context of a traditional top-down analysis, we might well start with a DFD style context diagram showing external objects and data flows crossing the system boundary. The system is then the top-level object (layer) with operations defined by these data flows. Each operation is then examined to determine if it could be implemented by a lower-level object. This is only a first approximation. A better approach is described in detail in Chapter 7.

What happens when a component object needs to send a message outside its containing layer? While messages sent to layers are dealt with at the layer interface and delegated thereby to the components' operations along implemented_by links, it is less obvious what should happen when a component requires the services of an object outside its containing layer. Considering Figure 6.6, we can observe that there are two cases.

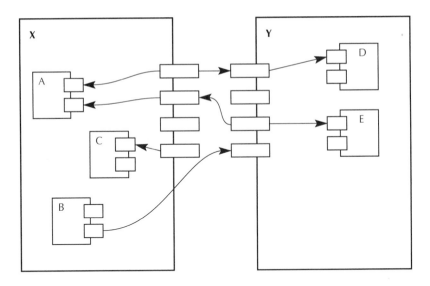

Figure 6.6 Layers and implemented_by links in SOMA.

Case 1 occurs when a class B with no implemented_by links needs the services of E, say. In this case, B should be removed from the composition structure since it implements no services for it. This may involve a minor redesign but is good practice in most cases.

Case 2 is the case where a proper component class B needs the services of either Y or E. Here B can send messages directly to Y, or to E via Y, but not to E directly. It is quite permissible to entertain a direct correspondence or collaboration but the semantics of the design should be examined carefully to see if the anomaly can be removed; for the diagrams may get a little messy. In other words, layers can contain object references in their components.

In short, inbound messages cannot penetrate a layer but outbound ones can.

Layers should be regarded in the same way as object wrappers; in other words, as high-level objects themselves. Such objects receive and send messages and, on receipt, delegate responsibilities to objects which they encapsulate. Dually, every object wrapper is a composition structure.

By default, the wrapper object's operations are the union of all its component object's operations. It is the responsibility of the wrapper object itself to resolve polymorphic references. For example, if two objects within the layer have the same operation and the sender has not specified which applies, a rule is required in the layer object to determine how to resolve the conflict.

SOMA layers are in some ways similar to de Champeaux's *ensembles*, RDD's *subsystems* and, but to a lesser extent, Booch's *class categories*.

There has been considerable interest in the object-oriented design community lately in the use of patterns for expressing design experience. Much of this work has been inspired by a study of Christopher Alexander's controversial work on design patterns in architecture. Patterns are micro-architectures: collections of objects and structural relationships that help to provide a common design vocabulary, support conceptual chunking, raise the level of abstraction and constitute a foundation for reuse at this higher level. Patterns can be modelled as layers by building a wrapper around an entire pattern or framework. In such a case, the wrapper consists of more than just a composition structure and often involves classification, composition and association linkages. If we follow Alexander's example, we would come up with a catalogue of reusable patterns and several research groups are attempting this at present. A notable one is the group led by Erich Gamma (1995) at UBILAB in Switzerland and, latterly, Taligent. The best way to deal with patterns is still a research issue. Section 6.8.2 offers some further discussion.

6.7 Finding objects

Objects can be identified using the methods of standard data modelling, those suggested by Coad and Yourdon (1991a), Firesmith (1993) or Shlaer and Mellor (1988), the textual analysis technique described in Chapter 7 or in any other way (perhaps from examining DFDs or Jackson event diagrams as suggested by Ince (1991)). SOMA adds object identification techniques taken from knowledge elicitation and HCI practice. Specifically these include: structured and focused interviews, Kelly grids, protocol analysis, topic analysis and task analysis. A new refinement technique called Analysis of Judgements is added. All these techniques are described in Chapter 7. These techniques are most helpful when a written requirements statement does not exist and interviews or workshops are necessary.

Where no specification exists, a critical technique used within SOMA is based on an extension and deepening of the Objectory idea of 'use cases'. A context diagram showing external objects and actors is constructed and task scripts prepared for each business process defined by a message interaction. Exceptions are defined as side-scripts. Task decomposition is performed and the resultant text is used to prepare class cards. These may then be used to conduct walkthroughs with users and analysts that effectively test the specification. The details of this method are given in the next chapter.

SOMA also uses techniques similar to those of RDD (Wirfs-Brock *et al.*, 1990) to identify objects and to refine their definition and organization when a written specification of requirements is available, notably the analysis of parts of speech in the text. This is a good way to start but requires the additional techniques of SOMA when the system is complex or semantics are important.

State models of systems can also be used to identify and refine objects as in OMT. The response of objects to system events can be designated by entity state change, state transition or life-history diagrams. The use of multiple techniques is recommended to boost confidence in their products; which should be the same. However, the default notation is that of Harel as extended by Rumbaugh *et al.* (1991) and discussed briefly in Section 6.11.

The SOMA notation is merely the final repository for all the information discovered and unifies the static object model with the dynamic behavioural model using assertions, rules and possibly STDs.

6.8 Structures

The structures to be identified are of four kinds: classification, composition, association and usage structures. The last three are often equated in other methods. Usage structures show the permissible message paths through the system and are less useful as a part of the static description of the structure of a system. We shall see in Chapter 7 how they may be combined with event traces to help understand the dynamic aspects and even animate the specification. Classification structures show inheritance of features and composition structures show the formation of aggregate objects and layers. Any other relationships are shown by the association structure or represented as objects in their own right.

6.8.1 Classification structures

The many object-oriented methods in existence still largely represent opinions or fragments of methods rather than complete, mature methods. Hybrid methods based on synthesized ideas from these suggestions, conventional methods, AI and semantic modelling are emerging. A rationalization of the current position is expected to happen soon with a few 'market leaders' emerging. There is no clear candidate for market leader yet. As an example of the confusion, consider the many notations for classification structures on offer. Just a few of these are illustrated in Figure 6.7.

The recommended SOMA notation for classification structures is shown in Figure 6.8(a). The bar above the diamond in Figure 6.8 (a) indicates the superclass side of the diamond. This means that the diagram can be inverted or rotated without losing its meaning. The notation inside the diamond is interpreted as follows. E/O stands for 'exclusive/optional' and I/O means 'inclusive/optional'. The term 'exclusive' indicates that each subclass's intersection with the other subclasses is empty, and 'inclusive' indicates that the subclasses may overlap. The 'optional' indicates that the list is not exhaustive; there may be more, as yet unidentified, subclasses. An M, for 'mandatory', would indicate that a member of the superclass must be in at least one of the subclasses; that is, the subclasses are an exhaustive list. The subclasses form a **partition** of the class if the symbol E/M appears. Note that stating that a classifi-

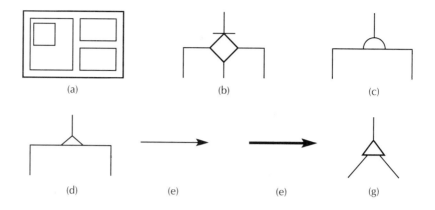

Figure 6.7 Some of the suggested classification structure notations: (a) Bachman, Ptech; (b) Chen, SOMA; (c) Coad/Yourdon; (d) OMT; (e) Booch; (e) MOSES; (g) OSA.

cation structure is optional (mandatory) corresponds to stating that the super-class is a concrete (abstract) class. That is, this information about the structure can be encapsulated in an object. It is not clear that this can be done with the exclusive/inclusive dichotomy. Therefore, it is recommended that overlapping subclasses are removed before the design is finalized. This can be done using multiple inheritance or by introducing a new subclass at the 1-ply level. For example, consider the curious situation in English motoring law where a driver can legally drive a three-wheeled car such as a Reliant Robin with only a motor cycle licence. As illustrated in Figure 6.9, there are two ways to remove optional-ity present in the model of 6.9(a): introduce either a new subclass of Vehicles as in 6.9(b) or a subclass of both Cars and Motorized Cycles as in 6.9(c). Removing optionality ensures that all model information is encapsulated by objects. Another solution is to introduce a new object to represent the association implied by the classification structure.

C++ programmers should note that SOMA superclasses correspond to what they will think of as **base** classes and subclasses to **derived** classes.

Note that multiple inheritance is permitted notationally but that the E/O–I/M notation is not used since it has little meaning in that case. Two (or more) bars indicate the superclass ends of the relationship. Multiple inheri-tance is dangerous because both name and value conflicts can arise. However, it is also semantically powerful and its use is not discouraged in SOMA. When we move to physical design it may be routinely eliminated.

Classification can be shown either in this manner, in some other nota-tion or, more simply, as simple trees or fern diagrams as in Figure 6.8(b). Fern diagrams should be avoided when there is a danger of confusing the semantics of the links as, for example, when we inadvertently mix up classifi-cation with composition.

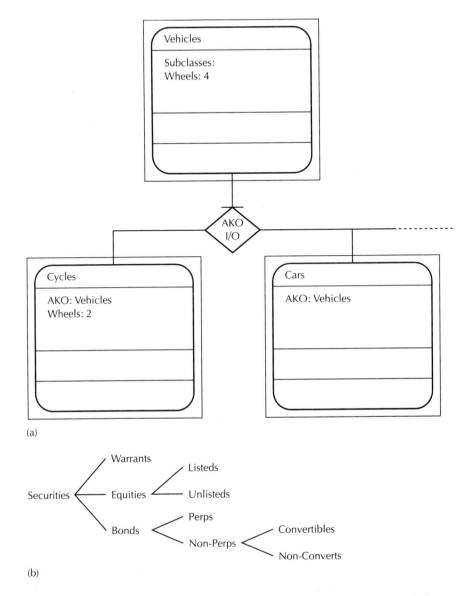

Figure 6.8 (a) Classification structure notation. Note the special attributes Subclasses: and AKO: (A Kind Of). (b) Informal fern diagram recording a classification structure.

An X against an attribute, operation or ruleset (on the left) records the fact that it may not be inherited from a superclass.

The attribute windows of classes that participate in classification structures must contain the special, possibly list-valued, attribute AKO: and possibly

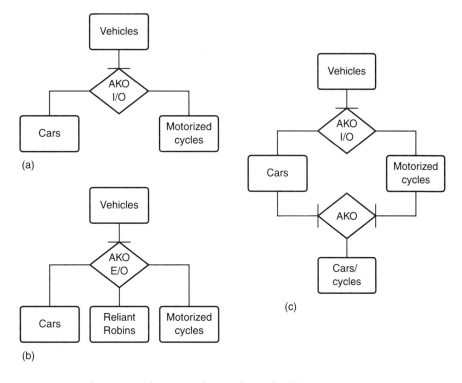

Figure 6.9 Alternative designs for a classification structure.

Subclasses:. Instances must contain the special attribute IsA: instead of AKO:. If desired, a distinction may be made between the special attributes Members:, which refers to instances and Subclasses:, although the context always makes this clear. Clearly, if the Subclasses: attribute is regarded as part of the specification, it compromises reuse, because every time a new subclass is added it must be changed. However, if we envisage automated support for this method this problem evaporates, since it is an entirely mechanical procedure to update the Subclasses: attribute automatically every time a member is added or deleted from the class. Strictly, Subclasses: is not part of the specification but merely a convenient navigational aid. This is exactly how *SOMATiK* manages to draw diagrams of the classification structure from the information contained in class cards. The subclass links are generated dynamically. The keyword Superclasses: is sometimes used instead of AKO:.

It may also be argued, by those committed to an object based approach to analysis, that inheritance is an implementation issue which should not enter into the analysis process, and that users may be confused by it and distracted from the goals of the system. This is a genuine argument but suffers from two weaknesses. First, it confuses the elicitation of requirements with the conceptual analysis process which seeks to abstract the key concepts of the application independently of the perceptions of users. In the latter, the structural features of the domain are revealed, including natural notions of specialization and generalization. Secondly, inheritance, and other, structures are an important part of the domain semantics; the way objects are classified defines the domain, and often the purpose, of the application. For example, the objects of sociology and history are the same, people and organizations, but in history we would not classify by socio-economic group but by social class or perhaps nationality. The structures represent the *purpose* of the analysis.

It is worth mentioning a distinction that has been made between classification and inheritance. Classification is usually thought of as the abstract act of placing instances into classes. Classifying the classes is then referred to as 'generalization'. 'Inheritance' is then the physical linking of the behaviour of a subclass to that of a superclass. These distinctions relate **exclusively** to the details of programming languages. They are of no concern whatsoever to the analyst. Therefore we routinely confuse them. In SOMA the terms inheritance or classification refer to **both** the AKO and IsA relationships within a classification structure. Based on this confusion, some methods consider inheritance to be purely an implementation technique and exclude it completely. My view is exactly the opposite; inheritance is only dangerous as an implementation technique. It is most useful in modelling the structure of the domain at the analysis stage; it provides richer semantics. In allowing a very relaxed view about overriding and multiple inheritance, where even instances can override features, SOMA can model systems to be implemented in prototype languages such as SELF (Ungar and Smith, 1987) as well as object-oriented ones. In this sense it could be argued that SOMA is not truly object-oriented, offering as it does a slightly more general model.

Classification, inheritance or generalization/specialization structures permit the analyst to record the semantics of classification. Inheritance is only used in this sense in SOMA and any kind of *ad hoc* polymorphism or inheritance merely for the purposes of code sharing is banned at the analysis stage. The notation for these structures follows the Chen style of ER modelling. Normally, multiple inheritance is conjunctive; that is, the subclass is a kind of all its superclasses. In very rare cases, disjunctive inheritance is useful. In this case, where the subclass is a kind of one of the superclasses, a double bar is used. This too can be named and annotated.

Implicitly all AKO relationships are many-to-one associations of a special kind denoting classification. However, including this redundant multiplicity information not only adds nothing to our understanding of the problem but is usually highly confusing.

Certainly the Chen style for dealing with multiple inheritance works much better than the Bachman style adopted in, say, RDD/CRC, ORACLE*CASE and Ptech where subclasses are shown by inclusion. This is even true for single inheritance when the hierarchy is deep and we have boxes, within boxes, within boxes and so on. Martin and Odell (1992) fudge this by allowing fern diagrams to be used as well as inclusion boxes in the Bachman style.

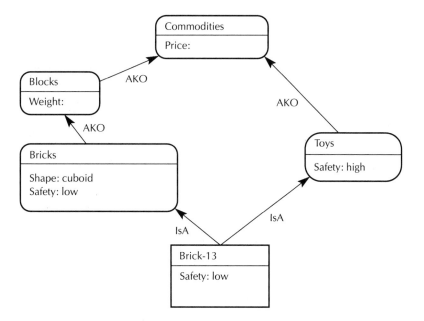

Figure 6.10 Are toy bricks safe?

As is often noted in the literature, multiple inheritance is powerful but dangerous. One particularly difficult related problem is distinguishing subclasses from rôles. For example, a person can be a student or an employee at various points in his or her life or might be simultaneously both. Should this be modelled by subclasses of People called Students, Employees and Student-employees? If so, there is soon an explosion in the size of the classification structure because every rôle that a person can adopt, and all the possible rôle combinations, can be added to the structure. Almost an infinite regress! One alternative is to model these subclasses as rôles. However, this introduces additional complexity since, now, instances of People need to track the rôles they occupy. The whole issue is still a research topic and, pending its resolution, I recommend extreme care in the design of classification structures with multiple inheritance.

Figure 6.10 shows another use of multiple inheritance that is appropriate for attaching 'adverbial' features to classes or instances. This style is widely used by Eiffel programmers. I have chosen the more pathological design involving multiple IsA inheritance rather than the more usual approach that would involve a class called ToyBricks. The structure addresses the safety of toy bricks using a rule: SafetyFirst. Toys are safe in the hands of children, a British Standard says so; bricks are not, especially if you have a greenhouse. The conflict is resolved by the rule that all conflicts on the Safety: attribute should inherit the 'lowest' value. The notation used in this diagram is informal.

6.8.2 Composition structures

Composition structures show how objects are assembled from component objects. Any composition structure is potentially a layer. Classification structures are viewed as orthogonal to these and are not layers, nor are they usually shown on the same diagram as composition. Messages arrive at the outside of layers and are delegated to sub-objects via implemented_by links. Messages can arrive anywhere in a classification structure but do so most often at instances. Thus, in usage structure diagrams, classification structures may be expanded but composition structures may not. An exception to this rule is made when we are describing patterns, as discussed below.

The attribute windows of classes or instances that participate in composition structures must contain the special attribute Parts: and possibly APO:. Exactly the same remarks apply to the APO: attribute of parts as apply to the Subclasses: attribute of superclasses. They are navigational aids which must be updated automatically when the Parts: attribute is added to or subtracted from, otherwise every time a composite object was restructured the specification of its parts would have to be altered. The E/O, E/M, I/O and I/M notations may be used but parts do not usually overlap.

It is important to understand that composition is not the same thing as 'has-a' as it is commonly understood in programming. An object is often thought of as the composite of its attributes; thus a car *has-a* colour and *has-a* engine. In SOMA, composition is to be thought of as physical composition and not as attribution in this way. An example may help. It might be said that I am part of my family because my family is composed of my mother, wife, children and aunts. It might also be claimed that the handle is part of my suitcase. To see that these part-of relationships are different, consider what can be deduced if I travel from London to Zurich. If the suitcase handle goes with me then (unless I deliberately detach it) the whole case goes too. However, my family may stay behind. SOMA composition structures have the same semantics as the suitcase and not the family. The other kind of composition is modelled using either attribution or association; attribution being – after all – only a special case of association. This, of course, applies to layers as well because layers stand at the top of composition structures. If the layer is implemented on a new machine so are all its component objects. The layer is thus the unit of delivery for its components.

Other notations interpret all composition links as instance-level connexions. I have occasionally found it useful to permit a class-level interpretation as well. In Figure 6.11(b) a particular wheel (an instance) may belong to only one cycle – at any one time. However, that type of wheel (its class) may be a part of several models or types of bicycle as shown in Figure 6.11(a). At the instance level, for every wheel there is at most one bicycle that it is part of. However, at the class level, for every wheel type there may be many bicycle types that incorporate it. Since this may be confusing and is certainly difficult to give a concrete interpretation to, it is considered that rules should be used to record such constraints – although the diagram may be sketched as an *aide-mémoire* during analysis. The rules window of Frame in this case could have a rule of the form: Can be fitted to Cycles A, B or C. The problem with this is that

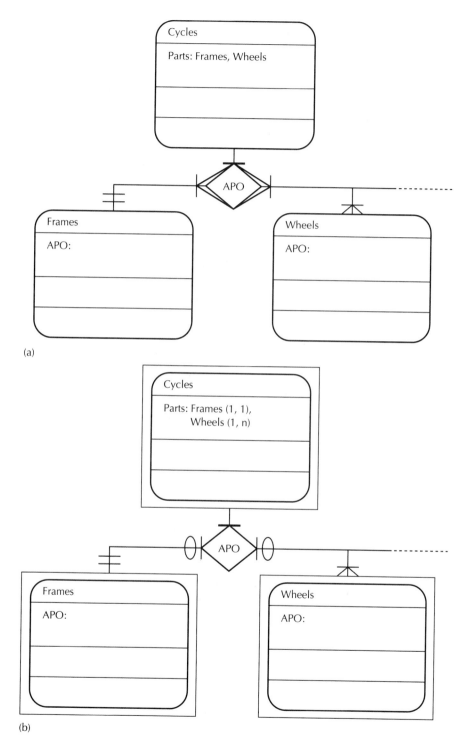

(a)

(b)

Figure 6.11 Composition structure notation. Note the special attributes Parts: and APO: (A Part Of) which records the structural link at either end. (a) Class level; (b) instance level.

encapsulation is compromised and therefore it is better to create an association, or even a separate *relationship* object, to contain the rule. Similarly, at the instance level it is improper for the Frame to know how many Cycles it is part of. However, the information may be important as, for example, when an electron in a molecular binding is simultaneously part of two or more atoms. In these rare cases it is probably best to annotate the parts in the composite objects as 'shared with ...'. The above notation is merely a temporary step towards recording this information on class cards. *SOMATiK* generates these diagrams from class cards and, additionally, can show an expanded composition structure that takes account of composition links that are implicit because of inheritance. The details are given in Appendix A.

Athough we normally try to exhibit classification and composition structures separately in SOMA, they do interact. In particular, if a superclass C has parts then these parts are inherited as parts of all subclasses of C unless overridden explicitly. Likewise, associations and usage connexions will be inherited by subclasses. When we convert classes to types (see Chapter 12) such overriding is forbidden and we only permit the addition of new parts to subclasses. Bapat (1994) formalizes the rules for combining classification and composition structures clearly but, in doing so, violates encapsulation by including rules that assume that classes know their subclasses.

Another place where these two structures interact is in recursive structures such as binary trees and lists. My recommendation is to use only the primitive elements of the notation in the 'pattern' for recursive composition shown in Figure 6.12, which indicates that a list is recursively composed of an atomic head and a tail which is itself a list. Note that this pattern is quite general and occurs for lists and for program blocks in almost exactly the same form. The list and the block patterns are regarded as whole objects or layers and the pattern merely describes their internal structure. Patterns such as this are common in object-oriented analysis and should be recorded as discovered. See Coad (1992) and Madsen *et al.* (1993) for further discussion of the concept of a pattern. As I have said, they can be wrapped and treated as layers. SOMA recommends that a wrapper offering the services of a binary tree as a deliverable layer be constructed. This makes pattern reuse somewhat easier but there are still many unresolved research issues surrounding the design and reuse of patterns. BETA is a pattern-oriented language in a sense that makes patterns a generalization of classes but it is still unclear to many of us what this conception has to do with the patterns of Coad for example. My colleague John Taylor points out (in his forthcoming thesis) that the homomorphisms of OMT are also a form of pattern. Much current work on patterns has been inspired by the work of Alexander and his colleagues (Alexander 1964, 1979; Alexander *et al.*, 1977) in architecture where the notion is quite vague. SOMA will be improved in this area as research continues.

Coad's method (Coad and Yourdon, 1991) was one of the first to reintroduce to OOA the idea that semantic associations between objects should be recorded. This at first seems to compromise reuse but, as Jim Odell has

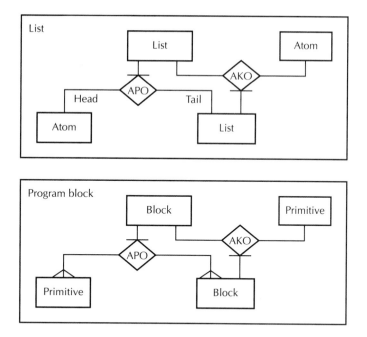

Figure 6.12 Recursive composition (binary tree) patterns.

pointed out: 'The state of an object is the collection of associations that an object has.' (Martin and Odell, 1992). This is equivalent to saying that the object's state is its set of types but the alternative view is often far easier to work with. The main problem with most OOA/D methods is that they have very little to say about system dynamics, inter-object constraints, system control parameters, and the second-order structure of objects. Typical of second-order structures are inter-attribute constraints. Pre- and postconditions can be used to model the temporal constraints on individual methods, but system-wide constraints or those that apply to the object as a whole, rather than to its methods, are difficult to express in this way. It can be done but it's hard.

In practice, the interpretation of the world in terms of composition structures is problematical. Neophytes often confuse composition with classification and draw them all mixed up on the same diagram. A little mentoring can soon correct this but there is a deeper difficulty. The problem is that the phrase 'part of' does not have a unique meaning. It can mean that an attribute is part of an object, that an employee is part of a company and that a wheel is part of a car – and all these meanings are different. Odell (1994) classifies APO relationships according to three decisions: whether they represent a structural relationship (configurational), whether the parts are of the same type as the whole (homeomeric) and whether the parts can be detached from the whole (invariant). This evidently factors APO into eight types. He then discusses six of them and names his different interpretations of composition as follows.

(1) Component-integral APO (configurational, non-homeomeric and non-invariant)
(2) Material (configurational, non-homeomeric and invariant)
(3) Portion (configurational, homeomeric and non-invariant)
(4) Place-area (configurational, homeomeric and invariant)
(5) Member bunch (non-configurational, non-homeomeric and non-invariant)
(6) Member-partnership (non-configurational, non-homeomeric and invariant)

In SOMA we only use configurational, invariant composition. A good rule of thumb to use to identify it is to ask whether if the component moves the whole moves as well. For example, if a firm's general manager flies from London to Madrid the company is not said to have moved. This is better handled by the WorksFor association. In fact, all other types of so-called composition are handled by either associations or attributes (which are merely a special case of associations in SOMA). Thus, we must now examine the modelling of associations.

6.8.3 Associations

Composition and classification structures are merely special kinds of association between objects. Other kinds of associations and their static semantics must be catered for. Connexions of this sort are called **associations**; that is, structural relationships other than usage, classification or composition. In some cases these associations have properties and should be expanded into objects in their own right. In others, the association may be so important for the application (for example, kinship in anthropology) that a fourth or fifth structure needs to be added to the model. Data semantic links indicating multiplicity and modality may be used on composition structure links. Note especially that the term **relationship** is reserved in SOMA for objects with no operations, often introduced to simplify an object model by removing associations. Associations are merely logical pointers to other objects, as we shall see in Section 6.9.1. Note that when a relationship is represented explicitly with its own attributes the normal four-window object icon is used but, following Desfray (1992), we do not permit relationships to have operations.

Now we must face the question of whether a particular concept is to be modelled as an object type or as an attribute of another object. The usual data modelling considerations apply and, generally, objects with one or very few features are better treated as attributes of other objects. The guidelines for identifying objects given in Chapter 7 are helpful in this context. It is also worth remarking that, as with sound data analysis practice, object ownership and validation should be specified as clearly as possible, as discussed in Section 6.9.1.

Normalization into third normal form provides valuable guidelines in making the decision about whether to treat something as an object or as an attribute. The normal form is 3NF which eliminates most redundancy. However, normalization is definitely not part of the object model and should only be used as an heuristic guide. ER models tend to produce 3NF relations. Here too it will be found that what is most natural tends to look like 3NF. The rule is: model the real world and think about potential redundancies and anomalies. Conventional normalization only considers associations. In object-oriented analysis normalization must take place with respect to all four structures.

When existing data models are available as a starting point for analysis they should usually be de-normalized first. The thing to look out for is long compound expressions or names that mean little to users. Such entities usually arise from attempts to remove many-to-many associations. This is not only unnecessary in an object model but positively harmful, since it breaks the common understanding of models by users and developers.

Objects should be concise but meaningful. More than about 30 operations and attributes indicates an object that is unlikely to be reusable. On the other hand too few operations and attributes indicates that the object may be better modelled as an attribute. The software engineering principle of maximizing cohesion and minimizing coupling may also provide important clues as to what is an object versus what should be an attribute. This principle may be generalized by saying that objects should be connascent (or born together) (Page-Jones, 1992).

Associations are discussed further in Section 6.9.1.

6.8.4 Usage structures

Usage structures record the message passing topology of the system or, equivalently, the visibility or client/server relationships. The objective is to minimize the 'homology' or complexity of the structure and this homology may be a useful metric to collect. The homology is found by counting the number of 'holes' in the structure; regarding double-headed arrows as two single-headed arrows. In Figure 6.13 the homology is 2. This structure generalizes the HOOD Seniority hierarchy. Purely hierarchical usage structures have a homology of zero.

It is quite permissible to build separate behavioural models for objects and for their interactions. Local state transition diagrams may be embedded in the objects as discussed in Section 6.11. Possible notations and approaches to behavioural modelling include those of Booch'93, OMT, SSADM ELHs (Entity Life Histories) or Martin and Odell's Object Behaviour Model notation. This means that existing CASE and diagramming tools can be used for this activity if *SOMATiK* is not. The results are consolidated using SOMA notation.

Individual messages may be shown explicitly with labels in the very early stages of analysis. The formal diagrams, however, are compiled under the rule

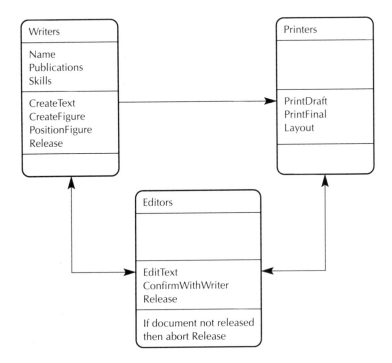

Figure 6.13 A fragment of a Usage structure. Writers may ask a printer to print a draft and editors may ask them to print a final copy. Writers can release text to an editor and editors check changes with the author who can approve them. Not all attributes, operations and rules are shown.

that an arrow joining two icons represents the possibility of any message being passed, the actual legal messages being determined from the operations window of the receiver. These arrows are thus equivalent to usage structures or client/server relationships. Illegal polymorphic messages must be explicitly declared in the operation description, attribute facets or as a comment in the rules window. For example, it may be necessary to permit 'user' objects to send messages to 'employee' class objects, but to forbid the user to discover an employee's age. It is proposed that the tools which support SOMA should include facilities for dynamic simulation of events/messages using an augmented Petri net; augmented because each object needs to stack the tokens that it has passed. Failing this, manual walkthroughs or state diagrams are to be used. *SOMATiK* currently animates models by compiling the features of classes, though this is not supported by the version provided with this book.

We will see later, when we come to deal with SOMA class cards, that the usage structure of a model is entirely encapsulated by the objects if we permit operations to display their servers. This permits usage diagrams to be reconstructed entirely from the class descriptions and thus increases the level to which the principles of encapsulation are adhered to compared to other methods. *SOMATiK* allows its users to browse models, using automatically generated diagrams, in any of the four structures: classification, composition, association or usage.

⊟ 6.9 Responsibilities

Each object has responsibilities: **responsibilities for knowing** and **responsibilities for doing**. Attributes and, more generally, associations and Parts: links are responsibilities for knowing. Operations are responsibilities for doing. AKO links have a combined nature. This section specifically examines the responsibilities defined by attributes and operations and looks at their facets.

6.9.1 Attributes

Attributes are often discovered using standard data modelling techniques. Two special list-valued attributes are used: Superclasses: and Parts:. The AKO (or Superclasses) attribute contains the superclass names for the object. The Parts attribute contains a list of objects that compose the object. Recall that, where automated support is available, the dual attributes, Subclasses: and APO:, may be employed to aid navigation through the model but these must be updated automatically otherwise reuse is compromised.

During analysis we are only concerned with public attributes. The internal data structure and private attributes will be specified later.

There are various common, useful annotations on attributes that are supported directly by the notation. These are as follows.

- $ before an attribute name indicates a class attribute. Its absence indicates an instance attribute. A class attribute is a property of a collection of the class's instances such as the maximum height of People. An instance attribute may have a different value for each instance such the height of a person.
- × before an attribute name indicates that it cannot inherit its value.
- / before an attribute name indicates a derived (that is, inherited) attribute.
- Every attribute has a type, which is either a primitive type (integer, date, and so on) or a user-defined object type or class. When the type is a class, there can be cardinality information indicated. This is an association (see below).
- We sometimes specify more than mere multiplicity and modality. Types are qualified as either {set}, {bag}, {ordered set} or {list}.
- Initial values and default values are shown as follows: attrib(type, n, m): init=x: default=y.
- Attributes can be variable/fixed/common/unique. **Fixed** means that the value may not change during the lifetime of the object. Different instances

may have different values and we need not know what these values are. **Variable** is the opposite of fixed and is the default. **Common** attributes require that all instances have the same value, again without necessarily knowing what it is. **Unique** attributes are the opposite of common ones; each instance has a different value. A well-known example is a primary key in a database table. The default is neither common nor unique. The notation is one of the following: {variable}, {fixed}, {common}, {unique}, {fixed,common}, {fixed,unique}, {variable,common}, {variable,unique}.

- Security level may be specified.
- Ownership may be specified.
- Null values may be permitted or not. If not, the facet NON-NULL is set true. For associations this is shown by a minimal cardinality of 1; for example, WorksFor(Depts.,1,n).
- Valid range constraints may be specified; for example, age >16.

The above attributes of attributes are called **facets**. Facets, therefore, are a gloss on each attribute together with information on ownership, nullity, valid range, defaults, computation, derivation, security, visibility, class/instance applicability and so on, in so far as these are not derived from the type. Attribute facets include also pre- and postconditions on get and put operations.

In SOMA, every attribute has a type which must be a valid user-defined or primitive object type in the system. The analyst is free to decide what is primitive but must list these. Typical primitives will include real, integer, string, list, date and so on. Attributes also store associations. For example, if we have the semantic relationship which says that employees must work for exactly one department while departments may employ zero or more employees, then we might record

WorksIn: (DEPTS,1,1)

as an attribute of EMPLOYEES and

Employs: (EMPLOYEES,0,n)

as an attribute of DEPTS or produce the equivalent 'crow's foot' diagram. In fact, we regard attributes as split into two classes: **pure attributes** and (attributes representing) **associations**. The associations of pure attributes are not shown in the association structure diagrams, mainly to avoid clutter. The default cardinality for a pure attribute is (0,1); if the attribute is non-null this is shown as a facet.

The extent to which such associations compromise reuse has been widely debated, but the requirements of commercial systems development seem to have brought the consensus round to their acceptance, and associations are even part of the OMG Abstract Object Model. SOMA's associations are equivalent to what are called *rôles* in many conventional data modelling approaches.

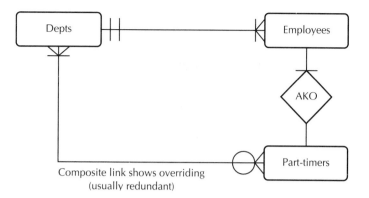

Composite link shows overriding
(usually redundant)

Figure 6.14 Overriding the default semantics given to a composite classification link. In the absence of the override the default would state that part-timers worked in zero-to-one departments.

This means that a SOMA association is a pointer to another class that is encapsulated. There are no associations that stand outside of classes as such.

These linkages are inherited along classification links in the following default manner.

Superclass	Subclass
One-to-many	Zero-to-many
Zero-to-many	Zero-to-many
One-to-one	Zero-to-one
Zero-to-one	Zero-to-one

These default assumptions may be overridden. In the case of overriding the diagrams must show any replaced composite links as in Figure 6.14.

6.9.2 Operations

In its approach to specifying operations, SOMA borrows almost everything from other object-oriented and conventional methods. STDs may be used to specify operations, as in OMT. Even SSADM (or Jackson) Entity Life Histories (ELHs) may be employed. DFDs may be used as follows. Take a data store and find the objects that encapsulate it. Identify the immediately linked processes as candidates for operations. Repeat this for each data store and refine the results. SOMA is deliberately neutral on the technique to be used because in this way practitioners may build on their previous experience. The philosophy of SOMA is that the conventional structured techniques are used internally on an object-by-object basis and not for global system description.

The latter is the function partially of the usage diagrams in the object model but chiefly of the event traces produced at the requirements capture stage and described in Chapter 7. However, cross-checking the products of a global DFD with the operations identified within SOMA can act as an additional check on completeness and is not discouraged where doubts exist.

Just as attributes have facets so operations have facets too. Each operation is associated with the list of messages it sends and the servers it sends them to. It may also invoke a sequence of other public operations as subroutines, the list of these being a facet. As we shall see, other facets are assertions such as preconditions and some class invariants can be expressed as facets of a single operation.

When the behaviour of the object is very complex, state transition diagrams have proved an effective tool for identifying operations. All the traditional techniques for specifying computer systems are also to hand for the specifier of each operation: data flow diagrams, Petri nets for concurrent operations, decision trees and even functional decomposition.

It is essential to make a distinction between operations that apply to instances, such as calculating a person's age from their date of birth, and operations that apply to entire classes, such as calculating the average age of all employees. If the distinction arises then these types of operation are called **instance operations** and **class operations**, respectively.

Operations have a parameter list and a return type. Assertions (pre-, post- and invariance conditions) may also be attached to each operation and are inherited. The operations of layers potentially have an 'implemented_by' attribute. As with attributes, a $ before the operation name indicates a class operation, an × before an operation name indicates that it cannot inherit or that it overrides and a / indicates a derived operation. Other facets of operations include security level, ownership information and assertions.

6.10 Rules and rulesets

In performing object-oriented analysis and building a model, a large number of lessons can be learned from AI systems built using semantic nets and from semantic data modelling. Specifications that exhibit reusability and extensibility are all very well but do not necessarily contain the meaning intended by the analyst or the user. To reuse the specification of an object we should be able to read from it what it knows (attributes), what it does (operations), why it does it and how it is related to other objects. It is my position that this semantic content is partly contained in the structures of association, classification, composition and usage and by the rules which describe the behaviour.

Most notations for composition or parts hierarchies do not take account of search strategies. This is not merely an implementation issue but a question of the application semantics. Inheritance hierarchies use the knowledge implicit in them in a manner analogous to search, and search can occur in a backward or forward chaining manner, just as in expert systems. Backward chaining descends the hierarchy, looking for values, while forward chaining assembles properties from the components of the hierarchy.

The fact is that all semantics compromise reuse. For example, inheritance does so; and so does anything that makes the *meaning* of an object more specific. In system specification, both aspects are equally important and the trade-off must be well understood and managed with care, depending on the goals of the analysts and their clients.

In my opinion, one of the most serious defects of most methods of object-oriented analysis is their lack of support for global control descriptions and business rules.

Object-oriented methods may obviously be extended to deal with multiple inheritance. This extension must include provision for annotating the handling of conflict arising when the same attribute or operation is inherited differently from two parent objects. It must also permit different semantics for subclasses that partition their superclasses into an exhaustive set of subclasses and those that are incomplete, in the sense that presently unspecified subclasses may still be added.

The obvious suggestion to cover these declarative semantics is to add rule-sets to SOMA objects that can not only disambiguate multiple inheritance but also define priority rules for defaults and demons. (A demon is a method that wakes up when needed; that is, when a value changes, or is added or deleted.) That is, these rules can determine how to resolve the conflict that arises when an attribute inherits two different values or perhaps specify whether the default value should be applied before or after inheritance takes place or before or after a demon fires. They may also specify the relative priorities of inheritance and demons. Business rules specify second-order information, such as dependencies between attributes; for example, a dependency between the age of an employee and her holiday entitlement. Lastly, global class invariants and pre- and post-conditions that apply to all operations may need to be specified as rules. A typical business rule in a personnel application might include 'change holiday entitlement to six weeks when service exceeds five years' as a rule in the rules window of the Employees object. With this extension the notation can cope with analysis problems where a relational or deductive database with object-oriented features is envisaged as the target environment.

One must also be aware of the need to decide whether rules belong to individual operations or to the object as a whole. There is no reason in principle why operations cannot be expressed in a rule based language and this is possible in *SOMATiK*. However, the distinction to be made here is not the form of expression but the content of the rules. Rules that relate several operations do not belong within those operations and rules that define dependencies between attributes also refer to the object as a whole. Conversely, rules that concern the encapsulated state of the object belong within one of its operations. The most important kind of 'whole object' rules are control rules, which describe the behaviour of the object as it participates in structures that it belongs to: rules to control the handling of defaults, multiple inheritance, exceptions and general associations with other objects.

The Rules activity is one of the most novel aspects of SOMA. It enhances object models by adding a set of rulesets to each object. Thus, while an object is normally thought to consist of Identifier, Attributes and Operations, a SOMA object consists of Identifier, Attributes, Operations and Rulesets. **Rulesets** are composed of an unordered set of assertions and rules of either 'if/then' or 'when/then' form. This modelling extension has a number of interesting consequences, the most remarkable of which is that these objects – which are local entities – can encapsulate the rules for global system behaviour; rather as DNA is supposed to encapsulate the morpheme.

Another consequence is that rulesets can be regarded as objects for expert systems developments. In that case, one natural approach is to regard ruleset objects as having a small number of attributes and operations. For example, we might have the attribute Goal_variable: and the operation Backward_chain inherited, of course, from the general ruleset object.

As with attributes and operations, the interface of the object only displays the name of a ruleset. In the case of a backward chaining ruleset this might well consist of the name of the value being sought; for example, If Route: needed SEEK Route:.

Rules may be of several different types. For instance, we may have triggers, business rules and control rules. Business rules typically relate two or more attributes and triggers relate attributes to operations. For example:

> Business rule:
> > If Service_length > 5 then Holiday=25
> Forward Trigger:
> > When Salary + SalaryIncrement > 20000 run AwardCoCar

The above simple business rule is interesting because we could evidently implement it in two completely different ways. We could place a precondition on getHoliday that always checks Service_length before returning the value. Alternatively, we could place a postcondition on putService_length that detects whether Holiday should be changed on every anniversary. Clearly, the former corresponds to lazy and the latter to eager evaluation. The important point here is that we should **not** be making design decisions of this nature during analysis. Using a rule based approach defers these decisions to a more appropriate point.

Quite complex rules can be expressed simply as rulesets. For example an InsuranceSalesman class might contain the rules for giving the best advice to a customer in the form:

If client is retired and Client.RiskAverse: is false
>   then BestProduct: is 'Annuity'
If client is young and Client.RiskAverse: is false then
>   BestProduct: is 'Endowment'
If Client.RiskAverse: is true then
>   BestProduct: is 'Bonds'
If Client.Children: > 0 then
>   Client.RiskAverse is true

The rules fire when a value for BestProduct: is needed. Note that these rules do not compromise the encapsulation of Client by setting the value of RiskAverse in that object. The salesman is merely making an assumption in the face of missing data or prompting the Client for that information. If the Client.RiskAverse: attribute is already set these rules never fire. Note also the non-procedural character of this ruleset. The rule that fires first is written last. The ruleset executes under a backward chaining régime to seek a value for BestProduct as explained in Chapter 5.

Rule based systems are non-procedural. That is, the ordering of a set of rules does not affect their interpretation. Rules may be grouped into rulesets which concern the derivation of values for one object. In some environments, such as KEE, rules are each *bona fide* objects, but this approach begs the question of the relationship of a rule to another object.

Most expert system shells and environments encourage the developer to write the rules first and only later identify the objects used by the rules. This enforces a top-down approach and can be useful as a discipline but contradicts an object-oriented approach.

Control rules are encapsulated within objects, instead of being declared globally. They may also be inherited and overridden. The benefit of this is that local variations in control strategy are possible. Further, the analyst may inspect the impact of the control structure on every object – using a browser perhaps – and does not have to annotate convoluted diagrams to describe the local effects of global control. Genuinely global rules can be contained in a top-level object, called 'object', and will be inherited by all objects that do not override them. Just as state transition diagrams may be used to describe the procedural semantics of operations, so decision trees may be found useful in describing complex sets of rules.

Rules are used to make an object's semantics explicit and visible. This helps with the description of information which would normally reside in a repository, such as business rules for the enterprise. It can also help with interoperability at quite a low level. For example, if I have an object that computes cube roots, as a client of that object it is not enough to know its operations alone; I need to know that what is returned is a cube root and not a square root. In this simple case the solution is obvious because we can characterize the cube root uniquely with one simple rule: the response times itself twice is equal to the parameter sent. If this rule is part of the interface all other systems and system components can see the meaning of the object from its interface alone, thus removing some of the complexities of repository technology by shifting it into the object model.

The rules which appear in the rule window may be classified into several, not necessarily exclusive, types, as follows.

- Control rules
- Business rules
- Exception handling rules
- Triggers

Recall that assertions are also attached to each operation and are inherited. Another way of classifying rules and rulesets is into the following six kinds.

(1) Rules that relate attributes to attributes. Example: If Service >5 then Hols=Hols+1. This could be expressed as a postcondition on put.Service causing put.Hols(Hols+1) or as a precondition on get.Hols.

(2) Rules that relate operations to operations. These are naturally expressed as assertions rather than rules anyhow.

(3) Rules that relate attributes to operations. Example: These may be expressed as if_needed (pre.get) or if_changed demons (post.put) or as pre- or postconditions.

(4) Control rules for attributes. Example: behaviour under multiple inheritance conflicts and defaults (preconditions on gets).

(5) Control rules for operations. Example: behaviour under multiple inheritance conflicts (postconditions on gets).

(6) Exception handling rules. Example: overheated sensor (invariance or postcondition on temp).

Let us examine a simple but amusing example involving control rules for multiple inheritance and the default values of attributes. Suppose that we wish to construct a text based adventure game of the type represented by Colossal Cave. We usually have the following sorts of objects: locations, actors and things. The game has locations that may contain movable objects (we'll call them 'things' to avoid confusion) listed in their contents attribute or have mysterious properties described by operations. The attributes of locations also describe the various entries and exits and where they lead. There are players and the computer pretends to contain an anthropomorphic guide who will describe your current location and, if you ask it to eat the snake, say, will reply to the effect: 'I just lost my appetite'. These actors may be conveniently regarded as persons and fitted into a classification structure as shown in Figure 6.15. Note that the guide is not allowed to pick up objects (indicated by the ×) but inherits the ability to move from place to place. Players can issue commands such as 'take gem', 'go west' or 'hit troll with bucket'.

Consider the Things structure now. Things can be classified into treasure, which has a default value of ten points, weapons, which do not, and utility

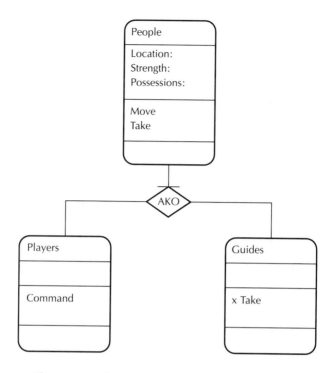

Figure 6.15 The actor classification structure of Quest.

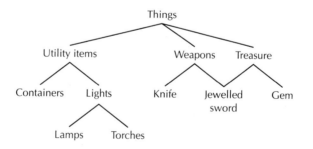

Figure 6.16 The classification structure of Things.

items such as food, bags and the like. A provisional classification structure for Things is shown in Figure 6.16, where it can be seen that multiple inheritance has intruded; the jewelled sword is both treasure and a weapon. Treasure has positive value in points, and weapons have zero value. So what is the value of the jewelled sword, which could inherit from both weapon and treasure?

There are several strategies for handling inheritance conflicts of this type. The system may report the conflict to the user and ask for a value, and this is the most common strategy. Unfortunately, stopping runs in a batch environment is usually more than merely annoying; it is costly. All other approaches require that the system is coded with some of the semantics of the application. Touretzky (1986) and others have suggested various 'shortest path' (or longest path) strategies based on the idea that the most direct inheritance represents the most specific knowledge. This can be useful but the assumption is not always justified and the strategy breaks down when the path lengths are equal. Other work by Touretzky (Horty *et al.*, 1990) suggests that conflict implies ignorance and means we should inherit the null value 'unknown'. The problem with this is that it reproduces all the logical problems that arise with null values in databases, but in some applications it makes sense. It may also lead to run-time errors. If possible, the inheriting object can be given the answer in advance and told, by the default control rule, for example, not to allow inherited wealth to override existing resources. Lastly, in the case of attributes rather than operations, the inherited values can sometimes be combined. One could, for example, take the average or weighted average of two numerical inherited values. Lenzerini *et al.* (1991) provide a survey of work in this general area of the interpretation of multiple inheritance lattices, now called 'terminological logic'. Section 6.12 outlines a completely different scheme for combined value inheritance of this type. It also shows how to implement partial inheritance (inheriting something to a certain extent – a bit like inheriting your mother's singing voice) and even how to inherit partial properties (like being a bit rich) using notions from artificial intelligence and fuzzy set theory. But we still have not resolved the problem of the jewelled sword. A good practical suggestion in this case is to embody the rule 'If conflicts occur on the Value: attribute, combine values by taking their maximum' in the Thing class (Figure 6.17). The jewelled sword inherits this rule. This ensures that the sword gets its points and can still kill the troll.

Integrity rules are regarded as part of the data semantics and stored as part of the association information.

Control rules **concern** the operations and attributes of the object they belong to. They do not concern themselves. Thus, they cannot help with the determination of how to resolve a multiple inheritance conflict between rulesets or other control strategy problem related to rulesets. This would require a set of meta-rules to be encapsulated and these too would require a metalanguage. This quickly leads to an infinite regress. Therefore, in SOMA, multiple inheritance of rules does not permit conflict resolution. A dot notation is used to duplicate any rulesets with the same name. Thus, if an object inherits rulesets called POLICYA from two superclasses, X and Y, they are inherited separately as X.POLICYA and Y.POLICYA. The case of fuzzy rules is slightly different since fuzzy rules cannot contradict each other, as will be explained later. Therefore multiply inherited fuzzy rulesets with the same name may be merged. In both the crisp and fuzzy cases, however, the careful user of the method should decide every case on its merits, since the equivalent naming of the inherited rulesets could have been erroneous.

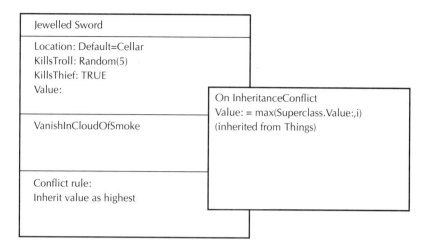

Figure 6.17   SOMA object notation including a conflict-breaking rule.

It is sometimes possible, in simple cases, to specify rules that must be obeyed by all control strategies for multiple inheritance. In the case where objects are identified with only abstract data types – that is, constructed types representing relations, say, are not permitted – we have a clear set of three rules for inheritance:

(1) There must be no cycles of the form:
     x is AKO y is AKO z is AKO x
     This rule eliminates redundant objects.
(2) The bottom of an AKO link must be a subtype, and the top must be a subtype or an abstract type (that is, not a printable object; not an attribute).
(3) It must be possible to name a subtype of two supertypes. This rule prevents absurd objects, such as the class of all people who are also toys.

These rules are commended as design checks.

As we have seen, control rules are not the only rules in an application. We have mentioned business rules already. In both cases, encapsulating these rules in objects makes sense and enhances reusability and extensibility. System-wide rules belong in the most general objects in the system; that is, the top of the hierarchy (or hierarchies if there is no catch-all class as there is with Smalltalk's 'object'). They are propagated to other parts of the system via inheritance. All kinds of rule are stored in the rulesets of the fourth window of the object icon.

OMT's qualifiers may be expressed as rules. For example, consider the many-to-many association between DOS files and directories. The Filename qualifier reduces this to a many-to-one association. In general, qualification only partitions the sets. This is because qualification is relative; there is a degree of qualification. To avoid confusion SOMA uses rules such as 'Every file in the ListOfFiles attribute must have a unique name', a rule encapsulated in Directory. If FileNames is an attribute this can be avoided by writing FileNames[set of names] as opposed to [bag of ...] or [list of ...].

Rule based extensions to object-oriented analysis help enrich the semantics of models of conventional commercial systems. This makes these models more readable and more reversible; more of the analysts' intentions are evident in the model. SOMA also provides a truly object-oriented approach to the specification of advanced database and knowledge based systems.

Recently, researchers have begun to apply this kind of rule based idea to program browsers. These researchers believe that developers know much about their code that cannot be expressed formally, which leads to time being wasted searching for implicit relationships. They suggest that the code should be related to a descriptive level that can be searched and manipulated. For example, the CogBrow research system supports operations such as: 'Find all the routines written last week by J. Smith and change every occurrence of GOTO 32767 to GOTO END:'. Similarly assertions and rules can be manipulated as if they were at the descriptive level. There are also very recent attempts to apply objects with rules to object-oriented network modelling (Bapat, 1994).

It may be enlightening to know that I was first motivated to add rules to the Coad/Yourdon method in 1989 when using it, not to describe a computer system, but to build a model of an organization. This kind of activity, known these days as enterprise modelling or business process re-engineering, brings to the fore the need to record business rules, often expressed at a high level or vaguely – just the sort of thing knowledge based systems builders are used to.

6.11 State model notation

For objects with significant complex state SOMA permits the use of state transition diagrams (STDs) using either the notation of Booch (1994) or Rumbaugh *et al.* (1991), or entity life histories (ELHs) as found in the SSADM and JSD methods if these are more familiar. These diagrams are used to capture the dynamics of individual objects and are related to the object model as effective specification of operations and their assertions. The recommended notation is that of OMT and this is what is described briefly in this section. It is recommended that the technique is used sparingly as we believe it will not be of use for the majority of objects that occur in MIS systems and that its prime benefits arise during physical design – see Chapter 12. Another problem with over-zealous use of STDs is that they can become very complex very quickly. However, for some objects with complex life histories the technique is invaluable for capturing information about both the business and the system. A good example of an object where the technique is suitable is a loan application.

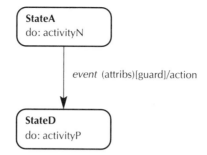

Figure 6.18 States and transitions.

However, the very act of representing this business process as a class is highly questionable in itself. It is often better to capture this kind of information in the Task Object Model which then refers to classes such as loans. The individual circumstances will dictate the best approach.

An object's significant states are determined by key arrangements of its attribute values. These and the valid transitions between them are captured by a state transition diagram. Figure 6.18 illustrates the basic notation. States are represented by rounded rectangles labelled with their names. Transitions are arrows connecting states. Events that cause transitions to occur are written next to the arrows. Events may have attributes. For example, thinking of a calculator object, the event of pressing a key may have the attribute key_number. This avoids the need to have a separate event for each key. Events may have guards or preconditions. A guard determines a logical condition that must be true before the transition can take place. An action is a function that is executed, effectively instantaneously, after the transition occurs. States may have activities. These are functions that begin execution as soon as the state is entered and continue executing until completion or until the state is left, whichever is the earlier. A guard may mandate that the state may not be left until an activity is completed.

Henderson-Sellers (private communication) points out that novices often misuse and overuse activities. They effectively use their STDs as DFDs in this way. The use of activities is not recommended in SOMA.

Figure 6.19 gives a simple example showing part of the life history of a pop-up menu. Initial and final states are shown as filled circles and ringed filled circles respectively as shown in this example.

States may be nested and partitioned into concurrent states. Figure 6.20 summarizes the rest of the notation.

STDs describe the local dynamics of each object in the system. We still need some techniques to describe global behaviour. The main means of doing this is covered in our discussion of event traces in the next chapter. However, the use of rulesets helps to encapsulate locally some aspects of global behaviour, as we have seen.

Figure 6.19 An example.

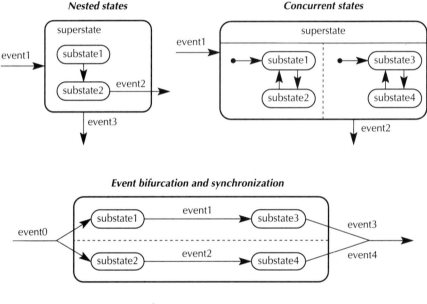

Figure 6.20 STD notation.

6.12 Fuzzy extensions

This section describes the fuzzy extensions to SOMA. This part of the method may be adopted optionally and readers with a strong aversion to such radical and dangerous ideas may safely skip this section, unless they read it for its discussion of how to overcome some problems with multiple inheritance.

In SOMA an object may be a fuzzy object. A fuzzy object may be fuzzy in three senses: it may have attributes that take as values fuzzy sets, it may contain fuzzy rulesets and it may have superclasses from which it inherits only partially. A fuzzy object can be fuzzy in any one, two or all three of these senses. Fuzzy objects in an object model have particular value when defining fuzzy rule based systems or when building business process models where fuzzy

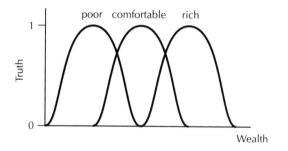

Figure 6.21 Fuzzy term set for the variable 'wealth'.

concepts are normal. The theory of fuzzy objects is described in the appendix to Graham (1994a) and is summarized here.

A fuzzy set is a function f:X → I whose codomain is the unit interval, I. It may be interpreted as a linguistic value over the variable represented by the domain. For example, if the domain, X, represents wealth (over a monetary scale) we can introduce fuzzy sets to stand for the imprecise linguistic terms 'rich', 'comfortable' and 'poor' as illustrated in the diagram in Figure 6.21. The unit interval (vertical axis) is used to represent the degree of truth, so that 'poor' is fully true for wealth zero but falls off as wealth increases until eventually a point is reached when it is entirely untrue; has zero truth. Note that in this model one can be simultaneously both poor and comfortable but to differing degrees. Fuzzy sets are conveniently represented pictorially in this way. They may also be represented as vectors of truth values.

The operations of propositional logic are defined for fuzzy predicates as follows.

$$f \text{ AND } g = \min(f,g)$$
$$f \text{ OR } g = \max(f,g)$$
$$\text{NOT } f = 1 - f$$

Implication is then defined in the usual way, by:

$$(f => g) = (\text{NOT } f) \text{ OR } g = \max(1-f,g)$$

Given a term set of permissible linguistic values, it is possible to extend it using the propositional operators and the fuzzy operations known as *hedges* introduced in Chapter 5. As examples, the hedges 'very' and 'quite' are often defined by:

$$\text{VERY } f = f^2; \qquad \text{QUITE } f = \sqrt{f}$$

Thus, expressions such as 'very rich or not very poor' receive an interpretation as a fuzzy set.

6.12.1 Fuzzy rules

Given these basic definitions it is possible to approach the problem of representing inexact inferences as fuzzy rules. The two kinds of statements we may wish to use are assertions of the form 'X is A' and rules of the form:

'If X is [not] A [and|or X' is ...] then Y is B'.

X, X' and Y stand for objects and A and B stand for fuzzy sets. Simple syllogisms such as *modus ponens*:

X is A
If X is A then Y is B
Y is B

can be handled easily.

For a simple example of fuzzy inference, consider the rule:

If X is A then Y is B.

The fuzzy sets A and B are illustrated in Figure 6.22. If the input is the value x from the domain X then the first step in the inference is to determine the truth value of x: its compatibility with A. In Figure 6.22 (a) this is seen to be 0.8. Therefore, the fuzzy set B is truncated at this level. The output from the inference is this truncated fuzzy set, shown as the shaded area in Figure 6.22 (b).

Inference may be performed over fuzzy rulesets using either forward or backward chaining as discussed in Chapter 5, although forward chaining, one-shot régimes are the most common and well understood currently. In a SOMA object's ruleset we might find the following ruleset for determining a consumer product's price.

PRICE = *LOW*
PRICE = *ABOUT* (2*DIRECT.COSTS)
IF OPPOSITION.PRICE IS *NOT VERY **HIGH*** THEN PRICE = *ABOUT*
    (OPPOSITION.PRICE)

The fuzzy terms are italicized and the primitive fuzzy terms are in italic bold. Each primitive term requires that a truth vector (graph) be stored. The manipulation of this example is explained further in Chapter 8.

6.12.2 Defuzzification

In case it is not convenient to work with fuzzy sets as output values, the result may be **defuzzified** to return a scalar value. There are a number of ways this can

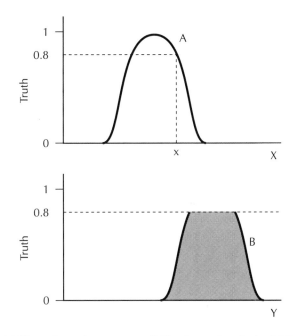

Figure 6.22 (a) The value x has a compatibility (or truth value) of 0.8 with the fuzzy set A. (b) The fuzzy set B is truncated at the truth level of x.

be accomplished. We will need to know about two. The 'mean of maxima' (or maximum) method involves returning the scalar in the domain of the resultant fuzzy set that maps to the arithmetic mean of its maxima. The 'centre of moments' (or moments) method returns the average of all domain values weighted by their truth in the output fuzzy set; in other words, the centre of gravity of a notional cardboard cut-out of the graph of the fuzzy set. The appropriateness of these methods in different applications is discussed exten- sively by Graham and Jones (1988). Basically, the moments rule is best for control applications where a smooth variation in output is desired, and the maximum method for decision support applications where discrete jumps between output states are preferable.

If a fuzzy set is required as output, but some regularity in its form is desirable, then a method known as linguistic approximation may be invoked. This involves the predefinition of an allowed 'term set' of fuzzy sets over the domain, such as the one given in Figure 6.21. In the case of fuzzy numbers (fuzzy subsets of the real line) an example term set might be {tiny, small, medium, large, huge}. The term set may be extended by fuzzy set operations (for example, to include 'not very small'). Linguistic approximation returns the term 'closest' to the resultant fuzzy set, according to some stated measure of distance.

6.12.3 Fuzzy quantifiers

Fuzzy quantifiers are represented by words such as 'most', 'almost all', 'some' and so on, as opposed to the crisp quantifiers 'for all' and 'there exists'. They often occur implicitly in natural language. Thus, 'birds fly' may be interpreted as 'most birds can fly'. Zadeh (1982) introduced rules of inference and a formal semantics for such statements. A typical rule of inference for this system is:

$$\frac{\begin{array}{l} \text{Q1 A are B} \\ \text{Q2 (A and B) are C} \end{array}}{\text{Q1} \otimes \text{Q2 A are (B and C)}}$$

where the Qs are fuzzy quantifiers, interpreted as fuzzy numbers, and $\otimes$ stands for the product of fuzzy numbers. For example, this justifies the syllogism:

$$\frac{\begin{array}{l} \text{Most (about 90\%) birds can fly} \\ \text{Most (about 90\%) flying birds have feathers[4]} \end{array}}{\text{At least many (about 81\%) birds have feathers}}$$

6.12.4 Fuzzy attributes

The attributes of a fuzzy object may contain fuzzy sets (vectors of truth values) as values. Consider the class of vehicles as a fuzzy object. Our general knowledge about the attributes of vehicles can be summarized in Figure 6.23. This object has four fuzzy attributes, each defaulting to the fuzzy set 'high'. The bracketed expressions indicate the type of the value; either [list], [text], [fuzz], [real], or some user-defined abstract data type. A list of text items, for example, is shown as (text,0,n).

6.12.5 Fuzzy inheritance

The degree of inheritance from the class(es) in the superclasses list may be specified as a number between 0 and 1 in square brackets after the superclass name. If no value is given the default value of [1.00] is assumed. A smaller number indicates partial inheritance of attribute values or defaults. These numbers are interpreted as certainty factors and are attached as such to all crisp attributes and operations inherited, though not to rulesets to avoid problems with the type theory. When a fuzzy attribute is inherited it is attenuated according to the following scheme, which includes the possibility of multiple inheritance.

---

[4] One of my reviewers wanted an example of a flying bird without feathers. Next time we meet I intend to chuck him some plucked capons.

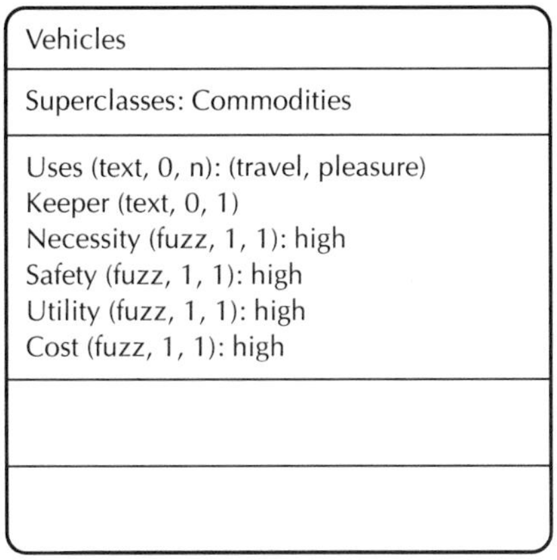

```
┌─────────────────────────────────────────┐
│  Vehicles                               │
├─────────────────────────────────────────┤
│  Superclasses: Commodities              │
├─────────────────────────────────────────┤
│  Uses (text, 0, n): (travel, pleasure)  │
│  Keeper (text, 0, 1)                    │
│  Necessity (fuzz, 1, 1): high           │
│  Safety (fuzz, 1, 1): high              │
│  Utility (fuzz, 1, 1): high             │
│  Cost (fuzz, 1, 1): high                │
├─────────────────────────────────────────┤
│                                         │
├─────────────────────────────────────────┤
│                                         │
└─────────────────────────────────────────┘
```

Figure 6.23 A class with fuzzy attributes.

The fuzzy single inheritance scheme merely insists that a fuzzy attribute of a class inherits the fuzzy set from the superclass truncated to the truth level represented by the certainty factor of the inheritance link. If there is more than one superclass, and thus multiple inheritance, the union of all the separately inherited fuzzy sets is taken, each truncated at the level defined by the certainty of the link along which it was inherited.

An example may help to clarify this. Consider the partial inheritance network shown in Figure 6.24. Here a sailing dinghy is regarded as a vehicle that is slightly dangerous and as a leisure item too. We have used the shorter term 'toy' for leisure item. Now, it is usual to regard vehicles as major, and therefore costly, purchases. Toys and leisure goods in general can normally be relied upon to be safe and of low cost. This is shown by the default values for Cost: and Safety:. To say that a dinghy is a vehicle does not do justice to our normal conception of a vehicle, which probably has four wheels; nor is it fully reasonable to assert without qualification that a dinghy is a toy. This is modelled here by restricting the degrees to which dinghies can inherit from their superclasses, as indicated in the figure. In this particular case the designer, rightly or wrongly, has decided to emphasize that dinghies are quite capable of capsizing by stating that a dinghy is a dangerous thing with especially high risk. However, it is not as dangerous as a hang-glider so the inheritance from this class is limited to degree 0.6. Of course, this is a highly artificial example developed solely for the purpose of explaining the mathematics of fuzzy inheritance. I hope the reader will bear with me in this and begin to see how these kinds of models of usuality could be effectively used in business modelling; a topic we return to in Chapter 8.

Since a dinghy is a vehicle the Safety: attribute inherits 'medium', but as this is only true to the extent 0.8 the fuzzy set is truncated at this level. It also

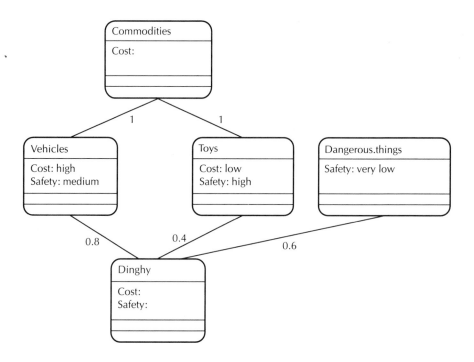

Figure 6.24 Partial inheritance network for Dinghies.

inherits the value 'very low' from Dangerous.things, but only to degree 0.6. The inheritance path from Toys gives the value 'high' in degree 0.4. These fuzzy sets are combined with the union operator as shown in the diagram in Figure 6.25(a). If this were the final result of some reasoning process the resultant fuzzy set would be defuzzified (in this case with the mean-of-maxima operation) to give a numerical value for the term 'safety'. Alternatively linguistic approximation could be applied to return a word corresponding to a normal, convex fuzzy set[5] approximating the returned value. This would return *medium* in this case. In a different application, the moments defuzzification method might be applied. This would return a lower value than *medium* for Safety:. This is a control decision that I feel should be left to the discretion of the user or systems designer and encapsulated locally within the rules window. The other diagram in Figure 6.25(b) shows the fuzzy set for the dinghy's cost. In the absence of evidence to the contrary, Dinghies inherit both these values. Here the maximum defuzzification method gives *high* and the moments method gives *fairly high* as illustrated by the pointers in the figure. They point at the centroid of the returned fuzzy set in the case of the moments method, though this set is not shown.

---

[5] That is, fuzzy set which attains the value of 1 somewhere (normal) and which has only one peak (convex). The fuzzy sets of Figures 6.21, 6.22(a) and 6.27 all have both these properties.

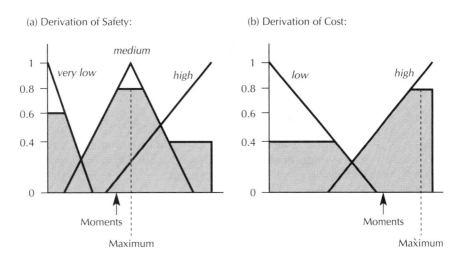

Figure 6.25 (a) Inherited fuzzy set for the safety of dinghies; (b) inherited fuzzy set for the cost of dinghies.

Thus the system is able to deduce correctly that dinghies are costly items that are of only average safety.

The details of the control régime under which fuzzy inheritance takes place may be modified from the default régime given here. For details see Graham (1994a). The repository for this control information is the *rules* window of the object, where the declarative semantics are encapsulated. For example, the choice of the maximum or union operator may be regarded as problematical because of the difficulty in assigning a definite semantics to the disjunction operation, OR, in normal speech. However, the system proposed here should allow for this by the provision of a control parameter, or rules, which would allow users to specify the alternative minimum operation to deal with applications wherein the natural interpretation of the combination of values is different and perhaps represents the possibilistic view that only evidence receiving support from all sources should be inherited.

It is worth remarking that all object-oriented, frame and multiple inheritance systems pose a similar dilemma. A property, such as dangerousness, can be associated with an individual either by inheritance or by explicit inclusion in the object's descriptor. A way round this problem is suggested in Section 6.12.10.

The moments method of defuzzification is the more appropriate one in the example discussed here. This is because we were dealing with the usuality of properties which are subject to combination in reaching a 'balanced view', rather than ones which contribute to either/or decision making. There could be problems if we had mixed objectives in our use of the object-base. We would at least have to type the AKO links – using the rules window – were the two strategies to be required over the same object-base.

I have thus presented, via a very simple example, the basic theory of fuzzy objects in SOMA and explained its logic of inheritance. I have concentrated on attributes but operations can have inheritable possibilities attached and rules in SOMA can be fuzzy rules of the sort found in languages such as REVEAL (Graham and Jones, 1988).

Usage structures may not be fuzzified and I can think of no safe way of, or practical use for, fuzzifying composition structures.

Association structures may be fuzzified by attaching a certainty factor to their links or including fuzzy attributes in objects that stand for associations. The syntax consists of allowing two values between 0 and 1 in the association descriptor, representing the minimum and maximum certainties, in place of the first numerical term. A possible practical application of fuzzy associations is to 'dotted line' relationships in organizations, where the responsibilities of certain specialists to technically related parts of an organization may override or mingle with those of the formal reporting hierarchy. One application of such an object-base is to assist with the decision as to whom should be consulted when the specialist is asked to work overseas for a year. For example, the association WorksFor between Employees and Departments could be written:

WorksFor(Depts,0.5,1,n)

meaning that certainties as low as 0.5 may be attached to the several departments that an employee works for. In the case of a particular employee, we can write:

WorksFor: Sales [0.7], Production [0.8]

indicating the strength of the reporting lines. Obversely, no employee may be allowed to report fully to any one department. Here we could write:

Worksfor (Depts,0,0.8,n)

Another application concerns the construction of formal models of the sort of loose–tight properties of organizations referred to by Peters and Waterman (1982). It is my belief that there are a tremendous number of opportunities for the application of fuzzy objects. Among the most promising are enterprise and strategic business modelling.

6.12.6 Fuzzy objects, fuzzy quantifiers and non-monotonic logic

We can now explore the application of fuzzy objects to one of the classical problems in inheritance, using non-standard quantifiers instead of non-monotonic logic.

Zadeh's theory of fuzzy quantifiers lets us express one of the classical motivating problems of non-monotonic logic as 'Most birds can fly'. It is a part of the folklore of fuzzy sets that this can be neatly expressed with fuzzy

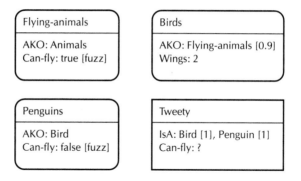

Figure 6.26 Fuzzy objects for non-monotonic logic.

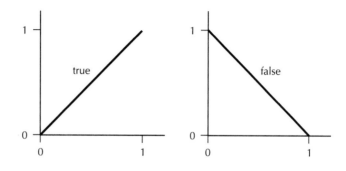

Figure 6.27 The fuzzy set 'true' is given by x=x and 'false' by x=–x.

inheritance; thus a fuzzy objects approach is indicated. The object-base is shown in Figure 6.26.

The fuzzy sets involved are illustrated in Figure 6.27. The answer is that Tweety is a bird and can't fly. So far this is the same result as that suggested in McDermott and Doyle (1980) – but we can do better: penguins do sort of fly (they make fluttering movements when diving or running) and the fuzzy set shown in Figure 6.28 preserves this information in a way. Another approach to this problem would be to use analogical reasoning, but this is often a very complex approach.

It is useful to interpret a fuzzy AKO link as a most/some type fuzzy quantifier. AKO links may be used (or misused) for a variety of conflicting purposes. A good design theory would force us to state the interpretation of the inheritance links and not mix them up. An alternative is to permit fuzzy objects to have a number of 'typed' inheritance links. Then inheritance could take place through a manifold of different networks.

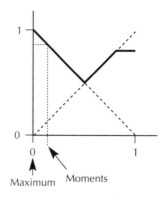

Maximum Moments

Figure 6.28 Fuzzy set for the compatibility of the statement 'Tweety can fly'. Under the maximum rule the answer is 'no' while if the moments rule is used it is 'a little'.

6.12.7 Control rules for fuzzy multiple inheritance systems

Let us summarize the control régimes available within the theory of fuzzy objects. These are global rules only if stated within the rules window of the most general object, if there is one. Otherwise, they may be subject to local variations.

(1) The default régime: If an attribute is filled, don't inherit into it. If it isn't then combine the truncated inherited attributes with the maximum operator. For non-fuzzy variables the maximum of the certainty factors represented by the AKO values is attached to the inherited value. Multiple inheritance of non-fuzzy values may result in multi-valued attributes (lists).

Different fuzzy logics may be used according to the application at hand. The maximum operator may then be replaced with the appropriate t-conorm. The maximum (or conorm) operator may be replaced for individual AKO attributes by the minimum (or corresponding norm). The choice of maximum corresponds to regarding conflicting values as alternative viewpoints. The choice of minimum corresponds to maximal caution and the view that the conflicting sources complement each other.

(2) The Fuzzy Closed World Assumption: Inherit all defined values and perform a union. Some theory of attenuation may be added. The control strategy precludes exceptions, but this is sometimes what is required. For example, when we reason that dogs have four legs because they are mammals and that humans are an exception, having only two, we are plumping for naive physics in contradistinction to a mature biology. Humans (normally) do have four legs; it is merely that two of them have become adapted to other purposes. From such a viewpoint, we want an inheritance mechanism that propagates the mammality in spite of the human exception; that takes account of both factors.

Each régime bifurcates because one of the maximum or moments methods of defuzzification must be selected, unless linguistic approximation is employed. This gives the system designer a choice from at least 24 control régimes. Thus, the array of permissible control régimes is characterized by the following decisions.

(1) Should defined attributes inherit?
(2) Should multiple inheritances be combined with union or intersection?
(3) Which fuzzy logic is appropriate?
(4) Which defuzzification method is to be used?

6.12.8 Design theory for fuzzy objects

In this section, I examine some of the problems that arise in the design of fuzzy object systems, and suggest some design guidelines.

Fuzzy objects are not alone in raising general problems in terms of multiple attribute or property inheritance. Touretzky (1986) lists the analogous problems with crisp inheritance systems and suggests some very reasonable ways round them in terms of a lattice-theoretic semantics. It is not just on theoretical grounds that this approach offers some benefits. There are some problems that Touretzky's approach does not address. What is required is a procedure that determines whether an object-base is 'complete' in this sense. We need to develop a design theory for general object-bases. This would appear to be a very difficult problem, since the recognition of a 'good' expansion is clearly a question of relevance. The absence of such a theory forces one to adopt some method of default reasoning under Reiter's closed world assumption (not the fuzzy version mentioned above).

The analogous question of completeness hangs over all attempts to structure knowledge and data. Even in conventional entity-relationship data models it is recognized that a sound design is achieved only by the exercise of great skill. Decomposition is assisted by a theory of normal forms, but completeness can rarely be assured when the model is of a real, dynamic system.

6.12.9 Objects versus attributes

A major problem in the area of design criteria arises when we have to decide whether the degree to which an object (whether instance or class) has a property is determined by inheritance or by attribute filling (which in turn can result from inheritance). Thus, the two objects in Figure 6.29 are equivalent in all except syntax. The problem is to decide when to choose between the alternative formulations. I will call such objects **tautological**. They are a particularly nasty kind of accidental object.

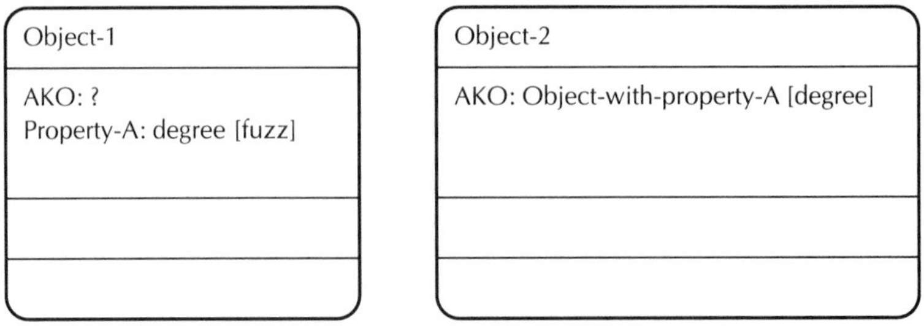

Figure 6.29 Representing tautological objects.

This is nothing more than the class-attribute problem of database design. Making the choice correctly remains a matter of skill and judgement. As a step towards a solution of the problem, the status of such 'tautological objects' is discussed below.

This problem also raises the question of the status of the two kinds of fuzziness: the fuzziness subsisting in the way classes (or instances and classes) are related, and the fuzziness inherent in predicates of description (attributes). It is necessary to ask if we are committing the unforgivable sin of mixing different kinds of uncertainties. This is clearly a danger with poor designs. On the other hand, it may be argued that more expressive power results from allowing the programmer to mix both forms as convenient.

6.12.10 Tautological objects and maximal decomposition

What, we may ask, is the status of tautological objects like the one in Figure 6.30?

These objects are recognizable as having only one non-AKO attribute with a meaning predicate and value corresponding exactly to the object's name. The AKO attribute also contributes nothing new. The specification of the object asserts that a dangerous object is an object that has the property of being dangerous to the degree 'high' or more.

In crisp systems we would automatically disallow such perversions. But, in the dinghy example given in Section 6.12.5, if we disallow all tautological objects on principle, then the only way the low value for safety can ever get into the attribute is if we put it there. This could accord with intuition, because there is really no *a priori* reason (at least not within the confines of our given object-base) why we should think a hang-glider dangerous; it just **is**. This is a convenient way of resolving the problem, which incidentally begs the same question for the design of crisp object systems. On the other hand it is sometimes unnatural not to include such objects: an elephant is a grey object; a grey object is a drab object. Once again, this issue of the difference between the essential and the accidental comes to the fore.

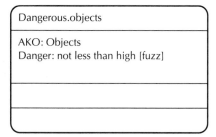

Figure 6.30 A tautological object.

One interesting angle on this problem is that the presence of a tautological object in a design invariably indicates the presence of a personal construct of the kind used by Kelly grids, for example Danger–Safety, so that the presence of tautological objects in a design naturally results from using the methods of knowledge elicitation derived from Kelly grids. Kelly grids and essential objects are discussed in Chapter 7.

Other structures which one would naturally disallow include cycles. In the crisp case, the problem raised by the example discussed immediately below does not arise, since a loop of the type below always represents equality and the network may be collapsed. In the case of fuzzy objects it is harder to decide whether there is a need for such relationships.

For example, the phrase 'Most men are avaricious' may be represented by fuzzy objects of the form shown in Figure 6.31. This pair of fuzzy objects contains an irreducible cycle. Crisp inheritance systems usually demand acyclicity. This is certainly computationally convenient, but no theory exists to say that it is strictly necessary for coherent inheritance, except for the collapse argument given above. The problem just pointed out is, however, special to the fuzzy case; because, for fuzzy objects the cycles do not collapse. One way to remove the problem is to disallow the cycle and expand the network to include a new

Men		Greedy.men
AKO: Greedy-men [0.8]		AKO: Men [1]

Figure 6.31 Cycles in fuzzy inheritance.

object representing 'avaricious entity' (for example, a petrol-hungry car). Then, a greedy man is avaricious [1] (or has the attribute avaricious filled with 'high') and a man [1], and a man is avaricious [0.8] and there are no cycles. In doing this we have broken the no-tautologies rule though. Thus, there seems to be a trade-off between cycles and the use of tautological objects.

The intimate relationship between acyclicity in a design and the presence of tautological objects suggests the following design rules (DR).

DR1 Tautological objects should be introduced to break cycles.

DR2 Tautological objects should be used to prevent users asserting a property for an object explicitly. This has the effect of preventing update anomalies where two objects would inherit the same value from the tautological object but may be assigned different values by the user.

DR3 Otherwise, tautological objects should be avoided.

6.13 Deliverables

The deliverables from object modelling are object descriptions in the form of class cards together with diagrams of the four basic structures: classification, composition, usage and association. The format for class cards is given in Chapter 7. Objects may be instances, classes or layers. If there are patterns combining more than one structure, diagrams of these should be delivered as well. Each class card shows superclasses, parts, responsibilities (attributes and operations) and rulesets. Objects are classified into concrete and abstract and among interface, application and domain objects. If there are any state transition diagrams, these are deliverable. For each responsibility its facets should be shown. These include constraints for attributes and assertions for operations.

Chapter 9 gives full details of the SOMA project structure including all activities, tasks and deliverables.

6.14 Summary

This chapter introduced the object modelling features of SOMA, which combines objects with rules. It was argued that AI has a lot to offer object technology and vice versa. In particular the strong encapsulation of object technology, combined with the semantic richness of rule based systems, offers a powerful set of techniques for both specification and prototyping of conventional, object-oriented, database and knowledge based commercial systems.

Though object modelling is not the first thing a developer does it is a prerequisite of all analysis and implementation activities.

The basic philosophy of the method was reviewed and compared with 'structured' approaches and other object-oriented methods. We also reviewed the OMG reference model for object-oriented analysis and design and saw that SOMA covers all the issues of that model plus coordination and reuse.

The activities within SOMA object modelling, in no particular order, are as follows:

- Identify objects.
- Identify layers.
- Identify association, usage, classification and composition structures.
- Add attributes to objects.
- Add operations to objects.
- Add rulesets to the objects where appropriate.
- Add state models for objects with significant, complex states.

Each of these was described in detail. Objects are either classes or instances. They have an identifier and features. The features are attributes or associations, operations and rulesets. Attributes are special cases of associations. Features have facets. For example, attributes may have constraints and operations may have assertions and servers as facets. Associations are pointers, encapsulated within the objects and equivalent to 'rôles' in structured methods.

Layers are a key, novel feature of SOMA. They are composite objects that are used as the architectural unit of delivery and reuse. Layers are *bona fide* objects.

SOMA offers the modeller four orthogonal structures rather than a hotch-potch of structural relationships that are to be combined in a single diagram. Notations for the structures and for various feature annotations were described in detail.

Rulesets consist of sets of rules written in a non-procedural language and subject to various expert systems control régimes. They enable business rules to be captured in a fashion accessible to users. The rules are encapsulated and may be inherited. This permits the modelling of complex control régimes. State models may be used to describe the life histories of individual objects.

The fuzzy extensions to SOMA were described in some detail. These have applications in expert systems and in business process re-engineering.

Object-oriented analysis is a key software engineering technology for the 1990s. The enrichment of the object model with rules helps insulate developers against changes in future implementation technology due to greater reversibility. The ability to use the same analysis techniques for conventional, advanced database, object-oriented and knowledge based systems is of great benefit in terms of organizational standards and training costs.

⊟ 6.15 Bibliographical notes

The object-oriented analysis and design methods discussed in Section 6.4 and in other places in the chapter, along with many others, are surveyed in Graham (1994a). Readers wishing to gain more detail about other approaches to object-oriented analysis and design should consult one or more of Booch (1994), Jacobson *et al.* (1992), Henderson-Sellers and Edwards (1994), Martin and Odell (1992), Rumbaugh *et al.* (1991) and Wirfs-Brock *et al.* (1990). Graham (1994a) provides an overview of these and a guide to the literature. Also the current journals, including *Object Magazine, J. Object-Oriented Programming (JOOP), Report on Object Analysis and Design (ROAD)* and *Object-Oriented Systems*, in which new material is appearing constantly, are a must.

An alternative approach to associations, but one that I think violates encapsulation, can be found in Ross and Kilov (1994).

7

Requirements capture and analysis

Burrow awhile and build, broad on the root of things.
R. Browning (Abt Voglar)

But men may construe things after their own fashion,
Clean from the purpose of the things themselves.
W. Shakespeare (Julius Cæsar)

All existing object-oriented design and most object-oriented analysis methods make the assumption that a written requirements specification is available at the outset and that business priorities and feasibility are issues that have already been hammered out. This is a major assumption and, if true, it is likely that the requirements capture work has proceeded using functional decomposition techniques that will present fundamental, latent incompatibilities with an object-oriented approach to development. In order to obtain the full benefits from the object-oriented metaphor, it would be better if the approach were applied from the outset.

To obtain requirements one may either guess at them (not recommended), conduct interviews or run workshops. Currently, workshop based approaches to rapid development are popular and have proved effective. This approach is commonly called Joint Application Design (JAD) because users are heavily involved with developers throughout the process. Equally often, the approach is referred to as Rapid Application Development (RAD) because it is usually associated with rapid, incremental delivery of software components.

Before requirements capture can begin, analysts must have a clear understanding of object modelling and the principles behind object-oriented software engineering. This is because if such an understanding is not present, the whole elicitation process may be structured in such a way as to ensure that the model produced is not object-oriented; if you do not know what you seek then you will not find it. The danger is that questions will be asked based on an incremental, functional decomposition that is formulated in the analyst's mind as discovery proceeds and based on the existing functional practices of the business rather than on essential business processes and goals. Users can be easily led along such a path even when they start with their own, business-oriented, mental object model – as they often do. The analysts may construe things after their own, functional fashion instead of going to the roots of the user's conception of the world. Of course, object-oriented analysts also construe the world in their own, biased manner but it is assumed that an object-oriented description is required and, I would argue, such an object-oriented model will map more closely onto the conceptual structures of a user than one based on functional specialization. This view is supported by modern management theory and practice, where it is found that models of business processes based on communicating actors are both more stable and more flexible than those based on functional views of organizations.

The last chapter began our exploration of SOMA by expounding the object modelling component of the method in some detail. That is not obviously the logical place to have begun, since requirements capture evidently precedes object modelling. However, SOMA applies the object metaphor consistently to every activity of development including requirements capture, which is the main subject matter of this chapter, and even to its life-cycle model. Thus, we need to be conversant with object modelling before we can understand how to build an object-oriented requirements model. This chapter also discusses key object identification techniques and the conduct of interviews and requirements workshops.

7.1 Object-oriented analysis methods

7.1.1 Object modelling

Requirements capture is a form of knowledge elicitation. Before we can capture knowledge we need some form of representation. An object-oriented approach dictates that the representation should be in the form of objects, so we shall assume that the representation as described in Chapter 6 is adopted, though any notation such as that of Rumbaugh *et al.* (1991) – with suitable extensions – can be used. If a CASE tool is used this may restrict the notation available but most object-oriented notations will be compatible with the approach described herein, if suitably extended. The extensions that are required principally concern the way subsystems, associations and rules are represented and various annotations that should be made to attributes and operations. Note that these remarks apply to notations rather than methods *per se*.

Some authors have observed that an object-oriented approach to analysis and *a fortiori* requirements capture is a nonsense on the grounds that analysis should be independent of technology. These people assume that object technology is the same as object-oriented programming. They deduce that object-oriented analysis is a tool and that representing knowledge with this tool is therefore implementation dependent. A philosopher would be able to deduce from this that representation in natural language is also forbidden; because language is a tool, albeit a very fundamental one. This argument, and there are many variants of it, is arrant nonsense. First, object orientation is a representational metaphor quite independent of object-oriented programming languages *per se*. Second, representation in terms of objects (including concepts) is fundamental to human cognition. Provided that the semantics are rich enough (and not all methods are ideal yet) there should be nothing not representable in this way.

7.1.2 The process of object modelling

Most existing approaches to rapid application development are based on functional decomposition and relational entity modelling techniques that are fundamentally incompatible with the object-oriented perspective. They need modification to be compatible with an object-oriented approach to system development but need not be abandoned completely.

Developers trained and steeped in traditional methods have two ingrained reactions to a problem: if it can be represented as a static entity they want to normalize it and if it can be regarded as a function they want to decompose it. This is almost an instinctive reaction and an outlet needs to be found for this urge. It has been found that a workshop that ends with a very good object model can easily lead to the production of documentation in the form of normalized entity models and hierarchical, functional decompositions. This can be discouraged by education but it is hard to prevent completely. One, rather devious, technique is to allow developers to decompose but to do so within the task domain rather than during object modelling *per se*. This gives them a suitable feeling of closure without violating the principles of object orientation. That is not to say that they need not understand the object-oriented approach thoroughly, only that their natural, functional reflex is inhibited.

This approach leads to a novel view of the whole requirements capture process as an iterative process moving from task analysis through object modelling to detailed design and implementation modelling. A Task Object Model (TOM) represents business processes, goals and tasks and *not* functions. The new view of development can be illustrated schematically as shown in Figure 7.1. As with all 'waterfalls' there can be elements of the task object model that are not discovered until the analysis and implementation models are built. Incidentally, I begin to feel that we should ban the word 'functional' from the development vocabulary as it is so overlaid with meaning, nuance and emotion.

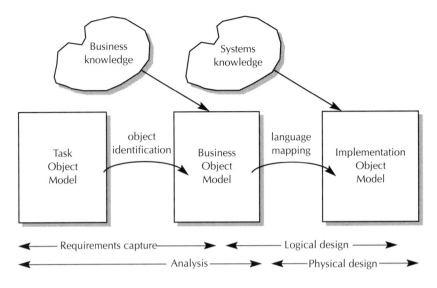

Figure 7.1 Stages of object-oriented development.

The process begins with interviews or a workshop involving people with knowledge of the business. A Task Object Model is constructed to represent the business processes involved. A process is composed of messages that represent 'semiotic acts': conversational acts that are triggered by events and imply commitment to a contract. The goals of these messages are expanded into task scripts that represent stereotypes of the tasks that the system must help the user perform. Note that this is not the same as tasks that are carried out **for** the user or use scenarios representing actual cases. The model is one of humans using tools, not of automata replacing people. Note also the stereotypical nature of the tasks. Placing emphasis on these interpretations turns out to be remarkably important in practice. Since the task scripts consist of sentences, a linguistic analysis can be performed on them to reveal business objects and begin the construction of a Business Object Model (BOM) using the techniques of Chapter 6. This too requires sound knowledge of the business at hand. If a sufficiently high-level language is available one can implement directly from the BOM. However, for low-level languages it is recommended that a detailed design notation be used for the implementation model. Again, a manual transformation process is involved – this time one that requires deep knowledge of information technology. This transformation converts the Business Object Model into an Implementation Object Model (IOM – pronounced YOM). I have used the Booch'93 notation for constructing models where the target language was C++. However, other suitable notations and methods are candidates for IOM representation. For a 4GL, or even Smalltalk, I am inclined to think that the step is only necessary for systems of great complexity. The IOM is discussed further in Chapter 12.

The task object model delivers an object model in the full sense but the objects in it represent users' tasks and not domain and application objects. As we shall see, a textual analysis of the task model helps discover these business objects. Lastly, the business object model is modified to a model that can be expressed in the semantics of some particular language or design notation. Booch'93 can, for example, represent preconditions but cannot represent rules. Thus, part of the conversion is the mapping of rules to assertions. Ambiguities in the BOM with respect to the language syntax must now be eliminated and any loss of expressiveness noted to ensure traceability. A further step could be to create a suite of mappings to different object-oriented design notations, following Desfray's (1992) idea of hypergenericity or, equivalently, Shlaer and Mellor's (1992) idea of recursive design.

There is no reason why this model should not be applied to business and enterprise modelling as well as systems modelling. There are really no significant changes. The language referred to need not be a programming language but a set of business imperatives. Anything with precisely defined semantics will do. This is discussed further in Chapter 8.

The SOMA approach to object modelling uses deliberately imprecise, though quite rigorous, semantics. This may be justified by the observation that precise semantics entails commitment to a particular logic and that it is known that all logics have a restricted expressive power. For example, what can be expressed in non-monotonic logic or fuzzy logic may be practically impossible or very difficult to express in first-order predicate calculus. Human reasoning is inherently imprecise and, the more detailed the understanding, the fuzzier it usually gets (Kosko, 1993). Our object model must capture the detail of even the vaguest requirements, although later the imprecision must be removed in order to implement on a machine. Some requirements are too vague even for this approach and may only be discovered after a prototype has been presented for critique.

7.2 The requirements capture process

The SOMA requirements capture activities commence with a discussion of the nature of the business problem and the objectives of development. This may take the form of interviews but it has been found that workshops are usually far more effective. The techniques are similar in either case. In a workshop the workshop facilitator will write up a mission statement for all to see and amend. Specific objectives are then sought and examined.

In SOMA no activity is allowed to produce a deliverable without it being tested. This principle is applied to the objectives by seeking a measure for each objective. For example, if our business is running an hotel and an objective is to provide a high quality service then the measure might be a star rating system as provided by many tourist boards or motoring organizations. Of course, there are cases where a precise measure is elusive. The minimum requirement is that it must be possible to prioritize all the objectives. A formal preference grid can be elicited by asking that each pair of objectives be ranked against each other. In workshops, this is too time consuming and a quicker, more subjective technique is needed. One way to come quickly to the priorities is to allow participants to place votes against each objective. I usually permit each person a number of votes corresponding to about 60 % of the number of objectives. Sometimes two rounds of voting should be done, under different interpretations, and the results added to reach a final priority score for each objective. An example of two possible interpretations that can be combined is:

(1) Vote from your point of view as an individual user;
(2) Vote from a corporate viewpoint.

Another pair might be:

(1) Vote from the supplier's viewpoint;
(2) Vote from the customer's viewpoint.

The results often generate further useful discussion.

An objective that cannot be measured and/or prioritized must be rejected or, at least, consigned to the mission statement. The priorities are a key tool for project management since they determine what must be implemented first from the point of view of the business sponsor. Technical dependencies must also be allowed for, of course. Often a discussion around these issues elicits new objectives, clarifies existing ones or leads to their recombination or even placement in the overall mission statement. Issues that cannot be resolved are recorded with the names of the people responsible for resolving them. Specific assumptions and exclusions should also be recorded.

Once the objectives are clear, measured and prioritized an **external context model** is built showing all typical messages between the business and **external objects**; its customers, partners, suppliers, and so on. Only when the business is understood completely in its external context is a business support system (usually a computer system) introduced. The context is shrunk to that of this business support system and **actors** introduced. These actors are usually the operatives of the business adopting particular rôles. Messages representing typical communication between actors and external objects and between actors and the business support system are now sought. This constructs the **internal context model** and leads to an analysis of tasks and the construction of a Task Object Model (TOM) in the form of a set of task scripts recorded on **task cards**. The participants in the workshop then carry out the transformation to the Business Object Model and produce class cards for all business objects. Once again, everything must be tested; so the class cards are distributed to the participants and a walkthrough conducted where every message in the TOM is exercised by the virtual machine that the class cards represent, using the participants as the hardware.

Quite a lot of correction and debugging of the cards takes place during the walkthrough and the results are recorded in the form of event traces that are similar to the interaction diagrams of Booch (1994). These event traces are regarded as test scripts and as reusable business processes composed of reusable task scripts. In practice the same processes come up in workshops over and over again. Thus our repository stores not only business objects but also task scripts. These can be incorporated with the new processes and objects discovered in future workshops. The *SOMATiK* tool automates much of this process (see Appendix B). Finally, we compare our business objects against our original objectives to help prioritize the implementation schedule and decide on time-box sequencing.

Subsequent sections of this chapter look at this activity in detail. The rôle of the facilitator and that of other workshop participants is discussed further in Chapter 9.

7.3 Context modelling and the environment model

The construction of a task object model (TOM) begins with the construction of a model of the business environment called the **external context model**. We will assume, unless otherwise stated, that the analysis is being carried out during a RAD workshop. The most common context modelling technique for conventional developers is to use a level-0 data flow diagram (DFD). An extension and generalization of this approach carries over to object-oriented projects, provided that there are major changes in interpretation. No changes to elicitation techniques are necessary, but the facilitators and analysts must understand that it is objects with responsibilities that are being sought ultimately and not functions. Data flow is far too restrictive a notion.

The interactions are better regarded as message flows between the system object and the external objects, which may be **actors** (that is: users playing a particular rôle), external systems or anything else that interacts with the system. Up to the point where actors are introduced we are dealing with the external context model and thereafter with the **internal context model**. Both models are models of message passing. The messages carry data in **both** directions, making them more general than data flows, and are interpreted on the model of Searle's speech acts, although they are more general than mere conversational acts because more than words can be involved. The correct term seems to be **semiotic acts**. In other words, a message implies a commitment and some sort of return value type, even if that type is void. No message is sent without a reason or cause.

It is important that message flows are related to events at this stage. Often a message is sent as the result of a task being performed. In the case of our business objects this is done by the operations of an object. In the case of the

Message name	Trigger event	Source	Target	Information sent/received	Expected result	Goal

Figure 7.2 Message table.

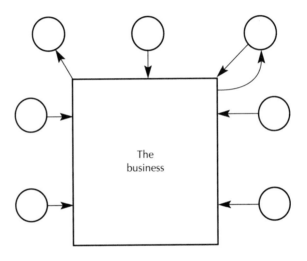

Figure 7.3 Context modelling, stage 1: find connexions with external entities and systems. This is referred to as the **external context model** or **environment model**.

external objects we usually don't have much information about their specification and behaviour. Therefore, the result of their tasks may appear to us as events. Further, messages are sent in order to achieve **goals**. The need to achieve these goals leads to the need to perform **tasks**. Thus a message going from A to B starts with a triggering event and goal, sends data to B and is only complete when a reply or handshake of the correct type is returned. In this sense, messages model primitive transactions.

The format for the message table should be as shown in Figure 7.2. There is one message row for every interaction on the context diagrams. An external context diagram is illustrated in Figure 7.3. This diagram only shows the immediately proximate external objects. This is all that is required for straight information system development. As we shall see in Chapter 8, it is permissible to extend the message model further into the outside world when we wish to re-engineer business processes.

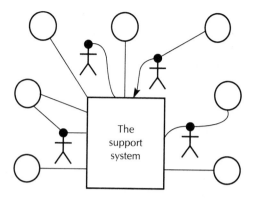

Figure 7.4 Context modelling, stage 2: identify **actors**: users adopting a rôle. This is referred to as the **internal context model**.

Every message is regarded as an implicit closed loop and the most important ones usually originate outside the context. The expected result may be void, as with the broadcast messages from a data feed such as Reuters. When using flip charts in a workshop, diagrams need not show every such relationship between clients and servers – as long as the message table is complete. That is, where there is more than one message flow between the same source and target then only one arrow need be drawn. *SOMATiK* users tend to produce more complete diagrams at this stage.

A distinction between temporal and external events is often useful and this is indicated by the nature of the trigger event; 'every Friday', 'customer action', 'when the index records an uptick', and so on. The characteristic feature of the message is its goal; why the message is being sent and what the sender hopes to achieve.

As an example, consider a counterparty who phones an equity trader to make a sale of equities. We might then record the message as 'external sale request' between counterparty and trader and specify that counterparty identity, instrument, limit price and quantity are passed as parameters. The result is a trade confirmation and an instruction to the Settlements department. The trigger is random action by counterparty. This example is not intended to be complete. Note further that messages can be classified. External sale requests could be for equities, bonds, foreign exchange and so on. This should be exploited by the facilitator and scribe to reduce the number of tasks in the model, elicit more of the environment model objects and find gaps in the model.

The method recommended is for the facilitator to use a flip chart diagram to lead discussion while the scribe records the information in message table form, as in Figure 7.2, pointing out any omissions as necessary.

There are three stages to context modelling. As indicated by Figures 7.3 and 7.4, the first two are to identify significant external objects and communication with the business, regarded as a system, including both manual and automated operations, and then shrink the context so that human users are seen as communicating with a support system or computer system. Once the external environment has been discovered the second step mainly involves identifying the actors. **Actors** are *users adopting a rôle to interact with the system for some purpose*. There may be many users who adopt the same rôle and vice versa many rôles played by one user. These actors now communicate with the support system as external entities. The question is: what sort of people or systems will make use of any proposed system and how will they expect it to behave? In other words, what responsibilities does the system have towards its users? The third stage is to complete the message flow table. The goals in the message table are then the starting point for the discovery of task scripts and the construction of the Task Object Model.

During these stages it is important to find out about the likely skills of the proposed users and describe the skill profiles of the actors. Later these skills can be related to those required to carry out the lowest-level tasks in component task scripts.

The external context model provides a framework for modelling the network in which the business operates. Internal context models will normally remove references to external objects that do not communicate directly with the support system; for example, a customer who deals through an agent and whose details are not recorded. However, when a business process re-engineering exercise is being run these out-of-scope objects will be retained in the project model as discussed in Chapter 8.

The most important messages are usually those sent by the actors to the system. For example, a trader may ask 'what is my position?'. Note that the message source is the trader, even though the data flow is substantially from the system to the trader; this is a closed loop. Every such message has a goal and this must be discovered because it then becomes possible to ask what task must be performed for the system to assist the user in accomplishing this goal. As we will see later, the elicitation of the goals completes a description of the system's scope. Now a more detailed task analysis begins to build a requirements model.

▤ 7.4 Task analysis: task scripts, subscripts, component scripts and side-scripts

Jacobson's (1992) use cases offer a clue as to how one can proceed from here. However, the use case idea has a number of weaknesses, not least that the phrase 'use case' often leads to confusing, and rather too sibilant, sentences; being – I guess – a literal translation from the Swedish. Further, it appears as if use cases are new, whereas there are several related ideas within computer science already. Firstly, they resemble the process bubbles of a DFD. Secondly, use case descriptions are reminiscent of the stereotypical scripts of Schank and Abelson (1977) discussed in Chapter 5. Lastly, use cases resemble the tasks of hierarchical task analysis which is widely, if not universally, used in HCI design. We will use the term **task script** to emphasize these honourable forebears. In doing so we can draw on the riches both of script theory, which has direct implications for object modelling of stereotypical behaviour or business processes, and of HCI, where it is known that tasks can be recursively decomposed and that objects are usually found during this process. We retain the idea from Jacobson that the task scripts will be used as the basis for test scripts later on. The most remarkable observation that can be made about this synthesis of ideas is that task scripts can be regarded as objects that may participate in classification, composition and usage structures. Furthermore, every task script is related to a goal that its execution facilitates. Task scripts are prototypical. Adams and Corriveau (1994) have also observed that replacing use cases, which are interpreted as scenarios of actual usage, with stereotypical scripts is beneficial. They describe and animate the scripts using regular grammars while I use declarative rules for the same purpose.

A major advantage of the task script approach is the reduction in the number of scripts compared to use cases. This results from the changed interpretation. A script is typical rather than actual behaviour. Exceptions are handled by side-scripts. Another key advantage is harder to prove but very evident in practice. Some early users of Objectory reported (at a birds-of-a-feather session at Object Expo Europe 93) that use cases were very good at describing the user interface and the more superficial aspects of a system but less good for getting to the internal complexity. Experience with SOMA indicates that task scripts overcome this problem. Nigel Backhurst (personal communication) reports that he compared SOMA models with a few existing models built using Objectory and found this view vindicated. My experience on about ten projects is the same.

Task scripts are primarily used to discover business objects and retained for testing purposes. However, they are objects in their own right, albeit in a different domain. Because of this, task scripts may be organized into composition, classification and usage structures. The components of a script are arrived at by using task analysis and are called **component scripts**. This is where the hierarchical decomposition takes place down to the level of atomic tasks that refer directly to objects and their operations. Classifying scripts into more specialized versions gives rise to **subscripts**. When exceptions require the flow of control to be redirected to a script dealing with a special case, the latter is dealt with by a **side-script**. It is important to emphasize that task scripts deal with business processes and not business functions in order to avoid the danger of capturing the requirements in the form of narrow functional specializations which are often present in the existing organization.

For each incoming message flow in the context model, it should be established what the rôle player or external agent would normally expect to happen in the form of a stated goal and a script beginning with an event. For example, when a 'request to raise invoice' event occurs in an accounting system, the actor who does this might expect the system to check the credit limit and, if OK, print the invoice, send it to the client, file a copy and send a confirmation. No more detail is required at this stage and it is probably sufficient that the system has a 'produce invoice' operation attached to some object responsible for invoicing.

For each goal there must be a task script. Ideally the script is expressed as a single sentence of the form Subject Verb Direct.object [Preposition Indirect.object]. Example task scripts of this form are:

The trader enters the counterparty details
The system manager changes the authorization of the trader
The user selects Edit using the mouse
The driver turns left using the wheel

We will refer to such sentences as **SVDPI sentences**. Clearly, rearrangements of this form are likely and permissible. We can also annotate task scripts with props[1] and these are likely to be objects in the BOM. Props are indirect objects implied by the action but not mentioned explicitly in every case. The driving sentence could be rearranged as:

The driver uses the wheel to turn left

and one of the props in this case could be the road.

Each script states what the system is **normally** expected to do. However, to emphasize exceptions it is advisable to record side-scripts corresponding to exceptional conditions. To reduce the number of scripts we have to deal with, we classify them and link them to associated task scripts.

During external context modelling we look at the external interactions. Now let us look at the interactions internal to the business area and posit a 'system' within it. The diagram in Figure 7.5 shows a fragment of the internal context model for a financial trading system.

Exploring the 'capture deal' script further reveals that there may be a 'check position' component script and that various objects are required to implement the script. This component script does not record an exception. The script might read: 'To confirm a *deal* the trader enters the *counterparty* and *security* details and checks the limits on his *position*. If the limits are OK the deal is struck and confirmed'. Here there are at least four objects (in italics). Implicitly, for a computer system, there is also a 'screen' object handling the interaction.

An exception or side-script is also useful. For example, the 'settle trade' script might read 'on receipt of ticket, match trade and record data'. When the match fails, a side-script such as 'alert exception manager and print letter' must

---

[1] The word **props** is used here in its theatrical sense.

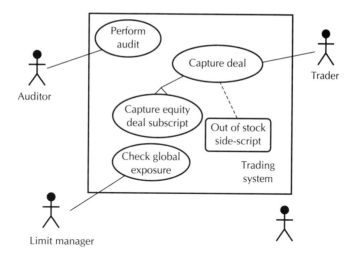

Figure 7.5 Context model for a trading system with task scripts added.

be added. Figure 7.5 shows a side-script for what do to when you have sold something that you do not have. Component scripts form a recursive hierarchy while side-scripts define a usage structure and help to discover event traces.

Task scripts may be classified just like objects. For example, a script for 'capture equity trade' may inherit features from 'capture trade' and add extra features specific to equities, as illustrated in Figure 7.5. Subclassifications of this sort are referred to as **subscripts**.

Tasks may have **attributes**, such as the relative complexity of the task, and **associated tasks**. Associated tasks are rarely used in practice, though I have used a 'similar to' association.

In summary:

- Task scripts may be one sentence or an essay.
- Task analysis should be used to decompose complex scripts into component scripts.
- Atomic scripts should be in SVDPI format ideally.
- There may be subscripts (for example, pay_gas_bill as a subscript of pay_bill).
- There may be side-scripts dealing with exceptions.
- Textual analysis can be used to find objects and operations.
- Task attributes and associations should be recorded, if known.

It should be apparent that task scripts are being modelled as objects and given classification, composition and usage structures corresponding to sub-, component and side-scripts respectively. These three structures correspond to the views taken in use case analysis, task analysis and script theory respectively.

It is necessary to realize that these objects are not objects in the problem domain but in the domain of task modelling; they are nevertheless objects – though they do not usually have significant operations other than their ability to deal with exceptions.

Tasks are carried out in order to achieve goals. Goals are desirable states to be achieved. Preliminary scoping elicits goals for each message. Analysis discovers the tasks behind them. Further analysis discovers the business objects mentioned in the task scripts.

The end product of this activity will be a set of high-level business objects and their responsibilities together with a message list as above. We may also have elicited some composition and classification structures and these should be recorded. Techniques for extracting these objects from the task scripts are described in Section 7.5. Any objects mentioned in discussion should be recorded uncritically for later analysis.

A notation similar to the class cards used for object modelling is recommended for recording the tasks. Thus, a task is represented by a task card with a similar structure to a class card, as shown in Figure 7.6. It is beneficial to record two rather special attributes for all tasks: Time taken: and Complexity:. These have applications in business process re-engineering.

As explained in Chapter 6, high-level objects are sometimes aggregates of lower-level objects and may represent departments, service providers and the like. Such an object is called a layer. A typical layer will be a department, organization, existing system or (rarely) a conceptual structure. Organization into layers can proceed bottom-up by assembling objects that have been discovered to participate in composition structures or merely identified directly. Doing the latter imposes a top-down decomposition to make the problem more tractable but corresponds well to the notions of subsystem, subject or layer found in various object-oriented analysis approaches. A layer will be a composition structure that will be more fully explored during a RAD workshop to identify how high-level operations are implemented by low-level components of the structure.

A matrix of events and objects affected is produced and, if time permits, risk identification is attempted at this stage.

7.5 Identifying objects

Once the task object model has been built we have a textual source that can be mined for objects, attributes, operations, structures and rules. However, it is

Task name	
	Abstract/Concrete
Task body	
Supertasks	
Component tasks	
Associated or analogous tasks	
Task attributes	
Time taken:	
Complexity:	
Exceptions	Side-scripts
Rules	

Figure 7.6 A task card.

always possible to pre-empt this process by skilful questioning during a workshop or even a one-to-one interview. The techniques involved in successful interviewing are also useful for the analyses of the protocols contained in task scripts and so we will present them first.

7.5.1 Techniques for leading group discussions and interviewing

In interviews and group discussions it is possible to identify and detail objects and structures using a number of discussion and questioning techniques. These enhance a basic analysis of the text produced during the task modelling stage. This section reviews some techniques that are useful in interviews and can also be applied to leading group discussions.

It is normal and enlightening to divide interviews into structured and focused interviews. Typically structured interviews are at a high level of generality and take place earlier in the discovery process. A structured interview aims to grasp an overview of the topic which is broad but shallow. It will result in elicitation of the key objects and concepts of the domain but not go into detail. In a workshop this corresponds to running a scoping session, where the same techniques can be used.

Focused interviews or detailed workshops go into the detail of one area and are typically narrow and deep. During the elicitation process it is essential to search for reusable elements – the grey rectangles in Figure 7.7. Analysts should select the area that gives either 80% of the benefit or 80% of the predicted complexity or reuse potential as the first area to explore – preferably both. This, ideally, corresponds to about 20% of the scope of the system. This broad and shallow followed by narrow and deep scenario corresponds closely to the approach that should be followed during prototyping.

Structured interviews follow a plan that should be prepared in advance and state the objectives of the interview. At the start of the session, participants

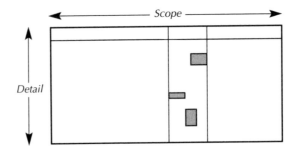

Figure 7.7 Narrow and deep versus broad and shallow approaches to interviews and prototyping.

Table 7.1 Types of probe.

Probe type	Example
Definitional	What is a ...?
Additive	Go on ...
Reflective	What you're saying is ...
Mode change	How would your colleagues view that?
	Can you give a more concrete example?
Directive	Why is that?
	How?
	Could you be more specific?

should agree an agenda. Then, for each agenda topic, interviewers or workshop facilitators ask questions, put out **probes**, review the results at each stage and move to the next topic. Finally, one must review the overall results and compare them with the plan, asking whether the objectives have been achieved. If not, the exercise can be repeated. It is essential that questions are open rather than closed. Open questions do not permit an answer such as 'Yes' or 'No' that closes further discussion or elaboration. Probes are merely particularly useful types of open question. Table 7.1 sets out some probe types with examples. Probes use all six question words alluding to by Kipling in the quotation at the head of Chapter 8.

Focused interviews are less easy to describe in abstract. Their form depends more on the domain in question. However, techniques such as teachback, repertory grids and task analysis are commonly the ones used. Teachback involves interviewers presenting their understanding to the users formally and receiving corrections thereby. The other techniques are described below.

A good interviewer or facilitator plans and prepares sessions and sets clear objectives. However, adaptability is the key skill and one must be prepared to adapt or even abandon a plan that is not working. Some domain knowledge is prerequisite to facilitate open discussion as is a good understanding of object-oriented technology itself, especially object modelling.

7.5.2 Task analysis

This section contains guidelines for object identification based on the formal deliverables from task modelling, while the next gives techniques for going beyond this.

Several of the methods which have been developed by knowledge engineers trying to elicit knowledge from human beings with the aim of building expert systems can be used to obtain concepts in any domain. These concepts often map onto objects. This is not the place for an exegesis on methods of knowledge acquisition but I will mention the usefulness of methods based on Kelly grids (or repertory grids), protocol analysis, task analysis and interviewing theory. The use of the techniques of Kelly grids for object identification is explained in the next section. Protocol analysis (Ericsson and Simon, 1984) is in some ways similar to the procedure for analysing parts of speech outlined in Section 7.5.4. Task analysis can reveal both objects and their operations. Knowledge engineers look for if/then rules in the verbal protocols. Task analysis is often used in user interface design (Daniels, 1986; Johnson, 1992).

Broadly, task analysis is an approach to knowledge elicitation that involves breaking down a problem into a hierarchy of tasks that must be performed. The objectives of task analysis in general can be outlined as the definition of:

- the objectives, or goal, of the task;
- the procedures used;
- any actions and objects involved;
- time taken to accomplish the task;
- frequency of operations;
- occurrence of errors and exceptions;
- involvement of subordinate and superordinate tasks.

The result is a task description which may be formalized in some way, such as using flowcharts, logic trees or even a formal regular grammar. The process does not however describe knowledge directly. That is, it does not attempt to capture the underlying knowledge structure but tries to represent how the task is performed and what is needed to achieve its aim. Any conceptual or procedural knowledge and any objects that are obtained are only elicited incidentally. This is why a transformation of the task object model based on business knowledge, as shown in Figure 7.1, is required.

In task analysis the objective constraints on problem solving are exploited, usually prior to a later protocol or text analysis stage. The method consists in arriving at a classification of the factors involved in problem solving and the identification of the atomic 'tasks' involved. *Atomic* (in the context of user interface design) indicates that the task has been decomposed into component scripts that are described at the level of basic system or screen interactions. In this way atomic tasks correspond loosely with the 'logical business transactions' of Mark II function point analysis (Symons, 1989) and the number of atomic tasks is a basic metric to collect. The categories that apply to an individual task might include:

- goals;
- time taken;
- how often performed;
- type of type;
- exceptions;
- procedures used;

- actions used;
- objects used;
- error rate;
- constraints (sometimes – erroneously – known as non-functional requirements);
- position in task hierarchy.

This implies that it is also necessary to identify the actions and objects in a taxonomic manner. For example, if we were to embark on a study of poker playing, we might start with the following crude object model structure.

Objects: Card, Deck, Hand, Suit, Player, Table, Coin
Actions for Player: Deal, Turn, See, Collect

One form of task analysis assumes that concepts are derivable from pairing actions with objects; for example, 'See player', 'Deal card'. Once the concepts can be identified it is necessary to identify plans or goals (win game, make money) and strategies (bluff at random) and to use this analysis to identify the knowledge required and used by matching object–action pairs to task descriptions occurring in task sequences. As mentioned before, this is important since objects are identified in relation to purposes.

The approach to cognitive task analysis recommended by Braune and Foshay (1983), based on human information processing theory, is less functional than the basic approach to task analysis outlined above, concentrating on the analysis of concepts. The second stage of their three-step strategy is to define the relations between concepts by analysing examples, then to build on the resulting schema by analysing larger problem sets. The schema that results from this analysis is a model of the knowledge structure of an expert, similar to that achieved by the concept sorting methods associated with Kelly grids, describing the 'chunking' of knowledge by the expert. This chunking is controlled by the idea of expectancy according to the theory of human information processing; that is, the selection of the correct stimuli for solving the problem and the knowledge of how to deal with these stimuli. This approach is akin to the ideas of object modelling due to the concentration on the analysis of concepts and relations before further analysis of functions/tasks.

The method of hierarchical task analysis can be better understood through the use of an example. Figure 7.8 is based on a project concerned with the selection of input technology for a financial trader. The overall task to be described is that of recording a deal when the trader, in this case an equities trader, agrees to buy from or sell to some counterparty.

The diagram in Figure 7.8 is to be interpreted from the top level, which represents the overall task of striking a bargain and recording it, downwards and from the left-hand side. Note that the hierarchy is represented as a network at some points. This is only to avoid repetition of common subordinate operations and recursion.

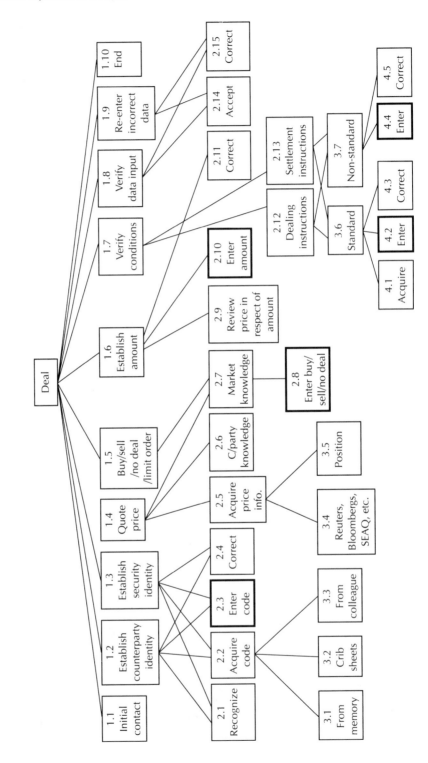

Figure 7.8 A task decomposition of an equity trader's dealing task.

We decompose the top-level task into ten steps starting with the initial contact. This task is atomic with respect to the problem but complex. It does not impinge on the deal capture process and so is not expanded further. This, of course, refers to the receipt or initiation (usually over the telephone) of a communication in which a dealing situation is identified. Once this complex activity is initiated the next step (possibly carried out in parallel) is to establish to whom the dealer is talking, and it is here that computer systems have a rôle to play. Thus, this task requires further decomposition. For example, 2.1 could refer to recognizing someone's voice or spotting their identity from the lights on a dealer board. Next, the counterparty identity must be validated as an authorized one by finding its code. This can be done either from the dealer's memory, from a paper list kept at hand, from a screen display or by calling out to a colleague who, in turn, may have all these resources available. Thus, there are recursive processes implicit in the diagrams but which have not been expanded. If the code is not obtained either the process can terminate (1.10) or a new code can be created. Having acquired the code it must be entered into the record keeping system, computerized or manual. This is the first point where there is significant interaction with the technology of deal capture, and the heavily drawn box indicates this interface. Further decomposition in terms of *inter alia* finger, arm and eye movements is not shown in the diagram precisely because it will now depend on the selected technology. The code must now be validated and if incorrect we either return to 2.1 or correct the entry (2.4) before re-entering stage 2.3. At this point we can return to level 1 and proceed to a similar process in order to identify the instrument being traded. Notice that this process revisits stages 2.1 through 2.4, which explains the tangle of descent paths in the diagram. The remainder of the diagram may now be interpreted in a similar fashion.

Note incidentally that 2.8 descends from 1.5 directly and that 1.8 refers to the verification of the entire transaction.

It will be seen that most of the tasks involve complex cognitive processes, especially perhaps 1.1, 1.4, and 1.5. However, the benefit of the task analysis is that it enables abstraction of those tasks where there is an interface with the deal capture technology from this background.

This rather detailed example is included here to give a feel for the practical problems in applying task decomposition. It should be clear, in particular, that there is value in using task analysis for designing systems and user interfaces but I would assert that other applications where it is necessary to conceptualize procedural knowledge can benefit from the approach. The example also shows the way in which task analysis can reveal the presence of objects, such as price information and settlement instructions, quite incidentally to its analysis of tasks. Thus, in applications where the functions are more immediately apparent to consciousness than the objects and concepts, task analysis is a useful way of bootstrapping an object-oriented analysis. This is often true in tasks where there is a great deal of unarticulated, latent or compiled knowledge. Task scripts are deepened into task analysis tree structures where this is helpful.

Task analysis will not help with the incorporation of the many psychological factors which are always present in deal capture or similar processes, and which are often quite immeasurable. Other incommensurables might include the effects of such environmental factors as ambient noise and heat, and the general level of distracting stimuli.

Readers familiar with Jackson Structured Design may notice a similarity between the task decomposition of Figure 7.8 and a JSD entity structure diagram. It could have been obtained from considering the time-ordered actions of the life history of a 'deal'. Any common subtree can be 'dismembered' (to use the JSD term) and regarded either as a separate group of actions or as a new object in its own right. It can then become the result of a JSD 'operation' or, in other words, a SOMA operation. The striking thing about this observation is how it shows that different disciplines within IT keep reinventing the same wheel under different names.

In some ways it could be held that the use of a formal technique such as task analysis in the above example can add nothing that common sense could not have derived. However, its use in structuring the information derived from interviews and workshops is invaluable for the following reasons. Firstly, the decomposition of complex tasks into more primitive or unitary actions enables one to arrive at a better understanding of the interface between the tasks and the available implementation technology, as will be seen in the above analysis. This leads to a far better understanding of the possibilities for empirical measurement of the quality of the interface. The second factor is that the very process of constructing and critiquing the task hierarchy diagrams helps to uncover gaps in the analysis, and thus remove any contradictions.

SOMA uses task analysis to capture the objects implicit in descriptions of key business processes, which are modelled as networks of semiotic acts (messages). Tasks are represented by scripts in SVDPI format and regarded as objects that participate in classification, composition, usage and association structures.

We now turn to methods borrowed from knowledge engineering which address the object identification and structuring problem more directly.

7.5.3 Other techniques

Basden (1990a, 1990b) suggests, again in the context of knowledge acquisition for expert systems, a method which may be of considerable use in identifying objects and their attributes and operations. He offers the example of a knowledge engineer seeking high-level rules of thumb based on experience (heuristics). Suppose, in the domain of gardening, that we have discovered the rule: 'Regular mowing produces good lawns'. The knowledge engineer should not be satisfied with this because it does not show the boundaries of the intended system's competence – we do not want a system that gives confident advice in areas where it is incompetent. We need to go deeper into the understanding. Thus, the next question asked of the expert might be of the form: 'Why?'. The answer might be: 'Because regular mowing reduces coarse grasses and encourages springy turf'. What we have obtained here are two attributes of the object 'good turf' – whose parent in a hierarchy is 'turf', of course. Why does regular mowing lead to springy turf? Well, it helps to promote leaf branching. Now we are beginning to elicit operations as we uncover more 'causal' knowledge. To help define the boundaries, Basden suggests asking 'what else' and 'what about ...' questions. In the example we have given, the knowledge engineer should ask: 'What about drought conditions?' or 'What else gives good lawns?'. These questioning techniques are immensely useful for analysts using an object-oriented approach.

One of the most useful knowledge engineering techniques for eliciting objects and their structures is that of Kelly, or repertory, grids. These grids were introduced originally in the context of clinical psychiatry (Kelly, 1955). They are devices for helping analysts elicit 'personal constructs'; concepts which people use in dealing with and constructing their world. **Constructs** are pairs of opposites, such as slow/fast, and usually correspond to either classes or attribute values in object-oriented analysis. The second dimension of a Kelly grid is its **elements**. These usually correspond to objects. Elements are rated on a scale from 1 to 5, say, according to which pole of the construct they correspond most closely to. These values can then be used to 'focus' the grid; a mathematical procedure which clarifies relationships among elements and constructs. In particular, focusing ranks the elements in order of the clarity with which they are perceived and the constructs in order of their importance as classifiers of elements. The details can be found in any decent book on knowledge acquisition; for example, Hart (1989), Graham and Jones (1988).

To illustrate the usefulness of Kelly grids, suppose we need to interview a user. The technique involves first identifying some 'elements' in the application. These might be real things or concepts, but should be organized into coherent sets. For example, the set {Porsche, Jaguar, Rolls Royce, Mini, Driver} has an obvious odd man out: Driver.

The use of the Kelly grid technique in its full form is not recommended. However, questioning techniques based on Kelly grids are immensely powerful in eliciting new classes and attributes and extending and refining classification structures. There are three principal techniques:

- Asking for the opposites of all elements and concepts
- Laddering to extract generalizations
- Elicitation by triads to extract specializations

Considering Figure 7.9, we might have discovered that SportyCars was a key class. Asking for the opposite produced not 'Unsporty' but 'Family' cars; not the logical opposite but a totally new class. Thus, asking for the opposite of a class can reveal new classes.

Concept	Elements					Opposite
	Rolls Royce	Porsche	Jaguar	Mini	Trabant	
Economical	5	4	4	2	2	Costly
Comfortable	1	4	2	4	5	Basic
Sporty	5	1	3	5	5	Family
Cheap	5	4	4	2	1	Expensive
Fast	3	1	2	4	5	Slow

Figure 7.9 A Kelly grid. Scores are between 1 and 5. The left-hand pole of the concept corresponds to a low score for the element and the right (its opposite) to a high one. The grid is not focused.

In laddering, users are asked to give names for higher-level concepts: 'Can you think of a word that describes all the concepts {speed, luxury, economy}?' might produce a concept of 'value for money'. This technique elicits both composition and classification structures. It generally produces more general concepts. Asking for a term that sums up both Fast and Sporty we might discover the class of 'ego massaging' cars for example.

Elicitation by triads is not a reference to Chinese torture but to a technique whereby, given a coherent set of elements, the user is asked to take any three and specify a concept that applies to two of them but not to the third. For example, with {Porsche, Jaguar, Mini}, top speed might emerge as an important concept. Similarly, the triad {Mini, Jaguar, Trabant} might reveal the attribute CountryOfManufacture: or the classes BritishCar and GermanCar. As a variant of this technique, users may be asked to divide elements into two or more groups and then name the groups. This is known as card sorting.

All these techniques are first-rate ways of getting at the conceptual structure of the problem, if used with care and sensitivity. Exhaustive listing of all triads, for example, can be extremely tedious and easily alienate users.

Object templates, which are similar to SOMA class cards, have been used in knowledge acquisition for expert systems for many years. Filling in the templates is a structured method for gathering semantic information which is of general applicability. The knowledge engineering approach emphasizes that classes should correspond to concepts held by users and experts. High-level classes represent abstractions that may be reusable across several similar domains. The abstraction 'object' is universal in all domains while 'account' is usable across most financial and accounting applications. 'Mortgage account' is more specialized and therefore reusable across a narrow set of applications. The key skill for analysts seeking the benefit of reuse is to pitch the abstractions at the right level, and this can be very difficult for some people. Prototyping and interaction with users and domain experts all help to elicit knowledge about objects.

7.5.4 Textual analysis

Existing documents and the results of the task analysis should be examined with a view to discovering as many object-types and operations as possible. Where there are legacy systems, there may be old design documents, code documentation, manuals, and fault reports and even proposals may be of limited use.

The main technique used within SOMA is textual analysis of the task scripts and other documents. Subsequently, questioning and discussion is used to refine the model and produce classification, composition and other structures which in turn are used to refine the model further.

It is beneficial to make a preliminary list of objects and operations based on their text prior to RAD workshops, if time permits. This would be used to kick-start object identification and there is a well tried and fairly mechanical means for doing this known as Textual Analysis (Abbott, 1983). Roughly speaking, nouns are candidate objects and verbs are candidate operations. These should be listed fairly uncritically as a basis for discussion. During discussions the aims will be to:

- eliminate duplicates,
- classify objects as within or outside the system,
- eliminate 'accidental' objects and demote to attributes,
- insert relationship objects (if any),
- detect nouns used as stand-ins for verbs.

Where possible, the objects identified should be assembled into classification and other structures. These are then used to refine the understanding of the objects in the system further. Table 7.2 contains much more detail than would normally be required. It is usually sufficient to work from the guideline that nouns are objects and verbs are operations. However, the complete table is included for reference and guidance in those rare and tricky situations that can arise.

The initial object model that is produced from an analysis of the text contained in all the task scripts that have been produced is written on class cards. It may be incorrect at this stage and a walkthrough will reveal many bugs. For example, some classes should have been modelled as attributes and vice versa. A common problem is deciding whether there should be a generalized 'server' object or whether services should be distributed among classes.

The Analysis of Judgements technique (Graham, 1994a) can be applied to improve matters slightly prior to a walkthrough. This technique involves extracting and classifying 'judgements' from the text or the discussion. The aim is to focus on essential, rather than accidental, objects with respect to the domain in question.

This allows us to distinguish between genuine high-level abstractions such as Man and completely contingent ones such as Purple Objects. Objects may be judged according to various, historically determined categories. For example,

Table 7.2 Guidelines for textual analysis.

Part of speech	Model component	Example
Proper noun	Instance	J. Smith
Improper noun	Class	security
Doing verb	Operation	buy
Being verb	Classification	is an
Having verb	Composition	has an
Stative verb	Invariance-condition	are owned
Modal verb	Data semantics, precondition, postcondition or invariance-condition	must be
Adjective	Attribute value or class	risk free
Adjectival phrase	Operation Association	the employee who works in Payroll the employee who got a rise
Transitive verb	Operation	enter
Intransitive verb	Exception or event	depend

'this rose is red' is a judgement in the category of quality. The important judgements for object-oriented analysis and their relevant uses are those shown in Table 7.3.

The categorical judgement is the one that reveals genuine high-level abstractions. We call such abstractions **essential**. Qualitative judgements only reveal contingent and accidental properties unlikely to be reusable but nevertheless of semantic importance within the application. Beware, for example, of abstractions such as 'red roses' or 'dangerous toys'; they are qualitative and probably not reusable without internal restructuring. Objects revealed by qualitative judgements are called **accidental**. Accidental objects are mere bundles of arbitrary properties, such as 'expensive, prickly, red roses wrapped in grease-proof paper'. Essential objects are universal, in the sense that they are (or belong to) classes that correspond to objects that have already been identified by human practice and are stable in time and space. What they are depends on human purposes; prior to trade money was not an object. Reflective judge-

Table 7.3 Analysis of judgements.

Judgement	Example	Feature
Categorical	Fred is a man	Superclass
Quality	This ball is red	Attribute
Reflection	This herb is medicinal	Association
Value	Fred should be kind	Ruleset

ments are useful for establishing usage relationships and operations; being medicinal connects herbs to the sicknesses that they cure. Value judgements may be outside the scope of a computer system but can reveal semantic rules. For example, we could have, at a very high business analysis level, 'employees should be rewarded for loyalty', which at a lower level would translate to 'if five years' service then an extra three days' annual leave'.

Attributes are functions that take objects as values; that is, their ranges are classes. They may be distinguished into attributes whose values are abstract (or essential in the sense alluded to above) objects like employee and those with printable (that is, accidental) objects as values, like redness. Crudely, attributes take their ranges in primitive data types and associations take their ranges in user-defined classes.

Objects should have a purpose expressed by the goals of their operations and their overall goals. This can be accomplished by specifying postconditions and rulesets. These conditions should be stated for each operation and for the object as a whole in the ruleset window of a SOMA object.

A concept should be abstracted as a class if:

- several interesting things can be said about it as a whole;
- it has properties shared by no other class;
- there are statements that distinguish this class from some larger class it belongs to;
- the boundaries of the concept are imprecise;
- the number of 'siblings' (for example, complementary classes whose union is the natural generalization of this one) is low.

A useful rule of thumb for distinguishing essential objects is that one should ask if more can be said about the object than can be obtained by listing its attributes and operations. It is cheating in the use of this rule merely to keep on adding more properties. Examples abound of this type of object. In a payroll system, an employee may have red hair, even though this is not an attribute, or be able to fly a plane, even though this is not an operation. Nothing special can be said about the class 'employees who can fly' unless, of course, we are dealing with the payroll for an airline. What is essential is context-sensitive.

Very long operations, objects with hundreds of attributes and/or hundreds of operations indicate that you are trying to model something that normal mortals couldn't apprehend in any conceivable perceptive act. This indicates that you haven't listened to the users.

It is not only the purposes of the immediate users that concern us, but the purposes of the user community at large and, indeed, of software engineers who will reuse your objects. Therefore, analysts should keep reuse in mind throughout the requirements elicitation process. Designing or analysing is not copying user and expert knowledge. As with perception, it is a creative act. A designer, analyst or knowledge engineer takes the purposes and perceptions of users and transforms them. S/he is not a *tabula rasa* – a blank sheet upon which knowledge is writ – as older texts on knowledge elicitation used to rec-ommend, but a creative participant.

To summarize:

(1) Textual and protocol analysis are used to extract candidate classes, attrib-utes, rules and operations from the decomposed task scripts. An additional step attaches the attributes, operations and rules to the objects.
(2) Repertory grids, card sorts, laddering, and so on are used to discover associations and classification and composition structures. The original objects are critiqued on the basis of this new knowledge. A mnemonic for the use of repertory grid techniques may be stated as follows:
   - Ask for the opposite of everything and discard logical opposites.
   - Ask for the general names for groups of two or more objects.
   - For every triad of objects ask for a property that two have and the other does not. Do this for each pair in the triad.
(3) Class cards are prepared for each class identified.

7.5.5 Further guidelines

Some common-sense guidance on object identification is worth including at this point.

- A good reusable object represents something universal and real.
- An object is a social animal; its methods may be used by other classes. If not, ask what its function is or delete it from the model.
- Although an object should not be so complex as to defy comprehension, it should encapsulate some reasonably complex behaviour to justify its existence.
- An operation that doesn't make use of its current class's own attributes is probably encapsulated in the wrong object, since it does not need access to the private implementation.
- Avoid accidental objects.

Measuring the quality of an abstraction is very difficult. Guidelines can be taken from an analogy with the design of machinery. As with a machine, there should be a minimum number of interchangeable parts and the parts should be as general as possible. Suggested criteria, with their corresponding metrics, include several from the field of object-oriented programming:

- Interfaces should be as small, simple and stable as possible.
- The object should be self-sufficient and complete; the slogan is: 'The object, the whole object and nothing but the object'.
- Objects must not need to send lots of messages to do simple things. In other words, the topology of the usage structure should be simple.

Similar guidelines apply to operations. Operations too should be simple and generative. For example, the operation 'add 1' generates an operation 'add *n*' for all *n*. Look for such commonalities. They should be relevant; that is, operations must be applicable to the concept, neither more specific nor more general. Operations and methods should depend on the encapsulated state of the containing object, as mentioned above. A very important principle of object orientation is the principle of loose coupling or the *Law of Demeter* which states that 'the methods of a class should not depend in any way on the structure of any class, except the immediate (top-level) structure of their own class. Further, each method should send messages to objects belonging to a very limited set of classes only' (Sakkinen, 1988). This helps classes to be understood in isolation and therefore reused.

Analysts should avoid objects arising solely from normalization or the removal of many-to-many relationships. The rule is: if it's not a real-world entity then it's not an object. For example, the many-to-many relationship between ORDERS and INVOICES may be removed by introducing a new class ORDER-LINE. This is fine, the lines are real things; they get printed on the invoice. On the contrary, there seems to be no such natural object that would remove the many-to-many relationship between cars and the colours they may be painted or products and the regulations that apply to them.

Analysts should not be expected to get it right first time. They never do. This is the mistake of the waterfall model – and we know all too well that the costs of maintaining incorrectly specified systems are high. Prototyping and task-centred design, if properly managed, allow the analyst to get it right – but third time round. We will examine this and the management of prototyping in Chapter 9.

7.6 Building the object model

The objects identified so far may now be assembled into a business object model and other structural features added. This model may show up incompleteness but analysts are to be warned to resist the temptation to normalize unnecessarily. Many-to-many relationships may be tolerated. First normal form is quite irrelevant in object-oriented analysis. As mentioned already, the golden rule is: 'If it isn't a real-world thing or concept then it's not an object'. This rule must not, however, be interpreted as saying that domain-specific abstractions are not permitted. What is in the 'real world' depends on the purpose of the development. For example, a programmer might regard a stack as a real-world object and an accountant may deal with an object called 'goodwill'.

Workshops and interviews may have identified layers as composite structures and some of their operations. It should be established by which objects inside the layers, if any, these operations are implemented.

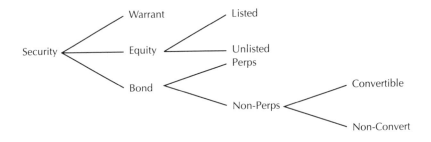

Figure 7.10 A fern diagram for the class Security.

Production of an object model proceeds roughly as in conventional entity modelling but operations and possibly rules will be added to the entities both at this time and later. The first step is to add to the object model those objects identified in the context models using textual analysis.

Following the identification of an object-type such as 'securities' we must now ask: 'Are all securities handled in the same way?' – which will help us to discover the classification structure of securities. Similarly, given three objects of a type we should ask, for instance, if the users can think of a property that equities and warrants share but that bonds do not. Maybe the answer is that bonds are always 'listed' on the stock exchange. This helps to discover both subclasses and attributes and can be repeated for all object triplets. It is also often useful to ask for the opposites of concepts as they are not always logical opposites. For example, the opposite of an equity may be considered to be a bond. This is a useful questioning technique for discovering more specific object-types or even attributes. A useful technique for discovering generalizations is to ask, say,: 'Is there a concept that covers the situation where a counterparty doesn't have the funds to settle and the one where settlement fails due to a non-existent counterparty?'. The answer may produce an object called something like 'settlement failure' at a higher level of generality. What we are doing here is applying one of the object elicitation techniques of SOMA: the method of repertory grids.

In a trading domain, for example, we may well end up with a structure of the sort shown in the fern diagram in Figure 7.10. Note that Coupon is an attribute of Bond but not of Perps[2]. Any instance of Perps will inherit the Coupon attribute and the 'gross yield to redemption' operation.

It is important to avoid mixing classification structures like this with composition hierarchies. For example, a warrant could be viewed as a composite instrument consisting of an equity and an option. This is **not** the same as equity inheriting from warrant. Beginners often suffer from this confusion and even experts slip up occasionally.

---

[2] A **bond** is an interest-bearing instrument. Its **coupon** is the amount of interest paid at the predefined times, usually every six months. **Perps** is short for perpetuals; these are bonds that do not mature and effectively pay a perpetuity, a perpetual annuity.

Producing a sound reusable structure is hard. It should not be expected that a RAD workshop will produce a perfect version first time. Subsequent analysis is usually necessary to refine the model and its structures.

7.7 Refining the task scripts to identify responsibilities

Now we have some objects (nouns) we must identify their responsibilities (that is, the services they provide to other components or actors or the operations (methods) they can perform). To do this we may examine the verbs present in the scripts. These operations must then be attached to a suitable object-type. The guiding principle is encapsulation; objects should contain and hide their data behind their operations. For example, a share register hides registrations behind an interface that permits it to send certificates to new registrants, pay dividends and so on. In RAD workshops, the functions will be tied to these and further objects.

Key questions that should be asked are:

- Who is involved in an interaction to carry out the responsibility?
- What exceptions may occur? (For example, credit limit exceeded.)
- What services (operations) must be provided to execute the interaction?
- Which objects may provide such services?
- Which data does a service need to access? (These data should be encapsulated by the object to which the operation is tied, if possible.)

The task scripts that were identified during context modelling should be further refined and checked for completeness. Have all potential actors and uses been identified? Have all important exceptions been covered sufficiently? The task scripts should be further examined for objects and operations and the operations attached to the objects where possible.

Task scripts may be decomposed into component scripts using hierarchical task analysis. The level of detail to which this is done depends on the purpose. If the user interface is being designed then quite a low level is appropriate. For business requirements analysis this is less likely. In either case the component scripts will offer a further source of nouns and verbs. The rule is that task scripts should be decomposed to the level where further decomposition fails to reveal objects relevant to the purpose; that is, to atomic level.

Objects should be classified into interface objects (if any) and system objects. System objects should be further divided into **application objects** and **domain objects**. Domain objects are persistent and likely to be fairly stable in structure throughout the lifetime of the application, though their instances may change rapidly. Typical examples might include Share-Register, Client-Database, Parts-Inventory, and so on. Application objects are more volatile. They contain operations that are not firmly tied to long-term stored data. Making this separation helps with the maintainability of the system in future and corresponds to the traditional notion of data independence. For those familiar with Sybase and roughly speaking, a Sybase server table with stored procedures will correspond to a domain object. A Sybase client would normally store the operations of application objects.

Each operation can now be provided with a process description exactly in the manner of conventional top-down methods but these **must** be attached to an object. This also provides a further check that no operation has been missed.

Rules and constraints that connect attributes and operations to each other and specify things like conflict resolution strategy are also written down. This was explained in detail in Chapter 6.

Existing systems are best regarded as entire objects that can send or be sent messages. During implementation this may require the construction of an object wrapper around each such system or the use of an object request broker.

For a system where declarative rules are important, such as mortgage lending or trade matching in a settlement system, this step is highly significant for two main reasons. Firstly, recording the rules to which an object must conform directly as rules matches the way users think about the problem and is far easier to use as a communication tool. The alternative would be to record these rules as preprocessing steps within procedures, which is much harder to understand and, worse, makes implicit assumptions about the style of implementation. Secondly, where there is a corpus of declarative knowledge expressed as rules it may be advantageous to implement these rules directly in a knowledge based systems component of the final system, with considerable benefits in terms of both rapidity of development and maintenance, as regulations, say, change in future. Objects with many rules can be implemented directly as the rulesets of an expert systems development tool.

It is recommended that a simple IF/THEN syntax is used to record rules as described in Chapter 6. Recall that the ordering of a set of rules is not significant. If it is, in the real world that is, then an operation should be defined instead.

If an expert systems implementation is not desired then the rules can be converted to assertions and then operations, quite mechanically, at design time.

7.8 Creating class cards and walking through the system

SOMA class cards are inspired by the idea of CRC cards. CRC stands for Classes, Responsibilities and Collaborations and is a form of Responsibility Driven Design (RDD) in wide use. It emphasizes the behaviour of objects as a set of responsibilities. Responsibilities break down into **responsibilities for knowing** things and **responsibilities for doing** things. The former correspond to attributes and associations and the latter to operations. Collaborations are mentions of the server objects with which an operation must collaborate, or send messages to, in order to complete its duty. Note that all links are one-way in object-oriented analysis. Associations are *from* an object and not *between* objects. Similarly, encapsulation dictates that objects do not record information about their clients.

CRC cards are replaced by larger, more detailed SOMA class cards. When used as the basis for a walkthrough, they help to **test** and **debug** the model. Class names corresponding to some of the nouns in the task scripts are written on standard-sized sheets of paper; A4 or Letter, say. Other nouns and adjectives are recorded as attributes. The verbs in the scripts lead to operations. In practice a class card can cover more than one page, in which case they are stapled together. For each entity in any existing ER model, we create a card and add its responsibilities. These objects come from the preliminary analysis, brainstorming and the examination of the task scripts. Next, it must be established which objects collaborate with each other to carry out each operation identified. During this process an attempt is made to organize the cards into classification and composition structures and this information too is written on the cards. Interviewers and workshop facilitators will use several questioning techniques to elicit these structures, including the ones based on repertory grids, teachback, probes and so on, as covered above. In workshops, I have now adopted the practice of letting users and domain experts carry out this task. The developers will then look over the results and apply basic object-oriented principles before the model is used in a walkthrough.

Classes are either application or domain objects as described above. Classes are either abstract or concrete. Abstract classes have no instances. Financial_security is likely to be an abstract class since every security is of some lower-level type, either a bond or an equity, say.

Attributes have a type which is an object-type or a primitive; for example, DoB(Date). Where the type is a class we regard the attributes as associations. Attributes that represent associations have multiplicity and modality constraints; for example, WorksIn(Dept,0,1). It is important to note that relationships are to be regarded as one-way pointers **out** of the object and not as two-way links between objects. If a two-way link is required then an object representing the relationship must be defined, especially if the relationship itself has attributes.

If known, we may classify the classes as abstract or concrete and as one of application/domain/interface. Associations are the attributes with type and multiplicity information written next to them. Operations that are procedurally linked are shown indented under the name of the grouped operation. These 'subroutines' can receive messages in their own right. For each operation, servers are shown with the messages actually sent to them in the form:

Class name	Abstract/Concrete
	Domain/Application/Interface

Superclasses
Parts
Attributes and associations

Operations	Servers-messages

Rulesets

Figure 7.11 A class card.

server1-message, server2-message, ...

Finally, any constraints and rules that the objects are subject to should be recorded on the cards. It does not matter if the information on the cards is incomplete or even incorrect at this stage. A walkthrough will debug the model and complete it. The format for a SOMA class card is shown in Figure 7.11.

At this point rôle-play should be carried out. Each participant takes one or more class cards and acts its part. The facilitator issues events based on the message table and task scripts and the messages are passed round verbally noting changes of state on the back of the cards. In this way the responsibilities and collaborations are 'debugged' and issues exposed. Whether this works well will depend on the personalities of the participants to some extent but I have never seen it fail. Errors in the model are corrected there and then, the participant who has the card writing any changes on it after some discussion. The scribe consolidates the changes later or, if using *SOMATiK*, there and then. This activity **tests** the model and **proves** that all task scripts can be executed successfully. The facilitator is 'the user' and the other participants are 'the system'. It is important to tell the participants at the outset that objects can only respond according to what is actually written down on the card rather than what ought to be there.

Starting with a triggering event, the facilitator asks if any object can help him with his current goal, such as *register sale*. If not, a new responsibility must be added. If so, he throws a coloured beanbag to the participant holding the card. This person may either return the bag to the facilitator along with information gathered from her own resources (attributes or operations) or she may pass the bag to a named server for the operation requested. The bag must always re-traverse the route by which it reached its destination; you cannot return the bag to someone who has not thrown it to you. The facilitator must ensure that the bag only moves according to these rules. Sometimes a concurrent process needs to be spawned. In such a case the facilitator produces a differently coloured beanbag and gives it to the person spawning the new process. It then follows its own path and returns to its point of origin.

As I have said, it must be emphasized that the 'virtual computer' is stupid and can only do what is actually written on the class cards and not what *should* be the case. Lots of pauses for correction and even heated discussion are quite normal. A ten-minute rule prevents such discussion going on for too long and unresolved points are recorded as open issues. The approach enforces the testing-first philosophy of SOMA. Prototypes are an extension and refinement of the same principle: that specifications should be tested.

It may be objected that all this could take a long time for a large system. Actual experience shows this not to be a problem. First of all, really large systems must be broken down into layers by a preliminary analysis. After this, the first few scripts take a long time but subsequent ones are dealt with very quickly. The reasons for this include the practice effect that derives from participants getting better as they understand the approach. However, the main reason appears to be the reuse of fragments of scripts. People are soon able to say: 'We don't need to explore that path; it will be just like path X'. In case any information is lost in this way, it is advisable to videotape the sessions and for the analysts to do a 'private' walkthrough later.

The output from this stage is the completed class cards and a series of event traces. A useful notation for recording event traces has its origins in the

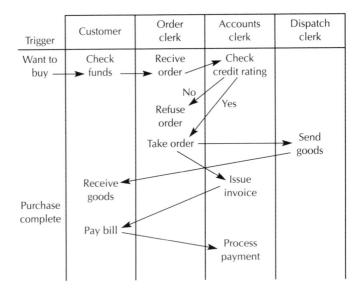

Figure 7.12 Incomplete event trace for a mail order goal.

document flow diagrams of early systems analysis. Lorenz (1993) proposes a similar notation. The objects and actors are written across the top of a large page and the triggering event is noted to the left. Figure 7.12 shows a very simple and incomplete example concerned with mail order. Descent of the columns underneath the objects represents the passage of time. The arrows indicate the flow of messages. The arrows in an event trace may be annotated with comments indicating decision processing, temporal constraints and so on. For example, we could add 'if limit exceeded' to the arrow from CheckCreditRating to RefuseOrder and 'after pay day' to the initial flow from the customer. An event trace is a representation of a business process composed of several messages or semiotic acts. It appears that the content of an event trace is the same as that of an interaction diagram in the sense of Jacobson *et al.* (1992) or Booch (1994), especially when a 'script' is added as Booch recommends. One difference is that the decision processing is written next to the arrows. This is often easier to do than scripting in the hurly-burly of a workshop and users find the notation easy to interpret. Scripts may also be written in the left margin if so desired. Another difference is the interpretation of the event trace as stereotypical, as with task scripts. Concurrent threads of control require more than one colour for the arrows and decisions.

Event traces are deliverable and will be used as test scripts for the working system as it is produced.

To me, this rôle-playing game and the whole approach to workshops has always been rather obvious. However, recent experiences have taught that it may not be so. There are a significant number of people to whom I have explained the approach, in training courses or in person. The majority of them, when they actually get the chance to take part in or observe a real RAD workshop, go through an 'Ah yes!' transformation and will often say that they never really understood how it worked until they observed the complex group dynamics and the inexorable progress towards a thoroughly tested specification. One such commentator said to me that he could 'see the shared understanding building, almost physically, in the room'. This may be an extreme way to put it. I prefer 'It works'.

7.9 Objects with complex states

Object-types should be divided into those with complex, significant states and others. Where the states are complex, a state transition model should be used to discover further operations. As an example, a trader probably does not have significant state – his behaviour only depending on his position (which he may not encapsulate) – whereas a mortgage application may have significant state and a device such as a funds transfer system (SWIFT, say) always will.

Whether the STD technique is useful depends largely on the application. A trade is a likely candidate for having a complex life history in this way whereas a security is not. A state transition diagram is a good way to identify the responsibilities of an object like 'trade' and check for completeness. The walkthrough establishes the global dynamics of the whole system while this technique looks at the internal dynamics of a complex object.

As discussed in Chapter 6, the notation for state models is that of Harel (1987) as presented by Rumbaugh *et al.* (1991).

Detailed state models should only be attempted in a workshop session if time permits. It is more usually deferred until the Rapid OOA and/or OOD activities.

7.10 Setting priorities and running object-oriented RAD workshops

7.10.1 Business objectives

After establishing the basic mission of a project, the first task of either interviewing or a RAD session is to set the primary business objectives. Although it does not derive directly from the object-oriented focus, it is beneficial if

	Objective 1	Objective 2	Objective 3	Total
Object 1	76	30	80	186
Object 2	88	30	50	168
Object 3	15	40	5	60
Total	179	100	135	

Figure 7.13 Object/Objective matrix.

participants are encouraged to suggest how the attainment of each objective could be measured. For example, system cost-effectiveness is measured by net present value (NPV). It is often hard to find such measures for objectives but a formal step which asks people to think about the question helps considerably. Rubin and Goldberg (1992) make a similar point.

A similar enhancement to the objectives stage asks participants to try to prioritize the objectives. This technique, sometimes called Expected Value Analysis, involves placing a rough forecast of the benefit expected to be derived from achieving each objective. Further, it tends to reveal grouping among objectives: when one objective cannot realize its benefits without another being also achieved, say. The most important benefit of this prioritization is that, in later project phases, it enables project managers to place emphasis on the critical modules. This is especially important where prototyping or rapid development is contemplated. The priorities should therefore be traced through to objects or modules wherever possible. Once objects, and especially high-level layers, have been discovered these should be scored against the objectives. This will typically happen after context modelling, task script analysis and walk-throughs have been completed, as described above. The objects/layers with the highest scores have *ceteris paribus* the highest development priority. Total scores for the objectives will confirm or deny the original business priorities or may be used to apply weighting to the horizontal scores, or used directly as illustrated in Figure 7.13. In the diagram, Object 1 clearly has a high priority while Objectives 1 and 3 can be mostly satisfied by delivering Objects 1 and 2.

7.10.2 Running the workshop

We have already discussed the rôles of the facilitator and other participants in workshops. A more complete discussion of rôles and responsibilities is given in Chapter 9. Therefore only a few remarks need be made here.

All participants in a RAD workshop should understand the approach being adopted in outline. The introductory session should explain the order of events, the techniques that will be used and the expected results. The workshop is usually divided into a scoping session which can last from half a day to a day or longer. Scoping elicits a set of key business objectives with measures and priorities that are crystallized into a mission statement or project charter. A first-level context model is built that contains descriptions of external objects and internal actors and their interaction with the existing and proposed system. This is expressed in a message table that contains the goals of each prototypical interaction but not the tasks needed to accomplish the goals. Unresolved issues, exclusions and assumptions are also recorded. After the scoping is thus complete, the detailed workshop can proceed. This starts with the set of goals produced so far, checks them for completeness and enhances them with task scripts that describe how the users perceive that the goal might be accomplished; that is, what has to be done to achieve the goal. Facilitators must zealously crush attempts to describe a systems solution here – it is what has to be done that is required, not how it is to be done.

Another recommendation, which does not derive specifically from object technology, is that an attempt be made to identify a 'lead user' who would resolve disputes where consensus proves difficult. The lead user should command the respect of all other users and business area representatives.

7.10.3 Deliverables from RAD workshops and preliminary analysis

The philosophy of this approach is to minimize deliverable products. Every deliverable should be immediately or subsequently useful to someone involved with delivering a product to users. The lists of deliverables given in Chapter 9 are therefore to be regarded as check-lists. Almost anything can be omitted at the discretion of the project manager but a (possibly one-line) justification must be sought for each deliverable omitted. Some deliverables are more mandatory or more optional than others and this is indicated in the discussion of deliverables in Chapter 9. The most important deliverables have been discussed extensively above. They include the mission statement and prioritized objectives together with the reusable components: task scripts, class cards and event traces. Perhaps the most important deliverable is the signature of the sponsor to confirm that the tested model is an adequate representation of the requirement and the potential solution.

7.11 Summary

This chapter exposed one of the most important and novel aspects of SOMA: its approach to requirements capture and analysis. Most methods of object-oriented analysis are weak in the area of requirements capture and usually assume that a written requirements document already exists. The danger here is that such documents often contain implicit functional decomposition assumptions that interfere badly with the task of generating a truly object-oriented specification.

We saw that a business or a computer system should first be modelled in terms of the tasks that it helps users with and the fundamental business processes that these tasks enable. The Task Object Model produced is then transformed into a Business Object Model using textual analysis and a number of knowledge elicitation techniques.

It was shown how to capture and test objectives in a RAD workshop before moving on to build a context model. The context model is a model of message passing and every message has a trigger and goal. Data flow in both directions along the message and the model generalizes data flow in this way. Goals are resolved into task scripts which are decomposed to atomic level. The tasks can be regarded as objects in the task domain and participate in all four structures of an object model. They are recorded on task cards. Task scripts generalize Jacobson's use cases and are influenced by the theories of task analysis and stereotypical scripts in AI. The former emphasize the relation of tasks to goals and the decomposition of those tasks to primitive units. The latter place the stress on tasks as prototypes for business processes. This enables us to view the task model as a *bona fide* object model and to view tasks as plans for work-flow execution. The latter emphasizes the character of object-oriented methods as techniques for modelling and simulation, rather than procedural descriptions of businesses.

At first sight the similarity of task scripts to use cases is more apparent than the differences that exist. Therefore it is worth clarifying that the stereo-typical nature of scripts is what makes them into classes in the TOM. They represent tasks that are *understood* and that may describe processing deep inside the system rather than merely the tasks at the interface. The emphasis on tasks as stereotypes controls a potential explosion in the sheer number of scenarios.

Various object discovery and elicitation techniques were reviewed in detail, including structured and focused interviews, probes, task and topic analysis, Kelly grids and textual analysis. When objects have been extracted from the task model they are recorded on class cards. Rôle-play is then used to test and debug both the task and business object models and to produce event traces that form the basis for later system testing.

The business objects are related to the objectives via a matrix, which helps set implementation and development priorities. The chapter ended with a discussion of the conduct of RAD workshops and deliverables.

☰ 7.12 Bibliographical notes

There have been many influences on the work described in this chapter, though I think it remains unique. The most influential works in the object technology literature are Jacobson *et al.* (1992), Lorenz (1993), Rubin and Goldberg (1992) and Wirfs-Brock *et al.* (1990). The influences from Shank and Abelson's script theory and work on HCI have been acknowledged in earlier chapters.

8

Strategic modelling and business process re-engineering

I keep six honest serving men
(They taught me all I knew);
Their names are What and Why and When
And How and Where and Who.

R. Kipling (The Elephant's Child,
Just So Stories)

Object technology started out as a new perspective on programming and slowly extended its reach into the whole of computing: design, databases, interfaces, networking and analysis. It is now being increasingly realized that the object-oriented perspective can be applied to far more general systems than computers.

Carl von Clausewitz (1968) defines tactics as 'the theory of the use of military forces in combat' and strategy as 'the theory of the use of combats for the object of the War'. In our present context this translates into the view that **tactics** is *the method of organizing teams to carry out particular activities, tasks or processes* and **strategy** becomes *the method by which these activities, tasks or processes are combined to achieve the firm's objectives*. In this chapter the emphasis is on objectives; in the next it is the method of combination that will occupy us mostly. Clausewitz also points out that 'it is easier to make a theory for tactics than for strategy'. For that reason perhaps, strategic and enterprise-level modelling has been largely ignored in previous work on object-oriented methods or, if not ignored, presented quite separately from the treatment of analysis or design.

The OMG reference model for object-oriented analysis and design offers a category entitled 'strategic modelling' where the intention is to use object technology to model information systems (IS) strategy. This chapter describes how SOMA can be used to model the firm and its IS components at this level, but goes further. We will see how SOMA can be applied to modelling the whole business network in which the company operates. The remarkable thing is that the modelling and requirements capture techniques explained so far require no modification to do this, although perhaps the emphasis is different. In order to deal with strategic imperatives and business policies that are expressed in vague terms we make far more use of the rule based and fuzzy extensions.

We begin by looking at enterprise-level modelling of companies, showing how the techniques are applied and extending their use into business process description and re-engineering. Next, a framework for strategic modelling is provided, based on a novel object-oriented extension of Zachman's framework for information systems. The issue of business process re-engineering is then re-examined in more detail. Finally, we consider the policy modelling aspects of SOMA.

8.1 Object-oriented enterprise modelling

Enterprise models should provide a foundation for sharing computer models of the business and data across the organization and provide a basis for system development, policy decisions, change management and decision support. They are built to enhance the dialogue between IS workers and those in the business itself. A precise model helps form a clear, mutual understanding of the nature of the business and validates the developer's understanding for the sponsor. Such a model also provides the starting point for business process re-engineering.

As we have seen in the last chapter, a business can be regarded as an object communicating with other objects in the external environment it inhabits; customers, suppliers, regulators, and so on. The processes of these business objects are implemented by objects within the business, including human actors and the tools used to support their activities. We can model the goals of actors and the tasks they use to accomplish them as a Task Object Model and model the objects that the tasks refer to and their interrelationships as a Business Object Model. The object modelling approach is quite general and can be thought of equally as a system model, an enterprise model or a business process model. This is tantamount to a general systems theory view of things and reminiscent of the approach taken in Checkland's (1981) Soft Systems method. The only difference therefore between an object model of a computer system and a business process model is the subject matter, which means that this can be a very short section since most of the material has already been covered. We will dwell briefly on the different emphasis that an enterprise modelling view entails and compare object-oriented enterprise modelling with the usual data-oriented approach.

Most enterprise models are little short of corporation-wide entity-relationship models. Although there are sometimes process descriptions attached, these are decoupled from the data model and often have no real structure as a whole. The commonest approach is that based on Martin's

Information Engineering (IE) which mandates a data model and a functional decomposition linked by a CRUD-like matrix. The functional decomposition militates against reusability and the business rules are arbitrarily scattered across the two models. Hardly any importance is placed on how the business operates or should operate. Both the data and functional models tend to replicate the historical structures of the business. Further, there is no ability to simulate, though recent tools, such as OMW, have begun to correct this using object-oriented techniques on top of IE. The development of complete IE models, because of these problems, can take up to five years before they become useful. Despite this critique, many of the skills acquired by experienced IE enterprise analysts do carry over to object-oriented enterprise modelling.

The most important thing about an enterprise is what it does for its customers. Michaels (1992) distinguishes between **end-use customers**, who pay for the end product or service and are usually outside the business, and **interim customers**, who are part of a chain of value-adding processes leading to the end product. The customers of most IS departments are interim customers in this sense and, as Michaels points out, the term *end users* can be misleading. Thus, requirements capture is centred around the needs of interim customers in internal departments. For this reason, enterprise data models are usually focused on the data structures of concern to these functionally defined components of the business and will typically duplicate data within systems that do similar things. This redundancy is clearly at odds with the principle of object identity and any kind of philosophy of reuse. Three things are necessary to overcome this problem. First, an enterprise object model must be based on the principles of object technology: encapsulation, inheritance and identity. Second, a reuse culture, especially at the specification level, must be established. Third, requirements capture must be focused on the needs of the end-use customers and examine the whole value chain leading to the satisfaction of their needs. The last point leads us to an examination of object-oriented methods for business process re-engineering, which is dealt with in Section 8.3, though I will observe here *en passant* that a SOMA event trace can be regarded as a description of a process chain if objects are identified with agents carrying out a business process. The whole issue of reuse will be dealt with in Chapters 9 and 11. Here, we consider the nature of an object-oriented enterprise model.

An object-oriented model differs from a conventional one in that business models are composed (rather than decomposed) from simpler, reusable ones. This ought to be both simpler and less expensive. More importantly time-to-market should be dramatically reduced. Simulation is a natural feature of object models and this helps to support business process re-engineering. The semantic richness of object-oriented models helps communication between developers and users as does the unnormalized character and terminological uniformity of these models.

The objects in a SOMA object model (including the actors and external objects) can be regarded as processors within a model of the business just as easily as they can be seen as the components of a computer system. From this point of view each method of an object can be thought of as doing three things: consuming resources, adding value and taking a certain amount of time to do so. A business process model thus can simulate the value added by the execution of a particular task script, the time taken, the resources (cost) consumed or all three. The model can then be modified to discover whether predicted process improvements are realized.

A SOMA enterprise model is constructed in exactly the same way as a system model. The Task Object Model (TOM) records the generic tasks of actors within the business as usual, but the business can now represent the whole corporation or business area rather than an individual service-providing organization and the message interface into the environment represents services to end-use customers. A Business Object Model (BOM) for the whole enterprise will include individual functional units that are layers within this object model. It is my strong belief that attempts to construct such models at one sitting are doomed to failure. Rather, the strategy should be to extract and refine a domain model from individual projects as they are run. The domain objects, as we shall see in the next chapter, are collected and organized into a repository that gradually becomes representative of the whole organization. Periodically business process re-engineering exercises will criticize and refine this model based on changed definitions of the business and changes in the environment. The main and most evident difference between the high-level view (that is, looking at the names of entities only) of a typical corporate data model and a SOMA domain model is that the naming will be closer to the terminology of the business due to its de-normalization.

Thus, we have seen that a SOMA enterprise model is identical in form to any other SOMA model though quite different in content. As we shall see later, the details of requirements capture may vary because the enterprise-wide view and the end-use customer are emphasized. We now turn to a general framework for understanding enterprise models.

8.2 The Zachman framework

The Zachman information systems framework (Zachman, 1987; Sowa and Zachman, 1992) is widely used as a means of providing structure for IE style enterprise modelling. It is based on the idea – by analogy with the building trade – that the various participants in development – planners, architects, owners, constructors, and so on – have different, unique perspectives on the system corresponding to their different rôles. Figure 8.1 illustrates the framework. The business (or equivalently enterprise) model perspective is a row of the framework corresponding to the owner's view of things.

The Zachman framework thus consists of six rows representing perspectives, views of – or arguably stages in – systems development, progressing from

	Data	Functions	Network	People	Time	Motivation
Scope/Objectives	List of entities	List of processes	List of locations	List of organizations	List of events	Strategy Goals, etc.
Business model	ERD	Process flow diagram	Logistic network	Organogram	Business schedule	Business plan
Information systems model	Data model	DFD	Distributed systems architecture	HCI architecture	Process structure	Knowledge architecture
Technology constrained model	Data design	Structure chart	Systems architecture	HCI design	Control structure	Knowledge design
Detailed representation	Database description	Program source	Network architecture	Security, etc.	Interrupts etc.	Knowledge base
Working system	Data	Functions	Comms	Organization	Schedule	Use

Figure 8.1 The original Zachman framework with sample representations in each cell (adapted from Sowa and Zachman, 1992).

initial scoping to implementation, and a number of columns. The columns are variously cited as being to do with different questions that may be asked or different components of the entire model. Each cell is regarded as corresponding to a particular representation. Zachman originally posited three columns labelled Data, Function and Network. Network stood for the more general concept of Location and he observed that they corresponded to the question words What, How and Where respectively. This led him to postulate three more columns corresponding to the other three question words and he eventually labelled these People(Who), Time(When) and Motivation(Why). Sowa and Zachman (1992) showed how the model may be formalized using Sowa's (1984) conceptual graphs and introduced a meta-model of the contents of each cell using an ER modelling formalism. For example, the What/Scope cell may contain a list of things important to the business while the *How/Information systems* model cell may contain a data flow diagram. One is tempted, in migrating to an object-oriented view of things, merely to substitute an event trace or usage structure diagram here and proceed by remapping the other cells. However, things are not so simple; various attempts to make the framework object-oriented have disagreed and there have even been attempts to extend to seven columns (for example, Loosely, 1992).

The mapping of *What* to *Data*, *How* to *Process*, and so on is obviously not an exact one but it is still an interesting and useful viewpoint on the semantics of the framework. Figure 8.2 shows a skeletal version of this view of the

	What	How	Where	Who	When	Why
Scope/Objectives						
Business/ enterprise model						
Information systems model						
Technology constrained model						
Detailed representation						
Working system						

Figure 8.2 A more general view of the framework.

framework. The mapping will vary unless a theoretical framework is applied. I think that the problem lies in the very general interpretation given to words like *what* and *how.* In an object-oriented framework, as in the world, processes and data are not separated. If we ask *what* something is, the answer must encompass how it behaves as well as what constitutes it. In that case we must ask what *how* corresponds to. The solution is to place the columns in a more logical sequence reflecting the process of requirements capture, analysis and implementation, as we shall now see.

Zachman's work grew, I suspect, largely out of IBM's attempts to rationalize and generalize Information Engineering approaches within the AD/Cycle and Information Warehouse concepts. It was logical to begin with data and functions as the primitive steps because that was how software engineering was supposed to proceed then. For the object technologist things are different and, with SOMA, a perfectly logical way to begin requirements capture is to ask: why? That is, we begin by asking for the goals behind user interactions, or customer interactions in the case of the enterprise model.

Asking *Why* corresponds to establishing the objectives of the business and the support systems and finding the goals of each interaction. It also means asking for global objectives first. Next we must ask for the goals of particular users. Goals are achieved by carrying out tasks. Tasks are the 'how' of goals just as critical success factors (CSFs) are the 'what' of global objectives. Asking *What* corresponds to finding external and business objects, including their behaviour. Asking *Who* means establishing the actors. Asking *When*

	Motivation	People	Tasks	Objects	Network	Motivation
Scope/Objectives	Goals Objectives	Actors	TOM with goals	Key terms	Messages	Constraints
Business model	Goals Objectives	Actors	TOM with scripts	BOM	Structures	Event traces
Information systems model	Goals Objectives	Actors	TOM with scripts	BOM + interface objects	Structures	Event traces
Technology constrained model	Goals Objectives	Actors	TOM with scripts	OOD model (IOM)	Structures	Event traces, STDs
Detailed representation	Goals Objectives	Actors	Test scripts	Types/ classes	Pointer structures, class specs	STDs, Event traces
Working system	Goals Objectives	Users	Test runs	Code	Code	Benchmarks

Figure 8.3 An object-oriented version of the framework.

implies placing constraints on the execution of operations and finding other temporal constraints. *Where* is a bit more tricky because the structures of object-oriented analysis show communication at both the logical and physical (for example, geographical) levels. Thus *Where* encompasses where in the system and where in the world. The former is primarily shown by the four structures in the BOM, but mainly the usage structure. Physically the usage structure translates into a model of distributed system or network architecture. The breakthrough in going from the original to the object-oriented version of Zachman lies in realizing that *How* corresponds to the task domain. *When* encompasses the dynamic models of individual objects and the flow of events through the system as well as the various temporal constraints imposed by the business or the implementation.

The object-oriented version of the framework in shown in Figure 8.3. The remarkable thing is that the framework largely collapses to a point in terms of representation, showing how object models can be used to express different viewpoints and perspectives using a uniform representation. The whole Motivation and People columns collapse to representations in terms of goals/objectives and actors. The other columns require modifications for early and late rows. Overall, the number of required representations is dramatically reduced.

This framework can help us understand object-oriented and rule based approaches to information systems far more clearly. It provides both a basis for understanding the complex interconnexions between different descriptions of the same system and a context for managing change. The object-oriented version shown in Figure 8.3 already makes it clear that there are fewer kinds of description to worry about, thus reinforcing the argument that OO gives better traceability through a continuum of representation while showing that transformations are still necessary. In a sense the framework largely collapses into a single representation that is used to explore the different viewpoints of system constructors. Some columns have only one representation, though it may vary as to level of detail, and none have more than four. The framework acts as a kind of completeness check on our understanding. It also clarifies the views taken by the various players in information systems development and/or business process re-engineering.

Zachman and his followers have established a set of rules for interpreting and using the original framework (see Bruce, 1992). These may be summarized as follows.

Rule 1. The columns have no ordering. No one column is more important than another but focusing on one may have significant practical implications.

Rule 2. Each column represents a unique model.

Rule 3. Each column is unique although they are interconnected.

Rule 4. Each row represents a unique perspective.

Rule 5. Therefore, each cell is unique (no item should show up in more than one cell).

Rule 6. Each row is a complete model from the row's perspective.

Rule 7. The logic is recursive and generic.

The only rule that might be affected by the revised, object-oriented framework is Rule 5. Obviously objects show up in several columns apart from *What*; that is, with structures, goals, and so on. However, they do not appear as objects *qua* objects so that the rule may remain if so interpreted.

Brown (1992) suggests that rules (that is, condition/action pairs) are the substance of the *When* or *Time* column. I have already shown in Chapter 6 that rules are better encapsulated within objects. However, global 'when' rules of this sort do exist and, in SOMA, are viewed as belonging to a special system-wide policy object. This object can then be viewed as the repository for the *When* column descriptions of conditional action. This begins to lead to the view that every column contains an object model in a separate domain.

Rule 1 is only partially violated by my reordering of the columns. I am suggesting that the emphases or focuses on the columns referred to in the rule are related and loosely sequenced – as are the rows.

Rule 3 suggests that there are interactions between columns or second-order aspects of the framework. This is true and is part of the reason why a mapping between the six question words and the six columns must never be exact or stable. Some examples of these second-order aspects are to be found by examining the sample question types given in Table 8.1.

Table 8.1 Interactions between question types.

Question type	Meaning in SOMA model
For what?	Relates purpose to object (goal-task- object)
With whom?	Usage structure
With what?	Tasks
When used	Event trace
Why him?	Actor-message-goal

Shelton (1993) offers a slightly different, but still useful, object-oriented interpretation of the Zachman framework. Effectively, he refines the What/Object column into three categories corresponding to what he calls Business, Application and Foundation objects. Shelton's business objects correspond to my domain and application objects. Foundation objects correspond to the implementation classes found in many class libraries; stacks, list, canvases, and so on. His Application objects are the components that make up an application, such as subclasses inheriting from Smalltalk Model, View and Controller classes. Each of these categories is relevant at a different stage of development or to different viewpoints (rows) in the Zachman framework. Figure 8.4 illustrates the incidence of these categories in the Zachman row model and Shelton's rather clearer interpretation of the row names.

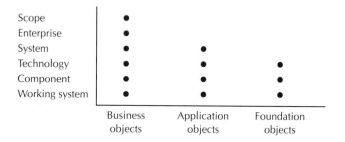

Figure 8.4 Shelton's object categories in the Zachman framework.

In more recent work, Shelton (personal communication) has regarded business objects as corresponding to the composite of the What, How, When and Why columns of the framework. He models Where and Who by what he calls Core Location and Core Organization models of his Object-Oriented Business Engineering method. Shelton regards my version of the Zachman framework as at a higher level of abstraction because it fails to emphasize that business objects are the only ones pertinent to enterprise modelling, although he does apply the framework to all three types of object. My solution to this problem is contained in the separation of concerns represented by the transition to the SOMA Implementation Object Model illustrated in Figure 7.1 and discussed further in Chapter 12.

More importantly, Shelton (1993) offers some useful advice on how to go about object-oriented enterprise modelling (OOEM). He says:

'The scope for OOEM ranges from a single business object to a vertical slice of the business. The former is self-explanatory: customer for instance. The latter differs from an IE business area in that it is not aligned with either the organization or any top-level business function from the Business Function Decomposition model. It is, however, a bounded area that has business meaning and encompasses exactly the business problem or opportunity at hand. As such the vertical slice of the business becomes the scope for a complete effort from enterprise modelling through business object implementation. *Scope should be as small as possible.* Avoid scopes like 'sales and marketing' or 'flight information' in favour of 'customer buying trends' or 'air route yield management'. Scoping is a skill driven by the caveat: think small. *OOEM models can (and should) be composed incrementally*: do not expand the scope simply because it is not all inclusive. *The whole enterprise model should be constructed incrementally.*'
[Emphasis added.]

The framework now lets us describe our abstract models of systems completely but there is third dimension that it ignores. Most IS organizations also have a framework that describes their infrastructure of hardware, operating systems software and networks and many nowadays define a standard applications architecture consisting of fielded and projected applications. My version of the object-oriented Zachman framework is intermediate between these two and deals with the logical structure of both. Although the *detailed representation* and *working system* rows could be thought of as describing the infrastructure and applications frameworks, this fails to capture important links between the abstract models and applications that are important for reuse. The framework must therefore be completed by a device that records which objects implement which tasks, which design objects correspond to which analysis objects, which source code objects implement the design objects, the objects out of which each application is built and the platforms on which the objects and applications run. Thus there is a set of cross-reference tables that represents relationships among the rows and the columns. These matrices are summarized in Table 8.2. In this table it is assumed that the Booch design method is used for implementation modelling and physical design. Collecting this information is essential if the full benefits of reuse and reduced maintenance costs are to be derived from object technology. Other useful cross-references may be stored if desired.

Table 8.2 Cross-reference tables for reuse.

Item type	List of related items
External object	SOMA task objects invoked
Actor	SOMA task objects invoked
SOMA task object	Object mentioned/used
	Application used in
	Actors and external objects used by
SOMA business object	Related tasks
	Application used in
Booch object	Related SOMA objects
	Application used in
Coded class	Related Booch or SOMA objects
	Platform implemented on
	Application used in
Application	Platform implemented on
	Related SOMA task objects, SOMA business objects,
	Booch objects and coded objects
	Actors and external objects used by

This provides a complete framework within which we can operate and evaluate our strategic modelling. We are now well equipped to consider the use of SOMA for business process re-engineering.

▤ 8.3 Modelling and re-engineering the business

Once we have an object model at our disposal we can use it to implement some automation of existing processes but this may merely reinforce some inessential, wasteful or counterproductive practice. As we saw in Chapter 1, it is beneficial to review all business processes to see if they are necessary to meet the objectives of the organization. This has led to considerable benefits for companies like Ford, Mutual Benefit Life and Xerox. Mutual, for example, reduced the time taken to issue policies from 24 days to four hours. Embarrassingly, at least for the proponents of BPR, Mutual was close to bankruptcy within months of this success. This, I think, was because they concentrated on cutting the costs of a wasteful business process that was not at the core of their business rather than on improving a central one.

The seminal works describing and abstracting from such case histories emphasize the obliteration of unnecessary tasks (Hammer, 1990) or the improvement of the process and enforcing the appropriate work flow (Davenport and Short, 1990). Other exponents of business process re-engineering (BPR) such as Peters (1992) extol the benefits of using the techniques to flatten organizational structures, shorten command chains and empower workers by providing access to the information resources of the company. There are

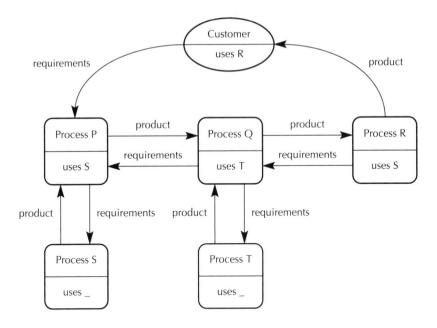

Figure 8.5 A conventional process chain model.

two complementary influences that lead to the need for business process re-engineering: changes in the needs of customers and changes that exploit the possibilities of new technology.

A business object model may be regarded as a simulation of the business. As such, the model may be altered and different strategies tried before implementing them. There are several tools available for this kind of simulation, such as ICL's ProcessWise, and some are based on the metaphor of objects. They have been discussed in Chapter 4 already. Usually they allow delays to be incorporated into the objects that represent processes so that bottlenecks can be uncovered by simulation runs. However, the way in which business rules and especially policy rules are incorporated into these tools leaves much to be desired. Rules are expressed procedurally or separated from the objects so that they cannot be inherited. They are also crisp rules whereas most policy is expressed in a fuzzy manner by business managers. This section shows how semantically rich SOMA models can be used to provide very effective object-oriented simulations. The next discusses the use of fuzzy rules to model vaguely expressed policy. *SOMATiK* too can be used for business process modelling, as we shall see in Chapter 13.

Most process modelling methods proceed by building a model consisting of a number of processes and contingent flows between them representing the value chain (Porter, 1980). It is the entire value of the chain that must be optimized, rather than the efficiency of any individual process, if the customer and

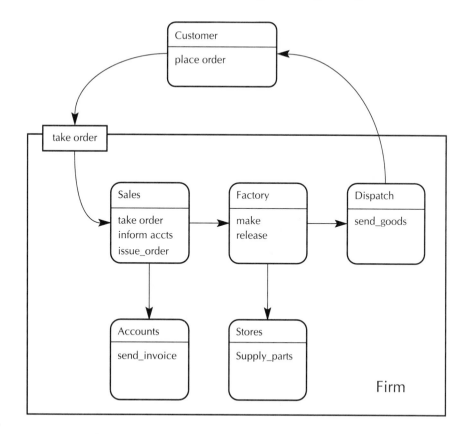

Figure 8.6 The equivalent SOMA business process model.

the firm are to benefit. Each process represents an activity that the firm performs as some part of creating a product to be sold to a customer. Each step adds value to the product and its output may be delivered to another internal process or interim customer or to the actual customer. A typical process chain model is illustrated in Figure 8.5. Notice that the customer tells requirements to P but receives the product from R of whom he is a client. It may be helpful to think of P as taking the order, Q as a manufacturing process and R as dispatch. S could be the accounting function and T some subsidiary manufacturing process of the stores. This would certainly not happen in an object model. However, there is a sense in which the process chain is a completed message circle. The solution to the dilemma is to realize that this circle can be represented by an event trace.

    This leads us to an object model and a set of event traces that represent process chains based on the model. We now have the choice of redefining the process chains using the same objects or, more radically, restructuring the object model itself. Figure 8.6 shows the object model underlying the same process in the form of a SOMA usage structure. The event trace is implicit. It is left as an exercise to the reader to sketch it out and suggest any improvements in this simple process.

From this model we can see how rules could be used to control a simulation. We can regard the customer as a goal-seeking agent trying to fill his need for some product or service. The rule processor searches for a supplier (there is only one here) who can satisfy the demand and its 'take order' operation is regarded as a goal for the firm. To take the order, its rules say certain things must happen, such as recording the order, ordering its manufacture and informing Accounts. There must be a confirmation from Dispatch and only then is the task complete. This is simple to express as rules and to execute under a backward chaining régime.

The SOMA approach to a BPR exercise is much the same as its approach to other requirements capture and analysis exercises set out in the previous two chapters and in Chapter 9. We first examine the communication with the customer and the goals underlying it to obtain a message table and associated task model. Objectives are prioritized as are the tasks (processes) to be redesigned. A business object model is produced from the TOM as usual, but concentrating on the abstract objects of the business rather than any proposed support system; support systems may be added later. Each operation of each object is assigned values for value added, time taken and cost, wherever possible. Dependencies are examined and the total value chain optimized. It is useful to challenge each operation and its location within the model by asking the following questions.

- Why is it done
- Who does it?
- Who benefits?
- Where is it done?
- How long does the whole task take?
- Where are the delays?
- Is there a similar operation for another object?
- Do we have anything similar (tasks or objects) in the repository?
- Can the structures be simplified?
- Where could technology be applied?
- What does the customer value most?

If an operation is not used it can be removed. Simulations and what-ifs will show up deficiencies and suggest improvements. The main thing is to approach the problem with an open mind, and a well-run brainstorming session can help immensely.

One of the mistakes that can easily be made is to focus on re-engineering wasteful processes without due regard to their importance to the organization. Keen and Knapp (1995) argue that business processes can be seen as assets or liabilities. Asset processes add value as well as consuming resources, while liability processes merely consume resources. For example, the process of providing cars adds value for a company such as Hertz but the process of insuring their cars does not. As time passes, asset processes can become liabilities. A good example here is IBM's unique approach to marketing, which was an asset in the 1970s but appears to be a major liability now. We can also distinguish between processes that contribute to the fundamental mission of a company, processes that are not mission-critical but have a major impact on efficiency and those that are merely necessary, background processes. Re-engineering should focus on the asset and mission-critical processes.

There are many re-engineering strategies available to organizations. Processes can be streamlined, abandoned, outsourced, franchised or invented. Some companies have converted liabilities into assets by making a product out of a process; for example, an airline's own reservation system might be sold to other airlines. Invention is often the result of observing the processes of companies in other industries; for example, Hertz have the car engine running when the customer arrives but the average hotel makes you wait 15 minutes to check in. This kind of creative thinking is greatly assisted (though not replaced) by the availability of a sound modelling technique to enable various strategies to be explored.

Short and Venkatramen (1992) suggest that redesigning the internals of a business is not enough and that we should look at changing the way the business is embedded in the nexus of interactions in its market and change the customer/supplier relationship thereby. They give an example where a value added network enabled a hospital supplier (Baxter Healthcare) to completely alter the traditional rôles of manufacturer, distributor, purchaser and so on, with Baxter able take on many of the internal logistic operations of hospitals as well as acting as supplier and distributor. This they characterize as economies of scope rather than economies of scale. If this kind of exercise is to be undertaken then our SOMA object models must reach out into the world and include objects that do not communicate directly with our business. There is no technical obstacle to this, though some modellers will have to abandon many long-held prejudices about the scope of their endeavours. Shelton's remarks, quoted above, are particularly pertinent to this point. Here again the trick is to focus on what is important to the customer and articulate the object model around critical tasks in the market as a whole.

SOMA avoids characterizing processes sequentially, as do many of the existing approaches. Sequential or procedural characterizations usually only work well for paper-oriented processes. Where people are involved, we need to emphasize the contracts that are involved in communication of the process. The focus on semiotic acts in the context model, as explained in Chapter 7, helps to capture the more subtle aspects of processes.

☰ 8.4 Business policy and fuzzy models

Business policy is set and followed in an uncertain world. The sources and kinds of uncertainty are manifold. They include:

- Lack of understanding.
- Conceptual error, uncertainty in judgement, lack of evidence, unreliable sources of data and information or lack of certainty in evidence. These and the imprecision of natural language and sensory apparatus all lead to variation in degrees of belief. A definition may be linguistic, and the possible data values will then have to be selected from a set of linguistic descriptors. For example, in a determination of a patient's clinical symptoms, the degree of pain present can only be described in terms such as 'slight pain', 'severe pain', 'very severe pain' and so on.
- Conflicting or complementary sources of facts.
- Hidden variables producing apparent randomness.
- The existence of exceptions.
- The energy required to obtain certain data.
- Random events leading to variation in the degree of likelihood.
- Variation in the degree of possibility or necessity.
- Instrumental or experimental error, faulty sensory equipment leading to variation in the degree of precision. This is, of course, the standard situation in scientific measurement, and is managed on the assumption that errors of observation are normally distributed about the true value of the observed variable.
- The abundance of irrelevant data leading to variation in the degree of relevance.
- Variation in the extent to which a proposition holds.
- Variation in the degree of truth or provability of a proposition.
- Variation in the degree of the mandate for performing some action.
- Variation in the degree of compulsion or duty.

To arrive at a decision in the presence of absolute certainty with respect to all the relevant facts and considerations is a luxury rarely afforded to human beings. Assumptions must be made about data that are not available, about events that may or may not have occurred, and about consequences likely to flow from a given decision.

Many of these assumptions may be made unconsciously or subconsciously. Some may be made explicitly, with whatever degree of justification may be adduced. Mathematics may be prayed in aid of some assumptions made on statistical bases. Otherwise, rules of thumb and accrued experience serve as a guide.

Traditionally, systems analysts are taught to 'prefer a fact to an opinion' and to remove all inexactitude from specifications. This is a good principle but can be taken too far. Zadeh's Principle of Incompatibility (Zadeh, 1973) states that:

'As the complexity of a system increases, our ability to make precise and yet significant statements about its behaviour diminishes until a threshold is reached beyond which precision and significance (or relevance) become almost mutually exclusive characteristics.'

Zadeh's original motivation came from attempts to construct numerical controllers for complex electronic equipment. This was recognized as a difficult problem because, partly due to the Law Of Requisite Variety (Ashby, 1956), as the controlled equipment became complex the controller became so even more rapidly. So much so that the controllers were either ineffectual or so complex as to defy the understanding of their designers. Zadeh formulated this in his Principle.

One way round the contradiction is to represent vague, imprecise human knowledge directly rather than mediating with some artificial representation such as a precise formula. In the context of automatic control, it turns out that a human operator formulates a control policy as 'when the gauge shows hot, I have to turn this knob down a little bit' rather than as 'when the temperature increases beyond 98.4 the input is reduced by 4.7%'. This is the approach taken by fuzzy set theory. It can be applied as readily to business policy as to industrial controllers.

Here is an example of the policy adopted by the product manager of a fast-moving consumer item such as washing powder; the same one used already in Chapter 5. It is expressed particularly succinctly but represents a fairly accurate picture of how such prices are set in practice.

1. OUR PRICE SHOULD BE LOW
2. OUR PRICE SHOULD BE ABOUT 2*DIRECT.COSTS
3. IF THE OPPOSITION.PRICE IS NOT VERY HIGH THEN OUR PRICE SHOULD BE NEAR THE OPPOSITION.PRICE

There are several things to note about this policy. First, it is expressed in vague terms and yet would be perfectly understandable to any other product manager as a basis for action. More remarkably perhaps, this is executable code in a language called REVEAL. This is possible because REVEAL uses fuzzy sets to implement the linguistic terms such as LOW. It is worth studying exactly how this code is implemented.

First, two fuzzy sets called LOW and HIGH are defined as vectors over the scale of relevant prices for washing powders. These are illustrated in Figure 8.7(a) and (b). 'Very' is an operator that takes the square of every point of the curve representing the fuzzy set. The result VERY HIGH is also shown in 8.7(b). The words OUR, SHOULD and THE are declared as noise words. BE is a synonym for IS and NEAR means the same as ABOUT.

Statement 1 in the policy means that the price should be as compatible as possible with LOW; that is, the price ought to be zero. This contradicts the assertion that it should be twice direct costs, a result of the need to turn a

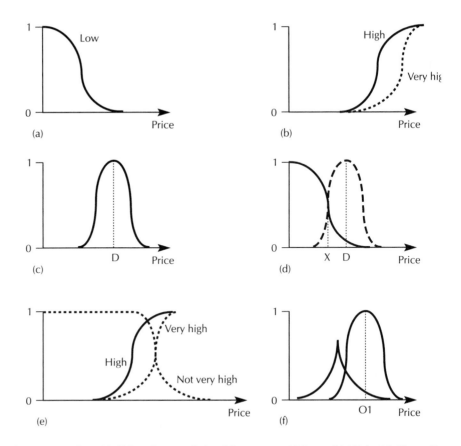

Figure 8.7 LOW, HIGH and some derived fuzzy sets. (a) Low. (b) High. (c) About D. (d) Low and about D. (e) NOT VERY HIGH = 1 − HIGH^2. (f) Low and about D and near O1.

profit based on experience. The remarkable thing is that the fuzzy policy will automatically resolve this contradiction by taking the price that gives the maximum truth value for the intersection of the fuzzy sets. This is labelled X in Figure 8.7(d). The peaked intersection now represents an elastic constraint, or feasible region, for price. Figure 8.7(c) shows the fuzzy set ABOUT 2∗DIRECT.COSTS.

Rule 3 must now be interpreted. We take an actual value for opposition O and compute how true NOT VERY HIGH is for it. This truth value is T. The fuzzy inference rule is interpreted as truncating the output fuzzy set NEAR OPPOSITION at the level T. We now arrive at the result by taking the union of LOW AND ABOUT D with this truncated set. D stands for 2∗DIRECT.COSTS here. Finally, if we want an actual value for PRICE rather than a fuzzy set, we must defuzzify. In this case we choose the mean of maxima method to do this. Figure 8.8(b) and (c) illustrate that there are two cases. As the value of T exceeds

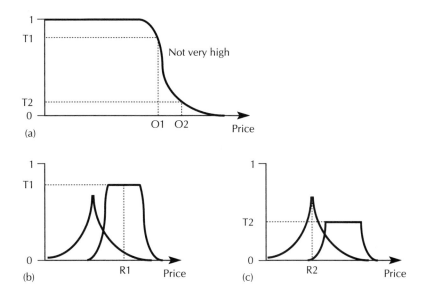

Figure 8.8 Fuzzy inference. (a) T*i* is the truth of NOT VERY HIGH for O*i*. (b) Case 1: T*i* > max A. (c) Case 2: T*i* < max A.

the maximum truth in the feasible region there is a sudden jump in output from R2 to R1. This models exactly what happens in real life; decision output is discontinuous. In process control, smooth output is required and the centre of moments defuzzification rule would be used.

The purpose of this example is to show how fuzzy rules, used to capture business policy, can be made to provide quite precise, although perhaps nonlinear and complex, models of behaviour. In SOMA, rulesets are embedded in objects and can be inherited. Business policy can be modelled in this way and fuzzy rulesets are permitted. One may either create a special purpose 'policy' object to which all other objects refer or distribute the policy to the pertinent objects. Which is best will depend on the application.

The use of fuzzy rules, and indeed of rules in general, is optional in SOMA. They need not be used and may only be used rarely. It is my belief and experience however that when they are needed they provide a very powerful modelling technique that helps build a common, shared understanding between users and developers.

8.5 Deliverables

SOMA enterprise models have the same set of deliverables as other SOMA models. It is likely that more information about customers will be present in the form of external objects and objects representing actors. For BPR use, there may be additional external objects and interactions. The objects may additionally have information on the resources consumed, value added and the time taken by each of their operations. Cross-reference tables as in Table 8.2 should be produced where appropriate.

The details of the deliverables from SOMA activities are discussed in the next chapter. Since business process re-engineering and strategic modelling are merely treated as the same approach applied to different subject matter there will be few changes except those that follow from the fact that a system is not produced. Further, the reports may be written for a different audience and this may affect the prose style somewhat.

8.6 Summary

Strategic and enterprise-level modelling have been largely ignored in previous work on object-oriented methods. This chapter described how SOMA can be used to model the firm and its IS components at this level and be applied to modelling the whole business network in which the company operates. The remarkable thing is that its techniques require no modification.

We began by looking at enterprise-level modelling of companies, showing how the techniques are applied and extend their use into business process description and re-engineering. Next, a framework for strategic modelling was provided based on a novel object-oriented extension of Zachman's framework for information systems. The issue of business process re-engineering was then re-examined in more detail. Finally, we considered the policy modelling aspects of SOMA.

A business can be regarded as an object communicating with other objects in the external environment it inhabits. The processes of businesses are implemented by objects within the business. We can model the goals of actors and the tasks they use to accomplish them as a Task Object Model and the objects that the tasks refer to and their interrelationships as a Business Object Model.

The most important thing about an enterprise is what it does for its customers. We should distinguish between end-use customers and interim customers. The customers of most IS departments are interim customers in this sense. Thus, requirements capture is centred on the needs of interim customers in internal departments and enterprise data models usually focus on functionally defined data structures and will typically duplicate data within systems that do similar things. An enterprise object model must be based on the principles of OT: encapsulation, inheritance and identity. A reuse culture, especially at the specification level, must be established. Requirements capture must be focused on the needs of end-use customers and examine the value chain. An object-oriented model differs from a conventional one in that business models are composed (rather than decomposed) from simpler, reusable ones. This ought to be both less expensive and simpler. More importantly, time-to-market should be dramatically reduced. Simulation is a natural feature of object models and this helps support BPR. The semantic richness of OO models helps communication between developers and users as does the unnormalized character and terminological uniformity of these models.

The objects in a SOMA object model (including the actors and external objects) can be regarded as processors within a model of the business. Each method of an object can be thought of as doing three things: consuming resources, adding value and taking a certain amount of time to do so. A business process model thus can simulate the value added by the execution of a particular task script, the time taken, the resources (cost) consumed or all three. The model can then be modified to discover if predicted process improvements are realized.

The Zachman framework is widely used as a means of providing structure for IE style enterprise modelling. It consists of six rows representing perspectives, views of – or arguably stages in – systems development, progressing from initial scoping to implementation, and six columns variously cited as being to do with different questions that may be asked or different components of the entire model. Each cell is regarded as corresponding to a particular representation. Previous attempts to make the framework object-oriented have disagreed. This framework can help us understand object-oriented and rule based approaches to information systems far more clearly. The remarkable thing about the object-oriented Zachman framework is that it largely collapses into a single representation. It acts as a completeness check on our understanding and clarifies the views taken by the various players in information systems development and/or business process re-engineering. Zachman and his followers have established a set of rules for interpreting and using the original framework. Only some rules are affected by the revised, object-oriented framework. Enterprise models should be constructed incrementally.

Once we have an object model at our disposal we can use it to implement some automation of existing processes but this may merely reinforce some inessential, wasteful or counterproductive practice. It is beneficial to review all business processes to see if they are necessary to meet the objectives of the organization. The seminal works on BPR emphasize the obliteration of unnecessary tasks or the improvement of the process and enforcing the appropriate work flow. Other exponents of BPR extol the benefits of using the techniques to flatten organizational structures, shorten command chains and empower workers by providing access to the information resources of the company. There are two complementary influences that lead to the need for business process re-engineering: changes in the needs of customers and changes that exploit the possibilities of new technology.

A business object model may be regarded as a simulation of the business. The model may be altered and different strategies tried before implementing them. *SOMATiK* can be used for business process modelling.

Most process modelling methods proceed by building a model consisting of a number of processes and contingent flows between them representing the value chain. It is the entire value of the chain that must be optimized, rather than the efficiency of any individual process. Each process represents an activity that the firm performs as some part of creating a product to be sold to a customer. Each step adds value to the product and its output may be delivered to another internal process or interim customer or to the actual customer. The process chain is a completed message circle and can be represented by an event trace. We now have the choice of redefining the process chains using the same objects or, more radically, restructuring the object model itself. Rules can be used to control a simulation. We can regard the customer as a goal-seeking agent trying to fill his need for some product or service.

The SOMA approach to a BPR exercise is much the same as its approach to other requirements capture and analysis exercises. We first examine the communication with the customer and the goals underlying it to obtain a message table and associated task model. Objectives are prioritized as are the tasks (processes) to be redesigned. A business object model is produced from the TOM as usual, but concentrating on the abstract objects of the business rather than any proposed support system; support systems may be added later. Each operation of each object is assigned values for value added, time taken and cost, wherever possible. Dependencies are examined and the total value chain optimized. The main thing is to approach problems with an open mind. A well-run brainstorming session can help immensely.

Redesigning the internals of a business is not enough. We should look at changing the way the business is embedded in its market and change the customer/supplier relationship thereby. If this kind of exercise is to be undertaken then our SOMA object models must reach out into the world and include objects that do not communicate directly with our business.

Business policy is set and followed in an uncertain world. The sources and kinds of uncertainty are manifold. To arrive at a decision in the presence of absolute certainty is a luxury rarely afforded to human beings. Traditionally, systems analysts are taught to remove all inexactitude from specifications. This is a good principle but can be taken too far. Fuzzy set theory can be applied as readily to business policy as to industrial controllers. Fuzzy rules, used to capture business policy, can be made to provide quite precise, although perhaps complex, models. In SOMA rulesets are embedded in objects and can be inherited. Business policy can be modelled in this way and fuzzy rulesets are permitted. One may either create a special purpose 'policy' object to which all other objects refer or distribute the policy to the pertinent objects. The use of fuzzy rules is optional in SOMA. They need not be used and may only be used rarely. When they are needed they provide a powerful modelling technique that helps build a common, shared understanding between users and developers.

SOMA enterprise models have the same deliverables as other SOMA models.

≣ 8.7 Bibliographical notes

The Zachman framework was originally presented in Zachman (1987) and extended by Sowa and Zachman (1992).

Ivar Jacobson is preparing a book on object-oriented business re-engineering that uses use cases as the principal modelling approach. It will be published by Addison-Wesley in 1995. The books by Hammer and Champy (1993) and Davenport (1993) are accessible references on business process re-engineering in general. Other material can be found in the management science literature, notably the *Harvard Business Review* and the *Sloan Management Review*.

Earl Cox's recent book on fuzzy logic (Cox, 1994) studies the pricing model discussed in this chapter extensively, though he attributes its origins incorrectly. To set the record straight, it was not – as Cox says – developed for a UK consumer goods company but was developed by Peter Jones as an example for a REVEAL tutorial. Undoubtedly, Peter drew on his earlier experience at Unilever but it was not used by that company so far as either of us knows.

9

Life cycle

The golden rule is that there are no golden rules.

G. B. Shaw (Man and Superman)

This chapter provides a detailed exposition of the SOMA life-cycle model, which is a non-procedural, object-oriented model of development activities. The method also incorporates an evolutionary, rapid development philosophy. First, we look at the requirements of an object-oriented method in general and review existing life-cycle models for both conventional and object-oriented methods.

9.1 What must an object-oriented method do?

For a system to be successful it must satisfy the requirements of three kinds of stakeholder: project sponsors, system users and system support personnel. It is unlikely that the requirements of these three groups will coincide exactly. In particular, if a system is to make the transition from a concept and plan to an industrial-strength application supporting the business then the requirements of group one – the project sponsors – must be completely satisfied. Once the system is live this group of people will judge the system based on the evidence they receive from group two – the users. The users' view of the system will be more favourable if the system is easy to use, performs to business needs and the support they receive is prompt and effective. However, before the system is live the project sponsors have little evidence on which to judge the future success of the project. Specifically, all they have available to them is the track record of the development team and the arguments put forward in favour of the system in the preliminary documentation.

Development organizations migrating to object technology need to recruit and hold on to the best developers in IT and produce both systems and documentation of the highest quality, usability and clarity. Their methods need to reflect existing practice – that is, what is actually done successfully now – rather than impose bureaucratic 'structured' methods that few developers will understand the need for. Such methods are only beneficial in the presence of unskilled developers.

Computers provide solutions to problems specified by industry and commerce as a whole. In theory, a new development should be a new solution to an unsolved problem. In practice, the solution may already exist but not have been adequately communicated to interested parties. In either event, there will be uncertainty present in the analysis and design of a new system. Effective analysis and design will rapidly reduce this uncertainty to manageable proportions. Use must be made of existing and established technologies and systems in order to manage this uncertainty successfully. Specifically, use must be made of stable platforms as a foundation for development at the outset, as well as throughout the life cycle of a project. Booch (1994) quotes Gall on this subject:

> 'A complex system that works is invariably found to have evolved from a simple system that worked ... A complex system designed from scratch never works and cannot be patched up to make it work. You have to start over, beginning with a working simple system.'

We should build evolutionary systems in an incremental fashion, not offer 'big-bang' solutions. Such an approach not only follows the guidelines alluded to by Booch and Gall but also allows the users and sponsors to comment on the intermediate products and have a greater input into the design of a system throughout its development cycle.

Sponsors should be made aware of the management of uncertainty and the approach of building evolutionary systems. Statements of such aims should be made in project proposals and systems analysis reports. In addition, specific statements of what will constitute a deliverable after each evolutionary cycle should be made. This should tie in with close user and sponsor involvement in the prototyping, systems design and construction phases. While this is already standard practice within some successful systems in existence, it should be adopted as a conscious policy by all organizations.

The difficulty in implementing such a policy is that the level of user or sponsor involvement will vary according to the product being developed. Many windows-based GUI designs lend themselves readily to user/sponsor involvement and comment. In addition, the tools available to support the development of these GUIs enable rapid implementation of cosmetic changes in response to user requests. However, it may be more difficult to generate the same level of user enthusiasm for complex transaction processing and computation with no graphical representation of the processes. Nevertheless, closer user involvement throughout the development of a project should be formally encouraged. Closer user involvement raises the profile of the development organization, gives greater visibility of developers to the user and sponsor communities and enables more open and effective communication between the development organization and these communities. This will enable users to articulate their needs more clearly and developers to understand them more precisely. This will result in the development organization delivering systems that the business **needs**, not what the business wants nor what the developers think it should have.

Despite what I have written about structured methods above, a good system development method must enforce a reasonable level of discipline on developers without hampering their productivity by unnecessary bureaucracy and endless deliverables that do not contribute to the product. Neither should it assume that it has all the answers, because there will be situations and types of system that have not been foreseen. A method should contribute to the business goal of continuous process improvement. This means that some means of measuring the output and efficiency of the process must be mandated, so that it is possible to discover the existence and the amount of any improvement. Productivity is enhanced when the imperatives of the method correspond to the steps that an ideal developer would take in the real world, under pressure, without the benefit of the method. Deliverables should be natural, essential and actually used by someone for some valuable purpose. Many existing structured methods mandate deliverables that may only be used under certain circumstances or that are really only there to cover managers against potential criticism. Methods adopted by governments are often the worst offenders in this respect because it is too often the case that *being seen* to do the job properly is more important than doing the job properly, for both civil servants and politicians.

A method should contribute to meeting real business needs by helping to ensure that quality is maintained and enhanced, requirements are captured accurately and fully, needs are not swamped by wants, deadlines are met and developers are productive. It should encourage the creation of flexible systems that can evolve with the business at minimal cost. It must help to control and shorten time-to-market in the sense that users should not have to wait for years for the system that they have specified while the inexorable changes in requirements march on.

The method proposed in this chapter shortens time-to-market through the use of an evolutionary development approach based on time-boxes, so that important layers of the system can be delivered in a maximum period of six months. Less important modules can be delivered and incorporated later. This approach recognizes that it is unrealistic to expect all of a huge, complex system to be built in the twinkling of an eye and that some systems just will not decompose in this way. I would not, for example, wish to travel on an aeroplane whose in-flight systems had been only 80% delivered. However, it is my observation that the majority of commercial systems will yield to this approach.

An object-oriented method should enhance productivity through direct support for and encouragement of a reuse culture and the use of appropriate and powerful development tools (see Chapter 3 for what constitutes a good tool). Of course, the cost of the development and the tools must be offset against the benefits derived in the end product. Taking the view popularized by Booch (1994), that object-oriented development is mainly justified by allowing us to manage complexity better, this whole argument amounts to building more valuable, bigger, trickier systems faster. The quality of the systems must be maintained too and this means that product as well as process and accounting metrics should be collected. The best of methods is of no use if developers find its imperatives onerous; they will inevitably devise ways of avoiding them. A good object-oriented development method should be small, simple, usable and *used*.

This chapter presents the SOMA software development life-cycle model. It is a truly object-oriented process model that addresses these issues.

9.2 Life-cycle models

This section provides a critical review of software engineering life-cycle models and suggests guidelines for an object-oriented life-cycle model that meet the above criteria.

9.2.1 Waterfall and V models

There have been several suggestions as to how IT projects should proceed, based on analogies with other industrial or natural processes and structures. The oldest and best known is the waterfall model which is often justified as being equivalent to the process model of the construction industry. The idea is that only after a complete set of requirements has been defined can analysis begin. After analysis is complete, and only then, logical design may commence and so on. Iterations are sometimes permitted but should be avoided since the cost of iteration is high and increases as the backward move crosses more phases of the life cycle, as indicated by Figure 9.1.

Closely related to waterfall models are the so-called 'V' models. These relate testing substages to the earlier waterfall stages; unit testing tests the code, integration and stress testing tests the design and, finally, acceptance testing and post-implementation reviews test the analysis and requirements. The later a test failure occurs, the more costly the fix.

It has been argued that the waterfall model was never put forward by software engineers as a prescription for system building but that it was designed by suppliers to control delivery and payment schedules. Once an external contractor had produced the analysis report it could be paid for the work. Naturally, buyers often felt that once they had paid for something it ought to work, so that redoing the analysis was resisted unless the supplier would do so at no charge; something that they were – equally naturally – reluctant to do. This led to contractors inventing rigorous methods to maximize the completeness of each phased deliverable, even unto the time-honoured practice of stating that if the customer didn't explicitly state it then it wouldn't be done – even if it was evidently needed. These methods

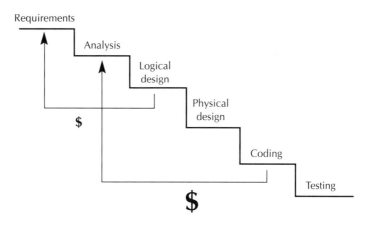

Figure 9.1 The waterfall model with iteration. The greater the number of stages reworked, the greater the cost.

consisted mainly of heuristics and manual instructions or check-lists. Current pressures indicate a widely agreed need for more flexible approaches that permit prototyping and rapid development in a highly iterative manner.

9.2.2 The X model

Hodgson (1991) has proposed an extension of the basic V model that takes account of reuse, called the X model. It is illustrated in Figure 9.2 with a few terminological changes for greater clarity.

The model emphasizes the way that components and frameworks move in and out of the repository using an analogy between accounting and computing. This model is certainly an improvement over the traditional V model and does throw light on the reuse issue. However, it is fundamentally a waterfall and I consider all such models inadequate for modern object-oriented development because they fail to deal with prototyping and iterative development.

9.2.3 Spiral models

Barry Boehm of TRW is credited with the first formalization of an iterative process model. His key idea was that software development should be risk and product driven. A modernized representation of his spiral model is given in Figure 9.3. This is interpreted as follows. Development begins with a survey and review of the existing situation in the business with due regard to existing systems. The situation must be monitored and measured so that an analysis of

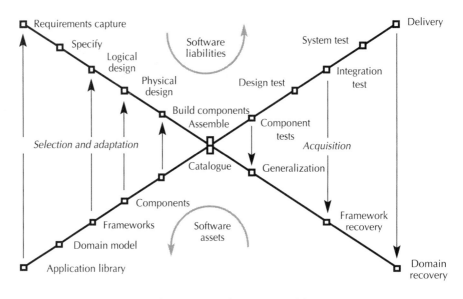

Figure 9.2 Hodgson's X model.

the risk of proceeding with any change can be made. If the positive risks out-weigh the negative ones sufficiently, the next stage is to plan what is to be done. Doing it implies that a mini-waterfall process takes place. This could represent the complete development, a prototype, a pilot or an incremental deliverable component of the final system. Next, the situation should be reviewed to establish if further development is required and, if so, plan the next step. This process can be repeated indefinitely or a number of times fixed in advance. Clearly, it is more general than the waterfall model. Some critics have argued that it is really a linear process with repetition rather than a gen-uinely iterative one (Henderson-Sellers and Edwards, 1994). Indeed, it can be viewed as little more than a wrapped-up waterfall but the emphasis on risk and producing usable products at every stage makes it quite different. Boehm (1981) points out that the model is inappropriate for putting work out to con-tract with external suppliers.

9.2.4 The fountain model and MOSES

Brian Henderson-Sellers and Julian Edwards (originally of the University of New South Wales but now at the University of Technology, Sydney and Object-Oriented Pty respectively) are the originators of a life-cycle model that uses an analogy with fountains rather than waterfalls. In this model the spiral

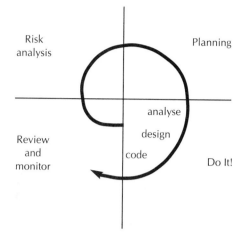

Figure 9.3 A modern version of the Boehm spiral model.

model is implicit and it emphasizes that phases overlap, that layers and subsystems emerge at various points in the development and that the development of individual components is uneven. It permits a division between domain and application objects and is designed to encourage reuse. The deliverables pass up the middle of the fountain, building on the existing reuse pool at the base and falling back into it as they are completed. The simile includes the idea of intermediate catchment basins. New components rise up through testing and program use into maintenance and further development. Both new and existing components may pass through a generalization and re-evaluation phase before falling back into the reuse pool.

There are three routes through the fountain model corresponding to the situations where: (1) all classes are new and pass through all life-cycle phases; (2) some reuse is possible so that classes are modified, messaged and subclassed rather than designed and built and (3) systems are merely assembled from existing classes based on a thorough domain analysis. The first scenario corresponds to the organization that is naive in object-oriented methods and the last to one which is unlikely to be achieved even in dynamic user organizations in the foreseeable future. The fountain model is a useful metaphor but contains insufficient detail to guide the development process on its own. In the sequel we will incorporate its ideas into a more prescriptive but flexible approach.

The process model described in this chapter is much influenced by that of MOSES (Henderson-Sellers and Edwards, 1994). Waterfall and V models divide the development process up into stages based on the unnatural functional division of labour whereby business analysis is separated from systems analysis, the latter from design and so on. The MOSES model offers an iterative

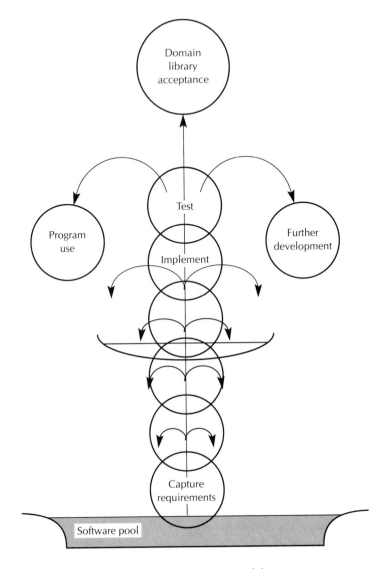

Figure 9.4 A fountain model.

cycle where the division of labour is based on a temporal split. This model is illustrated in Figure 9.5. It divides the product development life cycle into two periods designated as growth and maturity. The growth period corresponds to initial product creation and the maturity period to traditional maintenance. However, the concept of maintenance is regarded as substantially obsolete because it is more correctly viewed as continuous enhancement within an object-oriented, reuse-aware culture. In this spirit the Maturity Period is divided

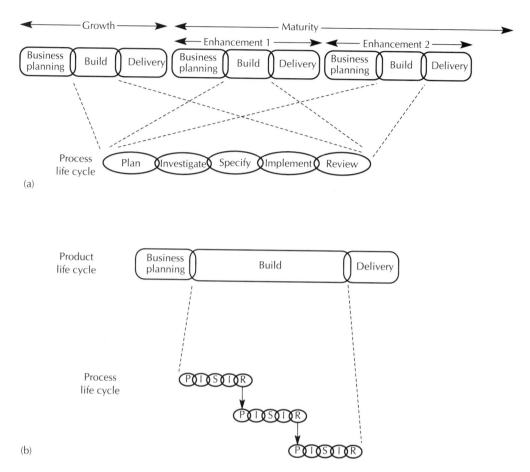

Figure 9.5 (a) The relationship between the growth and maturity periods of the product life cycle and the embedding of the process life cycle within its build stage. (b) Iterated process life cycles within the build stage. Each 'necklace' corresponds to a prototype iteration and each build to a time-box.

into a sequence of Enhancement Periods within which some of the growth period stages are rerun but with different emphases.

MOSES prescribes a product life cycle divided into planning, build and delivery *stages* and a process life cycle divided into five *phases* as shown in Figure 9.5. The process 'necklace' is reapplied on a smaller scale to each successive enhancement. Within each phase, MOSES prescribes a number of techniques and activities. MOSES claims to be a method that can be tailored to meet the needs of particular companies. Just such a tailoring is described in this chapter, but I have had to reorganize some activities more radically than mere tailoring would imply. Furthermore, MOSES is only one among several influences on the method.

In my interpretation, business planning encompasses feasibility studies, strategic planning, risk analysis, initial project proposal, cost-benefit analysis and management approval. It establishes the need for a system and its potential impact on the business. Critical success factors (CSFs) should be established at this stage. MOSES recommends that a business planning report containing the results be delivered but, in my opinion, a standardized, one-page project proposal should be the only mandatory deliverable. This can be supported by appendices with supplementary data such as cost-benefit analyses and the results of feasibility studies. The amount of effort devoted to cost-benefit analysis and feasibility will very greatly accordingly to the nature of the project and the amount of technical and commercial risk. A feasibility study is, in effect, a very rapid systems analysis and outline design. In a rapid development culture this will almost certainly form a part of the process of providing a systems analysis report as described in Section 9.4. It encompasses the consideration of the existing architecture and reuse. The build stage comprises the construction of a system with tested code as both end point and deliverable. In the delivery stage this code is rolled out to the user and acceptance testing and training completed. The build stage could consist of one or more time-boxes or, in rare cases, a big-bang approach may have to be adopted. The model applies to the life cycle of entire projects or to that of individual classes and layers. In my approach, risk analysis is not restricted to the business planning stage but is continuous throughout all stages and phases, as in the spiral model.

MOSES defines the activities appropriate to the process phases using a table similar to Table 9.1. The planning phase is a reprise of the business planning stage with a shorter-term focus. Investigation involves collecting existing textual sources, previous models and existing reusable class descriptions, running interviews or rapid application development (RAD) workshops and establishing scope and constraints. This process continues into the specification stage where again RADs are used and analysis performed. A system analysis report is produced from the first iteration. Later iterations may involve designs that take account of computer constraints. Implementation converts the object model representing the

Table 9.1 Simplified MOSES process model stages and activities.

Phase	Activities
Planning	Estimation, scheduling, objective setting, resource commissioning, risk analysis
Investigation	Requirements capture, information gathering, problem understanding, scoping
Specification	Analysis, high-level logical design
Implementation	Low-level physical design, coding, testing
Review	Quality audit, project plan assessment, metrics assessment, tests against task scripts

logical design to a physical design that is usually language specific and moves on to code production. The design model must include decisions on database storage, conversion of classification structures into inheritance networks, use of public/private/protected/friend, and so on, implementing composition structures, concurrent inter-object communication and architectural considerations. Unit and integration tests are performed here too. Review involves further testing and both product and process quality assessment.

We do not follow this model exactly because the investigation process takes place both within and outside of the time-boxes. RADs gather requirements that apply to all the iterations within at least one time-box; but each user review within the time-box is capturing additional requirements – at least in principle. If we admit that planning is primarily objective setting and scheduling then it is also clear that objective setting takes place during RADs and is only modified during time-boxes. Review too is split between the time-box (scenario (script based) testing) and the evaluation stage (which corresponds to MOSES' Review). Section 9.3 defines the SOMA time-box approach in detail.

The project should produce a quality plan and this is the right place to place a plan of the iterations through the process. We will refer to this as the time-box plan. RADs result in requirements statements and will include a Task Object Model and a Business Object Model along with statements of mission and objectives. An important deliverable is the set of event traces produced by walkthroughs. Ideally, all deliverables will be captured electronically by a CASE tool such as *SOMATiK*. The latter generates all graphical deliverables and collects all metrics automatically. The task model is the basis for a test plan.

9.2.5 Fractals, conches and ammonites

Other variants on the spiral and suggestions intended to support prototyping and/or RAD abound. McGregor and Sykes (1992) describe a fractal model due to Forte and based on the observation that development is self-similar at various levels of granularity: class, layer, system, and so on. Henderson-Sellers and Edwards (1994) criticize this approach on the grounds that fractals are infinitely recursive and deterministic because, they claim, development is not. However, I find the analogy useful and would expect to see use made of it in future methods. The issue of determinism is always contentious; cf. arguments about hidden variables in quantum physics and open and closed system arguments in cybernetics.

There are a number of variants on the spiral model in the literature such as the 'conch' model, which is really only a different, and more detailed, diagrammatic representation of the spiral; in fact, Boehm's original representation had such a shape. Figure 9.6 shows an example of this kind of representation of an object-oriented development process in the form of an ammonite.

My own experience with this kind of model soon showed that, while the metaphor was of some use, it did not give real guidance on what to do. Something

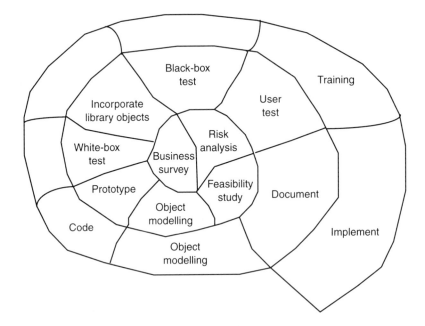

Figure 9.6 An ammonite model for object-oriented development.

better would have to be developed. The remainder of this chapter describes the result of my efforts to arrive at a truly object-oriented life-cycle model. This approach has by now been used for a large number of commercial projects.

9.3 RADs, time-boxes and evolutionary development

Rapid Application Development or RAD, as a development approach, began to be popular in the late 1980s but its origins remain obscure. The Joint Application Development (JAD) workshop technique used at IBM was certainly an influential component. Rapid prototyping had been used for years and also penetrated the RAD approach. James Martin is sometimes accused of first coining the phrase but the earliest formal declaration seems to be the Ripp (Rapid Iterative Production Prototyping) method developed at El du Pont de Nemours and sold later under the catchy slogan: 'Your system in 128 days – or your money back'. Ripp was followed by many proprietary imitations and now every consultancy has its own version and name. What they all have in common is the use of workshops and time-boxes. A 'time-box' sets a rigid limit to prototype iterations to ensure management control over prototyping. A small team is mandatory and the tested prototype is both end-point and deliverable. RAD methods vary in the extent to which users participate in the pro- totyping process and the kind of tools used. Some, as with Ripp, insist on the use of 4GLs and repositories. Others emphasize CASE tools and code genera- tion. SOMA emphasizes building a bridge between the understanding of users and developers and integrating their effort.

Prototyping and RAD are highly beneficial, whether object-oriented tools are in use or otherwise, and there is a growing amount of empirical evidence for this. Scott Gordon and Bieman (1993) report that ease of use and correct requirements capture are unarguably improved, based on a study of 34 projects. There is some evidence that maintainability is improved but only when throw- away prototypes are not allowed to evolve into the final product. These authors found no support for 'the common notion that rapid prototyping cannot be used for developing large systems' and recommend that an object-oriented approach is used within a disciplined framework such as that used in Hekmatpour (1987) and the one presented in this chapter. When RAD workshops are used, costs are often lower than those implied by multiple interviews with users and much time is usually saved. They give structure to the requirements capture and analysis activity but are dynamic, interactive and cooperative. They involve users and often cut across organizational boundaries. RAD workshops help to identify and prioritize needs and resolve contentious issues. User ownership of the end product is promoted from the beginning and the analysis process gets a healthy kick-start. Decisions and compromises are agreed and recorded during RAD workshops and the first workshop is the first opportunity to begin managing both users' expectations and their attitudes to change.

The time-box technique offers the following benefits. It imposes manage- ment control over ripple effects and uncontrolled iteration. Control is achieved by setting a rigid elapsed time limit on the prototyping cycle and using a small project team. Furthermore, it has a usable system as both the end-point of the process and its deliverable. There is no distinction between production, evolu- tion and maintenance as with conventional approaches, which usually ignore maintenance costs during project justification.

The time-box tackles the following management issues:

- Wants versus needs – by forcing requirements to be prioritized by negoti- ation between users and developers. Users and the project team are forced to concentrate on the real needs of the business.
- Creeping functionality – in the traditional life cycle the long delay between specification and delivery can lead to users requesting extra fea- tures. The use of a time limit reduces this tendency.
- Project team motivation – the developers can see a tangible result of their efforts emerging.
- The involvement of users at every stage reduces implementation shock.

The approach reduces time-to-market, not by a magic trick that makes hard things easy but by delivering an important usable subset of the entire system in no more than a few months.

It is absolutely critical to maintain credibility, build on success and manage expectations during the RAD process. This is achieved by several means. Users should be warned that a quickly developed prototype may conceal much complexity. A working system will take time in proportion to the complexity of the tasks it assists with. Equally, users should be stimulated by many small, incremental deliveries. With SOMA, they agree prioritized objectives and developers should show that corners that are cut to keep within time limits are low priority corners. Developers can thus afford to accept reasonable changes to requirements, provided that existing, low priority requirements can be eliminated by mutual agreement based on the priorities. This expectation management is a key task for the project manager. If it is neglected the project will usually fail.

The technique prevents paralysis by analysis, errors due to delay, spurious requirements and implementation shock. It usually motivates teams better than the waterfall approach ... but some systems just can't be built this way; for example, most of us would be uncomfortable about flying in a jumbo jet whose control systems were at the prototype stage or had only been partially delivered. This does not mean that RAD cannot be applied to real-time systems. In such cases the techniques are applied to development on the test bed but only fully tested systems are put into service.

One possible criticism of RAD is that its benefits may derive largely from the Hawthorne effect observed on many O&M studies, whereby merely paying more attention to users and developers makes them more productive regardless of the techniques used. It can also be argued that highly trained and motivated users and developers are the cause of the success, since many RAD-aware companies are also innovators with skilled staffs. I cannot disprove either of these assertions but remain confident of the utility of RAD nevertheless.

SOMA offers a synthesis of RAD and OT. In one company I have been involved with, both RAD and object-oriented programming had been introduced simultaneously but separately, with considerable and beneficial effects on productivity in each case. The RADs gave many of the benefits mentioned above but, unfortunately, they were run using structured techniques and typically produced normalized entity models and huge functional decompositions. The developers were prone to saying 'nice pictures', filing them somewhere and then going off to find a user who could help them prototype something. The SOMA life cycle model was developed, in part, to help this company reconcile RAD with OOP.

9.4 The SOMA process model

The remarkable thing about most published object-oriented analysis and design methods is that their life-cycle models remain thoroughly procedural. Some are nothing more than 'structured' methods with objects added to the entity model. I would include OMT, Shlaer/Mellor, FUSION, Objectory and perhaps even MOSES in the latter category. The MOSES life cycle is more iterative and recursive than the others and its phases may be executed in any order but even that method retains a procedural flavour because it has 'phases'. Other methods have no life-cycle model at all and the remainder have a very weak one; for example, Booch'93. Successful object-oriented RAD requires the total abolition of the notion of development 'phases'.

The SOMA method defines projects as networks of activities that have dependencies but no explicit sequence. An activity produces a result which must be a tested result. In particular we test objectives by measuring them and requirements object models by walkthroughs. Task scripts are captured very early on and are used as test scripts. This helps address the debugging problem in a tool independent fashion and places the emphasis on quality first. This tested time-box (or 'right on time') philosophy means that it is quite permissible and safe to write the code before the design is done – or vice versa if that's how you like to work. Both business objects and task scripts are accumulated in a repository for reuse in subsequent workshops and projects. It is not so much that OO enhances RAD with additional benefits or vice versa. It is more that modern IT requires the benefits of both techniques applied in such a way as to be consistent with one another. Structured RADs with OO programming can be dangerous. The main benefit of the combined approach is that it makes it possible to move to specification level, rather than code level, reuse. No CASE tool known to us supports such an approach adequately, which is why *SOMATiK* was produced.

In SOMA, there is not a series of 'phases' but there are activities, both bounded and unbounded. Bounded activities are time-boxes, limited by predetermined periods of elapsed time. Some unbounded activities are continuous but must still pay attention to cost control by setting and meeting objectives. Others are embedded within bounded activities and the project manager is required to balance their time and resource consumption within the overall bounded activity.

Activities are objects with operations defined by their deliverables. Each dependency is a guarded message so that all message sends are 'guarded' by the defined tests. Each guard is a ruleset or assertion. Each rule is implemented by a test. Activities are the building blocks of the stages of a project.

The stage model is inspired largely by that of MOSES. There are three stages: Propose, Build and Implement. The most complex of these is Build. Activities produce deliverables. Activities consist of tasks. Developers and users adopting rôles are responsible for carrying out tasks and producing deliverables. This recursive composition hierarchy is illustrated in Figure 9.7. Each activity has the same high-level structure in that its tasks will always accomplish five higher-level tasks: Plan, Investigate, Specify, Create and Review. This view leads to some very noticeable departures from existing practice, most notably that Design is no longer a separate phase but is embedded with the Specify and Create tasks of the time-box activity. Analysis spans Investigate

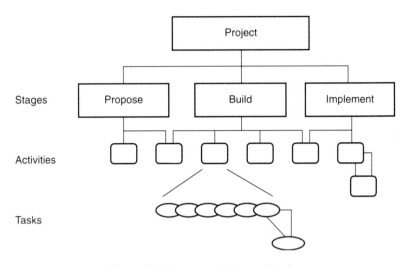

Figure 9.7 Stages, activities and tasks.

and Specify within each activity and runs through activities such as RAD workshops, Rapid OOA and the time-box. Review and testing are carried out within every activity.

The principles that are applied are:

(1) Quality first: everything is tested as it is created, removing the need for post-implementation reviews, though these may be held at the instigation of the IT or the user department.
(2) Continuous improvement: based on reuse of software and specifications and on measurement of the products and processes.
(3) Minimum time-to-market: through the use of the RAD approach.
(4) Flexibility and robustness: through a total commitment to object technology throughout the life cycle.

The philosophy behind the SOMA method is encapsulated in the diagram of Figure 9.8 in which the core intra-project activities are represented in the left-hand column and extra-project activities in the right-hand, shaded area.

Our process model is one where evolutionary prototyping and rapid development are the rule rather than the exception. Throwaway prototypes may also be produced during the Project Initiation, RAD Workshops or Rapid OOA activities.

The IT organization is subject to its overall strategy. Management controls financial allocations to projects at a high level and their decisions enter the project planning activity box and initiate RAD workshops aimed at establishing the scope of the application and the goals of the users of each of its features. These are followed by intensive RAD analysis workshops which

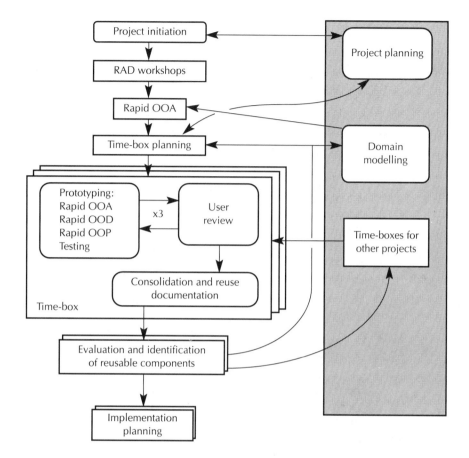

Figure 9.8 The SOMA life-cycle model.

deliver task scripts, event traces and an outline object model and then by a more thorough and critical rapid systems analysis which refines that model and produces a complete report on the systems analysis. For simpler systems this Rapid OOA activity may be entirely embedded within the workshop activity; there is always some degree of overlap. Output from the RAD workshops and subsequent analysis goes into the project planning activity because the planners must be made aware of the resource requirement that the preliminary scoping implies. Secondly, the trustees of the domain model need to examine the Business Object Model to see if there are any existing class descriptions in their repository that match, so there is communication with the class librarian.

In Figure 9.8, each box in the diagram represents an **activity**. Boxes with sharp corners represent activities bounded by elapsed time. Every activity has completion criteria so that its output is tested.

Every activity's completion is a milestone and results in fully tested output and deliverables. Output is that which is inevitable but not delivered to anybody beyond the producers. Deliverables are seen by others and are classified as optional, recommended and mandatory. **Mandatory** deliverables must be delivered in all circumstances. **Recommended** deliverables may be omitted provided that their omission can be justified. **Optional** deliverables may be omitted at the discretion of the project manager. Completion criteria always include tests of the products of the activity. Tasks, documentation and activities are thus marked as M, R or O. This structure may be applied recursively to substages, subtasks and subactivities.

Project initiation is usually quite informal. It is the process of 'coming up with an idea'. It can be driven strategically or be the result of a developer prototyping an idea in spare time. It results in a proposal that is tested by management approval.

The next step is requirements capture using interviews or workshops including or followed by more detailed analysis. These activities use the techniques expounded in Chapters 6, 7 and 8. Workshop results are tested by walkthroughs using rôle-playing and by user and sponsor sign-off, as is the systems analysis report.

Normally, RAD workshops and interviews are a precursor to rapid development. The deliverables from requirements capture should form input to a planning process which will set up a project lasting about two or three months' elapsed time, during which a small team will prototype the objects representing the objectives with the highest priority. Evaluation of the prototype should be based on the views of an independent evaluation team and upon the task scripts developed in the context model.

There are plans and estimates at various levels. At the highest, there should be a plan covering the entire scope established and perhaps recording the predicted tasks concerned with linking to other systems and the timing implications of dependencies on undelivered components in other systems. Within this plan there will be an overall iteration plan. Then there is a plan for each time-box. The extent to which these plans are formal deliverables is questionable. They should exist but may be recorded in minutes of meetings or as common agreements among teams. In that sense they may not be 'delivered' to anyone but the originators.

Time-box Planning first plans the overall structure of time-boxes to be used, based on the priorities already identified, and then each individual time-box. Time-boxes may run sequentially, in parallel or both. For complex project structures the project plan should explain how results are to be coordinated. A formal approach to concurrent development such as the one suggested by Aoyama (1993) may be adopted for really complex projects.

The main time-box includes three unbounded activities that must be managed and juggled within the overall elapsed time constraint. Prototyping involves OOA, OOD, OOP and testing but in no predefined order. If the developers are more comfortable doing the design last, so be it. The only thing that matters is that the time-box produces and tests its deliverables. The proto-typing activity interacts iteratively with user reviews and produces a sequence of (about three or four) prototypes. The user review tests them and they test the user reviews, possibly leading to slight requirements or analysis modifica-tions. When this is complete the results must be documented and integrated with existing system components and the results of other time-boxes. Developers are responsible for identifying potentially reusable classes for transmission to the domain modelling team for generalization. The products of the time-box are tested using inspections and walkthroughs. A popular technique is that of Fagan (1974).

Reuse potential is confirmed during the formal evaluation review which decides whether to release, redo or abort this part of the project. Again inspec-tions and walkthroughs based on the event traces are the key testing tools.

The implementation planning activity can then proceed up to final deliv-ery. This involves further testing in the live environment.

The following subsections enumerate the stages, activities and deliverables of SOMA and indicate which deliverables are mandatory and which are optional. Our slogans are:

- right on time; and
- minimize deliverables! To paraphrase Einstein, there should be as few as possible, *but no fewer*.

OTHER LIFE-CYCLE ISSUES

The life-cycle model described above needs the right people to apply it and the right tools to support them. These skills and tools are different from the tradi-tional approach. The difference is that between the production line specialization of the third-generation method and the total systems responsibility of fourth-generation and object-oriented methods. When development takes months or years, there is little choice but to specialize, with expensive and experienced staff concentrating on the initial feasibility, design, and specification stages and tech-nical specialists concentrating on the coding and testing.

Assuming that a RAD approach to system development in general is to be adopted and that it is desired to maintain the object-oriented approach throughout projects then users must define and operate an object-oriented approach in each subsequent activity. A sound philosophy and approach to object modelling are required. These can only be acquired from experience, education, training or all three. Thus, it seems wise to establish an education and training programme early on which will:

- provide the basic awareness of object-oriented concepts;
- teach specific analysis techniques and notations;
- draw on the experience already within the organization.

Organizations migrating to OT should take steps to:

- establish a standard notation for object-oriented analysis and design;

- establish standard techniques for translation from analysis to construction;
- select a defined set of tools for programming and CASE;
- institute a management awareness and education programme;
- define the life-cycle approach to object-oriented development;
- institute a training programme covering object-oriented concepts and analysis and design techniques with special modules for RAD facilitators, scribes and analysts;
- institute a reuse programme.

These actions need not all be taken simultaneously. The exigencies of the situation will dictate the priorities. However, the awareness issues cannot be neglected at any point.

TIME LIMITS   SOMA imposes elapsed time limits on all rapid development activities apart from project initiation and domain modelling. Requirements capture and rapid analysis should take no more than four weeks. A one-week minimum may be expected. The time-box planning activity will normally last for between one and four weeks as well. Each time-box may last for between one and six months and a three-month period is to be considered normal. Evaluation and reuse analysis should never take more than two weeks. These limits are subject to an overall maximum of six months' elapsed time from the end of the workshops to implementation.

The optimum size of a project is between three and 12 man-months effort, with two to four people in the project team, and a duration of up to six months (but see next paragraph).

In order to maximize efficiency, provide predictable testing workloads and deliveries to users and focus development teams on achieving delivery dates, development projects are 'time-boxed'. A time-boxed project will ideally take from 60 to 130 days elapsed and will occupy two to three staff members. Where a project cannot be limited to this amount of effort because its requirements are too complex, the work is split into sections that conform to the above standard. Where the scope of a project is limited, so that the required effort is too little, a number of requirements will be bundled together to create an effective project. Note that ideally, in this case, all requirements should be related to each other and assigned a high priority by the user.

The procedures outlined in the remainder of this chapter are only relevant for projects that are expected to take more than three man months of effort.

The sign-off of the products of the workshops and especially the systems analysis document fixes both the project plan and the elapsed time limits on the project. Requirements may evolve but only within the limits agreed at this time. Failure on the part of users to attend RADs, user reviews, or sign off requirements will result in the cancellation of the project. This may only be avoided if a delay agreement is signed.

The development of any computer system is presented below as a set of activities with a subsection devoted to each one. The steps outlined are intended as statements of best practice for systems development and project management.

9.4.1 Project initiation stage and activity

The development process starts with business planning and the organization's strategy plan. A request from part of the business or even external legislation can initiate the process. The product is a project proposal document, which should be short and to the point. It should contain a statement of the broad project mission and cost and other constraints. The proposal should contain a problem definition stated in terms of business processes and commercial impact, the names of a sponsor, domain experts and key users, the broad scope of the project, a cost/benefit justification and the project completion criteria. It may also include cost-benefit, feasibility, risk and critical success factor appendices. These will be produced precisely when they are needed to obtain the sponsor's signature. A throwaway prototype may also be part of the proposal.

A proposal once agreed and approved leads to the running of a RAD scoping workshop and usually a detailed RAD workshop immediately following. There is no definite assumption at this stage that the solution will be computerized and the workshop is free to explore the possibilities of business process re-engineering.

The following tasks need to be carried out during this activity. Recall that M = Mandatory, R = Recommended and O = Optional.

TASKS

Define problem in business terms	M
Identify scope and specific inclusions/exclusions	M
Prepare justification for further investigation	M
Identify sponsor	M
Specify completion criteria	M
Estimate the size of the project in task points where possible	R
Estimate the cost of the next activity of the project and the costs of the complete project, including future running costs	M
Review and sign off the proposal document	M
Identify resources for next activities	M
Review existing systems and identify existing components for possible reuse, especially existing models	R
Schedule workshop dates and obtain commitments from participants	R
Obtain approval to proceed from sponsor	M

DELIVERABLES AND DOCU-MENTATION

The major deliverable is a project proposal document of as little as a page in length. For larger projects a quality plan is used to record progress through the various project stages, both in terms of expected and achieved dates and responsibilities. The **project proposal document** might have the following structure:

(1) Business requirement definition
(2) Scope
(3) Justification
(4) Sponsor
(5) Exclusions
(6) External constraints
(7) Completion criteria
(8) Projected cost of proceeding, including projected future running costs
(9) Training plan for RAD workshop personnel
(10) Glossary of terms

PREREQUISITES, COMPLETION CRITERIA AND TIME LIMITS This is an unbounded activity with no elapsed time limits or prerequisites.

9.4.2 RAD workshop activity: Subactivity I – Scoping

Rapid application development (RAD) is a technique designed to improve the quality and efficiency of systems analysis within the project life cycle. A team of systems and business experts attends workshop sessions to define the business area's requirements, using either a CASE tool or a combination of drawing and WP products to document them. A model of the users' tasks and a model of the business objects and their relationships are produced. This includes or is followed by a refinement of the business object model using rigorous object-oriented analysis: Rapid OOA. Where appropriate, package evaluation is performed during Rapid OOA with a list of appropriate packages determined at the end of this activity. Extensive user involvement is required. Rapid OOA can be entirely embedded within the RAD Workshop activity for simple projects.

While the time-box activity uses prototypes as an evolutionary technique to move the build forward through successive iterations, any prototype built during a RAD workshop will almost certainly have to be thrown away. This implies that expectations must be managed accordingly.

Scoping refines the mission into a project charter and defines the boundaries of the problem, issues that must be resolved, objectives, priorities and users' goals. It should also begin a review of business processes.

The product is a scoping document that should contain the project mission statement, objectives, measures and priorities. It should identify external objects and the main rôles in which users will interact with the system, the events that trigger these interactions and the information exchanged. For each interaction its goal should be stated. Assumptions, exclusions and outstanding issues are documented.

The RAD workshop that elicits the scope of the project is followed by one or more RAD workshops to elicit the detail. These are dealt with in the next subsection although they may follow on directly from the scoping workshop, possibly on the following day.

The objectives of the scoping activity are as follows:

- To establish a high-level understanding of existing and proposed business processes, the context in which they operate and their goals
- To establish the mission, boundaries and objectives of the project
- To set clear targets, priorities and acceptance criteria for a new system
- To review financial and business justification and identify other benefits
- To complete the activity in a short time scale via the use of intensive workshop sessions

A number of purely logistical tasks need to be remembered, such as booking a suitable venue and informing and briefing the participants, facilitator and scribe. Equipment and software should be prepared. In particular, a copy of *SOMATiK* or a similar tool and any existing repository classes and class cards should be available. Stationery such as flip charts, pens, overhead projector, blank foils, video/audio equipment, blank tapes, paper for printer and participants, pencils, glow pens, and so on must be remembered. There must be a supply of blank class cards or the means of printing them; for example, a laser printer.

It is advisable to begin sessions with an introduction to the approach being adopted.

TASKS

Arrange accommodation and facilities	M
Confirm availability	M
Collect relevant documents	M
Collect reusable object specifications from repository and other projects	R
Prepare agenda	R
Explain SOMA approach to participants including the responsibilities of sponsors and users	M
Establish and agree project mission, objectives and their measures	M
Record assumptions and exclusions	M
Identify open issues and responsibility for solving them	M
Produce external context model	M
Produce internal context model	M
Identify all significant messages	M
Establish the goal of each interaction	M
Agree implementation priorities by discussing measures and voting	M
Discuss reuse of existing task objects and candidates for future reuse	R
Sign off agreements and models	M
Produce and publish scope document	M
Review and approve scope document	M

DELIVERABLES AND DOCU- MENTATION

A **RAD scoping workshop report** containing the following:

(1) Management summary (R)
(2) Introduction (O)
(3) List of participants and date of workshop (M)
(4) Project name and mission (M)
(5) Assumptions and exclusions (M)
(6) Objectives, measures and priorities (M)
(7) Open issues and responsibilities for closing them (R)
(8) Security issues (M)
(9) A context model containing external objects, internal actors and the messages that are passed (M)
(10) A message table with the following contents for each message: message name, triggering event, source, target, information sent/received, expected result type, the goal of the interaction (M)
(11) Planned reuse of previous RAD workshop output including task models, business models, definitions and designs (R)
(12) User sign-off (M)

PREREQUISITES, COMPLETION CRITERIA AND TIME LIMITS

Project initiation should be complete and suitably approved before a workshop takes place.

The activity is complete when the report is produced and the user sign-off has been obtained. Objectives are tested by trying to apply measures and by voting. The mission and goals are tested against consensus.

Participants should review the documents produced to ensure that the scoping document provides a clear statement of the scope of the project, its objectives, reuse considerations, the model of the proposed business process and its actors and interactions and the goals of each interaction.

The scoping workshop will normally last one day or less unless the objective is to decompose a very large business problem into smaller components.

9.4.3 RAD workshop activity: Subactivity II – Detail

Detailed RAD workshops follow scoping workshops and refine the context model into a Task Object Model by identifying the tasks necessary to accomplish each goal identified in the former. These are decomposed, classified and related to exceptions. A textual analysis of the task scripts leads to the construction of a Business Object Model that comprises the business objects and their relationships, with further detail as appropriate.

The objectives of this activity are:

■ To produce a detailed statement of system requirements
■ To produce and test a set of task scripts in the form of a Task Object Model
■ To produce and test a Business Object Model

- To make further recommendations on the resources and equipment required
- To revise development and implementation plans

TASKS	Arrange accommodation and facilities	M
	Confirm availability	M
	Collect relevant documents	M
	Collect reusable object specifications from repository and other projects	M
	Prepare agenda	R
	Explain SOMA approach to participants including the responsibilities of sponsors and users	R
	Confirm results of scoping session	M
	Confirm project mission, objectives, measures and priorities	M
	Confirm assumptions and exclusions	M
	Confirm unresolved open issues and responsibility for solving them	M
	Confirm external and internal context models	M
	For each goal, produce a top-level task script	M
	Classify tasks and discuss exceptions to produce subscripts and side-scripts	M
	Decompose all task scripts to atomic component tasks	M
	Textual analysis of scripts to produce candidate classes and their cards	M
	Add repository classes to model produced	M
	Add structures to model and refine using repertory grids and/or card sorts if necessary	M
	Identify layers and implementation priorities	M
	Identify attributes and operations for each class	M
	Find rulesets	R
	Walk through all significant task scripts to produce event traces	M
	Produce object/objectives matrix	R
	Discuss reuse candidates	O
	Check open issues resolved	M
	Sign off agreements and models	M
	Produce and publish requirements definition	M
	Obtain approval for requirements definition	M

DELIVERABLES AND DOCUMENTATION

The **requirements document** has the following contents:

(1) Management summary (R)
(2) Introduction (O)
(3) List of participants and date of workshop (M)
(4) Project name and mission (M)
(5) Assumptions and exclusions (M)
(6) Objectives, measures and priorities (M)

(7) Open issues and responsibilities for closing them (R)

(8) A context model containing external objects, internal actors and the messages that are passed (M)

(9) A message table with the following contents for each message: message name, triggering event, source, target, information sent/received, expected result type, the goal of the interaction (R)

(10) For each goal, a task script together with a decomposition of the script into component scripts (M)

(11) A Task Object Model of the tasks (R)

(12) A Business Object Model in the form of a set of class cards (M)

(13) A list of objects to be reused from earlier projects (R)

(14) A set of event traces documenting walkthroughs (M)

(15) A set of metrics for the model (M)

(16) Planned reuse of previous RAD workshop output including business models, definitions and designs (R)

(17) Glossary of business terms and other business information (R)

(18) Business process definitions including security and controls, disaster recovery, business transactions with volumes and frequencies, expected response times, major interfaces to other systems, object ownership (R)

(19) Next steps and recommendations (O)

(20) User sign-off form (M)

PREREQUISITES, COMPLETION CRITERIA AND TIME LIMITS The main tests applied are the walkthroughs carried out by rôle-playing which test the Business Object Model principally but also the Task Object Model. Objectives are tested by trying to apply measures and by establishing priorities using such techniques as placing a number of preference markers against objectives. These are counted to establish the implementation priorities attached to the objectives.

The activity is complete when the report is produced and the users' sign-off has been obtained.

The requirements document should contain no ambiguities or contradictions. Each object in the Business Object Model should have an owner.

The detail workshop will follow the scoping session and normally last four days. For large projects several workshops may be required. The formal limits are from one day to four weeks. There are overall limits on the RAD workshop and Rapid OOA activities combined of between one day and four weeks elapsed. A one-week minimum may be expected and a RAD workshop activity total of less than three days should be formally justified.

9.4.4 Rapid object-oriented systems analysis

Analysis involves two stages, information gathering and modelling followed by model refinement. Usually the first stage is accomplished during a RAD workshop that produces a workshop report containing a user task model, task scripts and a preliminary, but tested, business object model consisting of completed class cards and event traces. The review of business processes should be complete by this stage. Each goal in the scoping environment model is resolved into the tasks that users expect to be performed in order that it be accomplished. This includes examination of system internals as well as mere interface behaviour though not details of how these internals may be implemented. This is an important extension over and above the suggestions of Jacobson *et al.* (1992) which tend to restrict the tasks (use cases) described to those of the actors. The tasks are organized into a full object model and the report should contain task cards showing all four structures of such a model.

The developers must now review the model for completeness and consistency and discover any logical dependencies or unrealistic features. The models in the RAD workshop report are thus refined into a systems analysis report, which also should include project plans and estimates.

The analysis report will contain both a task object model and a business object model including a message table/context model, task scripts, class cards, event traces, an objects/objectives matrix, priorities for layers and most of the other material that appeared in the RAD workshop report but with additional definitions based on a thorough and technically informed analysis of the problem that the hurly-burly of a RAD workshop does not always allow the leisure for. The task scripts are important as they form the basis of test scripts. During the preparation of the systems analysis report, preliminary decisions concerning reuse of repository objects will be made and these should be reported.

It is useful to base the analysis report on a standard document template. The advantages of using a template are that it supports faster document creation and should result in a better quality document because the information is presented once, and in the right context. It should speed and ease reviewing; the Fagan's inspection of such a document will be easier as the reviewers will have a better idea of what should be contained in each section, and information retrieval for future developers of the system will be eased. Ease of review of system documentation by external auditors is also enhanced.

The objectives of this activity are to confirm the task object model is valid, produce a business object model in sufficient detail to confirm the technical approach and identify critical areas of system performance and revise development and implementation plans.

This activity is embedded within the time-box activity as well as preceding it. In the simplest case it may be entirely embedded within a detailed RAD workshop.

TASKS

Review existing systems and identify existing components for possible reuse, especially existing models	M
Examine alternative solutions and select a preferred approach	R
Build a prototype, where appropriate	O
Resolve open issues	R
Confirm scope and objectives	M

Produce and publish systems analysis report   M
Obtain sign-off for the systems analysis report   M

If the analysis determines that a package solution is appropriate, a package evaluation should be carried out.

DELIVERABLES AND DOCU- MENTATION A major deliverable from this process is a specification suitable for use in systems development. The specification should comprise a physical prototype and its paper-based counterpart. The forms of expression of the prototype code and the paper model should be as close as possible to each other. This tends to indicate the efficacy of rule based prototyping environments and of object-oriented programming languages.

The main deliverable of this activity is a systems analysis report whose purpose is to model and specify the proposed system in detail and work out its costs and benefits, in order to enable a decision to be taken as to whether to continue to the next activity. This systems analysis report should contain the following sections.

(1) Management summary (M)
(2) Introduction (O)
(3) Existing system, including description of any shortcomings it has and running costs (O)
(4) System requirements in the form of a Task Object Model, Business Object Model and task scripts (M)
(5) Proposed system description and object model (including running costs and metrics) (M)
(6) Choice of technology, justifying any divergence from any existing IT strategy (M)
(7) An analysis of system-based risk including project risk exposures, assumptions and dependencies (M)
(8) Options considered (including business process re-engineering) (R)
(9) Future requirements (O)
(10) Appendices(M)
  ■ Development plan (O)
  ■ Estimates (M)
  ■ Computer resource requirements (R)
  ■ Planned reuse of objects (R)
  ■ Prototype (O)
  ■ Screen and report layouts (O)
  ■ Coding system to be used (M)

If third-party software is to be used, an invitation to tender and a hardware/ software/package evaluation document may be produced. If the project concerns enhancements to existing systems, one should institute proper source code control output from the existing system. It is beyond the scope of this text to give the details of such general software engineering tasks.

PREREQUISITES,
COMPLETION
CRITERIA AND
TIME LIMITS Project initiation and initial requirements capture activities must be complete prior to Rapid OOA.

The systems analysis report should contain a review of the impact of change on production systems, a development plan, including a projected end date, and an estimate of the metrics of the system including non-development costs.

The formal time limits are from one day to two weeks. There are overall limits on the RAD workshop and Rapid OOA activities combined of between one day and four weeks elapsed. A one-week minimum may be expected for the combined activities. Time used in this activity is to be deducted from the overall maximum of six months to implementation.

9.4.5 Time-box planning

The time-box plan outlines the activities and resources required to build an agreed part of the system by a fixed date. Time-box planning also involves estimating and resource and infrastructure procurement. The plan takes account of the overall project plan and should be sent to those responsible for the overall plan.

One or more parallel time-boxes are planned. Each time-box will ideally last around three months' elapsed time though this will depend on the tools used. There is also a higher-level planning context which plans or at least predicts sequences of time-boxes and considers the interrelationships with the domain model.

Deliverables and observable milestones should be agreed when the project plan is produced and reviewed regularly.

TASKS Tasks in the time-box planning stage include establishing the environment and bringing in specialists in, say, communications, operations and corporate data administration, if necessary.

Review the requirements discovered in the RAD workshops and review the analysis report	O
Review domain model and existing systems and identify existing components for possible reuse	R
Ensure participant training programme is planned	R
Apply source code control tools to existing system if proposed solution is a change to an existing system	M
Revise development plans	R
Identify impact of proposed change on hardware, including response times	M
Set the time-box objectives and publish them	M
Set the number of planned prototype iterations	R
Establish development team. Confirm the lead user, project manager, developers and the sponsor	M

Establish the evaluation team – sponsor, project manager, user representatives, facilitator, demonstrator/reader, corporate auditor, operations representative, librarian, legal expert, and so on.   M

DELIVERABLES AND DOCU-MENTATION

Time-box planning produces a time-box plan, including a Gantt chart, and an estimate in task points with resource requirements and delivery dates.

A short participant training requirements report should be produced to ensure that the costs, rôles, systems training and business training needs of systems and business participants are clearly understood and planned. Emphasis is placed here on requirements and testing. This report identifies the broad skills required to undertake the project, then the skill set of the individuals allocated to it, to identify the mismatch. Ensure that:

- staff members are named;
- training requirements are identified and scheduled;
- business and technical needs are covered;
- equipment can be obtained on time;
- inspections are included in the plan.

PREREQUISITES, COMPLETION CRITERIA AND TIME LIMITS

The project initiation and requirements capture activities should be complete and there should be a completed systems analysis report before starting this activity. The formal limits are from one day to four weeks. A one-week minimum may be expected. Time used in this activity is to be deducted from the overall maximum of six months to implementation.

9.4.6 The main build time-box

Once time-box planning is complete, the resources are available and the equipment and environment is commissioned, the main time-box may be entered. The developers immediately produce a first-cut prototype and may, incidentally, sketch out a design in the process. This is reviewed with users and typically is a broad and shallow prototype. User reaction is taken back to a second prototype and a deeper, narrower prototype produced. Here it is more likely – but still not compulsory – that a design document will be produced. If C++ (or indeed any complex or hybrid object-oriented language) is being used and the design is very intricate then the Booch design notation is recommended, possibly supported by a tool such as Rational ROSE. In many cases however, the code can be produced straight from the class cards in the analysis report. When this is done any design changes should result in new or revised class cards being prepared. This may affect the domain model and should be flagged for review at the evaluation stage. Prototyping iterations – each with a strong user involvement – should be limited to about three but the actual number is determined partly by the absolute time limit on the time-box: a maximum of six months. Adequate time must be left for tasks such as consolidation with the products of other time-boxes, database integration, documentation and the identification of candidate classes for reuse. Note that the developers are not responsible for creating reusable classes, only for identifying their potential, and that the latter is subject to review by the evaluation team.

This activity consists of a number of nested and iterated subsidiary activities as follows.

- Prototyping:
  - Rapid OOA
  - Rapid OOD
  - Rapid OOP
  - Testing
- User review
- Consolidation
- Reuse potential evaluation
- Documentation

Figure 9.8 illustrates this.

A waterfall or 'V' process model is traditionally used for applications with heavy transaction processing requirements to be implemented in conventional languages on centralized architectures. This approach is not appropriate for development of systems in which the major elements of functionality are in the interfaces with users or which are constructed as veritable models of parts of the business. Development of these and of distributed applications and those using object-oriented languages is better approached with a method based on object-oriented principles.

The objective of the prototyping technique is to provide the user with a system that is easy to use and to achieve this in as short a time as possible. The SOMA method achieves this by:

- extensive reuse of existing components where they exist;
- applying an interface style that is consistent with other applications;
- supporting user goals and tasks based on business processes rather than narrowly defined functional responsibilities;
- eliminating the large number of steps required in a full 'V' model process while still providing a disciplined framework within which to work;
- supplying management control by testing the products of every activity and imposing an elapsed time limit;
- imposing management control over ripple effects and uncontrolled iteration; and
- not requiring a distinction between production, evolution and maintenance as with conventional approaches, which usually ignore maintenance costs during project justification.

A computer system development project is divided into time-boxes to allow effective cost control and to ensure, as far as possible, delivery of predicted benefits within time and cost limits. At the end of each time-box, a number of walkthroughs, reviews and tests are performed to validate the product against earlier documentation, especially the project proposal. This evaluation allows both defect analysis and configuration control to take place at each stage. It provides data to allow a decision to halt the project to be taken if necessary. The time-box is followed by a formal evaluation as described in Section 9.4.10.

Prototyping, within large software projects, must be carefully controlled. Iteration cycles should be limited to about three by the project manager. Implementation independent documentation should be produced as far as this is possible. This should state clearly what features of the prototype users may expect to survive to the final version and which ones may have to be compromised. Object-oriented analysis and design notations should be used to record analysis and design decisions reached via the prototype.

Each time-box uses a small team of users and developers, working together, to carry out three activities: prototyping, review and consolidation. If there have been previous time-boxes or if there are objects within the scope of the domain model in the repository, these objects are integrated during consolidation. At the end of the time-box an evaluation team including personnel not on the time-box team evaluates the product against task scripts from the initial requirements capture and other quality criteria. The evaluation can approve and plan delivery or reject the deliverable; that is, the system.

Experience with prototyping suggests that small teams of four or five at the most are appropriate, with no specialization within the team (there are issues of seniority, and grades of responsibility, but that is a different matter). The staff are not analysts or programmers; they are system builders expected to develop all the skills needed for building systems from start to finish. One therefore needs to recruit project staff who possess skills or potential in coding, analysis (business and technical), and effective communication with users. This increases job satisfaction but, most importantly, minimizes the risk of misunderstandings arising from multi-stage communication down the 'production line'.

Building a prototype involves building an initial prototype, as discussed, testing its functionality and producing user documentation to guide users through the prototyping review process. An additional step is sometimes necessary to build in security and/or recovery features and complete design documentation. System and performance testing must be completed within the time-box. This involves testing prototype functionality, including (possibly simulated) interfaces with other systems, incorporation of library classes and sizing.

It is recommended that walkthroughs and inspections should be used wherever possible in the time-box. These enhance the prototyping life cycle because they improve the quality of work, highlighting errors early in development. They can also result in the cross-education of team members in the application. Also, application expertise is communicated, work take-over is simplified and technical progress is readily assessed.

One might ask how teams are to prevent endless prototyping. There may be the fear that users will get carried away, constantly changing and rechanging their minds, opening up the spectre of an endless, uncontrolled development. Another common problem is user disagreement flip-flop. This occurs when the team visits several users in turn and makes changes after each visit, without collecting the consensus. The changes made in response to the first user's comments may be reversed by a later user's comments. Such situations should not be allowed to arise, since endless prototyping translates very directly into bottomless budgets. Commercial constraints rapidly take over and it may be apparent to both users and system builders that enough has been learnt from the first few prototypes to make further interactions unnecessary and economically unjustifiable. Further prototypes may be built in exceptional circumstances if, for example, there is a change in the underlying business process or the object model has changed.

Other questions include how to know if the prototype is of sufficient quality. This can be determined by a number of factors; namely, conformity to company DP standards, user reactions, and logical arguments and explanations presented by users, project team members, and so on. Taking the question of user reactions first, the prototyping process helps set the right expectations. The prototype can, among its many rôles, be a superbly effective channel of communication between technical and non-technical teams. Providing the user realizes how much is missing from the prototype and the value of the missing parts, the close interaction between user and technical staff that takes place during prototype development can be used to communicate a much deeper understanding of the challenges and details of systems development than has been achieved in the past in most IT organizations. The communication is two-way, for the development team also learn a tremendous amount about the real user requirement; but the communication from the technical team to users is often overlooked. It can be a vital part in building a better working relationship.

Finally, how do the teams concerned know that the prototype is finished? Once the prime business processes represented as event traces have been prototyped, the requirements list can be signed off by mutual agreement with the users, leaving only the tidying up of loose ends.

Credibility is maintained by constant user involvement and candour on the part of developers. Other guidelines to be aware of may be summarized as follows.

- Define the time-box and project objectives clearly and objectively.
- Remain within the scope of the project where possible.
- Architecture is important; attend to it.
- Consider performance as early as possible.
- Use high-level tools and packages wherever possible.
- Manage the user review process so as not to raise expectations too high or reduce them too much.
- Impose an informal change control discipline on the user reviews.

■ Include conversion time in estimates where a throwaway prototyping approach is used.

■ **Never** keep a prototype that was intended to be discarded.

During the time-box an Implementation Object Model (including reused, interface and data management objects) is produced or refined where necessary. Whether the technical documentation includes a full Implementation Object Model (IOM) is at the discretion of the project managers involved. As a guide, one should be produced for more complex systems, but in cases where implementation from the Business Object Model is feasible even this is not necessary. The crucial thing is that all design decisions are traceable back to the Business Object Model, either via the IOM or directly. The time-box evaluation report must make traceability visible in the prototypes and/or their documentation.

Time-boxes include testing activities and should deliver test results against both task scripts and a technical test plan of the normal kind; that is, tests that answer the questions: Does an enhancement leave previous things that worked working? Does the system work well under stress and high volume I/O? Also deliverable from this stage are the source code and the executable system.

TASKS	Review the objectives and the analysis report	R
	Convert OOA to OOD and document design decisions. Modify the class cards if necessary. Produce a IOM for complex systems	M
	Review existing systems and identify existing components for possible reuse	M
	Prototype (system build) 2–5 iterations. Construct broad and shallow followed by deep and possibly narrow prototypes. Basics first, rare exceptions later!	M
	Conduct a user review for each prototype iteration	M
	Identify candidate classes for future reuse	M
	Attend to security, GUI, network, coding and other standards compliance	M
	Documentation	M
	Consolidation of results of other time-boxes and the class library	R
	Conduct a (Fagan's) inspection where appropriate	R
	Document defect analysis	R
	Test against requirements definition task scripts and a standard technical test plan	M
	Produce a user manual	R

Throughout these tasks, consider reusability.

DELIVERABLES AND DOCU-MENTATION Each of the time-boxes results in deliverables in the form of one or more of the following:

■ A system and its documentation
■ A specification/report, including defect analysis and other metrics
■ A set of candidate classes for reuse

**PREREQUISITES,
COMPLETION
CRITERIA AND
TIME LIMITS**

The system is complete when all the task scripts in the systems analysis report can be exercised successfully and all systems tests are passed satisfactorily. The activity is complete when the system, its documentation and the reuse candidate list are all complete and tested. The system will be integrated with all necessary components to be delivered. The following subsections give detailed completion criteria for the subactivities of the time-box.

Each time-box may last between one and six months subject to an overall limit that the time from the end of the RAD workshop activity to implementation is under six months. The ideal time-box lasts three to four months.

9.4.7 Rapid object-oriented design and programming within the time-box

**RAPID OOD
ACTIVITY**

The purpose of this activity is to establish that the documentation describes the system in sufficient detail for it to be supported by persons not involved in its creation, and that it states how the application fulfils the requirements of the project proposal.

The Rapid OOD activity follows completion of the Rapid OOA activity, normally within a time-box. It may precede or follow programming. During this activity computer system design is carried out to produce a computer solution in terms of program, database, interface and file specifications.

Only limited user participation will be required in this activity, although the user should take part in the review/test process at its completion.

The objectives are:

- To produce a technical design that meets the business objectives as simply as possible while taking account of performance, security and control requirements and system-based risks, quality, flexibility, ease of use and reuse;
- To specify technical details of how the system will operate in terms of program modules, files and database usage;
- To finalize the physical formats of input and output for all types of systems, including the conversation structure of interactive transactions for online systems, if appropriate;
- To estimate the likely utilization of hardware and software resources, identifying likely requirements for change.

**RAPID OOP
ACTIVITY**

This activity converts the model as designed into a working system or fragment of a system. The first prototype will generally be broad and shallow, covering the whole scope. Subsequent prototypes will extend earlier ones and treat all or part of the system in depth. Narrow and deep prototypes will be used to identify reusable components for subsequent iterations.

During this activity, individual programs are designed, coded and tested. These programs are then linked and their interfaces tested. Formal OOD may precede or follow coding. Users will have little input to programming and the associated testing processes but they will be required to specify the acceptance test plan, construct test cases and review the results.

The developers should be required to provide an environment that is as close as possible to the production environment. Acceptance testing is designed for users to determine that the system works as originally specified and satisfies the business requirement, using actual terms and procedures.

The objectives are:

- To design, code and test each program;
- To produce the necessary documentation for subsequent program maintenance and operational running;
- To ensure that objects and layers link together properly;
- To ensure that the system performs as specified, and meets the business requirement;
- To establish that any conversion programs are working as specified and can be implemented;
- To verify that the system works within hardware operating requirements;
- To establish that the completed system can be released to users for acceptance testing.

Use of testing aids is recommended during this activity where it is possible.

OOD TASKS

The detailed tasks depend on the method selected, the time-box iteration reached and the type of project but may include:

Convert OOA model by adding interface and implementation objects	R
Identify system components	R
Develop detailed physical design	R
Revise development and implementation plans, including hardware changes and impact on batch and online timings	R
Identify sources of existing data and method of conversion	R
Data modelling and database design	R
Develop program test plan and data	R
Produce system test plan	R
Produce acceptance test plan	R
Complete documentation and seek approval	R
Collect or generate metrics	M
Perform an inspection or informal walkthrough	R
Document and package objects developed	M

OOP AND TESTING TASKS

Select the section of the model to be coded	R
Code objects	M
Unit-test coded objects	M
Incorporate library classes and record design decisions	R
Create system test environment	M
Perform system testing on prototype, including external interfaces	M

Test against relevant task scripts and event traces	M
Review against coding standards	M
Review against interface standards	M
Design usability tests	R
Produce program and system test report	R
Create acceptance test environment	R
Produce user documentation	R
Stress test	R
Note potentially reusable objects	M
Collect metrics	M

DELIVERABLES AND DOCU-MENTATION

The major deliverables from the OOD activity are a system design report, unit test plan, integration test plan and acceptance test plan. Testing is dealt with more fully in Chapter 10.

The system design report should have the following contents:

(1) Management summary, including cost estimates	M
(2) Introduction	O
(3) System description	M
(4) Implementation Object Model	O
(5) Database design if appropriate	R
(6) Navigation requirements (access paths) and compiled queries	R
(7) Impact analysis, performance and capacity requirements	R
(8) Backup and recovery requirements	R
(9) Audit, security and control requirements	R
(11) Interfaces with system software and reusable components	R
(12) Appendices	
■ Database design/file descriptions	R
■ Record descriptions	R
■ Design decisions/sizing calculations	R
■ Test plan for systems design report	M

The major deliverables from the OOP activity are the prototype itself with system test report and technical documentation, including metrics.

PREREQUISITES, COMPLETION CRITERIA AND TIME LIMITS

The prerequisites are the completion of a systems analysis report and a Rapid OOA confirmation of it within the current time-box iteration. The time-box has started and the project infrastructure is in place. User reviews have been planned.

A design review confirms that the documentation is adequate for maintenance. Test the system design to ensure that the designed system meets the business and technical needs, the system is secure but not over complex, the project as designed is still justified in terms of costs and benefits and all functions have been addressed in the design, including hardware/operating software requirements.

The team should review the test plans and reports to ensure completeness. Available techniques for this include informal walkthroughs or Fagan's inspections for larger systems.

For the code, confirm that the test results are adequate and that both the product and the documentation conform to standards.

9.4.8 User review activity

This activity involves both developers and users. The tested prototype is demonstrated to the users and if possible exercised by them.

TASKS	Demonstrate prototype to users	M
	User exercises the prototype following event traces	M
	User exercises the prototype not following event traces	R
	Identify potential reuse	M
	Iterate through all users affected	R
	Report results of reviews	M
	Agree and sign off necessary changes	M
	Agree next iteration through Rapid OOP or that application is complete	M
	Produce a review report	M

DELIVERABLES AND DOCU-MENTATION The major deliverable is a review report, including agreements and sign-off. Its purpose is to confirm that the system, as coded, works as described in the project proposal in a pseudo production environment and that the documentation is to the users' satisfaction. The user manual should describe the procedures to be followed on and after implementation satisfactorily.

PREREQUISITES, COMPLETION CRITERIA AND TIME LIMITS Before starting, the coded prototype has been produced and all Rapid OOD/OOP criteria satisfied. Users must be available. On completion, confirm that all relevant event traces can be handled correctly and that the usability checks are satisfactory.

9.4.9 Consolidation, reuse evaluation and documentation

This activity takes place after a number of iterations through Rapid OOA/OOD/OOP/Testing and User Review. It consolidates the products of this time-box with those of earlier time-boxes or other projects and systems. It confirms the candidate classes identified as potentially reusable and consolidates user and technical documentation.

TASKS	Identify components to be assembled.	M
	Perform all Rapid OOP tasks on the complete system	R
	Confirm reuse candidates	M
	Produce user and technical documentation	M

Review user documentation with users on team	M
Confirm technical documentation	R
Estimate application impact on communications systems	M
Consider impact of actual system on batch and online response times	M
Perform inspection	R
Conduct defect analysis	R
Complete metrics	M

DELIVERABLES AND DOCUMENTATION

The main deliverables from this activity are a complete system ready for delivery and a set of technical documentation. The system will be fully demonstrable at this point. It should be checked that all task scripts can be exercised and all reports produced without error. All objects and design decisions should be documented. Interfaces to other systems will have been described. Any modifications made to the systems analysis report during the main time-box will have been documented. A design report will be included, preferably using a CASE tool. Links between code objects and design objects and between design objects and specification objects will have been described. There will be a conversion report where appropriate and a test report. A report on operational implications and required actions should be produced.

The user documentation should describe every user task. This document may also include sample screens and reports with a commentary on how they are used. There will usually be on-screen help for all user tasks and system features.

The implementation and conversion plan outlines the steps to be followed when cutting over to the new system. This should include specific details of tasks required of the organization's technical infrastructure group, if any. The plan should define the business processes that will be changed as a result of the implementation; that is, the boundaries of the change should be defined. Special consideration should be given to testing where a phased conversion is planned. Where there is an existing system, the plan indicates:

- satisfactory conversion criteria;
- the method to be used;
- work that is required to existing system prior to conversion;
- the layout of any reports required specifically for conversion.

PREREQUISITES, COMPLETION CRITERIA AND TIME LIMITS

As a prerequisite, the results of prototype iterations must be signed off for consolidation and delivery by the users on the time-box team.

All mandatory and recommended tasks listed in this subsection must be complete at the end of this activity. There must be a justification for any recommended tasks not included. Check that:

- the system runs in the target environment;
- test results are accepted by users;
- the product and its documentation are complete and conform to standards;
- metrics are within acceptable ranges (to detect collection errors);
- all relevant event traces can be handled correctly;

- usability checks are satisfactory;
- time-box team user sign-off is complete;
- documentation is complete and conforms to standards;
- conversion plans are satisfactory.

9.4.10 Evaluation

The final evaluation, or acceptance, activity is the formal review of the system and documentation of the lessons learnt. It is a simple matter just to demonstrate the system or current increment, but to do so is a one-way process, for the most vital element in the whole prototyping approach is obtaining and exploiting user feedback. It is therefore very important that users recognize the need and plan for enough time to review the results properly. Thus the review process needs to be highly organized and may, though rarely, become a major logistical exercise. The review should primarily allow the project sponsor to agree that the deliverables have been produced according to the requirements definition, analysis and time-box planning documentation. However, representatives from all the users who may be affected by the system need to be present, so that all aspects of the system can be reviewed and feedback obtained.

The activity is most important. Here it is decided whether the time-box deliverables are adequate and that implementation should proceed or that the work needs to be redone or even abandoned as infeasible. The evaluation team must involve the sponsor and personnel not on the time-box team. Reference should be made during evaluation to the quality plan, which should have stated what elements of the method would be used and what deliverables mandated. There should be reference back to existing architectures, networks, operations and hardware. Suitably knowledgeable people should be co-opted if necessary.

Fagan's inspection technique (Fagan, 1974) may be used where appropriate and coding standards reviewed. The team will need to be assured that testing was adequate by reference to both the task scripts and normal system test plans. More details of this technique are given in Section 9.5.1.

Evaluation for each time-box produces an evaluation report that includes reuse recommendations, including reuse candidates approved, a quality report and an outline implementation plan. The report should confirm the results of the tests against task scripts and consolidate all metrics from this and earlier time-boxes. The objectives of an evaluation are:

- To authorize the project to continue, or not;
- To authorize delivery of the product of a time-box, or not;
- To confirm potential reusability of components identified as reusable within the time-box;
- To review stage tolerances, security issues and provide data for audit;
- To act as a collection point for project metrics;

- To review progress on both the current activity and the whole project against plan;
- To review and approve any exception plans;
- To review the plan for the next stage;
- To identify the effect of both current and potential problems and plan remedial action if necessary.

Efficiency will be enhanced by the reuse of software. Some organizations have made designers responsible for packaging code so that it can be reused as many times as possible in subsequent projects. The problem with this is that well-constructed, reusable classes take time and care to produce; and this presents a contradiction to the philosophy of rapid development within a time-box. Developers should be required to consider code reuse specifically for each project but only in so far as they identify reuse *potential*. The evaluations have the task of confirming candidate classes for reuse. These should be passed to a specialist class constructor for refinement, generalization and testing, then be reissued to projects. Class constructors could be evaluated on the number of times their classes are reused, the number of defects in them reported or on productivity improvements resulting from their reuse.

As part of the evaluation process, defect analysis takes place. The volume of defects identified should be compared to industry standards and past performance in order to track improvements in quality and accuracy in specifying and coding systems. Object-oriented software metrics should be used to measure changes and trends in productivity levels. The number of atomic tasks supported is taken as the equivalent of traditional logical business transactions. Atomic tasks were defined in Chapter 7. Usability metrics should also be collected where possible; for example, time to complete a task, time to forget, and so on. Comparisons of reliability (mean-time-to-fail), cost and programming efficiency (task points per man-month development time) will be made, amongst others. Reuse metrics will also be collected where appropriate; including number of classes reused and number of (candidate) reusable classes created. Metrics for each project must be completed before the project goes live, and must be maintained at each stage of the life cycle.

The project plan and quality plan should be made available. A nominated scribe should record the project name, stage being assessed and date of the meeting. The following points should be covered:

- status of deliverables against plan;
- cross-reference to previous system life-cycle activities;
- total man-months actual against plan;
- quality assurance undertaken, sign-off and use of methods compared to quality plan and standards;
- review exception plan, if any;
- named person responsible for change control;
- risks and dependencies, one-page review;

- review tolerance for next stage;
- named senior user;
- user deliverables.

TASKS		
Confirm candidates for reuse library identified by the developers and suggest new ones	M
Check that tests are adequate	M
Check that performance is adequate	M
Check that appropriate standards have been followed	R
A usability check should have been carried out	R
Check that the architecture is maintainable	R
Review issues of security, recovery, and so on	M
Review the user manual	R
Review the conversion plan	R
Review the acceptance test plan	R
Reveal and report further requirements	O
Decide between redo, release or abort	M
Confirm deadlines	M
Confirm technical solution	R
Initiate implementation	M

DELIVERABLES AND DOCUMENTATION

The main result of this activity is a decision as to whether to release, repeat or abort the time-box based on the above criteria, together with the minutes of the review.

PREREQUISITES, COMPLETION CRITERIA AND TIME LIMITS

This activity takes place after the end of a time-box.

All mandatory and recommended tasks listed in this subsection must be complete. There must be a justification for any recommended tasks not included. The completion criteria for earlier activities should have been met.

All parties must agree that the review is complete or decide by simple majority in case of dispute. In the latter case, senior management and the project sponsor must give their approval.

Review the time-box products to ensure that:

- the program documentation is complete and the program test plan has been executed correctly;
- completion criteria have been achieved for both unit and program testing and the programs are now ready for acceptance testing;
- the programs are maintainable;
- operation of the system has been successfully demonstrated;
- the techniques used and the documentation conform to standards;
- all required metrics information is complete;
- reuse candidates are acceptable;
- the justification from the project proposal remains valid;
- there are no decisions or items pending;

- security policies have been adhered to;
- relevant legislation has been adhered to.

This activity should never take more than two weeks and should typically last less than a day.

9.4.11 Implementation planning

If the time-box products are released, the implementation planning activity can begin. Implementation issues include the following:

- Training
- Education
- Change management (through the sponsor)
- Hardware and software resources
- Environment/locations
- Support

The objective of this activity is to ensure that all necessary activities are completed prior to the system starting live operation. It involves three groups of tasks concerned with implementation planning, training and installation.

The implementation planning activity really begins within the RAD workshop activity. Implementation planning is concerned with ensuring that all necessary activities are complete prior to going live.

The objectives are:

- To ensure that the production environment has been set up;
- To provide for, and ensure, complete and accurate file conversion and take-on;
- To convert to the new system;
- To provide support and assistance at and beyond changeover to the new system;
- To obtain formal acceptance of successful system implementation;
- To ensure that the change management organization has been informed of impact of proposed changes.

TASKS

Complete implementation plan	M
Complete training plan	R
Data take-on	R
Prepare beta test plan	O
Complete beta tests with selected users	O
Complete usability tests	R
Review beta and usability test reports	R
Create change management record of change	M
Establish that approval given for implementation	M

Ensure users and developers are trained for the new system	R
Establish that metrics are complete for project	M
Establish operational environment	M
Perform take-on and conversion	M
Test and approve conversion	M
Arrange support for users of new system	M
Install system	M

DELIVERABLES AND DOCU-MENTATION   A formal document from the user accepting the new system and an implementation pack are the chief deliverables from this activity.

PREREQUISITES, COMPLETION CRITERIA AND TIME LIMITS   Sign-off from the evaluation stage is prerequisite, although much planning may have been completed earlier.

On completion, review the implementation of the system and ensure that:

- the system has been accepted by both the users and the IT organization;
- the appropriate hardware/software has been installed;
- the network has been installed (if required);
- production libraries have been set up;
- all special stationery has been approved and obtained; and
- all required system documentation is available and conforms to standards.

This activity is constrained by the overall six-month limit but should take less than two weeks.

9.4.12 Project planning activity

Project planning comprises two types of activity, the detailed planning of an individual time-box, which was dealt with separately in Section 9.4.5, and the planning of a whole project composed of several time-boxes. This latter activity cannot be separated from the need to balance the resource requirements of the development department as a whole. Where there is only one time-box, these activities are combined. This chapter considers the planning activity as one that starts from global and site considerations and apportions work to various time-boxes given the discoveries and imperatives of the earlier activities: project initiation, RADs, OOA and other time-boxes and their plans. In parallel with this activity, the identification of potentially reusable classes from the repository is conducted.

Project planning involves two separate but related planning activities: planning the project itself and working out the implications of this project on other projects in the organization and resolving issues of interaction. The second issue is closely related to domain modelling and is considered with that topic in the next section. This section concentrates on the planning of the application. The project manager must plan checkpoints for integration with other projects, infrastructural services, and so on.

Project planning starts when the project proposal has been signed off by the user sponsor and the project manager responsible. The proposal should be submitted to the appropriate management for prioritization. Metrics should be updated at every phase of the project. A cut-over plan will also be prepared for use during the Implementation Planning activity.

The project manager is responsible for ensuring that initial user training is performed, because it has a direct impact on the success of the implementation. S/he will be in the best position to determine who actually does the training, which may well be one of the full-time users seconded to the project team or the supplier if it is a package solution. The project manager should decide.

However, users also have an interest in ensuring that training is done, so they are not absolved of all responsibility. Users also have responsibility for ensuring that their requirement is defined in terms of content and attendance. They are also required to release the staff at the appropriate time. This should be BEFORE implementation. Post-implementation training is the responsibility of the user group.

TASKS	Allocate priority to project – then according to the given priority:	M
	■ Allocate resources	M
	■ Define a high-level plan	M
	■ Decide on time-box decomposition, concurrency and sequencing (with reference to project planning team)	M
	■ Define training requirements and gain approval for cost from project sponsor	M
	■ Schedule and implement training plan	R
	■ Complete quality plan, where appropriate	M
	■ Plan checkpoints for integration with other projects/ infrastructural services, and so on.	M

In the initial stages of a project, estimating tools should be used to determine size in terms of both elapsed days and task points where possible.

Projects should be set up on an appropriate planning tool so that management can review the progress of all projects in each group's portfolio. Time should be recorded against each project. One person in each project team should be designated as the person responsible for change control. This will be the project manager by default. Changes include correction of errors and alterations to the specification.

DELIVERABLES AND DOCUMENTATION The key deliverables from this activity are the project proposal and a quality plan.

The proposal provides sufficient information for management to prioritize the project and allocate funds. A high-level project plan enumerates, sequences and sizes the time-boxes and indicates any parallel running. It includes information on projected costs.

The quality plan identifies the major milestones in the project, how quality is assured, methods used (for example, review methods) and how changes are to be controlled. The quality plan should list CSFs, major milestones, inspection and change control methods, metrics to be collected and the criteria by which the project will be judged.

PREREQUISITES, COMPLETION CRITERIA AND TIME LIMITS   Project planning is a continuous, unbounded activity with no specific time limits.

9.4.13 Domain modelling and repository administration activity

Before entering the time-box planning stage, due consideration must be given to the context of the time-box within some overall project plan and to the relationship of the objects to be constructed within the time-box to those in the corporate object library and domain model. Berard (1993) defines a **domain** as 'a well-defined set of characteristics which accurately, narrowly and completely describe a family of problems for which computer application solutions are being, and will be, sought'. Domains include graphical user interfaces, decision support systems, financial trading systems, and so on. McNicoll (quoted by Berard) defines **domain analysis** as 'an investigation of a specific application area that seeks to identify the operations, objects and structures that commonly occur in software systems within this area'. Domain analysis is the basis for building so-called application frameworks and many class libraries. Domain modelling is especially important for an object-oriented approach. This is because of the importance of reuse in motivating the adoption of object technology.

Interviews and workshops may lead to the discovery of new domain objects and it must be decided whether the extra expense of preparing them for inclusion in the library is justified. This applies to specifications as well as code modules. On the other hand, the domain model may already include components that can be used in the time-box to enhance the quality of the deliverables and speed up the process. Domain analysis is best separated from application systems analysis because development pressures make it hard to abstract from immediate concerns to truly flexible, complete and application independent components. Further, it is hard for a development team to see the broader issues within the organization and, of course, producing reusable components often requires more effort and may slow down projects unacceptably. Ways must be found to inform teams regularly about the contents of the domain model and advise them on what could be profitably used. The solution is to create a separate team of domain modellers, class librarians and component 'salesmen' or 'reuse consultants'. The individuals on this team must be committed to the object-oriented viewpoint, have first-class analysis skills, be very familiar with the business and know what is in the existing library and how to use it well. Often development team training can be made the responsibility of this team, especially in the areas of software architecture and reusability. They are also a potential source of quality reviews to estimate whether reuse principles have been applied properly and as fully as practicable. Domain models may also form the basis of business process re-engineering efforts.

Domain modelling is the continuous activity of defining and refining the objects that represent the business regardless of the particularities of applications. It is closely related to the issue of repository management, to which we will return in Chapter 11.

It is beneficial to divide analysis into various layers. In particular, SOMA separates domain analysis from application analysis. These are parallel activities. Domain modelling covers those objects and structures that concern all of the business and not those areas that are peculiar to an application. The boundary is fuzzy but the principle is clear. Domain objects are potentially reusable and, as such, deserve greater care in analysis, design and implementation. They should be improved by experienced developers, but these people need to be freed from the concerns of project deadlines while they are re-engineering and improving domain classes. Candidate classes for reuse are checked out of the applications, improved and checked in to the repository for subsequent use by projects.

The domain model is a Business Object Model (BOM) consisting of domain objects, application frameworks, task scripts and so on. It is owned by the whole business and has the same general character as a conventional entity-based enterprise model. It is unlikely that it will work well without some sort of computerized repository. That repository should be capable of storing, without loss of detail, context models, message tables, task scripts, class descriptions and structures. It should compute metrics automatically and provide both keyword and hierarchical browsing facilities. *SOMATiK* does all this.

Information from the domain model and rapid analysis provide input, along with company-wide project planning imperatives, to the time-box planning activity. This activity involves deciding if the project can be divided into different segments that can be implemented independently or almost independently. The layers identified during analysis are the obvious basis for this fragmentation. In some cases, the time-boxes will have to be run sequentially and in a certain order due to dependencies. In others, it will be possible to run parallel time-boxes if resources permit or delivery dates so imply. Otherwise, the aim is to build the layer with the highest priority first – and the priorities have been established at the first RAD workshop if all has gone well.

TASKS	Repository administration	Project team
Respond to requests for information from project teams	Y	
Check in candidate classes for inspection	Y	
Inspect candidate classes and structures	Y	

	Repository administration	Project team
Examine repository for similar or identical classes	Y	Y
Inform project manager that registered candidate has synonyms	Y	
Report incomplete project models to project manager	Y	
Rework class definitions and add to repository	Y	
Build and document links to code level classes	Y	Y
Publish changes in domain model to all projects	Y	
Attend project meetings to advise on reuse of repository classes	Y	
Maintain register of applications, specification objects, design objects, code objects and their linkages	Y	Y

DELIVERABLES AND DOCUMENTATION Every class defined in a RAD workshop or time-box and approved as a reuse candidate at the evaluation stage should be examined for potential addition to the repository. A report on the result is transmitted to the originating project manager. The repository itself documents the inclusion of classes and the links between applications, specifications, design objects and code objects. The linkages will be recorded in the following form, as a textual annotation to each object and application.

Application	■ List of specification objects in the systems analysis report ■ List of design objects ■ List of code objects used
Specification object	■ List of equivalent objects in the design ■ List of applications that use the specification
Design object	■ List of code objects that implement the design ■ List of related specification objects
Code object	■ List of design objects implemented by the code object ■ Applications that use this object

PREREQUISITES, COMPLETION CRITERIA AND TIME LIMITS The task is never complete, has no prerequisites and there are no time limits.

▤ 9.5 General project management tasks

A diagrammatic representation of the project life cycle relating the different activities of the SOMA system development life cycle was given in Figure 9.8. The associated project management tasks are briefly covered together in this section and under the individual activities discussed already.

A project manager is usually appointed to run each project. This person needs to initiate the project, plan first RAD workshops and likely subsequent development, create a high-level project plan, initiate the RAD process, obtain commitment from users for dedicated resources for the project and estimate costs for the development. S/he should use an estimating model to verify the estimated costs.

There are certain activities within a project activity that are associated only with the start of that activity. The manager should verify that approval was previously given to proceed to an activity and that its prerequisites are met. The latest version of the project plan must be reviewed and any changes published and authorized. S/he should ensure that project members are aware of the objectives of the activity and its deadlines. The procedures to be adopted for agreeing changes in the project will have been documented in the quality plan.

All project leaders should submit regular progress reports for their manager, at least monthly and possibly verbally. The project leader should update reports of planned progress against actual, forecast and performance metrics.

The project manager should ensure that the procedures for change management are followed, ensure requirements changes follow change control procedures and evaluate the impact of each change on the project.

Milestone reviews should be held throughout the activity. Material divergence from planned time frames should be reported to the project manager and the sponsor.

The project sponsor should ensure that the evaluation follows each main time-box activity in the project. This is a formal process of approval for the project to proceed to the next activity (or not, as the case may be).

A project is complete when it has concluded its implementation stage or when it has been terminated. Project completion will trigger changes to the status of the project in various project tracking systems.

9.5.1 Fagan's inspections

The purpose of inspections is to review the output from activities to identify defects. Fagan's inspection is a formal peer review of a document. It is a useful technique intended to identify defects, but not to provide solutions. The inspection team comprises the following:

- the moderator; an independent person, specifically trained in the rôle, who ensures that practical arrangements have been made for the inspection and that all participants are prepared and involved;
- the reader; to present the report being investigated;
- the person responsible for the code or document;
- the person responsible for input to the code or document;
- the person responsible for using the product under inspection.

Fagan's inspections can be performed on all major documents and systems produced from the systems development process. These include the systems analysis report, systems design, code, and the various test plans. Inspections take place as part of a process to instil a quality culture and will provide support to the assessments performed at the end of each project activity. Each document should be inspected before the sponsor's approval or sign-off. It is pointless to perform inspections after sign-off.

All participants should have been trained in Fagan's inspection technique. Inspections usually take no more than two hours but participants should have made themselves aware of the systems and products involved beforehand, as well as having read the document to be inspected. Defects will be identified in the meeting, however.

The output of the inspection process is a defect list. The defects are reworked by the person responsible for the document with the moderator following up to ensure completion. There would usually be one inspection meeting per document. A second inspection may be required if the moderator deems this necessary. The moderator is also responsible for maintaining control sheets for inspections held to be used in the collation of Fagan's inspection metrics; that is, analyses of defects found during the inspection process.

⊟ 9.6 Rôles, skills and responsibilities

This section details the responsibility to the project of each rôle in which people interact with the project. It provides definitions of all rôles referred to elsewhere in this book.

9.6.1 Project rôles

The **project sponsor** is the individual user who is responsible for the project, has authority to approve initial and continued expenditure on it and authority to approve implementation of any changes to production systems. The sponsor pays the bills and is thus of key importance. S/he should be kept informed of all significant milestones and involved in review points, especially evaluations. The sponsor will sign off each RAD workshop, analysis document, time-box deliverable and change of plan.

Responsibility for day-to-day management of a project is given to a **project manager or leader** from either the development department or a user department. The project manager may be a developer as well. S/he should possess all key project management skills and be responsible for steering committee and sponsor liaison. Project leaders are responsible for the technical and commercial success of the project, and for maintaining quality standards through the development. Both may act as **time-box managers**.

Specific responsibilities of project managers include: ensuring all work carried out is covered by defined tasks as contained in the plans for the project; reviewing the proposals with specific reference to exposure to risk; ensuring all methods used by the individual team members are appropriate and are consistent with the project's overall objectives for quality, cost and duration; checking the quality of their own work before indicating its completion; ensuring that all necessary communication channels with other groups have been established; identifying and resolving issues and problems that influence the quality, duration or cost of the project as a whole; considering the implications of the new system on the production environment; managing changes requested by users; and diagnosing and resolving problems.

9.6.2 Developers

The **developer** has a key rôle in the process. The developer's skill set may/must include C++, Smalltalk, O/S skills, client management, finance, pragmatism, GUI design, project management, database techniques and object-oriented analysis/design. In SOMA the developer is **not** responsible for making classes reusable but only for spotting opportunities for reuse. Evidence shows (Henderson-Sellers and Edwards, 1994) that practice helps developers do this earlier in the process. There are not analysts, designers, coders, and so on. There are just developers. This implies that horizontal stratification is the order of the day rather than vertical structuring. Standard career grades are obsolete. This does not imply that there is no division of labour or that special skills are not exploited. It does imply a flat organizational structure and a flexible approach.

Domain analysts in the reuse team need broad business knowledge and the skills and dispositions of the systems programmer; an impossible combination it seems. The job should rotate until suitable staff are discovered by trial and error. Domain analysis for reuse is a long-term investment that will pay off when RAD workshops begin to use its products. At the outset there may be only small visible benefits.

9.6.3 Users

Best practice in system development places emphasis on Rapid Application Development (RAD); hence the degree of user involvement will be high. In order for the RAD process to be successful, users must also supply a number of devoted resources, ones that are aware of the business requirements relating to the development.

Users are responsible for approving progress at major project milestones, in that the project sponsor has to sign off documentation at the end of each activity. Users have to perform acceptance tests, having previously written the acceptance test plan based on the event traces produced in RAD workshops. They should be made responsible for generating test data for this activity.

Users agree to the project being migrated to the production environment by a mutually agreed date and decide whether the cut-over has been successful.

The user is no less important than the developer. Users ideally need computer awareness, management skills, enthusiasm and commitment. However, we recognize that only unskilled users are not busy and that project involvement will not always be full time. It must however be a committed and planned involvement.

A **lead user** should be appointed to resolve disputes. This person will be one respected by other users and need not always be the most heavily involved in terms of time spent.

The project manager should possess all key project management skills and be responsible for user and sponsor liaison.

9.6.4 RAD workshop rôles

The participants in a RAD workshop are the sponsor, users, the facilitator, the scribe, the project leader and the team members. In addition, observers may attend the workshops (which provides an excellent forum for training) where they may have contributions to make in specific but limited areas of expertise.

The **scribe** is an experienced systems analyst – who must understand SOMA and object modelling – who documents the requirements during RAD workshops using *SOMATiK* or otherwise.

The **sponsor** is a senior executive responsible for the business area under review. His role is to:

- approve the cost and results of the workshop;
- ensure the appropriate participants are selected and committed;
- resolve issues that cannot be resolved during the workshop.

The sponsor should attend the scoping session but does not need to attend the detail sessions.

The core team is made up of developers and between three and nine key business users who are experts in the business area being analysed. Their rôle is to provide the business requirements in the RAD, as directed by the facilitator, and to verify that requirements are correctly documented.

The **facilitator** is an experienced business analyst who:

- conducts the scoping and detail RAD sessions;
- ensures the requirements are captured in a structured way, so that they are complete and consistent;
- ensures the right level of detail is achieved for input into the next project activity.

Effective facilitators require a rare combination of skills. They must be knowledgeable in the method – SOMA in this case – and about the business, at least to the extent of being comfortable with the terminology and familiar with the main concepts. Presentation and communication skills are key. They must be assertive but know when to keep in the background and just listen. They have to be able to encourage diffident participants and give them confidence while knowing how to deal with troublesome personalities, often very senior ones, without upsetting or belittling them. An important technique for doing this and for closing down redundant discussion is to explain at the beginning of the workshop that there will be a ten-minute rule. This means that, at the facilitator's discretion or at the request of other participants, any topic that has been discussed for too long is placed on the open issues list for later resolution by fewer people. A sense of humour helps put people at ease and the facilitator should not be afraid of quips and even risqué remarks, as long as this does not get out of hand. The key skill is that of being able to pull out the essence of an argument and see its principal contradictory elements quickly. My approach is always to look for two opposites in analysing anything and then explore the dialectic and mediations between them. With practice this can be done very quickly. Figure 1.5 showed the structure of this thought process as applied to object-oriented concepts; the pattern is the same for any discussion. Probably, the only way to learn to be an accomplished facilitator is by apprenticeship. Perhaps some people are just born and grown as natural facilitators. Certainly no one ever trained me; I learnt through practice, theory and imitation. Perhaps a study of group dynamics would be a useful background; it is certainly very important. The ten-minute rule can be applied to defuse group dynamics conflicts.

Voting is an important way of reaching consensus but should be handled carefully. A vote is not indicative of the truth, merely of the current conjuncture of opinion. The results of voting should be presented as such: softly and as a guide only. The facilitator is responsible for obtaining the sponsor's and other users' sign-off. This too requires a combination of tact and determination. I present the group with a form offering a single choice between 'I agree that this model is a good representation of the requirements' and 'I **strongly** disagree ...'; nothing in between will do.

The facilitator is responsible for maintaining the time-box discipline within the workshop and should have approximate time targets for each step on the agenda and a clear mental model of what will happen and where delays are likely. The facilitator must be aware of the tasks of the scribe and clarify issues or slow the pace for him when necessary.

Potential indicators of a poor facilitator include any tendency to be a bully or autocrat, timidity, lack of confidence when presenting, fixed ideas, inability to sit back and listen, any tendency to sycophancy in the face of senior management, lack of awareness of general and specific business issues and general lack of authority or charisma. Curiously, you cannot discover these faults reliably without watching the person actually do the job. Interviews and – especially – psychometric tests are of little use.

9.6.5 Mentors

When an organization is beginning the move to object technology as a whole or just to a new technique, method or language, it is highly likely to benefit from employing a **mentor**. This is someone who understands the new skill, can explain it and, preferably, has done it before. This person is often a consultant from outside the organization but this need not be so. A mentor must be prepared to teach by doing and by demonstration as well as by running courses. The developers must also be prepared to learn by apprenticeship.

Particular classes of mentor include language specialists, system architects, methodologists and integration specialists. A number of small companies now offer mentoring services.

A project with a mentor on it may not produce an ideal product. The mentor may not be perfect. However, the key benefit comes from the learning experience itself and even if the mentor's ideas and the product produced are totally discarded and rewritten successfully at a later stage, the mentoring must be seen to have been a success.

9.6.6 Other rôles

The **change controller** has the key rôle of ensuring the continuing integrity of systems as they are upgraded. Other key rôles include the **support** team that provides backup, assistance, and continuing training and ensures that the required infrastructure is present. Representatives from other functional areas such as the security and legal areas may also become involved.

Evaluators need reuse awareness and both technical and business skills. Some evaluators must not have been part of the project team and can benefit from training in inspection techniques such as Fagan's inspections if these are used.

☐ 9.7 Hacking as a structured activity

If one of the most fundamental principles of object technology is encapsulation then can we not deduce that undisciplined hacking can after all be permitted within our organized approach? The argument is that since an object is defined by its specification and contract alone the implementation can change without impact on other systems components. Therefore, we do not care exactly how an object gets implemented as long as it meets the specification and goes fast. This is where the talented hacker comes in. S/he can write really clever, efficient code; and who cares if it looks like spaghetti, contains no comments and is unmaintainable. We won't maintain it; we'll subclass from it if we need refinements. If not, we'll throw it away and hire another hacker to reimplement. Thus, the rôle of the undisciplined genius – the hacker – is restored to its rightful place in software engineering.

There are some organizations where this argument could actually be applied and I would not dismiss the argument completely. However, the major flaw is that it is not always possible to create variants by subclassing alone. More usually an abstract superclass must be created by generalizing the code. This involves examining the code and understanding it. For any large organization this means that some standards must be applied because developers will have to understand, at some point, someone else's code.

This point aside, there is another way in which SOMA supports what would usually be regarded as hacking as a structured activity. Within the main time-box it is supposed that OOA, OOD and OOP all go on, but no order is imposed. This means that it is perfectly permissible to do the design **after** writing the code. This assumes that the requirements capture activities are complete but not that the requirements are complete. In that sense, analysis too can follow coding as we go through successive prototype iterations. The testing and evaluation of the time-box products ensure that this practice is valid. As long as the tests are passed, we need not care how the products were arrived at. The time-box itself controls any tendency to creeping functionality. Thus, we have imposed perfect management controls on a total unstructured creative process. Our 'hackers' can work in the way they find most productive while not endangering the quality or maintainability of the product.

I rest my case.

☐ 9.8 Summary

This chapter gave a detailed exposition of the SOMA life-cycle model, which is a non-procedural, object-oriented model of development activities that also incorporates an evolutionary, rapid development philosophy. First, we looked at the requirements of an object-oriented method in general and reviewed existing life-cycle models for both conventional and object-oriented methods.

We concluded that waterfall, V, spiral and other conventional life-cycle models were not suitable for object-oriented development. The influence of the MOSES life-cycle model on SOMA was discussed.

The SOMA life cycle model was summed up completely up in Figure 9.8. The model is composed of objects that represent activities that communicate by sending messages in the form of output and deliverables. Each deliverable is tested as it is produced. Section 9.4 gave the details of the prerequisites, tasks, time limits, completion criteria and deliverables for each activity. The chapter also covered the general project management issues and rôles involved. It concluded by asking whether hacking could be regarded as a respectable activity in an object-oriented organization.

9.9 Bibliographical notes

The work of Henderson-Sellers and Edwards (1994) has influenced the treatment of the software development life cycle given in this chapter greatly, though the approach is quite different from their MOSES in the end. The other chief influence has been the enormous amount of work done on RAD methods since their inception at DuPont, most of which seems to be unpublished. The SOMA approach to objectives and their measurement was strongly influenced by the idea of critical success factors. Only as this book was going to press did I discover that this folklore idea was originally due to Jack Rockart of the MIT Sloan School of Management. The interested reader might like to look up his 1979 paper in the *Harvard Business Review*.

10

Metrics, estimation and testing

πάντον χρημάτον ἀνθροπον μέτον εἰναι (Man is the measure of all things).

Plato (Theaetetus)

This chapter deals with the issues of measurement and evaluation which arise in software development. Cost estimation is essential for anything but the most trivial project. If we are to make estimates we must make measurements and use these as input to models whose output is the estimate. Thus our first topic is software metrics wherein we have a chance to review conventional approaches briefly. Conventional estimation models are then also briefly discussed before moving on to discuss specifically object-oriented metrics and models. This material leads to an exposition on the metrics collected within SOMA and the justification for them. Having built a system, measurement may not stop; for we must test it. The second subject, therefore, of this chapter concerns testing and quality assurance and the particular approach to it taken by SOMA developers.

10.1 Metrics, measures and models

In mathematics, a **metric** is a function d of two variables that satisfies the following conditions for all x, y and z:

$$d(x,y) = 0 \Leftrightarrow x = y \qquad \text{(Zero)}$$
$$d(x,y) \geq 0 \qquad \text{(Non-negativity)}$$
$$d(x,y) = d(y,x) \qquad \text{(Symmetry)}$$
$$d(x,z) \leq d(x,y) + d(y,z) \qquad \text{(The triangle inequality)}$$

For example, the distance between two points in ordinary geometry is a metric. A **measure** is a non-negative numerically-valued function μ defined on a ring[1] of sets (usually the power set of some set) satisfying the following properties for all non-intersecting subsets A and B:

$$\mu(\varnothing) = 0 \qquad \text{(Zero)}$$
$$\mu(A \cup B) = \mu(A) + \mu(B) \qquad \text{(Additivity)}$$

The use of the terms *metric* and *measure* in computer science is not usually as precise as this and the terms are even used interchangeably by some commentators. Henderson-Sellers and Edwards (1994) point out that many writers on software engineering metrics confuse the two concepts and it is most usually measures that are being discussed. To fit in with current usage we will not always bother to make the distinction here where no confusion can arise. A measure can be regarded either as a function of a metric (for example, complexity or quality) or as a simple numerical value – such as the length of a journey – measured in some agreed manner. This manner is referred to as the measurement scale. Measurement scales can be nominal, ordinal, interval, ratio or absolute. A nominal scale merely provides a label for each item and is not a true measure on the above formal definition. Ordinal scales provide information about ordering but not the distance between two values. Interval scales are ordinal and, additionally, provide a uniform interpretation of distance. A ratio scale is an interval scale with a zero point and an absolute scale permits simple counting. Usually, ratio or interval scales are considered to be the best ones to use in software engineering studies because ratio scales permit the computation of significant ratios, so that we can talk about one project being three times more complex than another, and interval scales at least let one measure progress in a uniform manner. For a simple example, degrees Fahrenheit is an interval scale whereas degrees Kelvin is a ratio scale. Counting beans is done on an absolute scale. Having agreed to use different scales, such as source lines of code (SLOCs) and function points, software engineers should not mix them together. If this happens there is a danger that they will not be comparing like with like or that the units of the compound measurement will be meaningless.

Measures should thus be at least additive and on an ordinal scale. Metrics should also permit their automatic collection wherever possible.

Models are predictive equations usually based on measures. The usual type of model is one that predicts costs or durations for projects based on a measure such as function points or SLOCs. These models are often derived as simple linear functions derived from a scatter diagram of empirical project data. The slope of the line is often regarded as the measure of developer productivity. Such models usually relate process and product metrics, the best known being COCOMO (Boehm, 1981) and SLIM (Putnam, 1978). We will return to models in Section 10.2.

---

[1] A ring is a mathematical structure with operations analogous to addition and multiplication. In the case of the ring of subsets of a set these operations are intersections and union. See Dugundji (1966) for an introduction to the mathematics of metric spaces and Halmos (1950) for an exploration of measure theory.

Metrics are a useful but crude and fallible tool for the estimator. In one well-known study it was found that the most significant predictor of programmer productivity was whether the room had a window, a nominal metric. This also points up the rôle of human factors in productivity, which is too often ignored in metrics studies.

We recognize several different kinds of, or uses for, metrics. **Product metrics** measure properties of the thing being produced: its size, complexity or quality. **Process metrics** measure the process by which the product is created: costs, duration of stages, and so on. Arguably, we could also distinguish **quality metrics** as a separate category because they exist for both the product – ease of use, learnability, and so on – and the process – auditability, repeatability, and so on. Another possible distinction is the separation of **accounting metrics** from other process metrics.

Arthur (1985) suggests the following 11 quality metrics:

- correctness (measured by fault counts)
- efficiency
- flexibility
- integrity
- interoperability
- maintainability
- portability
- reliability
- testability
- usability
- reusability

to which I would add completeness, describability, extensibility, robustness, security and perhaps elegance. These may be further divided, and Browne (1994) for example offers the following division of the usability metric to which I would add only transferability and understandability:

- productivity
- learnability
- user satisfaction
- memorability
- error rates in use

Product, or structural complexity, metrics divide into intra-module complexity metrics, which evaluate properties of individual modules, and inter-module metrics, which concern the relationships between them and emergent complexity arising from their combination. In our present context this boils down to looking at intra-object metrics versus inter-object metrics.

Typical intra-object metrics include SLOCs per method, function points, numbers of attributes and methods, and cyclomatic complexity of methods. Inter-objects metrics include fan-out, depth of inheritance and so on.

Complexity resides both in systems and in the problems that they help to solve. Card and Glass (1990) call the latter *functional complexity* but I prefer Henderson-Sellers and Edwards' (1994) *problem complexity*. The latter writers point out that simple problems should have simple solutions and suggest as a design quality check that problem complexity should indeed be evaluated and compared with design complexity. Designs may have both static and dynamic complexity. Code complexity is usually measured by McCabe's (1976) **cyclomatic** complexity and **essential** complexity measures, although there have been other suggestions such as Halstead's (1977), which is based on counts of operators and operands in a program. Cyclomatic complexity is equivalent to the number of binary decisions made by the program plus one, and is a measure based on the Euler number of topology or graph theory. It was originally developed in connexion with attempts to test linearly independent program paths exhaustively and has been extended by Henderson-Sellers and Tegarden (1992) to deal with object-oriented systems. Henderson-Sellers and Edwards (1994) suggest that it could also deal with the measurement of use cases and note that it is closely connected with fan-out and fan-in measures. This point obviously requires further exploration but it is not discussed further herein.

Some metrics, such as cyclomatic complexity or SLOCs, can only be collected from written code and are therefore only useful as *post facto* checks. For estimating we require that metrics are collected from the specification. At the code level it is often useful to collect physical metrics such as the size of executables in bytes, the size occupied on disk, task image sizes and raw performance measurements. These will help to see if object-oriented programming is actually delivering any worthwhile benefits.

The complexity of objects, as opposed to methods, is largely concerned with estimating cohesion and coupling. Card and Glass (1990) are largely concerned with non-object-oriented systems and thus only data coupling, D_C. They define it as the number of variables entering or leaving a module. Structural coupling is defined as the number of subroutine calls. They can then define **system complexity** as:

$$C_S = S_C + D_C$$

Henderson-Sellers and Edwards (1994) extend this formula to:

$$C_S = S_C + D_C + \max(C_h) - C_h$$

where $D_C = \dfrac{\displaystyle\sum^{n} \dfrac{IO}{(fanout + 1)}}{n}$

C_S = system complexity
S_C = structural inter-module coupling (number of control flow connexions or messages)
D_C = data coupling (number of I/O variables)
C_h = semantic cohesion

In object-oriented systems D_C is largely irrelevant. Cohesion is high but so may coupling be. An uncoupled system just would not work. Some work suggests that the equivalent of reducing coupling for object-oriented systems is reducing fan-in.

Obviously it is much harder to measure semantic cohesion than the other factors and, for the present, this must rely on subjective estimates. Myers (1979) defines cohesion by insisting that modules (read objects) offer multiple services each with a single, specific function and have all conceptually related, data-related and resource-related functions hidden inside. Obviously, this notion of conceptual relationship is very difficult to formalize and measure. For this reason most tools collect structural rather than logical complexity. The trouble with this is that structural and semantic cohesion are quite different. This arises when people try to decompose many-to-many relationships between objects such as PRODUCTS and REGULATIONS and end up with structurally cohesive but semantically nonsensical objects such as REGULATION-PRODUCT-INCIDENCES or some such travesty of style and good sense. A similar problem arises in relation to conceptual and implementation inheritance.

The **fan-in** of an object with respect to a structure is the number of objects from which control is passed to the object. Its **fan-out** is the number of servers that it uses or points at via this structure. An object may not know its fan counts. For example, in a classification structure, objects do not know how many subclasses they have; their fan-out. It requires an external agent to count them. Similarly, objects are ignorant of their superparts in composition structures; their fan-out again. In association and usage structures objects do not know their fan-in; who sends them messages. It is generally considered in conventional software engineering circles that low fan-outs are highly desirable (Card and Glass, 1990; Berard, 1993). It is harder to see that this applies to all four structures in an object-oriented system; especially those of classification and composition. High fan-ins are desirable as they may represent reuse but they still increase complexity. Henderson-Sellers and Edwards (1994) point out that it is unlikely to be able to achieve both high fan-in and low fan-out simultaneously since 'the cumulative values must be equal'. We should note that the usual notions of top and bottom are not invariant with respect to fan counts among the four structures of a SOMA model.

Henderson-Sellers and Edwards (1994) suggest that complexity arising from message connexions is less important than that arising from subroutine calls. However, unnecessary usage coupling should be avoided. Inheritance coupling may be simultaneously a good and bad thing. It simplifies the conceptual structure but may add to maintenance difficulty. In C++ the situation is even more complex with the need to distinguish between public, protected and friend coupling.

The cognitive complexity model of Cant *et al.* (1992) (see Henderson-Sellers and Edwards (1994) for a summary) deals with the complexity of the processes that programmers use in understanding code rather than with intrinsic features of the code itself. It relies on measuring the effort that it takes to trace and understand chunks of code. Henderson-Sellers and Edwards (1994) provide a useful discussion of how such metrics can be used to understand and classify object-oriented systems. However, the computation is exceedingly complex – the equation involves about 40 variables – and an exposition is beyond the scope of this text.

Process metrics include running costs, maintenance costs and analysis, design, coding and testing costs, the latter being often grouped as production costs. Such cost metrics can be expressed in either units of money (real or inflationary), units of elapsed time or units of effort (man-hours). Normally cost can be computed from effort by a simple algorithm but one should beware of overheads and the cost of hardware, class libraries and other non-labour costs.

In an object-oriented project the appropriate process metrics to collect, where feasible, are likely to be:

- total development time;
- time spent on particular activities;
- development time per object (per method);
- time to 'modify' reusable classes;
- time to generalize classes for library adoption;
- time saved by reuse;
- quality assurance costs;
- time to implement each (atomic) task script (task point).

Process metrics can be related to each other; for example, low analysis cost implies high maintenance cost. Accounting metrics should include the costs and benefits associated with the whole product, each object and each activity. Cost metrics include development costs, maintenance costs, retraining costs, NPV of benefits and the ROI (return on investment) arising from the use of object technology defined as

$$R = \frac{\text{Savings from reuse}}{\text{Costs of generalization}}$$

where the reuse cost is the cost of finding the classes and the generalization cost is the extra development effort required to gain admission to the library. How these costs are to be measured is open to debate. It may depend largely on the costing and time recording régimes in force in the organization. Henderson-Sellers and Edwards (1994) argue that an extra term in the above formula is needed to account for bigger classes costing more to generalize. This leads them to the rather obvious conclusion that the reuse savings should exceed the generalization costs for benefit to be achieved and this provides a yardstick for estimating when reuse is like to be beneficial (Henderson-Sellers, 1993).

Having discussed metrics in general, we now turn to some conventional estimating techniques.

▤ 10.2 Estimation techniques

Most traditional estimation methods rely on either experience, using comparison with similar projects, or metrics that depend on first estimating the number of lines of code to be produced. Wellman (1992) gives an example of an heuristic approach based on check-lists. Neither method is appropriate for the estimation of object-oriented systems. The heuristic methods will not work, simply because there is not yet enough experience of this kind of project in the world, and some people claim they lead to bias even in conventional projects. Secondly, the measure of lines of source code also relies on experience and is impossible to use except for a language, such as COBOL, in which many applications have been written within the same industry or organization; nor do SLOC measures isolate environmental factors that may vary regardless of the nature of requirements. The obvious unit of estimation for object-oriented programming, or design for that matter, is the object. A concrete technique with appropriate metrics for object-oriented estimation has been proposed by Laranjiera (1990).

Nearly all the models used for estimation take SLOC estimates as input and can be classified into static and dynamic and single or multivariate categories (Londeix, 1987). Single variable, static models are of the form:

$$E = aL^b$$

where E is effort, L is in kiloSLOCs and a and b are empirically derived constants. Multivariate models such as COCOMO (Boehm, 1981) are weighted sums of such terms. Dynamic, multivariate models, such as Putnam (1978), contain several interdependent variables.

The Putnam model assumes that a project is the superposition of several curves representing the effort expended on solving individual problems. This is described by a differential equation whose solution relates productivity, total effort and time. The model depends on initial size estimates like COCOMO. One needs to provide estimates of SLOCs, manpower build-up, peak manning constraints and so on.

Clearly there is a need for methods that do not depend on size estimates. One of the most popular estimating methods of this type in recent years has been function points analysis to which we now turn in more detail.

10.2.1 Function points

The only conventional estimation technique that is usually considered likely to be useful for object-oriented systems is Function Points Analysis, developed by Albrecht (Albrecht, 1979; Albrecht and Gaffney, 1983). They introduced the technique as a method of system size measurement, taking the view that sizing

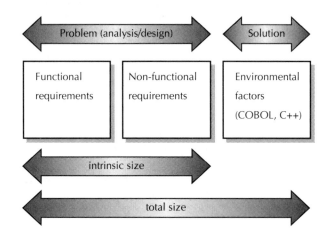

Figure 10.1 The domain of Function Points Analysis is the problem space.

has an intrinsic and extrinsic component. The intrinsic size was related to the scope and complexity of the requirements but the actual size of the solution could be influenced by many unpredictable environmental factors including the implementation language and platform. The aim was to isolate these environmental factors and predict system size from a problem description consisting of functional and non-functional requirements. Then the impact of productivity tools can be measured and compared. These concepts are illustrated in Figure 10.1. The Albrecht method involves counting external input, output and enquiry operations, external interfaces and internal files. These are weighted according to the type of system, which may be of high, medium or low complexity, and then adjusted according to the development environment being used. In an object-oriented system there may not be files but merely persistent objects and it is difficult to see how to apply the technique. However, none of the other conventional measures look so easy to adapt to object technology and several attempts have been made.

An enhanced version of FPA, known as Mk II FPA, was developed by Symons (1985) and is used as a standard by the British government though not widely outside Europe. In this version the estimator measures the surface area and processing complexity of a system. Surface area is the quantity of data crossing the system boundary and is measured by a count of variables appearing on screens and divided into input and output variables: N_i and N_o. Processing complexity counts 'logical business transactions' that represent units of function triggered by single events. Clearly, these may correspond to our task scripts or Jacobson's use cases in an object-oriented context. The complexity measure is the number of references to primary business entities (objects): N_{er}. It is apparent from this and from experience that FPA is only appropriate for data-rich systems and cannot be applied in, say, real-time contexts or to functionally rich problems such as weather forecasting or option pricing. Weightings are applied to each factor to give an estimate of system size using the formula:

$$Size = W_i * N_i + W_{er} * N_{er} + W_o * N_o$$

where the weights used for conventional systems are usually taken to be as follows: $W_i = 0.58$; $W_{er} = 1.66$; $W_o = 0.26$.

Feature points (Jones, 1988) were invented to overcome the objection about real-time or functionally complex systems but are not widely known. This method uses a weighted count of algorithms to capture internal complexity.

One problem with applying FPA to object-oriented systems is that one has to divide data and functions in order to do the counting, effectively requiring that an object-oriented description be re-engineered to a conventional one. This problem could perhaps be overcome if we interpret logical business transactions as task scripts (event traces) rather than as 'functions'. Tasks are already separate from the objects that they refer to.

A second problem relates to the measurement of reuse because it cannot be separated from other factors. Again we could possibly measure the reuse of task scripts, but not that of objects, using this approach.

A third difficulty in practice is that function point counting is laborious and diverts developers from productive work. If they are developing modern systems they often fail to see the relevance of the exercise. For example, if there is to be a standard graphical user interface one might ask how many function points the 'Undo' feature represents. From one point of view it scores zero because Undo does not do anything. From another it counts double the score for the whole system since almost every function must now keep an audit trail. Similarly those building client/server systems, expert systems, network routing packages or business simulations will generally find it hard to interpret the counts consistently and fairly in their contexts. Within my recent experience a function point enthusiast was observed to score the same system differently on two occasions.

Browne (1994) suggests using a separate count, based on Mk II function points but scoring different features, to estimate the effort required to build the user interface. However, Browne's assumption is that the interface can be totally separated from the rest of the system and will be built by a separate team, a dichotomy that I cannot support for both theoretical and practical reasons. His *interaction points* are weighted and adjusted counts of the numbers of input windows, output windows, pop-up windows, pushable icons and (menu) operations. The core system still has to be measured by some other technique such as ordinary function points analysis.

An extreme view, which I sympathize with, holds that object-oriented systems have no 'functional' aspects. They are composed of objects that behave in certain ways and from which functions are merely emergent.

Intuitively this is the most appealing of all the conventional estimation techniques but it is clearly not ideal either in MkI or Mk II form and collecting function points is a labour-intensive task loathed by most developers. The method may give a rough first estimate if used with care and judgement. Its main advantage is that it enables migrating organizations to compare their performance with the rest of the industry and with other migrants. Below we suggest a solution that effectively automates function point collection and abolishes it at the same time.

EMPIRICAL EVIDENCE

In a case study carried out by KPMG an attempt was made to discover whether counts of typical object-oriented metrics such as number of methods, parameters, messages, attributes, and so on were correlated with function point counts derived from a functional description of the same system. The application was an information system for car dealerships and was suitably data rich. In this case there was a high correlation between function points and the number of classes and the number of methods. They did not correlate with the number of messages. This is not surprising given the observation that the number of messages need not correlate with the number of task scripts.

Empirical evidence concerning object-oriented projects is still hard to come by but more and more projects are currently being reported in the literature and at conferences. Experience at the Swiss Bank Corporation suggests that a move to object-oriented programming alone can generate significant productivity gains. Mark I function point counts, independently audited by CSC Index, showed annual 50% productivity gains over a period of two years. However, as well as a move to Objective-C and C++ from COBOL, there was a move to distributed hardware and a flattening of the management structure along with other management changes that would have influenced the outcome. Praxis Systems (Rawlings, 1991) have also reported measurable improvements based on function point counts. They found a 290% gain on one project using Objective-C and a specification written in Z. The higher gain is accounted for by the use of pre-existing product-quality class libraries whereas Swiss Bank Corporation was also developing libraries from scratch.

10.3 Metrics for object-oriented systems analysis

The MOSES method (Henderson-Sellers and Edwards, 1994) collects metrics as part of its quality evaluation activity to permit code testing and reuse assessment. It collects intra-object metrics concerned with size and complexity, inter-object metrics concerned with coupling and metrics concerned with cognitive complexity. MOSES is one of the most complete methods yet published in respect of metrics yet it remains consciously tentative in its prescriptions. We have already discussed many of the ideas of MOSES in the foregoing, including cognitive complexity.

The intra-object metrics are size, average operations per class and average method size (in SLOCs). Size is defined as:

$$W_A * A + W_M * M$$

where A is the number of attributes and M is the number of operations or methods. W_A and W_M are empirically determined weights. W_A is expected to be close in value to 1 and W_M in the range 5–20. Complexity is measured by a variant of McCabe's cyclomatic complexity (McCabe, 1976).

The inter-object metrics are average system fan-out, depth of inheritance and the 'reuse ratio' of the number of superclasses to the total number of classes. Average system fan-out does not distinguish between the different structural relationships that objects may enter into. MOSES also permits the collection of the metrics suggested by Chidamber and Kemerer discussed below.

Chidamber and Kemerer (1991) offer six collectable metrics as follows.

- **Weighted methods per class** (WMC) is the sum of the static complexities of the methods of a class. If the complexities are taken to be unity this reduces to a simple count of methods. They do not state how the complexity is to be determined and presumably it could be a subjective estimate or a formal measure like cyclomatic complexity. This is an intra-object metric.
- **Depth of inheritance tree** (DIT), an inter-object metric that should more properly be called depth of inheritance network, is the maximal length of a chain of specializations.
- **Number of children** (NOC) is the fan-out in the classification structure: the number of subclasses. Of course, this is a global metric since classes do not know their children. It is not made clear whether this metric allows for dynamic classification schemes where NOC can change at run time.
- **Coupling between objects** (CBO) is a count of the non-classification structure couplings. It fails to make a distinction between association, composition and usage, effectively treating them all as messaging. This is an inter-object metric.
- **Response for a class** (RFC) is a measure of the structural coupling of the class and the most novel of the six. It counts the number of methods available to the class either directly within it or via one message to another class and could be regarded as closely related to the fan-in of the usage structure. RFC should be minimized.
- **Lack of cohesion in methods** (LCOM) is also innovative though the definition in the original paper is ambiguous. It measures the non-overlapping of sets of instance variables used by the methods of a class. An alternative, operational definition is: the percentage of methods that do not access an attribute, averaged over all attributes. The lowest, and most desirable, value of LCOM occurs when all the methods use all the instance variables and the highest when no instance variable is used by more than one method. This measures structural cohesion but not logical or semantic cohesion and there may be no correlation between the two. High LCOM may be an indicator of the need to split up a class but this should never be done automatically or without due reference to semantic cohesion as discussed above.

These metrics constitute one of the soundest and most practical suggestions to be found in the literature and have been quite widely adopted. For example, the McCabe Tools software product collects five out of six of them, adds more and provides an additional degree of structuring. This product divides its 13 object-oriented metrics into four categories: quality, encapsulation, inheritance and polymorphism. The encapsulation metrics are LCOM together with measures of the features of the class that are public and protected (Pctpub) and the number of accesses to these features (Pubdata). Inheritance measures are the number of root classes (Rootcnt), fan-in, NOC and DIT. Polymorphism is measured by WMC, RFC and the percentage of calls not made to overloaded modules (Pctcall). Quality is measured using the maximum cyclomatic and essential complexity of a class's methods and the number of classes that depend on descendants.

These metrics are also said to be founded on a sound theoretical basis in measurement theory and mathematics. The basis used is Wand's version of Bunge's mathematical ontology (Wand, 1989). Here, the work is less than convincing because this ontology itself suffers from some grave philosophical defects. It is atomistic; it conceives things as reducible to irreducible components. Further, it probably cannot stand up to the phenomenologist critique that an object's identity is independent of its properties (that is, they could all change). Whether the demolition of the base affects the correctness of the superstructure is equally arguable. Having arrived at the proposed metrics by an incorrect route need not mean that they are flawed. Chidamber and Kemerer are currently conducting empirical studies to validate their work and this will be a sufficient basis for the present, given the generally immature nature of the field. There is a good deal of empirical work being done at organizations like IBM's Hursley laboratories, KPMG, Praxis and the University of Technology, Sydney. It will be interesting to compare the results when they are available. In the meanwhile life must go on and metrics must be defined and collected.

As remarked above, in some systems NOC may vary at run time due to dynamic classification. I would suggest that max, min, mean and mode values for NOC should be collected in such circumstances.

Coupling depends on interaction. One is tempted to suspect that the type of interaction matters. My solution is to collect separate metrics for all the structures of an object model: classification, composition, usage and association. This view can be applied to fan-out and fan-in and to RFC.

Cohesion based on LOCM is purely structural cohesion. It is logical or conceptual cohesion that matters most from the point of view of reuse. I am also concerned that only instance variables are referred to in these metrics. Class variables should not be excluded from the definition since they contribute to complexity and cohesion.

An intriguing possibility is to attempt to unite coupling and cohesion as is done in Page-Jones' *connascence* metric (Page-Jones, 1992). This generalizes

Constantine's classic notion that good design minimizes coupling and maximizes cohesion by defining connascence[2] and three different kinds of encapsulation. Level 0 encapsulation represents the idea that a line of code encapsulates a certain abstraction. Level 1 is the encapsulation of procedures into modules and level 2 is the encapsulation of object-oriented programming. Two elements of a system are connascent if they share the same history and future or, more exactly, if changes to one may necessitate changes to the other. Good design should eliminate unnecessary connascence and minimize connascence across encapsulation boundaries and maximize it within them. For level 0 and level 1 encapsulation this reduces to the principle of coherence and cohesion. In general, inheritance compromises reuse. The connascence principle tells us that inheritance should be restricted to visible features or that there should be two separate hierarchies for inheriting the implementation and the interface. It would also discourage the use of friends in C++. Page-Jones classifies several kinds of connascence as name, type, value, position, algorithm, meaning and polymorphism. Polymorphism connascence is particularly interesting for object-oriented design and is closely related to the problems of non-monotonic logic. For example, if FLY is an operation of BIRD and PENGUIN is a subclass of BIRD then FLY may sometimes fail and sometimes succeed. This causes maintenance problems should the system be changed. I think that rules, as in SOMA, may be used to avoid this problem, as may the fuzzification of objects and inheritance discussed in Chapter 6. It is not yet clear how connascence could be measured in practice.

Another attempt to unify coupling and cohesion can be found in Cox and Novobilski (1991) where a hardware analogy is used to show how different levels' objects coexist inside an application.

In SOMA attribute values can be fuzzy sets and inheritance links can have a certainty factor attached. It is unclear whether this fuzziness of attribute values or classification increases or reduces complexity according to the metrics discussed so far. Intuitively one would expect fuzziness to reduce complexity since it does so in other areas of application; for example, a fuzzy process controller needs fewer rules than a numerical one. The same question arises for multiple inheritance. It is likely that the use of multiple inheritance will reduce WMC but increase some of the inter-object metrics.

Another open question is whether cohesion metrics can be made to deal with the fact that a whole may be greater (more cohesive) than the sum of its parts.

Metrics are often related to reward structures. Those used to measure domain class developers may not be appropriate to application developers and vice versa.

---

[2] Literally, connascence means being 'born together'.

☰ 10.4 The SOMA metrics

As we have seen, SLOC measures are poor estimating tools because they are highly language, environment and programmer dependent and estimation is most needed before any language decisions have been made. Function point counts, which address these points, suffer because of the labour-intensive process required to collect them and their poor mapping onto object-oriented systems, event driven systems, real-time systems, computationally intensive systems, GUIs and the like. What is required is a code independent measure that can be collected at the requirements capture stage and onwards and which correlates well with the business benefits to be delivered. Fortunately the SOMA Task Object Modelling activity suggests just such a measure and this measure has the additional benefit of being able to be counted automatically. The measure is the number of **task points**.

Task points represent atomic tasks that the system will help the user carry out. This includes autonomous tasks carried out within the system *en route* to the accomplishment of externally visible tasks. A task is **atomic** with respect to a problem if further decomposition would introduce terms inappropriate to the domain. For example, the register deal task might be decomposed into sub-tasks such as send confirmations, check positions and so on. We could go on decomposing until a level is reached where further decomposition would introduce sentences such as 'press key with finger'. The nouns are no longer in the trading domain, though they may well be in the domain of user interface design. This is a clear rule, though it relies on the fuzzy evaluation of whether a term is a term of a domain or not. In practice, it is nearly always obvious when to stop decomposing. The atomic tasks are the leaf nodes (terminals) of the task tree (network) and the count can be automated by counting the classes with no parts.

Task points obviously correspond to business tasks. The size and complexity of the task network may also be significant. Fortunately, the task model is an object model and the usual complexity metrics, such as fan-outs and depths, can be obtained. Some combination of these metrics ought to correlate with cost of build and, one hopes, with benefit delivered. As experience accumulates we should be able to interpolate a model line that relates task points to effort. Since we know that function points are correlated to effort also, we should be able to multiply the coefficients and generate a function point synthesizer as the composite of the two estimating functions. This would enable automatic generation of the function point equivalent of task points and support comparison with other industry metrics programmes. Of course the function points would have to be counted manually and independently audited for a while to validate the model. Since *SOMATiK* collects task points – along with all the other SOMA metrics – automatically, I hope that its users will form a club to collect their metrics to speed up the calibration process.

The metrics collected by SOMA are based on those of MOSES, the work of Kemerer and Chidamber and the original contribution of SOMA itself. Measures such as WMC are not quite sufficient to capture the complexity of a SOMA object since it does not allow for complexity due to rulesets. Our metric allows for this but does not measure the effect of assertions where they are used. This is open to discussion since clearly some assertions stand for rules and should be counted. On the other hand this is more difficult to automate and one could argue that attribute constraints should be counted too. I propose that the following metrics should be collected by all object-oriented projects. In every case collections can be made automatic by appropriate software such as *SOMATiK* at the requirements and analysis levels and proprietary software (for example, McCabe Tools) at the code level.

For the BOM the metrics are:

BM1 The weighted complexity WC_C of each class C, defined as:
$$WC_C = W_A*A + W_M*L_M*M + W_R*N_R*R$$
where
A = number of attributes
M = number of operations/methods
R = number of rulesets
N_R = number of rules per ruleset * average number of antecedent clauses per rule
L_M is the proportional excess of SLOCs per method over an agreed, language dependent standard (say 17 lines)
W_A, W_M and W_R are empirically discovered weights

BM2 The fan-outs and fan-ins for all four structures together with their averages.

BM3 The structure depths for the two acyclic structures: Dclass and Dcomp. This generalizes DIT.

BM4 The numbers of abstract and concrete classes.

BM5 The numbers of interface, domain and application objects incorporated into a project.

For the TOM the metrics are:

TM1 The number of external objects in the context model.

TM2 The weighted complexity WC_T of each task T, defined as:
$$WC_T = W_I*I + W_E*E + W_R*N_R*R$$
where
I = number of indirect objects per task
E = number of exceptions
R = number of rulesets
N_R = number of rules per ruleset * average number of antecedent clauses per rule
W_E and W_R are empirically discovered weights, which may be zero if empirical study shows that a factor such as I has no effect.

TM3 The fan-outs and fan-ins for all four structures in the task object model together with their averages; for example, number of exceptions (side-scripts) per task (usage fan-in).

TM4 The structure depths for the two acyclic structures: Dsub and Dcomp. This generalizes DIT.

TM5 The number of atomic tasks; that is, those with no component tasks. The leaf nodes of the task tree. (Task points.)

This last metric is the most important and most novel SOMA metric. It offers a potential replacement for function points as a measure of overall complexity with the added benefit of automated collection. Furthermore, it can be collected earlier in the life cycle; that is, at requirements capture. It is assumed that each task is expressed in SVDPI form. It also assumes some skill and consistency on the part of developers in identifying when atomic task level is reached. It is recommended that one person – the class librarian is ideal – examine all task models with this in mind; at least at the beginning. Eventually, the cultural norm should be established and consistent.

Other metrics which may be collected are as follows:

- homology of usage structures;
- cyclomatic complexity of methods (at coding stage);
- at the later stages of analysis/logical design, the number of interface objects.

It is proposed that, once sufficient data have been collected, effort estimation will be based on the model:

$$E = a + pT^k$$

where E is effort in man-hours, T is the task point count, p is the inverse of productivity in task points per man-hour (to be determined empirically) and k and a are constants; a may be thought of as start-up and constant overhead costs. Productivity will itself be a function of the level of reuse and may depend of the ratio of domain to application objects in the BOM and on the complexity of the BOM based on weighted class complexity, fan measures and so on. Much empirical work remains to be done in this area. In theory, function points can be computed directly from task points using these two estimating functions.

10.5 Testing techniques

Testing object-oriented systems is simultaneously the same and different from testing conventional systems. The same disciplines must be applied to the testing of units and assemblages and to release control and configuration management. However, the traditional V model of testing wherein deliverables are tested in reverse order to their production is quite inappropriate and object-oriented developers are in a far better position to test things as they are produced. The V model assumes that the whole system is specified before its subsystems, top-down. Object-oriented systems may also be specified, bottom-up, from reused classes which are tested before the whole system, as assembled, is completely specified. Equally, the overall system design can be tested by simulation long before any objects are coded, which is possible because of the continuum of representation on object-oriented development. This gives object-oriented development a distinct 'quality first' flavour compared to conventional approaches that apply quality assurance *post facto*. Further, object technology permits the user interface aspect of the system to be tested together with the operational components rather than separately as must be the case with conventional approaches (cf. Browne, 1994).

In this section we will take a brief look at the topic of testing in general before exposing the approach adopted within SOMA.

10.5.1 What does testing mean?

Testing is normally divided into **validation** (has one produced the right thing?) and **verification** (has one produced it right?). Validation is the process of comparing the end product with the true requirements of the users. Verification is the process of detecting faults and deviations from the expectations of the developers when they set out to build the system. The latter is often confused with checking the end product against the original specification. The former is only possible when the requirement can be articulated, which in some cases is not until after the system is built. In SOMA the only method for validation is the execution of prototypes either in the form of working code or in the form of simulations, as with CRC style walkthroughs with class cards. Verification on the other hand relies heavily on test scripts and conventional regression, stress and structural testing techniques.

The objective of verification is the discovery of faults in the code, the design or the specification that could cause the system to malfunction or fail. I will refer to all three aspects as 'the code' for brevity. Faults can be discovered by inspecting the code or running it to provoke failures and then trying to isolate the segment containing the fault. When a fault is corrected the system must be re-inspected and re-executed to ensure that no new faults have been introduced. This is also the case when a new feature is introduced. Tests of this kind are referred to as **regression tests**. It is beneficial to construct an automatic test harness for regression tests. The simplest and most powerful way to do this is to record all input events (keystrokes for example) during tests and the corresponding output. These events are then replayed to the modified system and the output from the two runs is compared. Any differences must then be examined to see if they are due to failure or not. There are many software tools on the market nowadays to help with this kind of testing. It is advantageous if these testing products run on separate hardware to avoid the possibility of them interfering with the test results themselves.

10.5.2 Types of test

There are several different types of tests and testing techniques that we shall need to know about. **Unit testing** tests the behaviour of each module, subsystem, method, object or layer. Perry and Kaiser (1990) discuss object-oriented unit testing in some detail. **Integration tests** test that assemblies of tested units do indeed work together as planned and with no unexpected side-effects or failures. Integration testing will be easier if formal contracts for class interfaces have been specified using assertions and/or rules. According to Jacobson *et al.* (1992) unit tests for object-oriented systems are much harder than for conventional systems because the structure of the whole program is flatter, and control flow and state are distributed. Conversely, they claim, integration tests are easier. Unit tests are further complicated by inheritance and other forms of polymorphism. For example, if a fault is suspected in a subclass we cannot assume that the fault is not inherited from some distant superclass. Clearly superclasses should be tested first to minimize this risk. Similarly, components should be tested before layers and servers before clients. Task scripts enable us to perform integration tests not only on the code but on the earliest object models produced by the analysts. However, it is clear that integration tests must follow the completion of unit testing of the components to be integrated.

    Black box (or specification) testing tests only the interface of a unit and asks whether it behaves as expected. Internal failures that lead to correct behaviour are not detected. For example, if unnecessary looping does not slow the system down below acceptable limits then it is not a fault, even though it does slow down the system unnecessarily. **White box** (or structural) testing does not accept this lax attitude and looks at the internal construction of the module. These tests attempt to exercise as many paths through the module as possible, though exhaustive coverage is seldom possible or practical. A rough guide to the number of paths is McCabe's cyclomatic complexity, which measures the number of linearly independent paths; though there may be many combinations of these. The tests should attempt to execute every line of code at least once. If possible, paths should be grouped into equivalence classes that can be tested as if one path. Jacobson *et al.* (1992) point out that polymorphism makes it harder to count the number of paths through a code module which in turn makes it harder to be sure that test coverage is complete; every sequence of mouse clicks is a potential path. Their solution is to use their use cases (task scripts in this book are a generalization) to represent potential paths through the system.

    Since object orientation emphasizes the interface rather than the implementation of objects, it might be expected that black box testing techniques, where only the specification is used to construct tests, would suffice. This has been found to be empirically false in studies carried out at Hewlett Packard (Fiedler, 1989), where white box testing, which examines the implementation, was shown to increase the number of defects detected significantly. This implies that class designers and implementers must be intimately involved in the testing at the white-box stage, as independent testers may be unfamiliar with the way low-level functions work.

Acceptance testing involves running the system under the conditions in which it will actually operate when delivered and is usually done by the users themselves. Acceptance testing can be partial or full scale. Partial tests only exercise a part of the system, usually a complete layer.

Beta tests are carried out on complete systems by selected users prior to release and are a form of acceptance test.

Stress testing exercises the system under abnormal loads, usually very high input transaction levels. It is normal to recruit many experienced and inexperienced users to carry out a stress test on a multi-user system. This, of course, can be expensive and should be planned carefully. Running several task scripts concurrently is a form of stress test.

Performance tests are specifically designed to find out if the system will perform at the required speed and resource utilization levels under load and are a special case of stress tests.

Boundary value tests seek to make the system fail by entering erroneous values. For example, asking a system to compute the logarithm of a negative number, increase the salary of an employee not yet hired or register a car that has not yet been manufactured. Boundary value tests usually involve partitioning the input data into equivalence classes such as negative, zero and positive numbers. A combination of stress and boundary value testing that I have always favoured involves leaning on the keyboard with your elbow, clattering keys at random and clicking the mouse furiously all over the screen, preferably all at once and with all mouse key combinations being tried. This is best done during complex operations. I have always called this **the elbow test**. A variant on this test is to try to use the system in exactly the same way as you already use another familiar system even if this is not expected to work; for example, test Lotus AmiPro as if it were Microsoft Word by trying to do things that work in Word. If they should be done in a different way, the system should help you discover that way if the interface is well designed. In that sense, this sort of test is a usability test.

Usability testing is becoming increasingly important as GUIs proliferate and systems become more complex and more central to business success. Microsoft, for one example only but to its credit, has invested huge sums in the construction of usability laboratories where users of systems under design are observed and measured. Testing documentation is part of usability testing. A reading of Browne (1994), Thimbleby (1990) and the material in Chapter 3 suggests the following checks on usability in the context of UI design, though they are applicable more widely.

- Is the interface consistent?
- Are tasks grouped in a logical manner?
- Is the user's memory overloaded or is too much information presented at once?

- Are all actions reversible?
- Can the user curtail a session and safely resume it later?
- Is the user comfortable with the terminology?
- Is adequate feedback provided? Is there a sense of completion?
- Are there unnecessary modes? Are all modes indicated clearly by colour changes, and so on?
- Does use of the system either lead to the user acquiring a model of the underlying model or make such a model unnecessary?
- Is the help system usable at all levels of skill?
- Are all task scripts supported as described and without backtracking?
- Does the system ask for information in an illogical order or require users to key information already deducible?
- Have applicable standards been adhered to?
- Can the user explore the system's functions without penalty?

These questions should certainly be asked of object-oriented systems.

Task script walkthroughs and simulations are a prime means of testing object-oriented systems, although they could be used on conventional ones in principle. These are discussed in the next section.

10.5.3 Testing object-oriented systems

Good practice dictates that everything that is produced should be checked for defects as it is produced, applying, thus, a 'quality first' philosophy and removing the need for extensive post-implementation reviews. This applies especially to object-oriented systems because objects can be tested as specifications, designs or coded modules, as can entire assemblies in the form of layers. Many of these tests will need to be planned at the outset of the activity that produces the thing to be tested, or at the start of the project stage. Testing resources must be allocated, testing tools purchased and test harnesses built. Integration tests especially need planning since often equipment must be commissioned to provide a realistic test environment.

Testers of object-oriented systems should follow the usual, good, conventional testing practices (see for example Myers (1979)). These have been summarized in the foregoing subsection. State matrices and decision tables remain useful. The main difference with object-oriented testing is that unit testing begins far earlier in the life cycle.

A **test plan** should be created and should state the tests that will be performed, the data that will be used and the criteria for passing each test. The plan should enumerate and explain the types of tests and, if possible, give examples. It should explain exactly how to apply the tests. Testing should result in a **test report** that records the results of each test whether successful or not. The report should include failures and their suspected causes.

Task script walkthroughs and simulations can be applied from the RAD activity onwards. In RADs we walk through the BOM by getting users to play the rôle of each class card. The facilitator issues an event to a class with an appropriate operation, and this class must then pass control to any necessary servers of that operation. Errors are removed at this stage by merely amending the cards in pencil. This process results in an event trace for each external stimulus issued. The event traces constitute the core of a test plan for the system as designed and coded. Each event trace must be performed by the system to pass this test. A degree of bloody-mindedness helps when performing these walkthroughs. You should attempt to issue unlikely events or misinterpret messages by sticking pedantically to what is written on the cards. You should also apply boundary value tests to task script tests as you would to coded systems. Try to exercise as many paths as possible, focusing on the normal paths first, then the exceptions. Automatic execution of the task scripts or event traces is possible when a CASE tool such as *SOMATiK* is available.

Not only does testing start early and continue throughout the Build stage, it never stops. A system in its maturity period is tested every time it is used. Change reporting and control mechanisms exist to manage the reporting and correction of post-implementation failures. Task scripts passing through a failure point should be re-exercised.

Inheritance is a feature that characterizes object-oriented systems. When a superclass is altered we must retest all its subclasses and when a subclass is changed we should retest the inherited operations as well as the new ones. One problem is that an inherited method may not work in the context of the subclass even though it worked properly in the superclass, meaning that the entire structure should be integration-tested top-down. This can happen when the subclass has different values for attributes that the method uses and if multiple inheritance conflicts or overriding have modified the methods in some way. One way to test new subclasses (Brown, 1993) is to test the superclass, test the subclass with stubs substituted for inherited features and finally test the two with the stubs removed.

With an object-oriented language, testing should have been carried out during coding as each class is completed, preferably by a separate team. This includes integration testing; testing either each layer or the whole system with the new classes added. Thus the testing is largely completed by the evaluation stage, which must only look for unexpected effects of the system working as a whole.

The SOMA life-cycle model implies that the sequence:

(1) prototype,
(2) white box test,
(3) incorporate library classes,
(4) black box test,
(5) document,
(6) train,
(7) user test,

is the norm.

The **project initiation document** is tested against the requirements of the stakeholders at a high level. Usually this is a combination of subjective approval and adherence to certain formal criteria such as contributing a certain return on investment or revenue stream, satisfying a known operational or statutory requirement and cost reductions of a certain size. If this document passes these tests the project may begin with workshops and/or interviews.

We test the **objectives** set during the scoping phase by defining measures for each of them. An objective is rejected if it cannot be measured at least on an ordinal scale; that is, prioritized with the other objectives.

During the analysis workshops we test the **specification** using voting and rôle-playing. Walking through the task scripts tests both them and the objects they refer to. It results in event traces that will be used at later stages. Automatic scenario generation makes it possible to test more than the most important task scripts and will usually be accomplished by the animation of event traces. This technique corresponds to white box testing the class descriptions. Repository objects may be incorporated at this stage but any changes to them are accomplished by subclassing and the new subclasses must be tested for defects in their additional or overriding features.

We unit test the objects as they appear. Unit testing examines the interfaces for logical cohesion and completeness. Walkthroughs also contribute to these tests. Such testing is an integral part of the rapid analysis activity. Users, analysts and sponsors must agree that the final BOM produced is a good model and that all classes are described and described correctly and completely. The test of this is user sign-off.

Once **the time-box** commences there should be informal project team reviews at each prototype iteration. These reviews are very much like Fagan's inspections, though less formal. The documents to be examined are the analysis model, if revised, the design model, the code and the system itself. Designs should conform to architectural standards and code to coding standards. Interfaces should be evaluated against standards in force such as CUA or OSF-Motif. Usability tests, as above, should be applied to prototypes. At the code level, check that subclass protocols conform to those of their superclasses and that overriding of methods is correct. This is especially important for C++ projects.

Test every object as it is produced, and again as it becomes part of a classification or composition structure. Test the design using structured walkthroughs and Fagan style inspections. For objects with complex significant states, use state transition techniques to test for unreachable states, indefinite postponement and deadlocks. In some cases it will be appropriate to construct state models for combinations of objects. Measure complexity of analysis, design and coded models and make sure they are consistent. One should consider rewriting if the coded version of a class is significantly more complex than its design model version. The measures of complexity are those given in Section 10.4. Watch out for classes, methods, and so on of unusual size. Also check performance and memory usage. Beware of classes whose functionality overlaps. Test layers as if they were single objects.

At the last iteration some stress testing must also be performed. This is followed by the consolidation of the results of this time-box with previous or parallel ones. Normal integration tests must now be performed and a formal Fagan's inspection performed on all relevant deliverables. The project manager should be satisfied that all task scripts can be correctly executed if specified in the test plan. Similarly s/he will have to be assured that the security policy has been complied with and that adequate documentation has been produced. For security reasons it should be checked that test routines have not been left in the final code.

The **evaluation** activity should now be a formality, checking that all the above points have been attended to but may involve a Fagan's inspection of deliverables if this cannot be shown to have already been done in the time-box. It should also include a demonstration that the system to be delivered can execute all the key task scripts without failure.

The **implementation** activity should create and obey release management controls.

Acceptance testing is carried out continuously since prototypes were released to users. This minimizes final acceptance testing workloads. However, some last-minute changes may be expected.

During **time-box planning** note that testing may account for 30–50 % of development time (Jacobson *et al.*, 1992).

Objects have been tested for implementation. If they are confirmed as candidates for reuse they should be tested again during generalization and release for reuse. This is the responsibility of **domain modelling**. Ownership and security issues will have to be revisited here too. Generally, the testing guidelines given above remain but there will be tougher standards for repository objects.

Myers (1979), Sommerville (1989), Perry and Kaiser (1990), Jacobson *et al.* (1992), Smith and Robson (1992), and Henderson-Sellers and Edwards (1994) constitute the most essential further reading on testing object-oriented systems.

10.6 Summary

This chapter covered the parts of SOMA concerned with metrics, estimation and testing. It began with a general review of software measurement theory and some remarks about the literature on object-oriented metrics. Next, we looked at the use of metrics in estimation and introduced the theory of function points with a discussion of the technique's strengths and weaknesses.

Section 10.3 discussed object-oriented metrics and introduced Chidamber and Kemerer's influential metrics for object-oriented programming. The next section defined the SOMA metrics and introduced the reader to the notion of task points: a potential replacement for function points whose collection can be automated.

The chapter concluded with a discussion of testing for object-oriented systems.

10.7 Bibliographical notes

Once again, I have to acknowledge my debt to Henderson-Sellers and Edwards. The treatment of metrics in this chapter owes much to their work and their book (1994) is highly recommended. Another important influence was the work of Chidamber and Kemerer (1991). Lorenz (1994) contains a large collection of useful but somewhat arbitrary OO metrics. Jacobson *et al.* (1991) influenced the treatment of testing given here.

11

Coordination and reuse

Again! Again! Again!
And the havoc did not slack

T. Campbell (Battle of the Baltic)

'In my youth,' Father William replied to his son
'I feared it might injure the brain;
But now that I'm perfectly sure I have none,
Why, I do it again and again.'

C.L. Dodgson (Alice in
Wonderland)

In this chapter, we will consider the relationship among parallel projects and time-boxes, issues of management and the thorny subject of how to encourage and manage reuse. The OMG reference model sees this topic as concerning the work done to link various subject areas, promote reuse and coordinate projects. It places these issues outside its scope but my experience is that they cannot be ignored and form, together with the general management issues, probably the largest single factor affecting the success of organizations migrating to object technology.

A software development organization must be able to manage its software assets, generalize them, manage changes to them and make them available across the organization. It must arrange for the delivery of components to be synchronized with each other and to meet real corporate targets. It must also ensure that deliveries actually meet strategic requirements. Many of the management issues raised here have been satisfactorily addressed in Chapter 9 by the SOMA process model. The latter showed how deliveries are matched to corporate targets and to requirements and Chapters 6 to 8 showed how the individual steps are accomplished. The outstanding issues then are cross-project coordination and reuse. We will concentrate in this chapter on issues related to reuse.

Reuse programmes are directed at the achievement of maintenance savings and quality improvements. In this chapter I will discuss the genesis of the reusable component and its location for subsequent reuse; how easy it is to find. I will argue for a software infrastructure group focusing on specification level reuse as an essential part of the reuse programme in every reasonably large development organization. Finally we look at the issue of coordination.

⊟ 11.1 Component management and reuse

Reuse is assembling all or part of systems from components that already exist. We should also consider re-engineering: disassembling a system and putting it together in a more robust and maintainable fashion. We need to consider how this assembly is accomplished and how the software assets are managed. The latter is the most problematical issue. Vince Jordan, Vice President of Object Technology for SHL, put it this way in *NeXTWORLD* (December, 1993):

> 'I find two underlying aspects of this technology striking: communication and collaboration. Objects in isolation, while useful, are rarely extensible. By itself, a timer object can track the passing of time – but only that. The same object, however, when collaborating with others, can generate powerful functionality: tracking patient histories, scheduling X-rays, initiating the movements of stocks and securities, providing automatic disaster recovery, managing entire networks. Unless an object is communicating with other objects, its usefulness is bound by what it alone understands and can accomplish. The same is true of people.'

> 'I have observed many object development efforts. Some fall far short of the promise, while others surpass the objective, accomplishing more than ever expected. When a spirit of communication and collaboration is absent or weak, even a highly skilled team of developers can miss the mark. Often, a group like this delivers the very results they were trying to avoid; using object technology poorly can, for instance, create unmaintainable legacy problems.'

For most developers, the tendency in the past has been to develop most things from scratch. This is because:

- the initial cost of investigating someone else's work is often high;
- there is uncertainty as to whether it will work;
- there is uncertainty as to who will fix it when it doesn't work;
- there is a tendency to chronic underestimation of how difficult particular tasks are.

Reuse, on the other hand, gives benefits in terms of faster development time, but only after the uncertainty in its usage and the management issues have been addressed. Object-oriented reuse can be **direct reuse** where a class is taken from a library and included in a project as it is and, most often, **indirect reuse** where project-specific subclasses are created. In the latter case, the library classes are never altered. All changes are made in the subclasses. Overriding can be used but care is appropriate as it can lead to confusion between the concepts represented by the library object and the actual use intended within the project. What should never be permitted is the copying and modification of library classes, though I have observed that this is a very common practice on several projects where the developers really ought to have known better.

Reuse is not new. Doug McIlroy proposed the idea of formal reuse as early as 1968. Function libraries and package software represent extremely successful examples of reuse and have done so for a long time. However, function libraries are often very hard to understand and use while packages operate at very coarse levels of granularity. The common practice of top-down decomposition into functions often leads to application-specific modules and tends to preclude functions written in-house from being reusable. The most widespread realization of reuse occurs when package software is employed. Compilers represent low-level reuse while payroll packages work at higher levels. The problem with packages is that their components are not reusable in themselves. We cannot easily extract the lexical analyser from a compiler or the tax routines from a payroll system. One of the key aims of migrating to object technology is to facilitate reuse at arbitrary levels of granularity, from stacks to application frameworks. Further, while reuse is possible with conventional approaches, the unique advantage of the object-oriented approach is that reuse is managed by contract. Reuse can be thus managed either at the code level or at the level of specifications. Remaining at the code level ignores this important advantage and is likely to lead to a petering out of the benefits accruing to us from reuse, as I will argue below.

Object-oriented reuse aims at fine-grain reuse based on an object's specification or contract. Even with object technology, reuse can still be problematical. Success requires organizational change, changes in the development process and investment. It is definitely not free.

A colleague of mine tells an interesting story about how a good class library régime can help avoid some of the pitfalls of reuse. Late in 1989 a formula was published for calculating the optimal flight path for an aircraft coming into land, given certain variables like wind speed, weather, and so on. Owing to bad printing of the formula in the publication, an eight was misread and entered into the formal documentation of the formula as a six. As the effect of this was minor, the mistake was not picked up for some time. It was only discovered after a number of complaints from maintenance crews about the level of maintenance required due to heavy landings. Three different projects had used the formula in developing software as part of landing control systems. Two groups used object technology in the form of C++; the third used C and structured methods. When it became clear that there was an error in the distributed version of the formula, all three groups were informed and instructed by the authorities that they had to correct all instances of the formula in their code. The first group had not used formal class library control approaches. It took them five weeks to find every incidence of the formula in their software, correct it and then recompile. The C group had embedded the formula in a set of library functions. They only needed to rework the library functions and recompile; about two days work. They completed the whole task in four days. The third group had placed the formula inside a set of specially constructed classes that were made available through a class library. The time taken to update the formula was half a day; to recompile, link and test, about the same. They were able to identify all the components affected, only needed to recompile those, then do a new build of the whole system. Total time taken: 1.5 days. This can only be attributed to good library control and configuration management. All three groups had systems of about the same size. What is most interesting is the estimated costs of the correction. Group 1's costs are said to be well in excess of one million DM. Group 2 incurred a cost of DM50,000. Group 3 reported their costs as DM2,500.

The key prerequisites to successful reuse are:

- senior management understanding of and support for the reuse programme;
- realistic estimates of the investment required for successful reuse;
- a life-cycle model that supports and encourages reuse;
- a library of reusable components; functions and classes;
- a means of documenting and accessing these components via their specification;
- suitable tools to support and facilitate the approach;
- a reward system that rewards both developers and reuse engineers for reuse;
- skilled, motivated developers.

The benefits include lower future maintenance costs, faster development and higher quality but not, in the majority of cases, lower initial investment.

11.1.1 Code-level versus specification-level reuse

It has been found that code-level reuse is possible for a limited time and on a limited scale. It is my considered belief that over longer periods and for larger libraries the key to reuse is to be found at the specification level rather than the code level, although code-level reuse is still important and must be managed. Objects should be identified by the contracts that they satisfy. These contracts are precisely the specifications of the attributes with their facets, the associations, operations, assertions and the rulesets that the requirements capture process generates.

Early adopters of object technology have encountered several problems with informal code-level reuse. As an example, one project I encountered had tried to invest in reuse by taking large parts of an existing NeXTstep application. The rework involved generalizing the existing code and documenting it took approximately two man-months. This was shorter than inventing the same techniques from scratch, but was definitely longer than having a central team separated from the project to do it. Suppose that work had been done by someone else centrally. A conservative assumption is that it would still have taken approximately the same amount of time: two man-months. Add a week for administration of a reuse library. Up to this point the investment in a centralized library function is one man-week in the red. Now consider the same parts being reused again. If one other project wants to reuse one of the classes and is unaware of the work on the first project, not sure whether to take this project's version or the original version, or not confident of the quality of either, then they may well spend an additional man-month taking either version and adapting it for their needs. In this case, the later project had produced a better, more reusable version of the same class and at least two other projects were using the original version. Unfortunately, this means that there were two different, and diverging, versions of the same class simply because there had not been time to reintegrate into the original project. Reintegration would have created a testing overhead that deadline pressures made intolerable. It is in these circumstances that a library could save time, and hence money. If the original project had promoted the class in question into a reuse library, which had then had the resources to improve and generalize it, then the second and subsequent projects could have taken it and generated a new improved version. This version could have been replaced into the reuse library for the other projects to use. The implication is that maintenance costs ought to be incurred once per reusable item rather than once per project, making investing in a library team cost-effective in time scales as short as two months. The presence of a centralized reuse team would have implied a one man-month saving due to rework of the class, minimal maintenance overhead due to library ownership of it and more reliable software due to benefits from bug fixes made in other projects.

Other work that has been done measuring NeXTstep projects also indicates that much potential productivity gain would come from centralizing code reuse. However, the question of how the code for reuse is to be identified is a separate matter to which we will return.

Reuse is not restricted, of course, to the NeXTstep environment. It is not even a unique result of using object technology. In the halcyon days of mainframes and before it was even commonly called reuse developers knew quite well that producing code that could be used across more than one subsystem required planning and resourcing centrally. In many organizations a code library was maintained and a team met every week to plan what modules could be coded in a reusable manner.

Some companies that have introduced centralized reuse libraries, such as British Telecom, report that the costs of maintaining the libraries have exceeded the savings from reuse (Software Futures, 1994). There are a number of possible explanations for this, including poor management, but the most likely ones for me are, firstly, that all these efforts have been focused at the level of source code and, secondly, the only repository tools available have been based on the structured view of the world. First Boston Corporation attributes massive reuse to the use of a custom written CASE tool (Banker, Kauffman and Zweig, 1993) but genuinely object-oriented reuse tools have yet to appear on any scale. *SOMATiK* is – to the best of my knowledge – one of the first, but I know that other companies have been working in the same general direction, especially those working in the field of business process re-engineering. My experience leads me to believe that massive productivity and quality improvements based on decentralized, informal reuse at the code level are possible over a period of two years or so; but a plateau effect then begins to set in which could forebode an actual decline. This corresponds to what Senge (1990) calls a 'limits to growth' feedback process wherein the volume and complexity of classes being produced, which is only possible because of reuse, limits the further growth of reuse. As Senge shows, 'pushing harder' against the limits of individual effort in relation to locating reusable objects can only succeed temporarily. The way to break out of the vicious circle is to move reuse to the specification level where the model complexities can be more easily managed. Other factors threatening the success of a reuse programme include loss of management support; the maintenance of multiple copies and variants of objects could soon lead to a 'legacy' problem and there is always the danger of being overtaken by the competition.

Without highly skilled and motivated developers and support staff, the support of a senior management team with strong leadership and clear vision, and good relationships with users, any reuse programme is in danger. Without a clearly defined method for application development and object-oriented analysis it is probably doomed.

Informal reuse relies on developers maintaining a grapevine of personal connexions spanning projects and sometimes geographical boundaries too. Developers may find it easier to write code than search for existing classes if there is no centralized repository and the grapevine is not forthcoming with intelligence of a suitable class. When code reuse is organized informally it is often hard to find objects and the problem increases over time and with the scale of the organization. Some reuse can be achieved by modifying source code from other applications but this leads to the danger of multiple versions of the same class and a potential maintenance nightmare. Another problem is that developers working in time-boxes have priorities other than creating reusable classes and generalizing them. This means that making them responsible for creating fully documented, reusable components is nothing if not voluntaristic. The biggest problem with informal reuse is that no one is responsible for measuring and increasing reuse or for the dissemination of information.

SOMATiK offers the possibility of reuse at the domain analysis and requirements specification level, having a repository of classes, task scripts and a glossary of business terms. It links the specification by cross-reference tables to code objects. It is also a business process re-engineering tool and a prototype generator in the sense that models can be models of processes, as we saw in Chapter 8, and they can be animated to show process paths, delays and bottlenecks.

Business processes themselves can be units of reuse. The reusable components stored by *SOMATiK* include task scripts (to be used later as test scripts), event traces and business terms (the glossary). By analysing the business processes rather than just the application we expect to get even greater benefits from the reuse programme, and get them sooner. *SOMATiK* relates business processes (event traces) to the tasks that compose them, these tasks to the specification objects that they refer to and these specification objects to actually delivered code via cross-reference tables. However, *SOMATiK* is not intended to be a source code management tool. A separate code library management tool will give additional benefits.

11.1.2 Logistics and management of the software infrastructure team

Most development departments have infrastructure support for such services as networks precisely because they can reuse them across many different systems. Why should code, design patterns, specifications or requirements be treated any differently? Surely they are, in a reuse-aware culture, a major part of the infrastructure of IT.

I believe that, for any reasonably large IT organization, having some developers not involved in directly productive development work will be more than offset by the savings gained from developers being able to use a set of well-documented, fully supported objects. I recommend the establishment of a small, full-time domain modelling and reuse team to produce, collect and maintain reusable code. This is effectively a software infrastructure team. It is not just a matter of objects; there are usually also libraries of conventional code, database scripts and so on, all of which can be reused. It would be a capital error to under-estimate the complexity of this task. It is the boring matters of documentation, configuration management and version control that are the key determinants of its success. A reuse or software infrastructure team focuses effort in the right place at the right time.

Domain modelling has been discussed already in Section 9.4.13. It plays an important rôle in component management and reuse. In this respect a key personality in the domain team is the **class librarian**. A key task of analysis, following initial requirements capture, is the identification of classes suitable for reuse that have emerged from the requirements and the discovery of existing components that can be used within the new development. The criteria that make an object reusable need to be established carefully since the costs of creating a reusable component are usually much higher than those for an application-specific one. The class librarian will provide valuable input to this process. Another key rôle is that of the **reuse engineer** or **toolsmith**. Such a person is devoted *inter alia* to quality, efficiency, reliability and maintainability. However, these characteristics are not always found together with deep application knowledge or the social skills of the business analyst. Thus, a third rôle needs to be catered for: that of the **application conscript**, a developer who works on the reuse team for short fixed periods. Reuse engineers have the same skill and dedication as systems programmers, though they are fully immersed in the object-oriented philosophy. However, they may not communicate well with users nor know much of the business at first. Colloquially they are sometimes referred to as 'hairies', after the stereotypical systems programmer with full beard, jeans, anorak and sandals. This gives us a mnemonic for the management approach: the 'hairies and conscripts' model. Some organizations use their annual intake of new graduate trainees to staff reuse teams. I would be wary of entrusting the creation of important business objects that are likely to be extensively used in critical applications to such neophytes. This approach therefore requires that the new talent is embedded within an existing skilled team.

Code libraries and domain analysis must be managed as an integrated activity. The librarian, or reuse administrator, is ideally placed to advise projects on existing, relevant parts of the domain model, suggest candidates for generalization and incorporate them seamlessly into the library.

Organizationally, there is a danger that, given immediate pressure to deliver, developers or their managers may abuse a relatively loosely defined resource. Creating a separate software infrastructure group is one solution to this problem, having it report directly to senior management is another. There is insufficient experience to pontificate on which approach is best and organizations will differ. *A priori*, I believe that the group needs to be separated from project teams so that personnel are not pirated by specific project managers.

The software infrastructure team, a technology-focused group, is responsible for maintaining and supporting *SOMATiK* (where used), maintaining its repository for use in RAD workshops, publishing information on reusable classes to project teams at both code and specification level and collecting and generalizing classes as they are produced in RAD workshops and projects at both specification and code levels. The group should work closely with every new project, initially through the offices of the RAD facilitator, capturing and generalizing every new class specification as it arises. A good, practical suggestion is that the librarian should meet with project teams on a regular basis, say at project meetings, to discuss reuse based on a walkthrough – or *SOMATiK* animation sessions when available. The rôles involved are as follows:

- management of the repository and the team;
- facilitation services for RAD workshops, BPR workshops, brainstorming and Fagan's inspections;
- generalization of candidate classes originating from projects or RAD workshops;
- testing these classes against technical and business criteria;
- maintaining the repository;
- publishing the reusable classes to projects;
- supporting the use of *SOMATiK*;
- freeing other developers to get on with the job.

This group should take ownership of the key objects that are used throughout the organization's systems and productize them. It should act as a centre of technical expertise, perhaps conducting one-day library awareness sessions for other developers who want to know what's available. It should be seen as a distributor of objects and seek general-purpose commercial objects. The rôle of the team could also encompass methods and reuse awareness training though the skill profiles are then slightly different.

Other key tasks include cross-project coordination, change management, ownership, version control and configuration management, control and ownership of reusable items (at whatever level), documentation and examples. The *SOMATiK* repository software mandates that there be an owner for everything in it. The repository manager will be able to change the owner manually.

The approach should evolve as the new team matures and gains experience. It would be wrong to fix it at too early a stage.

It is critical that the reuse team does not become an 'empire' with its own agenda. It must stay close to its interim customers, that is, the developers of projects, and thereby close to the demands of users. The hairy/conscript model helps this by bringing a constant stream of new business awareness to the work. However, the reward structure has to be treated with great care.

11.1.3 Rewarding for reuse

One of the most vexed questions we face is that of how best to reward people in the reuse culture. Traditionally, according to theory at least, programmers have been rewarded on the basis of productivity as measured by the number of SLOCs or function points they can churn out per annum. This militates against reuse, where the idea is to write as little code as possible. Of course, we can start to measure the number of SLOCs or function points reused and the ratio of this to new code and reward the developers on the basis of this ratio. This would give the biggest rewards to those who purely assembled systems but penalize the ones who write the new, creative stuff. Obviously, I think, this type of approach can never work in practice, as the correct balance could never be fixed. In practice, even in the presence of formal appraisal schemes, developers are rewarded on the basis of a number of highly subjective judgements made by their managers and colleagues; how well they did at the initial interview, whether the organization feels it wants to keep them, the state of the job market, the perception of their overall contribution to projects and so on.

It is easier to see that project teams as a whole can be rewarded on the basis of productivity, speed and quality. A team that understands and utilizes reuse is helped by finding fewer defects in library code but should be measured by defects in custom code **and** defects overall. Reusing classes reduces development time and increases quality. In this sense reuse is its own reward and every successful project that has reused code will further encourage reuse.

In an object-oriented organization there are two kinds of developer: the ones that build applications and the ones that generalize and refine classes for the library. For the former, I think that informal evaluations based on overall project work, subjective evaluations, time-to-market and defect levels are probably the only rational basis for reward. For the toolsmiths or reuse engineers a common suggestion is that they be rewarded on the basis of quality (reported defects) and the number of times that their objects are reused. A problem with this approach is that a developer could produce a very simple object, such as a date object, that is reused in every project henceforth and that saves a very small amount of effort in each case. Another developer might create a complex reusable framework that is reused only once but gives massive savings thereby. The first developer could retire on the proceeds while the second would have to struggle along to the next creative effort. Weighting the rewards according to the complexity metrics set out in Chapter 10 goes some way to addressing this conundrum but I still believe that it is too early to legislate exactly on how to reward toolsmiths. They will be judged informally in practice anyway.

Reward systems should be team and project based and remain flexible.

☰ 11.2 Class libraries and library control

As Prieto-Diaz (1993) points out, the problem of software engineering is not lack of reuse but lack of widespread, systematic reuse. Developers have been reusing code since programming began but they do it informally.

Strong and effective class library control is not always popular with developers and can be seen as a bureaucratic, expensive and unnecessary overhead by management. Backhurst and Chua (unpublished manuscript) have carried out informal surveys of several C++ projects using class libraries since the early 1990s. One project had over 120 developers working on it, in a number of independent teams. A series of problems had resulted in the attention of management being drawn to the class libraries in use throughout the project. Owing to the number of class libraries in use in this project and their size, it was not possible to check everything. Automatic means were used to identify class libraries used in code and scan the libraries to count the number of class definitions in each library. This resulted in the identification of 223 internally produced class libraries in use across the project. Within these there were 9127 classes. A random sample of 23 of the class libraries was taken for examination and found to contain 1239 classes. Examination of these classes indicated that in the case of 487 classes there was substantial duplication and of these 394 were pure duplication. This meant that 32% of the classes in the class libraries examined were duplicates and therefore redundant. An additional 8% were effective duplicates and could have been made redundant by better class management. The total redundancy represented in the class libraries examined was thus 40%. If the redundancy figure of 40% is extended across all 9127 classes, and there was no indication why this would not have been reasonable, it follows that 3650 classes in the class libraries were redundant. Observational evidence indicates that the average time required to develop one C++ class library component is at least a day. Given the current cost of skilled C++ programmers these researchers conclude that the wasted cash amounted to over a million pounds. It is tempting to conclude that these results were directly attributable to the management of particular projects. However, their observations of a number of projects in Europe led to similar results, with levels of redundancy in the class libraries as high as 67% in some instances. The development of redundant classes represents a major expense for developers.

Where central control is not provided, there are a number of identifiable symptoms. Unnecessary classes are developed and added to the library, classes within the library are not effectively used in the development of applications and effective maintenance of the class libraries is not possible, leading to major development problems.

There is an even more important reason for not developing redundant classes. One of the major reasons for using class libraries is to get effective reuse of components. If there is multiple redundancy in the class libraries, this is not possible. There is another major problem introduced into the class library by redundancy in that lack of a control over the library makes it impossible to identify dependencies between library classes. As a result, changes to base components in the library can have unexpected and costly results. These researchers conclude that the general level of class library control is 'at the best, abysmal, and often non-existent'.

The development of unnecessary classes has a direct impact in terms of the time and effort required to write the classes. There is, however, another problem. The more code in a program, the more likely it is that there are errors in the code. Unnecessary classes mean unnecessary code. This means an increase in the amount of code and so in the possibility of errors. The possibility of such errors in a development is a risk that can be avoided by careful control of the class libraries.

A common error in poorly managed class library environments is the lack of documentation that goes with the classes. Without proper documentation it is impossible for the developer to make the best use of the class libraries. There are two reasons for this. The developers may not know what is in the library. Consequently, they are likely to develop classes that replicate the functionality of existing classes in the library. Even if they know what classes exist in the library, they will probably be unable to identify the full functionality of the classes correctly or determine how they should be invoked. The second point is quite important. At one site investigated by Backhurst and Chua, an examination of code showed that developers were extensively reinventing functionality that was known to exist in the class libraries available. When this was investigated, it turned out that the developers knew of the classes but found them impossible to use because effective documentation was not available.

Management must realize that, although classes are being developed in-house, the relationship between the development user and the class developer is analogous to that of developers to end users. It is necessary for the class libraries to be made available with the same, or preferably better, documentation than would be expected with a commercially supplied product from an external source. Just because objects are internally developed is no excuse for poor documentation. The common answer: 'Well, Sue wrote it, and she is over there so we can ask her', is not a valid one. The life expectancy of a good class library is likely to be well beyond the employment expectancy of Sue, given that you are doing well to hold on to a good C++ programmer for more than a couple of years.

Class libraries need maintaining. An unmanaged library is virtually impossible to maintain. In a well-managed class library, every basic function should occur once only. Every other occurrence of that function should be acquired by inheritance. So, if there is a need to change the basic function, because of changes in hardware, say, then there is only a need to make changes in one place. That, of course, presumes that the principle of encapsulation has been correctly applied and that there is no need to amend the interface.

Where classes are developed at random and just added to the library, there can be no control over the use of basic functionality. You may find that the same basic functionality is implemented in several classes in a number of different ways. In this case you are faced with a major maintenance problem when it becomes necessary to amend the basic functionality.

There is a need to control class libraries. By implementing such control you can actually introduce a potential for cost reduction. This tends to imply that there is a need for a single person to take responsibility for the class library and the management thereof.

In their forthcoming book, which is based on studies of over 170 projects in Europe, Backhurst and Chua conclude that, for the handful of projects that had implemented reuse successfully:

> 'All the evidence we have acquired to date indicates that reuse is only successful when the reusable components are centrally owned and controlled under a Draconian régime. Whenever attempts have been made to introduce individual responsibility for components, or to allow flexibility in their control and management, chaos has resulted.'

Commercially available class libraries are available for most object-oriented languages. Arguably, there are over 100 such libraries available at the time of writing. Some languages, such as Eiffel and Smalltalk, come bundled with their own, very good and extensive libraries. Objective-C is most often used in the context of NeXTstep with its extensive library and application framework. Others, notably C++, require that a third-party library be selected. The Microsoft and Borland C++ compilers come with their own libraries which are effectively application frameworks, but the use of them can severely restrict inter-compiler portability. Third-party libraries for C++, such as NIH, InterViews, CommonView, ObjectCenter, USL's Standard Components, Rational's Booch Components and

Rogue Wave's Tools.h++, may be evaluated against the criteria of cost, performance, quality of documentation, comprehensiveness, design philosophy, robustness, learnability and ease of use. Most of these libraries offer support for fairly low-level programming and/or interface construction tasks such as basic algorithms and data structures. Korson and McGregor (1993) list 23 criteria that can be used to evaluate libraries of the type discussed. Currently, there are few commercial application-specific, vertical business libraries available. This is expected to change in the near future. Evaluation criteria will, of course, be different though the ones discussed will be included.

Very often a library that is suitable for one type of application may well be inappropriate for another class of problem. It is clear, for example, that the Microsoft Foundation Classes (MFC) for Visual C++ provide excellent insulation from the Windows SDK and are ideal for building applications such as word processors. One almost suspects that they could have been re-engineered from the code for Word for Windows 2.0. However, for applications with very different user interface requirements, such as a CAD system, it is less easy to see how to proceed. In building *SOMATiK* using an early version of the MFC this was found to be a problem, especially when the Application Wizards were used. This is one of the reasons why the version released with this volume has, in my opinion, rather too many modal dialogue boxes and, perhaps, violates some of the principles expounded in Chapter 3. Further, we found several compiler bugs but expect these to disappear in future versions of MFC. The commercial version of *SOMATiK* has resolved the issue of modal dialogue boxes.

Some of my friends who are expert C++ programmers tell me that the Booch Components are almost a work of art in terms of the design philosophy they incorporate. Portability is good, there is always a clear distinction between policy and implementation and the range of features is impressive. The library is also now available for Eiffel users. However, the performance and documentation are not quite as good as some of its competitors. The USL library is superbly documented and easy to learn and use. No one library can be said to be best in all respects and there seems to be a trade-off between performance and flexibility.

▤ 11.3 The process environment and tools

Reuse does not happen automatically. Objects may be reusable, but that is only their potential. To get the benefits of reuse, it is necessary to actually reuse the reusable. This means that the resource of a library of objects has to be carefully managed. The process of managing objects involves matching existing objects to requirements and, then, either reusing them or customizing them. If no suitable library class exists one will have to be built. New and customized objects then need to be examined for reusability by as many people as possible before being granted the status of library objects.

It is good practice to work within the context of a standard development environment comprising the following layers:

- Modelling
  - Business object models
  - Application object models
  - Foundation classes
  - Standard architectures
- Methods
  - Techniques and notation
  - Life-cycle model
  - Rôles
  - Team structures
  - Standards and metrics
- Tools
  - CASE tools
  - Project support tools
  - Standard metric collection procedures
  - Network management and security tools
- Authoring systems
  - GUI authoring tools
  - 4GLs
  - Languages
  - Databases
  - Application frameworks/class libraries
  - Networks

If possible, this environment should be standard across all projects.

11.4 Designing for reuse

Designing classes for future reuse involves generalization. No details specific to the application from which the class first arose should be allowed to persist in the generalized version. All the attributes and operations appropriate to a complete, general abstract type should be included. Facets and rules have a key rôle to play in ensuring the quality and reliability of the library class. Associations and attribute facets, such as valid ranges, specify the class's contract with respect to its data structure; operation facets such as assertions and the class's rulesets specify the contract with respect to behaviour and to interaction with other classes. Having a powerful set of contract specification tools such as rulesets is crucial in moving from code-level to specification-level reuse.

Class specifications that are candidates for reuse or those that have already been included in the library should have complete, precise and concise documentation. The form of documentation should be standard for the whole organization. The ideal form is that of the class cards given in Chapter 7. The same applies to reusable tasks where task cards offer a documentation standard. Source-code-level object documentation should also be standardized, though on a language-by-language basis.

Developers should keep reuse in mind throughout all stages from the requirements elicitation process onwards just as they must keep quality constantly in mind. Peer reviews and group work at regular intervals contribute greatly to the reuse culture. Reviews should always examine the issue of reuse explicitly. Teams should report reuse and extension problems regularly and use this to review the use of library objects.

Designing for reuse is not easy. The dangers are:

- over-generalization, leading to unbearably high infrastructure costs;
- the inclusion of application-specific ideas in a library intended for general use, leading to restrictions and delay in subsequent projects.

Unfortunately, I have no general prescription that will cure the disease or even alleviate the symptoms except the already-known requirement for skilled, creative developers.

Some guidelines for successful reuse at the design level can be given:

- Senior management commitment to the reuse programme and the funding that it implies is critical.
- Organizational changes are the hardest ones to make.
- Architectural reuse is more beneficial than simple component reuse or reuse by extending systems. We must base reuse on domain models of the business and/or on standard application frameworks such as GUI tools provide.
- Standard interfaces are critical.
- Browsing and search tools are indispensable for understanding existing designs and finding components.

Design-level reuse is best controlled within the context of a sound approach to specification-level reuse as discussed earlier in this chapter.

☰ 11.5 Repositories, frameworks and CASE tools

The usual understanding is that a **repository** is the database supporting a CASE tool and the developers of systems. The services associated with the repository – such as configuration management, reuse management, process management or quality control – are referred to as a **framework**. It is widely accepted that repositories are beneficial. The question is: what sort of repository is most beneficial? I would argue that an object-oriented repository is best for organizations where object-oriented development is used. Another issue is the openness of the repository. The repository should, ideally, conform to the standard. Fortunately, there are several standards to choose from! Well-known repository standards include Atis (A tools integration standard) and the Information Resource Dictionary System (IRDS) from the ISO. Amidst this plethora, the Portable Common Tools Environment (PCTE) standard seems to be emerging as the international *de facto* standard.

It is usually advisable to consider buying or building a tool to assist the library management function. I know of a number of organizations that have created their own tools in the absence of any suitable commercial library management tools; in one case, to my great surprise and successfully, using nothing more than an AS/400 database. The library components can be organized in a hierarchical manner or according to keywords. Research shows that a combined approach is beneficial. If a pure keyword approach is selected then standard information retrieval technology may be appropriate. Hypertext systems too may be used. I recommend a combined approach using a classification system using fuzzy sets as classifiers for suitable objects as exemplified by the manner in which *SOMATiK* handles things. This permits, in principle, both fuzzy matching on keywords and classification-based browsing. Some objects can be described precisely from the requirements, but others often have to meet requirements to a degree only. This is a subject that needs careful thought and investigation. It is generally acknowledged that existing tools are mostly inadequate. First Boston seems to have achieved their apparently massive levels of reuse precisely because they built a custom tool (Banker, Kauffman and Zweig, 1993) and did this without even the benefits of object technology.

SOMATiK provides a read-only repository containing classes, tasks, event traces and a glossary of business terms. It supports online reuse of these resources in RAD workshops. It also supports source/specification cross-referencing and the full animation of specifications.

11.6 Cross-project coordination

The process model described in Chapter 9 makes the assumption that time-boxes can be run in parallel. Clearly, this implies a means of dealing with the extra complexities of distributed, concurrent development. This section outlines the approach adopted within SOMA.

Aoyama (1993) describes a model of distributed, concurrent project management. He too suggests that object-oriented modelling could be used to take his models further. Centralized sequential development corresponds to the waterfall model. Its disadvantages include those alluded to in Chapter 9 already and long development times. Since it may also be hard to install large numbers of developers in just one office, there can be a distributed version that introduces additional problems of collecting and disseminating information

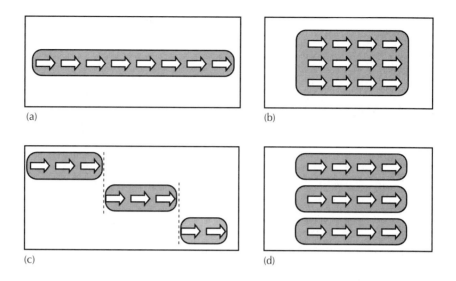

Figure 11.1 Four approaches to development. (a) Centralized sequential; (b) centralized concurrent; (c) distributed sequential; (d) distributed concurrent.

among distributed teams. Concurrent development shortens time-to-market drastically but creates new problems in terms of coordinating multiple, concurrent activities. When the development is distributed too, the complexity may be double that of centralized sequential developments. However, this is the ultimate model for downsizing the development organization and its processes. Figure 11.1 shows the four possibilities.

In previous chapters we have examined the decomposition of software into objects and layers. It is normally observed that project-level decomposition is more coarse-grained. In SOMA, however, the layer is the unit of decomposition at all levels and the time-boxes of Chapter 9 and the grey areas in Figure 11.1 correspond to each other and to layers. SOMA will support any of the models shown in this figure. However, if a concurrent approach is adopted there is additional complexity to manage.

We have a simpler problem than the one Aoyama describes because: (1) we have a single point of initial requirements capture; and (2) there is no notion of maintenance or enhancement as distinct from a project as such. We do still, however, have to coordinate across projects and time-boxes. The problem is to ensure that integration of time-box products is adequately planned for and that time-box synchronization is accomplished. The model we adopt is shown in Figure 11.2.

The diagram shows how the consolidation activity within each time-box integrates the results of other efforts to produce a product which is then subjected to evaluation. In some cases the time-boxes communicate directly and

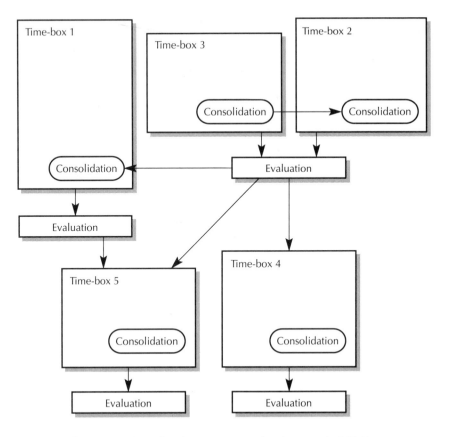

Figure 11.2 Coordinating concurrent development in SOMA.

informally, in others only after evaluation. If the products of the two final time-boxes interact there would have to be a combined evaluation.

To make it work and maintain consistent levels of quality, everyone involved must speak the same development language and that language must be sufficiently expressive, or semantically rich. SOMA is offered as the basis of just such a lingua franca.

11.6.1 Models of reuse

The outstanding coordination questions that we must discuss concern co-ordinating products from the repository, managing updates to the repository and releasing updates to the repository. Much of this has already been dealt with in Chapter 9 and we will only discuss the specific, additional issues raised by reuse.

Henderson-Sellers and Pant (1993) describe four different models of reuse coordination. In their **end-lifecycle** model the generalization activity is carried out after projects complete. My observation has been that there is a severe danger that this activity is omitted due to the demands of new projects for the newly released human resources who are the ones expected to carry out the generalization. Even if these resources are made available, as Henderson-Sellers and Pant point out, it is unlikely that the customer will be altruistic enough to fund the apparent extension to his project after he has taken delivery of a satisfactory end-product. The obvious alternative is to make developers responsible for creating reusable classes during the project. Menzies *et al.* (1992) call this the G-C1 model. I refer to it as the **constant-creation** model. The arguments for this approach are strong. The costs can be attributed to the customer during development. Furthermore, good developers have a tendency to produce reusable code 'as a silk worm produces silk'; as a by-product of what they are doing anyway. However, in practice this increases costs and increases time-to-market and is often the victim of time pressures within projects. Obviously, nothing should be done to discourage the production of high quality, reusable classes during projects but it cannot be enforced in practice. When this régime is in place we tend to observe a lot of source code copying and improvement rather than subclassing. To overcome problems with both these approaches Henderson-Sellers and Pant suggest two models, appropriate for small to average and very large companies respectively: the **two-library model** and the **alternative cost-centre model**. The SOMA version of the two-library model is illustrated schematically in Figure 11.3. Here there is a library of potentially reusable classes identified during projects and another of fully generalized and adopted classes maintained by the domain team. How an object's potential for reuse can be determined is almost impossible to legislate for. Business knowledge and development skills combine to determine the result in concrete circumstances. Developers will typically ask if the concept is important to the business, likely to be used in other systems, fundamental to technical components of applications and so on. Attentive readers of Chapter 9 will have already noticed that SOMA uses a two-library approach.

The only additional effort specific to the project in this approach is the recognition of potentially reusable classes and the extra cost is almost nil. As we have seen in Chapter 9, library components are scanned early in projects, from RAD workshops to prototyping in the time-box. If the classes identified in this way happen to reside in Library 1 then an additional generalization cost is incurred by the project, but this is entirely as it should be and the costs can be happily borne by the sponsor. The two-library model directly addresses the danger of over-generalization alluded to earlier.

The alternative cost-centre model involves creating and funding a separate cost-centre centrally. It is not funded by projects and initially runs at a loss, costs being recovered by selling classes to projects long-term. This model is only thought to be appropriate for very large organizations. SOMA is compatible with this approach too.

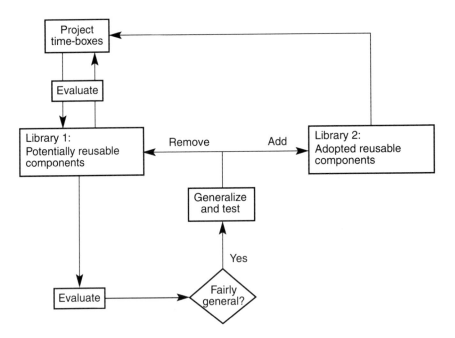

Figure 11.3 The two-library model of reuse.

⊟ 11.7 Summary

This chapter dealt with the relationship among parallel projects and time-boxes, issues of management and of encouraging and managing reuse. These issues constitute, together with the general management issues, probably the largest single factor affecting the success of organizations migrating to object technology.

Reuse is not new or a unique result of using object technology. Function libraries and packages represent extremely successful examples of reuse and have done so for a long time. The most widespread realization of reuse occurs when package software is employed. Top-down decomposition into functions leads to application-specific modules. Object-oriented reuse aims at fine-grain reuse based on an object's specification or contract.

The key prerequisites to successful reuse are:

- senior management understanding of and support for the reuse programme;
- realistic estimates of the investment required for successful reuse;
- a life-cycle model that supports and encourages reuse;
- a library of reusable components; functions and classes;
- a means of documenting and accessing these components via their specification;

■ suitable tools to support and facilitate the approach;
■ a reward system that rewards both developers and reuse engineers for reuse;
■ skilled, motivated developers.

The benefits include lower future maintenance costs, faster development and higher quality.

Reuse can be managed at either the code level or the specification level. Remaining at the code level is likely to lead to a petering out of the benefits accruing to us from reuse. The solution is to move reuse to the specification level. *SOMATiK* offers the possibility of reuse at the domain analysis and requirements specification level, having a repository of classes, task scripts and a glossary of business terms. It links the specification by cross-reference tables to code objects.

There should be a small, full-time domain modelling and reuse team to produce, collect and maintain reusable code. A key personality in the domain team is the class librarian. The criteria that make an object reusable must be established carefully. Another key rôle is that of the reuse engineer or toolsmith. This group should take ownership of key objects, act as a centre of technical expertise, be a distributor of objects, seek general-purpose commercial objects, manage the repositories and free other developers to get on with the job. The reuse team must stay close to its interim customers. The hairy/conscript model helps this by bringing new business awareness to the work. The reward structure must be treated with great care.

The problem of software engineering is not lack of reuse but lack of widespread, systematic reuse. Strong and effective class library control is not always popular with developers. The average time required to develop one C++ class library component is at least a day. Examination of OO projects has indicated substantial duplication and redundancy in class libraries.

Commercially available class libraries and application frameworks can severely restrict inter-compiler portability. Most of these libraries offer support for fairly low-level programming or interface construction tasks. Currently, there are few commercial application-specific, vertical business libraries available but this is expected to change. No one library can be said to be best in all respects and there seems to be a trade-off between performance and flexibility.

Designing classes for future reuse involves generalization. No details specific to the application from which the class first arose should be allowed to persist in the generalized version. All the attributes and operations appropriate to a complete, general abstract type should be included. Facets and rules have a key rôle to play in ensuring the quality and reliability of the library class. Having a powerful set of contract specification tools such as rulesets is crucial in moving from code-level to specification-level reuse.

Class specifications should have complete, precise and concise documentation. The form of documentation should be standard for the whole organization. The ideal form is that of class cards. The same applies to reusable tasks where task cards offer a documentation standard. Source code documentation should be standardized on a language-by-language basis.

An object-oriented repository is best for organizations where object technology is used. The repository should, ideally, conform to open standards. *SOMATiK* provides a read-only repository containing classes, tasks, event traces and a glossary of business terms. It supports online reuse of these resources in RAD workshops.

We discussed distributed, concurrent project management. Centralized sequential development corresponds to the waterfall model. Its disadvantages include long development times. Concurrent development shortens time-to-market but creates new problems in terms of coordination. When the development is distributed too, the complexity may double. We showed how the consolidation activity within each time-box integrates the results of other efforts to produce a product which is then subjected to evaluation. To make coordination work and maintain consistent levels of quality, everyone involved must speak the same development language and that language must be semantically rich.

We described four different models of reuse coordination: the end-lifecycle, constant-creation, two-library and alternative cost-centre models. SOMA uses a two-library approach and is compatible with the alternative cost-centre model too.

⊟ 11.8 Bibliographical notes

The literature on object-oriented library management and reuse is very young and there is little I can think of to recommend as further reading beyond the references already given in the text. McGregor and Sykes (1992) is an accessible reference that does discuss some of the issues of software reuse.

12

Moving to physical design and implementation

Deep in unfathomable mines
Of never failing skill
He treasures up his bright designs,
And works his sovereign will.

William Cowper (Olney Hymns)

This chapter deals with several issues related to the transformation from the SOMA Business Object Model to its Implementation Object Model. It makes the intrinsic assumption that existing methods of object-oriented design adequately cover the issues of designing for implementation in an object-oriented programming language. In my opinion the most complete of these methods is the Booch'93 approach and therefore I will use this notation exclusively for examples although it is intended that other methods could be used if desired. I do not intend to describe Booch's method in detail, since there is already a very good book doing exactly that (Booch, 1994). In some ways this could therefore be a very short chapter which says 'for anything complex or when using a low-level language such as Ada or C++, convert all SOMA representations to Booch'93. Otherwise implement directly from the SOMA models'. However, there are a few issues that deserve further attention that are visited herein. Furthermore, we should discuss exactly how SOMA constructs translate into specific language constructs or those of Booch when there is no direct equivalent.

The most evident SOMA construct to lack an equivalent in Booch'93 and, indeed, in most object-oriented languages is the ruleset. It is with this topic we begin.

12.1 Converting rules to assertions

Recall that, in SOMA, classes consist of an identifier, pointers to superclasses, pointers to component classes, attributes, operations and rulesets. Attributes may be simple place holders for objects or may denote relationships with appropriate multiplicity and modality information. Attributes are shorthand for their standard get and put operations. Operations may specify assertions of three kinds: preconditions, postconditions and invariance conditions. Attributes, operations and rulesets may be inherited. Note that the assertions attached to each operation are also inherited along with other facets.

Everything that can be expressed as rules can, in principle, be expressed as a combination of more formally expressed assertions: pre-, post- and invariance conditions and class invariants. However, doing so during the early days of analysis or logical design can be complex and unreadable for users. This prevents those vital bridges of understanding from being built and maintained. The advantage of rules is clarity and conciseness. However, there are cases where a simple assertion concerning an operation is more natural and clear than a ruleset. The analyst will be able to judge which is best in individual cases. An example I have used to illustrate the idea of rules is the ruleset with one rule about holidays which says that loyalty is rewarded:

If Service_length: > 5 then Holidays: = 25

where the standard holiday entitlement is assumed to be 20 days. As we have seen, this could be expressed as a postcondition on the length of service attribute, so that whenever its value changes in any way a method is called which updates Holidays:. This is really a postcondition on the method for putting length of service, not on the attribute itself. Alternatively, we could place a precondition on get(Holidays) that checks to see if there has been an anniversary since the last enquiry every time Holidays: is accessed and, if so, changes its value. Choosing between these alternatives corresponds to a choice between eager and lazy evaluation, which will have consequences for the relative efficiencies of enquiries and updates. Which is best will depend on the expected usage of the system and is indisputably a design decision. Using the ruleset defers this decision to a more appropriate point. Further, since these standard operations are not usually exhibited, this adds to the difficulty of maintaining their assertions and the rule's approach seems much cleaner on balance. Where formal correctness is an issue, rules should be avoided because of the possibility of side-effects and the lack of a formal proof theory. I find that this is rarely an issue for commercial systems where rules are usually the best form of clear expression for analysis purposes. However, while analysts need the clarity of rules, designers need the safety of assertions and may be worried by the possible side-effects of rulesets.

The fact that rulesets can be replaced by assertions in this case leads us to generalize the idea and assert that this can always be done, as I will explain in this section.

The decision to use the rule form may be easily reversed. Unless implementation is to be in a rule based language, SOMA designers will replace the rules with assertions during logical and physical design. This is more precise but less communicable to users so it is important to trace the conversion or even automate it. If the intention is to implement in a language such as Eiffel that supports assertions directly, this is the end of the story. However, most languages, including C++ and Smalltalk, do not have constructs that represent assertions directly. We either have to extend the language in some way or adopt a standard convention for coding these constructs. The obvious convention, taking C++ as a typical language, is to insist that every member function calls functions at the start and end of invocation to check that the preconditions and postconditions are satisfied and return an exception otherwise. This would have to be done individually for every member function to which an assertion applied. It is unlikely that one would be using invariance conditions with C++ since they apply solely to concurrent processes. However, these too can be simulated, as can general class invariants, by checking the state of variables at key points during execution. Clearly this can become very complex and we need some intermediate representation.

Several object-oriented design methods offer support for assertions and a few will even generate code based on them, thus saving the developer a great deal of work. SOMA object models that contain no rulesets or assertions can be implemented directly in most languages though I would advise against this in the case of low-level languages such as C++. If there are rulesets and a rule based language is used then there is no reason to use any other form of intermediate representation. This chapter concerns the many cases where we need to implement in a low-level language and thus need to convert rulesets to assertions and therefore need such a representation. It would be tedious to describe the approach using every object-oriented design method so I have chosen to use a good representative, Booch'93, to illustrate the entire discussion. This method has the additional benefit of being supported by a CASE tool that will generate C++ code: Rational ROSE. Several tools offer this capability now. Another example is IDE's Software through Pictures.

The conversion from rules to assertions may be conducted quite mechanically along the following lines. First, let us reclassify the types of rules in a manner useful for this exercise. Rules may now be viewed as falling into the following categories.

Type A rules: Rules that relate attributes to themselves. These are **not** rules but constraints on attributes and can be expressed as assertions about the standard get and put methods for each attribute. Usually they are preconditions on put.

Type M rules: Rules that relate operations to themselves. These are **not** rules but assertions concerning operations/methods.

Type AA rules: Rules that relate attributes to other attributes. These are expressed as pre- or postconditions on the put and get methods associated with one of the attributes. For example, the rule

Service: $> 5 \Rightarrow$ Hols: $= 25$

could be converted to a precondition on put.Service: which insists that put.Hols: fires and returns a value incremented by five whenever get.Hols: finds a value of 20.

Type MM rules: Rules that relate methods to methods. These are usually to do with sequencing and would be normally expressed as pre- or postconditions in any case.

Type AM rules: Rules that relate attributes to methods or vice versa. Rules that relate attributes to methods are triggers or preconditions and could be implemented directly as database triggers or preconditions or indirectly as special code. Rules that relate methods to attributes are invariance or postconditions.

Type CA rules: Rules that describe behaviour of attributes under global control strategies. These require specific code descriptions in many cases.

Type CM rules: Rules that describe behaviour of methods under global control strategies. These too may require specific code descriptions.

Type EA rules: Rules that describe exception handling for attribute values. If the language supports exception handling, these map directly to such language constructs. Otherwise, purpose-written code is required.

Type EM rules: Rules that describe exception handling for methods. If the language supports exception handling, these too map directly to such language constructs. Otherwise, purpose-written code is required.

Having converted all rulesets to the conventional form in this way, we can now convert to an object-oriented design method fairly directly since most other SOMA constructs find their equivalent therein.

12.2 Physical design and implementation in an object-oriented language using Booch'93

We have seen how to remove rulesets from the specification. Now let us consider the conversion of other aspects of a SOMA Business Object Model to a design notation that is highly suitable for modelling C++ implementations, Booch'93. Other design methods may be used but the enumeration of the correspondences for multiple methods would only add tedium rather than clarification.

It is often claimed that a major advantage of object-oriented methods over conventional or structured ones is that there is a continuum of representation from object-oriented analysis through to object-oriented programming.

Certainly there is some substance to this argument and we have seen how object-oriented representations can be used at every stage from requirements capture to logical design. This contrasts with the multiple representations of structured methods where we usually start with requirements statements in natural language, convert these to data flow diagrams and entity-relationship models for analysis and later introduce action diagrams, structure charts and the like for design. The costly overhead here arises from the need to maintain traceability and learn multiple notations. Object-oriented analysis certainly reduces these problems. However, there are still discontinuities, even if they are less severe. There is a semantic if not notational break between the TOM and the BOM in SOMA. The most severe and insuperable break appears when we move from models of the system to models of the implementation. Rather than the complete disappearance of all breaks, there is a shift of the breakpoint to the transition from logical to physical design. Offering a completely seamless representation would either restrict the expressiveness of our modelling language to those things that can be expressed in a programming language or impose very undesirable restrictions on our choice of the implementation technology. Though this break in continuity is real it is not very severe since we can use objects as our primary modelling construct either side of the break. The objects and structures in the Implementation Object Model, however, are interpreted far more rigorously. Classes must become types and inheritance rules are more restrictive, for example. We will look at this issue further in Section 12.6. The main task in going from logical to physical design is to re-express the model in a form suitable to the chosen language and platform.

Most SOMA constructs other than rulesets have direct equivalents or close equivalents in Booch'93. However, much more emphasis is placed on drawing diagrams rather than embedding text in class cards, so that many things that are written on class cards will convert to diagram icons. Fortunately, even here there is a direct correspondence. Classes and instances are merely shown by different icons, as illustrated in Figure 12.1. Abstract classes are adorned with an A as shown, concrete classes are not. There is no notion of the Application/Domain/Interface distinction but notes can be used to retain this information. Notes also correspond to the various description fields used in *SOMATiK* and to any textual annotation made on class cards. The information contained in the Superclasses: and Parts: lists must be converted to *inheritance* and *has* links on diagrams. Associations do not show direction as in SOMA so that both ends of such links must be in place on the SOMA class cards before the correspondence is exact. This completeness check may help the designer clear up any outstanding points concerning referential integrity. The multiplicity information converts directly. Usage links may be recovered from the server information on the class cards. Attributes and their types and defaults go across directly, as do operations with their return value types and arguments.

Booch'93 has many other symbols and these may be utilized to add detail to the design. It seems totally inappropriate to reproduce all of the Booch

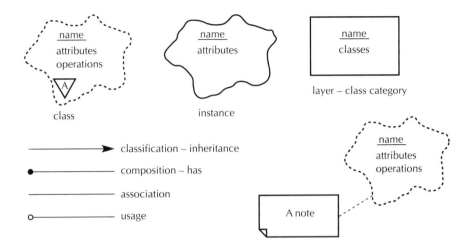

Figure 12.1 Booch'93 symbols and their correspondences to SOMA terms.

notation here since the user of the method will be better advised to study Booch's book to learn how to use the method to the full. I will assume that the reader of this section is familiar with Booch'93 and content myself with enumerating the correspondences between SOMA and Booch'93 constructs.

- Layers may be partially modelled by class categories with *has* links though the semantics are not quite as tightly defined. Implemented_by links can be (rather clumsily) modelled by usage links. There is also a correspondence here to the idea of *nesting*. Layers may also map onto subsystems.
- Booch rôles for associations are just SOMA associations.
- Relationships correspond to attributed associations.
- Event traces correspond almost exactly to interaction diagrams with scripts.
- Assertions and attribute constraints in SOMA correspond to constraints in Booch.
- State transition diagrams map directly to Booch's state machines but there are minor notational differences between Rumbaugh's notation and Booch's, notably the use of the history icon, which indicates that when a state with substates is returned to during processing the transition is to the state that the object was in when last visited. This is a useful enhancement.
- Message diagrams can be recovered from usage diagrams and event traces.
- Data flows can be recovered from message tables.
- Concurrency semantics and synchronization icons have no direct equivalent but may be recovered from event traces and rulesets.
- Time budgets correspond to SOMA delay annotations.

Much of the information on a class card is copied into a Booch *specification*. Booch'93 notions for which there is no SOMA equivalent are useful for detailed design. They include:

- Parametrized classes.
- Meta-classes.
- Class utilities.
- Export controls showing public, private, protected or implementation access. However, notes about private attributes and operations may be on the class cards.
- Static/virtual/friend properties.
- Physical containment adornments in Booch refer to language-specific issues such as call by value and call by reference. We have interpreted composition as true physical containment and used unadorned *has* links to represent it. Individual designers may wish to change this convention.
- Visibility types.
- Sequence numbers on message diagrams, though these may be recoverable from event traces.
- Keys have no counterpart in SOMA though they are easily recovered from any association.
- Module diagrams.
- Process diagrams.

Where stative classes – classes introduced to represent states – have been used, it is probably a good idea to remove them and formalize this information with a state diagram. A very common misuse of multiple inheritance occurs when it is used to model rôles or states. For example, if I have a Person class with subclasses for Employee and Student, I might be tempted to invent a subclass of both called Student-Employee. That is not too awful until I discover the Retired class and the class of people who are retired but take part-time employment, and so on. Fairly soon I will get a veritable explosion in the classification structure and it will quickly cease to have either meaning or value. One view of this problem is that classes like Employee are not genuine classes but rôles that instances of the Person class can adopt during their lifetime. The difficulty with this solution is that our implementation will now have to manage instances that must be constantly reclassified and may even admit of multiple classifications at any given point in time; as for example when Fred is a student and an employee simultaneously. Many languages do not support this approach well. I would like to be able to give a totally prescriptive solution to this problem. Unfortunately, it appears that no such solution is known, nor is one apparent. However, if one is aware of the problem one can redesign the model to avoid such constructions arising. This is especially critical in the implementation model but should really be done during business object modelling. Generally, the rule is to ask whether classes are being used to model genuine subtypes or to model rôles or states. In the latter case the structure should be redesigned or, at least, the classes marked as STATIVE for later removal.

Implementation modelling is nearly always complex and difficult in real applications. There are many things to be done. Objects must be assigned to processors and Booch'93 gives guidance on how to do this using processor diagrams. Decisions must be made and recorded about objects that will span processor boundaries, class libraries may be incorporated, interfaces to existing systems must be specified, hardware, networks, languages and operating systems must be selected and the costs and benefits assessed. It is not my intention to cover all these issues in detail in the chapter. They are adequately covered in many other books on software engineering and object-oriented software engineering already.

12.3 Implementation in a conventional language

Rumbaugh *et al.* (1991) and Meyer (1988) give good sets of guidelines for implementing an object-oriented design in a conventional language. The recommendations of this section are very similar.

Classes are converted to data structures appropriate to the particular language. In C these are structs, records for Pascal, packages or records in Ada, modules in Modula 2, arrays or common blocks in FORTRAN, and PIC definitions in the data division of a COBOL program. In BASIC, one has only arrays.

Operations, methods or messages correspond to function or subroutine calls. Instances correspond to storage allocated to global or stack variables.

Encapsulation must be enforced by good discipline. Access functions should always be used to update or retrieve data. Application functions are thus insulated from changes to the data structures. The access functions should not access data structures from more than a single class. Global variables should be avoided and scoping used as parsimoniously as possible.

Multiple inheritance should be removed. There are a number of ways in which this can be done but two of the obvious ones are indicated by Figure 12.2. On the left of the figure the suggestion is that the multiple subclass has the unique features it needs from Brick and Toy copied in and inherits their common behaviour from Object directly. The other suggestion is to create two subclasses with the appropriate features copied in where they cannot be inherited.

Single inheritance structures should be flattened. Each concrete class corresponds to a structure. Inherited operations are either reimplemented in each of them or, better, called as subroutines or functions.

Associations, concurrency and polymorphism must be implemented directly using whatever features of the language are available. Associations can be implemented either using pointers or as data structures (often relations) in their own right. In the case of polymorphism, method invocations can be resolved either at compile time by identifying the class to which each instance belongs or at run time by testing each instance. The latter is normally done using select/case statements or nested if/then/else clauses.

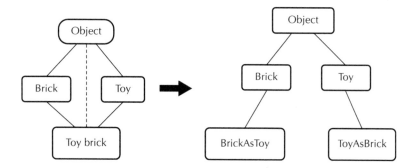

Figure 12.2 Removing multiple inheritance.

When implementation using a relational database management system is contemplated, there are some additional guidelines and correspondences. Classes become tables and instances tuples or rows. Associations, as we have seen, correspond to either tables or views. Views often arise as a result of the need to normalize objects before relational implementation. Object identity should be implemented using machine generated primary keys: surrogates. Sets of attributes should never be used as primary keys. Inheritance links are modelled as shared identifiers with a secondary index. Composition structures require joins as views. Advanced relational database products that support some object-oriented concepts obviously make this mapping a great deal easier.

Implementation in a conventional language used to be an important problem but more and more organizations are now switching to object-oriented languages. Implementation using relational databases, however, remains a key issue.

☰ 12.4 Code generation and class libraries

This section discusses the use of CASE tools that incorporate code generators and the use of class libraries during implementation.

12.4.1 Using code generators

CASE tools based on detailed, rigorous models can generate code automatically. Most current object-oriented CASE tools, however, will only generate class declarations and code stubs. This is labour saving but only relieves the developer of a small portion of the work. Full code generation is currently very rare and the theory of how to generate code for complete applications from an object model is not fully understood yet, though there are tools that do a reasonably complete job. We do know how to generate code on an object-by-object basis from state transition diagrams but often the construction of the diagrams with the necessary level of detail is as hard as writing the code itself. Further, there are dangers associated with code generation. If generated code is changed – as is often necessary, say, to improve run-time performance – then the specification will have to be changed and annotated accordingly. Extremely onerous management régimes then have to be enforced to make sure that this actually happens. Otherwise the potential for the divergence between code and specification is very great. Once the two have diverged, the specification becomes of little use except as an historical document. The alternative view is that code generators are merely equivalent to high-level, graphically based languages and that we should accept their performance limitations just as we once accepted the limitations of COBOL to get away from the intricacies of Assembler. My view is that this argument will gain credibility only when code generation technology improves considerably. By then we may have high-level languages *per se* that are easier to use and maintain than code generators.

Currently, code generation should be regarded as a useful labour-saving device rather than as a strategy for system building. Take the stubs and class declarations that come from your favourite code generator and fill the gaps with your own efficient, elegant, readable, robust code.

One way of improving your code is to use methods of great formality to express and model your design. In the next two sections we turn to a brief examination of some of the options available.

12.4.2 Integration of class libraries

At the implementation stage, developers must integrate in-house and commercial class libraries and frameworks. We have already discussed many of the issues related to this in Chapter 11. All that need be said here is that the use of class libraries often restricts portability and there may be some benefit in retrofitting specifications that correspond to library classes into the specification repository. This will help to support migration to different libraries. This said, the expense of doing this cannot usually be justified. Very often a class library will only be used for a defined layer such as the user interface. Quite often, the incorporation of these classes is done entirely during prototyping, with little guidance from the specification. Often the look and feel is so closely controlled by a GUI library that there is no need to formalize its use. Good examples of this are systems such as NeXTstep and Visual Basic where it is so easy to build the interface that a design is often not required at all. This does not, however, prevent developers from producing bad interfaces. The interface should be tested.

From the viewpoint of software economics it is best to include as many library classes as possible though, as I have said, this can compromise portability. This leads to the view that the best classes to reuse are those produced in-house. For most organizations migrating to object technology this will not be possible for some time and commercial libraries will be the only option.

Language-specific programming environments that include class library browsers are gradually becoming available. These not only support incremental linking and debugging but provide a sound framework for managing reuse. Such environments are similar in concept to *SOMATiK* but work at the code rather than the specification level. They are thus a valuable enhancement where *SOMATiK* is used. A typical such product is offered by Centerline Inc. in the context of the C++ language as part of the ObjectCenter product.

12.5 Modelling system dynamics

Up to now we have been restricted to the use of state transition diagrams and event traces for modelling system dynamics. The former specify the dynamics of individual objects and can express concurrency in so far as it occurs within objects. The latter specify global dynamics but have limited power, as described so far, in terms of concurrency. We allow coloured arrows on event trace diagrams but have not been very formal about their use. *SOMATiK* animations allow us to explore concurrency by simulation but this too is informal for some purposes.

If greater formality is required during implementation modelling in terms of concurrency there are several techniques that could be used. Jungclaus (1993) provides a highly formal treatment of the modelling of system dynamics in an object-oriented setting and discusses several of these techniques. A popular and perfectly acceptable technique is time threads. A less popular but interesting alternative is Petri nets.

12.5.1 Petri nets and augmented Petri nets

Petri nets (Petri, 1962; Peterson, 1981) were developed to model systems with interacting concurrent components based on events that trigger each other in a defined manner. Events have preconditions that determine when they occur and postconditions that determine their result. A Petri net model can be used to generate a simulation of a system or be analysed algebraically, though nothing can be proven about the program. The system can be examined under differing input régimes and execution efficiency estimated. This sounds remarkably suitable for describing object-oriented systems and especially for animating SOMA event traces, though we will see that there are some problems that mean that conventional Petri nets will not work unless augmented.

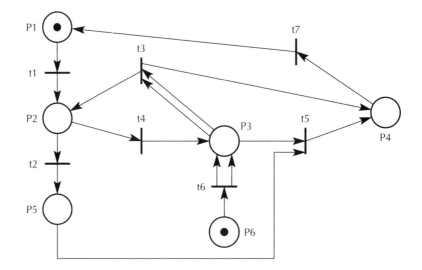

Figure 12.3 A marked Petri net (after Birrel and Ould, 1985).

A common version of Petri nets specifies five types of element: **places** representing states, **transitions** or events, **tokens, input** preconditions and **output** postconditions. Figure 12.3 shows a simple Petri net marked with tokens to show some initial state. The circles are places and the arrows represent input and output. Thick bars are transitions and the small filled circles are tokens. Input to a transition represents a precondition for the corresponding event and arrows leading away from the transitions represent postconditions. The presence of a token means that the state represented by the place is current. If all the places upstream from a transition are filled with tokens the transition can fire.

When transition t1 fires the token in place P1 is removed and a new one placed in P2. The token can be thought of as moving from place to place. Since t6 was also enabled, we end up with the marking of Figure 12.4. Note that the number of tokens at a place is equal to the number of input arrows.

The enabled transitions are now t2, t3 and t4. The next epoch enables t3 and t5 and we then get to the marking shown in Figure 12.5. The process terminates when there are no enabled transitions but may continue indefinitely. Note the implicit parallelism in the model; t2 and t4 in Figure 12.4 can fire in either order.

Unaugmented Petri nets do not model the time tokens spend in states. For this reason they can be non-deterministic. However, there are more complex versions that do measure time and impose time constraints on firing. Various other augmentations have been suggested. From a net we can construct a reachability tree and use it to answer questions about the system such as: 'What is the maximum number of tokens that a place ever has to hold?' or 'Are there unreachable states?'.

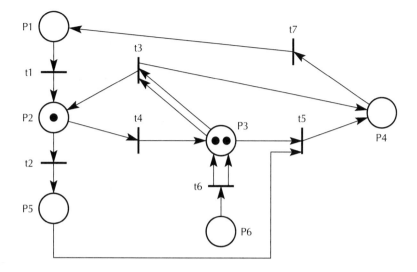

Figure 12.4 The same Petri net after two transitions have fired.

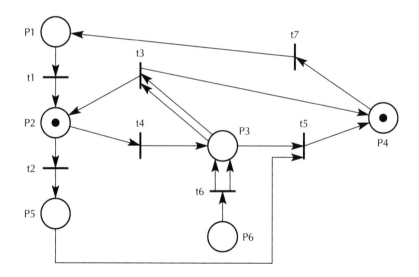

Figure 12.5 The same net after two more epochs.

From the viewpoint of object-oriented modelling, the problem with this technique is that places do not remember where tokens have been sent to. We would like to think of the marked places as states of objects and the token moves as message sends. However, messages imply an answer or handshake being returned. This implies that we must augment Petri nets so that the places remember the tokens that have been dispatched and the tokens can recall their history.

Define a **stacked Petri net** to be a Petri net where every place has a stack containing the places to which it has sent tokens that have not returned and been cancelled and where every token contains a stack containing the places it has visited since initiation. Stacked Petri nets could be used for animating SOMA event traces but this remains something that I have not yet implemented at the time of writing and a topic for future research.

What has been implemented is the animation of SOMA models in *SOMATiK*. This involves writing operations, assertions and rulesets in a formal but highly readable language, which makes it possible to compile the statements and execute the system. This is described further in Appendix A. The version of *SOMATiK* supplied with this text does not have this powerful feature.

12.6 Formal methods and logic

Formal methods have attracted increasing attention in recent years. Formal specifications of systems as complicated as CICS have been produced using mathematical notations based on set theory such as VDM and Z. The benefits are that the specifications are unambiguous and that proofs of correctness can be attempted. The disadvantages are the long learning curve, the mathematical skill required and the fact that the notation cannot be understood easily by users. Some would even argue that writing Z specifications is tantamount to coding the application. Further, formal methods fail to capture actual requirements whether overt or explicit. Programs can be proved correct with respect to specifications but not with respect to the needs of users.

Turing first suggested using formal logic to program computers as long ago as 1948. The idea was taken up by Dijkstra and Hoare in the late 1960s, who showed that the semantics of a programming language could be formally characterized and that specifications could be expressed in a formal language. Formal methods of specification have thus existed for some time and, contrary to one's naive expectations, are often used fairly late in the conventional development life cycle, after logical design. They are not intended to help with requirements capture and require considerable mathematical skill or a lengthy learning process. For these and other reasons they have not been popular for commercial software development despite numerous benefits. The chief benefits are:

- the possibility of formal proof of correctness;
- the removal of ambiguity from the specification;
- some limited forms of expression can be compiled into prototypes.

The most sophisticated approach of all is based on AI and proof theory. The philosophy here is that a program is identical to a proof of a theorem that represents the specification. Automatic theorem provers take the specification and search for a proof. If the search terminates the stored result is executable code.

There are problems with the approach. First, first-order predicate calculus may not be expressive enough to capture the specification, for example if vagueness is involved. Second, and more seriously, programming in logic is still programming. Formal logic is not itself entirely 'design free', for the very act of stating a problem in logic involves a commitment to certain positions about what can be expressed validly. This is why there are several different logics. Another problem is the need to retrain programmers in formal logic, which is a subtle and difficult subject to master.

Formal proof systems enable mathematicians to take a specification, expressed in a formal language based on logic or set theory, and a piece of source code and prove that the code meets the specification. Languages like Z and VDM start with a formal specification and then refine it into a program using mathematical transformations. It takes a great deal of mathematical skill and a great deal of time to produce these proofs of correctness for each transformation.

Formal methods address the problems of vagueness in specifications and of matching the semantics of specifications to those of source code. While the latter aim is laudable, there can be two views on vagueness: either it should be factored out by more formality or it is an essential component of the very act of description. For example, every user knows what an *adequate* response time is, but formal methods require that it should be expressed as so many seconds (or as a function returning so many seconds) to remove all vagueness. More seriously, a requirement for 'a friendly user interface' must be formally stated. I cannot think of a reasonable way to formalize friendliness, and incline to the opinion that vagueness is an essential feature of specification and should itself be captured in the formalism.

Because of the time- and skill-intensive nature of formal methods they are usually only considered worthwhile in safety-critical domains. However, the ideas evolved in formal methods can be adopted informally with considerable practical benefit in commercial systems, especially when combined with object-oriented methods.

Formal specification maps onto object-oriented design through the notion of a contract between client and server objects. This contract is expressible as pre- and postconditions and other assertions as described in previous chapters. In SOMA, assertions and class invariants, whether the result of rule elimination or not, may be specified in a formal language and its methods applied. It is neither feasible nor necessary to give the details of how to proceed further, as each language will use a different approach. We must however understand something about the possibilities.

12.6.1 VDM, Z and object-oriented extensions

The simplest form of formal specification uses a functional language and describes each function using nothing but logical assertions about the input and output of the function. A cube root function would be described as $f(x)$ where $x \in \mathbb{N}$ and $f(x) * f(x) * f(x) = x$, which are precisely the precondition that the input is a non-negative integer and the postcondition that characterizes the output. This is known as **axiomatic** specification.

Another approach involves describing the application in terms of a model of the logic. In the case where the logic is first-order predicate calculus the model is ordinary set theory. VDM, IBM's Vienna Development Method (Jones, 1980), was one of the earliest examples of **model-based** formal specification languages. Z (Hayes, 1987) is another. The main difference from the axiomatic approach is a greater emphasis on studying the states of the system and their transitions.

In Z, data structures and operations are specified by formal schemata that consist of a signature and a predicate (assertion) that constrains it. The signature specifies the type information. Z specifications are closely akin to specifications using STDs. Z uses both first-order predicate calculus and temporal logic.

Temporal or tense logic deals with the logic of locutions which involve time as explicated by tenses in natural language. For example, in normal discourse if Robert is alive, we can infer that Robert will have lived unless, of course, Robert is an immortal. There seems to be no way to express this in predicate logic; thus the need arises to find a suitable solution to the problem. Several suggestions have been advanced, such as using a many-sorted logic in which variables are intrinsically classified into 'sorts' such as instants, events, actions and so forth. There are various systems of temporal logic. All of them contain the tautologies of predicate calculus.

A very simple example of the application of temporal logic in a Z specification is the rule 'priority never increases' being replaced by the temporal logic formula:

$$\Box(\bigcirc(priority) \leq priority).$$

Here $\Box$ stands for *henceforth* and $\bigcirc$ for *next*. Other temporal operators include *eventually, iterate, before* and *until*.

It has long been thought that object-oriented programming languages and methods offer a basis for formalization based on contracts and that formal specification languages should be extended in this way.

There are several object-oriented extensions to such formal languages. These include MooZ (Meira and Cavalcanti, 1992), OOZE (Alencar and Goguen, 1991), Object-Z (Carrington *et al.*, 1990), Z++ (Lano and Haughton, 1992), Fresco (Wills, 1991) and VDM++ (Durr, 1992).

MooZ is an object-oriented extension of Z wherein a specification consists of class declarations that define templates for other classes as in Eiffel.

Object-Z is another object-oriented extension of Z and uses temporal logic to describe state transitions. It is probably the most widely used language among those discussed.

OOZE (object-oriented Z Environment) is an object-oriented language that uses Z notation. Its logical system is based on equational logic or order-sorted algebra and is a close cousin of OBJ3 and FOOPS. In OOZE some specifications can be executed.

Fresco is an extension of Smalltalk developed at Manchester University that introduces **capsules** that contain specifications, code and proofs. An unusual feature of Fresco is that types and classes are distinct notions in it. One of the motivations behind Fresco was the idea of using formal methods to overcome the problems associated with using large object libraries. The basic idea is that programmers need to know what the objects in a library do, so why not attach a formal specification to them so that one can prove theorems about them and even form composite objects constructed from them? The work depends on the notions of pre- and postconditions and effectively extends Smalltalk with these notions from VDM. This gives Smalltalk features which are provided in Eiffel.

VDM++ builds on the oldest of formal methods, VDM, by adding classes with assertions on methods. It uses a finite state machine notation in preference to any kind of temporal logic.

Object-oriented analysis methods are precursors to the use of formal languages. Formalizing operations implies building a mathematical model of their semantics. It is essential to eliminate rules and introduce assertions such as preconditions if standard logics are to be used. State Transition Diagrams may certainly be formalized using CSP. One could also represent each state as a set of instances currently in the state. Transitions are then modelled by the reclassification of instances from one class to another, with choices being made based on the instance's attributes and the states of other instances. BON (Nerson, 1992) is a particularly suitable method for this purpose as it expresses its assertions in a formal notation. However, the benefit of SOMA is that it is understandable and does not preclude the introduction of formality after the requirements have been clarified and the model explained to users and developers alike.

Lano and Haughton (1994) provide a first-rate comparison of several object-oriented specification languages and describe particular applications of these languages to expand the comparison.

A semi-formal approach to object-oriented modelling is provided by Ross and Kilov (1994). They concentrate on database modelling issues and introduce several formal rules for associations and, although they do not use the term, patterns. The approach makes use of contracts expressed by assertions to specify objects and associations. However, they regard associations as entities of a different type from objects and, in my opinion, this precludes their method from being described as object-oriented. I must admit, however, that there is a view in the pattern research community that supports this kind of approach. In SOMA, as we have seen, patterns are to be wrapped within layers that export the behaviour of the entire pattern and provide a basis for its reuse.

12.6.2 Type theory

Programs may be specified algebraically by declaring the features of an object and specifying relationships between them. Type theory is a form of algebraic specification that specifies programs in terms of types. Types have a **signature**, where the operations and their parameter types are laid out, and **axioms** that specify the relationships. In SOMA, the use of rulesets and assertions makes it possible to do this but the interpretation of inheritance is much looser than that found in type theory. It supports the idea of programming by contract, which interprets inheritance as meaning that every subclass fulfils the contract of its superclasses. Once classes have been converted to types in the Implementation Object Model, formal methods can be used to verify this.

A type is a template that is used to manufacture instances and the instances have all and only the features of their class. Types are substitutable, as defined in Section 12.7.

Type theories are closely related to formal methods and can even be regarded as programming languages. In that case programs written in these languages can be proved correct.

12.6.3 Intuitionistic type theory

The most successful proof theoretic methods are based on non-standard logics, such as the Martin-Löf intuitionistic type theory (Nordstrom *et al.*, 1990). This type theory was originally developed to clarify constructive mathematics or 'intuitionism', the philosophical school founded by Brouwer. If mathematics is not your forté you may comfortably skip this section.

Intuitionism takes a strong philosophical position within mathematics. For an intuitionist, semantics is identified with proof theory; so that the intension of $p \wedge q$ is that we have a proof of p and a proof of q and similarly for the other connectives. Quantification may only take place over a defined domain; thus we say 'for all x in X' rather than just 'for any x'. In more general treatments, quantification takes place over functions. Lastly, the proofs referred to must be constructive, which is actually not a very clearly defined term but for our purposes may be regarded as meaning that proofs must proceed in finite steps and abjure *reductio ad absurdum*. Thus Brouwer denied the validity of the hairy ball theorem when he showed that the only proof possible was by contradiction. (The hairy ball theorem assures us we all have a crown in our hair: every vector field on a sphere has a singularity.) In this approach we identify types with propositions or, in the model, with sets and functions or objects of a suitable category. The set of proofs of a proposition p is referred to as $O(p)$, the set of objects of type p. We then make the following identifications:

$$O(A \lor B) \quad \Leftrightarrow \quad O(A) + O(B)$$
$$O(A \land B) \quad \Leftrightarrow \quad O(A) \times O(B)$$
$$O(A \Rightarrow B) \quad \Leftrightarrow \quad O(A) \Rightarrow O(B)$$
$$O(\exists x\, A(x)) \quad \Leftrightarrow \quad (\Sigma c \in C)\, O(A(c))$$
$$O(\forall x\, A(x)) \quad \Leftrightarrow \quad (\Pi c \in C)\, O(A(c))$$

The basic operations are function abstraction and application, but the language differs from languages like LISP in not being type free, which has some important consequences for computational applications. It also differs from polymorphic, typed, functional languages like ML in that the evaluation of a well-typed program always terminates, which is not the case in ML. Further, type theory contains functions that are undefinable in ML and similar typed languages. This generality is needed to handle universal quantification. The statements of type theory,

A is a type
$A = B$
$a \in A$ (a is an object of type A)
$a = b$ in type A

can have different interpretations in set theory, proof theory or the theory of computation. For example, the third statement above could stand for:

a is an element of A
a is a proof of A
or   a is a procedure to compute A.

If we interpret A as a specification of a task and a as a program to carry it out then we can, following Martin-Löf, define a functional programming language and associated specification language and a formal means of deriving programs from their specification. These developments taken together make it possible, in principle, to create a new programming language that combines a powerful functional programming language that is intrinsically associated with a declarative specification language and a means of proving that programs meet their specification.

Type theory can be used for both program derivation from a specification and program verification, wherein an existing program is proved correct. Type theory is thus a programming language, a specification language and a programming logic. Programs can be generated from specifications using automatic theorem proving techniques but at present, and for the foreseeable future, this approach only works on trivially small problems.

One of the most important features of intuitionistic logic is its removal of the laws of the excluded middle and double negation. Fuzzy logic, though it supports the law of double negation, is less general but closely related to intuitionistic logic via topos theory (Stout, 1991), and this approach holds out the promise of being able to formalize the fuzzy rulesets of a SOMA model. My belief is that ordinary first-order predicate calculus will be inadequate to write a formal specification of the SOMA method because its semantics are flexible and vague although, I would claim nevertheless, precise. Intuitionistic type theory seems a reasonable candidate for formalizing SOMA. For the present though, this remains a rather obscure research topic. What we must do in converting from the Business Object Model to the Implementation Object Model in a formal context is convert our SOMA classes to types.

☰ 12.7 Converting classes to types

SOMA, as an analysis method, takes a very libertarian view on inheritance from permitting all manner of overriding even unto overriding by instances of their class's features, supporting multiple inheritance and even permitting fuzzy inheritance. Applied to physical design, this laxity can be dangerous. Up to now we have made no distinction between object types or classes and the abstract data types of programming. Now we come to implementation we may wish to distinguish them and tighten the interpretation of inheritance.

In some object-oriented programming languages, classes and types are regarded as the same thing. In others every class is a type but not vice versa. For example, in many languages real numbers are a type but not a class. When using such languages, in the Implementation Object Model we should remove overriding by redesigning the classification structures and keeping cross-reference tables of the correspondences for reasons of traceability. This is partly because overriding permits arbitrary modification of inherited features, which may lead to unsafe programs and reduce levels of code reuse.

Effectively, what we are doing is converting classes to types. Types obey Wegner and Zdonik's (1988) principle of **substitutability**, which states that every instance of a subtype can be safely used in any context in which an instance of its supertype would have worked. More generally this should apply to subtypes as well as instances. Substitutability can be verified mathematically by checking the type's contract; that is, assertions and constraints. Substitutability guarantees safety but still permits extensibility since features can be added. They cannot, however, be taken away or modified. This makes inheritance monotonic. Similarly, in the Implementation Object Model instances should be treated as having exactly the features of the class they belong to. BOM instances with overriding are replaced by new subclasses before the classes are converted to types.

☐ 12.8 Specification as implementation in a rule based system and the benefits of prototyping

This book has placed great emphasis on the benefits of both evolutionary delivery and throwaway prototyping. The need for throwaway prototypes to be reversible has also been stressed repeatedly. Throwaway prototypes should be regarded as executable specifications. It would be even better if our abstract SOMA business object models were fully executable and indeed *SOMATiK*'s animation features are a step towards this ideal. However, these features do not yet support the generation of screen designs and the other features of a fully working prototype – though this may change with future releases. For the present, it will still be necessary sometimes to construct separate prototypes following RAD workshops unless this activity can be reasonably combined with building the evolutionary prototypes. This will tend to arise when the requirements are unusually complex or poorly understood.

12.8.1 Prototyping and reversible systems

Frame based expert systems shells may be used to build, or at least prototype, conventional applications, and the experience of many people, myself included, suggests that this is enormously productive. One of the reasons for this is that rulesets are very easy to understand compared to conventional code. This makes the product rather more 'reversible' in that changes are easier to undo as well as to do. This makes the KBS shell approach attractive, but there is another reason why object-oriented developers are turning in this direction. To understand why you will need to know about a debate that has been going on in object-oriented circles for some years.

All object-oriented programming languages support single inheritance. Fewer support multiple inheritance, where an object may have more than one parent. Nearly all AI products allow multiple inheritance because of their need to express rich knowledge structures. For example, a guppy is a kind of fish and a kind of pet and inherits some features from both classes. The debate that has raged in object orientation about this issue arose because inheritance compromises that key aim of object technology: reuse. This is because if the superclass (pet) changes then so must everything below it (guppy, dog, and so on). This means that any other object depending on the services or definition of these classes may be affected. Thus, many object technologists and others (such as Michael Jackson) have eschewed inheritance as too dangerous. Others have suggested that it is too powerful to abandon but should be used with great care. Recently, Brad Cox, a pioneer of OO, was asked at a conference why his language, Objective-C, did not support multiple inheritance. His blunt answer was: 'I'm thinking of taking the single inheritance out.' His reason is the danger alluded to above, which arises mainly when inheritance is used for what object-orienteers call *ad hoc* polymorphism. This means that an object is declared as a sub-object of another merely because the super-object has some useful properties that the sub-object would otherwise have to reimplement and not because it is semantically a true subtype. Real (that is, not *ad hoc*) inheritance structures occur when the inheritance corresponds to a real-world classification structure.

Cox is one of several object technologists who are moving rapidly towards the view that inheritance, and especially multiple inheritance, is a powerful specification tool rather than an implementation technique. Classification structures can be flattened easily during implementation by (possibly automatically) repeating the shared code or using common routines. This leads such people to a search for powerful specification techniques and tools that support multiple inheritance but which can lead to an inheritance-free implementation in an object-based language. Thinking of these specification tools as (throwaway) prototyping environments leads rapidly to the conclusion, shared at least by Cox and the present author, that KBS tools are the ideal rapid prototyping and specification tools. What has been lacking is an implementation-independent notation for object-oriented analysis that supports rules. It is one of the aims of SOMA to fill this gap.

One great advantage of object-oriented analysis as an approach is that there is a smoother transition between analysis and logical design. The presence of techniques for representing association, classification (inheritance) and composition (part–whole) structures means that the method is far more capable of expressing concisely the semantics of the application. In a rule based approach, traceability is further supported because rulesets can often be read and understood and thus reverse engineering accomplished – because the designer's intention is written for all to see. Reverse engineering of COBOL or C++ code is downright impossible. Of course the purveyors of reverse engineering software tools will be worried to hear this. All their tools can ever hope to do is to extract the data structures from the code. The reason for this is that information about requirements and design – about the semantics of the application – is irretrievably lost during the transition to code unless the implementation language is knowledge rich.

My preferred approach to object-oriented systems development, whether of expert or conventional systems, has evolved into the following idealized scenario.

(1) Use both object-oriented analysis and knowledge acquisition techniques at the requirements stage.

(2) Prototype using an expert systems environment and use this to refine the analysis.

(3) Either evolve the prototype or design for implementation in a different language.

(4) Build wrappers for existing systems if an object-oriented language is to be used.

(5) If a non-object-oriented language is to be used, flatten inheritance structures in the physical design and convert classes to types. Retain the original structures in the specification and logical design for future migration.

SOMATiK offers a convenient means of animating a SOMA specification directly from the Business Object Model. This allows RAD analysts to take the specification and generate screens and database interfaces that enable the specification to run as a system.

12.9 Deliverables

The SOMA Implementation Object Model mandates a number of deliverables. These have been largely dealt with in Chapter 9 but a few comments are in order here. Depending on your choice of language and method there will be a model described using the notation of that method. Recall that the conversion to a design method is normally only required where a low-level language is used. I have chosen the Booch'93 model to do this. Also deliverable is documentation of the design decisions made during the model conversion and the reasons for those decisions. Examples include overriding removal, breaking classes into two or more, combining classes, use of library classes and so on. There should be a traceability report that includes code/specification cross-reference tables and class/type cross-reference tables along with any other useful traceability information. We tested our Business Object Model against the event traces produced during requirements capture; the Implementation Object Model should be similarly tested and inspected before being released.

We have discussed testing in sufficient detail in Chapter 10. After the code is produced it is highly beneficial to supplement the usual tests with usability studies based on real users and on UI inspections based on the principles expounded in Chapter 3 of this book.

This completes the exposition of SOMA as it is now. The approach continues to evolve and I intend to publish modifications from time to time to keep the method firmly in the public domain. The next chapter looks at some case studies and uses *SOMATiK* to build both task and object models.

☰ 12.10 Summary

This chapter described the key tasks that have to be performed in converting a SOMA Business Object Model to an Implementation Object Model or implementing it directly.

The method of mapping rules to assertions was described, as was a detailed mapping from SOMA to the Booch'93 design notation. The latter allows SOMA models to be enhanced to deal with language-specific constructs in C++ and similar languages. A CASE tool that supports Booch'93 can then be used to generate code.

Rules for implementing SOMA models in a conventional language were given, followed by a general discussion of the use of class libraries and code generators.

It was suggested that Petri nets could be used to model system dynamics and the idea of a stacked Petri net was introduced to this end. Next, we discussed the use of formal specification techniques and their relationship to the contracts of objects. Intuitionistic type theory was introduced as an example of a semantically rich formal notation. We then discussed the restrictions necessary to convert SOMA models to the type-theoretic interpretation of inheritance that might be required in some object-oriented languages.

We concluded with a discussion of executable specification using prototyping environments and knowledge based systems languages. The deliverables from a SOMA Implementation Object Model were enumerated.

☰ 12.11 Bibliographical notes

The Booch'93 method is described completely in Booch (1994). This book should be studied carefully by anyone wishing to make use of the mapping from SOMA to that method described in this chapter.

The recommendations given in this chapter on implementing an object-oriented design in a conventional language are very similar to those of Rumbaugh *et al.* (1991) and Meyer (1988).

Unfortunately, all the classic references on Petri nets, notably the one by Peterson, seem to be out of print.

Lano and Haughton (1994) provide a good survey of object-oriented formal specification methods but, sadly, provide little background of conventional formal methods. The reader will have to consult the extensive literature on this subject before reading their book.

13

Case studies

You know my methods. Apply them.

Sir Arthur Conan Doyle (The
Sign of Four)

This chapter presents a number of small case studies using SOMA and the
SOMATiK tool kit in order to illustrate the use of both. All of them are
based on realistic applications in some sense, though two are inward-looking
applications that describe aspects of SOMA using SOMA.

The disk supplied contains some of these models in the form of
SOMATiK project (.RAD) files for the reader to explore more fully. The
commentary in the text is therefore kept to the minimum necessary to
understand the modelling approach and the models in outline. None of the
examples is complete and the reader is encouraged to complete them as an
exercise in understanding both the method and the tool.

SOMATik is a very rapidly evolving product. The version used to prepare the artwork for this chapter and Appendix B was prepared with Version
1.00. Since then the code and the user interface has been substantially
improved and it was decided as we were going to press to deliver Version 1.20
with this book. I am convinced that this brings great benefits to the user but it
means that some of the screens will not look anything like those that appear in
the text. I have annotated the figures where this is important. Most of the
written instruction should still work but it is always better to explore the software when there is any doubt. The principle changes are:

- the introduction of an innovation in UI design: 'cut-away tab cards' for
  project details and for the task and class cards;
- new tools on the toolbar with ToolTips, notably the ObjectListings tool
  replacing the Objects menu;
- easier insertion of message links in the context diagrams;
- general improvements in dialogue boxes and the removal of some modes.

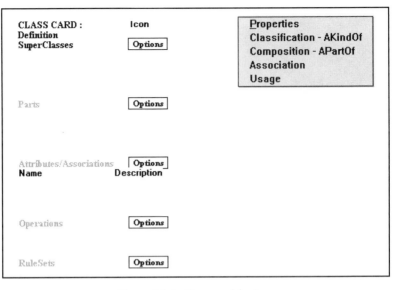

Figure 13.1 Class card for Icon.

13.1 SOMA in SOMA

If you really want to understand a method, object-oriented or otherwise, and check its completeness there are few better ways than to attempt to model the method using the method. I have done this and documented part of the model using *SOMATiK*. This section describes the task object model and business object model constructs available within SOMA and described in Chapters 6 and 7. For clarity of exposition, other aspects of SOMA are not included here.

In the *SOMATiK* model supplied on the disk included with this book there is no context or task model. The model consists entirely of class cards representing the SOMA concepts. The model is contained in a file called SOMA.RAD. Start *SOMATiK* and choose Open from the File menu. Open the SOMA.RAD project and select Class Objects using the ObjectsListings. A selection box listing the available class cards appears. Choose Icon from this list with the mouse and click OK. The class card shown in Figure 13.1 should now appear.

Left-click on the word 'Icon' and the pop-up menu appears from which one can choose to view the properties of the class or display its participation in the four object model structures graphically. The properties box merely gives a definition of Icon as 'An icon is anything that can be printed or displayed on screen.' and tells you that it is a concrete, application class. More interesting is the classification structure, which is displayed in Figure 13.2.

This diagram reveals that screen icons can be of two kinds: nodes and links. Nodes could be tasks, objects or actors. Objects can be instances, classes, layers or external objects. There are five kinds of link. Now click on Object and

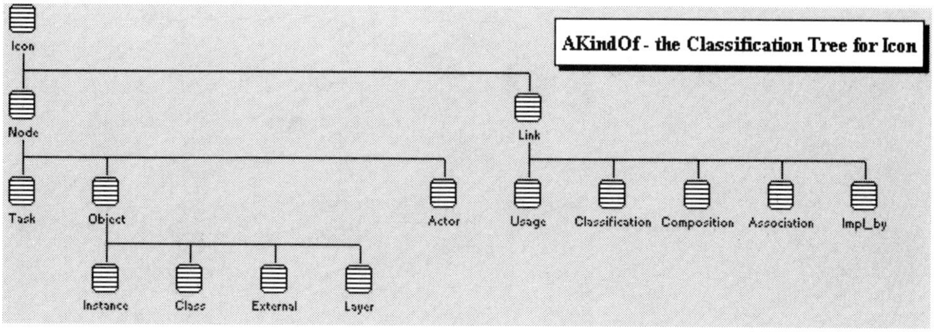

Figure 13.2 Classification structure for Icon (old layout).

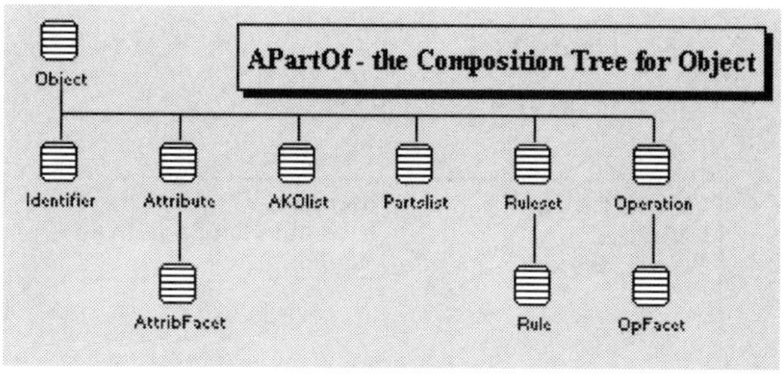

Figure 13.3 Components of Object.

select Composition. This produces the component structure for objects shown in Figure 13.3. Explore the model further using *SOMATiK* and complete it where necessary.

13.2 An object-oriented process model for migration

Chapter 9 described SOMA's non-procedural life-cycle model. This too can be represented as an object model in *SOMATiK*. The diagram of Figure 9.8 is fundamentally a SOMA usage structure, where activities are regarded as objects and activity dependencies as messages that convey information or cause activity initiation.

This model may be examined using *SOMATiK* and will be found on the disk supplied, in the file PROCESS.RAD. The internal context view, shown in Figure 13.4, is particularly simple. The business is the business of software development and the support system, represented by the screen icon, is the

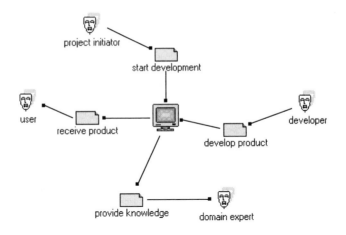

Figure 13.4 Internal context model for the SOMA process model.

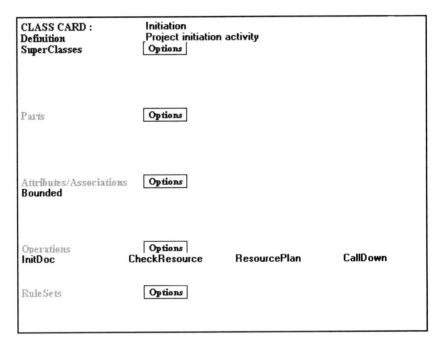

Figure 13.5 Class card for Initiation (old layout).

SOMA process itself. The TOM, too, is simple and has not been expanded in the supplied model. The interesting part of this model is the BOM, wherein the objects are the project activities.

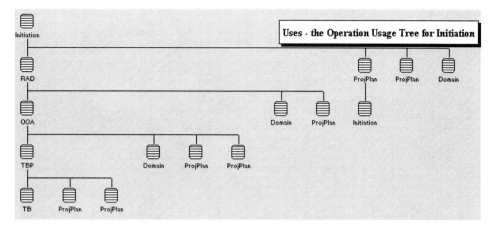

Figure 13.6 Activities downstream from Initiation.

Using the ObjectsListings tool of *SOMATiK*, select Class Objects and choose the Initiation object. The class card that is displayed is shown in Figure 13.5. It can be seen that Initiation has a number of operations. Clicking on any of them will take you directly to the activities that they collaborate with.

More interestingly, we can obtain a view of all the activities downstream from Initiation by holding the left mouse button down over the name of the class card and selecting Usage. The initial screen is shown in Figure 13.6. Then we can explore the process model by clicking on any of the activities, which will display its class card and provide details, if we then select Properties. Explore and complete this model using *SOMATiK*.

13.3 Building a simple trading system

Building on the illustrative example used in Chapter 7, this section presents a fragment of a financial trading system. For reasons of space only a fragment of this model is exposed here: the fragment concerned with deal capture. This submodel in fact appears in almost every trading system and provides an excellent illustration of how both objects and tasks can be reusable.

The scenario to be imagined is that a dealer (or trader) has already found an opportunity to deal in the foreign exchange (FX) market with a certain counterparty (another trader). Having struck a bargain verbally, the dealer is obliged to execute the deal within given counterparty limits and within her personal position limits. These limits and position represent the amount of risk or exposure that the trading organization is prepared to tolerate with respect to

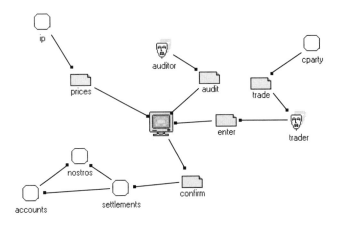

Figure 13.7 Context model for trade capture.

the creditworthiness of the counterparty and the chance of the currency falling in value, respectively. If these conditions are satisfied then:

- The dealer trades (buys or sells) with the counterparty at agreed terms and rates.
- A confirmation must be sent to the counterparty.
- The Settlements Department must be notified of the deal so that they can prepare instructions for the dealer's nostro banks. Settlements also provide settlement conditions and notify the Accounts Department of the deal.
- Accounts post on the deal date and on its value date.
- The dealer's position and the counterparty's limit availability must be adjusted to reflect the new position.

The first thing to do is to identify the key business objectives and the high-level structure of a simplified FX dealing system. Then one should find the key objects and their four structural relationships: classification, usage, composition and association. We omit a discussion of the business objectives and how they could be measured and prioritized for brevity. The modeller must now create a context model for this business system and the projected computerized support system. Such a model is shown in Figure 13.7. This model will be found on the disk supplied in the file TRADING.RAD.

The relevant external entities include those mentioned above and information providers (ip), such as Reuters, who provide online information on currency exchange rates and so on. The most significant actors in this model are the dealer and an auditor. We will concentrate on the tasks of the dealer, notably the deal capture task. The next step is to describe the messages, produce a message table and produce task scripts for the incoming message flows. Right-mouse over the enter message and select Task Card. This produces the task card shown in Figure 13.8, which shows that enter has five subtasks.

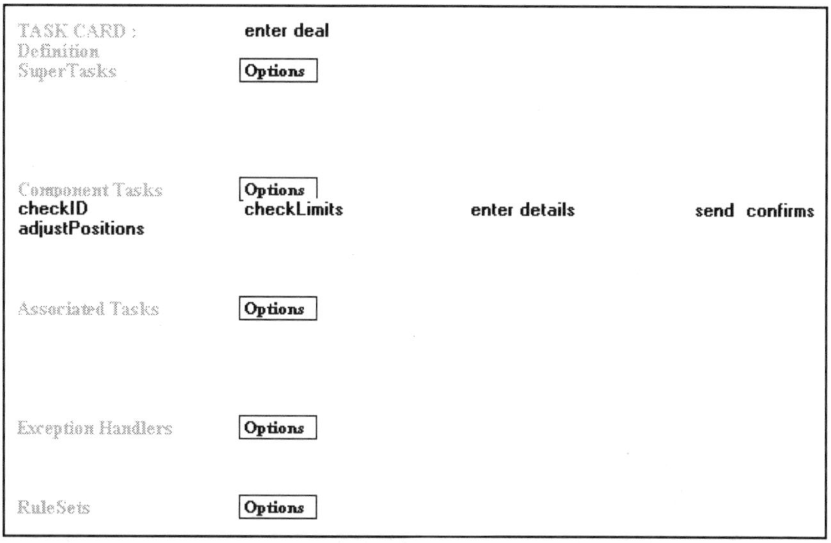

Figure 13.8 Task card for enter (old layout).

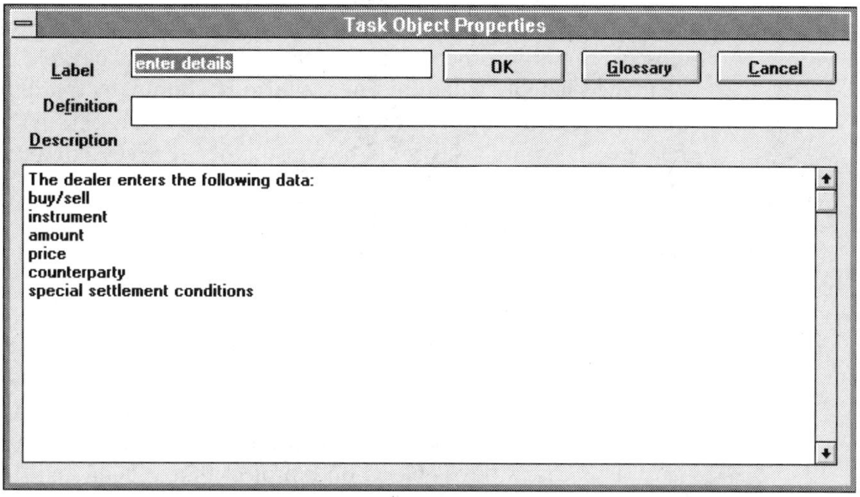

Figure 13.9 Task script for enter details.

Mouse-down over enter and select Composition to see the entire task tree. Select any of the leaf nodes of the tree displayed and select Properties. Choosing enter details gives the result displayed in Figure 13. 9.

Examining all the atomic task scripts in this way enables the use of textual analysis to find objects and operations. Note synonyms such as deal/trade and dealer/trader. The graphical views can be used as a sophisticated model browser or to analyse the structures, especially classification structures, further. The class cards can now be created and printed for use in a walkthrough. If you are able to do this, you could then produce an event trace for the system based on the walkthrough. The project supplied on disk has some class cards but they have not been fully completed. There are also glossary entries for Counterparty and Trader.

This model may be examined further using *SOMATiK*. It may be interesting to print the report for this project.

The FX deal capture process is very similar to other financial trading tasks and this provides an opportunity for reuse. What should be done is that the task scripts and objects should be taken by the reuse team for generalization and the generalized results placed in a *SOMATiK* repository for use by subsequent projects.

13.4 Building an order processing application

The last section described a financial application. This section describes an application that may be pertinent in almost every kind of commercial and industrial organization: order processing. This business process is usually closely related to other purchase ledger or accounts payable functions but will be treated here in isolation. The scenario is a company that buys various goods and services in support of its main business, the details of which are not relevent. The purchases could be consultants' services, computers, stationery or air-conditioning units. The modelling starts with the observation that people order things and that they may order from suppliers either outside the organization or within it. An internal order could be for a new computer system to be built by the IT department or as mundane as for a room reservation for a meeting. Order processing concerns all these things. At first sight one would think that order processing is quite different from foreign exchange trading but, even here, it turns out that cross-application reuse of tasks is possible. In particular, the reader may note the similarity in the following model between the order entry task and the deal capture task of the last section.

This case study is based on a project that I facilitated the workshops for. The original intention was to run three independent RAD workshops, on Accounts Payable, Order Processing and Invoice Processing. Owing to the need for certain people to attend specific sessions, it became necessary to amend the order so that Order Processing was done first. This turned out to be fortuitous as it became clear during the workshop process that there was a far higher interdependence between the operations than had been originally anticipated. Also a key factor which affected all the processes was the proof of delivery. As a result of these observations it was decided during the course of the first workshop that there was no need for a specific RAD session on Invoice

Processing, as the operational aspects of this had been covered in the Order Processing and Accounts Payable RAD sessions. However, there was a major requirement for ideas on how we could ensure proof of delivery. As a result it was decided to cancel the planned Invoice Processing RAD and replace it with a brainstorming session on proof of delivery. Effectively, we had combined systems analysis with business process re-engineering.

At the end of the workshop sessions it had become clear that there was a high degree of commonality between the object sets used by the elements. As a result the class cards of the objects identified were combined to produce one common set.

A fragment of the model of order processing may be examined using *SOMATiK* and will be found on the disk supplied in the file ORDER.RAD. There is a simplified context model and a detailed mission statement, and a set of sample objectives may be viewed by selecting Project Details from the Objects menu. Note that the model deals with requests for service and variations as well as firm orders. The context model shows how a requester sets up a request which goes to a supplier and sets up an order which goes to an authorizer. Feedback can take place between the requester and a service manager. The requester can request a variation on the order and can request a service report. Delivery can be confirmed either by the requester, the supplier, or on the arrival of the goods.

Initial discussion during the workshop identified the need to process enquiries about goods or services, requests for quotes for goods and services, and orders for goods and services. It became clear during the production of the internal context model that all three were different forms of the same basic object, a request. On this basis, it was decided that the emphasis of the workshop should move from order processing to request processing and that what was really needed was a request processing system and not an order processing system as such. Although the actual project went on to deal with the Account Payable system this case study is restricted to the processing of requests.

Only the messages 'quotation' and 'convert' have any substance in the model supplied. They show how the tasks of making an enquiry and converting it to a firm quotation are carried out. The objects implied by these tasks include Enquiry, Quote, Order, Authorization Manager, Requester, Product and Supplier. Class cards for these have been created in the sample project but are incomplete in detail and could be completed further by the reader. These, among others, were used to conduct walkthroughs in the workshops and Figure 13.10 shows sample event traces for the tasks of making an enquiry and converting it to a quote.

Exploring the model will also enable the reader to produce an entity model for this application. This needed to be done because the system was eventually implemented using relational databases. In fact the tools used were Microsoft Access, C++ and Sybase. My intention has been to give only the flavour of the example here. To complete the model would make it difficult to explore and probably not help because it is likely that any particular reader's

	Enquiry	Authorization manager	Requester	Product
Enquiry on cars			Call Enquiry	
	Create Request of type Enquiry		Request authorization	
		Check authorization of requester	Supply competence back to authorization manager	
		Check authorization of client		
		Return authorization result to requester	Check if a standard product	Look up product and advise requester
Completed			Identify request as non-standard so print out instructions on how to proceed	

(a)

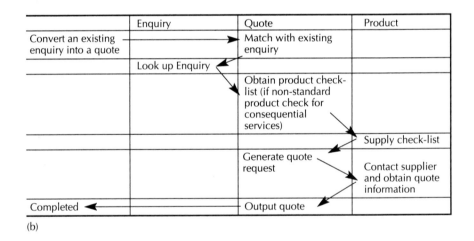

	Enquiry	Quote	Product
Convert an existing enquiry into a quote		Match with existing enquiry	
	Look up Enquiry		
		Obtain product check-list (if non-standard product check for consequential services)	
			Supply check-list
		Generate quote request	Contact supplier and obtain quote information
Completed		Output quote	

(b)

Figure 13.10 (a) Sample event trace: Making an enquiry. (b) Sample event trace: Converting an enquiry to a quotation.

application requirements will not match those of the organization using this approach. However, this case study gives a tiny glimpse of a large, real application of limited commercial sensitivity. Many of the applications that SOMA and *SOMATiK* have been applied to are not so readily exposed to the public eye owing to competitive considerations.

☰ 13.5 Other applications

The first actual, and possibly seminal, use of SOMA was in the context of what would be called today a business process re-engineering exercise. I was asked to examine whether the printing and publications department of a large Life office should move over to full electronic desktop publishing. Surprisingly or not, this was the organization's largest single department, producing policies and promotional material for hundreds of products. Working with a member of the firm's IT organization, I suggested that we should build a model of the production processes before and after the change and interviewed the key personnel. My colleague tried data flow diagrams and we found that they sometimes worked but, in many cases, were inapplicable or restricted expression. I then suggested using Coad/Yourdon notation. This was an immense improvement and much easier both to work with and to explain to the decision makers. However, there were a few cases where the data flow diagrams were better than the object diagrams and this troubled me. It turned out that if various extensions were made to the Coad/Yourdon notation then object modelling worked in all cases. The most notable of these extensions was the addition of rulesets.

Subsequent to this project I began to use the method on various assignments but without particularly explaining what I was doing to anyone. It was merely a way of proceeding for me. I also began to construct a version of the model of SOMA described above. This helped refine the method and acted as the foundation for a commercial course in object-oriented analysis and design. I soon discovered the need for some form of electronic support because of the painful process of drawing and redrawing object definitions and structure diagrams. A survey of the CASE tool market did not reveal a suitable product and I despaired slightly, but considered writing one myself. Eventually, I wrote the prototype of *SOMATiK* and started to use it to support my own model-building activities.

The first time the method was overtly used on a really large project the prototype was found to be useful but inadequate in some respects at this scale; unsurprisingly I think. My client was a software house extending a very large software product and migrating it to a new open environment from an RPG/AS400 implementation. The goal was a product that would run across several platforms including the original one and various UNIX machines and that would be enhanced early on with new management information systems features using a client/server architecture based on MS Windows client machines. The legacy system consisted of hundreds of millions of lines of code and existed in over 700 versions installed and maintained at customer sites around the world.

Another early user was a large Canadian bank that was building a sophisticated risk management system as an extension to an existing international banking package.

During this period a number of copies of the prototype were sent to people around the world who requested it. I never kept track of how they used it or the method but it is possible that SOMA was used at least partially by around a dozen of the sites that it was sent to.

The major use of the method has been within the Swiss Bank Corporation at its offices around the world. The bank is an advanced user of object technology and has been for some time. All new development within the International & Finance Division is based on RADs, object-oriented programming and distributed computing. Naturally, I am not at liberty to reveal the details of Swiss Bank's advanced applications but SOMA has been applied to around 25 projects at the time of writing. The applications cover both front and back office trading systems, office automation and work-flow, administrative and accounting systems and large database systems.

The final application that I want to mention is that SOMA was used and continues to be used to specify *SOMATiK*.

SOMA was created to address the deficiencies of other object-oriented methods and to support the real needs of organizations migrating to object technology. It is my sincere hope that this book will have convinced you sufficiently of its unique benefits to try it on a project. *SOMATiK* was created with similar aims and because no existing tool addressed the problems of reuse and object modelling properly. *SOMATiK* will undoubtedly have evolved a long way in the time between my writing these lines and your reading them. The free version reflects the state of the product in late 1994. Information on its current status may be obtained from:

Bezant Object Technologies
6 St Mary's Street
Wallingford
Oxon OX10 0EL
England
Tel: +44–(0) 1491–826005
Fax: +44–(0) 1491–825687
Email: 100073.1340 @ compuserve. com

APPENDIX A
Notation Summary

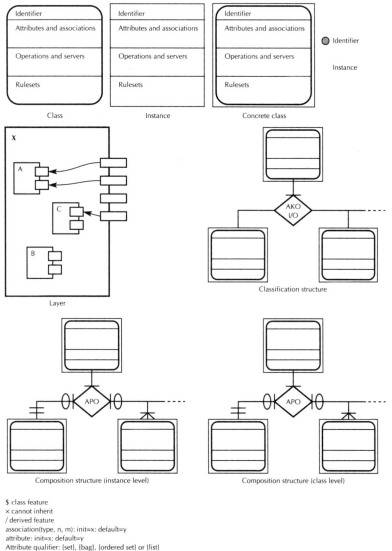

$ class feature
x cannot inherit
/ derived feature
association(type, n, m): init=x: default=y
attribute: init=x: default=y
Attribute qualifier: {set}, {bag}, {ordered set} or {list}
Attribute annonation: {variable}, {fixed}, {common}, {unique}, {fixed, common}, {fixed, unique}, {variable, common}, {variable, unique}
operation(server1-messageA, server2-messageB, ...)

Figure A.1 SOMA notation.

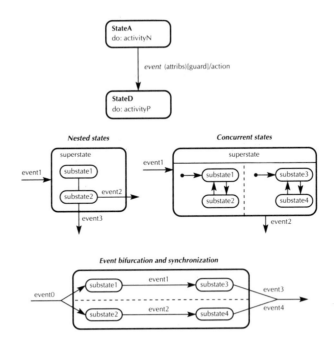

Figure A.2 State transition diagram notation.

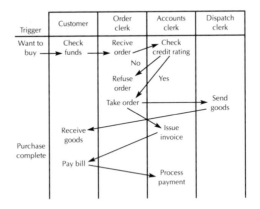

Figure A.3 Event trace.

Task name	Application/Domain/Interface
	Abstract/Concrete

Task body
Supertasks
Component tasks
Associated or analogous tasks
Task attributes
Time taken:
Complexity:

Exceptions	Side-scripts

Rulesets

Figure A.4 Task card.

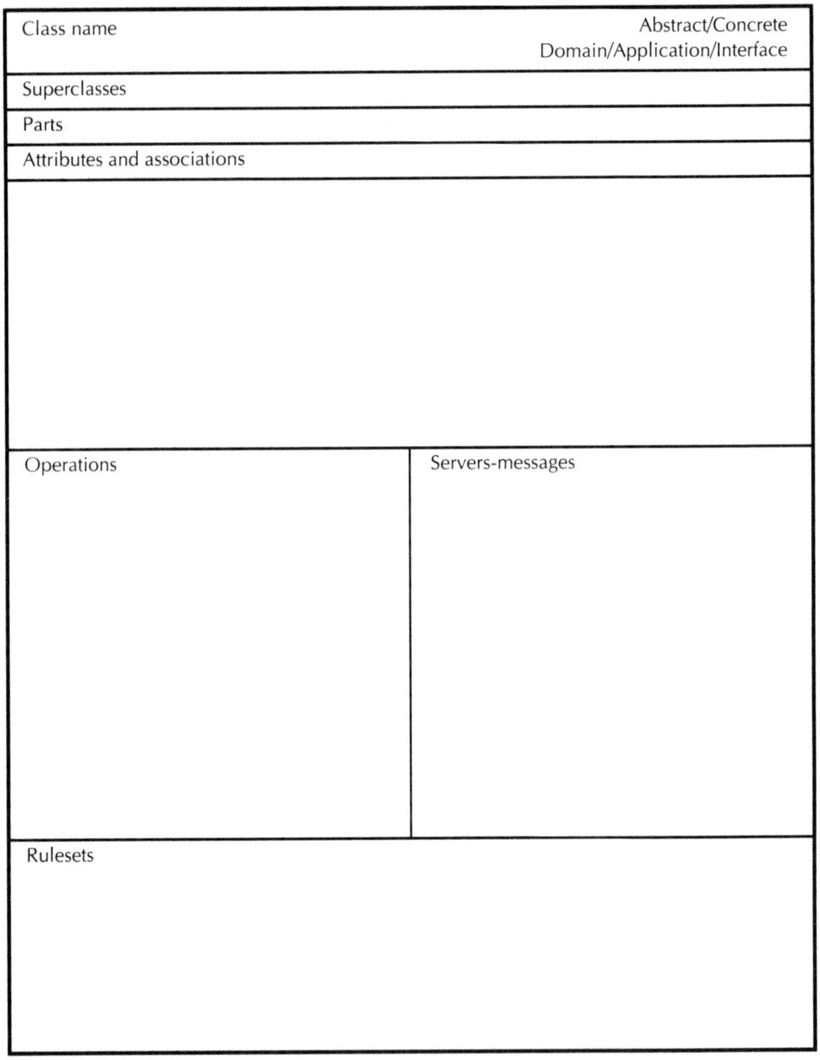

Class name	Abstract/Concrete
	Domain/Application/Interface
Superclasses	
Parts	
Attributes and associations	

Operations	Servers-messages

Rulesets

Figure A.5 Class card

APPENDIX B
Using the *SOMATiK* software tool

Again twelve stanzas. By this time the soma *had begun to work.*
Aldous Huxley *(Brave New
World)*

This appendix describes the *SOMATiK* software tool supplied with this book.

SOMATiK is a rapidly evolving product. The version used to prepare the artwork for Chapter 13 and this appendix was prepared with Version 1.00. Since then the tool has been substantially improved and it was decided to deliver Version 1.20 with this book to the benefit of the user. This means that some of the screens will not look anything like those that appear in the text. most of the written instructions should still work but it is always better to explore the software when there is any doubt. See also the remarks at the head of Chapter 13.

B.1 An overview of *SOMATiK*

B.1.1 Design objectives and restrictions

SOMATiK is specifically designed to support the execution and documentation of a RAD workshop and the initial stages of system analysis and design using the object-oriented approach. It also supports a corporate glossary, a central repository of class and task descriptions and models, metrics collection and much more. As such it follows closely the prescription laid out in this book. The version supplied with the book is restricted in the following ways. There is no compilation or animation, nor is there a repository that can be updated, though a small sample repository is supplied to show what can be done. Important features such as source code cross-referencing, event traces and object/objective matrices are not included in this version. A full commercial version is available from Bezant Ltd, whose address was given at the end of Chapter 13. A more up-to-date version of this user guide may also be obtained from them.

B.1.2 Deliverables

The SOMA approach to RAD workshops is discussed in Part II of this book. In particular, the deliverables from a workshop are defined in Chapter 9. One of the key objectives of *SOMATiK* is to provide support for the development of all these deliverables in an efficient and convenient manner. In addition, a number of other outputs are available including structure tree diagrams for all four structures, metrics tables, cross-reference tables for external objects, events, actors, tasks, classes, rulesets and attributes.

The deliverables may be generated in either or both of two formats: direct printed output, or as an ASCII file with associated Windows MetaFiles containing the graphical outputs. This second format is designed for export to an external word processor of choice for postprocessing and finalization of a formal RAD workshop document. The intent, however, is that the directly printed format should be sufficiently complete and well formatted to be completely suitable both as a working document and presented report. The limitation in the direct format is simply that *SOMATiK* does not purport to be a word processor, and the style specification implicit in the product cannot be amended by the user.

The degree of support provided for the outputs varies. At one extreme, input of the Introduction and Management Summary elements provides little other than a basic note-taking facility. If the intent of the user is to reprocess the output through another word processing system, it may be that the entry of these elements is left over to that phase. But the capability of entering the data is provided, so that the single RAD output file is capable of containing the results of the workshop in its entirety if so desired.

At the other extreme, the facilities of developing Task and Business Object Models, with the variety of hierarchy diagrams which are available, coupled with full consistency checking, provide facilities not available in other tools.

B.1.3 Support for reuse

Reuse of system components is provided through the medium of a repository. The details of a single workshop or project are stored in a *.RAD* file. Suitable elements of the RAD may then be copied into an external database termed a repository. This copying is a separate offline activity supported by an independent software component termed the *Repository Manager*. Selection of elements for transfer to the repository is a manual task. The *Repository Manager* is not supplied with this book.

Elements saved in the repository may then be copied into subsequent project files for reuse. *SOMATiK* provides the facilities for attaching to and browsing through a repository.

B.1.4 System requirements

SOMATiK requires an Intel PC or compatible with:

- an 80386 or higher processor with 4 Mb RAM and 4 Mb disk free;
- Windows 3.1 or higher;
- a mouse; and
- a printer with graphics capability (typically a bubble-jet or laser printer).

The requirements are reasonably modest by today's standards, and are intended to ensure that the system can be run from a standard laptop in the typical off-site location of a workshop.

The mouse is mandatory, since certain components of the drawing tools in the product absolutely require mouse input, and are not supported through keyboard accelerators. The reasoning here is that in the context of note-taking at a RAD, using a keyboard to drive graphics input would be so clumsy as to invalidate the purpose of the tool.

B.1.5 Using *SOMATiK* at a RAD workshop

The typical scenario for the use of *SOMATiK* is an off-site RAD, probably taking place in a hotel conference room, with one or two dozen participants. The **Facilitator** and the **Scribe** are the two key actors in assembling the RAD details into the final output from the workshop.

The facilitator is coordinating the session, maintaining the timetable and schedule, elucidating and clarifying points as they arise, and also note-taking on flip charts for the benefit of the participants.

Meanwhile, and in parallel, the scribe is taking down the proceedings on the computer, using the *SOMATiK* tool. How is the tool to be used, and how does it help the scribe and the facilitator in their activity? Explaining this is the purpose of this section.

OPENING UP THE RAD FILE

Use File New to create a new file

Create a new .RAD file for the project/workshop, and fill in the basic administrative details, list of participants and so forth. Generally, there will be an existing briefing document for the workshop with much of the material ready collated.

THE SCOPING SESSION

During scoping, the detail dialogues on the RAD Details area will be used extensively. Items will also begin to appear in the Glossary, and the Mission Statement, Scenario, Objectives, Exclusions, Assumptions and Open Issues areas will be filled in.

File Print Report... allows selective printing of parts of the project

The facilitator will be working on the flip charts in parallel. As the Objectives list begins to take shape, it is useful to make foils from time to time for projection (if a projection unit is not in use). During breaks, a hard copy of progress to date can usefully be printed and copied for circulation to the participants.

ENTITY IDENTIFICATION AND MESSAGE FLOWS

At the end of the scoping session, facilitator and scribe should review the project file, carry out any final edits, and produce the hard copy of the results to date for copying and circulation at the start of the next session.

The next stage of the workshop involves building the inventory of external objects interacting with the target system, and the overall nature of the message flows between them.

This is the role of the **External Context** component of the system, supported by the various **Table** facilities. Clearly, the *SOMATiK* graphics tool offers more flexibility in altering a diagram than working with a flip chart and pen, so use of overhead foils to keep displaying the up-to-date diagram is useful here with, once again, hard copy of the diagram and tables being provided for the users at break points in the session.

As more definition on the message flows emerges, and **actors** within the system are identified, focus can switch between the **External** and **Internal Contexts**, with the internal context providing a greater level of detail.

TASK IDENTIFICATION AND STRUCTURING

As the focus of the workshop moves to specific task identification, begin building a Task Object Model to capture the message passing relationships between *external objects*, *actors* and *tasks*. Open up a task card for each identified task, filling in its components, associations, exception handlers and general properties. Use the Task Tree facility graphically to depict these relationships.

Here again, feeding back output from the system to the participants can be valuable. Frequently, the scribe will be able to maintain a neater structure using the tool than is feasible on a flip chart.

The RAD Details area will also be in use here as further Open Issues and targets for their closure are identified, and further assumptions and exclusions become manifest.

At the end of this phase, prepare an updated copy of the proceedings showing the Task Table, Task Models, Task Cards and relevant Task Trees for distribution.

THE SEARCH FOR OBJECTS

The group activity of defining the classes implicit in the task structure is not directly supported by *SOMATiK* in its current form.

Once the manual activity has been carried out, though, the entry of data can proceed, and **Class Cards** and **Class Trees** can be prepared for the identified classes, and circulated.

REPORT FINALIZATION

On completion of the workshop, the report can be finalized. The **Introduction** and **Management Summary** sections can be written, and the completed workshop report published and circulated. This can be done either entirely internally in *SOMATiK*, or in conjunction with an external word processor of your choice.

⊟ B.2 *SOMATiK* User Guide

B.2.1 Using the RAD details

ACCESSING THE RAD DETAILS

All project details are saved on files with the extension .RAD

When a new project file (.RAD file) is created with the **File New** menu selection, or using the leftmost button in the **ToolBar**, the dialogue box shown in Figure B.1 is presented. This can be filled in partially or completely at this point. There is no explicit need to do so, however, because the RAD Details can be recalled at any time, either by selecting the **View Project Details** option from the menu, or by pointing at the system symbol in either the Internal or External Context and pressing the right mouse button.

The editable fields in the dialogue box are fairly self-explanatory. They are all pure text, and are not validated in any way. The values of the fields will appear in the printed report, sequenced as follows:

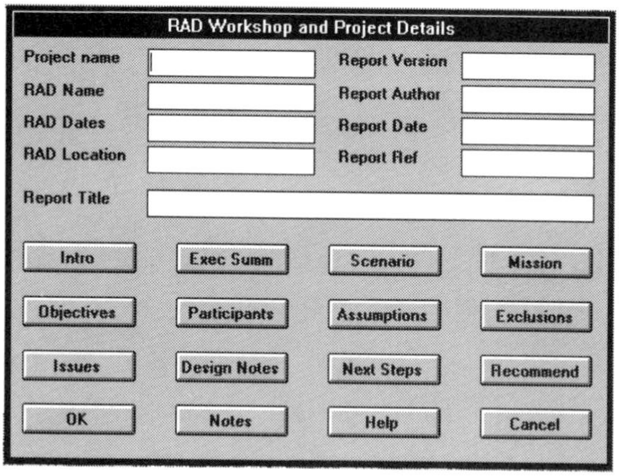

Figure B.1 RAD Workshop and Project Details Dialogue (old version).

Report Title appears a. in each page footer of the report.
Report Version, Report Date, Report Reference and **Report Auther** all appear in the reference fields of the report fly sheet.
Project Name appears as the left field in each page header of the report
RAD Name appears as the left field in each page footer of the report.

Full details on generating reports to file and printer are given in Section B.2.17.

USING THE RAD DETAILS BOXES

Below the edit fields lies an array of sixteen buttons. Twelve of these lead to further RAD details dialogue boxes. These again will appear in the printed report. The **Introduction** and **Management Summary** sections form sections one and two of the report; the remaining items are grouped into section three, the **Project Overview**.

The RAD details boxes are Introduction, Executive Summary/Scenario/Mission Statement/Objectives/Participants, Assumptions/Exclusions/Issues/Design Notes, Next Steps and Recommendations. Many of these dialogues will be used extensively during the first day (the scoping session) of a typical RAD. In particular, there will be considerable focus on the **Objectives** dialogue, which is one of the main purposes of the scoping session.

USING THE NOTEPAD

Experience shows that during this phase of the workshop, valuable points are frequently raised, which must be re-addressed later in the session, or on the following day, but may not be relevant to the main stream of the current discussion. For this reason, the **NotePad** facility of *SOMATiK* is made directly available from each of the dialogue boxes. As a side-point is raised, you can select the **Notes** button wherever you are, and record the item without losing context on the main thrust of the session.

USING THE GLOSSARY

In the same way, the Glossary facility is available everywhere, so that glossary items may be recorded in-line without losing context.

EXAMPLE RAD DETAIL: THE INTRODUCTION SECTION

A typical RAD Details dialogue box – the **Introduction Section** – is shown in Figure B.2. It consists mainly of a large edit control. The following remarks apply to this and to all other RAD Detail dialogues.

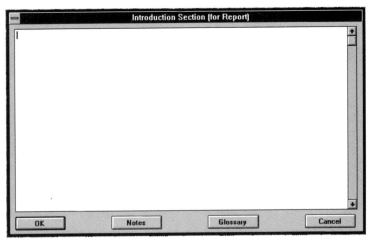

Figure B.2 RAD Details Introduction Section.

One of the design concepts of *SOMATiK* is that output of the final report is available through two routes – either directly from the system to a printer, or through ASCII and Windows MetaFiles to a foreign word processor of choice for editing and finalization.

SOMATiK automatically supplies section headings and numbering

If a direct report is to be produced, do not supply a section heading; this will be done automatically by the print routine. There are no internal facilities for selecting fonts and styles, but a standard set of these will be applied at print time to produce an acceptable standard of presentation.

Use the automatic word-wrap feature to ensure good formatting in the printer report

All *SOMATiK* multi-line edit controls feature automatic word-wrap, and this should be relied upon. If you use unnecessary **Return** keystrokes, you will see unwanted paragraph breaks in the printed report. Since the majority of word processors work this way, this rule of thumb also applies if you plan to export the data to your own WP for finalization.

Note the presence of the **NotePad** and **Glossary** buttons, for in-line access to these tools.

B.2.2 Components of the system

THE TOOLBAR   Many frequently used requirements are supported by the system **ToolBar**. By default, the **ToolBar** is displayed immediately below the Menu Bar. The display of the **ToolBar** can be toggled on and off by using the **View ToolBar** menu option.

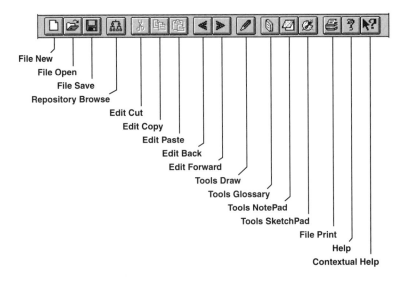

Figure B.3 The System ToolBar.

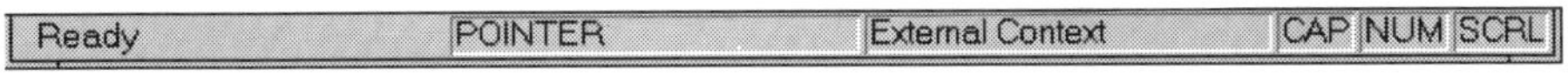

Ready   POINTER   External Context   CAP NUM SCRL

Figure B.4 The Status Bar (old version).

The equivalent menu options for each toolbar item are shown in Figure B.3. More details of the function of each of these options may be found in the *SOMATiK* Help file.

THE STATUS BAR

The **Status Bar** appears at the foot of the screen (Figure B.4). The display of the status bar can be toggled on and off by using the **View Status Bar** menu selection. It contains six fields. Reading from the left, these are as follows:

- The first field normally shows the word READY, indicating that *SOMATiK* is awaiting action on the part of the user. When a **Menu**, **ToolBar** or **ToolBox** selection item is depressed, this field contains a summary description of the function of the item currently under consideration for selection.
- The second field is only of use when *drawing* has been enabled. It displays the name of the currently selected drawing tool.
- The third field displays the name of the currently selected view.
- The fourth, fifth and sixth fields display the status of the **Caps Lock**, **Num Lock** and **Scroll Lock** keys respectively. If CAP, NUM or SCRL respectively appear in these fields, it indicates that the corresponding keyboard button has been toggled *on*.

THE TOOLBOX

A **ToolBox** of drawing tools is presented, with a range of tools available depending on the current context or view selected. As you switch contexts, the contents of the ToolBox will change automatically.

The **ToolBox** of drawing tools is selected and deselected using either

(1) the **View Drawing Tools** menu selection,
(2) the **Tools Enable Drawing** menu selection, or
(3) the **ToolBar** drawing tools icon.

The ToolBar button will be depressed irrespective of which method is used to invoke the ToolBox.

You can only use the ToolBox with a mouse

The **ToolBox** can *only* be employed using the mouse. No accelerator keys have been provided, mainly because as a graphics tool, to be employed in what is very much an online context at a workshop, it is hard to see how much value could be gained if control were applied using keyboard sequences.

The name of the current tool appears in the Status Bar

Tools are selected from the ToolBox by pointing and left-clicking with the mouse on the desired tool. The tool button will depress to indicate its selection. In addition, the second pane of the **Status Bar** will display the name of the currently selected tool.

The ToolBox can be located to a desired and convenient position on screen by pointing at its *caption bar*, pressing the left mouse button, dragging to the desired location and releasing.

The position of the ToolBox when *SOMATiK* is closed will be the start-up position the next time *SOMATiK* is invoked.

VIEWS, MODELS AND TABLES

A project file may be viewed in a variety of ways as its development progresses. Graphical views in a variety of styles and levels of detail are available, and the components that make up the project may be examined individually or through a spreadsheet-like format termed a *table*.

The available views are:

■ External Context
■ Internal Context
■ Project Details

These are selected through the **View** menu. The selected view is checked in the menu, and its name appears in the **Status Bar**.

The available tables are:

■ Entity Table
■ Actor Table
■ Message Table
■ Task Table
■ Class Table
■ Attribute Table
■ Operations Table
■ RuleSet Table

The table is selected through the **Tables** menu.

Alternatively, elements of the project may be viewed through the **Objects** menu, selecting the desired type. A pop-up dialogue offers the current list of elements of this type. New elements may be added, and existing elements deleted, using the **Delete** button.

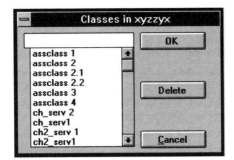

Figure B.5 Example Objects Selection Dialogue.

The *objects selection* dialogue is used extensively from all areas of the system for selection of components of tasks, classes and so forth. An example is shown in Figure B.5.

The **Objects** selection displays objects sorted alphabetically. The **Tables** selection displays them in the order of their creation.

B.2.3 Components of a project

The top level components of a project file are:

- The Project and System entities
- External objects
- Messages
- Actors
- Tasks
- Classes

The **Project** and **System Symbol** entities are created automatically, and cannot be deleted. They appear initially at the centre of the **External** and **Internal Contexts** respectively. They can be relocated at will.

Clicking on either of these symbols pops up the **Project Details** dialogue box, which can also be accessed through the **View Project Details** menu option.

Secondary components of a project file, which cannot exist except in the context of a top-level component, are:

- Attributes
- Associations
- Operations
- RuleSets

PROPERTIES OF COMPONENTS All of these components possess a set of *properties* which are accessed through the **Properties Dialogue** of the element. The properties dialogue can be accessed to expand or modify the properties as needed by:

- *right-clicking* on the element symbol in the context diagrams and selecting **Properties** from the pop-up menu which is presented;

- selecting the **Objects** menu option for the required type of object, and then selecting the object from the list presented;
- selecting **Tables** for the required type of object, and clicking on the selected object in the table.

The properties are:

- a Label
- a Definition
- a Description

Keep Labels short to avoid cluttering up the diagrams

The **Label** is a short description of the component. It appears beneath the representation of its component in all the graphical diagrams featuring the component. For this reason, the label should in general be kept rather short, and this is suggested by the narrow width on the *Label* field in all the dialogue boxes. A width restriction is not imposed, since there may be occasions when a wide label is appropriate – but obeying the indicated width is a good plan, since overlapping labels will obscure each other in the display, and in some of the displays there is no capability for altering the layout.

All labels must be unique within a project. Duplicated labels will be rejected immediately on entry.

Try to enter the Definition first, and then think of a good, short Label to encapsulate the definition

The **Definition** is a longer variant of the label, providing a one-line statement of the role of the element. All dialogue boxes support the definition field. When using *SOMATiK* in an active and flowing workshop, where speed of note taking is important, it is a good plan to enter the definition field first, and then perhaps the description, before considering the best short label to apply to the element. However, *labels* can always be altered at a later time if they are found to be too long for visibility in some contexts, so this is only a usage hint rather than a constraint.

Description fields in dialogues perform automatic word-wrap. Rely on this feature!

The **Description** allows a full description of the properties and purpose of the element to be supplied. It can be (within reason) as long as needed. One tip is to recognize that the *description* will be part of the printed report. Therefore treat the field in the dialogue box as if it were a word processor, and rely on the word-wrap facility which is built into the dialogue. Paragraphs in the printed report will be formatted and widowed based on paragraph markers. If you use the **Enter** key unnecessarily, just to mark end-of-line, it will spoil the look of your report, whether you print directly from *SOMATiK* or via an external word processing system.

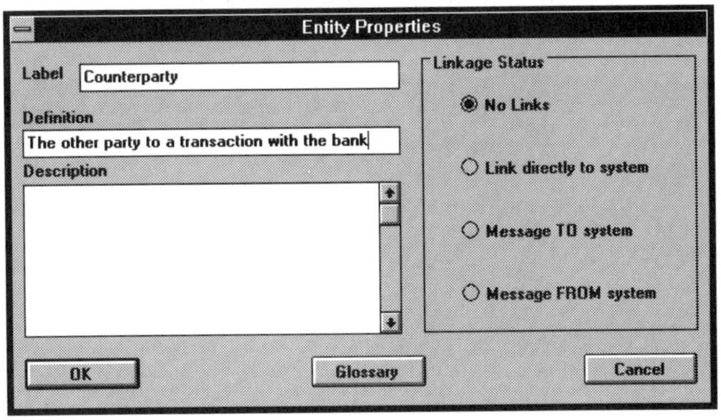

Figure B.6 Entity Properties Dialogue.

CREATING COMPONENTS

All components can be created in three alternative ways:

- by depositing their icon in the External and Internal Contexts (or the SketchPad),
- by adding them to the appropriate table, or
- by adding them to the object list in the **Objects** menu option.

In all cases, the **Properties Dialogue Box** for the component will be presented for filling in. This may be accessed again at any time, once again through the diagrams, through the tables or through the objects menu, for subsequent editing and completion.

EXTERNAL OBJECTS

External objects represent external bodies or organizations with whom the project and system have to deal. They are regarded as 'black boxes' by the project, with no recognition of their internal structure or methods.

External objects have the basic properties of all components, and in addition a *linkage status* which explains the relationship of the Entity to the system. The status may be:

- No link (there is no interaction between the system and the entity)
- Link directly to system (some linkage exists, but no known messages are passed; this is a very unlikely case)
- Message TO the system (the entity initiates the exchange of a message pair)
- Message FROM the system (the system initiates the exchange of a message pair)

This linkage status is selected by radio buttons in the properties dialogue box (Figure B.6).

ACTORS

Actors represent *users* adopting *roles*. On-screen, they are represented by the twin masks of ancient Greek tragedy and comedy.

They have the basic properties of all components and, in addition, the fields *User* and *Role* (Figure B.7).

MESSAGES

Messages transfer information between External objects and the System, or External objects and Actors. All messages are effectively message pairs, with an information context

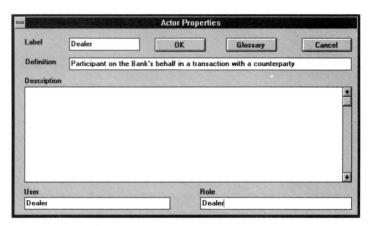

Figure B.7 Actor Properties Dialogue.

and an expected return value (which may be void). They are quite complex components with, in addition to the default properties shared by all objects, the following properties:

- Source (the Source of the message)
- Target (the Target of the message)
- Trigger (the Event or Task that triggered the outbound message)
- Goal (the objective of sending the message)
- Task (the task associated with achieving the goal of the message)
- Information Context (the information borne by the message)
- Return Value (the information context borne by the return message)

When a message is created, the associated task will also be created (after confirmation) if it does not already exist.

Note that there are in fact two variants of the message properties, depending on the context. In the overall External Context, only the basic properties are captured. It is in the more detailed Internal Context that the full details concerning the associated task are captured (Figure B.8).

Access to the Associated Task properties dialogue can be gained through the **Task** button in the Message Properties dialogue, or through all the other ways available for accessing task properties – the object list, the table and the diagrams.

TASKS

Tasks have a properties dialogue for capturing their basic common properties of Label, Definition and Description (Figure B.9), and in addition a **Task Card** which contains the full information regarding the task's internal structure and relationships. This Task Card is dealt with later.

CLASSES

Like Tasks, **Classes** (or **Business Objects** – the terms are synonymous in *SOMATiK*) obtain their properties at two levels: basic properties through the Properties Dialogue, and full details of the internal structure and relationships through the **Class Card**. **Class Cards** are dealt with later.

Class objects do not appear in the context diagrams. Thus they are created either through the **Objects** menu option, or through the **Class Table** option.

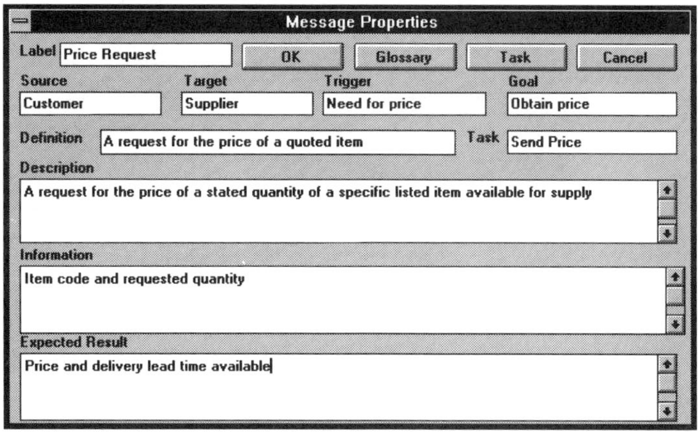

Figure B.8 Message Properties Dialogue (Internal Context View).

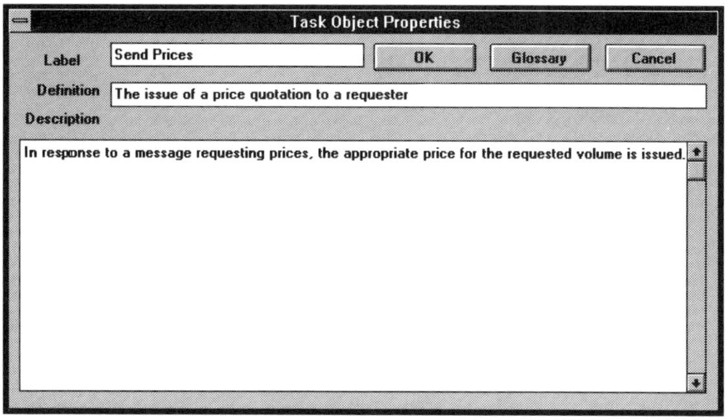

Figure B.9 Task Properties Dialogue.

In addition to the common properties, the class components are nominated as having a **Nature** which may be:

■ Abstract
■ Concrete

and a **Type** which may be:

■ Domain
■ Application
■ Interface

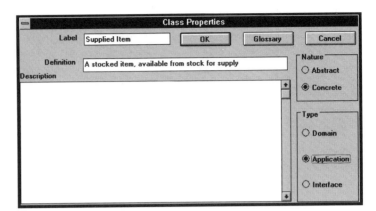

Figure B.10 Class Properties Dialogue.

These properties are selected with radio buttons. The Class Properties Dialogue is shown in Figure B.10.

B.2.4 Using the External Context

THE EXTERNAL CONTEXT TOOLBOX

In the External Context view, the following ToolBox is presented. Only two tools are available – the **Pointer Tool** and the **Entity Tool**. Use the **Entity Tool** to deposit new external objects in the context diagram by:

- selecting the tool,
- pointing with the mouse at the desired location,
- clicking with the left mouse button.

Use the **Pointer Tool** to move an existing entity by:

- selecting the tool,
- pointing with the mouse,
- pressing and dragging with the left mouse button.

CREATING AN EXTERNAL OBJECT

On selecting the Entity Tool, pointing and left-clicking with the mouse, a combo box pop-up shows the current list of known external objects, to which a new entity may be added. The Entity symbol is then deposited on-screen.

Entity names must be unique across the project (as must all component names be). Multiple copies of the same entity may be deposited in the Context Diagrams in the rare cases where this is an appropriate thing to do.

Right click to generate the Options Pop-up Menu

Having deposited an External Object in the diagram, its properties are accessed by pointing and *right-clicking* with the mouse. A pop-up menu offers the options

- Properties
- Delete

which are selected with the right button. Click elsewhere in the screen to dispose of the menu.

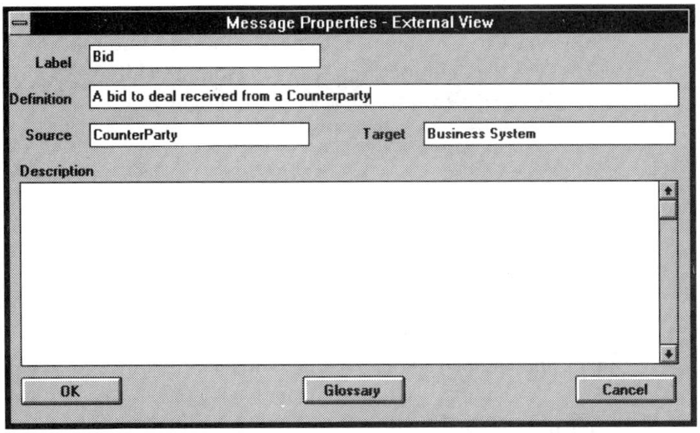

```
╔══════════════════════════════════════════════════════════╗
║  ▭         Message Properties - External View             ║
╟──────────────────────────────────────────────────────────╢
║   Label    │ Bid                        │                 ║
║                                                           ║
║ Definition │ A bid to deal received from a Counterparty │ ║
║                                                           ║
║  Source    │ CounterParty       │   Target │ Business System │ ║
║                                                           ║
║ Description                                               ║
║ ┌────────────────────────────────────────────────────┐ ▲ ║
║ │                                                    │   ║
║ │                                                    │   ║
║ │                                                    │   ║
║ │                                                    │   ║
║ │                                                    │   ║
║ │                                                    │ ▼ ║
║ └────────────────────────────────────────────────────┘   ║
║   ┌──────────┐        ┌──────────┐        ┌──────────┐    ║
║   │    OK    │        │ Glossary │        │  Cancel  │    ║
║   └──────────┘        └──────────┘        └──────────┘    ║
╚══════════════════════════════════════════════════════════╝
```

Figure B.11 Message Properties – External Context.

DELETING AN EXTERNAL OBJECT

Select **Delete** from the pop-up menu. Note that an entity (or any other component) cannot be deleted if there are active links with other components of the system in place. Remove these links first, after which deletion can take place.

MESSAGES IN THE EXTERNAL CONTEXT

If a new Entity is nominated as exchanging messages with the system, a **Message** icon will be deposited on-screen, with linkage lines in the appropriate direction between itself, the Entity and the Project Symbol.

The External Context **Message Properties Dialogue** will be displayed (Figure B.11), for entry of the message label, definition and description. The Source and Target of the message are of course already known to the system, and are displayed in the dialogue.

Subsequently, you can *right-click* on the message symbol to bring up the options pop-up menu, and select **Properties** from the menu to fill in or edit the basic description of the message. Further message properties will be added in the Internal Context.

Messages may be moved by selecting the **Pointer Tool**, pointing and *left-clicking* with the mouse, and dragging and dropping to the new location. The linkage lines will be moved as needed.

B.2.5 Using the Glossary

All properties boxes display the **Glossary** button, as a short cut for copying item definitions to the glossary. (Note that the glossary can be accessed at any time from the menus and the ToolBar, as well as the dialogue boxes.)

When, for example, an Entity Name should appear in the Glossary, proceed as follows:

(1) Mark the Label field with the mouse, or the **Shift** key and arrow keys.
(2) Type **Ctrl + C** to copy to the Clipboard.
(3) Click on the **Glossary** button; the Glossary dialogue will appear.
(4) Check that the definition does not already exist in either the *Repository* or *Project* glossaries, and if not:

(5) Click in the edit field at the top of the combo box.

(6) Type **Ctrl + V** to paste from the clipboard into the label field.

(7) Type the definition into the description field.

(8) Exit and return to the previous dialogue box.

B.2.6 Using the Internal Context

In the Internal Context, a larger range of drawing tools is available (Figure B.12). In addition to the Pointer and External Object tools which were available in the External Context, there are tools for depositing **Messages** and **Actors** in the drawing. There is also a **Link and Unlink** tool for creating and deleting links between these items.

MOVING FROM EXTERNAL TO INTERNAL CONTEXTS

Typically, external objects and messages will have been created in the External Context. On moving to the Internal Context, the presentation alters (Figure B.13). The linkage lines from messages to the project symbol which appeared in the External Context do not now appear, and the message icon has a red question mark on it.

The question mark appears because the message is not properly linked. A new linkage line must be created. This is because typically at the Internal Context level, an **Actor** will be invoked to be in receipt of the message.

Deposit an **Actor** on-screen by selecting the **Actor Tool** from the **ToolBox**, and left-clicking in the desired location. The familiar combo-box pop-up will appear, allowing you to select an existing actor or create a new one. Optionally now fill in the rest of the actor properties, and then select the **Link Tool**.

(1) Click first on the message. It will be outlined with a focus rectangle.

(2) Click now on the Actor. A link line from the message will be added.

(3) Typically, click again on the Actor. It will be outlined with a focus rectangle.

(4) Click now on the System Symbol. A link from the Actor to the System will be created.

The red question mark will disappear from the message icon.

EXPANDING THE MESSAGE PROPERTIES

Right-click on the Message Icon to display the **Options Pop-up Menu**. Select **Properties**, and the Internal Context Properties Dialogue discussed earlier will be displayed. This contains fuller details on the nature of the message, including its **Associated Task**.

Once this Task exists, the **Task** option will appear in the **Options Pop-up Menu**. This may be selected to view the Task Properties.

Figure B.12 The Internal Context ToolBox.

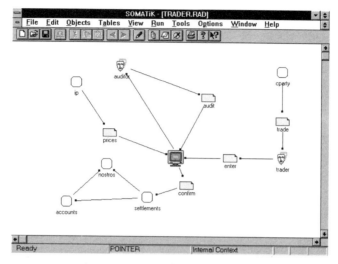

Figure B.13 Sample Internal Context.

B.2.7   Using the Task Cards

Each task in the system has a *Task Card* that shows all the internal structure of a task, as well as the standard *Properties Dialogue* which contains its standard fields common to all project entities.

A **Task Card** displays the following information about a task (Figure B.14):

- Name
- Definition
- Supertasks
- Component tasks
- Associated tasks
- Exception handling tasks
- Rulesets

Only the names of the various related tasks are shown. The task card can then be used to browse into further data on all of these items.

ACCESSING THE TASK CARD

The task card can be accessed:

- from the Internal Context diagram, by pointing and *right-clicking* on a message symbol. If the message has an *associated task* the task card for that task will be made available through the pop-up menu;
- from the **Objects** menu option, selecting the **Task Objects** option, and then selecting a task from the list offered.

ACCESSING TASK PROPERTIES

Point at the *task name* and left-click with the mouse. The **Task Properties Menu** will be shown. This allows access to all the various **Task Trees** to be discussed later and, as the first option in the menu, the **Properties** dialogue.

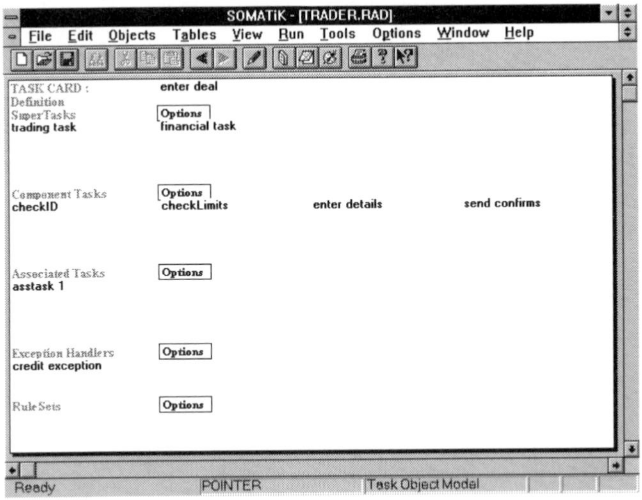

Figure B.14 Example Task Card (old version).

<table>
<tr><td>**ACCESSING**
RELATED TASKS</td><td>*Use **Back** and **Forward**
to switch quickly
between task cards*</td><td>Point at the selected task name and left-click with the mouse. Focus will switch to the task card for the selected task.</td></tr>
</table>

EDITING THE
TASK CARD

Point at the **Options** box associated with one of *Supertasks*, *Component Tasks*, *Associated Tasks* or *Exception Handlers*. Left-click with the mouse to bring up the **Task Options Dialogue** (Figure B.15).

The dialogue box title describes which subsection of the task card is being edited. In this example it is the *Component Tasks*. To the left of the dialogue box lies a combo box showing all the current tasks in the project. To its right lies a list box showing the tasks currently included in this section of the task card.

ADDING NEW
TASKS

Add to the list of tasks in the current subsection of the selected task by selecting with the mouse or arrow keys from the combo box list, and pressing the **Add** button. The selected element will be copied across to the list box showing the tasks included in this subsection of the task card. New tasks may be typed into the combo box, and after confirmation, the new task objects will be created, as well as being added to the current task card.

CONSISTENCY
CHECKING

Extensive consistency checking is carried out to maintain the integrity of the project task structures

When an existing task is selected for inclusion into the task card, an exhaustive check is carried out to ensure that this is a legal and sensible task to include at this point in the structure. For example, if task X has task Y as a Supertask, then it makes no sense also to include Task Y as a Component Task of task X. Other more complex but equally invalid relations will be detected; for example, the selected task may already be a component through inheritance, although this will not be obvious from an examination of the single task card for task X.

It might be thought that it would be easier and better to exclude from the list of candidate tasks all those tasks that may not be included in the selected location in the structure. To the designers, it seems that this is one of those cases where it is preferable to allow the user to attempt to include an invalid task, and then to explain why the task is invalid in this location. The fact that the user selected the invalid task may indicate that the user has started to 'lose the picture' of what tasks have already been created, and their relationships to each other, and that therefore it is beneficial to have this potential problem highlighted.

REMOVING AND SEQUENCING TASKS
Select the task in the list box. Then press the **Remove** button, and the task will be removed from the list. Note that this does not imply *deletion* of the task. It is still in the project, and can be added back to the current task card or a different one in the normal way.

A group of component tasks, associated tasks and so on form a set, and there is no ordering requirement imposed upon them. Having said this, the task card will often be more readable and meaningful if subtasks are displayed in a useful sequence. To alter the sequence, select a task from the list box and use the **Move Up** and **Move Down** buttons to move it to the desired location.

EXAMINING TASK PROPERTIES
Select a task from the list and press the **Select** button. The task properties dialogue will be displayed for examination and editing. Note that the *Task Card* for a task is accessed by clicking on the task name in the current task card.

ADDING RULESETS
A **RuleSet** is added in the same way as a task, by pointing at the **Options** box next to the *RuleSet* section header, left-clicking to bring up the menu, and selecting the **Add** option.

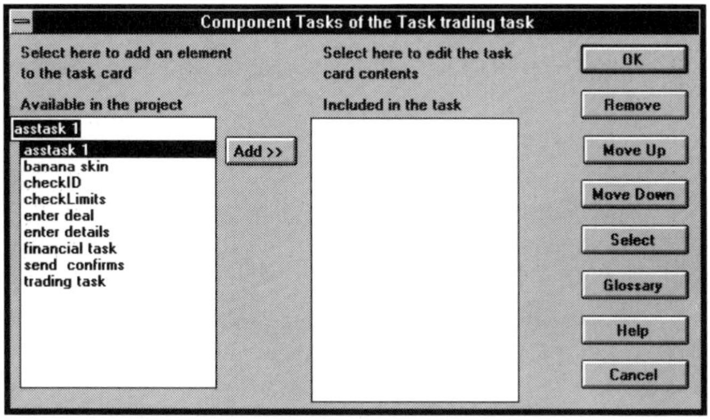

Figure B.15 The Task Options Dialogue.

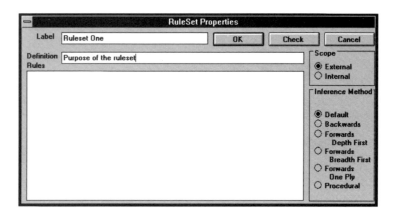

Figure B.16 RuleSet Properties Dialogue.

When selecting a ruleset, the **RuleSet Properties Dialogue** is opened (Figure B.16). The **RuleSet Properties dialogue** allows entry of the ruleset name and definition, and the body of the ruleset. At this phase of *SOMATiK* development, this body of rules is treated as pure text. Subsequent releases of *SOMATiK* will feature a rule compiler, which will allow rules entered in the ruleset to be parsed and executed.

In the supplied version, the radio button options have no effect, but their purpose is discussed here for completeness.

SCOPE
The Scope selection determines whether the ruleset is External or Internal. External rulesets determine the external behaviour of the task owning the ruleset. Rules expressed here typically govern the inheritance properties of the task: how to handle collision detection and disambiguation from multiple parents, whether inheritance overrides or adds to the primary list and so on.

Internal rulesets govern the internal behaviour of the task – they describe what the task does and how it is carried out.

INFERENCE METHOD
The **Inference Method** under which the ruleset can be executed is selected from:

- Default
- Backwards
- Forwards – depth first
- Forwards – breadth first
- Forwards – single ply
- Procedural

The default inference method is backwards chaining with 'opportunistic forwards chaining' (breadth first, unlimited depth).

A full discussion of inference methods is beyond the scope of this book. The interested reader is referred to Chapter 5 and to the references in the bibliography.

B.2.8 Switching Views – Edit Back and Edit Forward

As you change from one view to another, including **Tables**, **Task Cards**, **Class Cards** and **Sketches** as well as **Views**, a history is maintained of your progress. As a short-cut method of revisiting a previous view, select either **Edit Back** from the menu, or the **Back** button from the ToolBar. These options are enabled once you move from the initial view, and each time you select the option you retrace one step of the history until you reach the initial view, when the **Back** option is disabled.

As you retrace your steps, the retraced views are available through the **Edit Forward** menu selection and **Forward** ToolBar button, which are enabled once you have retraced your first step. Thus you can picture a sequence of views as being a tape, with a cursor that allows you to step back or forward through the sequence.

Edit Back can be selected by:

- using the **Edit Back** menu option
- using the **ToolBar Edit Back** button
- pressing **Ctrl + B**, which is an accelerator

Back |
Forward |

Edit Forward can be selected by:

- using the **Edit Forward** menu option
- using the **ToolBar Edit Forward** button
- pressing **Ctrl + F**, which is an accelerator

B.2.9   Using the Task Trees

To access a **Task Tree** either:

- click on the task name with the right mouse button while viewing the **Task Card** and select from the pop-up menu; or
- select a task from the **Objects Task Objects** menu selection to move to that task's **Task Card**.

In each of these cases, the task tree pop-up menu will be displayed. The pop-up menu offers:

- Properties
- Task Card
- Classification – AKindOf
- Composition – APartOf
- Association
- Exception
- Delete
- Remove

AKindOf shows the *Classification* structure for the task. It shows the *Supertasks* of the task, and for each of these, their supertasks, and so on. This is termed an *explicit*

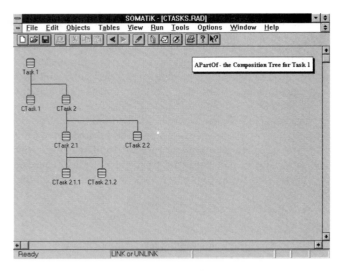

Figure B.17 Has as APartOf – the Component Tree.

tree since the supertasks are explicitly shown in the task card, and the tree can be explicitly followed from task card to task card. It also shows the *implicit* or *inverse* Classification Tree for this task. It shows those tasks that, in their task card, show the current task as a supertask; and for each of these tasks, further tasks that show each of them as a supertask in their task card – and so on. It is termed an *implicit* tree since it cannot be followed easily from task card to task card manually, requiring an exhaustive search of all the task cards in the project.

The other trees are grouped into similar explicit and implicit pairs. Thus **APartOf** shows the explicit *Composition Tree* for a task, and the corresponding implicit tree.

Association gives the explicit *Association Tree* and the implicit tree.

Exception gives the explicit and implicit *Exception Usage Trees*.

STRUCTURE OF A TASK TREE

The selected tree is drawn growing from the *Root Node* through as many generations of descendants as there may be. An example of a typical tree is shown in Figure B.17. Here the root task is *Task 1*. On its task card are shown *CTask 1* and *CTask 2* in the Component Tasks section, and these appear as the first *ply* of the tree. The tree shows that *CTask 2* has further components *CTask 2.1* and *CTask 2.2*, and that *CTask 2.1* has component tasks *CTask 2.1.1* and *CTask 2.1.2*.

BROWSING THE TASK TREE

Pointing at any node of the tree and pressing the left mouse button pops up the **Task Menu** which was discussed above. Thus it is simple to move from any task to any related task through the tree diagrams, examining the task cards, general properties or task trees at will.

Back and Forward allow you to scroll through a list of views, trees, cards and tables

This facility of browsing is made more powerful in conjunction with the **Back** and **Forward** feature discussed in the previous section.

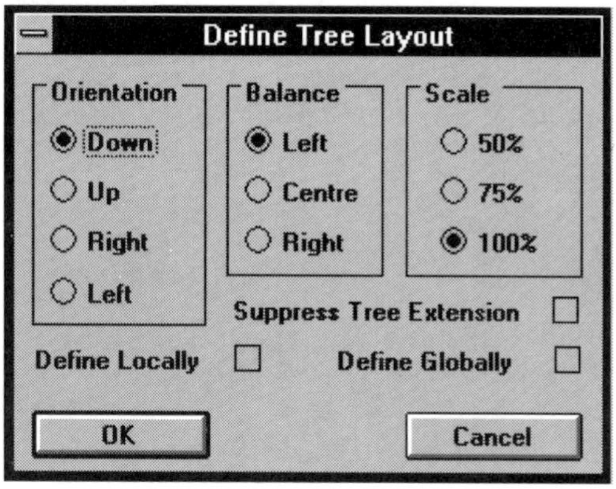

Figure B.18 Tree Layout Dialogue.

<table>
<tr><td>**MODIFYING A**
TASK TREE</td><td>To modify the presentation of Task Trees to suit your individual taste, select the **Options Tree Layout** menu selection. The **Tree Layout** dialogue shown in Figure B.18 will be presented. This contains three groups of radio buttons:</td></tr>
</table>

- Orientation
- Balance
- Scale

Orientation determines whether the tree grows *Down* from the top of the screen, *Up* from the bottom of the screen, *Right* from the left of the screen or *Left* from the right of the screen. There is no logical significance in the orientation, just a matter of taste. This feature is disabled in this version of *SOMATiK*.

Similarly the **Balance** selection determines whether the superior node is placed above its *left*most descendant, its *right*most descendant or *centred* over its descendants. Again, there is no logical discrimination amongst these choices.

Finally, **Scale** allows larger trees to be reduced in size to fit more data onto a screen without scrolling.

Check boxes allow the nomination of **Define Locally** and **Define Globally**. By default, tree layout selections apply only to the current tree in view. Selecting **Define Locally** makes the selections the new default for trees in the current RAD. Selecting **Define Globally** makes the selections the new default for *SOMATiK* itself.

<table>
<tr><td>**EXTENDED**
TREES</td><td>*Parentheses show that*
a task is inherited</td><td>If a given task has supertasks, then the Components, Associated Tasks, Exception Handler Tasks and Rulesets of these supertasks are inherited by the initial task. By default, these inherited tasks are displayed in the appropriate task tree, with their labels enclosed in parentheses.</td></tr>
</table>

These inherited tasks can be selectively viewed in the tree diagram. The Tree Layout Dialogue has a final check box labelled **Suppress Tree Extension**. If this is checked, then

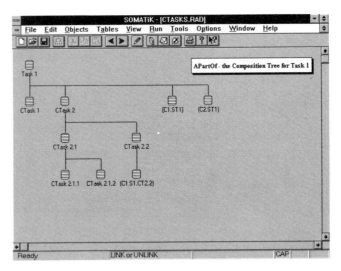

Figure B.19 An extended tree.

inherited tasks' components are not displayed in the tree diagrams. By default, inherited tasks are displayed.

The diagram in Figure B.19 shows the same tree as the first tree example in Figure B.17, but this time including the inherited components. *Task 1* is *AKindOf* task *S1*. (This would be apparent from an examination of the task card for *Task 1*.) The task *S1* has as components *C1.ST1* and *C2.ST1*, which can be checked by an examination of the task card for *S1*. These inherited components are shown as direct descendants of task *Task 1* when we draw the *APartOf* tree.

Likewise, the task *CTask 2.2* is *AKindOf* task *S1.CT2.2* and this task has a component task *C1.S1.CT2.2*. This inherited task therefore features in the tree as an immediate descendant of task *CTask 2.2*.

Note that inherited elements are distinguished by placing their labels in parentheses. Good practice suggests therefore that task names themselves should not be created with parentheses!

An alternative view of this task set is shown in the **Task Table** which is described in Section B.2.12.

B.2.10 Using the Class Cards

Each task in the system has a *Class Card* which shows all the internal structure of a task, as well as the standard *Properties Dialogue* which contains its standard fields common to all project entities.

A **Class Card** displays the following information about a class:

- Name
- Definition

- Superclasses
- Component classes (Parts)
- Attributes and associations of the class
- Operations of the class
- Rulesets

Only the names of the various related classes are shown. The class card can then be used to browse into further data on all of these items. An example class card is shown in Figure B.20.

The class card can be accessed from the **Objects** menu option, selecting the **Business Objects** option, and then selecting a class from the list offered.

ACCESSING CLASS PROPERTIES

Point at the *class name* and left-click with the mouse. The **Class Properties Menu** will be shown. This allows access to all the various **Class Trees** to be discussed later and, as the first option in the menu, the **Properties** dialogue.

ACCESSING RELATED CLASSES

*Use **Back** and **Forward** to switch quickly between class cards*

Point at the selected class name and left-click with the mouse. Focus will switch to the class card for the selected class.

EDITING THE CLASS CARD

Point at the **Options** box associated with each of *SuperClasses* or *Component Classes*. Left-click with the mouse to bring up the **Class Options Dialogue** (Figure B.21). The dialogue box title describes which subsection of the class card is being edited. In the example, it is the *Components* or *Parts* of the class. To the left of the dialogue box lies a combo box showing all the current classes in the project. To its right lies a list box showing the classes currently included in this section of the class card.

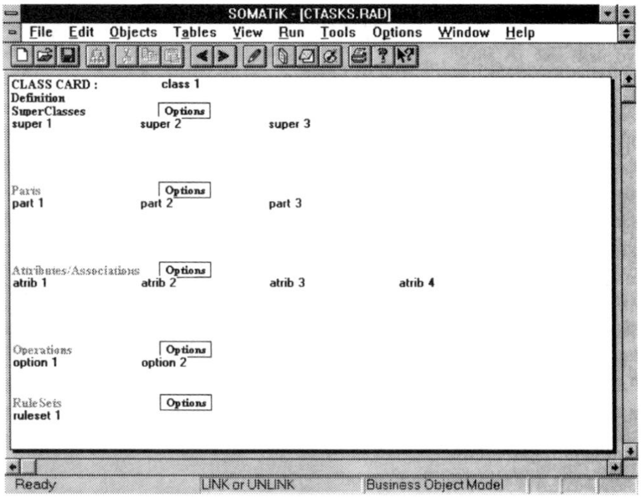

Figure B.20 Example Class Card (old version).

ADDING RELATED CLASSES

Add to the list of classes in the current subsection of the selected class by selecting with the mouse or arrow keys from the combo box list, and pressing the **Add** button. The selected element will be copied across to the list box showing the classes included in this subsection of the class card. New classes may be typed into the combo box, and after confirmation, the new class objects will be created, as well as being added to the current class card.

CONSISTENCY CHECKING

When an existing class is selected for inclusion into the class card, an exhaustive check is carried out to ensure that this is a legal and sensible class to include at this point in the structure. For example, if class X has class Y as a superclass, then it makes no sense to include Class Y as a Component Class of class X. Other more complex but equally invalid relations will be detected; for example, the selected class may already be a component through inheritance, although this will not be obvious from an examination of the single class card for class X.

It might be thought that it would be easier and better to exclude from the list of candidate classes all those classes that may not be included in the selected location in the structure. To the designers, it seems that this is one of those cases where it is preferable to allow the user to attempt to include an invalid class, and then to explain why the class is invalid in this location. The fact that the user selected the invalid class may indicate that the user has started to 'lose the picture' of what classes have already been created, and their relationships, and that therefore it is beneficial to have this potential problem highlighted.

REMOVING CLASSES

Select the class in the list box. The press the **Remove** button, and the class will be removed from the list. Note that this does not imply *deletion* of the class. It is still in the project, and can be added back to the current class card or a different one in the normal way.

SEQUENCING CLASSES

A group of component classes, associated classes and so on form a set, and there is no ordering requirement imposed upon them. Having said this, the class card will often be more readable and meaningful if subclasses are displayed in a useful sequence. To alter the sequence, select a class from the list box and use the **Move Up** and **Move Down** buttons to move it to the desired location.

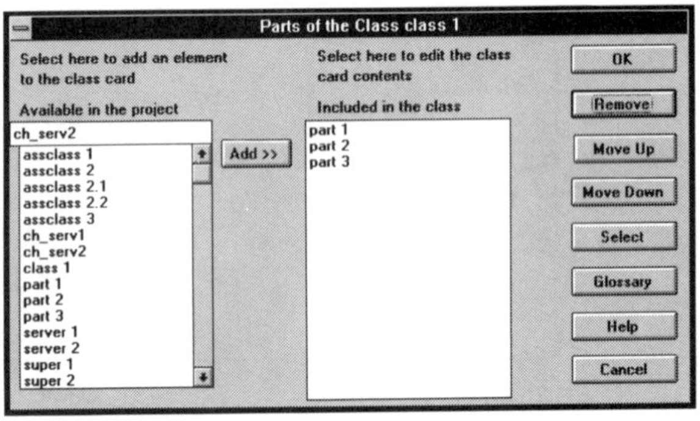

Figure B.21 The Class Options Dialogue.

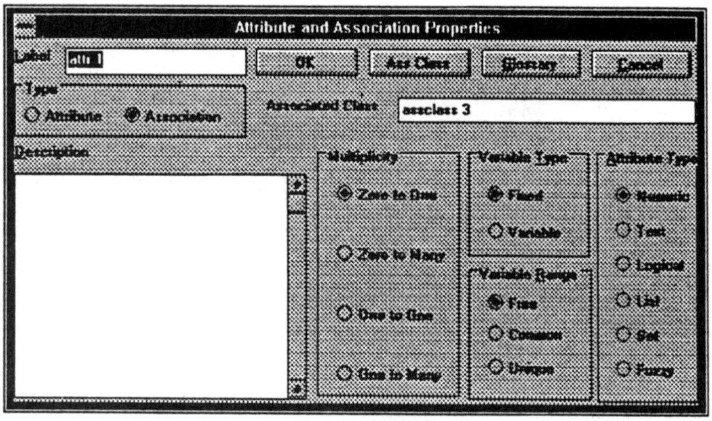

Figure B.22 Attributes Properties Dialogue.

EXAMINING
CLASS
PROPERTIES

Select a class from the list and press the **Select** button. The class properties dialogue will be displayed for examination and editing. Note that the *Class Card* for a class is accessed by clicking on the class name in the current class card.

ADDING
ATTRIBUTES
AND
ASSOCIATIONS

Attributes and associations are added in the same way as classes, by clicking on the **Options** box next to the *Attributes/Associations* header. The normal **Options** dialogue box is presented, this time showing all the *Attributes* in the project and in the class card. These can be added, removed and sequenced in the normal way.

However, an *Attribute* is not a class, and using the **Select** option brings up the **Attribute Properties Box** shown in Figure B.22. The key control in this dialogue is the radio button group below the *Label* field named *Type*. This determines whether the element is an **Attribute**, in which case it has its own static properties described below, or an **Association** in which case it has an *associated class* and a *multiplicity*. An element during its lifetime may change status from an attribute to an association or back as its definition develops.

For **Associations**, the *associated class* must be nominated using the **Ass Class** button to obtain the standard class selection dialogue box, through which new classes may be defined. Its **Multiplicity** of association should also be defined using the *Multiplicity* radio button group.

For **Attributes**, the *Variable Type*, *Variable Range* and *Attribute Type* parameters should be set using the appropriate radio group buttons.

Note that when **Associations** have been defined, the name of the *Association* will appear in the class card; but the name of the *Associated Class* will be used in the **Association Tree** diagram described below.

If the user wishes, the name of the association may be defined to carry the information. Thus if we had a class card for a class *employee*, we might define an association *WorksIn* which would associate the class *Department*, where an employee works in exactly one department. In the dialogue, this would be defined by setting the Type as Association, and Associated Class as Department, and the Multiplicity as One-to-One. If desired, the name of the association could be changed to *WorksIn(Department,1,1)* to indicate this directly in the class card.

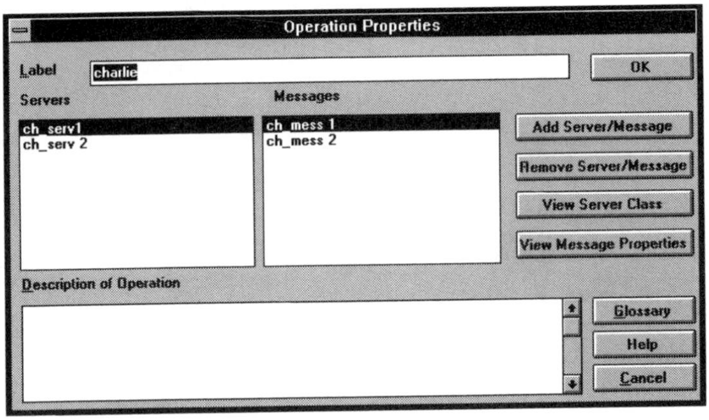

Figure B.23 Operations Dialogue Box.

ADDING OPERATIONS

Operations are added in the same way as classes, by clicking on the **Options** box next to the *Operations* header. The normal **Options** dialogue box is presented, this time showing all the *Operations* in the project and in the class card. These can be added, removed and sequenced in the normal way.

However, an *Operation* is not a class, and so using the **Select** option brings up the **Operations Properties Box** shown in Figure B.23.

An **Operation** executes by sending a *message* to a named *server*. The message is a standard *SOMATiK* message, and the server is a standard *SOMATiK* class object. An operation may be defined as sending a number of messages to a number of servers.

Thus, the dialogue box offers two linked list boxes, showing the list of servers employed by this operation, and for each server the name of the message to be sent.

A new server/message pair is added to the operation by selecting the **Add Server/Message** button. A standard class selection dialogue is then offered, allowing the selection of an existing (or the creation of a new) class to act as server. Immediately, a message selection box is offered to allow the specification of the corresponding message. The new server/message pair is added to the list boxes.

Server/message pairs can be removed from the list boxes by selecting a server and pressing the **Remove Server/Message** button. Note that removal does not imply deletion; the server and message still exist independently in the project.

Properties of the servers and messages may be examined by selecting a server or message as needed in the list boxes, and selecting the **View Server** or **View Message Properties** buttons, as appropriate.

Note that in the class card, the names of the operations are shown. However, in the **Usage Tree Diagram** discussed below, it is the names of the server classes which will appear.

ADDING RULESETS

A **RuleSet** is added in the same way as a class, by pointing at the **Options** box next to the *RuleSet* section header, left-clicking to bring up the option dialogue, and selecting the **Add** option. When selecting a ruleset, the **RuleSet Properties Dialogue** is opened (Figure B.24).

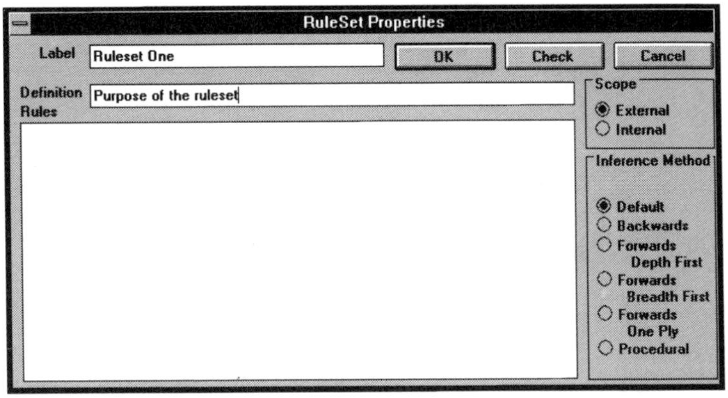

Figure B.24 RuleSet Properties Dialogue.

The **RuleSet Properties** dialogue allows entry of the ruleset name and definition, and the body of the ruleset. At this phase of *SOMATiK* development, this body of rules is treated as pure text. Subsequent releases of *SOMATiK* will feature a rule compiler, which will allow rules entered in the ruleset to be parsed and executed.

Currently, the radio button options have no effect, but their purpose is discussed here for completeness.

SCOPE

The **Scope** selection determines whether the ruleset is **External** or **Internal**. External rule-sets determine the external behaviour of the class owning the ruleset. Rules expressed here typically govern the inheritance properties of the class: how to handle collision detection and disambiguation from multiple parents, whether inheritance overrides or adds to the primary list and so on. Internal rulesets govern the internal behaviour of the class – they describe what the class does and how it is carried out.

INFERENCE METHOD

The **Inference Method** under which the ruleset can be executed is selected from:

- Default
- Backwards
- Forwards – depth first
- Forwards – breadth first
- Forwards – single ply
- Procedural

The default inference method is backwards chaining with 'opportunistic forwards chaining' (breadth first, unlimited depth).

B.2.11 Using the Class Trees

Class trees are made available by *left-clicking* on the name of the class, found at the top of the class card. This displays the pop-up menu shown in Figure B.25, which offers the options:

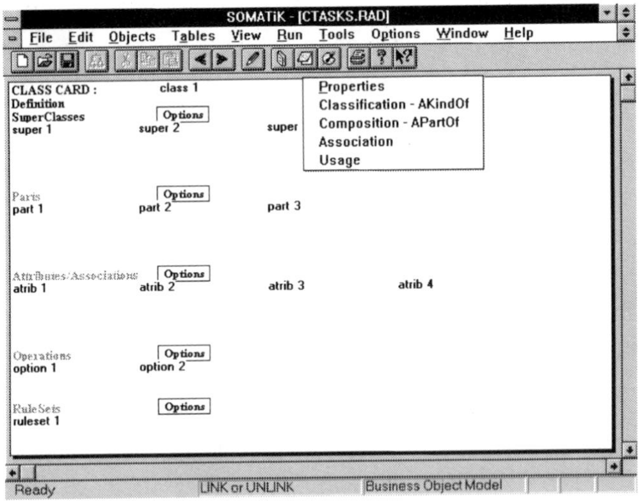

Figure B.25 Accessing class trees (old version).

- Properties
- Classification – AKindOf
- Composition – APartOf
- Association
- Usage

The **Properties** option simply displays the standard properties dialogue box for the current task. The other options lead to trees.

AKindOf shows the *Classification* and *Inverse Classification* structures – that is to say, the *SuperClasses* and the classes for which the current class is a *SuperClass* respectively.

APartOf shows the *Composition* and *Inverse Composition* structures – the classes that are *Components* and which have the current class as a *Component* respectively.

Association shows the *associated classes* of the current class – that is, the associated classes of the associations shown on the class card.

Usage shows the *server classes* of the current class – those classes which are employed as servers by the *Operations* of the class.

In all cases, the trees are extended to show the components of the components and so on.

In the example shown in Figure B.26, the class ZZ has five direct component classes and one of these classes has a further two components.

BROWSING THE TREE STRUCTURES

Pointing at an element in the tree and *left-clicking* with the mouse will display the pop-up menu shown in Figure B.27. This allows display of any of the trees propagated by the selected element, and in addition the ability to switch to its class card, or view its properties.

Use of the pop-up menu, particularly in conjunction with the **Edit Back** and **Edit Forward** facility, supports a convenient way of browsing through the structures.

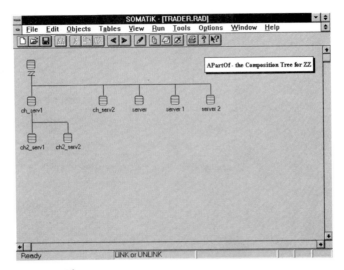

Figure B.26 A sample Composition structure.

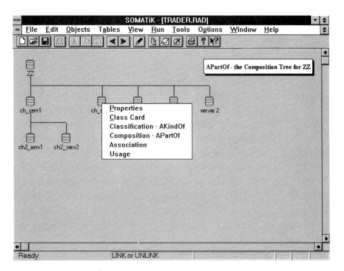

Figure B.27 Browsing structures.

B.2.12 Using the Table View

All elements of the system can be viewed in a tabular format. View the tables by selecting the **Tables** main menu option, and the appropriate table type from the list displayed.

All the system tables function in the same generic way. A list of all system elements of the selected type is displayed in spreadsheet format. A cell pointer, initially in

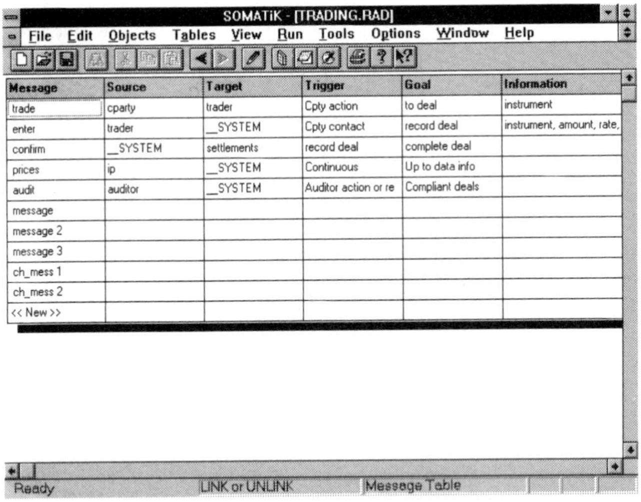

Figure B.28 Example Message Table. The other tables are of similar appearance.

row 1 column 1, can be moved using the cursor keys, or you can select a new cell using the mouse and left-clicking.

Left double-clicking or right single-clicking on the current cell opens up the element properties dialogue to present full details on the element.

Use scrolling in the normal way to view the parts of the table not shown on screen. The last row of the table contains the keyword <<*New*>> as an element name. Click on this row to add a new element of the current type to the project.

The **Message Table** displays all current messages in the project (Figure B.28).

The **Entity Table** displays all current external objects in the project.

The **Actor Table** displays all current actors in the project.

The **Task Table** presents the current complete list of tasks, ordered in the sequence of their creation. The *Name*, *Definition* and *Description* fields are displayed. Left double-click or right single-click on any row to bring up the Task Card associated with this task. From the task card, you can move to the general properties of the task, or any of its task trees, in the normal way. As always in table mode, the last row of the table supports the definition of new tasks.

The **Class Table** displays all the Business Class Objects in the project.

The **RuleSet Table** displays all the rulesets in the project.

The **Attribute Table** displays all the attributes in the project.

The **Operations Table** displays all the operations in the project.

B.2.13 Using the Glossary facility

The **Glossary** facility can be accessed from the **Tools Glossary** menu selection; or from the **Glossary** icon in the **ToolBar**; or through the **Glossary** button that appears in (nearly) all *SOMATiK* dialogue boxes.

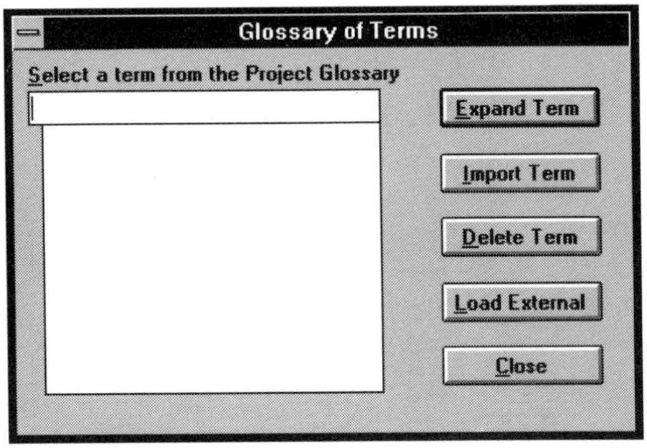

Figure B.29 Project Glossary Selection.

The Repository Glossary can also be accessed from the Browser

Two glossaries are available: the *Repository* glossary and the *Project* glossary. Items in the global repository glossary may not be edited or deleted, but may be copied into the local project glossary. It is the project glossary which is saved to the RAD file, and which appears in the printed report.

On selecting the glossary, the Project Glossary Selection dialogue is displayed (Figure B.29). The dialogue box contains a combo box and the following buttons:

■ Expand Term
■ Import Term
■ Close
■ Delete Term

The combo box presents a scrolling list of the items defined so far in the project glossary. Selection of a term is accomplished by double-clicking with the left button of the mouse or by using the arrow keys to scroll vertically through the list and the **Return** key to select an item. A new item may be typed directly into the edit box at the top of the combo box, or copied in off the clipboard using **Ctrl + V**.

The expansion and definition of a term may be inspected and amended via the Expansion dialogue box, which is displayed automatically when a term is selected in the manner just described, or when the Expand Term button is pressed. The expansion of the term can be entered and modified using the scrolling text box (Figure B.30).

The **Import** button refers to the ability to import a term from the *Repository Glossary*. *SOMATiK* must have the Repository loaded before this can be used. If the Import button is pressed without the Repository being loaded, a message box to this effect is displayed.

The **Close** button terminates the Glossary dialogue box.

The **Delete Term** button deletes the currently selected term from the combo box, after asking for confirmation.

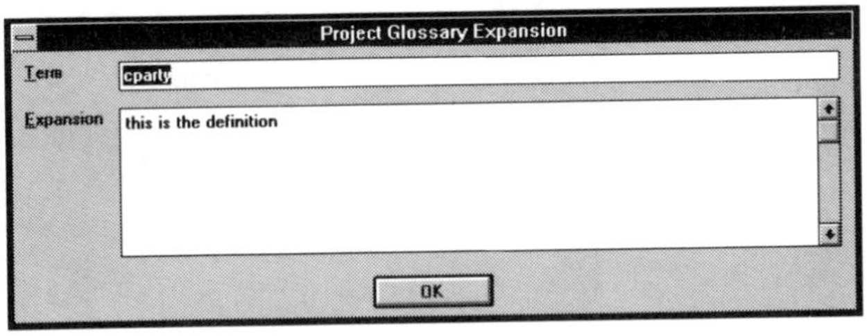

Figure B.30 Glossary Expansion Dialogue.

ADDING A TERM TO THE GLOSSARY

If *SOMATiK* has a Repository loaded, then the Repository glossary will be searched automatically whenever a term is added to the Project glossary. If the term is found in the Repository Glossary, a message box is displayed to inform the user and provide an opportunity to inspect the term and its associated expansion in the Repository and, if wished, to import them back into the project. Note that searching the Repository glossary is case-sensitive, so that 'counterparty' and 'CounterParty' are not the same thing. The user is not informed if the automatic search of the Repository glossary failed to find a matching term.

IMPORTING A TERM FROM THE REPOSITORY

Importing a term from the Repository Glossary is achieved by pressing the **Import Term** button on the Project Glossary dialogue box. If the Repository is loaded, this will result in the display of an identical dialogue box listing the terms contained in the Repository Glossary. Selection of a term in the Repository Glossary is achieved in the same way as before. The term and its expansion may be viewed by pressing the **Expand Term** button. Note that the term and its expansion are read-only. The term and its expansion may be imported back into the Project Glossary by pressing the **Import** button on the Repository Glossary dialogue box.

Updating the Repository Glossary is described in the Repository section.

B.2.14 Using the Repository Browser

AN OVERVIEW

The Repository is the name given to a collection of items defined during RAD workshops and subsequently archived, perhaps after modification. The Repository therefore grows in size over time. All types of item defined in *SOMATiK* can be stored in the Repository (External Objects, Actors, Messages, Tasks (including their associated RuleSets) and Business Objects (together with their associated Attributes, Operations and RuleSets). The Repository also has its own glossary of terms which can be imported back into projects.

Items stored in the Repository cannot be modified (although they can be imported into a Project and the imported version modified as required). Adding items to the repository is allowed provided the user knows the correct password.

LOADING THE REPOSITORY

Repository files have the extension .REP

This is achieved via the **File** menu, by selecting the **Repository Open** menu option. A **File Open** dialogue box is displayed to enable the Repository to be selected

by name. The Repository file has an extension of
.REP. Once loaded, Repository cannot be closed; it
remains loaded until *SOMATiK* terminates.

**INSPECTING
THE
REPOSITORY**

This is achieved in two ways:

■ Pressing the Repository button on the tool bar
■ Selecting the Repository Browse option of the File menu

Provided that the repository has been successfully loaded, either of these selections leads to the *Repository Browser*, a sophisticated dialogue box. This is shown in Figure B.31. The Repository Browser has the following parts:

■ A list of the available items
■ Classification data on each item
■ Means to select which items are displayed in the list
■ Buttons to achieve the following:
    – Close the Browser box
    – Obtain Help
    – Examine the details of an item
    – Import the selected item into a project
    – Examine the Repository Glossary
    – Modify the Classification data on an item

Items can be selected from the list of available items either by using the mouse or by means of the arrow keys to scroll up and down the list. Double-clicking with the left button results in the display of the Properties dialogue box for the selected item. The same effect is achieved by pressing the **Examine** button.

Note that the Properties dialogue box for the selected item is read-only, since items in the Repository cannot be modified.

**IMPORTING
FROM THE
REPOSITORY**

The selected item may be imported into the project by pressing the **Import** button. The names of items are required to be unique, both within the Project and within the Repository, and between Project and Repository. *SOMATiK* will therefore resist

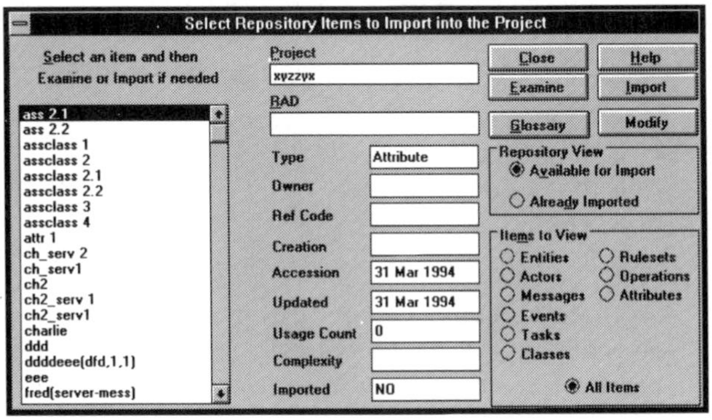

Figure B.31 Repository Browser.

attempts to import an item that has the same name as an item already in existence in the Project. The name of the project item should be changed before the import is made.

SOMATiK maintains a count of the number of times that each item is imported into a project. This count is shown under the name Usage Count in the Classification part of the Browser box. It is incremented each time the item to which it refers is imported into a project. Its value may only be changed by a user who has correctly quoted the password.

FILTERING THE DISPLAY

Which items are displayed in the list box is controlled by two settings: a major selection and a minor selection. These are effectively filters and are applied successively; the minor selection is applied to those items that were not filtered out by the major selection.

The major and minor selections are altered via the Radio buttons on the right-hand side of the Browser box. The major selection has two settings: list those items which are available for import, or list those items which have already been imported into the current project during the current *SOMATiK* session. When an item is imported, it is marked internally as such; it disappears from the Available List and reappears in the Imported List. The minor selection is according to item type.

CLASSIFICATION DATA

Classification data for the selected item is displayed in a column going down the middle of the Browser box. The Classification data consists of the following:

- The Project for which this item was originally defined
- The RAD workshop in which this item was originally defined
- The Type of the Item (for example, Actor, Entity, Task, and so on)
- The name of the owner of the item
- A Reference Code for the item (which will usually be assigned by its owner)
- The date when the item was created
- The date when it was first saved in the Repository (the accession date)
- The date of last update (that is, the date when the item's classification data was last changed)
- Its Usage Count
- Its complexity (a text string which can be used in any way you want)
- Whether or not it has been imported into the current project during the current *SOMATiK* session

The following items of classification data can be changed by a user who has correctly quoted the password for the Repository:

- The Owner
- The Ref. Code
- The Creation date
- The Accession date
- The Usage Count
- The Complexity

The **Repository Glossary** may be inspected by pressing the **Glossary** button. This gives rise to the **Repository Glossary Selector**, a dialogue box which is described in the previous section.

**MODIFYING
CLASSIFICATION
DATA**

Pressing the **Modify** button allows a user who has quoted the update password to change the classification data for the selected item. This is done via a dialogue box. Users who have not correctly quoted the update password will get an error message when they press the **Modify** button.

**CLOSING THE
BROWSER**

The **Repository Browser** is closed by pressing the **Close** button. This merely closes the Browser box; it does not cancel any imports which may have been made, nor does it close the Repository.

**CREATION
OF A NEW
REPOSITORY**

Repository files are password – protected against unauthorized update

Whenever *SOMATiK* is started, it creates an empty repository in memory. This can be saved if required via the **File** menu. Select the **Repository Update** option and then **Save Repository**. The user will be asked to allocate a password for the new Repository before it is saved to disc. The password may be up to twelve characters in length.

> *SOMATiK* will then ask for a name for the new Repository. This name must be unique; the new Repository is not allowed to overwrite an existing one having the same name. Having created the new, empty Repository on disc, *SOMATiK* then behaves as though this Repository had been loaded by a user in possession of the update password and the Repository may be modified by that user in the manner described below.

**MODIFYING
THE
REPOSITORY**

The Repository is password-protected. The password is a maximum of 12 characters in length. The following procedure is recommended:

(1) Run *SOMATiK* and open a Project file.
(2) Open the Repository from the File menu.
(3) Select the Repository Update option from the File menu, then the Add Project Items from its pop-up sub-menu.
(4) A dialogue box then appears requesting the password. This should be entered in the space provided.
(5) The Repository is then loaded and you have update rights to it.
(6) The Project Items Browser box is displayed.

Items from the project that are to be saved in the Repository are selected by means of the Items Browser. This behaves in a very similar manner to the Repository Browser and I don't propose to duplicate the description. The Browser box is shown in Figure B.32.

The principal differences between the *Project Items Browser* and the Repository Browser are as follows.

The Repository password can be changed when you select the Repository Update option on a second or subsequent occasion in the current *SOMATiK* session, after having correctly quoted it the first time.

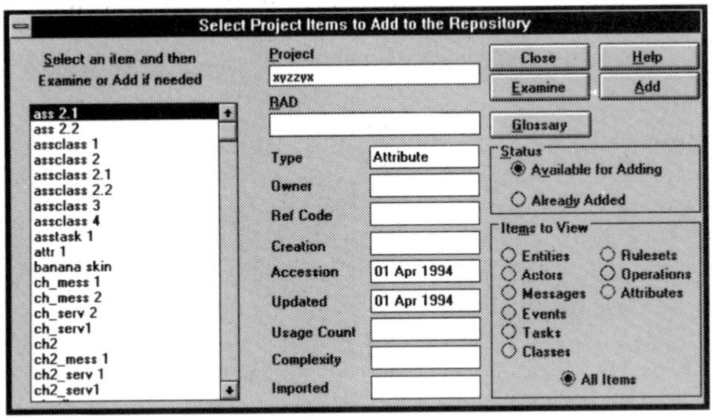

Figure B.32 The Project Browser.

The updated Repository can be saved by selecting the **Repository Update – Save** option from the **File** menu. You will be offered an opportunity to change the Repository password immediately prior to saving it. When a modified Repository is saved, *SOMATiK* changes the extension of the old Repository on disc from .REP to .BAK and then saves the modified Repository under the .REP extension, so that two generations of the Repository are kept. Any previous .BAK file is overwritten. You are advised to maintain independent backup copies of the Repository as it evolves. *SOMATiK* does not do this for you.

Pressing the **Glossary** button of the *Project Items Browser* displays the Project Glossary. A Term can be selected and the Save button pressed to save it in the Repository Glossary.

The selected item can be examined by pressing the **Examine** button. This results in the display of the Properties box for the item concerned. This item's properties can be modified.

After you have modified a Repository (added new items or new glossary entries), you will be offered a chance to save it there and then. If you have only a single change to make, you may wish to save at this point. However, if you have a series of changes to make, it would be sensible to save the Repository only after you have made the final change.

All fields of the item's classification data can be modified, with the exception of the *Item Type* and the *Imported* field. The fields are suitably defaulted.

The selected item is added to the Repository by pressing the **Add** button.

Project items are added to the Repository 'as is'; if you want to modify them in any way, you must do so *before* you save them, since repository items cannot be modified once added. The easiest way to do this is to create copies of the items and modify the copies prior to adding. Note that, in the case of Tasks and Business Objects which can form part of tree-like structures, all items in the trees are potentially imported as is. You should therefore prepare a tree of objects carefully in advance before adding. The same is true of any Operations, Attributes and Rulesets which are owned by an item being imported.

When a tree of items is being imported, you are offered the choice of whether or not to import each item in the tree. This includes Attributes, Operations and Rulesets.

If you don't want to modify the RAD file by making copies of the items to be saved, you can either:

- make another copy of the RAD file first and use that, or
- modify the RAD file and then exit *SOMATiK* without saving it.

A printout of the items in the Repository can be obtained by creating a new RAD file, opening the Repository and then importing the items to be printed. The resulting *SOMATiK* report will contain the details of the imported items. The RAD file can then be deleted (exit *SOMATiK* without saving). Note that the current version of *SOMATiK* does not provide any file locking of a Repository. The program assumes that the Repository on disk has not changed since it initially read it. If two users both load the same Repository at the same time and gain update access to it, the only arbitration between them is that provided by the Microsoft SHARE utility. It is recommended that a maximum of one user at a time be allowed update access to the Repository; this must be enforced manually/managerially. Future versions of *SOMATiK* will provide control of file contention.

B.2.15 Using the NotePad facility

Access to the **NotePad** is gained through the **Tools NotePad** menu selection; or using the **NotePad** icon in the **ToolBar**; or from the **Notes** button which is available in (nearly) all *SOMATiK* dialogue boxes.

The **NotePad** is a multi-page free-text edit facility (Figure B.33) for capturing points as they arise in the course of a RAD; these points may not fit into the current stream of discussion, but should not be forgotten. Thus typically notes entered into the **NotePad** will subsequently be expanded upon and moved into a more appropriate slot in the workspace; or used as an *aide-mémoire* to the facilitator to return to the topic at an appropriate time during the workshop.

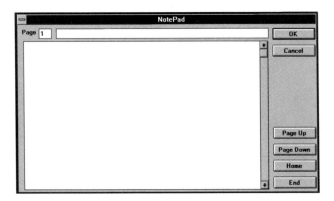

Figure B.33 The NotePad Facility.

NOTEPAD
PAGES

You can also use the equivalent keyboard buttons

As a small extra convenience, the **NotePad** is structured into ten sections or 'pages', although each of these 'pages' is free to be the equivalent of many physical pages in length. Optionally, each 'page' may be assigned a title for reference. So, for example, a user might label page 1 as 'General Notes', page 2 as 'Technical Points Raised' and so on. Use the **Page Up**, **Page Down**, **Home** and **End** buttons to move from page to page.

SAVING AND
PRINTING THE
NOTEPAD

The NotePad data are all stored in the RAD file. They do not appear in the printed report.

B.2.16 Using the Tools facility

STANDARD
TOOLS

The **Tools** menu offers a set of standard tools, comprising:

- the Drawing ToolBox
- the Glossary
- the NotePad
- the SketchPad

ADDITIONAL
TOOLS

Further tools of the user's choosing can be added to the list available. Select the **Options Add a Tool** menu selection. The dialogue shown in Figure B.34 will be presented. Use this to enter the Windows command line that you would use to invoke the tool from Program Manager. In **Menu Text** enter the menu prompt line you wish to have appearing in the Tools menu; use an ampersand character '&' to prefix the character in the prompt string which will be the menu accelerator and appear underlined.

If you wish to be prompted for arguments, check the **Ask for Arguments** check box; on selection of the tool, you will be prompted for its arguments.

There is also an option available to select the default **StartUp Directory** for the external application, which is typically of value when setting up to invoke a word processor or similar external tool, since this will be the directory utilized in the **Files** menu options within the application by default. This tool will be added to the **Tools** menu. All such additional tools will be saved on exit, and made available on start-up of *SOMATiK* thereafter.

In this way, for example, a preferred word processor can be plugged in to the system to facilitate transferring data. Often, a tool for shelling directly to DOS will be added (use the DOSPRMPT.PIF as the command target).

B.2.17 Using the Report Generator

Printer and Filed output is selected from the **File** menu using the three available options of:

- **Print...**
- **Print Preview**
- **Print Report...**

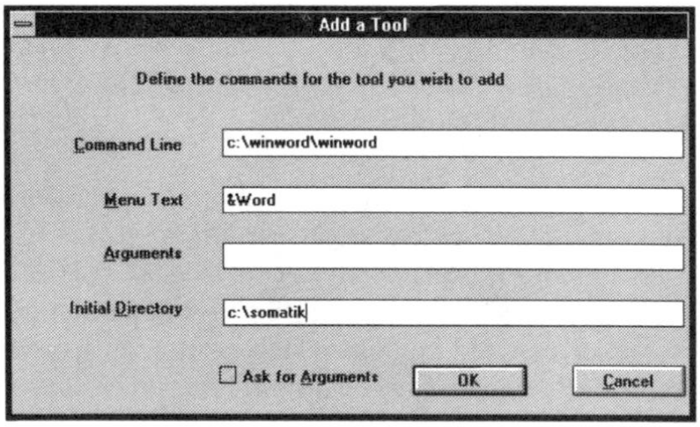

Figure B.34 Add a Tool Dialogue.

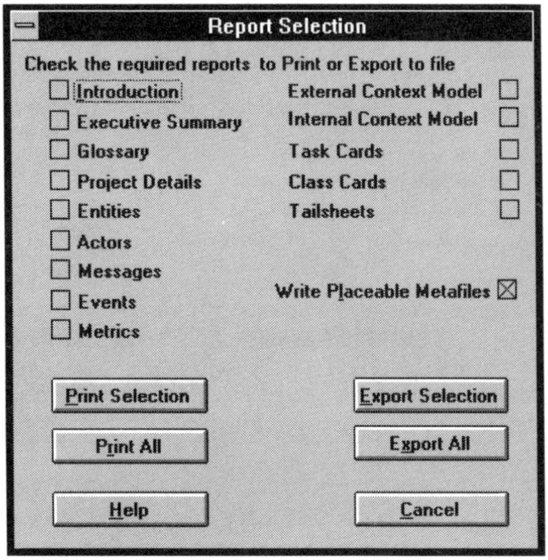

Figure B.35 Report selection dialogue box.

 Print and **Print Preview** produce a formatted report of the entire project structure. **Print Report** supports selective printing, and also the export of all or part of the project in ASCII format to a file for subsequent import to another word processor.

 Selecting **Print Report...** leads to the dialogue box shown in Figure B.35. This contains check boxes for each section of the formatted report. Check the subset of selections you wish to output. Then press **Print Selection** to output the subset report to the printer, or **Export Selection** to output to an ASCII file.

 If the entire report is required, the **Print All** and **Export All** buttons may be used as a short cut.

EXPORTING DIAGRAMS

Diagrams are exported in Windows MetaFile Format (.WMF files). These can then be imported into any Windows compliant word processor. The location of the diagram in the exported ASCII file, and the name of the associated metafile, is given in the text of the exported ASCII file.

PLACEABLE METAFILES

There are two supported formats of Windows Metafile: the standard format, and 'placeable metafiles' (otherwise known as Aldus Placeable Metafiles or .APM format). Various word processors are set up to deal with one or other of these formats. For this reason, there is a check box in the **Print Report...** dialogue for you to select which format of metafile should be output. Depending on your word processor, and its documentation, an experiment may be necessary to determine which type it expects.

B.2.18 Using the Metrics facility

Metrics for the current project are generated by selecting the **Run Metrics** menu option. All metrics are then computed, and presented on screen in tabular form. A partial example of a metrics report is shown in Figure B.36. The same report is available in the printed document.

Each measured attribute is presented with the following sample statistics:

- mean
- variance
- mode
- median

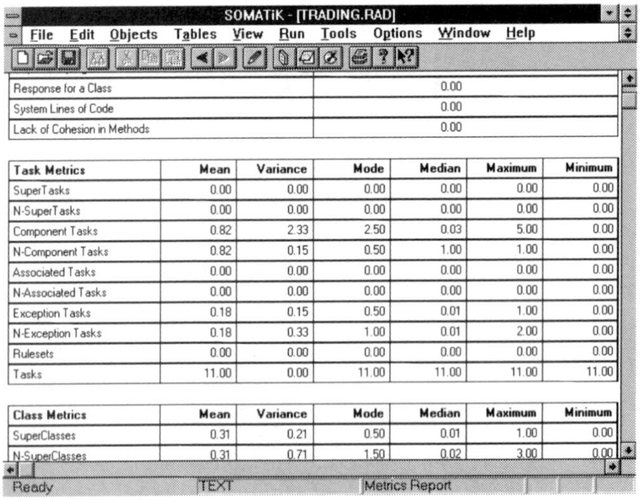

Response for a Class	0.00
System Lines of Code	0.00
Lack of Cohesion in Methods	0.00

Task Metrics	Mean	Variance	Mode	Median	Maximum	Minimum
SuperTasks	0.00	0.00	0.00	0.00	0.00	0.00
N-SuperTasks	0.00	0.00	0.00	0.00	0.00	0.00
Component Tasks	0.82	2.33	2.50	0.03	5.00	0.00
N-Component Tasks	0.82	0.15	0.50	1.00	1.00	0.00
Associated Tasks	0.00	0.00	0.00	0.00	0.00	0.00
N-Associated Tasks	0.00	0.00	0.00	0.00	0.00	0.00
Exception Tasks	0.18	0.15	0.50	0.01	1.00	0.00
N-Exception Tasks	0.18	0.33	1.00	0.01	2.00	0.00
Rulesets	0.00	0.00	0.00	0.00	0.00	0.00
Tasks	11.00	0.00	11.00	11.00	11.00	11.00

Class Metrics	Mean	Variance	Mode	Median	Maximum	Minimum
SuperClasses	0.31	0.21	0.50	0.01	1.00	0.00
N-SuperClasses	0.31	0.71	1.50	0.02	3.00	0.00

Figure B.36 Extract from the Metrics report.

- maximum
- minimum

taken over the population of members.

TASK METRICS
- The number of SuperTasks
- The number of tasks for which a task is a SuperTask (N-SuperTasks)
- The number of Component Tasks
- The number of tasks for which a task is a component (N-Component Tasks)
- The number of Associated Tasks
- The number of tasks to which a task is Associated (N-Associated Tasks)
- The number of Exception Tasks
- The number of tasks for which the task is an Exception Handler (N-Exception Tasks)
- The number of Rulesets
- The actual number of tasks (in this case, of course, the figures displayed for mean, mode, median, maximum and minimum are all equal to the number of tasks, and the variance is zero)

CLASS METRICS The same statistics as for tasks, but now counting the SuperClasses, Component Classes, Associated Classes and Server Classes. In addition, the number of Attributes, Operations and Rulesets is reported.

TASK TREE METRICS For each of the tree types:

- SuperTasks
- N-SuperTasks
- Component Tasks
- N-Component Tasks
- Associated Tasks
- N-Associated Tasks
- Exception Tasks
- N-Exception Tasks

the following statistics are presented:

- The number of nodes
- The number of non-terminal nodes
- The number of arcs per node
- The maximum depth of the tree
- The average fan-out
- The proportion of inherited nodes

CLASS TREE METRICS The same data structure as for task trees, this time counting SuperClasses, Component Classes, Associated Classes, Server Classes and their inversions.

SUMMARY METRICS A handful of summary metrics is provided. It is anticipated that this area of the system will be expanded as experience develops in future releases.

- The weighted methods per class statistic

SUMMARY
METRICS

- The average depth of all inheritance trees
- The average number of children

Place holders are provided for other statistics such as object coupling, system lines of code, and lack of cohesion in methods. Development of these statistics requires the provision of compilable code in the class descriptions.

UPDATES

For information on updates of this manual and of *SOMATiK* please contact Bezant at the address given at the end of chapter 13.

REFERENCES

Abbott R.J. (1983). Program design by informal English descriptions. *Comm. of the ACM*, **26**(11), 882–94

Adams G. and Corriveau J-P. (1994). Capturing object interactions. In *Tools 13* (Magnusson B., Meyer B., Nerson J.-M. and Perrot J.-F., eds.). Hemel Hempstead: Prentice-Hall

Agha G., Wegner P. and Yonezawa A., eds. (1993). *Research Directions in Concurrent Object-Oriented Programming*. Cambridge, MA: MIT Press

Albrecht A.J. (1979). Measuring application development productivity. In *Proceedings of the Joint SHARE/GUIDE/IBM Application Development Symposium*, Oct. 1979, 34–43

Albrecht A.J. and Gaffney J.E. (1983). Software function, source lines of code and development effort prediction: A software science validation. *IEEE Transactions on Software Engineering*, **9**(6), 639–47

Alencar A.J. and Goguen J.A. (1991). OOZE: An object-oriented Z environment. In *Proc. ECOOP'91* (America P., ed.). Lecture Notes in Computer Science 512. Berlin: Springer

Alexander C. (1964). *Notes on the Synthesis of Form*. Harvard: University Press

Alexander C. (1979). *The Timeless Way of Building*. Oxford: University Press

Alexander C., Ishikawa S. and Silverstein M. (1977). *A Pattern Language*. Oxford: University Press

Anderson J.R. (1976). *Language, Memory and Thought*. New York: Lawrence Erlbaum Associates

Andleigh P.K. and Gretzinger M.R. (1992). *Distributed Object-oriented Data-Systems Design*. Englewood Cliffs, NJ: Prentice-Hall

Aoyama M. (1993). Concurrent development process model. *IEEE Software*, July, 46–55

Apple Computer Inc. (1987). *Apple Human Interface Guidelines: The Apple Desktop Interface*. Cupertino, CA: Addison-Wesley

Arthur L.J. (1985). *Measuring Programmer Productivity and Software Quality*. New York: John Wiley & Sons

Ashby W.R. (1956). *An Introduction to Cybernetics*. London: Chapman & Hall

Austen J.L. (1962). *How to Do Things with Words*. Cambridge MA: Harvard University Press

Baecker R.M. and Buxton W.A.S., eds. (1987). *Readings in Human–Computer Interaction: A Multi-disciplinary Approach*. San Mateo, CA: Morgan Kaufmann

Banker R.D., Kauffman R.J. and Zweig D. (1993). Repository evaluation of software reuse. *IEEE Trans. on Software Engineering*, **19**(4)

Bapat S. (1994). *Object-Oriented Networks: Models for Architecture, Operations and Management*. Englewood Cliffs, NJ: Prentice-Hall

Barfield L. (1993). *The User Interface: Concepts & Design*. Wokingham: Addison-Wesley

Barr A. and Feigenbaum E. (1981). *The Handbook of Artificial Intelligence* (3 vols.). London: Pitman

Basden A. (1990a). Towards a methodology for building expert systems I. *Codex*, **2**(1), 15–19. Uxbridge: Creative Logic Ltd

Basden A. (1990). Towards a methodology for building expert systems II. *Codex*, **2**(2), 19–23. Uxbridge: Creative Logic Ltd

Beck K. and Cunningham W. (1989). A laboratory for teaching object-oriented thinking. In *OOPSLA'90 ACM Conference on Object-Oriented Programming Systems, Languages and Applications* (Meyrowitz, ed.). Reading, MA: Addison-Wesley

Berard E.V. (1993). *Essays on Object-oriented Software Engineering – Volume 1*. Englewood Cliffs, NJ: Prentice-Hall

Berliner H. (1981). The B* Tree Search Algorithm: A best-first proof procedure. In *Readings in Artificial Intelligence* (Webber B.L. and Nilsson N.J., eds). Tioga Publishing Company

Birrel N.D. and Ould M.A. (1985). *A Practical Handbook for Software Development.* Cambridge: University Press

Bobrow D. and Winograd T. (1977). An overview of KRL, a knowledge representation language. *Cognitive Science*, **1**(1), 3–46

Boehm B.W. (1981). *Software Engineering Economics.* Englewood Cliffs, NJ: Prentice-Hall

Booch G. (1994). *Object-oriented Design with Applications*, 2nd edn. Redwood City, CA: Benjamin/Cummings

Brachman R.J. and Levesque H.J. (1985). *Readings in Knowledge Representation.* Los Altos, CA: Morgan Kaufmann

Braithwaite R.B. (1953). *Scientific Explanation.* Cambridge: University Press

Braune R. and Foshay W.R. (1983). Towards a practical model of cognitive information processing, task analysis and schema acquisition for complex problem solving situations. *Instructional Science*, **12**, 121–45

Brice A. (1993). Using models in analysis. *Computing*, 27 May, 41

Brown R.G. (1992). Adding business rules to data models. *Database Newsletter*, **20**(6)

Brown W. (1993). Object-oriented testing. In *Proceedings of Object Technology 93*, BCS OOPS Group annual conference, March, Cambridge

Browne D. (1994). *STUDIO: Structured User Interface Design for Interaction Optimisation.* London: Prentice-Hall

Bruce T.A. (1992). Simplicity and complexity in the Zachman framework. *Database Newsletter*, **20**(3), 3–11

Brynjolfsson E. (1993). The productivity paradox in information technology. *Communications of the ACM*, **36**(12), 67–77

Butler A. and Chamberlain G. (1988). The ARIES Club: Experience of expert systems in insurance and investment. In *Research and Development in Expert Systems IV* (Moralee D.S., ed.). Cambridge: University Press

Cameron J. (1992). Ingredients for a new object-oriented method: Development process, shared object modelling and GUI design will integrate OT and MIS. *Object Magazine*, **2**(4), 64–7

Cant S.N., Jeffrey D.R. and Henderson-Sellers B. (1992). A conceptual model of cognitve complexity of elements of the programming process. *Inf. Software Technology* (to appear)

Card D.N. and Glass R.L. (1990). *Measuring Software Design Quality.* Englewood Cliffs, NJ: Prentice-Hall

Card S.K., Moran T.P. and Newell A. (1983). *The Psychology of Human– Computer Interaction.* Hillsdale, NJ: Lawrence Erlbaum Associates

Carrington D., Duke D., Duke R., King P., Rose G. and Smith G. (1990). Object-Z: An object-oriented extension to Z. In *Formal Description Techniques II.* Amsterdam: North-Holland

Champeaux D. de, Lea D. and Faure P. (1993). *Object-oriented System Development.* Reading, MA: Addison-Wesley

Charniak E. and McDermott D. (1985). *Introduction to Artificial Intelligence.* Reading, MA: Addison-Wesley

Checkland P. (1981). *Systems Thinking, Systems Practice.* Chichester: John Wiley & Sons

Chen P. (1976). The entity–relationship model: toward a unified view of data. *ACM Transactions on Database Systems*, **1**(1), 9–36

Chidamber S.R. and Kemerer C.F. (1991). Towards a metrics suite for object-oriented design. In *OOPSLA'91 ACM Conference on Object-oriented Programming Systems, Languages and Applications* (Paepcke A., ed). Reading, MA: Addison-Wesley

Chomsky N. (1980). *Rules and Representations.* Oxford: Basil Blackwell

Clausewitz C. von (1968). *On War.* Rapoport translation of 1908. Harmondsworth: Penguin Books

CLL (1987). *Leonardo Reference Manual.* Uxbridge UK: Creative Logic Limited

Coad P. (1992). Patterns in object-oriented analysis. *Comms. of the ACM*, Sept

Coad P. and Yourdon E. (1990). *Object-oriented analysis.* Englewood Cliffs, NJ: Yourdon Press/Prentice-Hall

Coad P. and Yourdon E. (1991a). *Object-oriented analysis*, 2nd edn. Englewood Cliffs, NJ: Yourdon Press/Prentice-Hall

Coad P. and Yourdon E. (1991b). *Object-oriented Design.* Englewood Cliffs, NJ: Yourdon Press/Prentice-Hall

Coleman D., Arnold P., Bodoff S., Dollin C., Gilchrist H., Hayes F. and Jeremaes P. (1994). *Object-oriented Development: The Fusion Method*. Englewood Cliffs, NJ: Prentice-Hall

Collins H.M. (1990). *Artificial Experts: Social Knowledge and Intelligent Machines*. Cambridge, MA: MIT Press

Computer Finance (1993a). Case study: Client-server costs. *Computer Finance*, **4**(4). London: APT Data Services

Computer Finance (1993b). Client-server costs on the decline? *Computer Finance*, **4**(6). London: APT Data Services

Computer Finance (1993c). Downsizing for right pricing. *Computer Finance*, **4**(7). London: APT Data Services

Cook S. and Daniels J. (1994). *Designing Object Systems*. Hemel Hempstead, UK: Prentice-Hall

Costello J. (1992). The shape of screens to come. *Computer Weekly*, 27th August

Coutaz J. (1987). *PAC, an Object-oriented Model for Implementing User Interfaces*. Laboratoire de Genie Informatique, University de Grenoble, BP 68

Cox B.J. and Novobilski A. (1991). *Object-oriented Programming – An Evolutionary Approach*, 2nd edn. Reading MA: Addison-Wesley

Cox E. (1994). *The Fuzzy Systems Handbook: A Practitioner's Guide to Building, Using and Maintaining Fuzzy Systems*. Boston: Academic Press

Dalton R. (1992). Predicting the cost of a sale. *Software Management*, March

Daniels J. and Cook S. (1993). Strategies for sharing objects in distributed systems. *JOOP*, **5**(8), 27–36

Daniels P.J. (1986). The user modelling function of an intelligent interface for document retrieval systems. In *IRFIS 6: Intelligent Information Systems for the Information Society* (Brookes B.C., ed.). pp. 162–76. Amsterdam: North Holland

Davenport T.H. (1993). *Process Innovation: Reengineering Work Through Information Technology*. Harvard: Business School Press

Davenport T.H. and Short J.E. (1990). The new industrial engineering: Information technology and business process redesign. *Sloan Management Review*, Summer, 11–27

Davis R. and Lenat D.B. (1982). *Knowledge Based Systems in Artificial Intelligence*. New York: McGraw-Hill

Desfray P. (1992). *Ingénerie des Objets Approche Classe–Relation Application à C++*. Paris: Editions Masson

DeSouza D. (1992). Dynamic modelling of object-oriented systems. In *Proceedings of OOP'93/C++ World, Munchen 1993*. New York: SIGS Publications

Devlin K. (1992). Logic and Information,

Diaper D. (1993). CSCW: Psychology, sociology ... and computing. *Computer Bulletin*, February, 22–5

Diaper D. and Sanger C., eds. (1993). *CSCW in Practice: An introduction and case studies*. London: Springer-Verlag

Dietrich W.C., Nackman L.R. and Gracer F. (1989). Saving a legacy with objects. In *OOPSLA'90 ACM Conference on Object-oriented Programming Systems, Languages and Applications* (Meyrowitz N., ed). Reading, MA: Addison-Wesley

Dreyfus H.L. and Dreyfus S.E. (1986). *Mind over Machine: The Power of Human Intuition and Expertise in the Era of the Computer*. Oxford: Basil Blackwell

Duda R., Hart P. *et al.* (1976). Development of the PROSPECTOR system for mineral exploration. SRI report projects 5822 and 6415, SRI, Palo Alto, CA

Dugundji J. (1966). *Topology*. Boston, MA: Allyn and Bacon

Durham A. (1992). *IT Horizons*, **1**(3)

Durr E. (1992). VDM++: A formal specification language for object-oriented designs. In *IEEE CompEuro 92 Proceedings* (DeWilde and Vandewalle, eds.). IEEE Press

Edwards J.S. (1991). *Building Knowledge Based Systems*. London: Pitman

Embley D.W., Kurtz B.D. and Woodfield S.N. (1992). *Object-oriented Systems Analysis: A Model-Driven Approach*. Englewood Cliffs, NJ: Yourdon Press

Englemore D. and Morgan A., eds. (1988). *Blackbroad Systems*. Wokingham: Addison-Wesley

Ericsson K.A. and Simon H.A. (1984). *Protocol Analysis: Verbal Reports as Data*. Boston, MA: Bradford Books

Ewald A. and Roy M. (1993). Why OT is good for system integration. *Object Magazine*, **2**(5), 60–3

Evans N. (1992). What are client server systems (1)? *Client Server*, **1**(1). Farnham: British Computer Society Client Server Group, ISSN 0966-7881

Fagan M. (1974). Design and Code Inspections and Process Control in the Development of Programs. *IBM Report IBM-SDD-TR-21-572*

Fichman R.G. and Kemerer C.F. (1993). Adoption of software engineering process innovations: The case of object-orientation. *Sloan Management Review*, Winter, 7–22

Fiedler S.P. (1989). Object-oriented unit testing. *Hewlett-Packard Journal*, April, 69–74

Firesmith D.G. (1993). *Object-oriented Requirements Analysis and Design: A Software Engineering Approach*. Chichester: John Wiley & Sons

Flint D. and Macdonald R. (1992). What are client server systems (2)? *Client Server*, 1. Farnham: British Computer Society Client Server Group, ISSN 0966-7881

Foley J., Kim W., Kovavavics S. and Murray K. (1989). Defining interfaces at a high level of abstraction. *IEEE Software*, **6**(1), 25–32

Forgy C.L. (1981). The OPS5 User's Manual. *Tech Rep CMU-CS-81-135*, Computer Science Dept, Carnegie-Mellon University

Forsythe R., ed. (1989a). *Expert Systems: Principles and Case Studies* 2nd edn. London: Chapman & Hall

Forsythe R., ed. (1989b). *Machine Learning*. London: Chapman & Hall

Friedman J. (1993). New options for object databases. *Object Magazine*, **2**(6)

Galitz W. (1981). *Human Factors in Office Automation*. Atlanta, GA: Life Office Management Association

Gamma E., Helm R., Johnson R. and Vlissides J. (1995). Design Patterns: Abstraction and Reuse of Object-oriented Design. To appear

Goldberg A. (1984). *Smalltalk-80: The Interactive Programming Environment*. New York: Addison-Wesley

Goldberg D.E. (1989). *Genetic Algorithms: in Search, Optimization & Machine Learning*. Addison-Wesley

Graham I.M. (1987). Expert systems find a ideal setting. *Banking Technology*, June

Graham I.M. (1991a). *Object-Oriented Methods*, 1st edn. Wokingham: Addison-Wesley

Graham I.M. (1991b). Fuzzy logic in commercial expert systems – results and prospects. *Fuzzy Sets and Systems*, **40**, 451–72

Graham I.M. (1991c). Corrigendum to fuzzy logic in commercial expert systems – results and prospects. *Fuzzy Sets and Systems*, **43**, 337–8

Graham I.M. (1992a). A method for integrating object technology with rules. In *Proceedings of Advanced Information Systems 92*. Oxford: Learned Information

Graham I.M. (1992b). Interoperation: Combining object-oriented applications with conventional IT. *Object Magazine*, **2**(4), 36–7

Graham I.M. (1993a). Migration using SOMA: A semantically rich method of object-oriented analysis. *Journal of Object-Oriented Programming*, **5**(9), Feb.

Graham I.M. (1993b). Migration strategies column. *Object Magazine*, **2**(5)–**3**(5)

Graham I.M. (1994a). *Object-oriented Methods*, 2nd edn. Wokingham: Addison-Wesley

Graham I.M. (1994b). Beyond the use case: Combining task analysis and scripts in object-oriented requirements capture and business process re-engineering. In *Tools 13* (Magnusson B., Meyer B., Nerson J.-M. and Perrot J.-F., eds.). Hemel Hempstead, UK: Prentice-Hall

Graham I.M. (1994c). On the impossibility of artificial intelligence. *BCS Specialist Group in Expert Systems Newsletter*, Summer

Graham I.M. and Jones P.L.K. (1988). *Expert Systems: Knowledge, Uncertainty and Decision*. London: Chapman & Hall

Grass J.E. (1991). Design archaeology for object-oriented redesign in C++. In *Tools 5: Proc. fifth international conference on Technology of Object-oriented Languages and Systems* (Korson T., Vaishnavi V. and Meyer B, eds.). New York: Prentice-Hall

Gray P.M.D., Krishnarao G.K. and Paton N.W. (1992). *Object-oriented Databases: A*

Semantic Data Model Approach. Englewood Cliffs, NJ: Prentice-Hall

Greenberg S. (1991). *Computer-supported Cooperative Work and Groupware*. New York: Academic Press

Guttman M., King J.A. and Matthews J. (1993). A methodology for developing distributed applications. *Object Magazine,* **2**(5), 55–9

Haack S. (1978). *Philosophy of Logics*. Cambridge: University Press

Halmos P. (1950). *Measure Theory*. New York: Van Nostrand

Halstead M.H. (1977). *Elements of Software Science*. Amsterdam: North Holland

Hammer M. (1990). Reengineering work: Don't automate, obliterate. *Harvard Business Review*, July–August, 104–12

Hammer M. and Champy, J. (1993). *Re-engineering the Corporation: A Manifesto for the Business Revolution*. NY: HarperCollins

Harel D. (1987). Statecharts: A visual formalism for complex systems. *Science of Computer Programming*, **8**, 231–74. Amsterdam: North Holland

Harmon P. and Taylor D.A. (1993). *Objects in Action: Commercial Applications of Object-oriented Technologies*. Reading, MA: Addison-Wesley

Hart A. (1989). *Knowledge Acquisition for Expert Systems* 2nd edn. London: Kogan Page

Hayes I., ed. (1987). *Specification Case Studies*. Englewood Cliffs, NJ: Prentice-Hall

Hayes-Roth F., Waterman D.A. and Lenat D.B. (1983). *Building Expert Systems*. Reading, MA: Addison-Wesley

Hekmatpour S. (1987). Experience with evolutionary prototyping in a large software project. *ACM Software Engineering Notes*, **12**(1), 38–41

Hempel C.G. (1966). *Philosophy of Natural Science*. Englewood Cliffs, NJ: Prentice-Hall

Henderson-Sellers B. (1992). *A BOOK of Object-oriented Knowledge*. Sydney, Aus: Prentice-Hall

Henderson-Sellers B. (1993). The economics of reusing library classes. *JOOP* **6**(4), 43–50

Henderson-Sellers B. and Edwards J. (1994). *BOOK TWO of Object-oriented Knowledge: The Working Object*. Sydney, Aus: Prentice-Hall

Henderson-Sellers B. and Pant Y.R. (1993). Adopting the reuse mindset throughout the lifecycle. *Object Magazine* **3**(4), 73–5

Henderson-Sellers B. and Tegarden (1992). The application of cyclomatic complexity to multiple entry/exit modules, *CITR Report 93/2*. University of NSW, Sydney, 1993

Hickman F.R., Killen J., Land L. *et al.* (1989). *Analysis for Knowledge-based Systems*. Chichester: Ellis Horwood

Hill R.D. (1986). Supporting concurrency, communication and synchronization in human computer interaction – The Sassafras UIMS. *ACM Transaction on Graphics*, **5**(3), 179–210

Hill R.D. and Hermman M. (1989). The structure of TUBE – A tool for implementing advanced interfaces. *Proceedings of Eurographics '89*. Amsterdam: North-Holland

Hodgson R. (1991). The X Model: A process model for object-oriented software development. In *Proc. of Toulouse '91, Toulouse, France*, pp. 713–28

Holsapple C.W. and Whinston A.B. (1986). *Manager's Guide to Expert Systems using Guru*. New York: Dow Jones-Irwin

Horty J.F., Thomason R.H. and Touretzky D.S. (1990). A skeptical theory of inheritance in nonmonotonic semantic networks. *Artificial Intelligence*, **42**, 311–48

Hughes J.G. (1991). *Object-oriented Databases*. Englewood Cliffs, NJ: Prentice-Hall

IBM (1991a). *Common User Access: Guide to User Interface Design*. Cary, NC: International Business Machines

IBM (1991b). *Common User Access: Advanced Interface Design Reference*. Cary, NC: International Business Machines

IBM (1992). *Object-oriented Interface Design: CUA guidelines*. New York: QUE

IEL (1986). *Crystal User Manual*. Richmond UK: Intelligent Environments Limited

Ince D. (1991). *Object-oriented Software Engineering with C++*. London: McGraw-Hill

Jackson P. (1986). *Introduction to Expert Systems*. Wokingham: Addison-Wesley

Jacobs S. (1992). What is business process automation? *Expert Systems Applications*, August, 5–10

Jacobson I., Christerson M., Jonsson P. and Overgaard G. (1992). *Object-oriented Software Engineering: A Use Case Driven Approach.* Wokingham: Addison-Wesley

Johnson P. (1992). *Human–Computer Interaction: Psychology, Task Analysis and Software Engineering.* London: McGraw-Hill

Jones C.B. (1980). *Software Development: A Rigorous Approach.* Englewood Cliffs, NJ: Prentice-Hall

Jones T.C. (1986). *Programming Productivity.* New York: McGraw-Hill

Jones T.C. (1988). A short history of function points and feature points. ACI Computer Services

Jungclaus R. (1993). *Modeling of Dynamic Object Systems.* Weisbaden: Vieweg

Keen P.G.W. and Knapp E.M. (1995). *Business Process Investment: Getting the Right Process Right.* Harvard: Business School Press

Kelly G.A. (1955). *The Psychology of Personal Constructs.* New York: W.W. Norton

Khoshafian S., Baker A.B., Abnous R. and Shepherd K. (1992). *Object-oriented Multi-Media Information Management in Client/Server Architectures.* New York: John Wiley & Sons

Korson T., Vaishnavi V. and Meyer B., eds. (1991). *TOOLS5: Proceedings of the fifth international conference on the Technology of Object-oriented Languages and Systems.* New York: Prentice-Hall

Korson T. and McGregor J.D. (1993). Technical criteria for the specification and evaluation of object-oriented libraries. In *Proceedings of Object Expo Europe 1993*, pp. 33–6. New York: SIGS Publications

Kosko B. (1991). *Neural Networks and Fuzzy Systems: A Dynamical Systems Approach to Machine Intelligence.* Englewood Cliffs, NJ: Prentice-Hall

Kosko B. (1993). *Fuzzy Thinking: The New Science of Fuzzy Logic.* New York: Hyperion

Koza J.R. (1992). *Genetic Programming: On the Programming of Computers by Means of Natural Selection.* Cambridge, MA: MIT Press

Lano K. and Haughton H. (1992). Reasoning and refinement in object-oriented specification languages. In *Proc. of ECOOP'92.* Berlin: Springer

Lano K. and Haughton H., eds. (1994). *Object-oriented Specification Case Studies.* Englewood Cliffs, NJ: Prentice-Hall

Laranjeira L.A. (1990). Software size estimation of object-oriented systems. *IEEE Transactions on Software Engineering,* **16**(5), 510–22

Laurel B., ed. (1990). *The Art of Computer Interface Design.* Reading, MA: Addison-Wesley

Lee G. (1993). *Object-oriented GUI Application Development.* Englewood Cliffs, NJ: Prentice-Hall

Lee S. and Carver D.L. (1991). Object-oriented analysis and specification: A knowledge based approach. *Journal Of Object-oriented Programming,* **3**(9), 35–43

Lektorsky V.A. (1984). *Subject, Object, Cognition.* Moscow: Progress Publishers

Lenat D.B. and Guha R.V. (1990). *Building Large Knowledge Based Systems: Representation and Inference in the Cyc Project.* Reading, MA: Addison-Wesley

Lenin V.I. (1964). The state and revolution. In *Collected Works Vol 25.* Moscow: Progress Publishers

Lenzerini M., Nardi D. and Simi M., eds. (1991). *Inheritance Hierarchies in Knowledge Representation and Programming Languages.* Chichester: John Wiley & Sons

Londeix B. (1987). *Cost Estimation for Software Development.* Wokingham: Addison-Wesley

Loomis M.E.S. (1991). Objects and SQL. *Object Magazine,* **1**(3), 68–78

Loosely C. (1992). Separation and integration in the Zachman framework. *Database Newsletter,* **20**(1), 3–9

Lorenz M. (1993). *Object-oriented Software Development: A Practical Guide.* Englewood Cliffs, NJ: Prentice-Hall

Lorenz A. and Kidd J. (1994). *Object-Oriented Software Metrics.* Englewood Cliffs, NJ: Prentice-Hall

Machiavelli N. (1961). *The Prince.* Translation by G. Bull. Harmondsworth: Penguin Books

Mackenzie K.D. (1991). *The Organisational Hologram: The Effective Management of Organisational Change.* Boston: Kluwer Academic

Madsen O.L. and Moller-Pedersen B. (1988). What object-oriented programming may be – and what it does not have to be. In *Proceedings ECOOP '88* (Gjessing and Nygaard, eds), Oslo, August. Lecture Notes in Comp. Sci. 322 Berlin: Springer

Madsen O.L., Moller-Pedersen B. and Nygaard K. (1993). *The BETA Programming Language.* Wokingham: Addison-Wesley

Magnusson B., Meyer B., Nerson J-M. and Perrot J-F., eds. (1994). *TOOLS 13.* Hemel Hempstead, UK: Prentice-Hall

Mandrioli D. and Meyer B. (1992). *Advances in Object-oriented Software Engineering.* Englewood Cliffs, NJ: Prentice-Hall

Marcuse H. (1955). *Reason and Revolution.* Oxford: University Press

Martin J. and Odell J.J. (1992). *Object-oriented Analysis and Design.* Englewood Cliffs, NJ: Prentice-Hall

Marx G. (1992). *Computerworld,* 20 April 1992

McCabe T.J. (1976). A complexity measure. *IEEE Trans. on Software Engineering,* **2**(4), 308–20

McCawley J.D. (1981). *Everything that Linguists have always wanted to know about Logic (but were ashamed to ask).* Oxford: Basil Blackwell

McDermott D. and Doyle J. (1980). Nonmonotonic logic I. *Artificial Intelligince,* **13**(1,2)

McGregor J.D. and Sykes D.A. (1992). *Object-oriented Software Development: Engineering Software for Reuse.* New York: Van Nostrand

Meersman R.A., Kent W. and Khosla S., eds. (1991). Object-oriented databases: Analysis, design and construction (DS-4). *Proceedings of the IFIP TC2/WG2.6 Working Conference,* Windermere, UK, July 1990. Berlin: Springer-Verlag

Meira S. and Cavalcanti A. (1992). Modular object-oriented Z specifications. In *Z Users Meeting 1990.* Workshops in Computing. Berlin: Springer

Menzies T., Edwards J.M. and Ng K. (1992). The case of the mysterious missing reusable libraries. In *TOOLS 9* (Meyer B. and Potter J., eds). Sydney: Prentice-Hall

Meyer B. (1988). *Object-oriented Software Construction.* Englewood Cliffs NJ: Prentice-Hall

Meyrowitz N., ed. (1987). OOPSLA'87 ACM Conference on Object-oriented Programming Systems, Languages and Applications. *ACM SIGPLAN Notices,* **22**(10)

Meyrowitz N., ed. (1990). *OOPSLA'90 ACM Conference on Object-oriented Programming Systems, Languages and Applications.* Reading, MA: Addison-Wesley

Michaels W.I. (1992). Re-designing customer driven IS processes. *Database Newsletter,* **20**(6), 1–12

Microsoft (1992). *The Windows Interface: An Application Design Guide.* Seattle: Microsoft Corp.

Miller G.A. (1956). The magical number seven, plus or minus two: some limits on our capacity for processing information *Psychological Review,* **63**, 81–97

Minsky M.L. (1985a). A framework for representing knowledge. In *Mind Design* (Haugeland J. ed.). Cambridge, MA: MIT Press

Minsky M.L (1985b). *The Society of Mind.* London: Heinemann

Minsky M.L. and Papert S. (1969). *Perceptrons.* Cambridge, MA: MIT Press

Moran T.P. (1981). The Command Language Grammar: A representation for the user interface of interactive computer systems. *IJMMS,* **15**, 3–50

Mullender S., ed. (1989). *Distributed Systems.* Reading, MA: Addison-Wesley

Myers B.A. (1991). GARNET. *IEEE Software,* **8**(2)

Myers G.J. (1979). *The Art of Software Testing.* New York: John Wiley & Sons

Nerson J. (1992). Applying object-oriented analysis and design. *Comms. ACM,* **35**(9), 63–74

Newell A. and Simon H.A. (1963). GPS: A program that simulates human thought In *Computers and Thought.* (Feigenbaum E.A. and Feldman J.A., eds.). New York: McGraw-Hill

NeXT (1991). *The NeXTstep Environment: Concepts.* NeXT Inc.

Nordström B., Petersson K. and Smith J.M. (1990). *Programming in Martin-Löf's Type Theory.* Oxford: University Press

Norman D.A. (1988). *The Psychology of Everyday Things.* New York: Doubleday

O'Connor P. (1991). A knowledge based trading system that management can trust. *Expert Systems User*, July

Object Management Group (1992). *Common Object Request Broker Architecture*. Framington, MA: Object Management Group

Object Management Group (1993). *Object-oriented Analysis and Design Reference Model*. Framington, MA: Object Management Group

Odell J.J. (1994). Six different kinds of composition. *Journal of Object-oriented Programming*, 5(8), 10–15

Open Software Foundation (1990). *OSF/Motif: Style Guide*. Englewood Cliffs, NJ: Prentice-Hall

Ovum Ltd (1992). *Workflow Management Software: The Business Opportunity*. London: Ovum

Paepcke A., ed. (1991). *OOPSLA'91 ACM Conference on Object-oriented Programming Systems, Languages and Applications*. Reading, MA: Addison-Wesley

Page-Jones M. (1992). Comparing techniques by means of encapsulation and connascence. *Comms. ACM*, 35(9), 147–51

Page-Jones M. and Weiss S. (1989). Synthesis: An object-oriented analysis and design method. *American Programmer*, 2(7), 64–7

Page-Jones M., Constantine L.L. and Weiss S. (1990). Modelling object-oriented systems: The Uniform Object Notation. *Computer Language*, Oct., 70–87

Perry D.E. and Kaiser G.E. (1990). Adequate testing and object-oriented programming. *JOOP*, 2(5), 13–19

Peters T. (1987). *Thriving on Chaos: Handbook for a Management Revoloution*. New York: Alfred Knopf

Peters T. (1992). *Liberation Management: Necessary Disorganization for the Nanosecond Nineties*. London: Macmillan

Peters T.J. and Waterman R.H. (1982). *In Search of Excellence*. New York: Harper & Row

Peterson J.L. (1981). *Petri Net Theory and the Modelling of Systems*. Englewood Cliffs, NJ: Prentice-Hall

Petri C.A. (1962). *Kommunikation mit Automaten. PhD dissertation*, University of Bonn

Porter M. (1980). *Competitive Strategy: Techniques for Analyzing Industries and Competitors*. New York: The Free Press

Prieto-Diaz R. (1993). Status report: Software reusability. *IEEE Software*, May, 61–6

Putnam L.H. (1978). A general empirical solution to the macro software sizing and estimating problem. *IEEE Trans. on Software Engineering*, July, 345–61

Quinlan J.R. (1979). Discovering rules from large collections of examples: A case study. In *Expert Systems in the Microelectronics Age* (Michie D., ed.). Edinburgh: University Press

Rawlings R. (1991). Some numbers from an object-oriented development. *Object-oriented Software Engineering*, BCS ITEXT 1991

Redmond-Pyle D. and Graham I.M. (1992). Object-oriented methods in Europe. Paper presented at Data Management '92, Bristol University

Reisner P. (1981). Formal grammars and human factors design of an interactive graphics system. *IEEE Trans. on Software Engineering*, 5, 229–40

Reiss S.P. (1991). Tools for object-oriented redesign. In *Tools 5: Proc. fifth international conference on Technology of Object-oriented Languages and Systems* (Korson T., Vaishnavi V. and Meyer B, eds.). New York: Prentice-Hall

Roach S.S. (1991). Services under siege: The restructuring imperative. *Harvard Business Review*, Sept–Oct, 82–92

Robinson J.A. (1965). A machine-oriented logic based on the resolution principle. *Proc. of the ACM*, 12

Ross J. and Kilov H. (1994). *Information Modelling: An Object-oriented Approach*. Englewood Cliffs, NJ: Prentice-Hall

Rubin K. and Goldberg A. (1992). Object behaviour analysis. *Comms. of the ACM*, Sept, 49–51

Rumbaugh J. (1993). Forceful functions: How to do numerical computation. *Object Magazine*, 6(6), 18–24

Rumbaugh J., Blaha M., Premerlani W. *et al.* (1991). *Object-oriented Modelling and Design*. Englewood Cliffs, NJ: Prentice-Hall

Sakkinen M. (1988). Comments on 'the Law of Demeter' and C++. *SIGPLAN Notices*, **23**(12), 38

Schank R.C. and Abelson R.P. (1977). *Scripts, Plans, Goals and Understanding*. New York: Lawrence Erlbaum Associates

Schneiderman B. (1992). *Designing the User Interface: Strategies for Effective Human Computer Interaction*. Reading, MA: Addison-Wesley

Schreiber G., Wielinger R. and Breuker J., eds. (1993). *KADS: A Principled Approach to Knowledge Based System Development*. London: Academic Press

Scott Gordon V. and Bieman J.M. (1993). Reported effects of rapid prototyping on industrial software quality. *Software Quality Journal*, **2**, 93–108

Searle J. R. (1969). *Speech Acts*. Cambridge: University Press

Senge P.M. (1990). *The Fifth Discipline: The Art and Practice of the Learning Organization*. London: Random House

Shafer D. and Taylor D.A. (1993). *Transforming the Enterprise through COOPERATION: An Object-oriented Solution*. Englewood Cliffs, NJ: Prentice-Hall

Shelton R.E. (1993). An Object-oriented method for enterprise modeling: OOEM. In *Proceedings of OOP'93*, Munich, pp. 61–70. New York: SIGS Publications

Shlaer S. and Mellor S.J. (1988). *Object-oriented Systems Analysis – Modelling the World in Data*. Englewood Cliffs, NJ: Yourdon Press

Shlaer S. and Mellor S.J. (1992). *Object-lifecycles: Modelling the World in States*. Englewood Cliffs, NJ: Yourdon Press

Short J.E. and Venkatramen N. (1992). Beyond business process redesign: Redefining Baxter's business network. *Sloan Management Review*, Fall, 7–17

Shortliffe E.H. (1976). *Computer Based Medical Consultations: MYCIN*. American Elsevier

Simon H.A. (1981). *The Sciences of the Artificial* 2nd edn. Cambridge, MA: MIT Press

Smith M.D. and Robson D.J. (1992). A framework for testing object-oriented programs. *JOOP*, **5**(3), 45–53

Software Futures (1994). Objects and Software Reuse: Dead on arrival at your company. *Software Futures*, **3**(3)

Soley R.M., ed. (1990). *Object Management Architecture Guide*. Framington, MA: Object Management Group

Sommerville I. (1989). *Software Engineering*, 3rd edn. Wokingham: Addison-Wesley

Sowa J.F. (1984). *Conceptual Structures: Information Processing in Mind and Machine*. Reading, MA: Addison-Wesley

Sowa J.F. and Zachman J.A. (1992). Extending and formalizing the framework for information systems architecture. *IBM Systems Journal*, **31**(3), 590–616

Stout L. (1991). A survey of fuzzy set and topos theory. *Fuzzy Sets and Systems*, **42**(1), 3–14

Suchman L.A. (1987). *Plans and Situated Actions: The problem of Human– Machine Communication*. Cambridge: University Press

Sun Microsystems Inc. (1989). *OpenLook: Graphical User Interface Functional Specification*. Reading, MA: Addison-Wesley

Symons G. (1989). *Software Sizing and Estimating: Mk II Function Point Analysis*. Chichester: John Wiley & Sons

Tanenbaum A. S. and van Rennesse R. (1985). Distributed operating systems. *ACM Computing Surveys*, **17**(4), 419–70

Taylor D. (1992a). *Object-oriented Information Systems: Planning and Implementation*. New York: John Wiley & Sons

Taylor D. (1992b). *Object-oriented Technology: A Manager's Guide*. Reading, MA: Addison-Wesley

Thimbleby H. (1990). *User Interface Design*. New York: ACM Press (Addison-Wesley)

Touretzky D.S. (1986). *The Mathematics of Inheritance Systems*. London: Pitman

Ungar D. and Smith R.B. (1987). Self: The power of simplicity. In *OOPSLA '90 ACM Conference on Object-oriented Programming Systems, Languages and Applications* (Meyrowitz N, ed.). Reading MA: Addison-Wesley

van Rijsbergen C.J. (1993). The state of information retrieval: Logic and information. *Computer Bulletin*, February, 18–20

Wand Y. (1989). A proposal for a formal model of objects. In *Object-oriented Concepts, Databases and Applications* Kim W. and Lochovsky F.H. eds, Reading, MA: Addison-Wesley

Wegner P. And Zdonik S. (1988). Inheritance as an incremental modification mechanism. *Proc. of ECOOP '88, Lecture Notes in Computer Science*, **322**, pp. 55–77, New York: Springer

Wiener N. (1948). *Cybernetics*. Cambridge, MA: MIT Press

Wellman F. (1992). *Software Costing: An Objective Approach to Estimating and Controlling the Cost of Computer Software*. London: Prentice-Hall

Wills A. (1991). Specification in Fresco. In *Object-orientation in Z*. (Stepney, Barden and Cooper, eds.). Berlin: Springer

Wilson P. (1990). *Computer-supported Cooperative Work*. Oxford: Intellect Books

Winograd T. and Flores F. (1986). *Understanding Computers and Cognition*. Reading, MA: Addison-Wesley

Wirfs-Brock R., Wilkerson B. and Wiener L. (1990). *Designing Object-oriented Software*. Englewood Cliffs, NJ: Prentice-Hall

Wirth N. (1976). *Algorithms + Data = Programs*. Englewood Cliffs, NJ: Prentice-Hall

Woolfe R. (1991). Managing and redesigning business processes to achieve dramatic performance improvements. *European Business Journal*

Xephon (1992). *The Mainframe Market Monitor*. Newbury, UK: Xephon

Young R.M., Green T.R.G. and Simon T. (1989). Programmable user models for predictive evaluation of interface designs. In *Human Factors in Computer Systems – CHI'89* (Bice K. and Lewis C., eds.). Reading, MA: Addison-Wesley

Yourdon E. (1992). *The Decline and Fall of the American Programmer*. Englewood Cliffs, NJ: Prentice-Hall

Zachman J.A. (1987). A framework for information systems architecture. *IBM Systems Journal*, **26**(3), 276–92

Zadeh L.A. (1973). Outline of a new approach to the analysis of complex systems and decision processes. *IEEE Trans. Systems Man. and Cybernetics*, SMC-3, 28–44

Zadeh L.A. (1982). A computational approach to fuzzy quantifiers in natural languages. University of California (Berkeley) *Memo. UCB-ERL M82–36*

NAME INDEX

A

Abbott, R.J. 301
Abelson, R.P 100, 200–1, 203, 211, 287, 317
Abnous, R. 124, 138, 163
Adams, G. 287
Agha, G. 163
Albrecht, A.J. 405–6
Alencar, A.J. 460
Alexander, C. 123, 232–3, 242
America, P. 529
Anderson, J.R. 171
Andleigh, P.K. 65, 163, 218
Aoyama, M. 360, 438–9
Arnold, P. 225
Arthur, L.J. 401
Ashby, W.R. 186, 335
Austen, J.L. 94

B

Bachman, C. 238
Backhurst, N. xiii, xiv, 287, 432–4
Baecker, R.M. 123
Baker, A.B. 124, 138, 163
Banker, R.D. 427, 438
Bapat, S. 163, 242, 258
Barfield, L. 19, 77, 99–100, 123
Barr, A. 173
Basden, A. 298–9
Beck, K. 530
Berard, E.V. 25, 388, 403
Berliner, H. 184
Bieman, J.M. 355
Birkbeck, S. xiii
Birrel, N.D. 456
Blaha, M. 45, 216, 225, 234, 258, 276, 277, 313, 452, 468
Bobrow, D. 188
Bodoff, S. 225
Boehm, B.W. 347–8, 353, 400, 405
Booch, G. 44, 218, 227, 232, 258, 276, 283, 312, 344–5, 445, 450, 468
Brachman, R.J. 211
Braithwaite, R.B. 185
Braune, R. 295
Breuker, J. 209
Brice, A. 45

Brookes, B.C. 532
Brouwer, 462
Brown, R.G. 326
Brown, W. 419
Browne, D. 88, 123, 401, 407, 415, 417
Browning, R. 277
Bruce, T.A. 326
Brynjolfsson, E. 139
Bunge, M. 410
Butler, A. 65
Buxton, W.A.S. 123

C

Cameron, J. 55
Campbell, T. 423
Cant, S.N. 405
Card, D.N. 402–3
Card, S.K. 103
Carrington, D. 460
Cavalcanti, A. 460
Chamberlain, G. 65
Champeaux, D., de 218, 232
Lea, D. 218, 232
Champy, J. 38, 341
Charniak, E. 174
Checkland, P. 320
Chen, P. 62, 238
Chidamber, S.R. 409–10, 413, 422
Chomsky, N. 165
Christerson, M., as Jacobson, I.
Chua, M. 432–4
Church, A. 171
Clark, D. xiii
Clausewitz, C., Von 319
Coad, P. 28, 218, 225, 230, 231, 242
Coleman, D. 225
Collins, H.M. 12, 38, 165, 211
Constantine, L.L. 411
Cook, S. 24, 55, 132, 159, 163, 225
Cooper, A. xiii
Corriveau, J-P. 287
Costello, J. 119
Coutaz, J. 104
Cowper, W. 445
Cox, B.J. 43, 411, 466
Cox, E. 341
Cox, G. 11
Crewe, R. xiii

D

Dalton, R. 119
Daniels, J. 24, 55, 132, 159, 163, 225
Daniels, P.J. 294
Davenport, T.H. 9, 38, 140, 329, 341
Davies, S. xiii
Davis, R. 187
DeBono, E. 11
Desfray, P. 218, 244, 281
Devlin, K. 139
Diaper, D. 143, 163
Dick, M. xiii
Dietrich, W.C. 43, 48–9, 51, 71
Dijkstra, E. 458
Dodgson, C.L. 423
Dollin, C. 225
Doyle, J. 269
Doyle, Sir A.C. 469
Dreyfus, H.L. 165
Dreyfus, S.E. 165
Duda, R. 173
Dugundji, J. 400
Duke, D. 460
Duke, R. 460
Durham, A. 140, 163, 215
Durr, E. 460

E

Edwards, J.M. 27, 68, 218, 225, 276, 348–9, 353, 393, 398, 400, 402–4, 408, 421, 422
Edwards, J.S. 210
Englebart, D. 73
Englemore, D. 71
Ericsson, K.A. 294
Evans, N. xiii, 133
Ewald, A. 147, 158

F

Fagan, M. 361, 381
Faure, P. 218, 232
Feigenbaum, E. 173
Feldman, J.A. 538
Ferreira, A. xiii
Fichman, R.G. 38
Firesmith, D.G. 233

Flint, D. 134
Flores, F. 94
Foley, J. 104
Forgy, C.L. 188
Forsythe, R. 210–11
Foshay, W.R. 295
Fowler, M. xiv
Friedman, J. 54

G

Gaffney, J.E. 405
Galitz, W. 96
Gall, J. 344
Gamma, E. 233
Gee, T. xiii
Gilchrist, H. 225
Glass, R.L. 402–3
Gödel, K. 219
Goguen, J.A. 460
Goldberg, D.E. 211
Goldberg, A. 104, 314, 317
Goodall, A. 211
Gracer, F. 43, 48–9, 51, 71
Graham, I.M. 3, 6, 38–9, 46, 54, 61,
    63, 71, 81, 113, 136, 159–60,
    175, 195–6, 206, 209, 211,
    217, 222, 261, 263, 267–8, 276,
    299, 301
Grass, J.E. 49, 71
Gray, P.M.D. 63
Green, R. 165
Green, T.R.G. 103
Greenberg, S. 163
Gretzinger, M.R. 65, 163, 218
Grotehen, T. xiii
Guha, R.V. 160, 188
Guttman, M. 130

H

Haack, S. 185
Halmos, P. 400
Hammer, M. 4, 9, 38, 140, 329, 341
Harel, D. 234, 313
Harmon, P. 39
Hart, A. 211, 299
Hart, P. 173
Haughton, H. 460–1, 468
Hayes, F. 225
Hayes, I. 460
Hayes-Roth, F. 210
Hekmatpour, S. 354
Helm, R. 233
Hempel, C.G. 185
Henderson-Sellers, B. xiv, 27, 68,
    218, 225, 259, 276, 348–9, 353,
    393, 398, 400, 402–4, 408,
    421–2, 441

Herakleitus 215
Hermman, M. 104
Hickman, F.R. 56
Hill, R.D. 104
Hoare, C.A. 458
Hodgson, R. 347
Holsapple, C.W. 188
Horty, J.F. 256
Hughes, J.G. 63
Huxley, A. 485

I

Ince, D. 233
Ishikawa, S. 123, 232–3, 242

J

Jackson, M. 465
Jackson, P. 210
Jacobs, S. 38
Jacobson, I. 21, 100, 143, 218, 276,
    286–7, 312, 317, 341, 406,
    416, 421–2
Jeffrey, D.R. 403
Jeremaes, P. 225
Jobs, S. 92
Johnson, P. 95, 103–5, 123, 294
Johnson, R. 233
Jones, C.B. 460
Jones, P.L.K. xiii, 6, 195–6, 211, 263,
    268, 299, 341
Jones, T.C. 407
Jonsson, P. *as* Jacobson, I.
Jordan, V. 424
Jungclaus, R. 455

K

Kaiser, G.E. 416, 421
Kaufmann, R.J. 427, 438
Keen, P.G.W. 332
Kelly, G.A. 299
Kemerer, C.F. 38, 409–10, 412, 422
Khoshafian, S. 124, 138, 163
Killen, J. 56
Kilov, H. 276, 461
Kim, W. 104
King, D. xiv
King, J.A. 130
King, P. 460
Kipling, R. 293, 319
Knapp, E.M. 332
Korson, T. 435
Kosko, B. 205, 281
Kovavavics, S. 104
Koza, J.R. 211
Krishnarao, G.K. 63

L

Lamb, T. xiii
Land, L. 56
Lano, K. 460–1, 468
Laranjeira, L.A. 405
Laurel, B. 122–3
Lee, G. 101, 105, 123
Lees, C. xiii
Lektorsky, V.A. 17
Lenat, D.B. 160, 187–8
Lenin, V.I. 141
Lenzerini, M. 256
Levesque, H.J. 211
Lewis, C. 542
Lewis, M. xiii, xiv
Londeix, B. 405
Loomis, M.E.S. 54
Loosely, C. 323
Lorenz, M. 225, 312, 317
Love, T. 43
Lyall, M. xiii

M

Macdonald, R. 97, 134
Machiavelli, N. 67
Mackenzie, K.D. 69
Madsen, O.L. 28, 242
Magnusson, B. 537
Mandrioli, D., *see* Meyer, B.
Marcuse, H. 185
Martin, J. 58, 113, 208, 225, 238, 243,
    245, 276, 320, 354
Martin–Löf, P. 462–3
Marx, G. 141
Marx, K. 125
Matthews, J. 130
McCabe, T.J. 402, 409, 416
McCawley, J.D. 176
McDermott, D. 174, 269
McGregor, J.D. 353, 435, 444
McIlroy, D. 425
McNicholl, D. 388
Meersman, R.A. 538
Meira, S. 460
Mellor, S.J. 225, 231, 281
Menzies, T. 441
Meyer, B. v, 149, 452, 468
Meyrowitz, N. 71
Michaels, W.I. 321
Miller, G.A. 82, 230
Miller, R.G. vi, xiv
Miller, S.K. xiv
Miller, S.T.G. vi, xiv
Minsky, M.L. 165, 186
Moller-Pedersen, B. 28, 242
Moralee, D.S. 530
Moran, T.P. 103
Morgan, A. 71

Mullender, S. 129,163
Murray, K. 104
Myers, B.A. 104
Myers, G.J. 403, 418, 421

N

Nilsson, N.J. 530
Nackman, L.R. 43, 48–9, 51, 71
Nardi, D. 256
Nerson, J-M. 461
Newell, A. 171
Ng, K. 441
Nordström, B. 462
Norman, D.A. 123
Novobilski, A. xiv, 116, 411
Nygaard, K. 28, 242

O

O'Connor, P. 119
Odell, J.J. 58, 113, 225, 238, 242–3,
  245, 276
Ould, M.A. 456
Overgaard, G. *as* Jacobson, I.

P

Paepcke, A. 539
Page-Jones, M. 410–11
Pant, Y.R. 441
Papert, S. 186
Paton, N.W. 63
Perrot, J-F. 537
Perry, D.E. 416, 421
Peters, T. 4, 8, 11, 13, 141, 268, 329
Peterson, J.L. 455, 468
Petersson, K. 462
Petri, C.A. 455
Piaget, J. 174
Plato 399
Porter, M. 330
Premerlani, W. 45, 218, 225, 234, 258,
  276, 278, 313, 452, 468
Prieto-Diaz, R. 432
Prosser, C. xiii

Q

Quinlan, R. 186

R

Radmore, R. xiii
Ramji, A-N. xiii
Rawlings, R. 408
Rechenberg, I. 211
Redmond-Pyle, D. 55

Reisner, P. 103
Reiss, S.P. 47, 71
Rhodes, B. xiii
Roach, S.S. 139
Robinson, J.A. 178
Robson, D.J. 421
Rockart, J. 398
Rose, G. 460
Ross, J. 276, 461
Roy, M. 147, 158
Rubin, K. 314, 317
Rumbaugh, J. 45, 218, 225, 234, 258,
  276, 278, 313, 452, 468

S

Sakkinen, M. 305
Sanger, C. 143
Schank, R.C. 21, 100, 200–1, 203,
  210, 287, 317
Schneiderman, B. 122–4
Schreiber, G. 209
Schwarb, R. xiii
Scott Gordon, V. 355
Searle, J., R. 94, 283
Senge, P.M. 428
Shafer, D. 163
Shakespeare, W. 215, 277
Shaw, G., B. 343
Shelton, R.E. 327–8, 334
Shepherd, K. 124, 138, 163
Shlaer, S. 225, 233, 281
Short, J.E. 9, 38, 140, 329, 333
Shortliffe, E.H. 173
Silverstein, M. 123, 230–1, 240
Simi, M. 254
Simon, H.A. 19, 165, 171, 294
Simon, T. 103
Smith, A. 141
Smith, G. 460
Smith, J.M. 461
Smith, M.D. 421
Smith, R.B. 27, 62, 238
Sommerville, I. 421
Sowa, J.F. 322–3, 341
Spock 27
Stevenson, R.L. 41
Stone, C. 149
Stout, L. 463
Suchman, L.A. 94, 123
Sykes, D.A. 352, 444
Symons, G. 294, 406

T

Tannenbaum, A.S. 126
Taylor, D.A. 4, 38–9, 163
Taylor, F. 141
Taylor, J. xiii, 240
Thal, B. xiii

Thimbleby, H. 20, 88, 90–1, 123, 417
Thomason, R.H. 256
Thyssen, U. xiii
Touretzky, D.S. 256, 271
Turing, A. 14, 171, 458

U

Ungar, D. 27, 62, 238

V

Vaishnavi, V. 435
van Renesse, R. 126
van Rijsbergen, C.J. 139
Venkatramen, N. 38, 333
Vilcius, A. xiii
Vlissides, J. 233

W

Walker, R. xiii
Walsh, J. xiii
Wand, Y. 410
Waterman, D.A. 268
Watson, R. xiii
Webber, B.L. 530
Wegner, P. 163, 464
Weiner, N. 188
West, M. 41
Wellman, F. 405
Welton, D. xiii
Whinston, A.B. 188
Wielinger, R. 209
Wiener, L. 225, 233, 276, 317
Wilkerson, B. 225, 233, 276, 317
Williams, K. xiii
Wills, A. 460
Wilson, P. 163
Winograd, T. 94, 188
Wirfs-Brock, R. 225, 231, 276, 317
Wirth, N. 6
Woolfe, R. 38

Y

Yonezawa, A. 163
Young, R.M. 103
Yourdon, E. 108, 218, 225, 233, 242

Z

Zachman, J.A. 320, 322, 323, 326,
  327, 341
Zadeh, L.A. 264, 268, 334
Zdonik, S. 464
Zemp, M. xiii
Zweig, D. 428, 438

SUBJECT INDEX

× 236, 247, 250
$ 247, 250
.RAD files 469, 471, 473, 477
/ 247, 250
{common/fixed/unique/variable} 247
3270 terminals 128
3NF – 3rd normal form 245
4GLs – 4th generation languages 42, 280, 355
abduction 184

A

absolute and relative truth 170
abstract classes 227, 309, 413
abstract data types 25, 58, 132, 464
Abstract Object Model *see* OMG Abstract Object Model
abstraction 13, 27, 28, 30
acceptance testing 417, 421
access functions 136, 452
access operations 25, 229, 248
access privileges 56, 136
accidental objects 271–2, 301–4
accounting metrics 401
accounting systems 4, 479
Action Technologies 144
actions 259
activated memory 82, 83, 85, 230
active data *see* triggers
active objects 130–2
active subject, rôle of 17
activities 259, 351, 352, 357, 359
Actor xii, 18, 108, 115
actors 100, 201, 282–3, 286, 315, 320
acyclic structures *see* SOMA metrics
acyclicity in inheritance 273–4
ad hoc polymorphism 238, 268
ad hoc queries 137
AD/Cycle 324
Ada 68, 445, 452
ADABAS ENTIRE 111
adaptable businesses 3–12, 17, 23, 35
adaptive fuzzy systems 205
ADS *see* AionDS
advanced relational database products 58, 61, 63, 217, 226
ADW 111
aesthetics 86, 87, 96
agents 61
aggregation *see* composition structures
AI – artificial intelligence 12, 39, 57, 61–4, 81, 165, 174–5, 224, 248, 459
AI Magazine 211
AI planning theory 100
AI products *see* expert systems development tools
AI Watch 211

AI, frames in *see* frames
AionDS 59, 207
airline reservation systems 16, 155
AIX 105
AKO – A Kind Of 236–8, 247
algebraic GUEPs *see* GUEPs
algebraic specification 462
allowed values *see* Leonardo
alternative cost-centre model of reuse 441
AM (Artificial Mathematician) 187
ambiguity 458
Amdahl 58
AmiPro 75
ammonite model 353
analogical reasoning 260
analogous tasks *see* associated tasks
analysis modelling 220
analysis of judgements 301–3
analysis report *see* systems analysis report
analysis *v.* design 221
Andrew toolkit 108
animation xi, 246, 419, 428, 430, 438, 455, 458, 465, 485
animation features of *SOMATiK see* animation
antecedent clauses 172, 413
anthropology 123, 142
AOM (Abstract Object Model) *see* OMG Abstract Object Model
APL 43, 67
APO – A Part Of 240
Apple Computer 14, 74, 104
Apple Lisa 73
application conscripts 429
application frameworks 117, 123, 389, 425, 454
application grids 141
Application Manager 111
application objects *see* Domain/ Application/ Interface objects
Application Wizards *see* Wizards
applications architecture 329
APPN protocol 145
approximate reasoning 205
APT Data Services 39
architectural design and reuse 437
architecture 375
ARIES expert systems project 65
ART, ART-IM and ART-Enterprise 59, 208
Arthur D. Little 75
artificial intelligence *see* AI
AS/400 machine 50, 438, 479
assembler 42, 43
assertions 59, 101, 169, 227, 229, 243 247, 250, 252, 303, 357, 413, 415, 446, 447, 450, 459
assertions and rules 281, 308, 445–8
asset business processes 333

associated tasks 289
association structures 244–5
association *v.* attribution 240, 244–5
associations – as violaters of encapsulation 242
associations 132, 224, 227, 244–5, 247–8, 276, 303, 309, 450, 452–3
associative knowledge 94
associative queries 136
associativity *see* GUEPs
assumptions 282, 315, 364
Atis 438
ATMs (Automated Teller Machines) 16
atomic tasks 101, 287, 294, 383, 412, 414, 475
atomism 410
attention, gaining *see* gaining attention
attribute annotations *see* facets attribute
facets *see* facets
attribute values 410
attributes 25, 26, 63, 200, 227–8, 247–9, 289, 303, 309
augmented Petri nets 246, 257–60
authentication 149
Automated Teller Machines *see* ATMs
automatic control 335
automatic function point collection 412, 414
automatic indexing systems 139
automatically generated diagrams in *SOMATiK* 247
axiomatic specification 460
axioms 462

B

Bachman notation 238
backtracking 183
backward chaining inference 168, 180–1, 191, 251, 262, 332
backward chaining under uncertainty *see* fuzzy backward chaining
band-width 15
banking 8
Banque Paribas 35
bargain *see* trade
base classes 235
BASIC 10, 452
Bass 119
batch 44, 46
Baxter Healthcare 334
Bayesian probability 168
bean bags 311
behaviour *see* operations
benefits–based pricing 412
BETA 242
beta testing 413

Beyond Inc. 142
BeyondMail 142
Bezant Ltd/Bezant Object Technologies xi, xiii, 480, 485
bi-directional search 183
binary large objects *see* BLOBs
BIS Banking Systems xiii
black box testing 416, 419
blackboard systems 43, 59–61, 71, 119, 204–5
BLOBs (binary large objects) 57, 138
blocking sends 129
Boehm's spiral model *see* spiral model
Boeing 35
boiled eggs 24
Boldon James 142
BOM – Business Object Model 218, 280–2, 288, 305, 320, 322, 325, 330, 331, 359, 366, 389, 413–14, 419, 445, 449
BON 461
Booch '93 method 68, 218, 245, 280–1, 328, 372, 445, 447–52, 467–8
Booch Components 50, 434–5
Borland 33, 35, 104
borrowing strategy 46, 47, 49, 52, 61, 76
boundary value tests 417, 419
bounded activities 357, 359
BPR – business process re-engineering 4, 5, 8, 22, 31, 35, 38, 140, 143–4, 226, 258, 284, 286, 320–2, 329, 332–3, 338, 341–2, 389, 428, 477–8
brainstorming 309, 333, 477
breadth-first search 183
British Airways 146
British Telecom 144, 249
Britvic 119
broad and shallow prototypes/interviews 292
broadcasting messages 26, 59, 61, 204
browsing facilities xi, 437–8, 476
build stage 357
business knowledge 280
business network 286, 319
Business Object Model *see* BOM
business objects 320
business policies 10, 330–1, 336–7
business process re-engineering *see* BPR
business processes and process modelling 9, 17, 21, 31, 100, 260, 268, 278–80, 283, 312, 320, 332–7, 373, 429
business rules 58, 62, 64, 65, 101, 218, 252–3, 321, 330
business simulations 208, 407
Butler Cox Foundation 15, 74
Byte 124

C

C 48, 50, 109, 150, 425, 452
C++ 20, 31, 49, 55, 63, 68, 108, 115, 150, 235, 280, 372, 408, 420, 425, 432–5, 445, 447–8, 455, 477
C++ class libraries 150
C++/Views 114
cable television networks 15
CAD/CAM applications 31, 33, 57, 58
Cairo 14, 75

call-back mechanism 204
Canadian Imperial Bank of Commerce xiii, 35
capsules 461
capturing requirements – *see* requirements capture
card sorts 304
Carnot project 159–60
CASE xi, 15, 16, 31, 34, 35, 47, 50, 58, 63, 100, 206–7, 245, 278, 355, 357, 362, 364, 381, 427, 437–8, 453, 479
case-based reasoning 75
CBO (Coupling between objects) 409
CBR Express 75
ccMail 77
CD-ROMs 107
Centerline Inc 50, 434, 455
centrality of tasks 100
centralized architectures 126–7
centralized computing 129, 137
centralized repositories or reuse libraries *see* repositories
centralized sequential development 438
CEO 149
certainty factors 168, 264, 268, 411
change control 396
change management 4, 67, 158–9, 355, 425, 431, 437
changing businesses 8
changing requirements 7, 30, 356
channel capacity 16
channel switching 92
chartism 60
cheating *see* reuse
Chen notation 238
Choreographer 109
chromosomes *see* genetic algorithms
chunks 82, 171, 230, 233, 295
CIBC *see* Canadian Imperial Bank of Commerce
CICS 14, 458
Civil Aviation Authority 35
class attributes 250, 410
class cards 230, 242, 246, 274, 290, 300, 308–10, 419, 449, 451
class categories 232, 450
class invariants 227, 250
class librarians 414, 429
class libraries 13, 50, 63, 426, 434–5, 453–5, 461
class library browsers *see* browsing facilities
class library evaluation 435
class library management and control 426, 432–4, 438, 444
class operations 250
class utilities 451
class variables 410
class-oriented 26
class/type cross reference tables *see* cross reference tables
classes 25, 26, 62, 227, 452, 461, 464
Classes Responsibilities and Collaborations *see* CRC
classes/instances 227
Classic Ada 63
classification 26, 28, 29, 139, 238
classification structures 82, 85, 99, 200, 234–40, 300, 306, 309, 420, 464, 466

classification-based browsing 438
classless inheritance 27, 62
CLG *see* Command Language Grammar
client/server computing *see* CSC
client/server relationships 245
clock synchronization problems 129
CLOS 60, 68, 207
closed world assumption 271
closure 86, 88
co-operating knowledge sources *see* blackboard systems
CO-OPERATION 130–1
co-operative processing 43, 61, 136
Coad/Yourdon method 225, 478
coarse grain reuse *see* granularity
COBOL 6, 10, 34, 42, 43, 67, 150, 408, 452
COCOMO 400, 405
CODASYL databases 6, 56
code generation 15, 355, 453–4
code level reuse *see* specification *v.* code level reuse
code libraries 427
code/specification cross reference tables *see* cross reference tables
CogBrow 258
cognition 167, 173, 279
cognitive complexity theory 403, 408
cognitive dissonance 86
cognitive psychology 82–86
coherent entities *see* object identity
cohesion *see* coupling and cohesion
collaborations 309
collaborative work and collaborative computing 139–146
colour 82, 96, 97
colour blindness *see* handicaps
command language grammar (CLG) 103
command languages 20
Commander 111
Common Lisp Object System *see* CLOS
Common Object Request Broker Architecture *see* CORBA
Common Object Services Standard *see* COSS
CommonView 104, 108, 434
communications technology 15
commutativity *see* GUEPs
competitive advantage 7, 8, 15, 33, 53, 136
compilers 425
completeness 271
complexity 4, 6, 7, 9, 11, 13, 17, 34, 67, 289–90, 345, 356, 402–3, 408, 410–12, 439
complexity metrics 402, 420, 432
component objects *see* composition structures
component task scripts 287–89
composite objects *see* composition structures
composition structures 28, 82, 230, 240–2, 309, 420
computer based training 107
Computer Finance 39
Computer Supported Co-operative Work *see* CSCW
computers, performance of labour by *see* intelligence (social nature of)
Computing 33
computing metrics automatically 526–7

concept classification 138
concept sorting 295
conceptual chunking *see* chunks
conceptual cohesion *see* logical cohesion
conceptual dependency theory *see*
        conceptual primitives in script
        theory
conceptual graphs 323
conceptual modelling 36
conceptual primitives in script theory 201
conch models 353
concrete classes 227, 309, 413
concurrency 132, 311, 447, 452, 455
concurrency semantics 450
concurrent development 360, 439
concurrent states 257
concurrent systems 42
concurrent threads 310–12
configuration management 414, 426, 429,
        431, 437
configurational composition 241–2
connascence 243, 410–11
conorms *see* fuzzy logic
conscripts model *see* hairies and
        conscripts model
consequent clauses 109
consistency 75, 76
consolidation activity 380–2
constant-creation model of reuse 441
constraints 55, 308, 310, 450
constructive mathematics 462
constructs *see* personal constructs
content and form 28
context modelling *see* internal and
        external context models
continuous speech recognition *see*
        speech recognition
continuum of representation in
        object-oriented methods 226, 326,
        415, 448
contracts 13, 216, 280, 415, 425–6, 436,
        459–62, 464
contradictions 17, 22, 27, 169, 395, 462
control régimes *see* control rules
control rules 252–4, 256
conversational acts *see* semiotic acts
Conversational Remote Job Entry *see*
        CRJE
convex fuzzy sets 266
Cooperative Solutions Inc *see* TP
        monitors
Coopers & Lybrand 157
coordination and reuse 220
Coordinator, The 144
CORBA (Common Object Request
        Broker Architecture) 11, 31, 45,
        46, 50, 57, 130, 146, 152,
CORBA 2 151
CorVision 111
COSS 152
cost estimates 333
cost metrics 404
cost-benefit analysis 352
coupling and cohesion 34, 245, 402–3,
        408, 410–11
CP/M86, 67
CRC cards 308
CRC/RDD 225, 238, 308
Create Read Update Delete *see* CRUD
        matrices

Credit Suisse 35
creeping functionality 355
critical success factors *see* CSFs
CRJE – Conversational Remote Job
        Entry 73
cross reference tables 338, 428–9, 438,
        464, 467, 485
cross-project co-ordination 431, 439
CRUD matrices 47, 224, 321
Crystal 188
CSC – Client Server Computing 16, 22,
        31, 34, 39, 53, 61, 62, 76, 81, 127,
        129, 131–7, 151, 157, 407
CSC Index 111
CSCW – Computer Supported
        Co-operative Work 128, 139–44,
        204
CSFs 324, 352, 387, 398
CUA 88, 105
cultural changes 35, 68, 158–9
cultural variations 97
customer service organizations 20, 81
Cybernetics 186, 353
CYC 160, 188
cycles in classification structures 271
cyclomatic complexity 402, 409–10, 414,
        416

D

Darwinian selection *see* genetic
        algorithms
data dictionary 57
data duplication 24, 26
data flow diagrams *see* DFDs
data flow models 45
data flows 450
data gloves 78
data independence 55, 308
data management strategies 46–8, 126–7
data modelling 320
data servers 125
data structures 6, 452
data-centred translation strategy 47, 52
data-directed inference 168
database management systems 6, 24, 47,
        55, 209, 479
database modelling 461
database server model 127
database servers 134, 136
database triggers *see* triggers
database wrappers *see* object wrappers
Dataflex 110
DB2 54, 57
DB2/CICS server 154
DBMSs *see* database management
        systems
DCA 11
DCE (Distributed Computing
        Environment) 135, 154
Dclass 413
Dcomp 413
DDE *see* Dynamic Data Exchange
de-normalized relations 56
deafness *see* handicaps
deal capture 297
DEC 50, 58

decentralization 4
decision support systems 263
decision trees 250, 253
declarative knowledge 94
declarative programming 173
DECnet 145
decomposing many-to-many relationships
        see normalization
deduction 184
default values 247
defaults 251–62
defects 432
defuzzification 196, 262–3, 264–5, 267, 337
delays 362
delegation 231, 232
deliverables, minimizing 315, 360–1
Demeter, Law of 305
demons 60, 168, 251
denormalization *see* normalization
depth of inheritance 401, 409, 412–13
depth-first search 182
deregulation 8
derived classes 235
description fields (*SOMATiK*) 449
design decisions 446, 467
design for reuse 437
design modelling *see* logical design
design patterns *see* patterns
design report 381
designable businesses 8, 11, 18
desktop metaphor 20, 21, 75
desktop publishing 478
determinism 353, 456
development life cycle *see* software
        development life cycle
development team 433
DFDs (data flow diagrams) 10, 48,
        224–5, 259, 287, 478
dialectics *see* contradictions
dialogue design 94–8
Digital Equipment Corporation *see* DEC
DIM – Document Image Management
        107, 140, 142
discourse analysis 94
disjunctive inheritance 238
distributed computing 12, 16, 31, 35,
        36, 41, 66, 67, 125–63, 204
Distributed Computing Environment
        see DCE
distributed concurrent development 438
distributed databases 133, 138
distributed front-end model 127
distributed object computing 130, 132,
        146–52, 159–60
Distributed Object Management
        Systems (DOMS) 50, 149, 150
Distributed Objects Everywhere (DOE)
        135, 152
distributed operating systems 126, 129
DIT (depth of inheritance tree) 409–10, 413
division of labour 141
document flow diagrams 312
Document Image Management systems
        see DIM
document interchange standards 11
documentation 23, 380–2, 417, 429, 431,
        433–4, 437
DOE *see* Distributed Objects Everywhere
domain analysis 388, 393

domain modelling 143, 361, 421
domain modelling and repository administration activity 388–90
domain modelling team 393, 429–30
domain objects *see* domain/application/interface objects
domain/application/interface objects 55, 56, 230, 281, 307, 309, 349, 388–9, 413–14
domains 388
DOME 50, 151
DOMS *see* Distributed Object Management Systems
dotted line relationships 268
downsizing 16, 41, 136
downsizing disasters 155–9
drag-and-drop 75
drawing diagrams rather than embedding text 219
Dsub 414
DuPont 354, 398
dynamic binding 26
dynamic classification 410
Dynamic Data Exchange (DDE) 118

E

E-mail 107
E/M *see* structure semantics
E/O *see* structure semantics
eager evaluation 252, 446
ease-of-use 74, 75, 85, 355
Easel 109
EDI – Electronic Data Interchange 15
education and training 33, 34, 68, 361–2, 392
Effect Correspondence Diagrams 224
efficiency 31
EFTPOS – Electronic Funds Transfer at the Point of Sale 15
Eiffel 31, 63, 68, 239, 434–5, 447, 460–1
elastic constraints 336
elbow testing 417
Electronic Data Interchange *see* EDI
Electronic Funds Transfer at the Point of Sale *see* EFTPOS
electronic mail *see* E-mail
elements of a Kelly grid 299
ELHs – Entity Life Histories 245, 258
elimination rules 176
embedded expert systems 43
embedded graphics 75
empowerment 4, 8, 22, 136, 141, 329
encapsulation 3, 24–9, 43, 63, 67, 167, 246, 249, 309, 411, 452
encapsulation metrics 410–11
Encina *see* TP monitors
end users 321
end-lifecycle model of reuse 441
end-use customers 321
end-user computing 137
endless prototyping 375
ENFIN 50, 104, 109
engineering databases 31
Enhancement Periods 351
ensembles 232
Enterprise Mail 142
enterprise modelling 220, 224, 281, 319–330

entity life histories *see* ELHs
entity modelling 279
entity-relationship diagrams/data models 62, 224
Epic/Workflow 144
epistemology 173
equal opportunity 91
Equitable Life xiii
ERDs *see* entity-relationship diagrams/data models
ergonomics 82
ES/kernel 205–7
essential and accidental objects 271–2, 301–3
essential complexity 402, 410
essential objects *see* essential and accidental objects
estimation 399, 405
estimation models *see* models
ethnomethodology 123, 142
EURISKO 187
evaluation activity 384–5, 421
evaluation team 360, 396
evaluations 361, 419
EVE *see* ISA
event driven dialogues 7
event driven interaction 22, 36, 81
event handlers 102
event traces xi, 259, 283, 311–12, 321, 331–3, 359, 407, 419, 429, 450, 455, 467, 478, 485
event traces, documenting walkthroughs with 310–11
events 257, 280, 283–4, 364
evolutionary delivery 10
evolutionary development 344–5
evolutionary prototyping 358, 465
exception handling 101, 201
exceptions 101, 252, 287, 335
exchange value 12
excluded middle, law of 176, 463
exclusions 282, 315, 364
executable specifications *see* animation
expanded composition structure 507–8
expected value analysis 314
expert modes *see* novice modes
expert system shells 58, 168, 173, 178, 189–92, 206, 226, 465, 467
expert systems 6, 14, 15, 17, 18, 22, 36, 38, 42, 58, 59, 61, 62, 64–5, 71, 95 100, 140, 165–211, 217, 252, 308, 407
expert systems development tools and environments 67, 206, 466
explanation facilities 95, 168, 173
explicitness 10
export controls 451
Express 111
extended relational databases *see* advanced relational database products
extensibility 12, 13, 18, 30, 33, 35, 63, 257
extension 42, 52, 53
external context diagram 282, 284
external context model 283, 286
external objects 282, 285, 315, 364, 413
external tasks 99

F

facets 227, 229–30, 248, 250
facilitators 311, 315, 395–6, 419, 430, 487

Fagans inspection technique 379, 382, 391–2, 420, 421
fan counts 401–3, 412–4
fan-in 403, 410
fan-out 401, 409, 412
fast-path developments *see* evolutionary development
fault diagnosis expert systems 107
fault tolerance 129
feasibility studies 352
feature points 407
features 227
feedback 428
fern diagrams 235, 238, 306
file servers 129, 134
Filenet 142
financial services organizations 153
financial trading 59, 119, 295, 473–6, 479
finding objects *see* object identification
fine grain reuse *see* granularity
First Boston Corporation 427
first normal form 47, 305
first order predicate calculus (FOPC) 281, 459–60, 464
flat organizational structures 4, 140, 329, 393, 408
flattening classification structures 452, 466–7
flexibility 13, 30, 34, 66, 358, 435
FOCUS 111
focussed interviews 292–3
focussing Kelly grids 299
Folder Application Facility 144
FOOPS 461
Ford Motor Co. 4, 5, 140, 329
Forests & Trees 108
formal logic 458
formal specification methods 14, 458–64, 468
FORTÉ 50
FORTRAN 10, 13, 43, 452
forward chaining 168, 178–80, 251, 262
fountain model 348–9
FPA *see* function points analysis
fractal model 353
frame slots *see* slots
frame-based expert systems 58, 61, 465
frames 27, 62, 63, 167, 199–200, 204, 206–7
frameworks 437
free software tool *see* SOMATiK
Fresco 460–1
friend *see* public/private/protected/friend
friend coupling 411
full-content information retrieval systems 138
function calls 26, 452
function libraries 425
function points 401, 405–8, 412, 414, 431
Function Points Analysis (FPA) 294, 405–8
functional decomposition 5, 51, 129, 250, 277, 279, 320, 356
functional decomposition *v.* reusability 321
functional languages 463
functional models 141, 320
functional specialization 4, 141, 143, 278, 287
fundamental analysis 60
funds transfer system 313

FUSION 223
fuzzifying composition structures 262
fuzzy associations 268
fuzzy attributes 264, 268
fuzzy backward chaining 196–9
fuzzy classification 226
Fuzzy Closed World Assumption 270
fuzzy controllers 42, 205
fuzzy expert systems 196, 206
fuzzy features of SOMA 320
fuzzy inference 195–9, 262, 264
fuzzy inheritance 139, 265–74, 464
fuzzy logic 262, 281, 342, 463
fuzzy matching 139, 438
fuzzy *modus ponens* 195
fuzzy multiple inheritance 264
fuzzy numbers 263
fuzzy objects 260, 264–74, 411
fuzzy policy 334–37
fuzzy quantifiers 264, 268–9
fuzzy relations 195
fuzzy rule-based systems 260
fuzzy rules 193–4, 205, 262, 268, 331, 337
fuzzy rulesets 139, 260, 262, 464
fuzzy set theory 193, 261–4
fuzzy sets 193, 260–1, 264, 411

G

G–C1 model of reuse 441
gaining attention 96
garbage collection 52
GARNET 104
Gemini 209
GemStone 54, 58, 63
General Electric 35
General Magic 74
general systems theory 320
generalization 349, 361, 436–7, 441
generalization costs 404
generalization/specialization *see*
        classification
generating code *see* code generation
Generative User–Engineering
        Principles (GUEPs) 88–93
genetic algorithms 187, 211
GeOde 111
geographic information systems *see* GIS
geometrical image transformation 45
get operations *see* access operations
GIE interface builder 160
GIS (geographic information systems) 31,
        57
glass teletypes 73
global behaviour and dynamics 252, 259,
        455
global class invariants 251
Global Financial Engineering 119
global system control 251–2
global variables 452
glossary 428–9, 476, 485
goal directed inference 168
goals 59, 99, 172, 279, 284–6, 288, 290,
        315, 320, 324, 358, 364
Goals Operators Methods and *see* GOMS
GOMS 103–4, 123
Gradygrams 44, 231
granularity 45, 51, 132, 171, 425
graphical front-ends 43, 76
graphical icons *see* icons

graphical user interfaces *see* GUIs
graphics tablets 78–9
Greek drama 123
group discussions 292
group dynamics 313, 395
group work 100, 437
groupware 87, 94, 139–44
growth period 350–1
guards 259, 357
GUEPs *see* Generative User-
        Engineering Principles
GUI authoring tools 67
GUI design *see* HCI design
GUI development tools 108–19
GUI frameworks 104
GUI libraries 50, 104, 454
GUI Master 109
GUI standards 104–6
GUIs 20, 31, 34, 36, 41, 49, 61, 63, 73–124,
        129, 344
Guru 188

H

hackers 397
hacking 397
hairies and conscripts model 430–1
hairy ball theorem 462
handicaps 94, 96
handshake (tandem) strategy 46, 47, 52
Harvard Business Review 342, 398
has (has-a) 240, 449–51
Hawthorne effect 356
HCI (human computer interaction) 20–2,
        142–3, 287, 317
HCI design 76–108
Hearsay II, 60
hedges 193, 261
help desks 18
Hertz 333
Hewlett Packard 35
hidden variables 335, 353
high level languages 12, 15
history icon 450
Hitachi *see* ES/KERNEL
Hodgsons X model *see* X model
Hollerith punched cards *see* punched cards
holonomic cube 9
Holos 111
homeomeric composition 243–4
homology 245, 414
homomorphisms (in OMT) 242
HOOD Seniority hierarchy 245
HP *see* Hewlett Packard
human computer interaction *see* HCI
Human Interface Guidelines see Apple
Hypercard 108
Hyperdesk 149–11
hypergenericity 281
hypermedia 42, 46, 87
hypertext systems 96, 438

I

I/M (inclusive/mandatory) *see*
        structure semantics
I/O (inclusive/optional) *see* structure
        semantics

IBM 14, 31, 33, 35, 43, 104, 144, 333,
        354, 410
ICL 35, 330
icons 20, 85, 93
ID3, 186
idempotence *see* GUEPs
identifying objects *see* object
        identification
identity *see* object identity
IDL 104, 148–9, 152
IE *see* Information Engineering
IEEE Expert 211
IEF 111
if/then rules 252
IIDL 150
ImageFlow 144
impedance mismatch 160, 207
implementation modelling *see*
        physical design
Implementation Object Model (IOM)
        218, 280, 328, 376, 445, 449
implementation planning activity 361,
        385–6
implemented–by links 230–1, 240, 250,
        450
import–export facilities 57
imprecision 281
IMS 6, 56, 57
incompatibility, principle of 335
incremental delivery 277, 356
induction 184–5
Inertial modes *see* modes
inference 175–200, 227, 262, 264
Inference Corp 75
inference engine 166–7
inference régimes 230
infons 139
information 169
Information Engineering (IE) 320–1,
        324
information hiding 27, 34
Information Resource Dictionary
        System *see* IRDS
Information Retrieval (IR) systems
        138–9
Information Warehouse 324
informed search 183
Informix 111
INGRES 49, 54, 58, 64, 108
INGRES Windows 4GL 110
inheritance 3, 13, 26–8, 30, 61–3, 65,
        67, 168, 237–8, 249, 251, 330,
        410–11, 416, 419, 434, 449, 453,
        462, 464–5
inheritance as compromiser of
        encapsulation/reuse 26, 249
inheritance conflicts *see* multiple
        inheritance
inheritance rules 257
initial values 247
input devices 78–80, 295
input modes *see* modes
inspections 361, 374
instance level connexions 240
instance operations 250
instances 25, 26, 62, 227–8, 238, 240,
        452, 464
instantiation 27
integration testing 415, 418, 421

integrity rules 55
Intellect 57
intelligence, social nature of 165–8
intelligent databases 138
inter-object metrics 401, 408, 411
interaction diagrams 283, 312, 450
interaction points 407
interactive dichotomizer algorithm
    see ID3
Interface Builder *see* NeXTstep
interface classes (CORBA) 148–9
Interface Definition Language *see* IDL
interface design principles 304–9
interface standards 74, 420
interfaces 25, 45
interference 83
interim customers 321, 431
internal context model 282–3, 286, 288
internal tasks 99
internalization 28
International Data Corporation 23
interoperability 35, 42–6, 53–8, 62, 74
interviewing 277, 280–91, 292
InterViews 434
intra–object metrics 401, 408
introduction rules 176
intuitionism 462
intuitionistic type theory 462–3
invariance conditions *see* assertions
invariant composition 244
inverted indexing 138
IOM *see* Implementation Object
    Model
Iona Technologies 50
Ipsys 111
IR systems *see* Information Retrieval
    systems
IRDS 438
IsA 237–9
ISA Limited xiii, 117
ISO 9126, 106
ISO 9241, 106
IT Horizons 211
ITASCA 54, 63, 160

J

Jackson Structured Design *see* JSD
JAD (Joint Application Design) 277, 354
job–shop scheduling 100
join operations 47
Joint Application Design *see* JAD
JOOP 276
Joshua 207
joysticks 78
JSD (Jackson Structured Design) 258,
    298
judgements *see* analysis of judgements

K

KADS expert systems development
    method 56, 209
Kappa 59, 63, 207
KBMS 59, 207
KBS (knowledge based systems) *see*
    expert systems

KEE 59, 207
Kelly grid technique 273, 295, 299–300,
    306, 309
Kerberos 154
keyboards 78
keys 451, 453
keyword based retrieval 138–9, 438
knowledge 169
knowledge acquisition *see* knowledge
    elicitation
knowledge analysis of tasks 21, 100, 104
knowledge base 166–7
knowledge based systems *see*
    expert systems
knowledge elicitation 165
knowledge engineering 21, 87
knowledge representation 173, 176,
    201, 205, 211
knowledge, social nature of 12, 39,
    175, 211
KnowledgePro 111
KPMG 408, 410

L

labour 21, 22, 165
laddering 299–300
language independence of methods 64,
    68, 217
language understanding *see* natural
    language
LANs (local area networks) 126
large systems and prototyping 357
latency 129, 132, 138
layers 132, 230–2, 240, 242, 290, 305,
    311, 349, 421, 439, 450
lazy evaluation 250, 446
LCOM (lack of cohesion in methods)
    409–10
lead users 315, 394
leadership 35, 67
learnability 74–5
legacy systems 31, 33, 35, 43, 45, 49,
    51, 53, 145
Leonardo 59, 63, 188, 191, 192, 207
liability business processes 333
Liant 114
librarians *see* class librarians
library classes *see* class libraries
library information management
    systems 107
linguistic approximation 263
linguistic variables *see* fuzzy sets
LISP 103, 463
local area networks *see* LANs
local dynamics of objects 259
localization 259
locating reusable objects 428
locational transparency 130, 132, 135,
    138, 148–9, 152
locking 134
locking delays 137
logic and inference 176–8, 281
Logica 80
logical business transactions 294, 406–7
logical cohesion 403, 410
logical design 220–1, 226, 446
London Ambulance Service 155
long term memory (LTM) 82, 85
long transactions 53

loosely bound systems 74, 116
Lotus 123 86
Lotus Notes 142
low level languages 280
LTM *see* long term memory
Lucas 144

M

MacApp 104
Mach kernel 14
machine generated primary keys *see*
    surrogate keys
Machine Intelligence News 211
machine learning 185–8, 201, 211
Macintosh 67, 73–5, 106
MagicCap 74
main build time-box 372–7
mainframes 16, 35, 39, 46, 66, 67, 75,
    125–6, 427
maintainability 355
maintenance 6, 12, 23, 24, 30, 35, 41,
    43, 49, 127, 134, 173, 349–50,
    426–7, 434, 439
management awareness programmes
    362
management commitment 437
management control over prototyping
    10, 354–60, 373
management information systems
    (MIS) 41
managing change *see* change
    management
managing expectations 355–6, 364, 375
mandatory deliverables 360, 362
many-to-many associations 245, 305
market share 7, 41
marketing strategy 32, 33, 194
maturity period 350
maximum (mean of maxima) method,
    see defuzzification
Mazda 4, 5, 140
McCabe Tools 410, 413
mean-of-maxima operation *see*
    defuzzification
measure theory 400
measurement 399
measurement scales 400
measures 399
mediations *see* contradictions
membership functions *see* fuzzy sets
memory characteristics 82–6
memory management 52
mentoring 34, 396
menu design 83
message diagrams 450
message passing 20, 22, 24, 28, 30, 43,
    45, 50, 60, 67, 81, 126, 130, 245,
    283
message tables 284–6, 311, 315, 333, 450
messages 28, 250, 280, 282, 309, 408
metaclasses 451
metaknowledge 169
metarules 256
methods 25, 63, 221
metric spaces 399–400
metrics 346, 381–3, 399–414, 422
MFC *see* Microsoft Foundation
    Classes

mice 73, 74, 78
MicroFocus 31
MicroFocus COBOL Workbench 113
Microsoft (MS) 33, 35, 50, 74, 104
Microsoft Foundation Classes (MFC) 50, 104, 435
Microsoft Windows *see* MS Windows
Microsoft Word *see* MS Word
migration strategy 34, 41–68, 75
Miller's law 230
MIPS 16
Miranda 26
MIS applications 58, 258
mission critical business processes 333
mission statement 281, 313, 315, 364
mixing up classification with composition structure 306
MkII FPs 406–7
ML 26, 30, 463
modal dialogue boxes 80, 90, 435
Model-View-Controller metaphor *see* MVC metaphor
modelling 21, 22, 205
models 400, 414
modes 89, 90, 93
Modula 2 452
modularity 34
module diagrams 451
modus ponens 177–8, 262
modus tollens 178
moments defuzzification method *see* defuzzification
MooZ 460
MOSES life cycle model 349–53
MOSES method 68, 225, 398, 408–9, 413
Motif 105
motivated developers 355
motivation 355
MS Access 108, 477
MS Office 75
MS Visual C++ 435, 477
MS Windows 20, 74, 75, 479
MS Word 105
multi–client/multi–server systems 127, 135, 137
multi–media 31, 108
multiple inheritance 207, 235, 238–9, 251–2, 254–57, 264–274, 411, 419, 451–3, 464–6
multiple inheritance conflicts 235, 252, 255–7
multiple versions 48
Mutual Benefit Life 140, 329
MVC metaphor 56, 102, 104, 135, 327

N

Nabisco 144
NAG FORTRAN library 42
name services 152
naming conventions 151
narrow and deep versus broad and shallow interviews/prototypes 292
National & Provincial Building Society 35, 144
natural language 81, 95, 139, 279

natural language query systems 57
NatWest Bank 81
nesting 450
NetGateway 153
Netware 109
network architecture 145
network bottlenecks and delays 135, 137, 157
network nodes 132
network operating systems 126
network routing packages 407
networks 5, 43, 61, 75, 144–6
neural networks 186, 205, 211
NeWI 48, 50, 150
NewWave 50, 149
Nexpert Object 59, 207
NeXT 104
NeXTstep 14, 50, 68, 74, 75, 105, 426–7, 434, 454
NeXTWORLD 424
NFS 109, 135
NIH library 434
NOC (number of children) 409–10
non-monotonic logic 268–9, 281, 407
NON-NULL facet 248
non-pre-emption 92
non-procedural (declarative) languages 167, 253
non-procedural data access languages 54, 55
normal fuzzy sets 266
normalization 47, 245, 279, 305, 322, 356, 453
novice and expert modes 89, 94, 95
null values 248, 256
numerical controllers 335
NYNEX 35

O

O2 111
OBJ3 461
Object Behaviour Model 245
Object COBOL 63
Object Expo conference 71, 123, 287
object identification 233, 290–305
object identity 25, 26, 28, 30, 63, 159, 227, 452
Object IQ *see* ES/KERNEL
object libraries 19
Object Magazine 71, 163, 276
Object Maker 111
Object Management Group (OMG) ix, 11, 33, 50, 146
Object Management Workbench 113, 207
object modelling 13, 220–279
Object PASCAL 63, 108
object request brokers 35, 45, 48–50, 53, 57, 61, 131, 138, 146–52, 308
Object Reuse Librarian (ORL) 206
Object SQL 54, 55, 58
object types 221, 464
Object Vision 108
Object Windows Library *see* OWL
object wrappers 35, 42–53, 55, 56, 59, 61, 64, 71, 75, 76, 128, 131–2, 136, 151, 205, 232, 242, 308, 467

object wrappers – concerns about data management 46–53
object-oriented analysis 46, 48–50, 59, 61–3, 136, 226
object-oriented analysis and design 31, 42, 66, 67, 226, 276
object-oriented COBOL 31
object-oriented databases 31, 35, 43, 45, 53–7, 61, 64, 71, 131–2, 136, 149
object-oriented enterprise modelling *see* enterprise modelling
object-oriented metrics 408–14
object-oriented modelling 128, 361
object-oriented network modelling 163, 242, 258
object-oriented process model 356–60
object-oriented programming 358
object-oriented programming languages 28, 31, 42, 53, 57, 61, 419, 445, 447–53
Object-Oriented Pty 348
object-oriented rapid application development 357–60
Object-Oriented Technologies Ltd 151
object-oriented Zachman framework 324–29
Object-Z 460–1
object/objectives matrix xi, 314, 485
Objectbroker 50
ObjectCenter 50, 434, 455
ObjectCOBOL *see* object-oriented COBOL
ObjectIQ *see* ES/KERNEL
Objective-C 14, 43, 63, 68, 408, 434, 466
objectives and measures 281–2, 313–15, 319, 356–7, 360, 364, 420
Objectivity/DB 54
Objectory 100, 287
objects 24, 25, 167, 227
objects, tautological *see* tautological objects
ObjectStore 54, 149
ObjectWise Ltd xiii
ObjectWorks 114
obliterating work 9, 330
ODBC 138
office automation 138, 479
OfficeVision 154
OLE 11, 50, 75
OMG *see* Object Management Group
OMG Abstract Object Model 220
OMG OOA/D Reference Model 219–20, 319
Omnis 108
OMT 225, 242, 258, 450
OMT qualifiers *see* qualifiers
OMW 207, 321
ontology 410
ONTOS 54
OOEM (object–oriented enterprise modelling) 328
OOPSLA 71, 123
OOZE 460–1
Open Client API 135
open issues 282, 315, 364
Open Software Foundation *see* OSF
open systems 7, 41, 61, 64
open systems standards 136

OpenLook 74, 105
OpenODB 54
OpenServer 138, 153
OpenStep 14, 106, 135, 152
operations 25, 26, 200, 221, 227, 247, 249–50, 309, 452
opportunistic chaining 181, 192
opposites (asking for) 299
opposites interpenetration of *see* contradictions
OPS5 180
optical fibre 15
optical storage 107
optional deliverables 360, 362
optionality, removing 235
Oracle 49, 54, 58, 108
Oracle Card 108
ORBIX 150
ORBs *see* object request brokers
order processing 476–8
organizational change *see* change management
organizational hologram 8
ORION object-oriented database 160
ORL *see* Object Reuse Librarian
OS/400 44
OSF (Open Software Foundation) 104, 105
OSF Motif *see* Motif
OT9X conference 123
output devices 79
output modes *see* modes
overlapping subclasses 235
overriding 26, 238, 242, 419, 425, 464
OWL graphical library 50, 104
ownership 244, 248, 250, 355, 421, 431

P

PAC 104
package evaluation 364
package software 425
packages 41, 43, 51
paper tape 73, 78
Paradigm Plus 111
Paradox 108
parallel processing 42, 60
parallel projects 423
parallel time–boxes 423, 438
parallelism 14, 126, 129, 135
paralysis by analysis 356
parametrized classes 451
partial inheritance 256, 260, 264
partial properties *see* fuzzy attributes
partitioned servers 127
partitions 234
Parts: attribute 240, 247
PASCAL 452
passive objects 130–1
pattern classification 187
pattern matching 183
pattern oriented languages *see* patterns
patterns 28, 123, 232–3, 240, 242, 274, 461
PCs 5, 14, 74
Pctcall 410

PCTE 438
Pctpub 410
peer-to-peer communication 127–8, 134–5, 145
pen computers 78, 79
Pepsi Cola 119
performance 54, 435
performance tests 417
Performing Rights Society 155
persistence 54, 55
personal computers *see* PCs
personal constructs 299
Petri nets 250, 455–8, 468
Pharos 81
phases 351, 357
phenomenology 410
physical design 220–1, 226, 235, 446–53
physical handicaps *see* handicaps
pilot projects 33
PL/1 43
plans 21
plug boards 73, 78
plural form for class names 228
PM *see* Presentation Manager
policy modelling 320, 331, 337
policy object 337
policy rules 330–1, 337
political economy 3
polymorphic languages 29
polymorphism 23–9, 89, 410–11, 416, 452
portability 435
Portable Common Tools Environment *see* PCTE
possibility 193
post-conditions *see* assertions
PostScript 11
potential reuse 441
power hedges *see* hedges
power law of practice 94
Powerbuilder 113
Praxis Systems 408, 410
pre-conditions *see* assertions
pre-emptive modes *see* modes
predicate calculus *see* first order predicate calculus
preference grids 282
Presentation Manager 20, 74, 105
pressure pens 78
primacy effects 85
primary keys *see* keys
priming 82–5
priorities 389
prioritization of objectives 282, 314–15, 356, 364
private *see* public/private/protected/friend
private attributes 247
private facets 229
Pro-Kappa *see* Kappa
probes 293, 309
procedural descriptions 21
procedural embedding 20
procedural knowledge 94
procedural life cycle models 356
procedures 168
process chains 330
process control applications 31, 128, 226, 263, 336, 411

process diagrams 451
process innovation 322
process management 437
process metrics 401, 404
process models 141
ProcessIT 144
processor diagrams 452
ProcessWise 330
product metrics 401
production rules 171
productions *see* production rules
productivity 3, 7, 12–17, 20, 23, 34, 35, 66, 67, 74, 81, 139, 217, 345, 408, 414, 427–8, 431, 465
program browsers 258
programmable user models 103
progress, sense of *see* sense of progress
project charter/mission *see* mission
project initiation 360, 362–4, 420
project leaders 393
project management 282, 391–2
project managers 393
project planning activity 359, 386–8
project proposal document 362
project rôles 392–6
project sponsors 392
Prolog 58, 91, 183
Prolog++ 207
proof theoretic methods 458–9, 462–63
props (theatrical) 101, 288
protected *see* public/private/protected/friend
protocol analysis 294
prototype languages 27, 238
prototypes 27, 62
prototyping 15, 18, 30, 64, 65, 87, 101, 103, 110, 217, 225, 281, 305, 347, 355–60, 364, 374, 376, 415, 419–21, 454, 458, 465–7
prototyping tools 466
provability 458
Prudential Assurance 155
Ptech 143, 207, 225, 239
Pubdata 410
public *see* public/private/protected/friend
public attributes 247
public/private/protected/friend 353, 403, 411
punched cards 73, 78
pure attributes 248
purpose 76, 238
put operations *see* access operations
Putnam model 405

Q

QBE (Query by Example) 90
qualifiers(OMT) 257–8
qualitative judgements 168
quality 13, 21, 30, 35, 346, 353, 357–8, 375, 415, 426, 428, 431, 436, 440
quality control 437
quality metrics 400, 410
quality plan 362, 383, 387
quantification over functions 225
question words 319, 323

R

RAD (rapid application development)
13, 30, 32–5, 144, 209, 277, 347,
353–60, 398
RAD facilitators *see* facilitators
RAD rôles *see* rôles
RAD scoping workshop *see* scoping
RAD workshop activity *see* RAD
workshops (RADs)
RAD workshop rôles *see* rôles
RAD workshops (RADs) xi, 283,
290, 352, 354, 364–8, 419, 430,
465, 485, 487
range constraints 248
Rank Xerox 144
rapid analysis activity *see* rapid OOA
rapid application development *see* RAD
Rapid object–oriented design *see*
rapid OOD
Rapid OOA (rapid object-oriented
analysis) activity 359, 368–71
Rapid OOD (rapid object-oriented
design) activity 377–80
Rapid OOP (rapid object-oriented
programming) activity 377–80
ratio scales *see* measurement scales
Rational ROSE 372, 447
Rdb 54
RDBMS (relational database
management systems) 453
RDD/CRC 225
re-engineering 34, 424
reachability trees 456
ready-to-hand tools 21
real-time systems 356
Realia 31
recency effects 85
recommended deliverables 360, 362
recursive composition 242
recursive design 281
recursive structures 242
referential integrity 449
reflexion 17
registered objects 61
regression tests 415
regular grammars 49, 287, 294
rehearsal 82
relational calculus 55
relational database management
systems *see* RDBMS
relational databases 5, 6, 42, 43, 49, 53–8
relationships 242, 244, 450
release control 414, 421
reliability 23, 436
Remote Database Access (RDA) 159
remote procedure calls *see* RPCs
repertory grids *see* Kelly grids
replication 127, 159
repositories xi, 31, 32, 50, 58, 107–8,
139, 219, 253, 322, 347, 357,
389–90, 427–8, 437–8, 454, 476,
486
repository classes 421
representativeness (task) 100
representing knowledge *see*
knowledge representation

requirements capture 21, 74, 100, 101,
277–317, 320, 355, 360, 458
Requisite Variety, Law of 335
resolution principle 178
response for a class *see* RFC
responsibilities 26, 247–9, 286, 307, 309
Responsibility Driven Design *see* RDD
restaurant script 100, 203
result returned *see* return value types
RETE algorithm 180
return value types 10, 283
reusability 30, 63, 65, 257
reusable business processes *see*
reusable task scripts
reusable code 18
reusable components 14, 388
reusable modules 3
reusable specifications 18
reusable task scripts 437
reuse 12, 13, 30, 32–5, 41–3, 45, 48, 51,
52, 56, 61, 66, 68, 216, 233, 328,
349, 357–8, 361–2, 366, 373, 382,
388–90, 393, 414, 423–38, 440–1,
444, 455, 464–5, 486
reuse administrator/engineer/librarian
429–30
reuse awareness 350, 431
reuse candidates 388, 421
reuse co–ordination 441
reuse evaluation 380–2
reuse libraries and repositories 56, 427
reuse management 437
reuse metrics 404, 407
reuse ratio 409
reuse team 427, 429
reuse tools 426, 428
Reuters 120
REVEAL 268, 336
reverse engineering 10, 47, 62, 466
reversibility ix, 31, 34, 64, 225, 258, 465
reversible descriptions 217
reversible prototypes 217
revolutionary prototyping *see*
throwaway prototyping
reward structures 35, 68, 411, 431
rewarding reuse 426, 431, 432
RFC (response for a class) 409–10
rightsizing 16, 22, 36, 66, 134, 136, 158
Ripp (Rapid iterative production
prototyping) 354–5
risk 117, 290
risk management systems 479
ROAD 276
robustness 358
Rogue Wave 437
rôle playing *see* walkthroughs
rôles 201, 239, 248, 282, 286, 450–61
Rooms 74, 83
Rootcnt 410
Rosette parallel computation manager
160
RPCs (remote procedure calls) 16, 132,
134–5, 147–8, 159
RPG 86
RTF (Rich Text Format) 11
Ruby xiii
rule induction *see* induction
rule–based languages 446–7
rule–based systems *see* expert systems

rules ix, 55, 58, 94, 167, 200, 216, 225,
227, 239, 250–8, 287, 308, 310,
320, 332, 345, 411, 413, 415, 436,
446, 458
rules, classification of 254
rulesets 200, 227, 230, 250–9, 303, 337,
357, 413, 450, 465, 479
RUMBA 157

S

safety critical systems 14, 459
SAS 111
Sassafras 103
satisfied users 19–21
SBC (Swiss Bank Corporation) xiii, 35,
479
scaleability 30, 132
scales *see* measurement scales
scenario modelling 141
scenarios representing actual cases *see*
use cases
scenes *see* scripts
schema evolution 53
scoping activity 286, 314, 364–6
scoping rules 452
scribes 285, 394, 396, 487
script theory 200–4, 289, 317
scripts 21, 27, 100, 101, 200–4, 287
SDLC (software development life cycle)
ix, 36, 343–98, 471–3
search *see* tree search
second order structure of objects *see*
rulesets
security issues 137, 421
security level 248, 250
SELECT 111
SELF 27, 62
self describing data 45, 46, 50
self-demonstrability 92
semantic cohesion 403, 409
semantic data modelling 62, 63, 225
semantic databases 64
semantic nets/networks 139, 200
Semantic Object Modelling Approach
see SOMA
semantic richness ix, 10, 13, 31, 34, 64,
217, 321, 440
semiotic acts 280, 283, 298, 312, 334
semiotics 94
sense of progress 78, 92
servers 246, 250, 309
set theory 460
SGML (Standard Generalized Mark–up
Language) 11
shared data 46
shared objects 55
shared understanding 22, 95, 313,
320–1, 337, 355, 446
shift hedges *see* hedges
SHL 424
Shlaer/Mellor OOA 225
short term memory *see* activated
memory
shortest path multiple inheritance
strategies 256
Shorthand 111
side effects of rules 446

side-scripts 203, 287–9
sign-off 360, 362, 368, 395
signature table 138
signatures 24, 315, 462
significant complex states 258–9, 313
SIGS Publications xiv
Simplify 108
Simula 63
simulation 21, 31, 321, 330, 415,
    418–19, 455
single inheritance *see* inheritance
skill acquisition 94
skills 68, 130, 392–6
SLIM 400
Sloan Management Review 342
Sloan School of Management 398
SLOCs (source lines of code) 400, 402,
    405, 412, 431
slots 60, 101, 168, 200–1
small teams 354, 374
Smalltalk 20, 21, 27, 31, 63, 115, 280,
    434, 447, 461
Smalltalk V x
Smallworld 57
sociology of knowledge 165
Soft Systems method 320
software development life cycle *see*
    SDLC
Software Futures 427
software houses 3, 18, 33, 34
software ICs 152
software infrastructure group *see*
    domain modelling team
Software through Pictures (StP) 447
Softwright Systems *see* NeWI
solid modelling systems 48
SOM object model 11, 152
SOMA vii, viii, ix, 27, 62, 68, 74, 94,
    100, 101, 139–40, 193, 200, 208,
    215–485
SOMA metrics xi, 412–4
SOMATiK vii, viiii, ix, 51, 139, 178,
    182, 208, 219, 237, 242, 246–7,
    251, 283, 310, 331, 357, 364,
    389, 412–13, 419, 428–31, 435,
    438, 455, 458, 467, 469–527
SOMATiK system requirements 486
source code management tools 429
source/specification cross-referencing
    xi, 438
spatial modes *see* modes
specification level *v.* code level reuse 13,
    32, 68, 357, 424–9, 436, 438, 457
specification libraries and repositories
    216, 454
specifications (Booch'93) 451
speech acts 94, 283
speech recognition 79
speech understanding systems 9, 60
spiral models 347, 353
sponsors 394
SQL 55–7, 127, 135
SQL Access Group 159
SQL Connect 135
SQL gateways 58
SQL Windows 108, 119
SQL3 55
SSADM 245, 258
stack variables 452

stacked Petri nets 458
Staffware 144
stages 351, 357
stakeholders 343
Standard Generalized Mark-up
    Language *see* SGML
standard interfaces 437
standards 11, 41, 58
Star interface (Xerox) 73
state diagrams *see* STDs
state machines 450
state transition diagrams *see* STDs
states 259
Statice 207
stative classes 451
STDs (state transition diagrams) 225,
    245, 250, 251, 258–9, 274, 313,
    420, 450, 454–5, 460–1
step-wise refinement 47
stereotypes 280
stereotypical behaviour 203–4
stereotypical exceptions 203
stereotypical scripts *see* scripts
stored procedures 56, 64, 135
StP *see* Software through Pictures
strategic modelling 220, 319
strategy 319
stress 74
stress testing 417, 419
structural cohesion 409–10
structural complexity metrics 403
structural testing techniques 415–16
structure depths 413–14
structure semantics (E/O etc.) 234, 240
structured interviews 292
structured methods 9, 31, 35, 61, 108,
    156, 208–9, 217, 344–5, 356, 425
structured techniques 15
structured walkthroughs 15
structures 234–47, 274, 287, 289, 410,
    413–4
Studio 111
STUDIO 88
style guides 105, 123
subclass intersection *see* structure
semantics subclasses 30, 237
subclassing 397
subject area layers 213–14
subroutines in SOMA class cards
    229, 250, 309
subscripts 203, 287, 289
substitutability, principle of 462, 464
subsystems 232, 450
subtypes 464
Sun 104
Superbase 108
superclasses 237
superclasses list 237
surrogate keys 453
surrogate objects 130
SVDPI (Subject – Verb – Direct.Object
    – [Preposition – Indirect.
    Object]) sentences 101, 288–9,
    298, 414
SWIFT funds transfer telexes 203
Swiss Bank Corporation *see* SBC 33,
    408
Sybase 49, 54, 55, 58, 127, 307, 477
Sybase Replication Server 160

Symbolics Inc 207
synchronization 450
synthesis 222
Syntropy 225
System Architect 111
system development life-cycle *see*
    SDLC
System Engineer 111
System Object Model *see* SOM
System W 111
systems analysis report 352

T

tactics 319
take-over data management strategy
    46, 48, 49, 51, 52
Taligent 14, 152
tandem (handshake) strategy 46, 49
Task Action Grammar 103
Task Action Language 103
task analysis 21, 78, 88, 99–101, 104,
    287–90, 293–8, 307
task attributes 289
task cards 282, 290
task centred design 21, 78, 86, 93, 97,
    305
task domain 279
task knowledge 100
task modelling 94
Task Object Model *see* TOM
task points 372, 412, 414
task scripts 143, 166, 280, 282–3,
    287–9, 292, 309, 311–12, 315,
    322, 357, 359–60, 366, 382, 389,
    407–8, 415–16, 418–19, 421, 428
task scripts, tests against *see* testing
task-action grammar *see* SVDPI
tasks 13, 21, 80, 99, 172, 218, 279, 281,
    283–4, 286, 290, 320, 429
Taunton Cider 154
tautological objects 271–4
teachback 293, 309
TeamRoute 144
technical analysis *see* chartism
Televerket 120
Temple Barker and Sloan 74
temporal logic 460–1
temporal modes *see* modes
ten minute rule 311
terminological logic 256
ternary approaches to OOA 224
test harnesses 415, 418
test plans 379, 418, 419
test scripts 13, 283, 287, 357, 415, 428
testing 12, 281–2, 309, 311, 346, 349, 353,
    357, 359, 366, 377–80, 382, 414–22
testing GUIs *see* usability testing
testing objectives *see* objectives
    and measures
testing tools 418
textual analysis 280–1, 289, 294, 301,
    366
thesaurii 138
third normal form *see* 3NF
throwaway (revolutionary) prototyping
    355, 358, 465
tightly versus loosely bound solutions
    116

time threads 455
time-box evaluation *see* evaluation
    activity
time-box managers 393
time-box objectives 375
time-box planning activity 360, 371–2
time-box sequencing 283
time-box synchronization 439
time-boxes 345, 352, 354–60, 374, 428,
    439
time-to-market 41, 68, 144, 345, 355,
    358, 432
time-taken: 290, 322, 333, 450
timing implications and limits 362, 368
TOM (Task Object Model) 101, 259,
    279–80, 286, 294, 320, 322, 333,
    366, 412–14, 449
toolbars 75
Toolbook 75, 108, 109
TOOLS conference xiv, 123
Tools.h++ 435
toolsmiths 429, 430, 433
top-down decomposition 290, 425
topic analysis *see* task analysis
topos theory 463
touch screens 78–9
TP monitors 137
traceability 218, 326, 376, 449, 464, 466
tracker balls 78
training *see* education and training
transaction processing 16, 125
transaction server model 127
transfer effects 75, 83, 85, 98
transition from logical to physical
    design 449
transitions 259, 456
translation strategy 46, 48, 49, 51, 55
tree search 182, 251
triads, elicitation by 299–300
triggering event 284–5, 312
triggers 55, 58, 60, 62, 64, 252
TRW 347
TUBE 104
Tuxedo *see* TP monitors
two-library model of reuse 441
two-phase commits 127, 159
type theory 449, 462–63
typed inheritance links 269
types 449, 462–3, 464
typicality (tasks) 100

U

UI *see* user interface
UI design 19, 67
UI principles 67
UIDEs 104
UIMSs 104
unary approaches to OOA 224
unbounded activities 357
uncertainty 168–9, 171, 173, 186, 334,
    344
understanding 200–1
understanding stories 200, 203
undo/redo facilities 75, 90, 407
Unify 111
Unilever 342
Union Bank of Switzerland 35

unique identity *see* object identity
UniSQL/X 54
unit testing 415, 418, 420
United Artists 35
units *see* frames
University of Technology Sydney 348,
    410
UNIX 14, 48, 479
usability 7, 34, 36, 67, 87, 88, 106
usability engineering 99
usability laboratories 417
usability metrics 98, 99, 382, 401
usability studies 467
usability testing 98, 99, 417, 420
usability workshops 98
usage 30, 450
usage structures 240, 245–7, 450
use cases 21, 286, 289, 341, 402, 406,
    416
use-value 12
user centred design 21, 78
user interface design 66
User Interface Management Systems
    see UIMS
user interfaces, graphical *see* GUIs
user interfaces *see* UI
user modelling 22, 87, 95, 103
user review activity 380
user reviews 361
user rôles 394
user test 419
users adopting rôles *see* actors
USL Standard Components 434–5

V

V process model 346–7, 349, 414–5
vagueness 459
validation 244, 415
value 21
value added 333
value chain 321, 331, 333
value conflicts *see* multiple inheritance
VAX™ computers 44
VDM (Vienna Development
    Method) 458–60
VDM++ 460–1
verification 415
VERSANT 54
version control 31, 53, 251, 431
Video animation 107
views 453
virtual reality 74, 108
virtual terminals 44
visibility 28, 245
VisiCalc 6
Visual Age 104
Visual Basic x, xiii, 102, 104–5, 109,
    114, 454
Visual C++ *see* MS Visual C++
visual programming 16
VisualWorks 50, 104, 109
VLSI design 58
voice input 79
voice storage 107
voice-mail systems 107
voting 282, 366, 395
VSF 111

W

walkthroughs 282–3, 310–13, 357, 360,
    368, 374, 415, 418–20
Wang 139
WANs 128
wants versus needs 355
waterfall models 35, 346–9
weighted class and task complexities
    (WC$_C$, WC$_T$) 413–4
weighted methods per class
    (WMC) 409–11, 413
Westinghouse 34
white box testing 416, 419
widgets *see* class libraries
winter olympics 154
Wizards 435
WMC *see* weighted methods
per class WNDX 114
Word for Windows 75
word processing 11, 87
work flow 13, 330
work-flow automation 139–44, 479
Workflo 142
working memory *see* activated
    memory
workshop activity *see* RAD
workshops
workshop facilitators *see* facilitators
    workshops 277, 280–1, 292,
    312, 313
workshops *v.* interviews 292
workstations 16, 46, 125
WORM (Write Once Read Many)
    devices 107
wrappers *see* object wrappers
wrapping legacy applications *see* object
    wrappers
WYKAIWYCU 92
WYSIWYCU 92
WYSIWYG 88, 92

X

X model 349
X Windows 20
X–Windows 74
X/Motif 74
X500 E-mail standard 130
XCON 188
Xerox Corporation 330
Xerox PARC 63, 73
Xerox Rooms *see* Rooms
Xerox Sigma 67
XShell 50, 61, 150
Xt Intrinsics 105
XVT 114

Z

Z 408, 458–60
Z++ 460
Zachman information systems
    framework 322–7, 341
Zinc 50, 104, 108, 114
zoomed in/out views 228